The
Course
of
Civilization

The
Course
of
Civilization

VOLUME ONE: TO 1660

SRIPTORVM PRINCEPS EGO NEC OBITVRA DEINCE

VIVS · Q VEM TIBI SEQVE DATVM MVNVS

Joseph R. Strayer

Princeton University

Hans W. Gatzke

The Johns Hopkins University

E. Harris Harbison

Princeton University

HARCOURT, BRACE & WORLD, INC.

New York and Burlingame

THE COURSE OF CIVILIZATION
VOLUME ONE: TO 1660
STRAYER, GATZKE, HARBISON

Printed in the United States of America

Library of Congress Catalog Card Number: 61–9181

[a·2·61]

MAPS BY J. P. TREMBLAY

TITLE-PAGE ILLUSTRATIONS

A warrior in lunge position, from the Aegina marbles, Greek, *ca.* 510 B.C.

A bodhisattva maitreya, or Buddhist messiah, from a Japanese Buddhist temple, early Heian period, 8th century.

The English scribe Eadwine, from the Utrecht Psalter, 12th century.

A *condottiere,* or professional soldier, painted by Antonello de Messine, Italian, 15th century.

Preface

This book is an attempt to interpret the course of civilization with the aid of the best historical research we know and in the light of the dominant concerns of our twentieth-century society.

We make no particular claims to originality of method or content. We have tried to seize on what seems important, to sketch the determining or enduring features of each age or society, not the random or colorful detail, even if hallowed by textbook tradition. We have asked ourselves constantly: What made this society what it was? Why did it grow? Why did it fade away? We have tried to focus on the deep and enduring human needs and how men satisfied them in each epoch: the need for food, clothing, and shelter; for community and political order; for peace—and for glory; for pleasure, for beauty, for salvation.

We have tried at every point to relate and to explain, to encourage the reader to think about what he is reading, to stimulate the bent of mind called historical-mindedness. We would like the student to come away from his reading with the feeling that history is not "all in the book," but that the book has got him interested in pursuing history—which, after all, meant "inquiry" to its Greek authors.

Text, illustrations, and inserts have all been shaped to this end. In the earlier ages, where perspective allows a more synoptic view, we have tried to "make sense" of a civilization or society as a whole, even at the risk of oversimplification. But we have often tried even here to suggest that the evidence is complex or that scholars disagree on some of our conclusions. Illustrations and inserts are meant to suggest the variety of evidence that is of service to historians. Captions for the illustrations have frequently been made longer than is customary, in an attempt to make the picture serve as a genuinely important source of knowledge beyond some point in the text. Selections from the sources or from other historical works included in the inserts are designed to extend the reader's insight into the text or to challenge his critical thought by suggesting contradictory viewpoints. As befits the importance of more recent events for understanding the achievements and forebodings of today, the narrative broadens considerably once it reaches the nineteenth century. As generalization becomes more difficult in the twentieth century, events are left more often to speak for themselves.

There are many acknowledgments we should make: to our teachers (some of whom warned us never to try to write a textbook), to our present colleagues (who have cheerfully borne our factual quizzes), and to the younger staff members of our undergraduate courses (who have mercilessly criticized every textbook we have ever used).

We are particularly grateful to Professors Franklin Ford of Harvard University, John A. Harrison of the University of Florida, Maurice D. Lee, Jr., of the University of Illinois, and A. Paul Levack of Fordham University, for their critical reading of the manuscript.

JOSEPH R. STRAYER

HANS W. GATZKE

E. HARRIS HARBISON

Contents

List of Maps

The
Course
of
Civilization

Introduction

This is a history of civilization, with emphasis on the civilization developed by the peoples of Europe. Like all histories, it must be selective. Incomplete as our record of the past is, it is still too full to permit discussion in a single book of all civilizations or even of all events in the history of one civilization. The principles which have guided our selection of topics may be indicated by a definition of our subject. We must answer two questions: what is civilization, and what has been the role of western civilization in creating the conditions which we find in the world today?

Civilization is derived from the Latin word for city, *civitas*. There is reason to emphasize this derivation, for every great civilization has had great cities, and the basic characteristics of civilization are easiest to observe in cities. Civilization is first of all *cooperation*—men working together to satisfy their material and spiritual needs. It requires *organization*—as soon as several people start working together there must be some sort of social, political, or economic pattern to regulate their activity. It encourages *specialization*—as soon as several people begin to cooperate in an organized way there are obvious advantages in dividing the work so that no one man has to do everything for himself. The

character of a particular civilization is determined by the type and degree of the organization and specialization of that civilization. Ten thousand Greeks living in a small city-state could accomplish much more than ten thousand Indians scattered through the forests of North America. A few hundred men specializing in science have done more to change our civilization in the last few centuries than millions of artisans working through past ages. Intensive organization and specialization can produce spectacular results, and they can also create spectacular problems.

Civilization requires faith in certain ideals and values as well as skill in organization and techniques. The immediate and direct advantages of organization and specialization are not very apparent to most people. Organization sets limits on personal freedom, and specialization makes a man dependent on other men who may not be wholly trustworthy. In the long run the advantages are greater than the disadvantages, but farseeing, enlightened self-interest is a very rare human quality, probably rarer than altruism. And if men hesitate to give up present benefits for advantages in their own future, they will be even more hesitant if the advantages are to be gained only by their descendants. There is always resistance to increasing the scale and scope of organization; there is usually resistance to new types of specialization. This resistance can be overcome only by belief that there is something more important than the individual—a religion which emphasizes cooperation, a divinely appointed ruler or ruling class, a nation which has become almost a divinity, a theory of society which has taken on the aspects of a religion. There is a close connection between the dominant beliefs of a people and the kind of civilization it creates.

Thus in studying the history of civilization we shall be studying, more than anything else, how and why men worked together. We shall be concerned with political history, because the political record helps us to understand why people have been more successful at some times than at others in organizing on a large scale, and why some types of organization have proved more effective than others. We shall be concerned with economic and social history, because economic and social organization has a direct effect on both political organization and the type and degree of specialization. We shall be concerned with the history of ideas and their manifestations in art and literature, because organization and specialization are possible only within a framework of accepted beliefs. The interactions among political organizations, economic institutions, and dominant beliefs determine the character and development of a civilization.

Western civilization is only one, and by no means the oldest, of the civilizations which have left a historical record. The earliest civilizations touched Europe and the West only slightly; they centered in the river valleys of Egypt, the Near East, and China. Only with the appearance of the Greek city-states after 1000 B.C. can we see the beginnings of a civilization which belongs to the same family as our own. The Greeks drew heavily on the older civilizations of their neighbors, but they reorganized their borrowed materials and added significant elements to them. Ideas and forms of organization which have remained important in western civilization for over twenty-five hundred years first appear in ancient Greece. The Romans followed the Greeks as the dominant people in the Mediterranean basin. Like the Greeks, they borrowed from their predecessors, rearranged the old materials in new ways, and added ideas of their own, especially in government and law. Roman civilization is the direct ancestor of the civilization of

modern European countries. There has never been a time, from the first conquests of the Roman Republic down to the present, when Roman law and Roman political ideas were not being discussed in some parts of the Continent.

Yet while there is unbroken continuity between the civilization of the Greeks and the Romans and that of the modern West, it is well to remember that continuity is not identity. Much has been added—for example, the ideas brought in by Christianity —and much has been changed. Greco-Roman civilization was neither western nor European; it was Mediterranean. It was most highly developed on the eastern shores of the Mediterranean, and it was greatly influenced by the Orient. France and Spain were colonial outposts which contributed little to Greco-Roman civilization; Germany, Scandinavia, and the Slavic countries were outside the limits of the civilized Mediterranean world.

This Mediterranean civilization ran into trouble in the fourth and fifth centuries A.D. The economic organization proved unsatisfactory, and loyalty to the political organization weakened. As the Roman Empire slowly crumbled, the unity of the Mediterranean basin was destroyed, never to be restored. The southern and eastern shores became part of an Arab empire, part of the non-European Moslem civilization. A remnant of the old Roman Empire, centering around Constantinople, became the Byzantine Empire. This Empire developed its own civilization—Christian in belief, Greek in language, but strongly influenced by the East in organization. Byzantine civilization made a great impression on the Slavic peoples of eastern Europe and had some influence on the Latin and Germanic peoples of the West. But it was never fully integrated with the civilization which grew up in western Europe. The western Europeans thought of the Byzantines as remote and somewhat untrustworthy relatives, who might hand out valuable gifts from time to time but who were too eccentric to live with. This attitude, in turn, has made it difficult to integrate eastern and western Europe, since the eastern countries borrowed much more from Byzantium than did those of the West.

With the Arab and Byzantine Empires developing separate civilizations, the western European remnant of the old Mediterranean world was thrown back on its own resources. These were at first not very great. Western Europe saved only a fragment of its Roman inheritance, and this Roman inheritance was itself only a fragment of the old Mediterranean civilization. Moreover, the Germanic peoples of northern and central Europe, who had never been included in the Mediterranean world, were for a time dominant in western Europe. They brought in some new ideas and institutions, but they were backward in both political and economic organization. They were slow in assimilating the fragments of Roman civilization which remained, and even slower in developing effective types of organization. In the same way, the Christian religion, which eventually had great influence on European civilization, was only slowly absorbed by the half-barbarized Latins and the half-civilized Germans. For six centuries Europeans struggled with the problems of assimilating the Roman inheritance, integrating Latin and Germanic peoples, and implementing the basic ideas of Christianity. Only when this triple task was done did western Europe at last achieve an independent and consistent civilization. Only then could it profit from its contacts with the more highly developed civilization of the Arab and Byzantine worlds.

Once it was established as a separate and viable entity, western European civilization developed rapidly. Many of our basic

institutions and ideas, such as those expressed in universities and representative assemblies, were worked out in the twelfth and thirteenth centuries. But this western European civilization was confined to a very small area. Its center was in the north, in a triangle bounded by Paris, Cologne, and London. The peripheral countries—Spain, Ireland, Norway, Sweden, Poland, Bohemia, and Italy—did not share in all the manifestations of this civilization, though they accepted its basic ideas. And beyond these countries the influence of western European civilization dropped off sharply. It had almost no effect on the Mohammedan countries, none whatever on the people of Africa and Asia who lived beyond the limits of the Moslem world. It had some impact on Byzantium, but not enough to erase the differences which separated Byzantium from the West. There were some contacts with Russia, but the Russians were far more influenced by the Byzantines. And the Mongol conquest of the thirteenth century weakened the few ties which the Russians had with the West and forced them to face east for two centuries.

Meanwhile, another group of civilizations had developed in the Far East, in India, China, and Japan. Each had its own characteristic values—religious in India, secular and political in China, military in Japan. All three tended to become somewhat self-satisfied and isolated; neither India nor China, for example, was as interested in foreign voyages in the sixteenth century as it had been earlier. In all three the economic system was still based largely on village agriculture. Finally, in spite of promising beginnings, none of the Far Eastern civilizations had developed a strong scientific tradition. These characteristics put the Far Eastern countries at a disadvantage in dealing with Europeans, who were deeply interested in strange lands and peoples, were beginning to develop an economy based on machine production, and were just about to make their first important scientific discoveries.

The great voyages of exploration and the great mechanical inventions, both of which began in the fifteenth century, enabled western European civilization to emerge from its narrow corner and to spread throughout the world. Eastern Europe gradually accepted much of the civilization of the West, though the process was never complete. Three new continents —North America, South America, and Australia—were occupied by Europeans, and a fourth, Africa, was dominated by them. Asia, with its old civilizations and its dense population, was not so easily overrun, but even Asia was profoundly influenced by the European impact. Thus, for the first time, all the peoples of the world were brought into contact with a single civilization. The results of this great experiment are only beginning to be apparent.

There is some justification, then, for the conventional division of history into Ancient, Medieval, and Modern. Ancient history deals with the period in which some of the basic elements of western civilization were developed and passed on to later peoples. But Ancient history must be focused on the Near East and the Mediterranean, not on Europe. It must give greater weight to Greece, Asia Minor, Syria, Mesopotamia, and Egypt than to Gaul, Britain, or Germany. Medieval history deals with the period in which a distinct western European civilization appeared. But this civilization was confined to a small part of the European peninsula, and it had little influence outside that area. During the Middle Ages each great region of the world had its own civilization, and no one civilization was able greatly to modify another. Modern history deals not only with the rapid development of western European civilization in its old homeland, but also with relations between that civilization and the rest of the world.

This growth and diffusion of western civilization has gone so far that we have perhaps entered a fourth period in its history. This period is marked by the appearance of distinct types of western civilization in the different areas occupied by Europeans, and, even more, by the revitalization of other civilizations following their contact with the West. Both the appearance of different types of western civilization and the revival of old civilizations are stimulating factors; they should help to prevent ossification and decay. Unfortunately, a stimulus can also be an irritant, and the reactions among competing civilizations may lead to efforts for mutual destruction rather than for mutual instruction.

The history of civilization begins in obscurity and ends with a question mark. Yet past experience is our only guide in solving present and future problems, and knowledge of our history may help us answer the great question with which we are faced today, that of the survival of civilization in any form.

1

The

Ancient

Near

East

Men of one kind or another have lived on this earth for hundreds of thousands of years, but historians can deal with only a tiny fraction of this period—the five or six thousand years for which we have written records. Thus in a sense all history is modern history. If we represented human existence on a scale of an inch to a thousand years, the line would be some forty to fifty feet long and the part for which we have written evidence would occupy only the last six inches. The early Egyptians are almost as remote from the first men as we are. This point is worth stressing because many basic human characteristics and skills were determined or acquired in the long ages which preceded the development of written records. It is an obvious mistake to believe that human society can be understood by studying only the events of the last fifty or hundred years. It may be just as much of a mistake to believe that the experiences of primitive man have left no mark on our behavior.

Early Man

The first manlike creatures may have appeared as much as a million years ago. They were not apes, though the apes and the earliest human types may have descended from a common ancestor. On the other hand, they were not men as we know them; they were not fully erect, and their brain capacity was smaller than that of our own species. Over many thousands of years, by stages that are still imperfectly known, early types of men developed. They used fire and tools, and they had the full-sized human brain, though their appear-

ance and posture were still not entirely like ours. Which of these early types of men was the ancestor of our own species is still uncertain; there may have been some interbreeding so that we are descended from several ancestral stocks instead of just one. In any case, the Cro-Magnon man, who appeared about twenty-five thousand years ago, was unquestionably a human being of our own species, and men of this type rapidly displaced or absorbed all the earlier species. All the present races of man belong to the same species. We can classify men by cultural characteristics, such as language, or physical characteristics, such as color, but none of these differences is as fundamental as that which separated Cro-Magnon man and his relatives from their predecessors. There has been no significant physical change in mankind since the first men of our species appeared. We can do more with what we have, but the equipment is the same.

Archaeologists can tell us a good deal about some aspects of human experience in the period before written records. They have established the main sequences in the development of human skills and they have developed remarkably accurate methods of dating certain early objects. For example, by determining the amount of radioactive carbon which remains in the charred wood of an early campfire they can fix the date of the fire within a range of a few centuries. But while they can tell us how people lived, they cannot explain why they lived as they did, or how they felt about the conditions of their life. Why, for example, did some men of the New Stone Age develop a remarkably expressive form of painting while others never experimented with the art? Why did some people domesticate animals while others failed to do so? What were the religious beliefs and social organization of the ear-

An early Egyptian king, Mykerinus, and his wife, ca. 2900 B.C. These figures are typical examples of Old Kingdom sculpture, which set a fashion that persisted for many centuries. Egyptian sculpture developed very early; its characteristic feeling of power and dignity is already evident here.

Painting of a bull by a Cro-Magnon man, from the caves of Lascaux, France, ca. 13,000 B.C.

liest settled communities? Such matters are obscure and are likely to remain so.

This is unfortunate, because it was during the long millennia of prehistory that man really became man. All the characteristics which differentiate him from the animals were established before written records appear. The most important and the most puzzling of these characteristics was language. There is no real evidence on the origin of language, and no theoretical explanation has ever been very satisfactory. But it was the decisive step in the development of mankind, for it made possible the preservation and the communication of experience and thus made it possible for each generation to go a little further than the one before. And without language there would have been none of the religious and political ideas which held early societies together.

In order to survive, early men must have lived together in some sort of small communities. There is evidence of this sort of grouping even for the hunting and food-gathering stages of human existence. It becomes much more apparent with the development of agriculture, when permanent village settlements were established. We know practically nothing about the organization of these early communities, though we may believe that it was not unlike that of primitive tribes which still exist. There were undoubtedly leaders, perhaps even hereditary chiefs, but there cannot have been any great specialization of functions or any elaborate framework of political institutions. But community and leader were the basic elements out of which all later institutions could be developed.

We are equally ignorant about early religion. It certainly existed and it was certainly important. It is probable that the art of the cave men had religious or at least magical implications. By portraying the animals they hunted, they may have sought to attract them to the region or to propitiate their spirits. There are some

10's of 1,000's of years to develop fine tools but after that, things went faster

early figurines which probably represent gods and goddesses. Formal burial also implies religious ideas. In any case, as soon as we begin to know much about an early society, we find that it already has well-developed religious beliefs. These beliefs inspire its art and its literature. Even more important, they are used to justify the growing complexity of its social and political organization.

It was probably during this same period that man developed an aesthetic sense, in the broadest meaning of the word. That is, he did certain things not because they were immediately useful, not because they were necessary for survival, but because he enjoyed doing them. Granted that early art grew out of religious beliefs, not all objects produced for primitive religious cults are beautiful. Some are roughly made; some are, by almost any standard, ugly. Others seem to show an effort to achieve beauty, to reach an aesthetic rather than a religious goal. In the same way, the polishing of certain stone tools did not make them more efficient; it simply made them better looking and more satisfying to the touch. Or, at a completely different level, it is hard to imagine a purely practical motive for domesticating the cat. This desire for satisfactions that are not entirely utilitarian has remained an important human characteristic and has been a more important influence in our history than we sometimes realize.

We are better informed about the development of tools and techniques. Man very early found how to use fire. Even earlier, he was using objects around him—branches and stones which had convenient shapes —as tools. The decisive step came when he began to make tools himself. This was a very slow process; it took tens of thousands of years to advance from the first crude stone hammers to the precisely made and beautifully finished tools of the New Stone

Age (ca. 10,000 B.C.). But once these first, difficult steps had been taken, progress became relatively rapid. Men apparently gained confidence in their ability to manipulate material objects; they could imagine and then make new and more complicated tools, weapons, and utensils. There was a technological revolution toward the end of the New Stone Age when pottery and textiles appeared, and when the great invention of the wheel was made. Shortly thereafter men discovered metals, probably as a result of accidental smelting when large fires were built on outcroppings of ore. When they learned to make bronze by alloying copper with tin and other metals, a new age began—an age of greatly improved tools and weapons. The Bronze Age (ca. 7000 B.C.) coincides with the first civilizations; it rapidly developed into the Iron Age (ca. 4000 B.C.) in regions where this metal was easily available. We are still in the Iron Age, and it is worth remembering that here again we are practically contemporaries of the first men who used metals. The rate of technological change has speeded up with every century, so that more has been done in the last seven thousand years than in all the ages which preceded them. It took far longer to make a simple improvement in a stone knife in the Old Stone Age than it took to advance from the first two-wheeled cart to the supersonic airplane.

During the New Stone Age two other important techniques were developed. In the first place, men learned how to domesticate animals. This meant a more regular food supply, more and better materials for clothing, and eventually an additional source of power to supplement human effort. Somewhat later certain wild plants, especially the ancestors of our food grains, were domesticated. Seeds were collected, were sown in specially prepared places, and were harvested at the most suitable

9

time. This was the invention of agriculture, which was to be for many years the chief occupation of the vast majority of mankind and which was an indispensable first step toward the building of civilization.

The First Civilizations

As men became more dependent on agriculture, they found themselves facing new problems. The period of the invention of agriculture seems to have coincided with a period of decreasing rainfall and of desiccation of many previously inhabitable areas. As a result, there were not many regions which had both adequate moisture and land that was easy to cultivate with primitive tools. Population tended to increase in these favored regions, and increased population meant that new land had to be brought into cultivation. Since the most easily cultivated fields—those that were neither too swampy nor too dry—had been the first to be used, each successive addition of crop-producing land required an increased amount of work. There had to be a group effort and a large-scale community organization to drain low-lying fields or to irrigate those that lacked water. Moreover, men who were dependent on agriculture could not move easily when unfavorable weather or unfriendly neighbors made life difficult. They had to preserve and protect their crops from wild beasts and predatory men, so the community had to develop a guard service, and eventually an army. Regular habits of life and the rhythm of the agricultural year led them to observe other regularities in nature and thus to piece together the beginnings of scientific knowledge. Organized, settled communities had more sense of continuity with the past than roving hunters or food-gatherers, more need to remember how particular problems had been solved before. These needs could be satisfied only by the invention of writing and the preservation of written records.

Thus the first communities which were organized enough to be called civilized appeared in river valleys, where people were almost entirely dependent on agriculture. The first civilizations become identifiable about 4000 B.C., and from these centers techniques of production and organization spread slowly to less-favored regions. But for many centuries the largest and most prosperous organized communities were in the Valley of the Nile, the Tigris-Euphrates Valley (Mesopotamia), the Indus River region of India, and the Yellow River Valley in China.

The early civilizations of the Far East and India will be discussed at length in Chapter 6. The earliest organized communities in these areas probably came into existence a little later than those of Egypt and Mesopotamia. Moreover, the first river-valley civilizations were relatively isolated from each other, and the sporadic contacts between them had, at first, little effect in modifying local patterns of living. India and China began to influence Mesopotamia and Egypt, and through them Europe, only after the civilizations of the Near East were well established.

The first European civilizations were heavily indebted to their predecessors in the valleys of the Nile and the Tigris-Euphrates, and in adjacent regions. At a time when European tribes were barely emerging from the New Stone Age, the peoples of the Near East had already organized large states, developed long-distance commerce, created religions of a high ethical and philosophical quality, laid the foundations of astronomy and mathematics, and produced remarkable works of art. The first civilized peoples of Europe profited greatly from their proximity to a region where many of the basic problems of

The Ancient Near East *ca.* 1000 B.C.

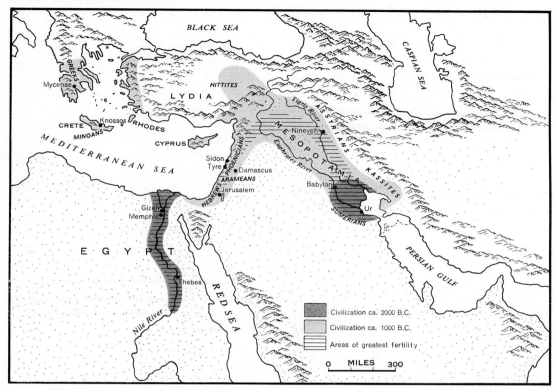

Civilization ca. 2000 B.C.

Civilization ca. 1000 B.C.

Areas of greatest fertility

0   MILES   300

organization and specialization had already been solved.

Both the Nile and the Tigris-Euphrates valleys offered everything necessary to support large and prosperous agricultural communities. The climate was mild. The soil was rich, and its fertility was frequently renewed by deposits of silt laid down by floods. Rainfall was scanty in both valleys, but the rivers offered an unfailing supply of water. Groups of a few hundred people could easily find sites safe from devastating floods but still well watered.

A regular supply of food, however, naturally led to a growth in population, and as expanding villages sought more land the water problem became more acute.

There was too much water in the low-lying plains near the river mouths and not enough in the higher lands remote from the rivers. Drainage and irrigation were necessary to increase the amount of arable land, and neither task could be accomplished effectively by small village communities. Since tools were primitive and animal power was still not very much used, thousands of men would be needed to dig a rather small canal. A village could not operate on this scale; larger organizations were required. The need to control the flow of water is one of the chief reasons for the appearance of the first kingdoms after 4000 B.C.

It would be interesting to know more about the origins of those kingdoms, for it has always been difficult to persuade men to give up a familiar pattern of life or to subordinate local interests to those of a larger group. Unfortunately, there is no direct evidence about the political ideas of this early period, and it is a little dangerous to reason back from the documents of a later period. But it seems fairly clear that religion was an important basis for political organization. Agricultural communities are especially dependent on and especially conscious of natural forces; from a very early date these forces were personified and worshiped. The sun-god or sky-god, the water- or river-god, the earth-god or the goddess of fertility, were appeased by elaborate rituals to insure that the weather would be good and the crops abundant. The men who knew how to deal with the gods (aided, perhaps, by skill in predicting weather and harvests) had great prestige and influence. They could demand obedience in the name of the gods and call their orders divine commands. And once an able leader had established a new and tighter form of organization in one center he would have a great advantage over other communities in his neighborhood. Thus many scattered villages might be combined under one man's control.

It is certain that the first rulers about whom we have any information relied on their religious position to enforce their political authority. The king might be the chief priest of the gods of his district; he might claim divine ancestry; he might even be considered a god himself. In any case, he was closer to the gods than were ordinary mortals. He knew what the gods wanted, and in their name he could demand the goods and the services which made it possible to establish governments, build cities, and encourage specialization in the crafts and arts.

Egypt

The earliest cities were in Mesopotamia, but the first great kingdom of the ancient world was in Egypt. There are several possible explanations of this different rate of political development, all connected with the geography of the two regions. Egypt, except for its seacoast, is surrounded by deserts, and for many centuries it was free from invasion and war. Thus, once the process of consolidation had started in

Ancient Egypt 1450 B.C.

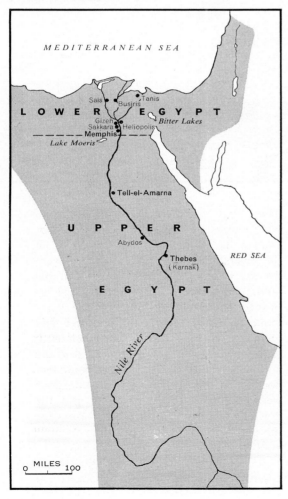

MEDITERRANEAN SEA

Sais • • Busiris • Tanis

LOWER EGYPT

Gizeh
Sakkara • • Heliopolis
Memphis
Lake Moeris

Bitter Lakes

• Tell-el-Amarna

UPPER

Abydos

• Thebes
(Karnak)

RED SEA

EGYPT

Nile River

0 MILES 100

Egypt it was not slowed down or reversed by outside forces, as it was in Mesopotamia. The Nile, even more than the Tigris-Euphrates, required large-scale planning if its waters were to be used effectively. In the long narrow upper valley there were no tributaries or branches; in order to irrigate any large amount of land, the water had to be led from the main stream and carried considerable distances. In the shorter but broader lower valley, or delta, the river divided into many channels and made much of the ground swampy. Local drainage was not very efficient because the ground was so flat. Here again only if several villages combined their efforts could they reclaim large amounts of land.

Egyptian Government

In the earliest period of Egyptian history there were many small kingdoms, but this phase lasted a relatively short time. Gradually they were consolidated, until at last a kingdom of Upper Egypt emerged in the long valley, and a kingdom of Lower Egypt in the delta. The two kingdoms were united about 3500 B.C., and from that time on Egypt almost always formed a single political and economic unit. On a few occasions weak rulers allowed the country to fall apart, but each time a new dynasty restored unity. In this respect Egypt differed markedly from Mesopotamia, where no large kingdom lasted for more than a few centuries.

Once established, the main features of Egyptian society changed very little during the thirty centuries which followed. A centralized government served by many agents controlled both the political and the economic life of the country. The supreme authority was the king, who was incomparably greater than any of his subjects and was on intimate terms with the gods; in fact, he was a god himself. He owned all the land in the country and could demand services from all men. He preserved the well-being of Egypt, and in return Egypt gave him wealth, power, and, as far as it could, immortality.

The Search for Immortality

The rapid development of royal power in Egypt is unusual; even more unusual is the early interest of the Egyptians in the afterlife. Other peoples came very slowly to the conviction that the individual personality could survive death, but the Egyptians believed wholeheartedly in immortality from the time of the first united kingdom. They wanted it passionately, and they feared that it was to be attained only through elaborate rituals and expensive funerals. Since they thought of the afterlife as a physical prolongation of life on earth, they believed that the body had to be preserved, and with it all the material things which might be needed on the long journey to the Land of the Dead. The soul had to be enlightened, guided, and interceded for with the gods—hence the great tombs, of which the pyramids are only the most striking example, the priceless furniture and elaborately decorated funeral chambers, the religious texts endlessly repeated on the walls of the tomb and on the wrappings of the body. A king could be reasonably sure of obtaining all this, especially if he began his preparations early in life, and the great men of his court had some chance, especially if they were aided by the favor of the king. But the ordinary Egyptian, for many centuries, had little hope. Only late in Egyptian history did religious ideas rise to a level where a few sacred texts rather than elaborate funeral furnishings were thought sufficient to ensure survival. With this lowering of funeral costs lesser men could at last hope to attain immortality.

This great interest in the afterlife obviously implied a great interest in religion.

Complete ? utter power of pharaohs

Egyptian Religion

14TH CENTURY B.C.

a. Morality and the Last Judgment in the Book of the Dead.

Hail to you, ye gods. . . . Behold, I came to you without sin, without evil, without wrong. . . . I gave bread to the hungry, water to the thirsty, clothing to the naked, and a ferry to him without a boat. I made divine offerings for the gods and food offerings for the dead. Save me! Protect me!

From James H. Breasted, *The Dawn of Conscience* (New York: Scribner, 1934), pp. 259, 284–85.

b. Monotheism in the hymn to the sun-god (Aton). This was written during the brief period when King Ikhnaton (1376–1362 B.C.) was trying to establish the cult of a single sun-god.

How manifold are thy works!
They are hidden before men.
O sole God, beside whom is no other,
Thou didst create the earth according to thy heart . . .
Thou didst make the distant sky in order to rise therein,
In order to behold all that thou hast made
While thou wast yet alone.
Shining in thy form as living Aton,
Dawning, glittering, going afar and returning.
Thou makest millions of forms
Through thyself alone.

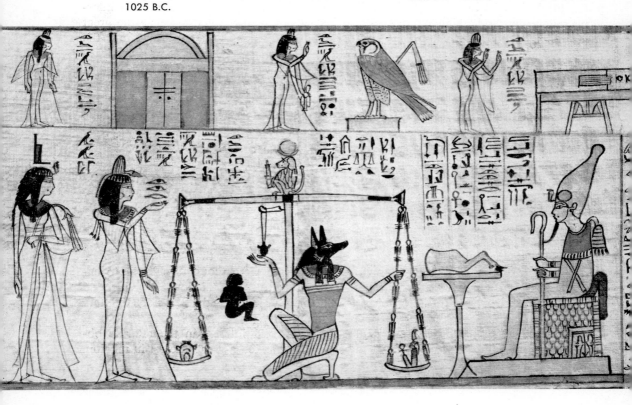

Book of the Dead: The gods judge an Egyptian princess. Osiris (seated) acts as judge, Anubis weighs the heart of the princess, Isis (extreme left) stands behind her. From a funerary papyrus of 1025 B.C.

Egypt had many gods and many temples, each with a large and well-organized priesthood. Each district had its own divinities, often represented in the form of animals, such as the bull, the crocodile, or the cat. The consolidation of the upper and lower kingdoms led to a merging of the local gods and the establishment of a small group of major divinities. Amen-Ra, the sun-god, eventually became the most important, but Egypt as a whole never reached the stage of monotheism, though some kings about 1400 B.C. grasped the idea. They were overridden by conservative priests, and Egypt reverted to polytheism. On the other hand, during the second millennium before Christ Egyptian religion did acquire an ethical content which was at first lacking. Wealth and semimagic rituals were no longer enough to ensure salvation, and righteous behavior became one of the necessary conditions for immortality. The gods were interested in human conduct; there was a final judgment in which the fate of each soul was determined. As more emphasis was placed on the value of ethical behavior, burials became less elaborate and costly, although Egyptians continued to spend more on funerals than most of their contemporaries in the Near East.

Artists and Artisans

Centralized government and a highly developed religion must have made the keeping of records necessary at an early date. The king wanted to know what his officials were doing; the priests wanted to preserve rituals which were pleasing to the gods. The Egyptians were one of the first peoples to develop a system of writing, but, as in several other fields, they failed to carry their invention through to its logical conclusion. Egyptian hieroglyphs were at first schematized pictures of concrete objects; then they were used to represent syllables and abstract ideas;

Egyptian scribes, ca. 1350 B.C. They are obviously in the presence of a great man and are writing to his dictation.

A hieroglyphic sign, more elaborate than most, meaning "millions of years," from an Egyptian shrine, ca. 500–350 B.C. Even at this late date, the convention is observed by which the torso faces the observer though the head is in profile.

tians than we have about any other people before 2000 B.C.

The king, the government officials, and the priests profited most from the centralized control of all aspects of Egyptian life. The common people, peasants and artisans, were protected, most of the time, from internal and external violence. This security, plus careful regulation of the waters of the Nile, assured them an adequate supply of food, but few of them had anything more than the bare essentials of life. Wealth was funneled to the king, who kept what he wanted and distributed the rest to his own servants and to the servants of the gods. It was this concentration of wealth that made possible the great buildings and the magnificent art of the Egyptian kingdom. The pyramids represent the labor of thousands of men for many decades; the great statues of kings and gods, carved out of the hardest stone, such as diorite, must have kept individual artisans busy for years at a time. Gold was scarce in Egypt, yet the few unpillaged tombs which have been discovered contain an almost incredible profusion of goldsmiths' work. Nothing was too good for the gods, and for the king, who was a god on earth.

In a country where monarchy and religion were both so venerated, art was solemn, massive, and monumental. Egyptian architects and sculptors often tried to produce their effects through sheer size and mass—witness the crowded pillars of the temple at Karnak, or the colossal statue of the Sphinx. They also had a sense of proportion and balance, and the style of much of their work is as impressive as its size. Rather formal and conventional at first, their sculpture and painting became increasingly realistic by the middle of the second millennium B.C. The actual features of many Egyptian kings and queens have been preserved in stone; they look down at us as individuals; not as general-

Hypostyle Hall, Temple of Amen-Ra at Karnak, built by Seti I and Ramses II, 13th century B.C. Notice how the huge, closely ranked pillars swallow up space and dwarf the observer.

but they never developed into an alphabet. Nevertheless, the Egyptians succeeded in writing down a great deal of their knowledge in this rather clumsy script: official records and long religious texts, stories, and semihistorical narratives. They inscribed the most important documents on stone; others they wrote on papyrus, the earliest form of paper, made from the reeds of the river swamps. Thanks to the dry, warm climate of the region, a great many of these records have survived, giving us more information about the Egyp-

The Sphinx at Giza, ca. 2900 B.C., with the pyramids in the background.

ized symbols of royalty. This much immortality, at least, the Egyptian rulers gained in their search for survival after death.

Egyptian artists and artisans had to solve many technical problems in order to work on the scale that they did. It is obvious, for example, that the pyramids could not have been built without using mechanical devices such as levers and inclined planes. The sculptors, who carved what were probably the first free-standing statues in the world, had to know something about the proportions of the human body and the techniques of cutting and polishing stone. Goldsmiths, painters, and glass-workers likewise had great technical skill. The Egyptians made very fine cloth; they

were also among the first to discover the art of making bronze tools and weapons. To use the waters of the Nile effectively, they had to work out many of the principles of engineering; to maintain permanent boundaries in fields which were regularly flooded, they had to learn something about geometry and surveying. They were early interested in developing a calendar based on the solar year, and what is perhaps the first recorded date in history comes from Egypt. If it has been correctly interpreted, it would be the equivalent of 4241 B.C. in our system of chronology.

Yet the Egyptians, after a remarkably early start, developed their ideas and techniques rather slowly, and were often

surpassed by their neighbors. Excessive centralization and the influence of a conservative and powerful priesthood discouraged innovation. Observance of established forms seemed to ensure the favor of the gods and the prosperity of the ruling classes. For example, there was a strong tendency toward monotheism in Egyptian religion about 1400 B.C., but when the king, Ikhnaton (1376–1362 B.C.), tried to make monotheism into an official religion, he was completely defeated by the priests of the old gods. Again, although Egyptian hieroglyphs started at a very early date, it was the Semites of the Sinai-Palestine region who developed an alphabet out of earlier forms of writing. The Egyptians must have known some principles of geometry and mechanics at the time of the building of the pyramids, but it was the Babylonians who laid the foundations of the science of mathematics. Even in art this conservatism is evident. Egyptian sculptors adhered to their old conventions, even when their technical ability made change possible. Thus sculptured bodies were always shown facing the observer, even when the heads were in profile. In short, Egyptian civilization was conservative and at times almost stagnant. It preserved a unique way of life, but it did not encourage new forms of organization or new ideas.

Mesopotamia

Civilization probably developed earlier in the Tigris-Euphrates Valley than in Egypt, but we know less about the early states of Mesopotamia than we do about the first Egyptian kingdom. There was no stone in the great Mesopotamian plain, and cities and monuments made of sun-dried brick did not survive as well as the stone constructions of Egypt. Moreover, there was less political stability in the Tigris-Euphrates region than in the Nile Valley. It was easier for small states to preserve their autonomy and to attain local self-sufficiency in the wide stretches of Mesopotamia than it was in the narrow Egyptian valley. Finally, the rich Mesopotamian plain, unguarded by deserts, was open to invasion on almost every side. To the east, north, and west lay regions which, though less fertile than the river valley, could still support fairly large human groups. The peoples of these border regions repeatedly attempted to settle in, or to conquer, the Mesopotamian plain. Archaeologists are only beginning to discover the great cities and kingdoms that were obliterated by war and forgotten by later generations. On the other hand, while war and conquest often caused a sharp decline in civilization, the constant influx of new peoples and new rulers had a stimulating effect. Not all invaders brought in new ideas and new techniques, but those who did ensured that the peoples of western Asia would be far less conservative and far more diversified in their ways of life than were the people of Egypt.

Early Mesopotamia   *ca.* 1900 B.C.

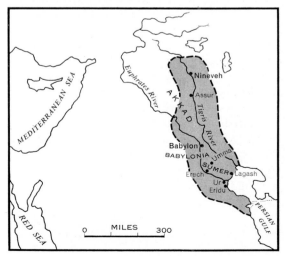

Early Political Developments

Civilization in Mesopotamia began with the appearance of small city-states. They were founded by people known as the Sumerians, who may have come from the hill region north of the Mesopotamian plain. The typical Sumerian city was fortified for defense; within its walls were the temples of the gods, the residences of the ruler and his assistants, the shops of traders and craftsmen. It was the religious, political, and economic center of the surrounding countryside, from which it drew its supplies. Every city had its god, who was the guardian of its welfare and the ultimate owner of its land. The ruler derived his authority from the fact that he was the chief servant of the god, but his power was more limited than was the power of the Egyptian king. Although theoretically all the land was owned by the city's god, there was in fact private property beyond the ruler's control. And, at least in the early period, the king had to pay some attention to the wishes of leading citizens, for he could not count on their unquestioning obedience.

This stage of small kingdoms, which came so early in Egyptian history that we have only fragmentary evidence of its existence, persisted for centuries in Mesopotamia. The cities remained independent, or loosely associated with one another; only occasionally was a strong ruler able to bring several of them under his control. After 2900 B.C. the king of Ur commanded the largest state, but his authority never extended throughout the entire valley.

The endless bickering among the Sumerian cities weakened them for attacks by their neighbors, the Semites. The Semites were probably living in the Tigris-Euphrates Valley before the Sumerians; certainly they were numerous in Syria and other border regions. From about 2600 to about 2000 B.C. there was a seesaw of

A Sumerian votive figure, ca. 3000 B.C.

power between Semites and Sumerians. First the Semites conquered and united most of the valley; then the Sumerians regained their independence, with Ur again the most prominent city; and finally a wave of Semitic invaders from Syria permanently ended Sumerian power. A new kingdom was founded which included all of lower Mesopotamia and even some of the adjacent regions, such as Assyria. The Semites established their capital at Babylon, and from that time on the lower Tigris-Euphrates Valley was known as Babylonia.

The wars that swept over Mesopotamia left individual cities in smoking ruins, but they did not alter the basic pattern of civilization. The Semitic conquerors took over the urban organization and the culture of their new subjects and made relatively few innovations. Thus, in spite of the rise and fall of individual kingdoms and the frequent movements of peoples, the old civilization of Mesopotamia was fairly uniform in all parts of the valley.

Mesopotamian Law

The most striking feature of this civilization was the rapid development of commerce and of law. Most of the people were peasant farmers, as they were in every other early civilization, but there were many merchants as well. With civilized and half-civilized peoples on every side, Mesopotamia had more contacts with and more influence on her neighbors than did Egypt. We know that goods from the Tigris-Euphrates Valley reached Syria, Asia Minor, and Egypt, and that the merchants of Mesopotamia probably traded with India as well. Moreover, although the power of the kings steadily increased, they did not attempt to monopolize trade and they respected private property. The very fact that men could acquire wealth tended to stimulate the growth of commerce.

The members of an active business community are constantly making and breaking contracts, setting up and dissolving partnerships, seeking and granting loans. In response to the need for rules to regulate these relationships, the Mesopotamians developed a system of commercial law. The individual had more initiative and freedom than he had in Egypt, but this meant that he was freer to do harm as well as good. In order to preserve social order, the kings found that they had to suppress violence and fraud, and even at times to protect the poor against the rich. Thus, we also find a system of criminal law taking shape, and we have several law-codes dating from the period from 2200 to 1900 B.C. The best known is the code of Hammurabi, who ruled the Babylonian kingdom about 1900 B.C. His laws are strict—they include the famous rule of "an eye for an eye"—

King Hammurabi receives his law-code from the sun-god Shamash, ca. 2100 B.C.

but they do attempt to grade penalties according to the seriousness of the offense. Burglary was punished by death, and simple theft by a heavy fine. "If a man steals from a priest or a prince, he shall restore it thirtyfold, but from a freeman, tenfold." The laws also reveal a rather complex society, with well-defined social classes and an active business life. The idea of justice is emerging, though still in rather crude form.

At a very early date the Sumerians developed an effective system of writing. They used a reed cut at an angle to make wedge-shaped marks on a tablet of soft clay; hence the writing is called cuneiform, from the Latin *cuneus* (wedge). Since it was difficult with these materials to make pictures corresponding to words, the Sumerians soon began to ascribe arbitrary values to certain signs. Each sign at first represented a word; then each one came to stand for a syllable. There were several hundred of these signs, but, while they were simpler than hieroglyphs, they never became a true alphabet. Nevertheless, cuneiform writing had one great advantage: it produced permanent records easily and quickly. For ordinary transactions the clay tablet was sun-dried; for important matters it was baked in a kiln. The thousands of tablets that have survived furnish us with information about every aspect of life in Mesopotamia—business, government, law, religion, literature, and science. Cuneiform writing survived centuries of conquest and migration, and it was used by most inhabitants of western Asia down to a few hundred years before the birth of Christ. This persistence was due in part to the intellectual prestige of the Babylonians, in part to their dominant position in commerce. But it was also due to the flexibility of a system of writing that could be adapted easily to new languages and new ideas.

Cuneiform clay tablet found in Egypt, ca. 2100 B.C. A receipt for oil to be used in a temple.

Mesopotamian Culture

The Mesopotamians made their chief intellectual contributions in literature and in science. Some famous stories appear for the first time in Sumerian or Babylonian epics—for example, the story of the flood which almost extinguished life on earth. In science, the Babylonians were especially interested in mathematics and astronomy. Their system of measurement, based on multiples and factors of sixty, still influences us today. We reckon twenty-four hours to the day, sixty minutes to an hour or to a degree of longitude, 360 degrees to a circle, and so on. They also were able to solve rather complicated arithmetical and geometrical problems, and apparently they even had some notions about algebraic processes. They based their calender on the phases of the moon, but realized that a year composed of twelve lunar months was too short, since the sun would not then be back in the position it had occupied when the cycle began. To overcome this difficulty they introduced an extra month from time to time, and so obtained a fairly close approximation of a solar calendar. They observed and noted the positions of stars and the movements of planets. Babylonian scientific texts are difficult to interpret, and we are still not sure of the Babylonians' level of accomplishment, but it is clear that other peoples of the ancient world, especially the Greeks, acquired their basic ideas of mathematics and astronomy from Babylonian sources.

In art and religion the early Mesopotamians were less imaginative than the people of Egypt. Their sculpture was neither monumental nor realistic; the figures are short and squat, with little of the majesty or the individualism of the best Egyptian work. Their architecture was more impressive, at least in size. They built luxurious palaces for their kings and great temples for their gods. Their most striking construction was the ziggurat, a sort of artificial hill dedicated to the chief god of the city. The ziggurat looked like a series of cubes of diminishing size placed on top of each other, with ramps or steps leading from one terrace to the next. On the flat top was the shrine of the god. These great mounds rising from the plain must have been very impressive; the Biblical story of the Tower of Babel, which almost reached heaven, probably describes a ziggurat and shows how this type of building struck a neighboring people.

Mesopotamians were a practical people, and their religion was concerned primarily with material well-being. If the gods were properly approached, they would protect the cities and ensure good crops. There was a good deal of magic and very little morality in religious observances. It was more important to know the right prayers and the right sacrifices than to lead an upright life. A few great kings and leaders might achieve real immortality in the heaven reserved for the gods, but the ordinary man could look forward only to a shadowy existence in the underworld. Thus the idea of future rewards and punishments played little role in Babylonian religion; the favor of the gods was manifested by success and wealth in this life, not in the next. Of the many gods and goddesses the most important ones controlled the weather and the fertility of land and animals. The belief that each king was the servant of some god was probably one reason for the growth of royal authority from 2900 to 1900 B.C. The victory of a king was a victory for his god, and the extension of the boundaries of a kingdom meant an extension of the area in which its god was recognized as the chief divinity. Thus the religious system eventually permitted social organization on a fairly large scale, since obedience to the ruler was obedience to the god and conquest was a sign of divine approval. But as political units grew larger and the authority of the ruler greater, there was less and less opportunity for the individual to exercise his conscience or his judgment.

New Peoples and Ideas in the Near East

After 1900 B.C., both the Egyptian and the Mesopotamian kingdoms were beset by a series of invasions. It is hard to discover the origins of the new peoples who appeared at this time, since most of them had not yet reached the city-building stage and left few traces of their early activities. They were probably border-dwellers, people who lived on the fringes of the great river-valley civilizations and learned enough from their contacts to organize and arm themselves. Egypt was conquered about 1800 B.C. by the Hyksos, or shepherd-kings, apparently a group of nomads who came into the Nile Valley through the Sinai Desert. Babylonia was temporarily occupied by the Hittites and was then (soon after 1800 B.C.) taken over by the Kassites, a hill people from the northeast.

Neither the Hyksos kings nor the Kassite invaders destroyed the civilizations of the lands they conquered. Attracted by the luxuries of the wealthy river valleys, they chose instead to preserve existing patterns of organization and production as far as they could. But if they were not destructive, neither were they constructive. Both Egyptian and Babylonian civilization stagnated under these foreign rulers. Only when the Hyksos kings were displaced by a native dynasty about 1580 B.C. did Egypt again play a major role in the Near East. Babylonia had even longer to wait, for the Kassite domination lasted until 1100 B.C.

But war and conquest were not the only signs of the spread of civilization beyond its old centers in the river valleys. Many peoples were now organizing on a large scale, building cities, making written records, and developing religious and artistic ideas. The oldest and in many ways the most interesting of these new centers of civilization was on the island of Crete. Here the Minoans (named for King Minos, who was famous in Greek legend) had developed a remarkably sophisticated and elegant way of life. Because the Minoans were closely connected with the Greeks and influenced early Greek civilization they will be discussed in more detail when we consider the origins of Greek society (p. 36). But it is worth remembering that Minoan civilization was flourishing before 2000 B.C., and that it remained vigorous while Egypt and Mesopotamia were in the doldrums of foreign rule.

The Indo-Europeans

It was also around 2000 B.C. that the Indo-European peoples first began to make contact with the old centers of civilization. The Indo-Europeans formed a linguistic but not an ethnic group—that is, they all spoke languages derived from a common stock, though they might be of different races. Since thought is greatly influenced by language, people who have similar vocabularies, grammars, and sentence structures tend to have the same ideas. This was roughly true of the various Indo-European-speaking groups, especially in such matters as religion and social organization. But the fact that they could understand one another better than they could their non-Indo-European neighbors did not mean that they cooperated any better. In fact, the peoples of the Indo-European language group have usually fought each other more energetically than they have complete strangers.

The original home of the first Indo-Europeans was probably the western Russian plain. From this center they spread

✧✧✧✧✧✧✧✧✧✧✧✧✧✧✧✧✧✧✧✧✧✧✧✧✧✧✧✧✧✧✧✧

Race

Race and language are not the same. This should be obvious, for not all who speak Arabic are Arabians and not all who speak English are of the White race. . . . A man's hereditary features and the language he speaks depend on two different sets of circumstances. His hereditary anatomy depends upon his remote ancestors, and his language depends upon the speech he heard as a child.

A race does not move forward as a whole. . . . Race is not a touchstone by which civilized people can be separated from uncivilized. . . . The lesson of history is that pre-eminence in cultural achievement has passed from one race to another, from one continent to another; it has embraced not whole "races" but certain fragments of an ethnic group which were for certain historical reasons favorably situated at the moment.

From Ruth Benedict, *Race: Science and Politics* (New York: Viking, 1945), Ch. 2, pp. 9, 18.

✧✧✧✧✧✧✧✧✧✧✧✧✧✧✧✧✧✧✧✧✧✧✧✧✧✧✧✧✧✧✧✧

out in all directions. They were among the first people to use horses in combat, which gave them an advantage in warfare, and they seem to have been skillful political organizers. They eventually assumed control of lands stretching from Ireland to India and imposed their language on their subjects. In this process of dispersion and mingling with other peoples their original language began to change, breaking up into a number of dialects which were the ancestors of Celtic, Germanic, Italic (Latin), Greek, Slavic, Persian, and Sanskrit (in India).

By the first millennium before Christ, Europe was almost completely occupied by groups speaking Indo-European languages. Only a few isolated islands of older languages survived. But the Celts in France and the British Isles, the Germans in Germany and Scandinavia, and even the Latins in Italy had little contact with the early civilizations of the East. On the other hand, the Indo-European groups who moved south and east had greater opportunities to learn. As they occupied Greece, and even more as they pushed into Asia Minor, Persia, and India, they had many contacts with Near Eastern peoples and they learned rapidly from them.

The first group under Indo-European leadership to play a prominent role in Near-Eastern affairs was the Hittites. Only in the last four decades have archaeologists produced solid evidence of their activities, and many details of their history are still obscure. They probably entered Asia Minor from the west and established a strong kingdom in the central part of the peninsula. Their first notable accomplishment was the great raid on Babylonia which so weakened that kingdom that it later fell to the Kassites. But the expedition was a raid, not a conquest; the Hittites withdrew to Asia Minor where they founded a powerful military federation. They probably took over existing communities and developed into a military aristocracy ruling a large native population. They

The Hittite and the Egyptian Empires *ca.* 1450 B.C.

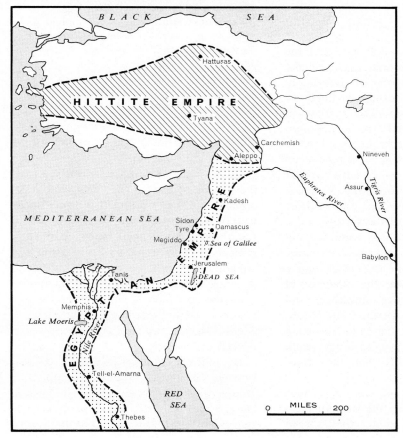

united under the leadership of their king in time of war, but otherwise they permitted a good deal of local autonomy.

Although the Hittites ruled only the central part of Asia Minor and northern Syria in the period around 1500 B.C., they were the strongest military power in the Near East. This predominance was due in part to their discovery of methods of smelting and working iron. Among the first people to make weapons of this metal, they had a distinct advantage over opponents armed only with bronze. They also may have introduced the horse to western Asia; at least they made effective use of horse-drawn chariots to break through the ranks of enemy infantry. These military innovations were eventually copied by their neighbors, and after 1500 B.C. the Hittites began to lose their dominant position.

The chief contributions of the Hittites were in the arts of war and politics. They built an effective army and found a solution, though only partially successful, to the problem of ruling an empire made up of many different peoples. Their sculpture was heavy and rough, but it incorporated certain motifs that spread throughout most ancient civilizations. Thus the long processions of figures, the winged lion, and the two-headed eagle were copied by Assyrians, Persians, Indians, and Greeks. Even in our own century the two-headed eagle was a symbol of empire for both Austria and Russia. Like their neighbors, they had many gods and goddesses, but their chief deity was the Mother Goddess of Asia Minor. Finally, the Hittites adapted and transmitted to western Asia Minor, and thus eventually to the Greeks, many of the ideas and techniques of Babylonia and its neighbors.

Other Indo-European groups, notably the Greeks and Persians, entered the Near East around 2000 B.C., but they were not yet strong enough to play a leading role in

A Hittite warrior.

the area. Instead, it was the revived Egyptian kingdom which challenged the power of the Hittites. In the sixteenth century B.C. the Egyptians drove out their Hyksos rulers and pursued them into Palestine and Syria. Perhaps they merely wished to crush their former masters; perhaps they hoped to establish a buffer zone to protect themselves from future invasions. In any case, the Egyptian kings were soon trying to add Syria to their dominions, and this bid for empire involved them in a long struggle with the Hittites. Neither side could win a complete victory, and in the end the contestants had to adopt the reasonable solution of dividing the disputed area between

The Near East *ca.* 1200 B.C.

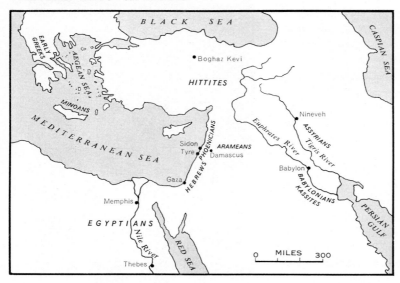

them. By this time both Hittites and Egyptians had been seriously weakened. The Hittite state collapsed soon after 1200 B.C., and Egypt entered a long period of decline.

The Semites: Small, Independent States

Disastrous as the Egyptian-Hittite struggle was to both participants, it probably stimulated the exchange of ideas and techniques throughout the ancient world. Egypt was less isolated than it had been before; it borrowed such devices as the war-chariot and in turn spread Egyptian culture through southern Syria. Neither the Egyptians nor the Hittites could ignore or annihilate the small states which lay between the heartlands of their empires. Each might form alliances with them, or reduce them to the position of subject principalities; each might try to stir up disaffection and revolt in states that joined the other empire. But such attempts required a knowledge of local conditions and a continuing diplomatic effort. The Tell-el-

Amarna letters, a collection of diplomatic documents of Egyptian kings of the fourteenth century B.C., show how internationalized Near Eastern society had become, at least at the level of the ruling classes. Though these letters were written by Egyptian kings to rulers in western Asia, the script is cuneiform, not hieroglyphic, and the language is Babylonian, not Egyptian.

This spreading of a common stock of ideas throughout the whole Near East, combined with the collapse of Egyptian and Hittite power, gave an opportunity to many of the smaller communities in the area to develop new ideas and techniques. Civilization was no longer confined to a few major centers. With the development of international relations went a rapid expansion of commerce, and all the Near East was tied together by trade routes. Small communities could now draw on the whole area for physical and intellectual necessities. The rise of three related peoples— the Phoenicians, the Aramaeans, and the

1 / The Ancient Near East

Hebrews—shows how important some of these small groups could be.

The Phoenicians were a Semitic people who settled along the Syrian coast before 2000 B.C., founded cities at such seaports as Tyre and Sidon, and gradually became expert in shipbuilding and navigation. Subject first to Babylonia and then to Egypt, their great opportunity came with the collapse of the Egyptian Empire in 1200 B.C. They expanded rapidly westward across the Mediterranean and founded many colonies (see map, p. 43) the most famous of which was Carthage, near modern Tunis. They pushed on to Morocco and Spain and then explored the Atlantic coasts of Europe and Africa. They traveled as far as Britain in search of tin, a voyage which many later Mediterranean seamen shunned because of the rough Atlantic waters. Later on they were hired by an Egyptian king to determine how far south Africa extended. According to tradition, they circumnavigated the continent and returned to Egypt by way of the Red Sea. Given their skill and determination, there is nothing improbable in this report. The Phoenicians were the great sailors of antiquity, even surpassing the Greeks, and it was not until the fourteenth and fifteenth centuries A.D. that European seamen began to equal their exploits.

The Phoenicians were also responsible for perfecting and popularizing the alphabet. They probably did not invent it, for the first attempts at developing a simplified system of writing seem to have been made by other Semites in the Sinai region. But the Phoenicians were quick to see the advantages of being able to express all sounds by means of a small number of characters, and they developed an alphabet of twenty-two letters which was copied by many other peoples. Even though it had signs only for consonants (the Greeks added the vowel signs later), the Phoeni-

cian alphabet was still a great improvement over cuneiform and hieroglyphic writing. It took less space, was easier to write and to read, and simplified the problem of adding new words and concepts to a language. Almost anyone could learn to read and write with an alphabet; both business and scholarship profited from being able to dispense with the specially trained clerks who had been needed for earlier forms of writing.

The Aramaeans, like the Phoenicians, were a Semitic people greatly interested in commerce. About 1600 B.C. they settled in southern Syria along the trade route which led from upper Mesopotamia to Egypt. One of their chief cities was Damascus. Just as the Phoenicians were the chief traders by sea, so the Aramaeans dominated the overland caravan routes. Because they played such an important role in trade, and also because they adopted the alphabet from their Phoenician neighbors, the Aramaean language became the international language of western Asia. It was used for business and diplomacy, and was even accepted as the mother tongue of neighboring peoples such as the Hebrews. Thus Jesus and the disciples spoke Aramaic rather than Hebrew. By the birth of Christ, the Aramaic alphabet and language had driven cuneiform and the older Babylonian languages out of much of the Near East.

The Hebrews were the third Semitic group to appear in the narrow corridor between the Syrian Desert and the eastern Mediterranean. They had been nomads, wandering in the desolate regions east and south of Palestine. Some of them probably entered Palestine directly from the desert, but according to tradition one group had lived in Egypt and had been led out across the Sinai Desert by Moses. Palestine was already occupied by other peoples—the Canaanites and Philistines—and the Hebrews struggled for many years before they could establish themselves in their new home. At first only a loose confederation of tribes, they had more success after they organized a kingdom under Saul and David (*ca.* 1000 B.C.). David's son, Solomon (*ca.* 960 B.C.), was so powerful that both the Phoenicians and the Egyptians sought him as an ally, but this brief period of political glory soon passed. After Solomon's death, the Hebrew kingdom split into two segments and neither had any weight in Near Eastern politics. The northern kingdom of Israel was conquered by the Assyrians in 721 B.C., and most of its inhabitants lost their identity as a separate people. The southern kingdom of Judah preserved a precarious existence until 586 B.C., when it fell to Babylonia. But by this time the people of Judah, the Jews, had developed such a distinctive religion that they could not be absorbed by their conquerors. Of all the peoples of the ancient Near East, they alone have survived as a recognizable group to the present day.

The survival of the Jews was due to the fact that their greatest and most successful efforts were devoted to religion, not politics. Like their neighbors, the Jews had had a tribal god, Yahweh or Jehovah, who was supposed to protect them and give them prosperity. Their religious practices were not at first very elevated; they appeased their god with sacrifices and the observance of certain taboos, and in return expected worldly success. But gradually they began to develop a higher concept of the relation between man and God. Though it was always a temptation in times of trouble to sacrifice to other gods in the hope of regaining divine favor, the Hebrews in the end rejected this practice. They remained true to Yahweh in defeat as well as in victory; they were the first people to develop a strict monotheism which left no place for other divinities. At the same time they be-

gan to think of their God as something more than a local deity walking in thunder on the Judaean hills. He became the Creator of the world, the Lord and Judge of all mankind. He was too great to be represented by images or appeased by semimagical rituals; he was Power and Justice which surpassed human understanding.

With this more elevated idea of God went a corresponding advance in ethical ideas. The Jews had long believed that right conduct was pleasing to God, but their idea of right conduct had been legalistic and formalistic. They had picked up the old Babylonian phrase of "an eye for an eye and a tooth for a tooth"; they expected earthly and immediate rewards in return for good behavior. But in the troubled times of the divided kingdoms, threatened by outside enemies and harassed by internal social pressures, they came to realize that formal justice was not enough and that worldly prosperity often went to evil men. They developed the idea of sin, of an inner weakness which was just as hateful to God as open lawbreaking. This was the period of the great prophets —Isaiah, Jeremiah, and others—who spiritualized the Hebrew idea of God and purified their ethical standards. They spoke of mercy and humility as well as justice; they urged the rich to be generous and the strong to be forbearing. "What does the Lord require?" said Micah. "Only to do justice and to love kindness and to walk humbly with your God."

This strong prophetic tradition ensured the survival of the Jewish religion even after Jerusalem had fallen and its people had been deported. Most other conquered and uprooted peoples quickly lost their faith and their identity, blaming their gods for their misfortunes and transferring their loyalty to the gods of the conquerors. But the prophets blamed the sins of the people and the iniquities of the rulers; they would

The Assyrian Empire *ca.* 700 B.C.

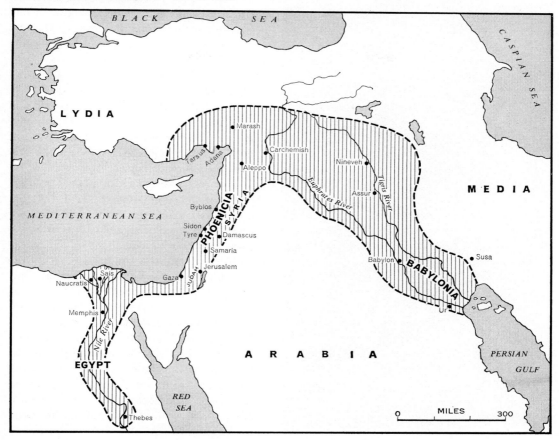

not challenge the will of God, whose ways passed human understanding. They saw hope for the future if the people, purified by tribulation, remained true to their faith. They began to speak of a Messiah who would come to redeem his people. Thus the Jewish community, scattered throughout the Near East, retained its belief. It became somewhat rigid in its ritual and legalistic in its moral code after the age of the great prophets had passed. But it retained its emphasis on the frailty and helplessness of man, on the omnipotence and loving-kindness of God, and on high ethical standards. Judaism influenced many people who were not Jews, and prepared the way for the rise of both Christianity and Islam.

The Rise of New Empires

The period of independent small states, which had followed the collapse of the Egyptian and Hittite empires, was succeeded in turn by a new period of empire-building.

The Assyrians

The first of the new empires was created by the Assyrians, a people who lived on

Bas-relief from Sargon's palace, 8th century B.C. Winged genie with eagle's head sprinkling lustral water to keep off demons.

and Egypt. They enforced their rule by a deliberate policy of frightfulness, enslaving and deporting whole peoples, and torturing and killing thousands of captives. The Old Testament speaks eloquently of the panic caused by the approach of the Assyrians: "the people coming from the northland . . . cruel and pitiless, the sound of them is like that of the sea when it roars, and they ride upon horses" (Jeremiah 6). It is equally emphatic about the tremendous relief which was felt when the Assyrian Empire collapsed.

The Assyrians were cruel and militaristic but not unintelligent. Realizing that they owed much to earlier civilizations, their kings made great collections of cuneiform tablets which included much of the knowledge of the Sumerians and the Babylonians. This interest in the past, this desire to preserve ancient knowledge, was not peculiar to the Assyrians. By the beginning of the first millennium B.C., most Near Eastern peoples realized that civilization had existed for a long time and that it was both interesting and profitable to consult old records. But the Assyrians, thanks to their wide conquests and efficient government, had greater opportunities to build up large libraries.

Assyrian sculpture reflects many of the characteristics of the people. Strong, harsh, and realistic, it delights in scenes of war, torture, and death. There are remarkably vivid pictures of the king and his army, and even more striking reliefs of the king hunting lions from his chariot. The human figures are somewhat stiff, but no artists have ever surpassed the Assyrians in depicting animals fighting, charging, and writhing in their death agonies. There is no serenity in Assyrian art, as there is in Egyptian; there is always tension, struggle, and a longing for power.

Overexpansion and the hatred of subject peoples brought an end to the Assyrian

the upper Tigris. The Assyrians had a basically Babylonian culture, but they developed a new technique of conquest. They built up the best army the ancient world had yet seen, with long-service professional soldiers and what were probably the first effective cavalry units. They used this army to terrorize and to conquer their neighbors. The growth of Assyria began about 1100 B.C., but the empire reached the height of its power only after 700 B.C. By that time the Assyrians held most of Mesopotamia, Syria, the Palestine coast,

Assyrian relief of King Assurbanipal hunting, ca. 625 B.C., from his capital at Nineveh.

state. There simply were not enough Assyrians to garrison an empire stretching from the Nile to the borders of Persia, and their systematic cruelty had made it impossible to control conquered peoples except by force of arms. The Babylonians, anxious to regain their old supremacy, led the uprising, assisted by the Medes, a group of tribes from the Persian border. Nineveh, the capital of Assyria, fell in 612 B.C., and the Assyrian Empire dissolved overnight.

The Decline of Egypt and Babylonia

For a few decades after the collapse of Assyria there was no dominant power in the Near East. Egypt regained its independence under its last dynasty of native kings, and the small states of Syria and Asia Minor enjoyed a brief period of prosperity. The revived kingdom of Babylonia was the strongest state in the region. Under Nebudchadnezzar its influence reached into southern Syria, where he put an end to the kingdom of Judah (586 B.C.) and carried the Jewish people off into captivity in Babylon.

There was a curious autumnal quality about this early sixth-century period. The peoples who had been shorn of their former greatness were all looking backward, remembering past glories, recording old traditions, reviving archaic styles in art. Even the Jews sat by the waters of Babylon and wept, remembering Jerusalem; their prophets had to struggle mightily to convince them that they had a future as well as a past. This concentration on the past reveals that the peoples of the ancient Near East had lost some of the originality and energy which had made them the leaders of civilization for over three thousand years. They had reached a plateau from which they could not rise, and they were soon to be overcome by peoples who had gone further in organization and specialization. For over a thousand years the old Near East was to be ruled by outsiders—first the Persians, then the Greeks, then the Romans.

It is interesting to speculate on the causes of the decline of Egypt, Babylonia, and related states, though the absence of detailed records of economic and social history makes speculation dangerous. It seems likely that the great weakness of these ancient societies was their failure

Persian sculpture from Persepolis, *ca.* 500 B.C. King Darius of Persia gives audience; his son Xerxes stands behind him.

to make adequate use of their human resources. The great majority of the population were peasants, cultivating the soil for the benefit of an upper class of kings, nobles, officials, and priests. The upper class was small, because the agricultural surplus was too meager to support many people in luxury. Nor was the upper class renewed from below, for the peasants had few opportunities to gain an education or to change their occupation. Few of them could be freed from the primary obligation of cultivating the land to serve in the army, to act as officials in newly acquired territories, or to devote themselves to industry and commerce. The remarkable success of small peoples like the Phoenicians and Aramaeans, who were primarily traders, demonstrated some of the opportunities which had been missed by the older, static, agricultural societies. The rapid expansion of the Hittites and the Assyrians showed what could be accomplished by using a larger part of the population as professional soldiers, though both these empires

eventually collapsed for lack of political skill. Now the ancient Near East was to be faced with people who combined several of these missing skills—soldiers and administrators like the Persians and the Romans, or soldiers and traders like the Greeks. Persia and Greece and Rome were far from being perfect societies, but at their best each gave more opportunities to more men to develop their abilities than had any large community before.

The Persians

The Persians, the first of these new rulers of the ancient world, were related to the Medes, who had helped overthrow Assyria. About 550 B.C. the Persian king Cyrus defeated the Medes and became king of both peoples. The Medes, well treated by their new ruler, accepted him without complaint, and the united kingdom of the Medes and the Persians became the strongest power in the Near East. Cyrus moved rapidly into Asia Minor and added this region to his kingdom; next he conquered Babylonia and thrust eastward to the Indus River. His son Cambyses completed the work of conquest by taking over Egypt in 525 B.C.

The Persian Empire was the greatest that had yet existed in the Near East; it was also the best organized. Darius, who succeeded Cambyses in 522 B.C., brought about this organization by establishing a pattern of government that was to be followed by all his successors, even by the Greeks, who ultimately destroyed Persian rule. This pattern of government combined a large degree of local autonomy with careful supervision by the central government. Each of the subject peoples was allowed to keep its own customs and religion and often its own local government. Thus the Jews were permitted to return to Jerusalem and rebuild their temple, and the Phoenician trading cities continued to be ruled by Phoenician merchants. Darius made no attempt to impose his language or Persian culture on subject peoples; Aramaic remained the ordinary language of business, and Egyptian and Babylonian artists represented Darius in the traditional garb of their own ancient kings.

But this tolerance of local diversity did not imply indifference on the part of the central government. The whole empire was divided into provinces, each with a Persian governor, or satrap, who was responsible for preserving order and obedience. An

The Persian Empire *ca.* 500 B.C.

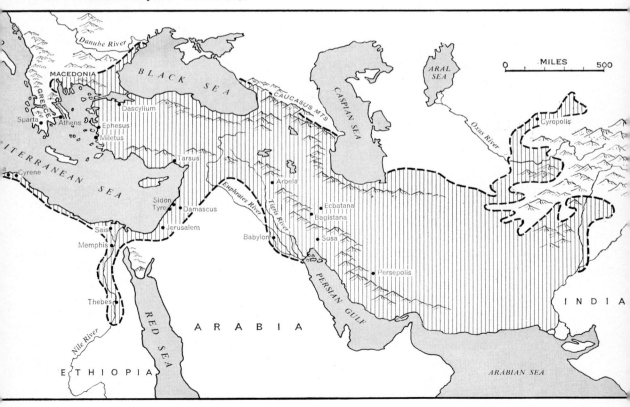

elaborate system of roads was built so that information would reach the central government quickly and troops could be moved rapidly to restless areas. A professional army was maintained, including large groups of mercenary soldiers. Military superiority was reinforced by political manipulation. The satraps supported pro-Persian parties among the local inhabitants, and received a good deal of backing from the rich, who profited from the existence of a great, peaceful trading area. These devices generally ensured peaceful acceptance of Persian rule. But when the Persians had to strike hard to repress rebellion or the threat of rebellion, they did not hesitate to take extreme measures. They deported whole nations just as their predecessors had done; they sent great armies on the long road to Greece to punish the Athenians for aiding rebellions in Asia Minor.

Persian Religion

One source of the Persians' assurance and zeal for conquest may have been their religion. The original Persian religion, like many others, began with the deification of natural forces. It eventually gave special prominence to the sun-god, Mithra, and told of his suffering, death, and resurrection. This again was nothing new, for many eastern religions symbolized the passage of the seasons from fall through winter to spring by telling of a god who was slain, buried, and rose again. But Mithra was more a soldier's god than most of his counterparts. He did not merely suffer passively; he struggled against the forces of darkness in order to protect mankind. Persian soldiers could believe that Mithra was a warrior like themselves, battling beside them in their long wars of conquest.

More sophisticated and spiritual than the popular religion of the Persians was the creed taught by Zoroaster, which was professed by the king and most of the leading families of the court. It is still not certain when Zoroaster lived—any dates between 1000 and 600 B.C. are possible. The religion that he taught may have been one of the forces which inspired Persian expansion, since it repeated and re-emphasized the old theme of eternal war between good and evil. But Zoroaster clarified and spiritualized this old idea in a way that gave it tremendous impact on Judaism, Christianity, and Islam. He taught that there was a god of good and light, Ahura Mazda, or Ormuzd, who was engaged in a perpetual struggle with a god of evil and darkness, Ahriman. Since both gods had taken part in creating the world, it was neither wholly good nor wholly evil. Man had free will, and could ally himself to either side. After thousands of years there would be a final struggle in which good would triumph. Those who had fought on the side of good would go to paradise (this is a Persian word); those who had aided evil would be consumed in fire.

Although Zoroastrianism never spread far beyond Persia, and is the creed of only a few hundred thousand people today, mostly in India, it nevertheless was one of the great religions of the world. Its dualism gave an easy explanation of one of the most difficult religious problems—how a good God can permit the existence of evil. While this solution was never accepted by orthodox Christianity, it became an ingredient of several Christian heresies. Popular concepts of the devil in the Middle Ages were not very far removed from Zoroaster's description of Ahriman. Even more influential were Zoroastrian ideas about a last judgment at which rewards and punishments would be meted out. These ideas were taken up by the Jews, who had originally had only vague notions about a future life, and through the Jews they influenced both Christian and Moslem beliefs.

Though the Persians made important innovations in government and religion, they accepted with little change most of the culture of their predecessors in the Near East. They were not particularly original in their art or their science; the first was full of Hittite and Assyrian influences, while the second was based almost entirely on Babylonian work. The Persians created favorable conditions for trade, but they were not themselves great traders, nor did they raise the level of economic activity in their empire. The bulk of the population continued to be peasants bound to the soil, and there was little large-scale industry. The Persians never learned to use their man power efficiently; in fact, as they ex-panded, opportunities for the ordinary man decreased. He became a peasant or a servant instead of a free warrior. This change had a bad effect on the army, which became more and more dependent on mercenaries, many of them not even subjects of the empire. Thus the Persian Empire, though better organized than any of its predecessors, had serious weaknesses— weaknesses that were sharply revealed when the empire came into conflict with the Greeks.

The Early Greeks and Minoans

Compared to the total population of the Persian Empire, the Greeks were a mere handful of people. Yet this handful

The Aegean World   second millennium B.C.

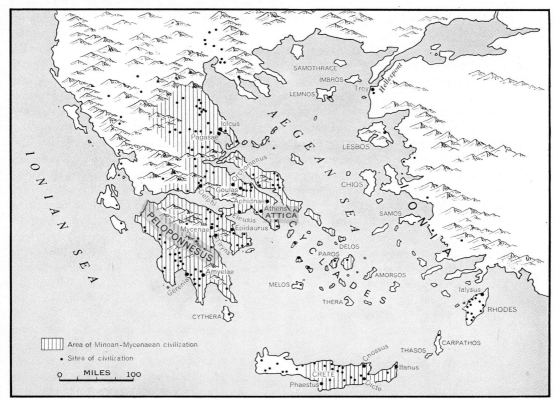

Area of Minoan-Mycenaean civilization

• Sites of civilization

0 MILES 100

checked the expansion of the Persian Empire, overthrew it, and established Greek rule in its place. This was one of the turning points in the history of Europe and western Asia.

The Greeks knew little about their own early history, and for a long time they were too unimportant to be noticed in the records of the great empires of the Near East. Our best information about the Greeks before 800 B.C. comes from archaeological discoveries, which often raise as many problems as they solve. This is especially true of the relationship between the early Greeks and the great civilization which centered on the island of Crete. Although there is important new evidence about this relationship, it has not yet been fully evaluated, and we cannot yet speak with certainty about this stage in Greek development.

The Greeks came down from the north, from Thrace and the region of the lower Danube; their original home may have been even farther away, on the plains of Russia. They spoke an Indo-European language and were part of the great wave of peoples of this linguistic group who spread through Europe and into the Near East during the second millennium B.C. The Greeks moved in small groups over a long period of time. Some of them reached the shores of the Mediterranean early in the second millennium; others were still pressing south after 1000 B.C. As a result, Greek groups that had settled in the Aegean area at an early date and had reached a relatively high level of civilization were repeatedly overrun by their more barbarous relatives coming down from the north. As a whole, the Greeks were a vigorous, warlike people, quick to fight with each other and their neighbors, and equally quick to pick up new techniques and ideas from the civilizations of the Near East.

As the Greeks pushed down into western Asia Minor and the Balkan peninsula, they came into contact with relatively advanced civilizations. The first Greeks in Asia Minor certainly had contacts with the Hittites and were probably tributary to the Hittite ruler. Later they fell under the influence of the Lydian kingdom, a rich and powerful state built on the ruins of the Hittite kingdom. Both Hittites and Lydians shared in the general civilization of the area and both developed new techniques of their own. Thus the Hittites, as we have seen, were probably the first people to use iron extensively, and the Lydians, as we shall see in the next chapter, were probably the first to coin money. Through political and commercial contacts with these peoples the Greeks learned a good deal about metal-working, building, and trade.

The relationship between the Greeks and the Minoan civilization on Crete is more difficult to evaluate. The inhabitants of Crete were a trading, seafaring people, much more individualistic than most of the mainlanders. This individualism is revealed in their art, which is full of lively, personal touches, and in their government, where the king's authority seems to have been limited by a large and powerful aristocracy. The royal palaces were built for comfort as well as ceremony; they had running water and drains, and many small rooms where people could be by themselves. Apparently members of the upper classes, as well as of the royal family, lived in these buildings. The Cretans had a strong feeling for elegance and a great interest in fashion; their women dressed well and ornamented themselves with beautifully designed jewelry. There were many Cretan cities, each with its own ruler, and the ties among them seem to have been very loose. At times the king of the great city of Knossos may have acted as a sort of president of a confederation, but he never became the absolute ruler of a unified empire.

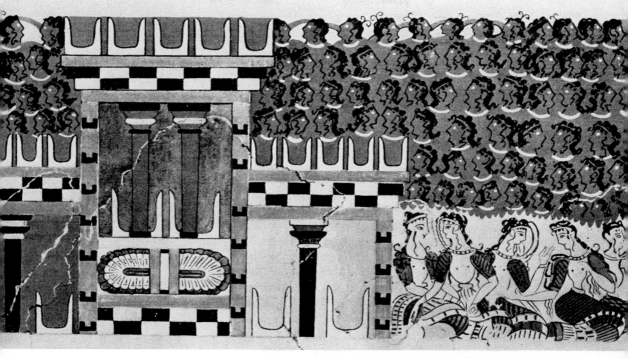

Cretan fresco of court ladies seated around a pillar shrine at a public festival, from the palace at Knossos.

This Minoan civilization, which was flourishing about 2000 B.C., dominated the entire Aegean basin and seems to have been strong enough to stimulate trade and maintain peace among the peoples of that region. The first Greek-speaking people, who reached the Aegean area about this time, must have been greatly influenced by the Minoan way of life. Early Greek communities, especially at Mycenae in the Peloponnesus, reproduced many aspects of Minoan civilization, though on a smaller scale and at a lower artistic and technical level. It seems very likely that Mycenae and its neighbors eventually became strong enough to attack Crete and to capture the city of Knossos. We know that Knossos was almost destroyed by an attack from the sea about 1450 B.C., and

we also know that one group of Cretan inscriptions, those of the so-called Linear B script, is written in an early Greek dialect. Finally, the last stage of Cretan civilization, which runs from the sack of Knossos to about 1200 B.C., shows a certain amount of barbarian influence and a decline from the splendors of the earlier period. It would appear that the Mycenaean Greeks took over Minoan civilization and kept it going, though at a lower level, until they in turn were crushed by a new and even more barbarous wave of Greek invaders. There are many doubtful points in this reconstruction, but one thing is certain: the earliest Greeks had many contacts with Minoan civilization and much of early Greek culture derives from the island of Crete.

Suggestions for Further Reading

1. Early Man

J. W. Swain, *The Ancient World,* Vol. I (1950), has very good material on neolithic and paleolithic man based on the latest archeological and anthropological evidence, a good introduction, with up-to-date bibliography. G. Fougères, *Les Premières Civilisations* (1926), is a more scholarly study of the same subject, with a thorough treatment of religion, art, and early communal life.

2. Egypt

The standard work on ancient Egypt is J. H. Breasted, *A History of Egypt* (1905), a fine study of the political, economic, and military conditions from the earliest times to the Persian conquest. Breasted's *The Development of Religion and Thought in Ancient Egypt* (1912) is valuable for an understanding of intellectual conditions. There are a number of fine studies of Egyptian art: C. Aldred, *Development of Ancient Egyptian Art* (1952), traces the development of Egyptian sculpture, painting, and architecture. W. S. Smith, *The Art and Architecture of Ancient Egypt* (1958), is a detailed study of Egyptian art by an outstanding authority, with good bibliographic material. The best study of one branch of Egyptian art is the beautiful Skira edition of A. Mekhitarian, *Egyptian Painting* (trans. S. Gilbert, 1954).

3. Mesopotamia

C. L. Wooley, *Dead Towns and Living Men* * (1929), is a study of archeological expeditions and discoveries in ancient Mesopotamia; a good starting point for study. The fascinating work of C. W. Ceram, *Gods, Graves, and Scholars* (1952), tells the story of early archeological expeditions in Mesopotamia. R. W. Rogers, *History of Babylonia and Assyria,* 2 vols. (1900), has detailed material on early expeditions in the ancient Near East and is a sound history of Mesopotamia. The beauty of Mesopotamian literature is brought out in S. N. Kramer, *History Begins at Sumer* (1956), which contains excellent source material for the political, social, and religious thinking of the Sumerians, the first people to keep written records; an exciting and valuable book. E. Chiera, *They Wrote on Clay* (1938), is a good account of Mesopotamian life and literature. A. Champdor, *Babylon* (1958), a fine commemoration of the genius of Babylon, reveals the impact of Babylonian culture on western Asia Minor. Perhaps the best treatment of the art of Mesopotamia is H. Frankfurt, *The Art and Architecture of the Ancient Orient* (1955).

4. Hittites Phoenicians and Hebrews

O. R. Gurney, *The Hittites* * (1952), is a good introduction to the social history of the Hittite peoples and their arts. A fascinating study of the archeological expeditions which uncovered Hittite civilization is C. W. Ceram, *The Secret of the Hittites* (1956), a well-illustrated book. The older work of J. Garstang, *The Hittite Empire* (1929), describes the history, geography, and culture of Hittite civilization but is less exciting reading than Ceram.

R. Weill, *Phoenicia and Western Asia to the Macedonian Conquest* (trans. E. F. Row, 1940), is a straightforward narrative of Phoenician history which gives a picture of

* Available in paperback edition. Bowker's *Paperback Books in Print* is a valuable guide.

the Mediterranean world of which Phoenicia was the center. The books by Swain and Fougères mentioned in Section 1 above have valuable material on the Phoenicians.

Probably the best account of the ancient Hebrews is that of A. Lods, *Israel* (1932), a study of the origin and development of the Hebrew religion based on literature, customs, and institutions. Lods combines wide learning, sound critical judgment, and a good prose style. G. Ricciotti, *The History of Israel* (1955), is based more on archeological evidence and carries the reader down to 135 A.D. The old study of H. H. Milman, *The History of the Jews,* 2 vols. (many editions), though somewhat superseded by recent archeological and scriptural research, is still valuable.

5. Assyrians and Persians

The titles by Swain, Rogers, Frankfurt, and Wooley cited above all have information on the Assyrians. W. H. Boulton, *Persia* (1935), surveys the rise and fall of the Persian Empire. A. T. Olmstead, *History of the Persian Empire* (1948), is a fine exposition of the intermingling of the cultures of the Persian Empire, together with a thorough treatment of political history.

6. Minoans and Early Greeks

There is good material on Minoan civilization in C. H. Hawes, *Crete: The Forerunner of Greece* (1911). A. J. B. Wace, *Mycenae: An Archaeological History and Guide* (1949), is a beautiful study of the artistic achievement of Minoan civilization. For studies of the early Greeks, see the titles mentioned after Chapter 2.

2

The Rise
and Spread
of Greek Civilization

The Greeks were the first inhabitants of Europe to dominate the eastern Mediterranean and to develop a civilization of their own. Although the Minoan civilization was flourishing when the first Greeks arrived, the Greeks were prevented from moving smoothly from the heights of that civilization to new achievements of their own. During the latter part of the second millennium B.C. new waves of Greeks came driving down from the north and hit the prosperous and flourishing cities of the Aegean in a series of disastrous invasions. The newcomers, in conquering a place for themselves, destroyed both the political and the economic organization of their

predecessors. Cities were ruined, trade slumped, the level of living fell off, and standards of artistic production declined.

Early Greek Society

This period of transition has sometimes been compared to the European Middle Ages, and, like the Middle Ages, the times following the invasions and the overthrow of the old order are obscure. When the Greeks re-emerge into the light of history after 1000 B.C., we find them established in small states grouped around fortified settlements. Each state has a king and a warrior aristocracy, supported by a popula-

tion of small farmers and herdsmen. This is the society described in the Homeric epics (though the actual siege of Troy seems to have taken place in the Minoan-Mycenaean period). It is not a primitive society, for many of the techniques of the earlier period survive, though sometimes in rather rudimentary form. But it is a society organized on a very small scale, a society in which personal relationships are far more important than institutions and laws. The family is a strong and cohesive unit, and the heads of the more important

Panathenaic procession, from the west frieze of the Parthenon, 5th century B.C.

❖❖❖❖❖❖❖❖❖❖❖❖❖❖❖❖❖❖❖❖❖❖❖❖❖❖❖❖❖❖

The Greek Army Prepares to Attack Troy

Agamemnon made no delay; he sent out the criers at once to sound the call for battle, and the army was soon assembled. He and his staff of princes were everywhere, arranging the men in their sections. With them went the goddess Athena. . . . Through the host she passed, dazzling them with the vision and filling each heart with courage to wage war implacable and unceasing. In a moment war became sweeter to them than to sail back safely to their own native land.

As a ravening fire blazes over a vast forest on the mountains, and its light is seen afar, so while they marched the sheen from their forest of bronze went up dazzling into high heaven.

As flocks of wildfowl on the wing, geese or cranes or long-necked swans fly this way and that way over the Asian meadows, proud of the power of their wings, and they settle on and on honking as they go until they fill the meadow with sound: so flocks of men poured out of their camp onwards over the Scamandrian plain, and the ground thundered terribly under the tramp of horses and of men.

From Homer, *Iliad*, trans. by W. H. D. Rouse (New York: Mentor, 1950), p. 31.

❖❖❖❖❖❖❖❖❖❖❖❖❖❖❖❖❖❖❖❖❖❖❖❖❖❖❖❖❖❖

families are nearly as powerful as the kings. They argue with and oppose their rulers; they cannot be commanded, but must be persuaded to obey. Lesser men, in turn, are not meek subordinates of the great. They recognize the warrior aristocracy as their natural leaders, but they debate and discuss plans before accepting them. If an aristocrat displays personal bravery, shrewdness, and ability in argument, he will enjoy a large and loyal following; if he lacks these qualities, he will exert little influence on his fellows. Altogether, we get the impression of an individualistic, vigor-

ous, adventurous people, fond of warfare and physical contests, clever with their hands and cunning in political intrigue, but not as yet interested in science and philosophy.

The period of migration and settlement of new waves of Greek-speaking peoples gradually ended after 1000 B.C. Petty wars continued, but they were not severe enough to prevent an increase in population. Greece itself is a hilly, rocky country with only small patches of good farm land; the western coast of Asia Minor, where many of the Greeks had settled, is not much better. The growing population soon began to make heavy demands on the meager food supply, and by the eighth century B.C. the Greeks either had to find new resources or perish. Situated in a region where it was easier to travel by water than by land, and with a maritime tradition inherited from Crete and Mycenae, they turned naturally to the sea.

The Greek "Commercial Revolution"

The sea offered two solutions to their problem. First, the surplus population could be sent out to colonize regions where there was still plenty of good farm land— Thrace, the coasts of the Black Sea, Sicily, and southern Italy. Second, the sea provided access to other settled communities which were glad to exchange their wares with those of the Greeks. Since the Greek peninsula is not well supplied with metals, imports of copper, bronze, and iron utensils must have been necessary from a very early date. After 800 B.C. the Greeks were carrying on both colonization and commerce with remarkable energy. Greek colonies ringed the Black Sea. They clustered so thickly in southern Italy that the region became known as a "new Greece." There were Greek outposts at the mouth of the Don in the Sea of Azov, at Marseilles near the Rhone delta in Gaul, and even in

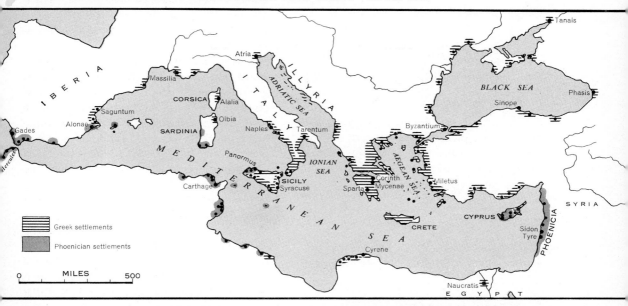

Greek settlements

Phoenician settlements

MILES 500

far-away Spain. Greek ships and Greek merchants were to be found in every Mediterranean port. Greek civilization was founded on commerce, which brought in new ideas and created a prosperous and active society which could use them.

But if colonization and commerce solved one economic problem they immediately created several new ones. The colonies were not subjects of the older states; they were completely independent communities which retained only cultural and sentimental ties with the founders. They could not be exploited as some modern colonies have been; the older settlements had to pay a fair price for the goods they imported. In commerce the Greeks obviously could not trade with non-Greek communities unless they had desirable products to offer in return. So Greek farmers had to begin raising cash crops—mainly wine and olive oil; Greek potters had to make thousands of great jugs in which these liquid products could be shipped; Greek artisans had to

produce wares which could be exchanged for the expensive goods of Egypt, Syria, and Mesopotamia. This dependence on production for distant markets completely changed the social and economic pattern of Greek society. A few isolated regions remote from the sea continued to be predominantly rural, with small villages, a self-sufficient agricultural economy, and a patriarchal government. But most of the old fortified settlements now developed into thriving commercial cities; the merchant became more important than the landowner; business relationships began to supplant old family and personal ties. This was the first of the great economic revolutions which have repeatedly transformed European society.

The invention of coined money, which occurred in Asia Minor (probably in Lydia) at about the beginning of the Greek economic expansion, speeded up and intensified the impact of economic change. Gold and silver had long been prized com-

43

modities, and the value of other goods had sometimes been expressed in terms of specific weights of these precious metals. But this practice was restricted to large-scale, long-distance trade; testing, weighing, and cutting a bar of gold or silver was too tedious for ordinary local transactions. Now men discovered that the metal could be cut up into bits and made ready long before actual business transactions took place. Small pieces of metal were stamped to show that the ruler guaranteed their weight and fineness, and the coins could then be used over and over for any sort of business.

Attic black-figured amphora, ca. 540–530 B.C. Ajax and Achilles are throwing dice. Achilles calls, "Four," Ajax, "Three." Signed "Exekias painted and made me."

The invention of coins was one of the great innovations in economic history, for it meant that exchanges and contracts were enormously easier to arrange. It also meant that remote impersonal relationships, based on the giving and taking of money, could be substituted for close personal dealings among neighbors. It added a new dimension to economic activity, and those who understood this new dimension profited from their increased freedom of movement. But money has always seemed mysterious to some people, and from the very beginning there were men who were lost in the new dimension. They did not know how to sell their goods and services for enough money to meet their needs. The small farmer could not sell his crop directly; it went to a middleman who gave him a low price and charged him a high one for the provisions he needed. But if it was hard to earn money, it was fatally easy to borrow. Small producers pledged their lands, and even their personal liberty, as security for repayment, and the class of hopeless debtors soon was larger than the class of successful businessmen.

The Greek Political Revolution

All these changes—the growth of trade and of cities, the increasing dependence on distant markets, the rise of a business class, and the impoverishment of the small farmer—put a strain on existing institutions. Many of the old monarchical governments, based on the support of a landowning, warrior aristocracy, were unable to adjust to the new situation. They neither understood, nor sympathized with, the needs of the businessmen in the cities; in fact, businessmen were often treated as inferiors because they had neither the military training nor the landed estates which qualified a man for full political rights. At the same time, the old-style monarchies were unable to deal intelligently with the problems of the small farmers and the other debtors, because they were at once too conservative to think of drastic solutions and too ignorant to know where to begin.

It is not surprising, then, that these changes in economic activity and in relations between classes eventually led to changes in political organization. The power of the kings declined, and the old landowning aristocracy and the new merchant class competed for control of the government. In the period of political disorder that followed, strong and ambitious men seized power. These were the "tyrants" who ruled many Greek states during the seventh and sixth centuries B.C. "Tyrant," to a Greek, simply meant a ruler who had seized power by force or intrigue. He might also be "tyrannous" in our sense of the word, since he was unrestrained by law and custom, but many tyrants were good and intelligent rulers. The better tyrants tried to lessen, or even abolish, the load of debt pressing on the poor. They recognized the importance of the business class, and adopted policies favorable to commerce. Most of the great Greek trading cities, including Athens and Corinth, were subject to tyrants at one time or another.

What is surprising is that tyranny, in most of the cities of ancient Greece, was only a passing phase, and did not develop into a new type of absolute monarchy. It solved some economic and social problems, but it offended the strong individualism and sense of justice of the Greeks. Even though they had shown no great devotion to their kings, they could accept monarchy. The ancient races of kings, descended from gods and heroes, were supported by religious tradition and long habit. But the tyrant was only a man like any other, and many Greeks were irritated to see an ordinary man dominating his fellows. Dictatorship, to them, could not be justified by the material benefits it conferred. Opposition to tyranny, even when it took the form of treacherous assassination, was always justified. The men who dared to attack a tyrant became heroes, whether or not they succeeded in their plot. Tyranny never managed to transform itself into a permanent monarchy, and in most cities it lasted only one or two generations.

But the ending of tyranny left the basic political problem unsolved. Backward and isolated districts could manage well enough with their ancient monarchies, but for most Greeks this form of government had proved inadequate. There was nothing in Greek political and religious tradition that made monarchy seem absolutely essential. Greek kings had never had the absolute power enjoyed by the rulers of Egypt and Babylonia; they had always been checked by the leading men of the community. In many states, even before the rise of the tyrants, the kings had steadily lost power and had been limited to ceremonial and religious functions. Greek religion had sanctioned the claim of certain families to the throne but had not given them divine attributes or unlimited authority. In fact, Greek mythology denied absolute power even to the chief god, Zeus. Though he was called "ruler of gods and men," he was bound by the decrees of the Fates and his wishes were constantly thwarted by the actions of his fellow divinities. Nor had he himself always been the chief god; tradition related that he had seized power in a revolt against his father, Cronos. Thus even in heaven there was no permanent, absolute monarchy, and the Greeks felt no compulsion to return to monarchy when they decided that they did not like tyranny. Greek individualism, always strong and now growing stronger, pushed in another direction.

These were the conditions which made possible the great Greek experiment—the establishment of a secular state with republican forms of government. All previous civilizations had been organized around the intertwined concepts of monarchy and religion. The Greeks dropped monarchy altogether and reduced religion to a form of civic patriotism. They directed their basic loyalty to the city-state, a small, closely knit community which satisfied all the material and spiritual needs of its inhabitants. The peak of Greek civilization was reached during the period in which the city-state was the dominant form of organization.

The City-State

The city-state never covered a very wide area; usually it was about the size of a small American county. It included farm lands and small agricultural villages, but its heart and center was the city itself, with its marketplace, its citadel, and its temples. Small in area, the city-state was also rather small in population. A large city-state might have several hundred thousand inhabitants, a small one not more than twenty-five to fifty thousand. Large or small, the citizens knew each other better and shared each other's experiences more fully than in any modern city of comparable size. There were no great office buildings in which business and political leaders could sit in seclusion guarded by cordons of secretaries and assistants. There were almost no large manufacturing establishments; most artisans worked in small shops open to the street. Even the home was not the citadel and refuge it is today. The ordinary Greek house was small and simple, a place to eat and sleep, not to live. Women might stay at home, but the men spent as little time there as possible. All public and private business was transacted in the open, in the streets and the market places, in the porches of the temples and law-courts. Playwrights gave their performances in unroofed theaters; teachers met their pupils in public gardens. Everyone had a chance to know everything that was going on in the city; there was little privacy and apparently little desire for it.

This intensely communal life was reflected in and strengthened by the activities of the city government. It performed all the normal functions of a government; it raised armies, administered justice, col-

A painting of a shoemaker's shop, probably done shortly before 500 B.C., from a Greek amphora. On one side a shoemaker prepares to cut a pair of soles for an Athenian lady, who is standing on a bench. On the other side are a helper and a spectator.

lected taxes, erected public buildings, and so on. But, more important, it determined the whole character of a citizen's life. As we have seen, the Greeks were facing serious economic problems; the way in which the government dealt with these problems could save or ruin whole classes of people. If it favored debtors, it gave small farmers a chance to survive as independent landholders; if it discouraged commerce, it ensured the domination of the landed aristocracy. Thus each class strove to win control of the government, and the group or groups which were successful used their power to preserve or improve their economic position.

Moreover, the government exerted powerful influence over education, religion, and the arts. More than any earlier people, the Greeks realized the importance of education and the contribution it could make to citizenship. In most places, the state took over the training of boys at an early age. This training included physical and military exercises and indoctrination in the religious and political traditions of the city. It might also include instruction in academic subjects. Each city tried to preserve its own way of life, its own particular social and political arrangements, by its system of education.

Religion in many ways extended civic education into adult life. Every city had a god or goddess who was supposed to be its special protector, though other gods were also worshiped. The city was closely identified with its protecting divinity, and public religious ceremonies were at the same time patriotic festivals. Since most of the people took part in the greater ceremonies, they shared the same religious-patriotic ideas and emotions. The state paid all the expenses of the cult; it built the temples and organized the festivals. Although there were priests who served the major gods, they had, in most cities, very little influ-

Statue of Athena as a warrior, in the archaic style, from Aegina, ca. 510 B.C.

ence. Political leaders often played a leading role in religious ceremonies; secular writers were deemed perfectly competent to discuss religious problems. The Greek

47

belief in oracles gave some political power to the priests of major shrines, but the divine messages were usually vague and obscure and frequently were interpreted by political leaders to suit their own policies.

Most artistic and literary productions—indeed, most amusements—had a religious connection, and were therefore supported by the state. Civic pride expressed itself in the building of temples adorned with masterpieces of Greek sculpture. The Homeric poems were prized as much for the information they gave about the gods as for their description of the heroic deeds of the early Greeks. The plays of the great Greek dramatists were written for religious festivals and were produced at state expense. Athletic contests were also held under religious auspices. Thus the citizen's leisure-time activities were controlled by the state and were affected by the character and policies of the government.

Living in tightly knit communities that affected their lives in so many ways, the Greeks naturally took a passionate interest in politics. It was not merely an inconvenience to have the wrong kind of government, or the wrong people in control; it was a catastrophe which made life hardly worth living. Today a man who is dissatisfied with his political environment may take refuge in private associations and activities, but this path seemed neither feasible nor desirable to most Greeks. The city-state was nation, hometown, church, club, college all in one. Only barbarians lived outside a city-state, and no Greek wanted to leave his native community. Yet a city-state might be so organized and governed that many of its inhabitants felt that it made a good, or even a satisfactory, life impossible.

This is why the Greeks worried so much about the constitutions of their city-states. A constitution was not just a set of rules defining and regulating political institutions; it was a way of life. Perhaps Americans can understand this point better than most Europeans, since we too believe that our constitution is the basis for our way of life. But our constitution forbids the government to interfere with certain activities, such as religion, whereas Greek constitutions seldom set any limits to the power of the state. The constitution determined the character of the government, and the character of the government affected everything that happened in the city-state. It favored some economic groups and hurt others; it encouraged some activities and discouraged others; it determined the nature of education, the goals of religion, and the forms of literary and artistic expression. The values and attitudes developed under a constitution such as that of Sparta were so different from those encouraged by the Athenian constitution that citizens of the two states could seldom understand each other's point of view (see p. 62). Thus changing a constitution meant revolution in the fullest sense of the word, as complete a change as would occur today if a country shifted from capitalism to communism.

Because the Greek city-state was such a highly integrated community, it could focus the energy of its inhabitants to a remarkable degree. There was none of the waste of human resources so typical of the monarchies of the ancient Near East. Most citizens were educated and were able to take an intelligent interest in the affairs of their communities. Most citizens lived in the towns where they had constant contact with one another and with visitors from other towns; they were not peasants living in isolated villages. True, slaves and foreigners were numerous in many Greek city-states, and both groups were excluded from many of the activities of citizens. Nevertheless in no previous society had such a large part of the population been able to participate in politics and in commerce, in art and in science. This explains why relatively small communities could accomplish so much. Even Athens, at the height of its glory, was a small city by modern standards, and yet the Athenian achievement equaled that of empires with millions of subjects.

But the Greeks paid a high price for this concentration of energy in the city-state. Because the city-state summed up all existence, it was hard for the Greeks to become interested in any larger organization. Because each city had its own character, it was suspicious of, if not hostile to, every other city. Thus cooperation among the Greek cities was always fragile and temporary, while wars were common. And when wars and revolutions weakened the Greek cities so that they were threatened by a foreign conqueror, the Greeks had no alternative to their traditional organization. They could not form effective larger units; they clung to their city-states to the end. The city-states' loss of independence in the fourth century B.C. was a tremendous psychological shock to the Greeks; it put an end to their greatest creative period. They had given their full devotion to the city-state, and when that passed there was nothing left to inspire them.

The Sixth Century B.C.

The first cities to reveal the Greek capacity for building a high civilization were those of Ionia, the western coast of Asia Minor. This region was closer to the older cultural centers of the Middle East and suffered less from the last waves of invasion than did the Greek peninsula. The nearby kingdom of Lydia, which, as we have seen, was one of the heirs of the Hittites, exercised a civilizing and stabilizing influence in the area. The Greeks of Ionia acquired much of the learning of the ancient Middle East through Lydia, and Lydian military power protected the Greek cities from other Asian kingdoms. In return, the Ionian Greeks probably acknowledged Lydian suzerainty in the seventh and sixth centuries B.C., but this very loose bond left them free to manage their own affairs.

Ionian Philosophy

According to tradition, Homer was an Ionian, and the *Iliad* and the *Odyssey* were certainly composed in this region either by Homer or by several other poets of the same name. But the real glory of Ionia was not its poetry—great as the Greek epics are. It was rather that in Ionia we find the beginnings of Greek philosophy and science. Here the Greeks first demonstrated their ability to take scattered facts, organize them, generalize from them, and so build up coherent bodies of knowledge and of theory. Their facts were not new; many of them came from Babylonia and other older centers of learning, or else were matters of common observation. Even some of their generalizations were not new, nor were the Greeks the first people to have abstract ideas, though some Greeks thought they were. But the Greek passion for generalizing, always trying to reduce observed phenomena to a few basic rules, always seeking first principles behind secondary effects, *was* new.

Archaic decoration from the cornice of the Siphnian treasury at Delphi.

Even the earliest Ionian philosophers showed this tendency to a high degree. They tried to explain the visible world in terms of the fewest possible basic principles —heat and cold, or fire, air, earth, and water, or the finite and the infinite. They tried to find regularities in nature. The first Ionian philosopher of whom we know very much, Thales of Miletus, is said to have predicted an eclipse in 585 B.C.* Other Ionians tried to find mathematical language in which to express their ideas about the nature of the universe and the regularities of nature. The first important Greek mathematician, Pythagoras, was an Ionian.

Much of this early work was overambitious and premature, for the Greeks were always ready to generalize, even when their knowledge of detail was insufficient. But the habits of thinking which these early philosophers developed lie at the foundations of all modern science. The early Ionian philosophers looked behind surface appearances; they sought simple explanations for complex phenomena; they began to develop the idea of laws of nature; they saw that mathematics was a powerful tool for solving problems and stating results. It was from these attitudes that Greek science developed, and Greek science became the model for all later scientific thought.

The Ionian cities, famous for their wealth as well as their intellectual activity, were great commercial centers that carried on trade throughout the Mediterranean world. Therefore, when the growing Persian Empire overthrew the kingdom of Lydia in 546 B.C., the Persian king was anxious to take the Greek coastal cities as well. The Ionians, no match for the military strength of the Persians, submitted at first with little resistance. But they resented Persian rule and eventually, in 499 B.C., they rebelled, with some assistance from Athens. Although the rebellion was a complete failure, it convinced the Persian king that he must conquer the European Greeks if he was to be secure in Asia Minor. This decision led to a long war between Greeks and Persians (see p. 54). Meanwhile Ionia, though still prosperous, was much more closely supervised by the Persians than before the revolt. With the loss of any real independence, the intellectual leadership of Ionia began to decline and Athens took its place.

Athens

The Greek cities on the European side of the Aegean had developed more slowly than those of Asia Minor, but by the sixth century B.C. many of them had reached a high level of civilization. This was especially true of Athens and the other cities situated on the bays and gulfs near the isthmus connecting the southern part of Greece (the Peloponnesus) with the rest of the country. Trade funneled into this area, both because it was a good distribution center for the rest of the country and because it lay at the end of the chain of islands which led to the coasts of Asia Minor. And with trade came new ideas, new techniques, and new economic problems, all of which stimulated the inhabitants of Athens and neighboring cities.

Outside this area of intense activity things moved more slowly. The Greeks who lived north and west of Attica (the Athenian peninsula) were less active in trade, less interested in new ideas; in fact, the Athenians looked down on their neighbors as simple, unsophisticated country folk. The southern part of the Peloponnesus was also backward in commercial and intellectual activities, though here the

---

* The Babylonians were probably able to predict eclipses from their astronomical tables at a much earlier date.

backwardness resulted from a deliberate attempt to adhere to the old way of life and to block disturbing innovations. In spite of different rates of development, all the Greeks felt that they had much in common, that they formed a group which was clearly set apart from the rest of the world. They spoke dialects of the same language; they worshiped the same gods; they formed leagues and alliances for common religious or political purposes. Their athletes and their poets competed with each other in the Olympic or Isthmian games; their writers drew their basic materials from the same stock of legends. The Greeks might quarrel incessantly among themselves, but they never surrendered their belief that they were one people, far superior to the outside barbarians.

Athens became the leading city of the commercial, innovating section of Greece, just as Sparta led the more rural, conservative groups. Because Athens and Sparta represented opposing patterns of Greek life, their rivalry dominates much of Greek history. But we should never forget that there were many other cities, such as Corinth on the Isthmus or Syracuse in Sicily, and that most of them did not go to the extremes of either Athens or Sparta.

Athens had been seriously disturbed by the seventh-century growth of population, shift to money crops, and increasing importance of commerce. Raising olives and producing wine for distant markets required large amounts of capital, and the small farmers had fallen into debt. The merchants fretted over the domination of the landed aristocracy, while the poorer classes in the city resented being excluded from political rights. It gradually became apparent that only two alternatives were open: to freeze the social structure through strong aristocratic government, or to democratize society through gradually extending political rights and economic safe-guards to the underprivileged classes. Athens chose the second road—perhaps because her leaders were eager to avoid civil strife, perhaps because she was so dependent on trade that she could not afford to snub her businessmen, perhaps because the need for larger military forces required the enfranchisement of new groups. Whatever the reason, the aristocracy lost its monopoly of political power during the seventh century. Well-to-do businessmen served in the army and became eligible for high office. During the sixth century Athens went even further and established a completely democratic government.

The first great reformer, Solon, was archon—that is, chief magistrate—of Athens in the 590's. He began by dealing with the farm problem, an issue that has plagued every civilized state since the beginning of history. As population increases and land becomes scarce, the small farmer almost always gets into trouble. Beset by bad weather, wars, and economic disturbances, he becomes dependent either on a military class which protects him or a business class which lends him money. Unless the government takes deliberate action to save him, he becomes a tenant-farmer or even a serf and thus is unable to participate fully in the life of his society. Solon saved the Athenian farmers, who were already treading this downward road, by canceling old debts, by forbidding slavery based on debt, by restricting mortgages on land, and by limiting the amount of land which could be held by any one individual.

Having secured the independence of the farmers, Solon was able to create a political system based on the participation of all free men. Every citizen was allowed to vote in the popular assembly, which made final decisions on important matters of policy. Every citizen also had a voice in choosing the chief administrative and judicial officers of the city. It is true that only the

Ostraka, or broken pieces of pottery on which citizens wrote the names of those they wished to ostracise from Athens, ca. 470 B.C. The names here are Themistokles, who was later recalled, and Kimon.

wealthy could be elected to important offices and that an aristocratic council retained a good deal of power, notably the power to decide what matters were to be presented to the assembly. It is also true that slaves, and foreigners living in the city, had no political rights, though they may have composed from one-third to one-half the population of Athens. Nevertheless, this was a more democratic form of government than had ever been attempted before by such a complex society.

Solon's reforms did not go far enough to prevent political unrest, and in the middle years of the sixth century Athens, like many other Greek cities, fell under the control of tyrants. But the Athenian tyrants were, on the whole, favorable to the poorer classes, and they preserved most of Solon's reforms. After they were expelled,

a new reformer, Cleisthenes, continued the trend toward democracy. His constitution, which went into effect in 502 B.C., gave every citizen equal political rights and also ensured that most citizens would hold public office.

Cleisthenes divided the population into ten tribes, so selected that each tribe was a cross section of the whole population. Fifty citizens chosen by lot from each tribe made up the governing Council of Five Hundred, which determined the policy of the state. Large juries of several hundred men, also selected by lot from the tribes, decided lawsuits. A general assembly of all citizens passed the laws. Only one vestige of special privilege remained: the highest offices—those of the treasurers and the generals—were restricted to the wealthier citizens. But even these offices were filled by popular vote, and, since they carried no salary, the poorer citizens could not have afforded to fill them even if they had been eligible.

The Athenian constitution thus gave every citizen both the right to participate in the government and the responsibility for seeing that the government did its work well. Almost every citizen took a passionate interest in politics, and, because the Greek city-state was such an integrated unit, in education, art, and literature as well. There were, of course, private interests and political factions; the Athenians could be as shortsighted, as selfish, as unreasonable as many modern voters. But for almost a century the Athenian system succeeded in releasing the energy of all citizens and in concentrating a good part of it on the common welfare. In the proud words of Pericles' Funeral Oration, the Athenian democratic constitution made Athens "the school of Greece" and the individual Athenian a man who could "adapt himself to the most varied forms of action with the utmost versatility."

In the earliest period of Greek history Sparta was not very different from other states in the peninsula, except that it had two kings at a time, instead of only one. Its political history followed the usual course, with the kings gradually losing power to a military aristocracy, and the aristocracy extending its ranks to take in most landowners. But once the landowners had gained control, they did their best to ensure that there would be no further change. Every innovation which might threaten their supremacy was either rejected or modified. A typical example is their attitude toward the new idea of coining money. They could not ignore the idea completely, but when it came to deciding what currency to use, they chose not gold and silver coins but iron bars! Clearly no great banking or merchant class could arise in a state with such unwieldy currency, and so the effects of the economic revolution were blunted. In the same way, Sparta, which had produced poets and artists in its early days, after 600 B.C. became hostile to most forms of art and literature, for they distracted attention from military training, the main objective of the state.

There was nothing unusual, to a Greek, in expecting all citizens to serve in the army, but for the Spartan citizen military service became the chief aim of existence. One reason for this emphasis may be the fact that a relatively small number of Spartans (perhaps no more than 25,000 families) were dominating a much larger number of subjects and allies. The lands of the Spartans were cultivated by Helots, a group of state slaves who had no rights and who were often cruelly treated. Beyond the Spartan lands were the communities of the "Neighbors," subject cities with limited self-government but completely dominated by Sparta in military and foreign affairs. Beyond these again were the

Pericles on Athens and Sparta

This oration, inserted by the Greek historian Thucydides in his *History of the Peloponnesian War,* does not give Pericles' exact words, but it does express admirably the pride of the Athenians in their city and its form of government.

We are called a democracy, for the administration is in the hands of the many and not of the few. But . . . the claim of excellence is also recognized, and when a citizen is in any way distinguished, he is preferred to the public service, not as a matter of privilege, but as the reward of merit. . . . Our city is thrown open to the world, and we never expel a foreigner or prevent him from seeing or learning anything of which the secret, if revealed to an enemy, might profit him. . . . In the matter of education, whereas the Spartans from early youth are always undergoing laborious exercises which are to make them brave, we live at ease, and yet are equally ready to face the perils which they face. . . . For we are lovers of the beautiful, yet simple in our tastes, and we cultivate the mind without loss of manliness. . . . Such is the city for whose sake these men fought and died; . . . and every one of us who survive should gladly toil on her behalf.

From Pericles' Funeral Oration, in Thucydides, *The History of the Peloponnesian War,* trans. by B. Jowett (New York: Random House, 1942), book II, Ch. 37.

cities of the Lacedaemonian League, a military alliance created by Sparta during the sixth century to enable her to control the Peloponnesus. The preservation of Spartan supremacy depended on the strength of the Spartan army, and the Spartan constitution was designed primarily to keep the army strong.

Although the Spartans regarded themselves as superior to the Helots and the

"Neighbors," within their own ranks they tried to secure complete equality. They retained their two kings as commanders of the army, and a council of the old noble families. But the real power lay in the assembly of Spartans of military age, and even more in the five ephors, magistrates elected by the assembly. The Spartans not only enjoyed equal political rights; as far as possible they were assured equal economic status as well. Each Spartan was given one or more Helot families to supply all his material needs and to leave him free for physical and military training. This training began at the age of seven, when the Spartan boy was taken from his mother. From that time until he was past fighting age he belonged to a military club which provided him with simple food and rough living quarters in a barracks. He had no home life; even after marriage he could visit his wife only occasionally and in secret. As part of the harsh, rigorous training, the boys and young men had to endure cold, hunger, and fatigue. The girls, up to the age of marriage, were also subject to intensive physical training. This system, which might be described as military communism, enabled the Spartans to create a community of warriors, by far the strongest fighting force among the Greeks.

It may seem strange that the other Greeks, who were so individualistic, admired Sparta, that even in Athens there were men who praised the Spartan constitution. But the weak spot in Greek individualism was lack of discipline, and, like many people, the other Greeks admired in the Spartans a quality that they themselves lacked. Even more, to all the Greeks the city-state was the center of existence, and the highest form of virtue was devotion to and service of the city-state. Here again the Spartans set an example unequaled elsewhere. Moreover, the Spartan rejection of wealth and luxury pleased many conservatives who were troubled by the rise of the business classes. The Spartans seemed closer to the heroic way of life recorded in the Homeric poems, which for many Greeks had the same authority the Old Testament had for the Puritans. Finally, the fierce egalitarianism of the Spartans harmonized with radical democratic thinking. If one forgot the slaves, which was easy enough for a Greek to do, one could argue that the Spartans had achieved complete equality.

The Fifth Century B.C.

Sparta and Athens were thus the natural leaders of the European Greeks when they found themselves threatened by the Persian Empire. As we have seen (p. 50), Persia had annexed the Greek cities of Asia Minor in the second half of the sixth century B.C., and these cities had later staged an unsuccessful revolt. Since Athens had supported the revolt, King Darius of Persia decided that he must add European Greece to his empire in order to preserve his rich possessions on the Asia Minor coast. He obviously could not send the entire Persian army to Greece, but he felt that a small expeditionary force landed in Attica would be enough to overcome weak and divided Greece.

The Persian Wars

Darius was very nearly right in his calculations. Most of the Greek cities remained neutral, and Sparta, though it promised aid to Athens, did not send its army in time. But the Persians had included no cavalry in their expeditionary force, and their light-armed infantry alone proved no match for the more heavily armed Athenians at Marathon (490 B.C.). Darius died before he could avenge the defeat, and only after ten years was his successor, Xerxes, able to resume the war.

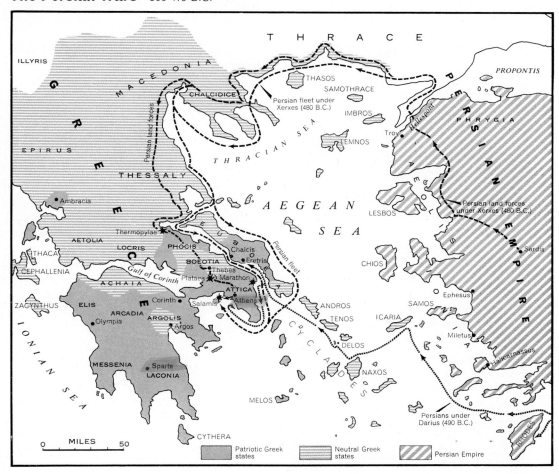

This time the Persians made a greater effort by marching a large army across the Straits, through Thrace and Macedonia, and down toward Attica. A fleet supported the army and kept it supplied with provisions. The success of the invasion was almost ensured when Sparta and Athens fell out over an Athenian plan to check the attack by concentrating all forces at the narrow pass of Thermopylae. The plan was rejected, and the Persian army swept into Attica. A small detachment of Spartans made a heroic and hopeless stand at the pass, but their bravery was small comfort to the Athenians who saw their fields plundered and their city taken and burned. The only thing that saved the Athenians in this dark hour was the fleet which their general, Themistocles, had persuaded them to build. There was some doubt as to whether the fleet should be risked in battle, but, under the urging of Themistocles, the Athenians finally decided to take the chance. Themistocles met the Persian fleet in the narrow waters of the Gulf of Salamis, where its superior numbers were of little use, and won a sweeping victory (480 B.C.). With the Greeks in command of the sea, Xerxes retreated with part of his army.

Next year, however, the Persians who had remained in Greece, reinforced by fresh troops, invaded Attica once more and completed the destruction of Athens. At this point the Athenians succeeded in convincing the Spartans to take a stand in central Greece rather than at the Isthmus of Corinth, which the Spartans preferred. Finally a large Greek army assembled under Spartan leadership defeated the Persians decisively at the battle of Plataea (479 B.C.). The invasions were not renewed, and for many years Greece was free from the threat of Persian domination.

This victory over the Persians stimulated the self-confidence and daring of the Greeks. A few small city-states had succeeded where the great kingdoms of the Orient had failed: they had thrown back the invincible Persian army. Now the Greeks were more confident than ever that they were destined for greatness, that their way of life was superior to that of all other peoples, that they could succeed in any enterprise they undertook. The century following Salamis and Plataea was the great period of Greek history, the period in which the Greeks made their indelible mark on the history of civilization. Released from fear of invasion, freer from the restraints of tradition and social stratification than any human group had been before, they molded their ancient Middle Eastern heritage into the forms that have influenced every subsequent civilization.

They dramatized their new self-assurance by transforming the defensive war against Persia into a war of liberation for the eastern Greeks. Athens, with the best fleet, took the lead in this new phase of the war; the Spartan army was of little use in campaigns against the Aegean islands and the coast of Asia Minor. After years of hard fighting the Greeks succeeded in freeing the islands and the Ionian mainland from Persian domination. The Aegean was now completely under Greek control, and with it the commerce of the Straits and the Black Sea.

The Age of Pericles

Athens profited most from this new situation. She had done at least as much as Sparta in repelling the Persian invasions, and far more than Sparta in the war of liberation. Most of the cities north of the Isthmus acknowledged her prestige and accepted her leadership. Athens could profit from the new opportunities for commerce as Sparta, still hostile to trade, could not. Able men from many other cities, especially men with new ideas to discuss and new projects to launch, flocked to Athens, drawn by her eminence and her wealth. Thus, more than ever before, Athens became the center of innovation and experimentation in the Greek world.

Athens was also fortunate in retaining a high degree of political stability during most of the fifth century B.C. The basic constitution stood unchanged, though the general assembly of all citizens assumed more power than before. This continuing approach to absolute democracy had one dangerous result: the citizens, jealous of men who seemed to usurp leadership, often forced them into retirement or exile. This was the fate of Miltiades, who won the battle of Marathon; of Themistocles, who built the fleet that triumphed at Salamis; of Aristides, who helped drive the Persians from the Aegean. But for several generations new leaders of equal ability replaced those who fell into disfavor. And for over thirty years (461–429 B.C.) the great statesman Pericles retained the confidence of the people and gave direction and continuity to Athenian policy.

The Athenians wanted their city to be

great and powerful; they also wanted to make it beautiful and to pay due honor to the gods who protected and symbolized the state. The devastation wrought by the Persians gave them an opportunity which seldom comes to the inhabitants of a great city: to replace the old Athens that had been destroyed, they could now erect new buildings balanced in design and grouped symmetrically on and around the central hill, the Acropolis. The rebuilding, which began immediately after the victory at Plataea, reached its height under Pericles and continued even during the dark days of the

Peloponnesian War when Athens was losing her political supremacy (see p. 62). Nothing indicates more clearly the Greek view of life and the way in which the city-state integrated all activities. To an Athenian it was natural to spend as much on art as on the fleet; in fact, there was much more argument in the assembly about military expenditure than about the cost of new public buildings.

During the fifth century B.C. Athens was the leader in Greek art as well as in Greek politics. This had not always been true; in the earlier period the Ionians had set the pace in art as well as in philosophy and science. But as the temples on the Acropolis reached completion, Athens became the marvel and the model of the Greek world. The buildings and the statues of the Acropolis were imitated everywhere—and fortunately so, for while the temples still stand much of the original Athenian sculpture has perished and is known only through copies made by later artists in other cities.

Greek art of the fifth century B.C. was an art that had solved its technical problems. Greek architects could combine their materials in many ways to produce buildings which were imposing and well-proportioned. Greek sculptors could represent all the details of the human body, clothed or nude, with absolute accuracy. This technical skill developed rather rapidly, perhaps because the Greek artists set limited goals for themselves. They were interested in the finite, not the infinite; they never undertook the hard task of giving visions concrete form. They were serene and confident; they idealized life here on earth, not life in a heaven about which they thought little. For the sculptor, the ideal man was a demigod and the god an idealized man. There was no sense of conflict in the Greek art of this period, no antagonism between the real and the ideal. Life in this world at its best could be beautiful and satisfying,

Pericles, the great Athenian statesman, d. 429 B.C. Copy of a contemporary bronze.

ZETVS ANTIOPA AMΦHION

Stele from the end of the 5th century B.C. Orpheus and Eurydice parting, Eurydice to return to Hades with Hermes.

and this was what they sought to represent.

These characteristics of Greek art are evident in the sculpture of the Parthenon (the temple of Athena on the Acropolis) carved by the great Athenian artist Phidias and his followers. They are also evident in Greek architecture, both in the temples of the Acropolis and elsewhere. Like the Minoans of Crete, the Greeks of the fifth cen- tury never sought to impress the beholder through mere size. Instead, they sought harmony and proportion; they built on a scale which could be measured and under- stood by the human eye. Their temples did not soar toward the sky like a Gothic ca- thedral nor did they dwarf the observer like an Egyptian temple. Instead, the archi- tect cut off a definite and limited segment

2 / The Rise and Spread of Greek Civilization

of space and organized it in proportion to the human body and the human understanding. The essential elements of a temple were the inner sanctuary, which housed a statue of the temple's god, and the outer porch, on one, two, or all four sides, where the worshipers could congregate. Reliefs were placed in the gable ends of the roof, and in a frieze which ran around the upper wall under the eaves. These reliefs represented the gods, and also the people of the city in their processions, their athletic combats, and their military exercises. Here again the Greeks did not distinguish between the religious and the secular aspects of life; rather, to them the noblest and best secular activity was a religious act.

This same restraint and sense of proportion is evident in Athenian tragedy, which also reached its height during the age of Pericles. The Greeks had long been accustomed to celebrate the festivals of their gods with semidramatic performances in which a single speaker told a story to which a chorus offered responses or comments. The Athenians transformed these rituals into full-fledged drama by adding a second, and then a third, speaker. This innovation enlivened the development of the story and allowed the introduction of opposing viewpoints. The stories were taken from ancient Greek legends, but they were used to

The Acropolis, Athens, as it appears today.

The Parthenon, southeast corner, 5th century B.C.

illustrate problems of human behavior in the present world. What is right conduct? Can man avoid the fate decreed to him? What should one do when law and conscience conflict? These are some of the questions asked by the great Athenian dramatists, Aeschylus (525–456 B.C.), Sophocles (496?–406 B.C.), and Euripides (480?–406? B.C.). And running through all the tragedies is the basic theme of harmony, moderation, recognition both of human potentialities and human limitations. The greatest sin is overweening pride, and the man who defies the gods and the mores of his society is doomed. The greatest virtue is fortitude, to play the role allotted by the gods, and to do one's duty without fear or wavering. Like Greek architecture, Greek tragedy was worked out within sharply defined limits according to clearly formulated rules. But unlike Greek architecture, it had an element of conflict and tension between aspiration and achievement, between the ideal and the actual.

Perhaps the best example of Greek tragedy for a reader in our own century is Sophocles' *Antigone*. It deals with a conflict which is acute today—the conflict between the demands of the state and the desire of the individual to obey a higher moral law. The nephew of Creon, King of Thebes, has been killed in an unsuccessful rebellion. Creon in his anger orders that the body be left to lie unburied in the fields, defying an old Greek religious tradition. Antigone, the sister of the victim, determines to give her brother a proper burial, even though Creon has decreed death to anyone who touches the body. As she says:

> I deemed not that thy decrees were of such force, that a mortal could override the unfailing and unwritten statutes of heaven. For their life is not of today or yesterday, but from all time. . . . Not through dread of any human pride could I answer to the gods for breaking their laws. . . . So for me to meet this doom is trifling grief; but if I had suffered my brother to lie unburied, that would have grieved me.*

Creon vainly tries to make her change her mind, but when she goes ahead with her plan he has her executed. He is re-

* *The Complete Greek Drama,* ed. by W. J. Oates and E. O'Neill, Jr., trans. by R. C. Jebb (New York: Random House, 1959), Vol. I, p. 434.

morseful later, but his remorse is not enough to prevent first the suicide of his son, who had loved Antigone, and then that of his wife. Creon had set his will against religion and conscience, and, as the chorus says at the end:

> Reverence to the gods must be inviolate. Great words of prideful men are ever punished with great blows, and in old age teach the chastened to be wise.†

The Peloponnesian War

The age of Pericles was ended by a war between Athens and Sparta which so weakened the Greek world that its old way of life was eventually destroyed. Perhaps most important among the complex causes of the war was the growing power of Athens and the jealousy which this power gen-

† *Ibid.,* p. 459.

Detail from an Attic cup, ca. 470 B.C. Oedipus, in traveler's clothes, tries to answer the riddle asked by the sphinx.

erated in Sparta and other states. Athens, at the head of a great alliance of mainland and island cities, had driven the Persians from the Aegean. But once the immediate threat had been eliminated, the alliance began to fall apart. The Athenians, quite rightly, believed that the Persian danger had not yet ended. In addition, they enjoyed the power which the leadership of the confederation gave them, especially as they now controlled the chief trade routes of the Aegean. When some of the cities tried to leave the alliance, Athens used force to keep them within its orbit. Thus an alliance of free cities was gradually changed into an Athenian empire. More powerful than her neighbors, Athens monopolized trade and annexed colonies which had been founded by other cities. Thus many cities which had no real sympathy with the dour Spartans were driven to join them in an effort to cut down Athenian strength. Since Sparta and her satellites in the Peloponnesus were the chief opponents of Athens, the war which resulted was known as the Peloponnesian War.

Fighting began in 431 B.C., and for a

An Athenian coin, 480–450 B.C. The owl is the symbol of Athena, the goddess of wisdom. The waning moon symbolizes Sparta.

while went in favor of Athens. But Pericles died early in the war, and with his passing some of the weaknesses of Athenian democracy began to manifest themselves. No real successor to Pericles appeared, and the Athenians failed to give consistent support to any one leader or to any one policy. They alternated between excessive boldness and excessive timidity; they made grandiose plans to dominate the Greek world and then failed to carry them out. As a result, they kept alive the fear of Athenian domination, which had inspired the alliance against them, but they were never successful enough to crush their opponents. The final collapse of Athenian power resulted from an attempt to conquer the city of Syracuse in Sicily. If Athens had succeeded in annexing Syracuse it would have dominated western trade as it already dominated the trade of the Aegean. But the Athenians failed to give full support to their fleet, and it was annihilated in Sicilian waters in 413 B.C. Now all that was needed to ruin Athens was steady pressure, which the Spartans supplied. They defeated the last Athenian fleet in 405 B.C. and forced Athens to sign a humiliating treaty the next year.

The Spartan victory ended the prospects for a united Greece, which might have been created under Athenian leadership and might have preserved for centuries Greek independence and the Greek way of life. Since the Spartans had claimed that they were fighting for the liberty of individual cities, they could not replace the Athenian empire with one of their own. They did try to install aristocratic governments which would favor them in most Greek cities, but even this policy they did not push vigorously. Thus, when Athens rejected its aristocratic government and returned to its democratic constitution, the Spartans made no objection. Their man power had been so reduced during the long war that they could not hope to preserve a purely military domination over the rest of Greece, and they had no skill in political manipulation.

The Fourth Century B.C.

As a result, the Greek cities remained weak and divided. Athens recovered to some extent and created new alliances with some Aegean cities, but it could no longer dominate the Greek world. Sparta continued to decline in military strength; it was finally defeated in 371 B.C. by Thebes, a city which had never before played an important role in Greek politics. But the Thebans, like the Spartans before them, were satisfied with local and temporary advantages and made no effort to unify the Greek states. In this confused and uncertain situation, Persian power in the Aegean began to revive. Even more important, the kings of Macedon started to plan the annexation of the Greek cities.

The Rise of Macedon

Macedon, on the northern shore of the Aegean, was a backward, rural region, full of good fighting men, but not very far advanced either economically or intellectually. Although the Macedonians were of Greek stock and had been influenced by Greek culture, the Greeks were not very eager to claim kinship with their remote country cousins. But Macedon was far larger than any Greek city-state; it had a strong army and a remarkably able king. Philip of Macedon created a new type of infantry formation, the closely knit phalanx which could break any contemporary army. With this powerful military force, he made his aggressive intentions unmistakably clear, and once more, as in the days of the Persian War, there was a great debate in Greece on how to meet the danger. The Athenian orator, Demosthenes,

urged union and defiance, but others suggested compromise and collaboration. As usual, the Greeks were unable to give full support to any one policy. They resisted to the point of provoking war with Macedon, but not to the point of concentrating their strength against the enemy. As a result they were defeated at the battle of Chaeronea (338 B.C.) and the Greek cities became appendages of the Macedonian kingdom. Philip, a great admirer of Greek culture, let them keep a large degree of local autonomy, but their real independence was lost. *very kind to Gr. organized well*

Greek Culture

The period from the Peloponnesian War to the victory of Macedon was a dark time for the Greeks. Yet the momentum of their earlier accomplishments was so strong that they continued to do important work in art, science, and philosophy. It is true that there was some decline in the quality of their sculpture; the serenity of the fifth century was lost and there was more emotionalism, more sense of strain, more recognition of human suffering. On the other hand, the end of the fifth and the first part of the fourth century saw the height of Greek philosophy and history.

The ascendancy of Athens had led to a remarkable concentration of Greek scholars and writers in the city. The old Ionian school of philosophy, which had dealt with abstract and speculative problems (see p. 49), had gradually given way to a new group of thinkers who were more concerned with questions of human conduct. These men were called Sophists, or "knowers," because they knew or pretended to know the answers to all questions. For the most part they were not Athenians, but many of them taught and lived in Athens. They were very popular with the young intellectuals, but they had a bad reputation among older and more conservative citizens. This was because they examined traditional standards and beliefs with a skeptical eye and attacked their opponents with the new, and therefore suspect, art of logic. Their reasoning was clever, but not always fair, which is why a tricky argument today is called "sophistical." Their basic viewpoint was entirely pragmatic. One of their favorite sayings was: "Man is the measure of all things"—that is, laws and morals are mere conventions made for human convenience, rather than permanent standards to which human behavior should conform. But while they stirred up controversy they did succeed in interesting the Athenians in problems of ethics, logic, and psychology.

The first important Athenian philosopher was Socrates (*ca.* 469–399 B.C.). He was certainly influenced by the Sophists, and his enemies always classed him with them. But although he used the logic of the Sophists to force his fellow citizens to re-examine their basic beliefs, he was not satisfied with negative or limited answers. He believed that there were permanent truths which could be discovered by human reason, that there were standards of justice and right conduct which all men would accept once they saw them clearly. He devoted his life to discussion and teaching, while fulfilling all his duties as a citizen. Unfortunately, the period of his greatest influence was at the end of the Peloponnesian War, when the Athenians, shocked by defeat, were suspicious of all innovators. Because he wanted young men to think for themselves instead of accepting traditional beliefs, he was accused of undermining religion and state. At his trial he refused to recant his convictions, and after his condemnation he refused to make any attempts to escape the death penalty. He felt that he must demonstrate by his death both the sincerity of his beliefs and the respect which he had for the laws of his country, even when they were applied unjustly.

Socrates' favorite pupil was Plato (427–347 B.C.); in fact, most of what we know about Socrates comes from the dialogues in which Plato reproduced and elaborated the thoughts of his master. Plato, like Socrates, re-examined accepted beliefs in order to arrive at ultimate truth. He drew a sharp distinction between the visible, material world and the realm of permanent, unchanging ideas. To him, ideas alone had reality; material objects were merely reflections of the ideas which existed in a higher world. For example, a chair could not exist unless there was already an idea of "chair-ness"; no man could be just unless he clearly envisioned the idea of justice; and justice itself was only part of the highest idea of all, the idea of the Good. Plato drew a sharp distinction between the intellect, or soul, which should be the ruling part of man, and the body and its appetites, which often led men astray. Perhaps influenced by speculations which had reached him from Persia and India, he believed in a judgment after death and a reincarnation of the soul in a better or worse condition according to its merits. His most famous work was the *Republic,* in which he began by trying to define justice and went on to describe an ideal commonwealth. This ideal commonwealth was both static and aristocratic. Justice and good government could be obtained through educating every man to do his duty in the station which his ability entitled him to occupy. Since only a few were qualified to be rulers, Plato was not very sympathetic to democracy; indeed, he had a certain leaning toward the Spartan system.

Plato's own emphasis on abstract ideas was exaggerated, and some of his followers pushed it to absurd lengths. But it did have the merit of strengthening the Greek interest in meaningful generalizations, and in counteracting the tendency of some of the Sophists to dwell on isolated and unrelated situations. Plato's most famous pupil, Aristotle (384–322 B.C.), tried to tone down some of the exaggerations in his master's thought, while preserving its more useful aspects. Aristotle taught that ideas were not independent entities, but rather that they were derived from concrete experience. And yet he urged just as strongly as Plato the need to generalize and to relate particular facts to enduring laws of nature.

Aristotle was the great organizer of Greek thought. He came at a time when the Greeks had already acquired a large amount of useful information, either from their eastern neighbors or from their own experience, and when they had begun to arrange this material in meaningful order. As we saw earlier, the chief intellectual contribution of the Greeks was this urge to connect isolated facts, to derive general rules from particular cases, to ask questions about the basic structure of the universe. Aristotle provided a powerful tool for use in the effort to classify and generalize from scattered facts.

This tool was logic, which Aristotle purified from the quibbles of the Sophists. He developed rigorous, consistent, and intellectually honest rules of logic and thus gave western thinkers an intellectual instrument they could use for work in every field. Aristotle's logical system was based too exclusively on sharp contrasts—A is either B or it is not B—and it permitted a certain amount of word-juggling. Nevertheless, it was not modified for over two thousand years, and it provided a highly effective way of classifying facts and deriving useful generalizations from them. Logic has been so bred into our intellectual system that we no longer study it as a separate subject, and we fail to realize how much our intellectual achievements owe to it. But when we contrast western thinking with that of the rest of the world we see the

❖❖❖❖❖❖❖❖❖❖❖❖❖❖❖❖❖❖❖❖❖❖❖❖❖❖❖❖❖❖

Plato's Parable of the Cave

Behold, human beings living in a cave, with its mouth open toward the light . . . here they have been from their childhood and have their legs and necks chained, so that they cannot move and can only see the wall of the cave. . . . Behind them a fire is blazing, and between the fire and the prisoners is a path. . . . Men walk along this path carrying vessels, and statues and figures of animals . . . [and the prisoners] see only the shadows which the fire throws on the opposite wall. . . . To them the truth would be literally nothing but the shadows of the images. . . . Now the prison-house is the world of sight, and the light of the fire is the sun . . . ; the shadows are the objects in the visible world, and the things which truly exist, of which the shadows are only a distorted representation, are the Ideas. The Idea of Good appears last of all and is seen only with an effort, and, when seen, is also inferred to be the universal author of all things beautiful and right . . . and the immediate source of reason and truth. . . .

Adapted from Plato, *Republic,* trans. by B. Jowett (Oxford: Clarendon Press, 1871), book VII.

❖❖❖❖❖❖❖❖❖❖❖❖❖❖❖❖❖❖❖❖❖❖❖❖❖❖❖❖❖❖

significance of Aristotle's work. Our theology, our law, our mathematics, and our science were all marked in their early stages by strict application of Aristotelian logic; their strengths and their weaknesses were those of the Aristotelian system.

In his books and public lectures Aristotle showed how his method could be applied. He discussed almost every subject of interest to the men of his day—constitutional law, ethics, biology, physics, astronomy, and philosophy. In preparing his work on law he studied the constitutions of hundreds of Greek cities, and his knowledge of biology was almost as extensive. In all his treatises he tried to derive general principles from the known facts and to make sure that his general principles were consistent with one another. Some of his generalizations dominated European thought for two thousand years. For example, he argued that the degeneration of one form of government gives rise to an opposing form: thus corrupt democracy produces dictatorship. Since all the simple forms of government—monarchy, aristocracy, and democracy—are subject to degeneration, the best government is a mixture of the three: a strong executive, an aristocratic council, and a democratic assembly. Equally fruitful was his distinction between Form and Matter, which stimulated thought about developmental processes in the universe. Thus the sculptor imposes Form on the Matter of a lump of clay; an acorn is a small bit of Matter but it has within it the Form of a large oak.

Aristotle tried to collect all available data on the subjects he studied, but in some fields he found that the data were insufficient to permit valid generalizations. This was especially true in the physical sciences, where the techniques of making exact measurements were lacking. In such cases Aristotle, like many of his Greek predecessors, made guesses based on analogy and intuition. Some of his guesses were helpful, if not accurate. Some, such as his theory of planetary motion, were definitely wrong. Unfortunately, in later ages Aristotle's authority became so great that some of his worst errors were accepted as demonstrated fact.

Yet with all their weaknesses, Aristotle's books were valuable, both as collections of facts and as statements of fundamental problems. For many centuries all western scholars had to begin with a study of Aristotle, and much of their work was merely a commentary on or an elaboration of his thought.

Aristotle, 384–322 B.C. Roman copy of a Hellenistic statue.

Besides the philosophers, Athens in the period around 400 B.C. also produced two remarkable historians, Herodotus and Thucydides, and a great playwright, Aristophanes. Herodotus, who wrote about a half-century before Thucydides, displayed remarkable narrative skill, but was more interested in telling a story than in reflecting on its meaning. His wide-ranging interests covered all the regions of the world which he knew, and periods of history so remote that he could describe them only by means of ancient legends. Herodotus tried to obtain the best information available, but in covering so much ground he inevitably had to use unreliable sources and second-hand evidence. He was also a thoroughly patriotic Greek, and in his account of the Persian Wars, the high point of his history, he probably exaggerated both the heroism of the Greeks and the weaknesses of the Persians.

Thucydides made a deliberate effort to avoid the faults of Herodotus. He believed that history should be more than entertainment: it should be a rigorously accurate description of human behavior which would be of use to any future generation encountering similar situations. In order to meet this standard of accuracy, he confined himself to his own country and his own period and as far as possible based his narrative on the evidence of men who had actually participated in the events he described. His history of the Peloponnesian War is a detailed account of the struggle between Sparta and Athens; it is completely dispassionate, even though he himself was an Athenian who had once commanded an Athenian army. Not content with a mere recital of facts, however, he tried to explain the motives of political figures and the underlying causes of political events. He set a high standard that was met by no ancient and by only a few modern historians.

Aristophanes (448?–380? B.C.) was a writer of comedies, most of them witty commentaries on events of his own day. He reflected many of the prejudices of his fellow Athenians; for example, Socrates appears in one of his plays as a ridiculous figure who talks learned nonsense. But Aristophanes had an honest dislike of humbug and official pomposity, and a sincere aversion to war. One of his most effective plays was an anti-war comedy (*Lysistrata*) in which the women of Athens persuaded their husbands to make peace by withholding their favors.

The Hellenistic Period

The Macedonian victory over the Greeks in 338 B.C. (see p. 63) began a new period of Greek history, a period in which Greek ideas spread throughout the eastern world while the Greek cities themselves were sinking into political insignificance. Philip had planned to attack Persia, which had regained a good deal of influence in the Aegean, as soon as he had united the Greeks under his leadership. He died before he could begin the campaign, but his plan was carried on by his son, Alexander, who ruled from 336 to 323 B.C. In a remarkable series of campaigns Alexander crushed the Persian Empire, annexed all its territories, including Egypt, and marched his armies to the region of the Indus River in northwestern India. His rule was accepted with little protest by all the peoples of the ancient Near East, and he controlled wider territories than had any previous conqueror.

Alexander's Empire

Alexander died before he could fully organize his empire, but he set two precedents which were to be followed by all his successors. The first was the founding of new Greek cities throughout his territories —for example, Alexandria in Egypt. These cities provided him with groups of Greek soldiers and officials in key areas and demonstrated the Greek way of life to his non-Greek subjects. Greek prestige was so high as a result of Alexander's victories that many of the leading men of other nations were anxious to imitate the Greeks, and those who settled in the new cities absorbed much of Greek culture. This Greek influence, however, was largely confined to the cities; throughout the Orient the

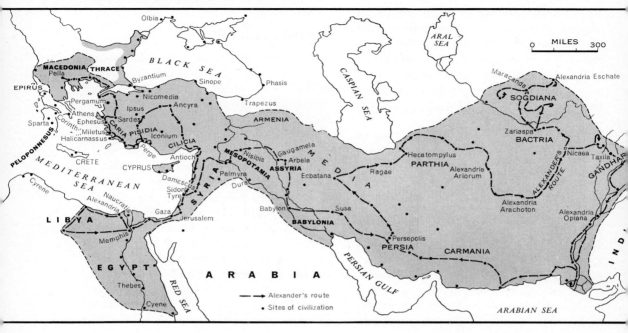

country people retained their old traditions and way of life.

The other precedent set by Alexander was his use of the ideas of absolute monarchy and the divine origin of the ruler—ideas familiar to most of the peoples of the ancient Near East. Absolutism was the only system of government which could have held Alexander's empire together. The Greeks had never succeeded in creating a political unit larger than the city-state, and even within the city-state they had not always secured unity and order. But Alexander had to claim that he was divine in order to make his subjects accept his absolute rule. A country like Egypt, which had been ruled by god-kings from time immemorial, would not have understood the claim of a mere mortal to authority. The Greeks, sorrowing over the loss of their freedom, derived some comfort from the fiction that Alexander was the son of Zeus. This theory justified, to some extent, the extraordinary power which Alexander wielded over the Greek cities.

The Successor States

Alexander left no heir to carry on his work. His generals quarreled over the succession and his empire fell to pieces as rapidly as it had been put together. Alexander's officers set up many independent kingdoms; in the end, the three most important were Egypt under Ptolemy, Syria and Persia under Seleucus, and Macedonia and Greece under Antigonus. These independent successor kingdoms were often bitterly hostile to one another, but they shared a common civilization. They were all dominated by Greeks and by those natives who had adopted Greek culture; they were all influenced by ideas which had come from Greece; they were all heavily dependent on international trade. This era in which the Near East was permeated by Greek influence is known as the Hellenistic period. It ended politically in 30 B.C. when Rome annexed Egypt, the last independent Hellenistic state. Culturally, it lasted far longer. Greek remained for centuries the language of scholars, traders, and administrators throughout the eastern Mediterranean. The cultural unity of the ancient Near East ended only when the followers of Mohammed conquered Syria and Egypt in the seventh century A.D.

The Hellenistic states seemed at first prosperous, powerful, and successful in their efforts to spread the Greek way of life throughout the Near East. But inherent weaknesses kept them from being entirely successful as economic, political, or cultural units. Their cities grew and their trade increased, but the gulf between rich and poor widened as profits went to a small upper class of rulers, administrators, and traders. The native populations showed little loyalty to the dynasties founded by Alexander's generals or to the Greek and imitation-Greek governing class. Rulers depended on small mercenary armies which could protect only the central part of their territories. Outlying districts such as Bactria, Persia, and northern Asia Minor soon became independent entities under native dynasties. The Jews under the leadership of the Maccabees gained their freedom after 167 B.C. Even the old Greek cities of the European mainland acquired a certain degree of independence and formed leagues which seriously limited the power of the kings of Macedon. None of the Hellenistic states ever became a strong political unit; they were all destined to fall to the expanding power of Rome.

The persistence of native loyalties and traditions which sapped the political strength of the Hellenistic states also prevented them from fully accomplishing their cultural mission. Alexander had

Alexander (left) defeats Darius III (right) at the battle of Issus. Roman mosaic from Pompeii, copy of a Hellenistic painting of the late 4th century B.C.

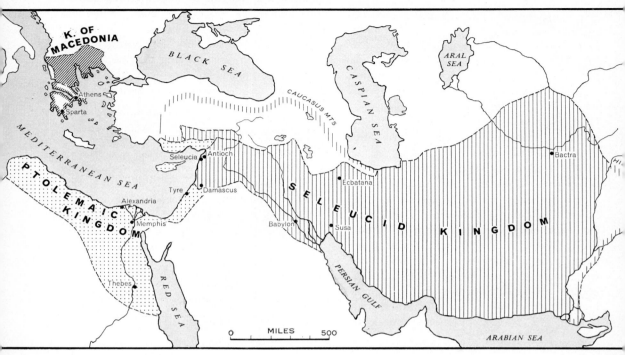

dreamed of a complete fusion of Greek and oriental civilizations, but the union remained imperfect. Outside the cities few people spoke Greek or adopted Greek ways of life or thought. The old native cultures smoldered beneath the surface; there was always a non-Greek way of doing things which expressed itself whenever the opportunity arose. Even after centuries of Greek cultural domination, Syria and Egypt retained their native languages, their religions, and their own forms of art. And the persisting antagonism between Greek and native had much to do with the eventual acceptance of Mohammedanism in the southern and eastern region of the Mediterranean.

Even within the Hellenized cities there was an uneven record of achievement. With the loss of political independence, the real Greeks had lost much of their self-confidence—their strong and assertive individualism. Once free men, they now bowed before kings along with the barbarians they despised. They had identified the good life with citizenship in an independent city-state; now the city had become a mere administrative unit in a great kingdom. And if the real Greeks were unsure and uncertain, the natives who imitated them were even more confused.

Greek art and literature never fully recovered from the collapse of the old city-state. In art there was both imitation of classical work and a continuation of the rather emotional style of the fourth century. In the end, however, the Hellenistic artists settled for a technically skillful, but not very profound, realism. Hellenistic writers also possessed high technical skill, but they failed in their attempts to deal with serious themes. Perhaps the most typical products of the age were the pastoral poems of Theocritus, which represented a flight from reality, and the farces of Menander, which dealt only with the surface of life. There were no great tragic poets, for tragedy depended on the belief that man was free to choose and to act at his own peril. Without that freedom, the wise and the good suffered equally with the evil and the stupid, and there was none of the stuff of tragedy in a universal calamity. History fared somewhat better. There were several competent Hellenistic historians, and there was one man of genius, Polybius, who in the spirit of Thucydides tried to discover the reasons for the growing power of Rome.

Philosophy

The highest achievements of the Hellenistic period were in philosophy and science, which had always been closely linked in Greek thought. The philosophers were painfully aware of the great problem of the age: what was the individual to do in a society in which individual effort seemed useless? It was difficult and dangerous to try to exert political influence in kingdoms run by irresponsible despots and their favorites. It was less difficult to accumulate wealth, but this, to many Greeks, was an inadequate goal. The old Greek religion was dying, and the new cults coming in from the Orient had not yet won wide acceptance among the upper classes; so the Greeks had no religious answer to their problem. The more thoughtful men turned to philosophy, and philosophers had a greater influence in the Hellenistic period than at any other stage in the development of western civilization.

Three important schools of philosophy grew up during the Hellenistic period: the Epicureans, the Stoics, and the Cynics, or Skeptics. The Epicureans taught that the chief goal of man was to avoid pain and to seek pleasure. They put at least as much stress on the first part of this formula as the second, and pointed out that political ambition, pursuit of wealth, and gross physical satisfactions in the end caused more pain than they were worth. The really wise man shunned politics and business; he found happiness in right conduct, serenity of mind, and moderation in all things. The gods cared nothing about human affairs and the wise man would do well to avoid involvement in them. Strong attachments to family, friends, or country meant unhappiness; it was best to live quietly on the margin of society.

The Stoics were nearly as pessimistic as the Epicureans, but they had a stronger sense of duty. They believed that there was a universal law and that all men, since they were equally subject to this law, were brothers. Right conduct was obedience to this law, and everyone, from slave to king, was capable of such obedience. A man must do his duty whatever and wherever he was. Like the Epicureans, the Stoics believed that power and wealth, human desires and human attachments, were dangerous. Public office was not to be sought, though it was not to be rejected if it came in the course of one's duty. But it was hard to live up to the Stoic code in public life. The ideal existence was that of the private citizen, free from public concerns and unaffected by external events.

The Cynics were the most pessimistic of all, and in their pessimism they reflected the insecurity and uncertainty of their age. According to their teaching, all knowledge and all beliefs were derived from sense impressions. But, since these impressions were fallible and contradictory, nothing could be known with any sureness, and one belief was as good as another. They took a certain pleasure in attacking the beliefs of others, but their final conclusion was much like that of the Epicureans and the Stoics. The wise man should not worry about transitory matters such as wealth, power, and fame; he should not try to set right a world sunk in hopeless ignorance. Peace of mind was the goal the wise man should seek, and peace of mind could be obtained only by withdrawal from worldly concerns.

These three philosophies discouraged the active and eager participation in community affairs which had marked the Greek city-state. Even for the Stoics, public service was a painful duty to be abandoned as soon as decency permitted. For the Epicureans and the Cynics public service was a positive evil, since it interfered with their ideal of the good life. These philosophical tendencies were reinforced by the mystical oriental religions which were spreading through the Hellenistic world. These religions had not yet reached their maximum influence, and will be discussed in more detail later (see pp. 143–44). It is enough to say that they all stressed salvation in a future life as compensation for the miseries of the present. Like Epicureanism, Stoicism, and Cynicism, they did not seek to reform a world which seemed hopeless, but rather to free the individual from that world.

It is easy enough to understand why, in an age of large states and absolute monarchies, individuals should feel discouraged and insignificant. But neither philosophic pessimism nor religious other-worldliness absorbed the interests of all men at all times; they had to do their jobs and earn their livings whether they thought they were important or not. Yet something important had been lost. That intensive use of human resources which had made the small city-state capable of great achievement was lacking in the Hellenistic kingdoms. This proved to be a serious weakness when they had to face the Roman Republic, a state marked by wide participation in politics and a strong feeling of responsibility for the public welfare.

Science

Many scholars would say that the most striking achievements of the Hellenistic age were in science. It is true that Hellenistic scientists performed some remarkable experiments and developed theories which foreshadowed the scientific achievements of the sixteenth, seventeenth, and eighteenth centuries. But we must not assume that science had the same significance to men of the third and second centuries B.C. as it has to us. Science in the Hellenistic period was an aspect of philosophy; purely speculative, it had little influence on ordinary life. Herophilus came very close to a complete theory of the circulation of the blood, but his work did little to change the practice of medicine. The principle of the steam engine was known, but it was used only for tricks of magic. Aristarchus developed a theory of the solar system with the planets circling around the sun, but only a few of his students accepted the new idea. The great majority of people, even of scholars, clung to the belief that the earth was the center of the universe.

In fact, the surprising thing about Hellenistic science was that so much of it was ignored or quickly forgotten. Even though it was encouraged by the rulers, notably by the Ptolemies of Egypt, it was not fully incorporated into the intellectual tradition of the Mediterranean world. Men reverted to the older doctrines of Aristotle, which remained the standard explanations of natural phenomena throughout the Roman and most of the medieval period. We have only fragments of the work of the greatest period of Hellenistic science, and this very fact shows how little attention was paid to that work.

Mathematics is the one notable exception. Euclid (*ca.* 300 B.C.), who built scattered propositions about geometry into a coherent system, has been studied from his day to our own. His books were not only the basis for all subsequent work in geometry; they were also considered for a long time a model for scientific reasoning in all fields. The mathematical formulas devised by Archimedes (287?–212 B.C.) for working out problems of physics and mechanics were more difficult to understand. People were more likely to remember stories about his setting Roman ships on fire with a huge burning-glass than they were to comprehend his rule for finding specific gravity. But Archimedes raised basic problems concerning mass, motion, and acceleration, and enough of this work survived to stimulate later scientific revivals.

Eratosthenes (third century B.C.), in one of the most striking experiments of ancient times, calculated the length of a degree on the earth's surface by observing how the height of the sun at noon varied between two towns lying on the same meridian. From this evidence he worked out an estimate of the earth's circumference which was very nearly right. (We are not entirely sure what the length of his unit of measurement was, but the most unfavorable interpretation would give him an error of about 10 per cent, and it may have been less.) Eratosthenes' estimate was remembered by later writers, and it may have eventually encouraged the fifteenth-century voyages of exploration by suggesting that the world was not impossibly large, and that the globe could be circumnavigated within a reasonable length of time.

But, as this last example suggests, while the work of the Hellenistic mathematicians and astronomers survived, it was many centuries before it inspired new investigations. The Romans, who became masters of the Hellenistic world in the first century B.C., saw little value in scientific inquiry, and little was accomplished under their rule. The intellectual heirs of the Hellenistic scientists were not the Romans, but the Moslem scholars of the tenth century A.D. and the western Christians of the thirteenth.

Suggestions for Further Reading

1. The Early Greeks

The classic epics of Homer, *The Iliad* * (trans. E. V. Rieu, 1950), and *The Odyssey* * (trans. E. V. Rieu, 1946), have played a great part in the foundation and evolution of western civilization. These poems are a mine of information about the early Greeks. R. Warner, *Greeks and Trojans* (1951), is an exciting prose account of the episodes of the Trojan War based largely on *The Iliad*. There is very reliable information on the private life of the Greeks in the seventh century B.C. in the poet Hesiod's *Works and Days* (trans. R. Lattimore, 1959); W. K. Prentice, *The Ancient Greeks* (1940), discusses political events at the time. C. E. Robinson, *A History of Greece* (1929), traces economic, social, political, and military developments among the early Greeks; a valuable introduction.

* Available in paperback edition.

2. The Greek City-States

There is excellent material on the origins and growth of Athens and Sparta in J. B. Bury, *History of Greece* (1901), and in M. L. W. Laistner, *A History of the Greek World, 479–323* B.C. (1936). Bury is somewhat more thorough, but Laistner is more readable and has a good critical bibliography. K. Freeman, *Greek City-States* (1950), pictures the Greek world through the study of nine important but lesser-known city-states. The social and constitutional history of Sparta is analyzed in the scholarly and interesting work of K. M. T. Chrimes, *Ancient Sparta* (1949).

3. Greek Science and Philosophy

The philosophical and scientific achievements of the Greeks have conditioned all subsequent western thinking. All the known Greek philosophers have now been translated in the *Loeb Classical Library,* and many important treatises are available in paperback.

The best study of early Greek philosophy and the birth of what we call science is J. Burnet, *Early Greek Philosophy* (rev. ed., 1958). There is valuable material on the Pre-Socratics in F. M. Cornford, *Before and After Socrates* (1950). E. Barker, *Greek Political Theory* (1948), traces the development of political thinking through Plato; an excellent analysis by an outstanding scholar and writer. A. E. Taylor, *Plato: The Man and His Work* (1926), is a provocative study of almost all aspects of Platonic thought. Taylor's brief monograph, *Platonism and Its Influence* (1929), is an inquiry into the relationship between Platonic philosophy and the modern world.

L. Robin, *Greek Thought and the Origins of the Scientific Spirit* (1948), traces the development of Greek science and has bibliographic material. There is an interesting description of Hippocratic medicine and Aristotelian biology in C. Singer, *A Short History of Biology* (1931). M. Kline, *Mathematics in Western Culture* (1953), is an exciting treatment of the influence of the Greek achievement on our civilization. Perhaps the best synthesis of Greek studies in philosophy and science is H. Marrou, *History of Education in Antiquity* (1948).

4. Athens and Sparta

Any study of Greek civilization should include Herodotus, *Histories* * (trans. A. Selincourt, 1951), which provides a wealth of information about the world that the Athenian Herodotus saw on his travels. Our chief written source for understanding Athens in the fifth century B.C. is Thucydides, *History of the Peloponnesian War* * (trans. R. Warner, 1954). This great historian gives a brief review of Greek history from 479 to 432, analyzes the ultimate causes of the war, and in so doing advances a significant philosophy of history. There is an excellent picture of Athens at the height of her political and cultural development in C. A. Robinson, *Athens in the Age of Pericles* (1959). The classic study of A. E. Zimmern, *The Greek Commonwealth* (1911), treats of political and economic conditions in fifth-century Athens in a very readable manner. Both H. Mitchell, *Sparta* (1952), and B. W. Henderson, *The Great War Between Athens and Sparta* (1927), discuss political affairs in Sparta in the period of the Peloponnesian War. The foreign policies which led to this war are analyzed in W. S. Ferguson, *Greek Imperialism* (1913). Ferguson stresses the continuity of constitutional development throughout the entire period.

5. Art and Literature

G. M. A. Richter, *A Handbook of Greek Art* (1959), which traces the evolution of Greek art in all forms, is a beautiful introduction to the artistic achievements of the

* Available in paperback edition.

Greeks. R. V. Schoder, *Masterpieces of Greek Art* (1960) is another good presentation of the material. Richter's *Sculpture and Sculptors of the Greeks* (rev. ed., 1950) combines tremendous knowledge of the subject with an exciting prose style, and contains good reproductions. There is excellent material on the slow development of architecture in A. W. Lawrence, *Greek Architecture* (1929), the standard work on the subject. The old work of W. J. Anderson and P. R. Spiers, *The Architecture of Ancient Greece* (1927), is sound and still valuable. Both A. W. Lawrence, *Classical Sculpture* (1944), and R. Lullies and M. Hirmer, *Greek Sculpture* (1957), show the Greek celebration of the human body.

The literature of the Greeks is easily accessible. The poets and dramatists are all in the *Loeb Classical Library*, and many are available in paperback. G. L. Dickinson, *The Greek View of Life* * (1951), is a very good introduction to Greek literature and thought; W. K. C. Guthrie, *The Greeks and Their Gods* (1950), is an excellent study of Greek religion and a valuable companion to the Greek classics. G. Murray, *Five Stages of Greek Religion* (1951), is also helpful for understanding drama and poetry. The best study of the Greek theater is probably H. D. F. Kitto, *Greek Tragedy* * (1939). W. Jaeger, *Paedeia: The Ideals of Greek Culture*, 3 vols. (trans. G. Highet, 1945), a study of the shaping of the Greek character, is a brilliant achievement by an outstanding authority on Greek life and thought.

6. Alexander and Macedon

The career of Alexander the Great has interested many historians. Plutarch's *Life of Alexander* * (many editions) is one of the chief sources. A. R. Burns, *Alexander and the Hellenistic Empire* (1947), is a balanced interpretation of Alexander's achievements. There is interesting material in both C. H. Robinson, *Alexander the Great* (1947), and W. W. Tarn, *Alexander the Great,* 2 vols. (1948); Tarn, who has devoted a lifetime of research to the subject, is the best guide. M. Cary, *A History of the Greek World, 323–146* B.C. (1932), which discusses political conditions, art, science, and economics, is the best general work on the Hellenistic period. H. Tarn, *Hellenistic Civilization* (1927), explores the evolution of Greco-Roman civilization. A fine short book on Hellenistic civilization is Bury, Bevan, Barber, and Tarn, *The Hellenistic Age* (1925), a readable and stimulating account by four leading authorities. The recent work of the English philosopher-historian A. J. Toynbee, *Hellenism* (1959), is an excellent assessment of the contribution of the Greco-Roman culture to the modern world.

7. The Hellenistic States

E. R. Bevan, *The House of Seleucus* (1902), and E. R. Bevan and J. P. Mahaffy, *Egypt under the Ptolemaic Dynasty* (1927), are sound and readable accounts.

8. Hellenistic Science

Most of the general works listed above have material on Hellenistic science. G. Sarton, *Ancient Science and Modern Civilization* (1954), a brief survey of all Greek science, is a good starting point for study. Sarton's *A History of Science* (1959), though intended for the specialist, is an interesting discussion of scientific developments in the last three centuries before Christ.

* Available in paperback edition.

3

Rome and the Unification
of the Mediterranean World

Although the peoples of western Europe had played no part in the development of the great eastern civilizations, they had not remained in a state of savagery, nor had they been uninfluenced by the ideas and techniques of their eastern neighbors. Before 1000 B.C. they had discovered how to domesticate animals, sow grain, shape pottery, and weave textiles. The Indo-European groups (Celtic- and Italic-speaking peoples, who entered Gaul and Italy during the second millennium B.C.) brought with them the use of bronze and began to smelt iron in some places not much later than the Greeks. The western Mediterranean was dotted with colonies settled by easterners who had brought their civilization with them. The Phoenicians had built cities in Spain; the Greeks had occupied large parts of Sicily and southern Italy; the mysterious Etruscans, possibly originating in Asia Minor, held the region just north of Rome. These settlements must have stimulated curiosity and inspired imitation. Thus, by the middle of the first millennium B.C., many of the peoples of western Europe had both the economic resources and the intellectual stimuli to build societies

more highly organized than those of the tribe or the village.

The first well-organized western states appeared in Italy, which was closer to the eastern Mediterranean than Gaul or Spain and had had longer contacts with eastern traders and colonists. All the major language groups of western Europe (Celtic, Germanic, and Italic) were of Indo-European origin, and hence were related to Greek. But the closest relationship was between the Italic dialects and Greek, a linguistic similarity that was reinforced by similarities in religion, society, and politics. Hence the Italians saw more of the Greeks than did their western neighbors, and were better able to understand the Greek way of life. Finally, there is some evidence that the population was denser in Italy than in Gaul or Germany or Spain. If it was, the Italians were probably under greater pressure to develop more complex forms of social organization.

The Early Roman Republic

These facts explain why city-states not unlike those of ancient Greece began to grow in Italy after 1000 B.C. But they do not explain why the Roman state rose so rapidly to become the strongest power in Italy. Rome had certain advantages—enough arable land to support a relatively large population, a good position on the main

---

Ruins of the Roman Forum. The Forum was the center of Roman life; it was both a marketplace and a meeting place and contained many of the principal public buildings of the city. In the foreground is the Arch of Titus.

north-south trade route, an easily defended citadel on the hills above the Tiber. On the other hand, it never had a very good harbor; it produced little that could be exported; and it was not a great trading center. Neither geography nor economics explains why Rome was able to break out of a ring of jealous neighbors and unite all Italy under its leadership. The rise of Rome was due almost entirely to the Romans' skill in political organization.

Down to 200 B.C. the one big business in Rome was government. There were a few great landlords, but even they were not wealthy by oriental standards, and most of the people were small farmers. When a business class did arise, around 200 B.C., it was occupied largely with government contracts. The only opportunity any of these groups had to increase their wealth and power was through wars of conquest. Successful wars meant more land for the farmers, and especially for the landlords, and more contracts for army supplies and public works for the businessmen. But to wage successful wars required constant attention to political and military problems.

The Romans devoted themselves with extraordinary single-mindedness to these problems, and their early history is largely a history of constitutional debates and wars of conquest. They were only slightly interested in the arts and sciences; it was a long time before they produced any literature they felt worth preserving. Nor did they spend much time on philosophical inquiry or religious speculation. Their gods were the founders and protectors of the Roman state, the embodiments of the virtues which made Rome strong. Mars, the god of war, rather unimportant in Greek mythology, was one of the chief Roman gods. Apollo, the patron of the arts, was slighted. For generations the ablest Romans devoted

An Etruscan sarcophagus, ca. 3rd century B.C.

themselves to politics, law, administration, and war, and their devotion set an indelible mark on Roman society.

The Romans were not only devoted to the arts of government; they also showed greater skill in these arts than any other Italic people. If we knew more about the Etruscans, we might find that they were partly responsible for this Roman expertness in politics. By 700 B.C. the Etruscans had developed a relatively complex and sophisticated civilization. Recent excavations have revealed the richness of their art; it seems likely that they were equally advanced in government. At any rate, Rome in the seventh and sixth centuries B.C. was under the influence of the Etruscans, and was governed for a while by kings who were probably of Etruscan origin. This experience may have speeded up developments which took place more slowly elsewhere.

Early Roman Government

During a period which stretched from about 600 B.C. to about 250 B.C., Rome went through a series of political changes which resembled those in the early Greek city-states. We have much legend and little evidence about this period, but certain broad facts seem clear. At first there was a king with supreme civil and military authority. He was overthrown, about 509 B.C., by an aristocracy, which for some time kept all power in its hands. These "patricians," who were large landowners and military leaders, dominated the much larger group of unprivileged "plebeians." Many plebeians served as tenant-farmers on patrician estates, or depended on the aristocracy for economic support and backing in lawsuits. But some were independent landowners, merchants, and artisans. This group of successful plebeians grew in size and in wealth, and soon after 500 B.C. began to demand a share of political power.

"The Orator," an Etruscan bronze statue, ca. 150 B.C.

At this point the Romans made their first important political decision. On the one hand, the patricians realized that they must make some concessions to the plebeians instead of trying to preserve all their privileges at the cost of disrupting the society and weakening the city. Like the Athenians, they needed the service of all free men if Rome was to be strong in war. On the other hand, the plebeians did not press for rapid, sweeping changes. They accepted a pro-

Roman territory ca. 326 B.C.

Rome and its allies at the start of the
Second Punic War, 218 B.C.

MILES
0   100

ALPS

RAETIANS   CELTS

CISALPINE   GAULS

Segusio   Vercellae   Mediolanium
Placentia   Cremona
Parma
Mutina   Po River
Bononia   AEMILIAN WAY

GAULA
CASSIAN WAY

Pisae   ADRIATIC SEA
Arretium   Ancona
Volaterrae   ETRUSCANS   Clusium
Tiber River   FLAMINIAN WAY

CORSICA   APPENNINE
Narnia
SABINES
AQUIANS
VALERIAN WAY
ROME   Alba   Tibur
Ostia   LATIUM   SAMNITES   Sipontum
APPIAN WAY   VOLSCIANS   LATIN WAY
APULIA   MESSAPIANS
CAMPANIA   APPIAN WAY   Brundisium
Cumae   Naples
MT. VESUVIUS   LUCANIA   GREEKS   Tarentum
SARDINIA   Salernum   Heraclea
Paestum   LUCANIANS

TYRRHENIAN

SEA   Croton

MAGNA

GRAECIA

AFRICAN   Messana   Locri
Panormus   Rhegium
MT. ETNA
SICILY   GREEKS   Syracuse
SEA

Carthage

gram of gradual reform, which took generations to accomplish. Only very slowly were the plebeians admitted to all offices; only very slowly did the Roman constitution become democratic. Changes which were compressed into a few decades at Athens took centuries at Rome. This avoidance of extreme positions, this willingness to compromise, this strong feeling of responsibility for the welfare of the city, remained typical of Rome during the period in which it rose to greatness.

The development of the Roman constitution between 509 and 287 B.C. illustrates this gift for compromise and gradual change. After the expulsion of the kings, the chief magistrates of the city were two consuls who shared executive power during their one-year term of office. They were elected by an assembly made up of all citizens but divided into groups based on social position and wealth. Each group had one vote, but since the wealthy landowners dominated a majority of the groups they controlled the election of consuls. Moreover, for many years only patricians were eligible for the office of consul. The same restrictions applied to lesser offices which were created during the fifth and fourth centuries B.C. to ease the consuls' administrative burden. Since each consul could veto the acts of his colleague, and since they held office for only a year, they could seldom make important policy decisions. General direction of the Roman government was in the hands of the senate, a large group of patricians from which the consuls were drawn and to which they returned when they had completed their term of office. The senate had to seek the assembly's approval for important legislation, treaties, and declarations of war. But since the system of voting by groups in the assembly gave preponderance to the wealthy, the proposals of the senate were almost always approved. Thus a few hundred patricians controlled every aspect of Roman political life.

The plebeians attacked this entrenched position by staging a series of sit-down strikes in which they camped on the Aventine Hill and refused to serve the patrician government. Without plebeian manpower, the patricians were helpless, especially as Rome was engaged in almost constant warfare with the Etruscans and nearby Italic peoples. This secession of the plebeians threatened the very existence of the Roman state, and the patricians could not risk refusing their demands. The plebeians first used this means of pressure soon after 500 B.C. in order to secure recognition of their tribunes, men elected by the plebeians as protectors of their interests. Eventually there were ten tribunes who gained a remarkably strong position in the Roman state, thanks to the steady support of the plebeians. Their persons were inviolate; anyone who attacked a tribune could be put to death without trial. The tribunes could veto the acts of the consuls or any other officials without giving a reason, and a tribune's veto could not be overridden.

The tribunes were elected by an assembly of tribes in which the Romans were divided into groups based on geographical district instead of relative wealth. The patricians did not participate in the assembly of tribes and hence could not control its vote. The tribunes used the assembly of tribes as a means of putting pressure on the senate; a resolution voted by the tribes and approved by the senate had the force of law. Before long, the patrician consuls found that it was more convenient to work through the assembly of tribes than through the older general assembly, for the assembly of tribes could be convened with less formality and could vote more rapidly. This development almost ended the power of the old general assembly, though it continued to meet for a few ceremonial affairs.

Finally, in 287 B.C., the plebeians insisted that their tribal assembly be given full legislative power, and they emphasized their demand by staging another sit-down strike. In the resulting discord, the ordinary magistrates were stripped of their power and full authority was turned over to a dictator for six months. The dictator ended the dispute by ruling that all measures passed by the assembly of tribes should have the force of law, even without senatorial approval.

In the meantime, the plebeians were also gaining access to all the offices of government. The first plebeian consul was elected in 362 B.C.; by 340 B.C. it was understood that one consul must be a plebeian and that both might be plebeians. By about 300 B.C. even the priesthood, the last stronghold of the aristocracy, was thrown open to plebeians. This was a major concession, because the Romans, following Etruscan precedents, would undertake no important business unless the auspices were favorable. The priests determined the auspices by watching the flight of birds or by examining the entrails of sacred chickens. Up to this time the priests, all of whom were patricians, had been able to block plebeian policies by claiming that the auspices were unfavorable.

This list of plebeian political victories might suggest that shortly after 300 B.C. Rome had become a complete democracy, like Athens in the fifth century B.C. Actually the reforms had not ended aristocratic control; they had merely changed the composition and the tactics of the aristocracy. The plebeians had made great social gains, for they could now hold high office and marry into good families. But this very mobility tended to deprive them of their natural leaders. The old patrician class was astute enough to accept the ablest and wealthiest plebeians as members of the senate and to merge with them in a new upper class which had nearly as much power as the old

patriciate. True, they had to pay a little more attention to political manipulation and had to give the poorer classes some share in the profits resulting from the rapid expansion of the Roman state. But political

❖❖❖❖❖❖❖❖❖❖❖❖❖❖❖❖❖❖❖❖❖❖❖❖❖❖❖❖❖❖❖

St. Augustine
on the Early Republic

These lines were written at the very end of the Roman Empire (*ca.* 412 A.D.) by St. Augustine. They are especially striking because Augustine, as a saint and a Christian, minimized the value of all worldly achievements. But he was sufficiently impressed by the Roman tradition to admit that the Roman state had been the best of all secular states.

Wherefore, when the kingdoms of the East had been illustrious for a long time, it pleased God that there should also arise a Western empire, which, though later in time, should be more illustrious in extent and greatness. And, in order that it might overcome the grievous evils which existed among other nations, He purposely granted it to such men as, for the sake of honor, and praise, and glory, consulted well for their country, in whose glory they sought their own, and whose safety they did not hesitate to prefer to their own, suppressing the desire of wealth and many other vices for this one vice, the love of praise. . . . So they despised their own private affairs for the sake of the republic, and for its treasury resisted avarice, consulted for the good of their country with a spirit of freedom, addicted neither to what their laws pronounced to be crime nor to lust. By all these acts they pressed forward to honors, power, and glory; they were honored among almost all nations; they imposed the laws of their empire upon many nations; and at this day, both in literature and history, they are glorious among almost all nations.

From *Basic Writings of St. Augustine,* ed. by Whitney J. Oates, Vol. II, pp. 75, 77. Copyright 1948 by Random House, Inc. Reprinted by permission.

❖❖❖❖❖❖❖❖❖❖❖❖❖❖❖❖❖❖❖❖❖❖❖❖❖❖❖❖❖❖❖

A citizen of the Republic (center), with two of his slaves whom he had freed. 1st century B.C.

manipulation was not too difficult, and the profits of expansion were great enough for everyone to share. On the other hand, as the state expanded, government became so complicated that the tribal assembly of citizens had neither enough knowledge to make decisions nor enough time to see that they were carried out. The members of the senate, however, served for life, and had both experience in politics and time to think about political problems. They thus retained control of the government in spite of the apparent triumph of democratic principles. For more than a century their dominance caused no resentment. Senatorial leadership was on the whole wise and efficient, and it produced such striking successes in foreign policy that most of the Romans were content.

The Roman Conquest of Italy

With its internal political problems under control, the Roman state expanded rapidly. The plebeians, satisfied with their gains, remained loyal citizens and devoted soldiers. The old patrician and the new plebeian senators worked well enough together so that there were few factional quarrels. Year after year there was remarkable continuity in Roman policy, and an equally remarkable willingness to allow experienced and responsible men to run the state. Both these sources of stability had been lacking in the Greek democracies.

Without this stability Rome could probably not have fought the innumerable wars that marked the early centuries of the Republic. Roman generals were not infallible; they lost many battles, and Rome itself was burned by invading Gauls in 387 B.C. But though a Roman general might lose a battle, the Roman army never lost a major war. One reason for the army's success was the stern discipline imposed by the consuls, who did not hesitate to use their power of life and death over the soldiers. Even temporary camps were always fortified, and there was no straggling on the march or wavering on the battlefield. More important was Roman skill in military organization. In the fifth century B.C. the Romans, like most of their contemporaries, drew their best troops from among the wealthiest citizens, the only ones who could afford long campaigns and expensive equipment. But the Romans soon saw that this policy wasted much of their man power, and by the early fourth century they were paying their soldiers and supplying the poorer citizens with arms. Now most Romans of military age could serve in the heavy infantry, the backbone of the army, and the reservoir of soldiers was so vast that no single defeat could exhaust it; new units could always be raised to replace those that were killed or captured. Finally, about the end of the fourth century B.C., the Romans developed a particularly effective military unit, the legion. The legion included about four thousand men (this number was later increased), and it had considerable striking power in a region where 15,000 men formed a large army. At the same time it was highly flexible, for it was divided into lesser units trained to maneuver independently.

This combination of discipline, large numbers of fighting men, and good tactical organization more than made up for occasional lapses in generalship. The Romans never accepted defeat, not only because they were courageous, but also because their military system made it unnecessary. They could always raise new armies and go on pounding their enemies. Stubborn perseverance won more for Rome than brilliant strategy; less well-organized states simply could not hold out against the relentless pressure Rome could exert.

Although Roman territory increased steadily after 500 B.C., it seems doubtful that the government of the early Republic had any long-range plans for expansion. Some things, of course, were obvious. Roman territory must be defended and dangerous neighbors pushed back. The other cities of Latium, the district immediately south of Rome, must not be allowed to combine against Rome, or to fall under the control of a hostile power. Following these elementary rules of political strategy, the Ro-

mans thrust the Etruscans back from the Tiber in the fifth century B.C. But then, with the Etruscans weakened, the Gauls, a group of Celtic tribes from the north, began to drive into central Italy. They took the city of Rome in 387 B.C., though not the citadel on the Capitoline Hill, and only after half a century of hard fighting did the Romans succeed in driving them back beyond the Apennines. But the ending of the Gallic threat removed one of the reasons for the close alliance that Rome had forged with the Latin cities. In 336 B.C. these cities allied themselves with the cities of Campania, the region between Latium and the Bay of Naples, and made war on Rome. This conflict ended in 334 B.C. with a complete Roman victory. Latium was incorporated into Roman territory and the Campanian communities became Roman allies.

For the first time in its history Rome was reasonably secure. It now controlled a solid bloc of territory running from southern Etruria to the Bay of Naples and reaching well back into the hills. Now that Rome was the strongest power in Italy, some Romans may have begun to dream of expanding their authority throughout the peninsula. In any case, the Roman penetration into Campania had already aroused the hostility of the Samnites, a central Italian people whose lands bordered those of Rome and who had hoped to take the coastal region around Naples for themselves.

In the Samnite wars, which lasted from 325 to 290 B.C., Rome completed its domination of the Italian peninsula. The Samnites, who were good fighters, twice inflicted severe defeats on the Roman army, but they were finally worn down by Roman persistence. In the last phase of the war the Samnites won support from the Etruscans and the Gauls, but this alliance, which might have been fatal to Rome a few decades earlier, came too late. All three peoples had been so weakened by Roman attacks that even their combined forces could not defeat the Roman army. A great Roman victory in 295 B.C. broke the resistance of the allies, and in the mopping-up operations Rome took control of all Italy between the Gallic holdings in the Po Valley and the Greek cities in the extreme south.

Now Rome entered into the wider political arena of the Mediterranean world. The Greek cities of southern Italy had close relations with the rulers of Sparta and Epirus, and had sometimes called on them for aid. The Carthaginians, who were established in western Sicily, were determined to prevent any strong power from gaining a foothold in southern Italy. Thus any further Roman expansion was certain to arouse the hostility of states far stronger than any Rome had challenged so far. Without the support, or at least the neutrality, of the Italians whom they had so recently subdued, the Romans could not hope to defeat such powerful enemies.

During the Mediterranean wars which filled the next centuries Rome did receive the loyalty of most Italians—another proof of Roman political skill. Stubborn and inflexible in making war, in making peace the Romans showed the same genius for compromise that had enabled them to solve their internal problems. On the one hand, they protected themselves against uprisings by annexing large portions of their enemies' land and by establishing strategic colonies throughout the peninsula. On the other hand, they allowed most of the Italian cities to retain local self-government within the framework of a permanent and unequal alliance with Rome. Rome assumed complete control of the external relations of the allied cities, forbidding them to form leagues with one another or to deal with outside powers. Rome could also call for military assistance from any ally, and in time of war allied troops were under the command of Roman generals. But the allies retained their own laws and institutions and had almost complete freedom in running their internal affairs. True, Rome encouraged its allies to establish aristocratic governments, but this policy strengthened rather than strained the alliance. Local aristocrats sympathized with the senatorial governing class at Rome and were enriched by their share of the booty from Roman wars.

Thus Rome had created a system of alliances not unlike that of the Athenian Empire. Why did the Roman system prove more durable? There were two reasons: First, Rome interfered less in the internal affairs of its allies and laid a lighter burden on them than did Athens. Thus Rome retained their loyalty even in times of danger and defeat. Second, Rome vanquished its great rival, Carthage, while Athens was defeated by Sparta.

The Carthaginian Wars

The Carthaginian wars grew out of Roman involvement in the affairs of Greek Italy. Following their usual custom, the Romans had allied themselves with one of the weaker Greek cities, thus arousing the hostility of Tarentum, the leader of the Greek communities. Tarentum asked for assistance from Pyrrhus, king of Epirus in Greece, who brought a first-class army to Italy in 280 B.C. Pyrrhus defeated the Romans in several hard-fought battles, and then won some striking successes over the Carthaginians in Sicily. But he could never solidify his position in Italy, for the Greek cities feared that he would become their master, and the Romans, with their usual persistence, kept on fighting in spite of his victories. Diverted by a chance to enlarge his possessions in Greece, Pyrrhus abandoned his Italian project and left the Greeks of Italy to their fate. Rome promptly overran the south, and by 270 B.C. had forced all the Greek cities to become allies.

Carthage and Rome had formed a temporary alliance when both were threatened by Pyrrhus, but the Carthaginians were not prepared to accept the Roman advance to the Sicilian Straits. Rome was the great land power of the West, while the Phoenician traders who had settled Carthage had long dominated the sea. Thanks to their naval power, they held most of the North African coast, southern and eastern Spain, Sardinia, Corsica, and the western half of Sicily. The Romans were no match for Carthaginian naval strength; in fact, they built their first fighting ships only after war with Carthage had begun. On the other hand, the Roman citizen-soldiers were more loyal to the state and probably better fighters, man for man, than the mercenaries whom Carthage employed. Yet the advantage was not entirely on the Roman side, for the Carthaginian generals were professional soldiers, while the consuls who commanded the Roman army were elected each year by the assembly. Although no man could become consul without extensive military experience, the assembly did not always choose able, or even competent, commanders.

And so the two powers stood evenly matched. In fact, it is surprising that the Romans were willing to risk a war with Carthage so soon after their conquest of southern Italy. Evidently some prominent Romans felt it an unwise move, for the Senate took the unusual step of referring the final decision to the tribal assembly. But the long series of victories had built up confidence in the destiny of Rome, and many Romans coveted the wealth of the Carthaginian empire. As deliberately as a people can, the Romans decided on a policy of expansion. They concluded an alliance with the Sicilian city of Messana, and the Carthaginians, provoked by this direct infringement of their sphere of influence, declared war in 264 B.C.

This first war with Carthage lasted from 264 to 241 B.C.* Rome's main objective was to expel the Carthaginians from Sicily, which meant that Carthaginian naval power had to be destroyed. With characteristic confidence in their ability to master any military problem, the Romans built a fleet. Although they had had almost no experience in naval warfare, they won their first sea battle with the Carthaginians. They won their second as well. Then they were beset by disaster as storms and the Carthaginian navy destroyed three of their fleets. But the Romans, as usual, would not admit that they had been worsted. Straining their resources to the limit, they built a fourth fleet, with which they won a decisive victory off the western tip of Sicily. This victory so weakened Carthage that it was never again a first-rate naval power.

Victory on land followed victory at sea. The Romans exploited their early naval advantage by landing an army in North Africa, the first time Roman troops had ventured out of the Italian peninsula. But the Carthaginians rallied, defeated the Roman army in Africa, and maintained their hold on western Sicily. Once Rome had gained final control of the sea, however, the fate of Sicily was sealed, for the Carthaginians could no longer support military operations there. Accepting defeat, they surrendered Sicily to the Romans and paid a large indemnity.

The long war with Carthage had revealed the strength of Roman political and military institutions. In spite of repeated defeats the Romans had always been able to keep an army in the field and a fleet at sea, and to retain the loyalty of their allied and subject cities. Further fighting during the next twenty years kept both their army and their navy at peak efficiency.

---

* The wars with Carthage are often called the Punic Wars, from Latin *Poeni* = Phoenician = Carthaginian.

The Gauls in the Po Valley, reinforced by new bands from beyond the Alps, posed a constant threat to the Roman position in northern Italy. The Romans defeated them and pushed them back into the upper Po Valley but could not entirely subdue them. At about the same time Rome fought a war with the semi-piratical kingdom of Illyria, on the east coast of the Adriatic, to protect the commerce of the Greek cities of southern Italy. The war brought no great territorial gains, but it did lead to alliances with various states on the Greek mainland, and hence involved Rome in the complicated politics of the Hellenistic world.

But the gravest threat during these twenty years came from the revival of Carthaginian power—this time in Spain. This was the work of Hamilcar Barca (who had been the ablest Carthaginian general in the First Punic War), his son-in-law Hasdrubal, and his son Hannibal. By exploiting the silver mines of Spain, the richest then being worked in Europe, they managed to build a first-rate army and to unite most of Spain under Carthaginian rule. Even if they had shown a smiling face they would have aroused Roman suspicions. Actually, they made clear that their intention was to avenge their defeat in the First Punic War. Rome reacted in a characteristic way by forming an alliance with Saguntum, a city well within the Carthaginian sphere of influence in Spain. Hannibal, now commander in Spain, took up the challenge by attacking Saguntum. So began the Second Punic War.

This war, which lasted from 218 to 202 B.C., was in many respects the most desperate war that Rome ever fought. Instead of waiting to be attacked, Hannibal marched a large army through Gaul, across the Alps, and into Italy. He was even able to take a few war elephants with him, much to the astonishment of the Gauls and the Italians. This march almost nullified the value of

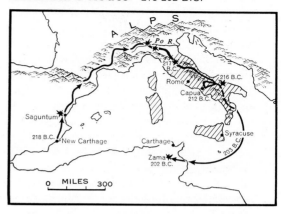

Hannibal's Route 218-202 B.C.

Rome's control of the sea, for as long as Hannibal could maintain an army in the heart of Italy the Romans could not exert their full strength in Spain or in Africa. Moreover, though Hannibal suffered losses in crossing the Alps, he found the Gauls of the Po Valley eager to swell his ranks in a new attack on Rome. The crisis in Italy also encouraged enemies of Rome on the eastern shores of the Adriatic, though their attacks were not very effective. Far more disturbing was the defection to Hannibal of cities in southern Italy that had remained completely loyal during the First Punic War. These defections enabled Hannibal to establish himself in the south, after his initial thrust at Rome had been deflected, and so prolonged the war for many years.

Hannibal had already displayed his boldness and skill in his march across the Alps; his campaign in Italy put him among the great generals of all time. A master of battlefield tactics, especially of enveloping maneuvers, he crushed one Roman army after another. For a long time the Romans could find no general to match him; to his brilliance they could oppose only their stubborn courage. They could not defeat him but they could contain him. By always having an army ready to meet him, they forced him to keep his own army together instead of dispersing it in a bid to control wider areas. By disrupting his lines of communication, they cut off most of his reinforcements and made it difficult for disaffected Roman allies to go over to his side. This policy of avoiding major battles while keeping constant pressure on the enemy was first developed by the Roman general Fabius (whence our expression, Fabian tactics), and it proved to be the only way of dealing with Hannibal. He maintained himself in Italy for almost fifteen years and devastated much of the south, but he never seriously threatened the city of Rome and he never occupied a significant amount of Roman territory. During most of the period he was confined to the south, where a few Roman allies, such as Syracuse and Capua, joined his cause. He would have been better off in the north, where he could have drawn reinforcements from Spain and the Gauls, but the Roman network of fortified cities made it difficult for him to operate there. Thus the Italian phase of the war settled into an endurance contest between Hannibal and Rome, and in such a struggle Rome had most of the advantages.

Moreover, the Romans carried the conflict to other areas. Though they suffered heavy losses in the fighting with Hannibal, they still managed, year after year, to keep an army in Spain. At first this force fared almost as badly as the Roman armies in Italy. But at last the Romans found a capable general, Publius Cornelius Scipio, who gained such success in Spain that the last Carthaginian army there decided to abandon the country and go to Hannibal's assistance. These troops succeeded in breaking through Scipio's lines and joining the Gauls in the Po Valley, but when they tried to march south they were almost annihilated by a Roman army. The defeat of this Spanish army, Hannibal's last hope for

reinforcements, made his position almost untenable.

After Scipio's conquest of Spain, he was recalled to head an expedition to North Africa. There he not only defeated a Carthaginian army but also succeeded in stirring up a rebellion against the Carthaginians. The situation was so desperate that Hannibal was recalled from Italy. In 202 B.C. he met Scipio at Zama and was totally defeated. In a peace which reduced Carthage to the status of an insignificant city-state, this once-great power surrendered all territory except for a small district surrounding the city, agreed to limit its navy to ten ships, and promised never to make war without Roman consent. Rome had defeated its only rival for supremacy in the Mediterranean. The Republic was to fight many wars in the centuries to come, but none of its future enemies would threaten the center of Roman power as Hannibal had done.

The Later Republic

After 200 B.C. Rome was the strongest power in the Mediterranean world. Total Roman resources in men and money may not have been greater than those of the major Hellenistic states, such as the Seleucid realm in Syria or the Ptolemaic kingdom in Egypt. But Rome made far better use of its resources than any of its opponents. The Roman political system still commanded the loyalty of both citizens and allies, which meant that Rome could use a far greater proportion of its available man power for military service than could the eastern states, which relied largely on mercenaries. Roman patriotism was still so strong that the state could make heavy financial demands on its citizens without risking rebellion. It would have required a coalition of all the major Hellenistic states to match Roman military power, and the one thing the Hellenistic states could never do was to unite.

Expansion East and West

The chaotic situation in the eastern Mediterranean in the second century B.C. invited Roman intervention. There was friction between the Seleucids and the Ptolemies, between the king of Macedon and some of the Greek cities striving to maintain a precarious independence, and between rival kings in Asia Minor. Kings and cities constantly sought allies, and it was only natural that some of them should turn to Rome. Once Rome had been drawn into this welter of conflicting ambitions, it could scarcely avoid annexing new territories. The Romans were too strong and too determined to endure the endless intrigue and the inconclusive wars which had kept the area in turmoil. They intended to protect their few faithful allies and to punish the much larger group of states which were constantly shifting their allegiance. On their first intervention in a troubled region they usually made an easy peace which preserved the independence of local rulers. But if the peace were repeatedly broken, they ended by annexing the lands of those who had attacked Roman allies or deserted the Roman cause.

The one exception to this rule was in Greece proper. By the second century most upper-class Romans had acquired a great respect for Greek civilization and a somewhat romantic desire to restore to the Greek city-states their old liberties. In spite of repeated disappointments Roman generals persisted in honoring the independence of the Greek cities. In return, the Romans expected the Greeks to recognize their hegemony in the area and to allow them to settle disputes among the Greek cities. Only when these hopes were destroyed did the Romans annex large amounts of Greek territory. And even then they extended nomi-

✣✣✣✣✣✣✣✣✣✣✣✣✣✣✣✣✣✣✣✣✣✣✣✣✣✣✣✣✣✣✣✣✣

A Greek Historian's Appraisal of the Roman Constitution
ca. 200 B.C.

In the following passage Polybius presents for the first time a fully developed theory of checks and balances.

The best feature of my work and the most instructive element in it is that it should enable students to know under what kind of constitution Rome brought nearly the entire world under its power in somewhat less than fifty-three years. . . . The Roman constitution had three elements, each of them possessing sovereign powers, and their respective share of power in the whole state had been regulated with such a scrupulous regard for equality and equilibrium that no one could say for certain whether the government as a whole were an aristocracy, or a democracy, or a despotism. And no wonder, for if we look at the power of the Consuls we should be inclined to regard it as despotic, if we regard that of the Senate, as aristocratic, and finally when we look at the power possessed by the people it would seem a clear case of democracy. . . . The result of this power of the different estates for mutual help or harm is a union sufficiently firm for all emergencies. . . . For when danger from without compels them to unite and work together, the strength developed by the state is extraordinary; everything required is unfailingly carried out by the eager rivalry of all classes to devote their whole minds to the need of the hour. . . . And when external alarms are past . . . if any one of the three classes becomes puffed up . . . and unduly aggressive, the mutual interdependence of all three and the fact that each one can be checked and thwarted by the others, must plainly restrain this tendency and so the proper equilibrium is maintained.

Adapted from Polybius, *Histories*, trans. by E. S. Shuckburgh (London: Macmillan, 1889), book VI.

✣✣✣✣✣✣✣✣✣✣✣✣✣✣✣✣✣✣✣✣✣✣✣✣✣✣✣✣✣✣✣✣✣

nal independence to Athens and Sparta as allies of Rome.

The decisive phase of these eastern wars took place between 200 and 167 B.C. By the latter date both the Macedonian and Seleucid rulers had been defeated, and the king of Egypt was entirely dependent for survival on the good will of the Romans. In spite of these victories, it took some time to convince the Hellenistic governments that Rome was indeed master of the East. The Macedonians, in particular, made repeated attempts to weaken Roman authority; their resistance ended only when Rome annexed the entire country. There was also trouble in Asia Minor, where Rome tried to prevent any ruler, even a friendly one, from gaining a dominant position. But by 146 B.C. it was clear that resistance to Rome was almost hopeless. Macedonia and most of Greece had been annexed, and the rulers of Asia Minor, Syria, and Egypt could make no move in foreign policy without inviting Roman intervention.

Meanwhile, Rome was conducting mopping-up operations in the West. The Gauls in the Po Valley, who for generations had threatened Rome's position in northern Italy, were finally subdued and their lands annexed. The people of Spain, who found Roman rule no improvement over Carthaginian, were a constant source of trouble, but their revolts had been checked by 133 B.C. The most spectacular victory was gained over Carthage in the Third Punic War (149–146 B.C.). There was no real need for this war, but many Romans resented the fact that their old enemy, though insignificant politically, was acquiring great commercial wealth. For years Cato, one of the leaders of the Roman senate, ended every speech with the words: "Carthage must be destroyed." The Romans nagged the Carthaginians into acts of defiance and finally into a hopeless war. Though the Carthaginians resisted with the courage of

desperation, in the end their city was taken and utterly destroyed. The Carthaginians were sold into slavery and their territory was annexed by Rome.

Political Problems

The long years of war and conquest had put a severe strain on the Roman political and social system. With every decade, new problems had to be solved and new responsibilities assumed. The Romans met these challenges successfully as far as the outside world was concerned. In spite of occasional weakness and stupidity and growing corruption, they had kept their political and military organization more effective than that of any of their opponents. But Roman citizens were beginning to lose their sense of community. A gulf was opening between the aristocracy and the rest of the population, between the few who profited and the many who suffered from the wars of expansion. Moreover, the loyalty of the Italian allies was weakening, for their autonomy had been impaired by the wartime demands imposed by Rome. Rome was becoming a colonial exploiter instead of the head of an alliance of self-respecting partners. Thus the sense of participation in a common effort, the feeling of common responsibility, which had been the strength of the Roman state and the Roman alliance system, was growing thin. After 146 B.C. Rome was threatened not by outside enemies, but by internal revolution.

The exigencies of war had in themselves generated political tension. During the Punic Wars and the period of expansion, Rome had to fight on many fronts and was in constant need of capable generals. The two consuls, even when aided by their chief subordinates, the praetors, could not command all the armies. This difficulty was overcome first by increasing the number of praetors, and then by calling former officials back into service. These men were given the titles of proconsul and propraetor; they had the power of command in remote areas but no authority in Rome. But sometimes there were not enough ex-magistrates capable of filling all these posts, and then the assembly voted extraordinary powers of command to private citizens. This was to prove a dangerous precedent, for it opened the way for demagogues to rise to power by bypassing normal constitutional processes.

Rome's far-flung victories throughout the Mediterranean raised another problem: how to govern the conquered territories. These areas, too remote to become part of the Roman city-state and too hostile to be accepted as allies, were organized as provinces, the first ones being Sicily and Spain. The Romans used the same formula which had proved successful in military operations: they named proconsuls and propraetors as governors of the provinces. With no professional civil servants to aid them in their task, these officials relied on military subordinates and young men of good family who accompanied them to gain political experience.

This improvised system of provincial government harmed both the Romans and their subjects. The proconsuls and propraetors served for very short periods, often no more than a year. Their chief duty was to maintain military security in the provinces with the least possible expense to Rome. They often knew little about the people they were governing, and in any case they had to promote the interests of Rome over those of the native population. At the best they kept peace and maintained security by levying heavy taxes and constantly interfering with local governments. At the worst they used their brief period of office to stuff their own pockets and the pockets of their friends with huge sums of money extorted from the provincials. Subject peoples felt they were paying a heavy price for the Roman peace which had been imposed on

them, and most of them tried to revolt at least once. The inhabitants of the Spanish peninsula rebelled about once every generation in the century following their conquest by Rome.

Problems in the provinces intensified problems at home. Many aristocratic Roman senators grew very wealthy through the exploitation of the provincials, thus sharpening the division between rich and poor. Competition for public office increased, for consuls and praetors knew that they would receive lucrative provincial commands when they had finished their duties in Rome. The temptation to resort to bribery and other abuses to win an election became almost irresistible. A class of wealthy businessmen arose who fattened on government contracts. These men were barred from the senate, and yet they had great influence. Power without responsibility made them even more corrupt than the senators. The poorer citizens gained little of the loot from the provinces, but they had to serve in the armies which maintained Roman rule. Their patriotism waned, and it was difficult to find troops to suppress the revolts in Spain about the middle of the second century B.C.

Back of all these political problems lay the same flaw that had wrecked Greek civilization. City-states that did not expand always ran the risk of being conquered or economically ruined by more powerful neighbors. But city-states that did expand always failed to develop institutions to assimilate their newly acquired territories into the old body politic. The central government remained that of a city-state, and the only people who could fully participate in it were those who lived in or near the capital city and who could attend meetings of local assemblies. Citizens who settled in remote districts were effectively disfranchised, and the inhabitants of allied cities, though they might preserve limited self-government, had no influence on general policy. The making of peace and war, military and financial exactions, commercial policy—all were decided by the people of the dominant city. No city-state ever tried the experiment of calling in representatives of colonies or allied cities to take part in deliberations concerning the empire as a whole. This is curious, because the principle of representation was not unknown in the ancient world. The Greeks had had leagues for common religious purposes in which the governing body was an assembly of delegates from each participating city. Later, in the Hellenistic period, certain Greek cities had formed similar leagues for political purposes. But neither Athens nor Rome followed these precedents; instead, each city tried to govern an empire through the institutions of a small town. Both cities failed, and in their failure they resorted to bribery at home and coercion abroad, thus alienating the great mass of citizens, allies, and subjects.

About 150 B.C., the Romans began to realize that they needed a thorough reform of their whole system of government. The problem was clear: how to combine the values of the city-state—citizen responsibility and participation in government—with the advantages of an empire—greater political security and economic opportunity. During the next century many attempts at reform were made, none of them successful, none of them far-reaching enough to have strengthened the Republic as a whole even if they had succeeded in their immediate aims. The tragedy of Rome lies in the fact that this political failure occurred at the time of greatest opportunity, when the whole Mediterranean world was being united into one state, and when the failure of the Greeks might have been repaired. The Romans struggled longer than the Greeks to preserve their republican institutions, but in the end they too took refuge in monarchy.

And while the Roman emperors were more successful than Hellenistic rulers in creating a viable state, they never succeeded in healing all the political and social cleavages which had developed in the second century B.C.

The Gracchi

The first moves for reform were triggered by the growing poverty of a large mass of Roman citizens. Small farmers had been injured not only by long periods of service in the army, but also by a revolutionary change in the production and distribution of their basic crop, grain. Roman roads were excellent, but Roman methods of transportation were poor. Small farmers, especially, found it difficult to get their produce to market. They did not use horses, partly because horses ate more grain than oxen and partly because the Romans never devised an efficient way of harnessing them. So the basic means of land transport was the two-wheeled oxcart, which moved slowly and held little. It was not profitable to carry grain any great distance by oxcart; fifty miles was the limit. And yet the best markets for grain were the big cities, especially Rome, which could easily be reached by sea. Sicily and other new provinces, whose land was more fertile than the districts near Rome, produced large crops of grain which were loaded on ships and sent to Rome.

Moreover, even the small farmer who was not ruined by the competition of imported grain found it hard to match the efficiency of the great estates owned by members of the senatorial class. These men had received more than their share of conquered land, and they could afford to buy slaves to cultivate their fields. The price of slaves was low, thanks to the unending Roman conquests, and Roman law did not yet protect them against cruel masters. In fact, slaves were often treated worse than domestic animals; they might, quite literally, be worked to death. Few small farmers could meet this sort of competition, and many of them had to mortgage or sell their land to wealthy neighbors. Often they could not even remain on their old farms as tenants, because the great landowners were shifting from grain production to the raising of livestock. And, since Roman ships were not designed to carry animals, the overseas competition which ruined the grain-producer did little harm to the cattle-raiser. But when a great estate shifted from grain to cattle its need for man power decreased sharply. A few slaves could watch the herds or flocks grazing on land which might have supported a hundred peasant households. The dispossessed farmers, unable to find work near their old homes, began to drift to Rome, where they joined the ranks of the urban proletariat—a mass of men without land and without permanent occupation.

Miserable though the Roman proletariat was, it still had potential political power. Most members of the proletariat were Roman citizens and could vote in the popular assemblies; in fact, they were far more likely to vote than were well-to-do citizens who lived outside Rome. The government tried to keep them from dominating elections by enrolling most of them in four urban tribes, leaving the other tribal votes in the assembly under the control of propertied classes. But this expedient did not always work, for the proletariat could intimidate voters by riots and violence. Moreover, there were many citizens of small or moderate fortunes who were jealous of senatorial domination and ready to ally themselves with the proletariat in order to limit the power of the ruling oligarchy. Most important of these were the "knights," men who had enough income to be rated as heavy-armed horsemen according to the old table of organization of the Roman army, but who actually formed the business class of Rome. The knights resented the social superiority of the senators and their disdain of business. The knights also feared the senators, since most knights held government contracts for army supplies or public works. They were not always very honest in these operations, and many of them could have been ruined by a senatorial investigation. Thus, as long as reformers respected the sanctity of private property, the knights were willing to join movements to curb the senatorial aristocracy.

The first leaders of the reform movement came, as is often the case, from the very class whose position was threatened. Tiberius and Caius Gracchus were sons of a consul, grandsons of the great Scipio who had conquered Carthage, members of the most exclusive group of the senatorial aristocracy. They would have held high office in any case; they did not need popular favor to enjoy a distinguished career. But they believed in the old Roman virtues of honesty, self-sacrifice, and devotion to the public good, and they saw those virtues threatened by the greed of the upper classes, the impoverishment of small farmers, and the resulting corruption of both citizens and government. They were influenced not only by their somewhat idealized picture of early Roman society, but also by their knowledge of the Greek political experience. The Gracchi belonged to a section of the aristocracy which had developed a great admiration for Greek culture, and they must have been impressed by the achievements of Athens under its democratic government.

The Gracchi decided that the best way to begin a reform movement was to redistribute the land. And they were convinced that the people most in need of assistance were the small landowners, who had given stability to the government and had furnished the largest part of the citizen army. If this group continued to be weakened, then Rome itself would be weakened. If it could be saved, as the small farmers of Athens had been saved in the sixth century B.C., then the government could safely be made more democratic and the army could be preserved.

This was a somewhat oversimplified diagnosis of the difficulties facing the Roman state. It is doubtful that a democracy of small Roman farmers would have been any more successful in running an empire than the Athenian democracy had been. But adequate or not, the reform program of the Gracchi never had a chance to prove itself. Tiberius Gracchus did succeed in 133 B.C. in getting a law passed that restricted the amount of land which could be held by one family, and in setting up a commission to redistribute surplus holdings. But the senate was outraged, not only by the act itself, which threatened the privileged economic position of the senators, but also by the methods used to pass and enforce it. Gracchus was only a tribune, and while a tribune technically had the right to propose a law to the popular assembly, recent practice had left the initiative in such matters to the senate. Moreover, Gracchus persuaded the assembly to revoke the powers of a tribune whom the senate had induced to veto the measure. This step, though perhaps justified by the spirit of the constitution (tribunes, after all, were supposed to protect the interests of the people), was probably contrary to the letter of the law. Furthermore, Gracchus tried to get elected as tribune for a second consecutive term, a violation of custom if not of law. This was the last straw for the senators, who stirred up an election riot in which Gracchus was killed. Apparently he had shocked so many respectable people that his murder prompted no strong protest. Yet by using violence to end political opposition the senate had set a dangerous precedent.

The reform party tried again in 123 B.C.,

when Caius Gracchus became eligible for the tribuneship. Caius revived his brother's idealistic schemes for land reform, but as a practical politician he saw that he must build an anti-senatorial party if his program was to have any lasting effect. He secured the support of the proletariat by a law providing for state distribution of grain at half-price. He courted the knights, or business class, by allowing them to form corporations to farm the taxes of newly acquired provinces. Each corporation paid the Roman government a lump sum, and was allowed to keep any surplus it could collect. A better inducement to dishonesty could hardly be imagined. For centuries the tax-farmers had a bad reputation; they were the "publicans" who are always coupled in the New Testament with "sinners." The knights were further favored by a law giving them control of the courts which judged official corruption. Thus corrupt tax-collectors would be judged, usually very leniently, by their fellow businessmen, while senators who tried to interfere with the tax-farming corporations could be convicted on trumped-up charges.

Much more statesmanlike was Caius Gracchus' proposal to extend Roman citizenship to inhabitants of allied and subject towns in Italy. This was, of course, a bid for the support of newly enfranchised citizens, but the policy was wise even if Gracchus' motives were not entirely pure. Unfortunately, the law was rejected, thus laying the foundations for a bitter civil war in the next generation (see p. 95). Equally unfortunately, Caius Gracchus' more demagogic measures, which he perhaps hoped would be only temporary, were continued after his death. Cheap food for the Roman mob and tax-farming in the provinces persisted as blights on Roman society for many generations.

The proletariat and the knights backed Caius as long as they saw immediate profit in doing so, but they failed him at the moment of crisis. Once again the senate stirred up riots against the reformers, and this time it was the Gracchans who shed the first blood. Now the senate had an excuse to declare martial law and thus to force Gracchus into open rebellion. His small group of followers was defeated and he committed suicide.

So ended in 121 B.C. the last hope for peaceful reform of the Roman Republic. Even though the Gracchan program was inadequate, it might have opened the way for other, more legal, reforms. As it was, the idealism of the Gracchi evaporated, while the bitterness created by their struggle remained. The popular assembly had been unable to protect its champions by legal means and a great political debate had been cut short by violence. Rome was now divided between the *Optimates,* or senatorial party, and the *Populares,* or popular party. But neither party stood for any principles; they sought only power for their leaders and spoils for their followers. The Republic was soon to be torn by a series of increasingly dangerous civil wars.

Marius and Sulla

The suppression of the Gracchi gave the senate an opportunity to reassert its control over the Roman state. But the senate did little to satisfy the desires of the poorer classes, and the commanders it appointed proved incompetent in the frontier districts. They failed to suppress a rebellion in North Africa and they were severely defeated by a combination of Gallic and German tribes in Gaul. These failures led to a revival of the popular party under Marius, a member of the middle class who proved to be a good army commander, though an inept politician. With the backing of the *Populares,* Marius was voted the command of the African army. He was so successful in suppressing the revolt in Africa that he was

then given the task of beating back the dangerous northern tribes of Cimbri and Teutones. It took him four years, but by 101 B.C. he had annihilated both tribes.

To win these victories Marius replaced the old citizen army with a force of professional soldiers. He enlisted volunteers, usually from the poorest classes, for periods of sixteen years. These men expected to be given grants of land on their discharge, and they looked to their generals, rather than to the state, to support their interests. The new army of long-service professionals was more efficient than the old army of citizen-soldiers who had served only a year at a time, but it was also more dangerous to the Republic. The professional soldiers obeyed their commanders without question, even to the point of attacking the legitimate government or massacring citizens whose only fault was belonging to the wrong party.

After defeating the northern tribes, Marius was in a strong position. He had a veteran army at his command and he had been elected consul for the sixth time, quite contrary to custom. His allies, the *Populares,* held most of the other important offices. But he had no program of his own, and he became frightened when his radical friends revived some of the Gracchan measures, such as cheap grain, free land for the poor, and citizenship for the allied towns of Italy. When the inevitable rioting began, Marius gave just enough help to the senate to enable it to defeat and massacre its opponents. This betrayal discredited him with both parties, and left the senate once more in control.

But again the senate proved unequal to its task. It stubbornly refused to make any concessions to the Italian allies, and so provoked a dangerous uprising, the Social (that is, Civil) War of 90–88 B.C. The Italian allies formed a confederacy, raised an army, and for more than a year held their own against the Roman armies. They began to weaken only when the Roman government offered citizenship to any inhabitant of Italy who would claim it. This act, which would have prevented the war had it been adopted in time, helped bring it to an end.

Overseas, the situation was almost as bad. Mithridates, ruler of the kingdom of Pontus in Asia Minor, took advantage of widespread discontent with Roman rule to start a rebellion in the western, Roman-held part of the peninsula. The Romans were massacred, and Mithridates extended his kingdom to the Aegean. This success encouraged the Greeks, in their turn, to rebel, and Mithridates sent his armies to assist them. The Romans were in danger of losing their entire eastern domain, but the Social War, and a new struggle between *Optimates* and *Populares,* kept them from taking effective action. Finally the *Optimates* won a temporary victory and sent their best general, Sulla, to the East.

Sulla soon hammered his army into a first-rate fighting machine, entirely loyal to him. He defeated Mithridates and broke the rebellion with a policy of pitiless repression. Rebellious Greek cities were devastated, and the population was ruined by heavy war indemnities. Greece never fully recovered its earlier prosperity.

Meanwhile, the *Populares* had regained power in Rome. This time they made little pretense of legality; they seized control of the government by force of arms and massacred the senators who opposed them. As before, they were unable to consolidate their position or to agree among themselves on a program. Marius, their nominal leader, died soon after his election to a seventh consulship (86 B.C.), and none of the men who succeeded him possessed his military ability. As a result, they were unable to prevent Sulla from landing in Italy when he returned from the East in 83 B.C. His veteran army quickly defeated the popular

forces and the Marian party was destroyed. Many were killed in battle; the rest were ruined by the new political weapon of proscription. Their property was confiscated and anyone was privileged to kill them on sight. Sulla had himself made dictator in 82 B.C. and proceeded to reorganize the Roman state.

Sulla's basic aim was to restore the authority of the senate. He restricted the power of the popular assembly and gave the senate veto power over its legislation. He limited the rights of the tribunes and decreed that election to the tribunate would bar a man from any higher office, such as the consulship. Finally, he curtailed the powers of the knights, enlarged the senate, and filled it with his own supporters. Sulla retired as soon as he thought the senate was capable of running the government (79 B.C.). He died the following year.

The Death of the Republic

Sulla had overrated both the ability and the character of the senate, which proved incapable of making policy or of controlling its military commanders. Individual senators sought their own profit rather than the good of the state and formed little cliques to share the spoils of office. As a result, the party of the *Populares* began to revive, and within ten years after Sulla's death succeeded in repealing much of his restrictive legislation. The power of the tribunes was restored, and the popular assembly once more became a rival of the senate. Roman politics grew shabbier and shabbier, with every election marked by bribes, riots, and threats of military coups.

Again threats from the outside intensified the trouble at home. Mithridates was rebuilding his power in the East, and pirates were terrorizing the Mediterranean. The Spaniards had rebelled once more, helped by exiled supporters of Marius. The land connection between Italy and Spain was still tenuous, for beyond the Rhone the Romans held only a narrow coastal strip. North of this strip, Gaul was full of restless Celtic and Germanic tribes which might at any time move south, as they had twice before.

Roman politicians were reasonably sure that their armies could defeat any of these enemies if they had enough time. They were also reasonably sure that any general left in command of professional soldiers long enough to complete his task would gain so much wealth and such authority over his troops that he could dominate Roman politics. Therefore, the most burning political conflicts in the decades after Sulla's death turned on the question of who was to hold important military commands. The stakes were so great that all precedents were disregarded; usually commands were awarded by special laws voted by the popular assembly.

The First Triumvirate

In this contest for power, Pompey, an old lieutenant of Sulla, at first seemed to have the advantage. He suppressed the revolt in Spain and then ended the pirate menace. These victories gave him so much prestige that he easily secured the command of Rome's eastern forces, although his predecessor had already deprived Mithridates of most of his power. Pompey finished the task and in his mopping-up campaigns brought all of Asia Minor and most of Syria under Roman rule.

These eastern campaigns carried Pompey to the peak of his power. But he was neither adroit enough nor ruthless enough to make himself complete master of Rome. Never having aligned himself consistently with either of the great parties, he never enjoyed the wholehearted support of either. Moreover, by disbanding his army on his return from the East, he deprived himself of his

Pompey, 106–48 B.C.

military power. And while he had eliminated several minor competitors in his rise to power, he was unwilling, for a long time, to risk his position in an all-out struggle with first-rate opponents. Instead, he preferred to make a deal with them, by which they shared political control of the Roman world.

Pompey's most dangerous rivals were Crassus and Caesar. Crassus, the less able of the two, had enormous wealth, which gave him great influence in the corrupt politics of Rome. He had gained some military reputation by putting down a rebellion of slaves and gladiators in Italy in 71 B.C. Gladiators, who fought to the death at public spectacles, were practically outcasts, and slaves stood even lower in Roman society. The fact that scattered bands of these men had been allowed to combine into a formidable army is proof of the ineptness of the authorities in Italy. Crassus, though no military genius, was more capable than his predecessors and soon put down the rising. The slaves were a mixture of all the peoples of the Mediterranean, united only by their desire to escape their miserable lot, and their internal divisions had as much to do with their defeat as the generalship of Crassus. Nevertheless, by freeing the landed classes from a danger to which they were particularly sensitive, Crassus strengthened his political position.

A far abler man and a far more dangerous threat to Pompey and the senate was Julius Caesar. The fact that he was an effective speaker and the nephew of Marius gave him the support of the *Populares*. And his skill as a military commander and his efficiency as an administrator made it difficult for his opponents to bar him from office. He had courage, ambition, and complete confidence in his destiny; he was always ready to take long chances, sure that his luck and his ability would pull him through. Caesar and Crassus had formed a working partnership, and it was this combination of Crassus' wealth and Caesar's ability that made Pompey agree to share his power. He formed a coalition with Caesar and Crassus in 60 B.C., and the combined political power of this First Triumvirate was so great that it dominated both senate and popular assembly until Crassus' death in 53 B.C.

The senate was distressed to see power slipping out of its hands, but it had no leaders who could oppose the Triumvirate. The ablest men on the senatorial side were the younger Cato and Cicero, neither of whom could muster popular support or military strength. Cato represented the best of the senatorial aristocracy; he was patriotic, courageous, absolutely honest, with a deep sense of responsibility. But he would not engage in corrupt politics; he would not evade the law even for worthy ends; he would not start a civil war even to save the values in which he believed. He was a perfect embodiment of the old Roman virtues,

but he was almost helpless in dealing with men like Pompey and Caesar.

Cicero was considerably more flexible than Cato, but if he lacked Cato's stubborn adherence to the letter of the law he also lacked Cato's courage. Not a member of one of the old ruling families, he was always a little unsure of himself. He was a great orator and writer, and his analysis of the Roman political situation was clear and accurate. He detested the corruption which prevailed in provincial government; he strove to end the factional quarrels which were leading Rome toward civil war. But, like many other men of thought, he found it hard to make quick and vigorous decisions, and he never commanded much popular support.

Cicero's moment of glory had come in 63 B.C., when he was consul. An unscrupulous senator named Catiline, allied with some of the more disreputable elements of the *Populares,* had formed a conspiracy to take over the government. In a great series

Cicero, 106–43 B.C.

3 / Rome and the Unification of the Mediterranean World

Caesar in Gaul 59-49 B.C.

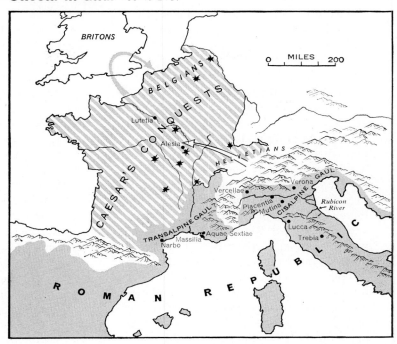

of orations Cicero had unveiled the plot and persuaded the senate to declare martial law. Catiline was killed in battle and many of his followers were executed. Cicero rejoiced that he had saved the Republic; actually, he had merely averted a minor danger, and in so doing he had won considerable unpopularity for himself and the senate. Many of the *Populares,* feeling that the repression of the conspiracy had been unduly severe, spoke out bitterly against Cicero. Crassus and Caesar themselves, who had supported Catiline earlier in his career, do not seem to have been especially disturbed by his plotting. As a result, one of the Triumvirate's first acts was to send Cicero into exile. Cato was given an official mission which removed him from Rome. With these two men gone, Pompey, Caesar, and Crassus stood unopposed.

The Rise of Caesar

The Triumvirate made Caesar consul in 59 B.C., but what he really wanted was a military command with which to enhance his reputation. With Pompey's support, a law was passed which gave him four legions and command of the Gallic provinces for five years. No Roman had ever gained much in Gaul except hard knocks—it was the eastern commands which had usually brought wealth and prestige. Pompey and the senate may have thought that by giving Caesar his command they had bestowed on him many troubles and little opportunity to increase his political strength. If so, they were mistaken. The Gallic command gave Caesar the reputation, the experience, and the army with which to dominate Rome.

Roman Gaul in 58 B.C. was divided into two parts (as Caesar did *not* say). Cisal-

99

pine or Italian Gaul, which included the old settlements of the Gauls in the Po Valley, was a fairly well settled and peaceful region, full of Roman immigrants. Beyond the mountains was the frontier region of Transalpine Gaul. It stretched from the Alps to the Pyrenees, but in the west the border remained close to the Mediterranean. East of the Rhone it nominally went as far as Lake Geneva, but Roman control of the northern mountain segment was precarious. Beyond the border of the Roman province were the "wild Gauls," a turbulent and warlike mixture of people. Most of them were of Celtic origin, but there were Germanic tribes in Belgium and in the upper Rhone basin. The Gauls were developing a civilization of their own, more advanced than most Romans were willing to admit, but they had not yet formed states with definite boundaries. Strong tribes tried to occupy the territories of weak ones, and the pressure of the Germans on the east added to the confusion. There was always a danger that their squabbles might spill over into Roman territories, as had happened several times before, and it was partly to avert this danger that Caesar was sent to Gaul.

Caesar certainly believed that offense was the best way to keep the Gauls off balance and to push the frontier tribes back from the southern coast. But it is doubtful that he planned the conquest of all Gaul at the very outset—this idea probably came to him only after the success of his first campaigns. He had the old Roman excuse for expansion: some of the weaker tribes had sought Roman support against dangerous neighbors and as Roman allies they had to be protected. This formula worked successfully during the early years of Caesar's command. He kept on acquiring new allies and marched deeper and deeper into Gaul to protect them. He defeated invading German forces and subdued the Belgians, the most warlike of all the Gauls. By the end of 56 B.C. almost all Gaul was under his control.

And during the next two years Caesar taught neighboring tribes not to interfere with his new conquests. To discourage German raids across the Rhine, he threw a temporary bridge across the river and marched his army up and down along the right bank. Even more impressive were his two expeditions to Britain. The first, in 55 B.C., was a mere demonstration, but the next year Caesar penetrated some distance into the country. He defeated one of the leading British kings, who promised to pay tribute; more important, he induced the Britons to cease aiding their fellow Celts in northern Gaul.

But the Gauls did not despair of regaining their freedom. A young leader named Vercingetorix organized a rebellion of almost all the tribes in 52 B.C., at a moment when Caesar was in Italy and his troops were scattered in winter quarters. Caesar was very nearly forced to abandon the country, but he managed to concentrate his troops and surround Vercingetorix and the main Gallic army in the fortress of Alesia. All attempts to relieve Vercingetorix failed and he was finally forced to surrender. By the end of the next year (51 B.C.), with the revolt completely suppressed, the Gauls accepted the domination of Rome. Caesar's lenient treatment of the defeated rebels was to win him their support in the following years.

Meanwhile the government of the Republic was tottering to collapse. The senate could not keep order, and demagogues with armed gangs disrupted the normal processes of government. No consuls could be elected in 56, 54, or 52 B.C. Pompey, Caesar, and Crassus had renewed their Triumvirate in 56 B.C., but each was more concerned with increasing his power than with ending the disorders. While Caesar was oc-

3 / Rome and the Unification of the Mediterranean World

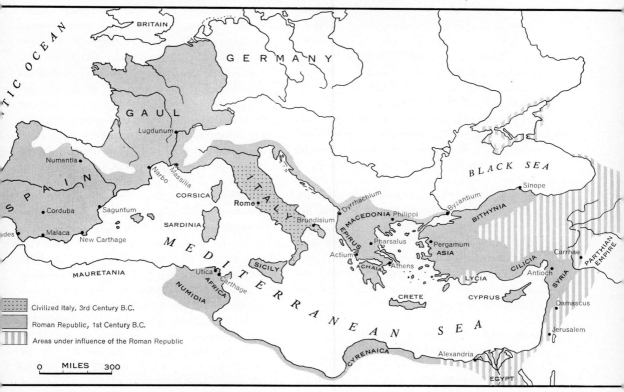

Civilized Italy, 3rd Century B.C.

Roman Republic, 1st Century B.C.

Areas under influence of the Roman Republic

0 MILES 300

cupied in Gaul, Crassus set out to the East to gain a military reputation to equal that of his colleagues. Eager to acquire glory, he led his army against the Parthians, a people who had taken over Persia when the Seleucid state collapsed. The Parthians waited until the army was deep in the Syrian desert and then cut it to pieces in 53 B.C. Crassus was killed and his lieutenant was barely able to hold Syria against Parthian attacks.

Only Pompey was left in Italy. Now the governor of Spain and Libya, he had also been empowered to supervise the shipment of grain to Rome, which gave him control of all the seaports. He had increasing support in the senate and had allowed Cicero to be recalled from exile, which gave him the backing of the ablest orator in Rome.

But for several years Pompey did little to check the factional fighting in the city. Perhaps he was waiting for the situation to become so desperate that all parties would turn to him to save the Republic.

In 52 B.C. his moment seemed to have come. Mob violence in the city reached such a pitch that the senate made him sole consul and empowered him to use his troops to restore order. The senate was entirely dependent on him, and many people began to refer to him as the *Princeps,* or First Citizen of the Republic. With his great military power and his control of several provinces, he was almost in the position which enabled Augustus, a few years later, to make himself emperor (see p. 110). But Pompey differed from Augustus

101

in two respects. First, he did not want to be bothered with the detailed work of government. He wanted to be an elder statesman who was consulted on all important matters but who worked through the old republican institutions. Second, he had a rival. Pompey could not really be First Citizen so long as Caesar, with his formidable army, held Gaul and the Po Valley.

Between 52 and 49 B.C. Pompey and Caesar fenced for position. Pompey was willing to make some concessions, but he was bent on stripping Caesar of his great military command. Caesar, on the other hand, knew that he would sacrifice his political career and probably his life if he did not retain control of at least part of his army. Cicero tried to arrange a compromise, but most of the senators were now wholeheartedly on Pompey's side and bitterly opposed to Caesar. They ordered Caesar to give up his command; when in January, 49 B.C., he refused, they declared martial law and placed Pompey in charge of the army in Italy.

Caesar Takes Power

Caesar accepted the challenge without hesitation. He immediately marched his troops across the Rubicon, a small river marking the boundary between Cisalpine Gaul and Italy. He moved so quickly and gained so much support in northern Italy that Pompey and the senate gave up hope of defending Rome. They fled to Greece and left Caesar in complete control of the Italian peninsula. This was the decisive action of the civil war. Caesar held the central position in the Mediterranean, while Pompey's supporters were scattered through the provinces. Caesar could draw on veterans of the Gallic War and fresh levies of Italians, while his opponents had to rely more and more on provincial troops and non-Roman allies. Caesar's quickness of decision and speed of attack enabled

him to make the most of these advantages. His enemies, never able to combine all their forces against him, were defeated piecemeal. Pompey was beaten at Pharsalus in Greece in 48 B.C. and was killed soon after. Next Pompey's adherents in Spain and Africa were crushed, and by 46 B.C. Caesar was complete master of the Roman state.

His rule was too short for all his plans to be revealed, but it is clear that he knew that the Republic was dead and that some kind of monarchy had to take its place. In its last days the old republican government had proved to be neither republican nor a government; it gave power and wealth to a few military leaders and demagogues but brought only violence to Italy and oppression to the provinces. Except for a few senators no one was really attached to the Republic. Reformers had suggested nothing to cure its basic weaknesses; the only choice seemed to be between more misgovernment under senatorial auspices or security under the rule of one man. Pompey had been unwilling to make this choice; Caesar, as usual, did not hesitate. Neither senate nor people dared oppose him; they voted him all the powers which he demanded. He had himself made dictator for life; he was given the power of a tribune and also held the consulship; he had authority to make war and peace and to appoint most public officials. Even more significant, he accepted divine honors. A temple was dedicated to Caesar and the goddess of clemency; the month in which he was born was named July (Julius); his image was set up in the temple of Quirinus. Since most of the eastern monarchies with which the Romans were acquainted were based on the fiction that their kings were of divine origin, it seems probable that Caesar was hoping to justify his assumption of a royal title in the same way.

Rome, however, was not quite ready to accept a king, and Caesar contented him-

Caesar on the Origins of the Civil War

Caesar no sooner heard of these proceedings [the raising of a senatorial army against him] than he appealed to his troops. After recounting in detail the wrongs he had suffered at the hands of his political opponents, he charged Pompey with having allowed his mind to be misled, and his judgement to be warped by the pernicious influence these men exerted upon him, owing to the petty jealousy he felt at his rival's reputation. . . . He called upon them now to protect from political adversaries the honor and good name of their commander, under whose leadership for nine long years they had fought with such brilliant success the battles of their country, during which time they had gained such numberless victories, and subjugated the whole of Gaul and Germany [west of the Rhine]. . . . Assured of the temper of his troops Caesar began his advance . . . as far as Rimini . . . [thus crossing the Rubicon, the frontier of his province, and defying the Senate].

From Julius Caesar, *De bello civili,* trans. by F. P. Long (Oxford: Clarendon, 1906), p. 7.

self for the moment with the title of *imperator,* whence our word emperor. This was a military title held by a victorious general until he made his triumphal entry into Rome. The fact that Caesar used it almost constantly emphasized the military basis of his power. And the fact that Caesar's successors were called emperors shows one of the weaknesses of the new system of government which was developing in Rome. The ruler was first and foremost commander of the army. If he lost military control, no civil authority could save him; if he retained military control, no civil authority could restrain him, even when he was guilty of the grossest abuses of power.

Caesar, as dictator and imperator, used his power wisely. In an effort to lessen the difference between the old Roman citizens and the inhabitants of the provinces, he reorganized the senate and admitted some provincial members, even some Gauls. He extended the franchise to many Spanish and Gallic communities, and settled veterans in the provinces. All these arrangements encouraged the spread of Latin civilization, since the surest way to gain citizenship was to adopt Latin speech and Roman customs. They also protected the provincials against misgovernment, for a Roman citizen with a senator to defend him could not be exploited with impunity.

In Rome Caesar tried to restore order by abolishing the political clubs which had often supported gangs of thugs, and by reducing by more than half the number of citizens entitled to receive cheap grain from the state. He may have hoped that this latter act would persuade some of the Roman mob to leave the city and seek employment elsewhere. Finally, by greatly increasing the number of elective offices—for example, there were now to be sixteen praetors—he reduced somewhat the acute competition for political power among ambitious men.

One of Caesar's minor reforms has survived, with little change, to the present day: his introduction of a new calendar. The old Roman calendar was based on the lunar rather than the solar year, and while the priests were supposed to adjust it from time to time by putting in an extra month, they did not always add it at the right time or with absolute accuracy. Caesar, with the advice of Greek astronomers, adopted the system which is still the basis of our reckoning of time: three years of 365 days each, to be followed by a leap-year with an extra day in February. This was very close to an exact reckoning, although a slight change was made in the sixteenth century to make

A head of Julius Caesar, 100–44 B.C., much enlarged from the original intaglio. It is said to be an excellent likeness.

the approximation to the real solar year even closer.

Caesar, assured of the support of the *Populares,* now tried to win the backing of at least the moderate *Optimates.* He had not been cruel in his treatment of the defeated aristocracy. Pompey had been killed by Egyptians with whom he took refuge and not by Caesar; Cato had committed suicide after the defeat of the senatorial army in Africa, though Caesar would have spared his life. And Caesar permitted the many members of the leading senatorial families who survived to return to Rome, some of them as members of his inner circle of advisers. These men must have had mixed feelings about their position. On the one hand, as members of a governing class, they could appreciate Caesar's military genius, political skill, and administrative ef-

ficiency. On the other hand, it was perfectly apparent that Caesar was bent on destroying the political system which had made them a governing class. This old system had not worked very well, but it had divided real political power among many aristocrats and nominal political power among all Roman citizens. Granted that senatorial rule had led to corruption, violence, and civil war, would not other dangers arise from concentrating all power in the hands of one man? Was not the loss of liberty, even the imperfect liberty of the last years of the Republic, too high a price to pay for security? Thus selfish class interests and attachment to old Roman traditions made it difficult for some senators to give their full loyalty to Caesar.

By the end of 45 B.C. a fairly large group of senators had formed a conspiracy to assassinate Caesar. The original leader was Cassius, a former supporter of Pompey, but Brutus, who had also been on Pompey's side, soon became equally prominent in the plot. Together they succeeded in recruiting other Pompeians and even some senators who had been in Caesar's party for many years. Their excuse for action was a proposal to grant Caesar the title of king, at least in the provinces. When he entered the senate chamber on the Ides of March (March 15), 44 B.C., the conspirators surrounded him and stabbed him to death.

Men like Brutus, who represented the best of the old senatorial class, were convinced that by assassinating Caesar they could restore the old constitution and liberties of the Republic. This was a fatal error; the senate had missed its opportunity to reform the government and since the time of Sulla had enjoyed no popular support. The majority of the Roman people had preferred Caesar to any of his opponents, and they were ready to follow any leader who promised to carry on Caesar's policies. The assassination merely postponed the formal ending of the Republic by a few years, at the cost of a new series of civil wars.

The Second Triumvirate

Mark Antony, who was consul at the time of the assassination, was the most influential member of Caesar's party left in Rome. By winning the support of the mob and of Caesar's old soldiers with his famous oration at Caesar's funeral, he prevented the senate from exploiting the dictator's fall. But though Antony could check the senate he was not yet strong enough to take over the government. He saw a potential rival in Lepidus, who had been Caesar's military lieutenant and who had an army camped near Rome. There was also Caesar's grand-nephew, Octavius,* a youth of eighteen, whom Caesar had adopted in his will and to whom he left most of his fortune. At first, Antony did not take the young man very seriously, though he knew that anyone with Caesar's name was a possible threat. While he assessed the balance of political and military power, Antony played a cautious game. The leaders of the conspiracy were given provincial governorships, Lepidus was sent to Spain, and Antony himself prepared to take over Gaul.

Since no one trusted anyone else, however, this lull soon gave way to a period of confused fighting in which leaders changed sides and armies deserted their generals almost every month. When the dust had settled, old adherents of Caesar were in control of most of the West and the eastern provinces were held by Brutus and Cassius. At the same time, Octavian's star was rising swiftly. Playing a shrewd and unscrupulous political game, he sided with the senate just long enough to show Antony

how dangerous an opponent he was, and then, when the senate tried to set him aside, he occupied Rome with his own troops. He was able to treat with Antony and Lepidus on equal terms when the three met in 43 B.C. At this time they formed the Second Triumvirate, and a plebiscite gave them authority to reorganize the Republic.

Actually the triumvirs were more anxious to punish their enemies, reward their friends, and snatch up provinces than they were to reform the constitution. It was easy enough to punish their enemies in Italy by either proscribing them or seizing their property. Among those put to death was Cicero, who had attacked Antony in a series of violent orations. The triumvirs turned over confiscated property to the soldiers who had supported them, and some entire towns were settled by veterans.

The worst enemies of the triumvirs, however, were overseas in Greece, where Brutus and Cassius had raised a large army. The triumvirs took their own troops across the Adriatic and met their enemies at Philippi in 42 B.C. In two battles they destroyed the senatorial army; both Brutus and Cassius committed suicide. This was the last major engagement with the old senatorial opposition. The civil wars were not yet over, but future battles were to be among the triumvirs themselves.

Following the battles at Philippi, the victors divided up the Roman world. Lepidus, who had proved neither trustworthy nor effective as a commander, was set aside and given only the small province of Africa. Octavian was left in real control of the West, while Antony remained in the East to put down the last flickers of resistance.

This proved to be a fatal choice for Antony. One of his problems was Egypt, still nominally independent under Cleopatra, the last descendant of the Ptolemies. Cleopatra had no military strength, but she was an attractive woman, and she was prepared

---

* When the legal formalities were completed, Octavius' name was officially changed to Caesar Octavianus. He called himself Caesar, which was now his official family name, but it will avoid confusion if we use his other name, Octavian.

to use all her feminine charms to hold onto her political power. She had already saved her throne by becoming Caesar's mistress when he landed in Egypt in pursuit of the fleeing Pompey. But while Caesar was sufficiently enamored of Cleopatra to leave her in charge of Egypt, he never made the mistake of basing his policy toward the Roman world on her desires. Antony did. Cleopatra became his mistress soon after the Philippi campaign and persuaded him to marry her in 36 B.C. Since Antony was already married to Octavian's sister, this hardly made for good relations between the two triumvirs. Moreover, Antony, as co-ruler of Egypt, was independent of all other Roman authorities, and he soon showed a desire to add other vassal kingdoms to his personal possessions. The final straw was Antony's decision in 34 B.C. to assign Egypt, Syria, Crete, and parts of Asia Minor to Cleopatra and the children she had borne him.

Octavian Gains Supreme Power

Octavian had been on the point of breaking with Antony several times during the decade after Philippi, but the fact that the two triumvirs still had common enemies restrained him. By 33 B.C. this was no longer the case. The last supporters of Pompey had been defeated; Lepidus had been forced into retirement; the eastern kings had been overawed by Antony. Octavian and Antony, realizing that the Roman world was not large enough for both of them, began to prepare for a showdown. Since Antony and Cleopatra had concentrated their forces in Greece, Octavian had to raise a powerful navy in order to attack them. His fleet won a decisive victory over the easterners at Actium in 31 B.C., largely because Cleopatra deserted Antony with her ships at the moment of crisis. In spite of her treachery, Antony followed Cleopatra to Egypt, with Octavian hard on their heels. Military resistance was hopeless and Antony committed suicide. Cleopatra resorted to her feminine charms once again, but this time she was dealing with a colder and more cautious man than either Caesar or Antony. When she found that she could make no impression on Octavian, she too committed suicide, and Octavian took over Egypt as his private estate.

The victory at Actium ended the long period of civil war which had sunk the Roman world in misery. It also ended the Roman Republic. Octavian, more cautious than his great-uncle, never thought of taking the title of king, and he formally proclaimed the restoration of the old constitution. But he took all real power into his own hands. There was no army to oppose him, no political leader to rally the discontented, no one who wanted to start again the bloody cycle of riots, proscriptions, and civil wars. Octavian was accepted as head of the state, and the Roman Empire was born.

Suggestions for Further Reading

Roman Civilization, Vol. I (edited N. Lewis and M. Reinhold, 1951), is an excellent anthology of source reading for this period. It is arranged chronologically and has material on virtually all facets of Roman life and culture from the founding of the city to the end of the Republic. There is valuable primary material also in *A Roman Reader* *

* Available in paperback edition.

(edited B. Davenport, 1951). H. M. Scullard, *A History of the Roman World, 753–146* B.C. (1951), is an up-to-date account of the early Republic. Although Scullard gives considerable attention to political and military history, his emphasis is on the social and economic life of the times. The monumental study of T. Mommsen, *The History of Rome* * (many editions), has material on government, the military, religion, agriculture, and the arts under the Republic. M. Cary, *A History of Rome* (1954), is a very readable work which covers all of Roman history and contains recent bibliographic material; Cary has important chapters on the Punic Wars, social conflict and the Gracchi, and Marius and Sulla.

F. de Coulanges, *The Ancient City* * (1864), a classic of French historical writing, is a scholarly study of the religious and civil institutions of ancient Greece and Rome. Coulanges makes a good case for the theory that religion dominated every aspect of life in the ancient world. There is a good picture of the gradual disintegration of Roman society in the first century B.C. in R. E. Smith, *The Failure of the Roman Republic* (1955). The best study of the period of transition between the end of the Republic and the beginnings of the Empire is R. Syme, *The Roman Revolution* (1939), an exciting work by a leading English classicist. Syme's short monograph, *A Roman Post-Mortem* (1950), is a valuable inquest into the causes of the fall of the Republic. R. H. Barrow, *The Romans* * (1949), analyzes Rome's achievement and her contribution to western civilization and gives a broad survey of the entire period.

* Available in paperback edition.

SENATVSPOPVL
IMPCAESARIDIV
TRAIANOAVGG
MAXIMOTRIBPOT
ADDECLARANDVM
MONSETLOCVSTAN

4

The Early Empire

Octavian, left in sole control of the Roman state, worked carefully and cautiously to solidify his position. Not wishing to break entirely with the past, he was quite willing to conciliate the upper classes by preserving old institutions. Consuls and praetors were elected year by year and went out to govern their provinces at the end of their term of office in Rome. The senate, purged of its recalcitrant members, continued to meet and consider important legislation. The popular assembly, shorn of most of its

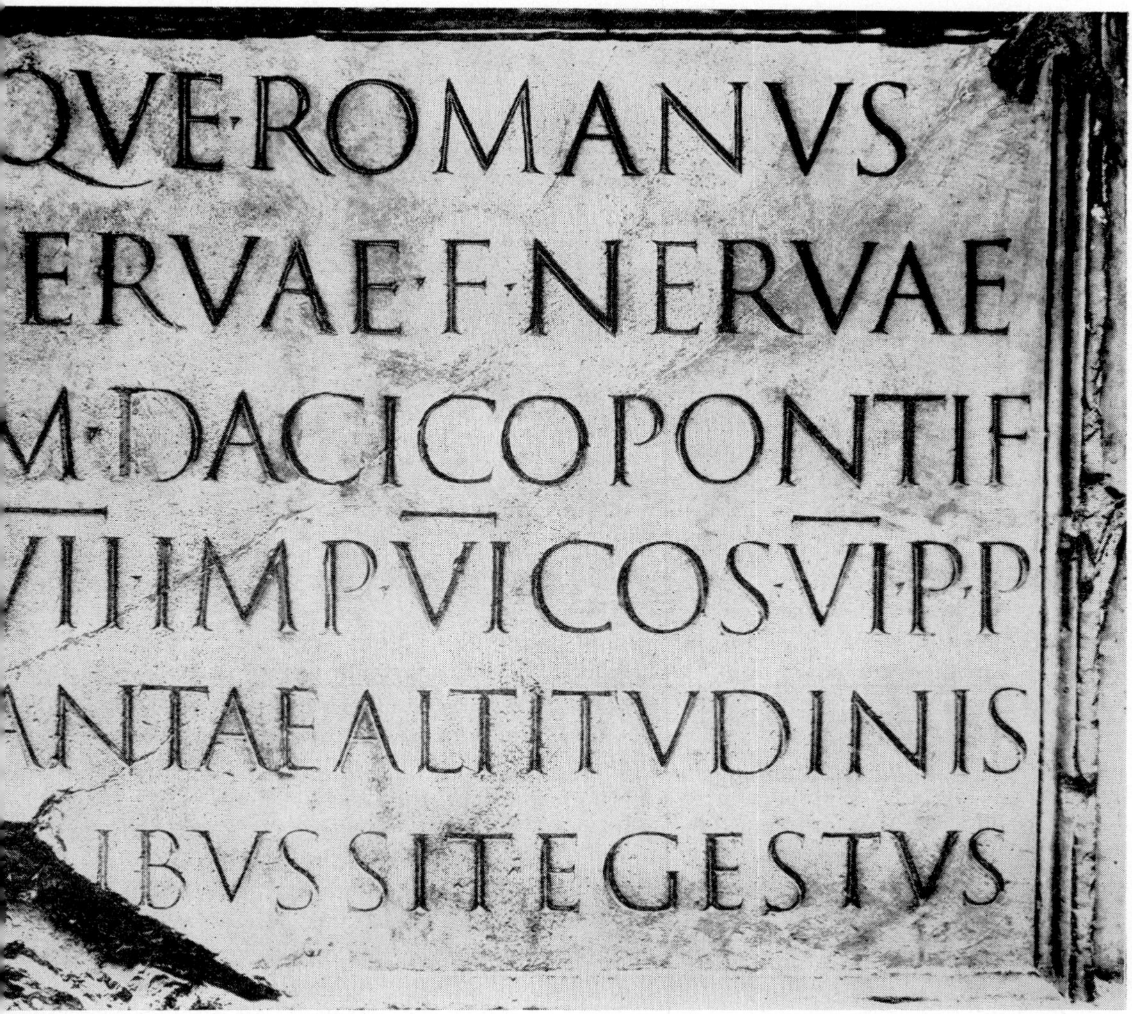

QVE ROMANVS
ERVAE·F·NERVAE
M·DACICO PONTIF
VIIIMP·VI·COS·VI·P·P
ANTAE·ALTITVDINIS
IBVS·SIT·E·GESTVS

power, continued to hold purely formal meetings at which it always approved what Octavian proposed. But the assembly had often been subservient to a leading senator or general in the past. In fact, many Romans believed that demagogic attempts to give the assembly control over policy had caused all the troubles of the last century of the Republic.

The Establishment of the Principate

Behind this façade of republican institutions, however, Octavian made all the basic policy decisions himself. He was the commander-in-chief of the army, and, like Caesar, he made the title of *imperator* a life-long personal possession. He retained

Inscription from Trajan's Column celebrating his victories, in the Roman Forum, ca. 114 A.D. "The senate and the Roman people to the imperator Caesar, son of the deified Nerva, Nerva Trajan Augustus conqueror of the Germans and Dacians. . . . " A fine example of formal Roman capitals.

direct control over all the provinces which required sizable military forces, turning over to proconsuls and propraetors only the secure inner circle of provinces which required no garrisons. He secured a permanent grant of the tribune's power, including the right to propose laws and to veto the acts of any other official. He spoke first in the senate, where no one ever dared to contradict him; he could make war and peace on his own responsibility; he had his own staff of officials and advisers, and they became the basis for an imperial bureaucracy. With all the key positions in Octavian's hands, even the most ardent republicans recognized that opposition was hopeless.

Octavian was something more than a military dictator, since some of his power was based on established civilian institutions. He was something less than a monarch, since sovereignty was not vested irrevocably in his person; at least in theory, his powers could have been curtailed or revoked at any time by the senate or by popular vote. Yet this possibility was purely theoretical, for he controlled all the political machinery which might have been used against him; in this respect he resembled an extraordinarily successful political boss. But no political boss has ever enjoyed the aura of sanctity and infallibility which surrounded Octavian; here he resembled an oriental monarch, or a Lenin or a Stalin in our own time. There is no ordinary word to describe his position, but most historians say that he established a "principate," the permanent rule of the leading man in the state.

His power was reflected in the titles that were heaped upon him: Imperator Caesar Augustus, Princeps of the Roman People, Father of His Country (*Pater Patriae*). Imperator referred, of course, to his military command, and Caesar to the power he had inherited from his great-uncle. As Princeps

Head of the Emperor Augustus, 20 B.C.

he was first citizen; *Pater Patriae* carried this idea a little further, implying that filial respect and obedience were due him. But the most difficult title to explain is that of Augustus, granted to him by the senate in 27 B.C. A title that could be used of gods as well as men, it implied awe and reverence and carried overtones of holiness, dignity, wisdom, and authority. An Augustus was no ordinary man, for there was a presumption that his acts were divinely sanctioned and inspired. To oppose Augustus was not only politically inexpedient, it was also immoral.

Augustus (to use the title by which he has been known ever since the senate's action) probably had no idea of developing a permanent and clearly defined concept of imperial authority. He was a practical and cautious man, more interested in the realities than in the theory of power. He knew what he wanted to do: to give peace and security to the Roman world and to restore public and private morality among the Roman people. He would allow no one and nothing to interfere with these ends, but he was quite flexible in his use of means. So long as the upper classes cooperated with him, he was willing to share responsibility and authority with them. He made extensive use of the equestrian order (the class of knights or businessmen), and able senators could still expect important posts in the government of Rome and the provinces. Tranquillity and order were far more important to Augustus than the creation of a monolithic autocracy.

The Military Policy of Augustus

During his principate (27 B.C.–14 A.D.) Augustus came very close to realizing his goals of peace and security. By keeping close watch on provincial authorities he greatly improved the government of the provinces. By showing little interest in acquiring new territories, he reduced the burdens and risks of war. In ending the rapid expansion of the Roman state, which had gone on for centuries almost without interruption, Augustus seems to have been motivated by his usual desire for order, security, and tranquillity. Rome already had enough; new conquests promised small profit and great risk. It was better to consolidate present territories and to secure the frontiers of exposed provinces.

This policy proved highly successful in the East, where the remaining vassal kings were either deposed or made completely obedient to Rome, and where a fairly stable frontier was established with the Parthian rulers of Persia. It proved less successful in the West, where the existing frontiers were hard to defend and where Germanic tribes showed an incorrigible tendency to raid Roman territory. Only after a long series of border wars was the Roman frontier pushed to the banks of the Rhine and the Danube, and even this line was not wholly satisfactory. It left an awkward angle between the north-flowing Rhine and the east-flowing Danube which could be exploited by the Germans and which greatly lengthened the line the Romans had to defend. To shorten his lines and bring the troublesome

❖❖❖❖❖❖❖❖❖❖❖❖❖❖❖❖❖❖❖❖❖❖❖❖❖❖❖❖❖❖

The Deeds of Augustus

This excerpt is from a long epitaph which Augustus composed for himself in his old age, and which was inscribed on brazen columns at Rome and copied in stone in many provincial cities. The only relatively complete copy which has survived is at Ankara (Ancyra). Note how Augustus poses as the preserver of the old Roman Republic.

In my twentieth year, acting upon my own judgment . . . I raised an army by means of which I restored to liberty the Republic which had been oppressed by the tyranny of a faction. . . . Those who killed my father [Julius Caesar], I drove into exile . . . and when they waged war against the Republic I twice defeated them in battle. . . . I have extended the boundaries of all the provinces of the Roman people. . . . I have reduced to a state of peace . . . the lands enclosed by the ocean from Gades [Cadiz] to the mouth of the Elbe. . . . I have added Egypt to the empire of the Roman people. . . . I accepted no office which was contrary to the customs of the country. . . . When I had put an end to the civil wars . . . I transferred the commonwealth from my own power to the authority of the Senate and the Roman people. In return for this favor I was given by decree of the Senate the title Augustus. . . . After that time I excelled all others in dignity, but of power I held no more than those who were my colleagues in any magistracy.

From Augustus, quoted in *Monumentum Ancyranum: The Deeds of Augustus*, ed. and trans. by William Fairly, *Translations and Reprints* (Philadelphia: U. of Pennsylvania Press, 1898), Vol. V, No. 1, pp. 12 ff.

❖❖❖❖❖❖❖❖❖❖❖❖❖❖❖❖❖❖❖❖❖❖❖❖❖❖❖❖❖❖

The German Problem
1st and 2nd centuries A.D.

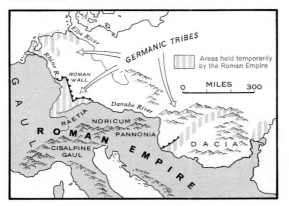

Germanic tribes under Roman control, Augustus wanted to push forward to the Elbe. His generals tried again and again, but they never had quite enough troops. Their last effort ended in disaster in 9 A.D. when the German leader Arminius (Herman) annihilated three Roman legions. Although Arminius has become a national hero of modern Germany, his fellow Germans killed him soon after his great victory. But he did convince Augustus that any further attempt to advance to the Elbe would be useless. Three legions were an appreciable part of the Roman army, which had only twenty-five legions in all. Augustus decided that it was not worth risking such forces to occupy a country which seemed to the Romans desolate, gloomy, and useless. The main Roman frontier remained on the Rhine and Danube, though Rome held outposts in the land just beyond.

Augustus also reorganized the Roman army. The main force was composed of the twenty-five legions, each now composed of about six thousand men. They were long-service, professional soldiers who were rewarded with large bonuses and, usually, gifts of land at the end of their enlistment. Numerous auxiliary troops raised from the subject peoples supported the legionnaires, though these troops were less effective soldiers. In a necessary, but dangerous, innovation Augustus created a praetorian guard of three thousand picked soldiers whose duty was to protect the emperor against risings in Rome. But, as Juvenal, a famous poet of the Empire, asked, who was to protect the emperor against his own guard? The praetorians, stationed in Rome, became a political force, and in the end they were as apt to make a new emperor as to protect an old one. Augustus completed his military reforms by establishing a regular navy to police the Mediterranean and put down piracy.

Morality and Patriotism under Augustus

On the whole, the policies of Augustus did bestow peace and security on the Roman world. They even revived somewhat the feeling of civic responsibility which had been one of the great Roman virtues under the Republic. Augustus found many men to serve him faithfully and to rule subject peoples impartially and justly. It was not mere flattery that led the official court poet, Vergil, to write that the rule of Rome was the rule of law and that the task of Rome was "to take pity on the helpless and put down the oppressor." But this was more true in the provinces than in Italy, and more true in Italy at large than in Rome. It was particularly true in the provinces for which Augustus retained sole responsibility; those in which he shared power with the senate were still subject to corruption and inefficiency. He could make the frontiers strong, but he could not cure the weakness in the heart of Rome.

This weakness has often been described as widespread immorality, and Augustus himself seems to have thought of it that way. But the problem was probably more complicated. The Romans had all the normal temptations to immorality and few of the normal restraints. The human tendency toward selfishness and irresponsibility is ordinarily held in check because one believes that there are certain things more valuable than the immediate gratification of personal desires. But many Romans had lost all sense of values, all belief in anything more important than themselves. Only naive idealists could believe in the Republic and in the possibility that it might one day be restored. The ordinary citizen living in Rome knew that he was devoid of political power, and even the upper classes realized that the emperor could snuff out what little authority they still possessed. In the old days, desire for fame and glory had spurred many men to heroism and self-sacrifice, but now all credit for military or political success went to the emperor. Roman religion, always formal and cold, had been further weakened by the century of civil war and contact with the East. During the wars the old priesthoods had been used for political purposes and were thus discredited; Julius Caesar, a notorious skeptic, had become chief priest (Pontifex Maximus) in order to advance his political prospects. Close contact with Greece and with Asia brought in knowledge of gods which, though they were identified with the Roman gods, were less abstract and more human. The Roman gods had at least represented the state and the virtues which had made the state strong. The new gods stood for no discernible values, and the Roman deities lost their meaning by being assimilated to them. In short, what the Romans needed, especially in Rome itself, was a new faith, and this Augustus only partially succeeded in giving them.

His official policy was to restore the old religion by reviving old ceremonies, purifying the priesthoods, and giving each district a special responsibility for some part of the official cult. Religious revival was to be accompanied by moral reform, especially in family life. Augustus had the necessary laws passed, but they were almost completely ineffective. The state cult was celebrated with somewhat more dignity and decency, but it is difficult to launch a religious revival by passing laws.

Unofficially, there was a widespread movement to build up a cult of Rome and of Augustus, a sort of religion of imperial patriotism. This movement had some chance of success, since it was based on widespread popular feeling. Many people were grateful to Augustus for restoring order, and the East, following the old Hellenistic pattern, was quite ready to deify its ruler. But while Augustus could encourage this cult in the provinces, he could hardly introduce it in Rome. It was associated with concepts of kingship, and in Rome Augustus was still officially only a magistrate with extraordinary powers. Moreover, though people felt it decent and proper to venerate their ruler, their sentiment was not very strong. Gratitude for good government was not the same thing as ardent patriotism, and the imperial cult struck no deep chords of emotion. Whatever religious feeling the Romans felt was turned toward the eastern faiths, which promised redemption and salvation to the individual, and which had little influence on political behavior. The cult of Rome and Augustus may have helped keep the provinces tranquil, but it did not inspire the revival of civic spirit and morality for which Augustus hoped.

For the ordinary individual, especially in the provinces, this lack of any strong loyalty or faith had as yet no serious consequences. The emperor devoted himself to maintaining order and tranquillity, and he had found able subordinates to carry out his wishes. Provincial municipalities still enjoyed self-government, and dedicated men could still look forward to useful and honorable careers in the service of their native towns. Many provincial landowners and businessmen looked no farther than this and were completely unconcerned with larger issues. This was even more true of the lower classes, who depended on the upper classes for their economic existence. Slaves, artisans, and peasants had to do their jobs whatever happened in Rome, and in ordinary times it mattered little what they believed.

This society, guided more by convention than by conviction, could remain stable only in the absence of difficult economic or political problems. In times of stress the lack of strong loyalties, the deficiency in spiritual resources, encouraged intrigues and *coups d'état*. The ordinary inhabitant of the Roman Empire felt no responsibility for its political or economic welfare; he would accept whatever was done by a handful of ambitious or unscrupulous men.

The Beginnings of Christianity

The religion which was finally to answer the longings of the great mass of the Roman population was founded under the early Empire. Jesus of Nazareth was born in the reign of Augustus, probably in the year 4 B.C.* His brief period of active teaching and the conversion of the first disciples came during the reign of Augustus' successor, Tiberius, from about 26 to 30 A.D. The Jews of this period had lost the independence which they had briefly gained under the Maccabees in the second century B.C. and were subject to Rome. But they still dreamed of a Messiah who would free them from foreign domination and prove to the whole world that theirs was the only true religion. When Jesus began teaching, many of the Jews accepted Him as the Messiah, especially since He

---

* Jesus' birth should, of course, have been put in the year 1 A.D. But the reckoning of years from the birth of Jesus did not begin until the sixth century, and by that time errors had crept into the generally accepted chronology.

quoted passages from the prophets which referred to such a mission. But most of these followers became discouraged when Jesus made it clear that His kingdom was "not of this world," that He was interested in a new view of the relation between God and man, and not in worldly politics. On the other hand, those who really understood His message were convinced that He was Christ, the Son of God, and that His teaching of the love of God and the brotherhood of man was the most important revelation which the human race had ever received.

The Romans had permitted the Jews to form a council to administer local Jewish affairs, and this council was dominated by the sect of Pharisees, who were strict upholders of the old Jewish Law. They were shocked by the claim of Jesus that He bore a new revelation which superseded the Law and even more by His assertion that He was the Son of God. As popular support dwindled they felt it safe to accuse Jesus of blasphemy and to condemn Him to death. The sentence had to be confirmed by the Roman governor, Pontius Pilate, who hesitated at first to do so. But he eventually acquiesced, perhaps because he wished to humor the Pharisees, perhaps because he feared, in spite of all evidence to the contrary, that Jesus had political ambitions. Jesus was crucified—a punishment reserved for criminals of the lowest classes—about 30 A.D.

Pilate and the Pharisees thought that this was the end of the matter. But the disciples, after wavering for a moment, remained faithful and were soon convinced that Jesus had risen from the dead and had appeared repeatedly to His followers. The Resurrection gave them courage and confidence; it was not a myth from the remote past, but an actual fact witnessed by living men. They began to understand the divine purpose: God had become man and had suffered on earth to redeem the sins of mankind; all who believed in Him would be saved by his sacrifice. Strong in this new faith, they began to make converts among the Jews of Palestine and Syria. At this time they began to be called Christians.

The new religion was at first only a Jewish sect, ignored by the rest of the world and bitterly opposed by many Jews. At this critical point the conversion of Saul of Tarsus enabled Christianity to break free from these limitations. Saul, though Greek in education and Roman in citizenship, was a passionately orthodox Jew who felt it his duty to persecute the Christians. In the midst of this campaign he was struck blind and dumb; on his recovery he announced his conversion to the faith which he had opposed. He took the new name of Paul, and promptly began preaching Christianity in the commercial cities of Asia Minor and Greece, and eventually in Rome itself.

Paul did two things which made Christianity attractive to the non-Jewish populations of the Roman world. First, he persuaded the early Christian leaders that it was not necessary to follow certain Jewish ritual practices; in other words, one could become a Christian without first having to become a Jew. Second, he began to explain Christian doctrine in terms which were understandable to men trained in Greek philosophy. He could not complete this task, but in his Epistles he began the work of building a Christian theology and philosophy which could appeal to men of all classes.

Meanwhile, other disciples were also spreading the faith outside Palestine. Peter, the leader of the group, may have come to Rome even before Paul, and very early tradition says that he was the head of the Roman Church and that he was martyred there. Other churches were established in Syria, Egypt, and, later, Gaul and Spain. At the same time stories of the sayings and doings of Jesus were collected and during the first century A.D. began to take shape as the Gospels. To these were added letters of the apostles, and so the New Testament was formed. By the second century there was general agreement that these books were divinely inspired, and Christian teaching was based upon them.

Christianity was a vigorous, active faith during the first century. At the same time its appeal was greatest to the poor and the downtrodden, to whom it gave consolation in this world and hope for a happy future life. It was strongest in the East, and among colonies of eastern slaves and workingmen in the West. Few members of the governing class had even heard of Christianity during the early years of its existence, and it had no influence on Roman government or politics until the end of the third century.

The Problem of Succession

The weak spot in the imperial political system first became apparent when Augustus began to cast about for someone to succeed him. Since he was not a king with hereditary powers, there was no reason to assume that his nearest heir would be accepted as his successor. But Augustus believed that only by perpetuating his system of government could he forestall a renewal of the civil wars, and his own career had shown him the strength of family claims. At his accession, when there was strong opposition to one-man rule, the fact that he was the grand-nephew and adopted son of Caesar had been a powerful political asset. How much stronger would be the position of the heir of Augustus, the emperor who had ruled without opposition for over four decades. To avoid chaos after his death, Augustus decided to choose a successor and to give him a share of imperial power.

But it was easier to decide on this policy than to carry it out. Augustus had no son— only a daughter, whose misconduct finally became so notorious that she was banished from Rome. Other relatives died young, and jealousy and intrigue sprang up among those who survived. In the end Augustus settled on his stepson, Tiberius, an able administrator, but an embittered man whom Augustus had passed over again and again in his search for a successor. This episode revealed a weakness in the imperial system which was never to be cured: the lack of definite rules of succession and the resulting danger that the imperial title could be seized through intrigue and violence.

Augustus, to insure that Tiberius would be able to take over the government when he died, had given him both military command and the power of a tribune. The smooth transition after Augustus' death in 14 A.D. showed how firmly established the imperial government was, and Tiberius made few changes in the Augustan system. He did end the popular assembly, which had lost all importance, and henceforward consuls and praetors were elected by the senate. Tiberius proved a careful and thrifty administrator and left a large surplus in the treasury when he died in 37 A.D.

But the problem of succession continued to plague the Empire. What had been merely a matter of family jealousies under Augustus boiled up into political intrigues and conspiracies under Tiberius. Each member of the imperial family tried to discredit the others, with some of the leading candidates being eliminated by poison. Tiberius, disgusted with the behavior of his relatives, retired to the island of Capri, a step which only made intrigue flourish the more. Conspiracies were now directed against the emperor himself, and the embittered old man began to suspect everyone around him. He had many senators and several members of his own family executed on rather flimsy charges of treason, and after his death the upper classes remembered him only as a morose and dangerous tyrant.

From 37 to 68 A.D. the problem grew more and more acute. There was seldom a desirable heir to imperial power, and when one did present himself he was usually removed by intrigue or assassination. The members of the praetorian guard, who made most of the choices, were easily satisfied. They wanted their candidate to have some connection with the ruling family and to be generous in his gifts to the soldiers; they demanded no qualities of intellect or character. Understandably, the insecure men they raised to power spotted conspiracies on every hand. They killed most of their rivals, squandered money on personal pleasures, and executed many senators, both because they feared plots and because they wanted to confiscate the senators' property. Caius Caligula (37–41 A.D.) and Nero (54–68 A.D.) were vicious men; Claudius (41–54 A.D.) was well-meaning but was dominated by an evil, ruthless wife. To calm their suspicions,

Nero, 54–68 A.D.

A ship with Roman soldiers, from the Arch of Titus, 81 A.D.

these rulers sacrificed capable generals and administrators like Corbulo, who had protected the East against the Parthians, and leading statesmen and philosophers like Seneca.

Nero, though perhaps no worse than some of his predecessors, offended the Romans by his cruelty and by his lack of dignity. He fancied himself a great poet and composer, and loved to give public exhibitions of his talents. When a disastrous conflagration devastated Rome during his reign, he was accused of having set fire to the city to provide a backdrop for his recitation of tragic verse. The story was almost certainly not true, but the fact that it could be told and believed is significant. Nero was worried enough to seek a scapegoat in Rome's tiny Christian community, which had been founded only a few years before. He accused the Christians of starting the fire and had a number of them executed.

As resentment against Nero rose higher, the legions broke into open rebellion. This was a new and ominous development. The praetorian guard had not been very wise in its choice of emperors, but at least it had always been able to agree on one man. But the scattered legions, stationed hundreds of miles apart, could seldom agree, and when each advanced the claims of its favorite general, civil war was inevitable. The result was the famous "year of the four emperors" (68–69 A.D.). Nero was easily overthrown, and then three army commanders in succession marched on Rome, claimed the imperial title, and promptly lost it to the next aggressor. The commander in the East, Vespasian, was wiser; he consolidated his hold over his own region and formed an alliance with the Danube legions before striking. This careful preparation proved its worth; by the time Vespasian's troops seized Rome all his opponents had shot their bolt and Vespasian was to stand unchallenged until his death in 79 A.D.

Roman Society in the First Century A.D.

The inhabitants of Rome must have found the first hundred years of the Empire a mixed blessing. The lower classes had lost all their political power, and the upper classes lived in constant fear of exile, loss of property, and execution. But the city of Rome was not the Empire, and the troubles of the inhabitants of Rome meant little to those who lived outside. To the provincials the Empire still meant peace and security; even the worst emperors had protected the frontiers, and their acts of tyranny had struck at the senatorial class rather than at the small landowners and business-men who formed the backbone of provin-cial society. Emperors scorned by the up-per classes in Rome were popular in the provinces. The Romans of Rome looked on Claudius as a pedant and a weakling, but to the inhabitants of Gaul he was a hero: he had conferred Roman citizenship on one of the largest Gallic tribes (the Aedui) and he had made the Empire's last great conquest by occupying most of the is-land of Britain. Even Nero had a consid-erable following in the provinces; the Greek East, especially, was pleased by his interest in art and literature.

The army, the real power in the Roman state, was far more in sympathy with the provincials than it was with the upper classes of Rome. Almost without exception, the army commanders believed in the ne-cessity of one-man rule. Bad as the em-peror might be, they much preferred a sin-gle source of authority to government by a divided and selfish aristocracy. Most of the soldiers and officers came from the provinces, and, like their fellow provincials, they were not greatly disturbed by the em-perors' mistreatment of the senatorial aris-tocracy. To a military man, imperial gov-ernment was a necessity, and while the army might turn against an individual em-peror it never thought of destroying the system.

Political problems, of course, never oc-cupy all the time of all the people, and many inhabitants of the Roman world busied themselves with other matters. The first century of the Empire saw a remark-able development of Roman commerce and industry and the spread of Roman agri-cultural techniques to the western prov-inces of Gaul and Spain. (This economic growth reached its peak in the next century and will be discussed in more detail on pp. 125–27.) Moreover, the greatest period in Roman literature and philosophy came during the troubled years which saw the end of the Republic and the establishment of the Empire. Romans, stimulated by contact with Hellenistic civilization and by the im-pact of rapid social and political change, were inspired to express their ideas in their own language and to create, for the first time, a Latin literature. Periods of upheaval and uncertainty often engender intellectual activity, and the Romans reacted vigor-ously to the great events of their day.

Latin Literature

Latin literature was modeled directly on the Greek example. The early Romans, as we have seen, were chiefly interested in war and politics; they tended to equate literary and artistic interests with moral and physi-cal softness. But this prejudice steadily weakened as they occupied more and more of the areas dominated by Greek culture. Aristocrats, especially, were impressed by the products of the Greek mind; by the end of the second century B.C. they were im-porting Greek slaves to teach their children and sending their sons to the East to study under famous Greek scholars. Soon Ro-mans began to try their own hand at philo-sophical and political essays, or encour-aged their dependents to imitate the Greek dramatists and poets.

The first products of this literary move-ment were not very distinguished, but those of the last century of the Republic were. The prose writers dealt mainly with history, political theory, and philosophy. Cicero (106–43 B.C.) covered the widest range; he published his orations and letters as exam-ples of an elegant and sophisticated style, and wrote extensively on constitutional theory, ethics, and philosophy. Caesar was perhaps the first general to realize that military communiqués could have both style and political purpose. His account of his wars in Gaul, which he wrote in terse, simple language in order to give them the widest possible appeal, was meant to convince the Romans that he was an invincible commander and a far-seeing statesman.

The poets of the late Republic were more concerned with expressing their personal feelings than with politics. Catullus (87–54 B.C.), in graceful lyrics about his love affairs, showed great technical skill in handling difficult meters. But the greatest poet of the Republic, and perhaps the most original of all Latin authors, was Lucretius (99–55 B.C.). In his *De rerum naturae* he expressed his personal philosophy and his view of the universe in verses of remarkable beauty and power. He drew many of his ideas from the Epicureans and from Hellenistic scientists, but the synthesis was his own. But Lucretius was too speculative to appeal to the practical Roman mind; he had little influence on his own generation and established no tradition.

With the exception of Lucretius, the Latin authors of the first century B.C. contributed few new ideas to the intellectual tradition of the West. They did, however, perfect the Latin language, which theretofore had had an uncertain grammar and a limited vocabulary. They fixed the grammar and imported or invented hundreds of new words, so that by the end of the Republic Latin had become a precise, efficient language. Since much of the world's thinking was to be done in Latin for the next millennium and a half, this was no mean achievement. These writers also introduced eastern ideas to the West in a form in which they could be assimilated. True, something was lost in the process; Latin was never able to reproduce all the subtle distinctions which could be made in Greek, and the Romans had little interest in the scientific and philosophical speculations of

✥✥✥✥✥✥✥✥✥✥✥✥✥✥✥✥✥✥✥✥✥✥✥✥✥✥✥✥✥✥✥✥✥✥✥

Lucretius on Atoms

If you think that basic particles can stand still, and by standing still can beget new motions among things, you are astray and wander far from true reasoning. For since basic particles wander through the void, they must needs all be carried on either by their own weight or by a chance blow from one or other. For when in quick motion they have often met and collided, it follows that they leap apart suddenly in different directions. . . . And to show you more clearly that all the bodies of matter are constantly being tossed about, remember that there is no bottom in the sum of things, and the first bodies have nowhere to rest, since space is without end or limit. . . . Beyond doubt no rest is granted to the first bodies, . . . some after being pressed together then leap back with wide intervals, some again . . . are tossed about within a narrow compass. And those which being held in combination more closely condensed collide and leap back through tiny intervals, . . . these constitute the strong roots of stone and . . . iron and others of this kind. . . . The rest leap far apart and pass far back with long intervals between; these supply thin air for us and the gleaming light of the sun.

From Lucretius, *De rerum naturae,* trans. by W. H. D. Rouse (Cambridge, Mass.: Harvard U. Press, 1937), book II, 11. 80–108.

✥✥✥✥✥✥✥✥✥✥✥✥✥✥✥✥✥✥✥✥✥✥✥✥✥✥✥✥✥✥✥✥✥✥✥

the Greeks. But something was also gained: Latin might be less subtle than Greek, but it was more powerful. Ideas which seemed a little flimsy in Greek acquired solidity and certainty in Latin. Few languages have carried as much conviction as Latin, which can make even the most obvious platitudes sound like profound truths. By borrowing from the Greeks, the Romans saved themselves a great deal of time and trouble; by putting what they borrowed into enduring form, they laid the foundations for much of the later literature of the West.

Under the Republic, the most gifted writers had come from a narrow circle of aristocratic families in Rome. By the time of the early Empire, literary activity had skipped the bounds of the city. The two greatest poets of the Augustan age, Vergil and Horace, came from small Italian towns and were of undistinguished birth. They were able to devote themselves to writing only because they were patronized by the emperor, or rather by one of his chief advisers, Maecenas. As a result, their work had something of an official flavor, and they were careful to celebrate the virtues prized by Augustus. Vergil (70–19 B.C.), in his long epic, the *Aeneid,* demonstrated that Rome had been founded under divine auspices, that its glorious destiny had long been predicted, and that its brilliant success was due to the virtue of its founders. But the *Aeneid,* with its mastery of the conventions and techniques of epic poetry, also demonstrated how well the Romans had learned from the Greeks. And with all Vergil's imitation and official moralizing, he was a real poet; he wrote some of the most effective lines which appear in the literature of any country.

Horace (65–8 B.C.) also wrote official poems on such occasions as Augustus' religious festivals, and he duly celebrated the heroic virtues of the early Romans. Just as Vergil praised the joys of rural life, so Horace wrote of his contented existence on his Sabine farm. This fitted in well with Augustus' theory that vice flourished in the cities and that the Romans could recover their lost virtues only by returning to the soil. But Horace was more than an official poet. He was a shrewd and experienced man who had risen from humble station to a position of prominence, a man who could see through hypocrisy and sham. At his best he was a keen observer of human behavior and a master of summing up his observations in brief and pungent statements.

The fate of Ovid (43 B.C.–17 A.D.), the third great poet of this period, shows why it was well to adhere to the official line. Ovid wrote some of the most graceful verse ever produced by a Latin writer, and he knew how to tell a story well. But he drew most of his material from Greek mythology and legend. There was little morality in these sources and Ovid did not bother to add any; he was frankly interested only in pleasure and a comfortable life. This attitude annoyed Augustus and probably explains why Ovid was banished from Rome to a very uncomfortable life on the remote shores of the Black Sea. His work remained popular, however, and provided the chief source of knowledge of Greek mythology for the Middle Ages and Renaissance.

Of the prose writers, the historian, Livy (59 B.C.–17 A.D.), best expressed the spirit of the Augustan age by summing up all the work of earlier annalists and historians in a monumental history of Rome. Much of his work has been lost, but what remains suggests that he was chiefly interested in celebrating the piety, heroism, and civic spirit of the early Romans. Again, this fitted in well with another of Augustus' aims: to bring about a moral and religious revival of Rome. Livy accepted legends uncritically

Vespasian, 69–79 A.D.

and explained everything in terms of the simplest personal or political motives. Nevertheless, he made his main point: that the greatness of Rome was based on fortitude, self-sacrifice, and a sense of responsibility. More than anyone else, Livy created the tradition that Roman character was the source of Roman strength, a tradition which was accepted without question for centuries after his time and which still impresses modern historians.

The Empire at Its Height

Vespasian's victorious entry into Rome in 69 A.D. marked a real change in the character of the Empire. Just as literary leadership had spread from Rome to the Italian municipalities (and eventually to the provinces), so political leaders now began to arise from a wider circle. Vespasian, the first emperor who was not a member of one of the old Roman aristocratic families, came from a middle-class family in a small Italian town. He cared little for the opinion of the upper classes; so long as he could administer the Empire efficiently and economically, it mattered not that elegant Romans called him a money-grubbing peasant. His predecessors had oppressed the senate; Vespasian ignored it. He still named individual senators to important positions, but he virtually abandoned Augustus' theory that the senate as a corporate body could have independent though limited power. Vespasian's common sense, his financial shrewdness, and his aloofness from the scandals and intrigues of high society helped to steady the Roman world after the unnerving events of Nero's last years. When Vespasian died in 79 A.D., both his sons were accepted as emperors without squabbling among rivals and without meddling by the army—the first time this had happened since the Empire was founded. The eldest son, Titus (79–81

Trajan, 98–117 A.D.

A.D.), was as capable as his father and considerably more popular. The second son, Domitian (81–96 A.D.), had inherited his family's administrative ability but was tactless in his dealings with subordinates and oppressive in his financial demands. He revived the old quarrel with the senate and executed many senators, while angering the army by heavy taxation of provincial subjects. But when a praetorian assassinated Domitian in 96 A.D. there was no repetition of the semi-anarchy of the year of the four emperors. Senators and praetorians agreed on selecting an elderly and upright gentleman, Nerva, as emperor, and Nerva made sure of the support of the legions by adopting an able army commander, Trajan, as his successor.

The "Five Good Emperors"

With Nerva and Trajan begins the period of the "five good emperors," which lasted from 96 to 180. Gibbon once wrote that this was the happiest period in the history of the human race; certainly it was the most prosperous and least troubled period in the history of the Roman Empire. All the old problems seemed to have been solved, and the ancient civic virtues of the

Hadrian's Wall, built 122–26 from the Irish Sea to the North Sea to protect the northern frontier of the province of Britain.

Romans were revived in the persons of the emperors and their military and civilian subordinates. Each emperor in turn adopted a worthy successor, and his choice was never seriously questioned. Thus Trajan (98–117) followed Nerva, Hadrian (117–138) followed Trajan, Antoninus Pius (138–160) followed Hadrian, and the adopted son of Antoninus, Marcus Aurelius (160–180), closed the line. This formula seemed to have all the advantages and none of the disadvantages of monarchy. The new emperor was always a mature man with wide experience of public affairs; he was selected because of his ability and not because of his family or place of birth. Trajan and Hadrian both came from Italica, a small town in Spain; the fact that an emperor could come from the provinces did

much to erase the old distinction between the Italian ruling group and the provincials.

The quarrel with the senate was also eased. Senators refrained from conspiring against the emperor and the emperor refrained from putting senators to death. The senate had no independent authority; in fact, it lost one of its traditional areas of influence when Italy was divided into districts ruled by imperial appointees. But the senate still functioned as a consultative assembly and as a high court, and senators filled many important offices.

Imperial Government in the Second Century

As the emperors took over more and more direct responsibility for the administration of the Empire, they found that they had to create a corps of permanent civil servants. The emperors of the first century had used senators and knights as governors and financial officers, but, since these men served only intermittently and for short periods, they could not provide the continuity needed for good administration. Therefore the emperor began to use members of his household to take care of his correspondence, his finances, and his records. Many of these men were freed slaves, despised by the aristocracy, and their growing power generated new friction between senate and emperor. Humble or not, by the time of Vespasian these civil servants began to be organized in regular governmental bureaus, such as a finance office and a secretariat.

During the second century Vespasian's successors enlarged and reorganized this rudimentary civil service. They were especially anxious to draw into it the knights, who ranked just below the senators in wealth and prestige. Hadrian built up a group of career officers whom he advanced from post to post until they reached the highest positions in the government. In his hierarchy of imperial procurators, men began in class four in minor posts in the provinces, and, if they proved able, were promoted grade by grade until they received a class-one appointment in Rome. By the end of the century these officers held all the significant administrative positions. Senators might still hold titular command, but the actual work was done by the imperial procurators. The emperors kept careful watch over these agents; Hadrian, for example, made two long tours through the Empire to inspect provincial government.

The emperors also protected the provinces against outside attacks. Trajan, the most military-minded of the second-century emperors, drove the Parthians out of the Tigris-Euphrates Valley and the northern barbarians from the Danube. It was during his reign that the Empire reached its greatest extent, with the conquest of Mesopotamia and Dacia (a large part of modern Rumania). Trajan's successor, Hadrian, was more defense-minded. He abandoned Mesopotamia and inaugurated the policy of building great lines of provincial fortifications, such as the wall across northern Britain. He also reorganized the army, not entirely for the better. His policy was to protect each province with troops recruited exclusively from the region, and to break up large units into small garrisons to man the frontier posts. This policy eventually reduced the legions to mere provincial militias, incapable of rapid or coordinated action. But during the second century the Roman army was still a magnificent fighting force. Under Marcus Aurelius, in the great wars against the Danubian barbarians, it fought for years in difficult country, far from its base of supplies, against a formidable enemy. Marcus wore himself out in the struggle, and the army

The philosopher-emperor Marcus Aurelius, 160–80. Head from a bronze equestrian statue.

suffered severe losses, but the Danubian provinces were protected. In fact, throughout most of the Empire, provincials could go about their business without worrying about invasion or war.

The Romanization of the Provinces

The main business of these provincials was to become Roman citizens. By accepting the way of life of either the Greeks in the East or the Romans in the West, they would first gain rights of municipal self-government and finally full Roman citizenship. The creation of the Empire speeded up this process in the West; there was less to be done in the East, which had been exposed to Greek influences long before the founding of the Empire. But the Romanizing of the West was almost entirely the work of the Empire; it was during the first and second centuries A.D. that Gaul and Spain were indelibly stamped with Latin civilization. There was nothing compulsory about all this; it simply became evident to the provincials that if they wanted to hold government jobs or trade with distant parts of the Empire they had better learn Latin and adopt Roman customs. Such a development takes time; this is why Britain, which was added to the Empire much later than Gaul or Spain, never became thoroughly Romanized and did not

The Roman Empire at Its Height A.D. 117

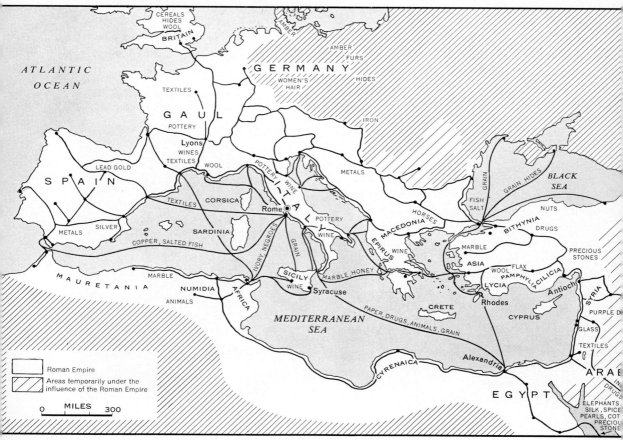

preserve its Latin culture after the fall of Rome.

One product of the Romanizing of the West was the building of towns. The Gauls and Germans of the western provinces had never known the intensive urban life of the East, living for the most part in scattered villages and hamlets rather than in cities. But the Romans could not conceive of organized life except in towns, which to them were essential as military, administrative, and economic centers. Everywhere they went they built towns and in so doing they spread Latin culture throughout the Empire.

As the provinces became more and more like Greece or Italy, there was less and less reason to treat them as backward and subject areas. Provincial towns were allowed to elect their own officials, whose jurisdiction extended to the surrounding countryside. The powers of these municipal officials were limited, and their chief duty was to collect taxes for the central government; but at least it was better to have a local man collecting taxes instead of some outsider. Thoroughly Romanized towns that managed to win the ear of the emperor might also be granted Roman citizenship. This process had begun under Claudius, but it was speeded up tremendously during the second century. By the end of that period some senators, many public officials, and almost the entire army came from the provinces.

Economic Activity

The growth of economic relations among regions also accelerated the spread of a uniform way of life throughout the Roman world. There had always been trade in luxuries between East and West; profits on such articles as silk, incense, and precious stones were great enough even in troubled times for merchants to brave the dangers of war and piracy. Under the firm peace established by the Empire, this trade burgeoned; now eastern businessmen became familiar with the meandering Seine and the ports of far-off Britain. But it was the trade in bulkier and less valuable commodities, which gave work to more people, that did most to bind the provinces together by ties of economic interest. For a while one of the great articles of trade was pottery. A real industrial center grew up around the Bay of Naples, and its products were shipped throughout the West. There was also a considerable trade in foodstuffs. Rome drew its grain from Egypt, and in bad crop years Gaul imported cereals from Britain. To a Roman, wine was as necessary as bread, and the provinces exchanged their favorite vintages or shipped them to the cold northern regions where no grapes would grow. All this trade taken together was not very extensive by modern standards, but it was enough to make the second century a prosperous period for many inhabitants of the Roman world.

Yet this commercial prosperity rested on an insecure foundation. The luxury trade was sure, but it supported only a few people. The trade in foodstuffs dwindled as Roman methods of agriculture spread to the provinces. For example, when Romans began to grow grapes in the French river valleys, a large part of the wine trade with Gaul disappeared. Rome, to be sure, still had to be supplied with grain, but since most of the grain came from Egypt, which was the emperor's private domain, and had to be sold to the Roman populace below cost, this operation was not apt to have a stimulating effect upon the economy.

The worst failure, perhaps, was in industrial production. The promising start which had been made around the Bay of Naples led to nothing, partly, again, because of the spread of Roman techniques to the provinces. For example, when manufacturing centers in southern Gaul began to produce pottery indistinguishable from Neapolitan ware, there was no longer any reason to pay the cost of transport from Italy. The failure in production also sprang from difficulties in distribution. Roman ships were not very large, but they could carry a considerable cargo economically; the trouble began when goods had to be moved by land. Roman roads were paved with large, flat stones, an excellent footing for marching legions but a poor surface for heavy wheeled traffic. Moreover, the Romans never discovered how to harness horses so that they could pull heavy loads. As a result, most land transport was in small, two-wheeled carts with a capacity of only four or five hundred

Triumphal arch and mausoleum near St. Rémy-de-Provence, 1st century A.D.

Arena at Arles, 2nd century A.D.

Aqueduct, Pont du Garde, near Nîmes, 2nd century A.D.

pounds. Communities which could not be reached by ship found it much cheaper to make their own goods than to import them overland.

Why did the Romans, practical and realistic as they were, fail to devise some means of lowering production costs and improving transportation? Though practical, the Romans were also very conservative, and both their practicality and their conservatism militated against inventiveness. They had little interest in science; it was the one branch of Greek learning which they failed to cultivate. Regarding scientific inquiry as mere speculation, they denied themselves the chance of making discoveries based on scientific theory. Their conservatism kept them from exploiting new techniques developed by artisans and engineers; what had been good enough for past generations was good enough for the present. Moreover, the Romans saw little point in labor-saving devices, since much of their work was done by slaves—and it was better to keep slaves busy and out of mischief. A good example of these attitudes is provided by the history of the water mill. The Romans knew how to build water mills, and in places like Rome the large population made them almost indispensable. But the Romans continued to grind their grain by hand in most parts of the Empire. True, the flow of Mediterranean rivers is very irregular, but that fact in itself does not explain the Roman failure to use water power. After all, they could have dammed some Mediterranean rivers to produce a fairly constant source of power, and not all Romans lived on the shores of the Mediterranean. In the rainy region of northern Gaul, where there were thousands of water mills in the Middle Ages, there were few in Roman times.

Roman Art and Literature

The same conservatism may be seen in the Roman architecture of the second century. But the Romans had made one significant architectural innovation—the round arch, which had not been used by the Greeks. The Romans found the arch very useful in bridging wide streams and in throwing aqueducts across deep valleys. With the arch and its logical development in a third dimension—the vault—they

127

constructed huge public buildings enclosing vast amounts of space—great structures like the Colosseum and the Pantheon. So enamored were the Romans of this architectural form that they built triumphal arches to stand by themselves as symbols of glory and victory. This impressive Roman architecture, though perhaps not as beautiful or well proportioned as the Greek, expressed the solidity and the far-reaching power of the Roman state. But once the Romans became fairly successful, they were satisfied and welcomed no further change. The new towns growing up all over the West were remarkably alike; the buildings might be larger or smaller, depending on local resources, but the pattern was the same.

Latin literature of the period after Nero was also conservative. Historians like Tacitus (55–118) bewailed the loss of liberty and the oppression of the senate under the evil emperors of the first century. Satirical poets like Martial (ca. 40–104) and Juvenal (55–138) attacked the vices of urban society. Both developed to the full the tendency toward terse, epigrammatic phrases inherent in the spirit of the Latin language. Tacitus was actually not a very good historian; strongly prejudiced in favor of the old aristocracy, he tended to explain everything in terms of intrigues among a handful of courtiers and sycophants. But few historians have written so well or had such a lasting influence. His pungent phrases have universal application; his description of one of the ephemeral emperors of the year 69 as a man who in the opinion of all was qualified to rule if only he hadn't tried it, would fit a good many politicians of the twentieth century. The satirical poets were equally gifted in depicting the unlovely aspects of high society. The fact, incidentally, that one of the ablest of these poets, Martial, came from Spain reflects the spread of Latin culture to the provinces and the suspicion with which many provincials looked upon the capital city.

Tacitus, Martial, and Juvenal, though conservative, at least wrote with biting energy. Pliny (61–113?), who published his letters on the model of Cicero, was considerably blander. He was a cultivated gentleman, well read in what were already coming to be considered the classics, somewhat interested in many things but not deeply engrossed in any one subject. He could tell a story in a clear and interesting way, as in his description of the famous eruption of Vesuvius which buried (and so preserved) the towns of Herculaneum and Pompeii. He was an honest and upright public servant, though a little deficient in imagination and power of decision. As governor of Bithynia under Trajan he annoyed the emperor by asking for advice on every difficult problem, notably on what to do with members of a peculiar sect called Christians who refused to perform the usual public sacrifices. Pliny was a useful official so long as he was dealing with familiar things, but he was at a loss when faced with innovations. If the rest of the civil service was like him, the chief danger which threatened the Empire in the second century was stagnation.

Latin writers, like Roman businessmen, were reluctant to experiment. Two promising starts were made at creating the literary form we know as the novel, one in the *Satyricon* by Petronius (d. 66), a courtier under Nero, the other in the *Golden Ass* by Apuleius (b. 124), who lived in North Africa during the second century. Both bear an extraordinary resemblance to the first novels in modern European languages; each describes the adventures of a hero whom misfortune dooms to wander among strange, often disreputable, people. Petronius described life among rich and vulgar freemen in Italy, Apuleius the society and religions of the East. But these works did not conform to Roman standards of elegance either in subject matter or in style, and were therefore neglected. Instead of developing the new genre, Latin writers turned to the past. Under Hadrian, whose reign marked a turning point in literature as in so many other activities, there was a wave of imitations of past masterpieces, often written in a deliberately archaic style. With the exception of Christian writers, who will be discussed in a later chapter (see pp. 163–64), Latin literature never recovered from this blight of imitation and adherence to conventional forms.

Roman Law

There was more vitality in Roman law. The long period of political stability and the interest of the emperors in good administration made the second century the decisive period in the formulation of Roman law. The Romans, like most other peoples, had started with a few simple rules of law which had been expanded by judicial interpretation and amended by legislation until they covered most of the ordinary problems which arose. But the Romans also had allied and subject cities, each with its own law, and the inhabitants of these cities frequently sued one another. Since it would have been manifestly unjust to insist that the law of any one city be followed in such cases, the Roman judges had to discover equitable principles which would be accepted by all reasonable men. The Stoic philosophy (see p. 71), which was held by most Roman jurists, helped in this quest; it was much easier to discover principles which were valid at all times and in all places if one were first convinced, as the Stoics were, that such principles existed. And once the principles were formulated in the late Republic and early Empire, they commanded such wide respect that they could be applied to all kinds of cases. It

seemed obvious that rules derived from the common experience of all peoples must be closer to the eternal law of nature than the peculiar and imperfect laws of a single city. Thus the Romans themselves began to prefer the general principles of the law of nations, as they called it, to their own municipal law, which was in many ways out of date.

It was not always easy, however, to discover exactly what the law was. It could be found in legislation, official decrees, judicial decisions, and the opinions and writings of famous lawyers. These scattered materials could be interpreted in several ways; there were, to use American terms, schools of "loose" and "strict" construction. During the second century the Romans tried to secure greater uniformity in the interpretation of the law. In the first place, some of the ablest lawyers produced textbooks which the courts accepted as authoritative. These textbooks did not eliminate all differences, but they greatly reduced the area of disagreement. In the second place, the emperor began to take almost complete responsibility for justice, as he did for other fields of administration. His own court was the highest authority; the praetorian prefect and the prefect of the City, under the emperor's direction, handled the most important cases. This concentration of judicial authority in the hands of the emperor and his appointees naturally led to a greater uniformity in interpreting the law.

We find a good example of both processes during the reign of Hadrian. For many generations the praetor's edict had been one of the chief sources of law. This was a statement by the praetor (who had been the highest judge under the Republic) of the rules of law which he would apply during his term of office. The edict had tended to become standardized over the years, but it was still not wholly official or completely set. Hadrian asked a leading

Ulpian on Justice

Ulpian was one of the great Roman jurists of the early third century A.D. These passages were quoted by Justinian's lawyers at the beginning of the *Digest,* an authoritative treatise on Roman law (see p. 224).

Justice is a constant and perpetual will to give every man his due. The principles of law are these: to live virtuously, not to harm others, to give his due to everyone. Jurisprudence is the knowledge of divine and human things, the science of the just and the unjust.

Law is the art of goodness and justice. By virtue of this we [lawyers] may be called priests, for we cherish justice and we profess knowledge of goodness and equity, separating right from wrong and the legal from the illegal. . . .

Roman lawyer to consult past records and prepare a final and authoritative version of the praetor's edict. This man, Salvius Julianus, produced a version of the edict which became an enduring part of the law.

This formulation of Roman law was one of the great achievements of western man. It was not perfect—no law is—but it was a great improvement over all earlier legal systems and has probably not been surpassed by any later one. It was based on principles of justice and equity—the Romans themselves described it as "the art of goodness and fairness," or "a continuing desire to give every man his due." It was comprehensive, flexible, and subtle; there were few situations which could not be brought under one of its rules. Though it did not eliminate class distinctions, it did admit that even the humblest men had some rights—for example, it protected slaves against cruel masters. The emperor, of course, could always override the law, and did on some occasions, but usually it was only powerful men

who had to fear this kind of injustice. The "five good emperors" seldom used this arbitrary authority; the second century was a golden age for the Empire precisely because it was an age of law. The Romans showed their best qualities of mind and character in their law, particularly during the second century. Justinian's great compilation (see p. 224), four hundred years later, was based largely on the work of the second century, and through Justinian Roman law has affected the jurisprudence of every country in the world.

The Greek East

Except in law, the eastern part of the Empire was much more vigorous than the Latin West. The easterners showed some tendency toward imitation and use of conventional forms, but even when they did, their work was often more interesting than that of their Latin counterparts. For example, the Greek Plutarch (46?–120?), in his *Lives* of famous Greeks and Romans, was not very original or profound, but the *Lives* are good reading. Greek scientists continued to produce useful and influential works, though they never quite reached the level of their Hellenistic predecessors. The Greek physician Galen (*ca.* 130–*ca.* 200) wrote a great summary of medical knowledge which was used as a basic text by schools of medicine for the next fifteen centuries, and Ptolemy the Alexandrian (second century) prepared a work on astronomy that had almost as long an influence. It was unfortunate that Ptolemy accepted an erroneous theory which placed the earth in the center of the solar system, but his explanation of the apparent movement of the planets made it possible to predict their positions with great accuracy.

The real genius of the East, however, lay in religion and philosophy. It was in the second century that the first Church Fathers, who all wrote in Greek, began to make Christianity acceptable to the educated classes by deriving a theology and a philosophy from Biblical texts. It was also the period when neoplatonism became more of a religion than a philosophy. Starting with Plato's belief in eternal, incorporeal Ideas (see p. 64), neoplatonists developed a whole system of intellectual or spiritual emanations. God, who was pure Spirit, generated lesser spirits who ruled the world, and the spirit which is in man. There were obvious analogies here with Christian doctrine, and neoplatonism helped prepare the way for the acceptance of Christianity.

The second century also saw the highest expression of Stoic doctrine, in the writings of the slave Epictetus (60–140) and the *Meditations* of the emperor Marcus Aurelius (121–180). Nothing could have illustrated more perfectly than the careers of these two men the basic Stoic doctrine that the man who understands the eternal law and who rules his own soul is unaffected by external circumstances. Marcus Aurelius took no pride in being an emperor; Epictetus felt no shame in being a slave. Each man simply did his duty as he saw it. This same spirit, which pervaded a large part of the Roman bureaucracy, helps explain both the good government and the remarkable legal achievements of the second century.

The Crisis of the Third Century

Many inhabitants of the second-century Empire thought they had found a permanent answer to all their social and political problems and felt confident that good government and prosperity would continue indefinitely. Actually the Empire rested on a narrow and precarious base, and with the death of Marcus Aurelius in 180 it entered a period of prolonged crisis. As we have seen, neither industrial production nor commercial exchange had increased during the latter part of the second century. This economic stagnation had two serious consequences: First, the growing tendency of the different regions of the Empire toward self-sufficiency carried with it a loosening of political bonds. The inhabitants of Syria cared nothing about the welfare of the people of Gaul, and a barbarian raid on Britain was of no concern to the inhabitants of Roman Africa. Second, and more important, the great majority of inhabitants of the Empire had no hope of improving their standard of living or of advancing to a higher social class. They carried the whole military and political structure of the Empire on their backs but gained very little by doing so. The peasants, above all, were cut off from the benefits of the society they supported; the Empire gave them peace, and that was all. If it failed to maintain peace, they had no reason to support the existing political system. The proletarians of the cities were in only a slightly better position. They enjoyed the games and spectacles staged by the upper classes, and in the largest towns they were provided with cheap grain. But their opportunities were limited and, like the peasants, they felt no great loyalty for their government.

The emperors of the second century had realized that the Empire rested on too narrow a base, that it had alienated most of its inhabitants. By granting local self-government and citizenship, and by expanding the civil service, they had succeeded in involving some members of the middle class in political affairs. But the Roman middle class was small and not all its members were capable of political activity. In politics as in economics, the Empire was not making the best use of its human resources.

Thus much depended on the ability and devotion of a small group of men—the emperor, the provincial governors, and the heads of the civil-service departments. If their efforts flagged, there was no reserve on which to draw—no other group which

Fourth-century mosaics of gladiatorial combat.

could be used to strengthen or reform the administration. And this narrow governing group, as so often happens, became increasingly conservative as the second century wore on. They were conscientious and honest, but they were satisfied with things as they were. They preferred to look back on a glorious past rather than ahead toward a dubious future. They were not the men to break through the economic and intellectual stagnation which had settled over the Empire.

Moreover, though the "five good emperors" had greatly strengthened civil administration, real power still lay in the army. Army officers were recruited from the same classes which supplied the civil servants; in fact, some army service in their early years was required of most members of the bureaucracy. But the men who remained in the army, the career officers, were contemptuous of the bureaucrats, especially when the bureaucrat had a soft job in Rome while the career officer was stationed in an uncomfortable frontier post. The soldiers had even less respect for civilians. They were recruited, for the most part, from the lower classes in remote frontier areas, the regions least prosperous and least touched by the spread of Latin or Greek civilization. If they showed any loyalty, it was to their general and not to the

Roman state; they could be used against other Romans just as easily as against barbarians. The army had fought hard and enjoyed few rewards during the second century. Both officers and men must have wondered at times whether they did not deserve a larger share of the profits of empire.

All these weaknesses were suddenly revealed during the third century when the problem of succession arose again in a particularly malignant form. A society solidly based on the participation of its members can endure a bad ruler without being shaken, but the Roman Empire lacked such a base. More than ever, it depended on the character and ability of the emperor; if he proved weak, stupid, or evil, the entire system was endangered. Unfortunately, Commodus (180–192) the heir of Marcus Aurelius, had all these defects. The first son to succeed his father in almost a century, he was a perfect example of the dangers of the hereditary principle. He was a superb athlete—his chief amusement was killing wild animals in public spectacles—but he was a whimsical and tyrannical ruler. There was general relief when he was assassinated in 192.

This relief was short-lived. The senate, in one of its last exercises of authority, joined the praetorians in trying to make an emperor, but the armies paid no attention to them. Each army had its own candidate for emperor, and, as in 68–69, the issue was finally decided by a series of civil wars. The general who eventually triumphed was Septimius Severus; he and members of his family or connections by marriage held the Empire for the next forty-five years.

The Army Takes Over

The period of the Severi launched the transition from the more or less civilian and bureaucratic state of the second century to the military dictatorships of the fourth. Septimius Severus and his heirs distrusted the old ruling classes and put more and more confidence in army officers from the frontier provinces. Senators were barred from army commands and hence from most provincial governorships. Many wealthy Roman citizens were arbitrarily arrested and executed, and there was a tendency to turn to the army instead of the courts to maintain internal order. And yet some of the best work in classical Roman law was done under the Severi. It is characteristic of the period that Papinian, one of the greatest Roman jurists, received the chief judicial post in Rome because of his learning, and

Statuette of a Roman eagle, 2nd or 3rd century A.D.

was then put to death on suspicion of treason.

Even more than their predecessors, the Severi effaced the distinction between Rome and the provinces. This was due, in part, to their tendency toward military despotism. If no one had any rights, then the inhabitants of Italy could not be particularly privileged. But it was also due to the Stoic tradition of the brotherhood of all men which had strongly impressed itself on Roman law. By the edict of Caracalla in 212, most provincials received the rights of Roman citizenship. This was only fair, since the emperors themselves all came from the provinces, and many of them had little or no Latin blood. One short-lived ruler, for example, Elagabalus (218–22), was of purely Syrian origin and was the hereditary priest of a Syrian temple-state. He owed his advancement solely to a connection by marriage with the imperial family.

The period of the Severi had its palace plots, its family intrigues, and its political assassinations, very much on the model of the first-century Empire. But the Empire as a whole did not suffer. The frontiers were defended and, if the provincials suffered from arbitrary government, at least they did not have to fear barbarian inroads.

Fifty Years of Anarchy

Not even this much can be said for the next group of emperors. With the death of Alexander Severus in 235, the armies seemed to lose all sense of responsibility. They spent more time fighting each other than foreign enemies; they left the frontiers undefended while their generals competed for the throne. During the fifty years from 235 to 285 there were twenty-six emperors and at least as many unsuccessful usurpers. A ruler who survived for as long as five years was exceptional. Rome never fully recovered from these years of military anarchy. The waste of human and material resources left the Empire of 285 far weaker and more impoverished than the Empire of 235.

No one has ever fully explained this act of political suicide. The fact that most inhabitants of the Empire had no political rights or responsibilities enabled the armies to abuse their power, but it is still difficult to understand why the armies behaved as badly as they did. It was not just a problem of overambitious officers. Again and again reluctant generals were forced by their troops, under threat of death, to proclaim themselves emperor. An army whose general was ruler of the Roman world could expect generous gifts of money and land, and this purely economic motive may explain the behavior of the soldiers. They came from the least-privileged classes and served long years for small pay; a gift of a few hundred dollars represented great wealth to them. But it is also possible that they were, more or less unconsciously, in rebellion against the whole structure of Roman civilization. The benefits of the Empire went almost entirely to the great landowners and ruling classes of the cities, while the army was made up of poverty-stricken peasants. Certainly there was no reason for the army to worry about the plight of the city-dwellers, and it may even have enjoyed their predicament.

In any event, the cities suffered during the third century. Germanic tribes pushed across the northern frontiers and even down to the Mediterranean, where they built a fleet to raid coastal settlements. The Persians attacked once more in the East, defeating a Roman army and taking an emperor prisoner. Towns far removed from the frontiers had to build walls to defend themselves; Rome itself was fortified by the emperor Aurelian (270–75). Commerce was disrupted by civil wars, by barbarian raids, and by fleets of German pirates in the Mediterranean. This, of course, increased the tendency toward local self-sufficiency and weakened the already tenuous economic ties between parts of the Empire. Economic localism was followed by political localism. In the middle of the third century Gaul had its own emperors, independent of the ruler in Rome. And along the Syrian border the vassal kingdom of Palmyra tried to take over a large part of the eastern provinces.

These attempts to split the Empire proved premature, but the weakening of the cities had disastrous political as well as economic consequences. In many respects the Empire had been a federation of cities, each responsible for the political and economic welfare of the surrounding territory. Now the cities, reduced in population, impoverished by fifty years of war, shrunk behind their encircling walls, were no longer able to perform their functions. Municipal government began to break down, and the central government had to intervene more and more in purely local affairs. The Roman senate had already lost all its power; now the municipal aristocracies began to suffer the same fate. The political basis of Roman society grew even narrower, for now all authority and all responsibility were concentrated in the hands of the emperor and his military and civilian advisers. There was no longer any sizable group of citizens who took an interest in public affairs. The imperial government received passive obedience, but no active support, from its subjects.

The third century was thus a period in which the Empire shrank in upon itself. It lost its outposts beyond the Rhine and the trans-Danubian province of Dacia. Trade and industry waned. War and a great plague in 252 ravaged the population. The overwhelming majority of Roman citizens no longer participated in any form of civilian political activity. Most of them were also barred from the army, the dominant politi-

****

The Empire in Decline

Musings of a trader as he revisits a provincial city in Switzerland in the third century. This passage is from a modern historical novel.

It was a pleasant town. Demetrius paused to look at the Treasury inside its stone wall, and the villas scattered within shady gardens. Yet each year they were a little more neglected; the temple yard had not been properly swept, a latch was hanging loose from a shutter, the gutter was choked by a dirty mass of what had once been somebody's garland. He wondered why the place had changed so much during the six years since his first visit. Then there had been chariots on the streets, and many wagons, an indefinable sense of the city being alive. Was the Empire too big? Yet it had been larger, and nobody had counted the provinces. Were the young so ungrateful? It seemed to him that there was just the same proportion of honest men and rogues as in his childhood. There was constant talk about invasion; nobody now was certain as to who was emperor of what, but the Treasury still functioned reasonably well, most roads got mended, trade went on, yet he could not deny the change. Something had happened; it was as if a sentry had been asked to keep one watch too many, and his fibre had snapped.

From Bryher, *Roman Wall* (New York: Pantheon, 1954), p. 124.

****

cal group, because soldiers were recruited almost exclusively from frontier regions. Nor was there any real hope for a better life in the future; the best one could hope for was to maintain the *status quo*. But even this was difficult—in the end it was achieved only by establishing an absolute monarchy and by imposing an almost military discipline upon the population. This was the policy of Diocletian, who became emperor in 284, and with his accession the period of the Late Empire begins.

Suggestions for Further Reading

1. Government

There is excellent source material on Roman political and social life in *Roman Civilization,* Vol. II (edited N. Lewis and M. Reinhold, 1955). This book covers subjects from political elections to the training of an architect and the practice of medicine. M. Hammond, *The Augustan Principate* (1933), is a careful analysis of the theory and practice of the constitution that Augustus established. R. Graves' novel, *I, Claudius* (1934), written as an autobiography of the Emperor Claudius, presents a fascinating picture of the early Empire based heavily on the *Annals* * of Tacitus. The best study of the first three centuries of the empire is probably M. Cary, *History of Rome* (1954), which is interesting reading based on sound scholarship, with up-to-date bibliographic material. H. M. D. Parker, *A History of the Roman World* (1935), has valuable material on imperial administrative policy. The life of a great emperor is told in the beautiful psychological novel of M. Yourcenar, *Hadrian's Memoirs* * (trans. G. Frick, 1954). *The Cambridge Ancient History,* Vols. X–XII, is the standard reference book for the political history of the Empire.

2. Art and Literature; Roman Law

F. Poulsen, *Glimpses of Roman Culture* (trans. J. Dahlmann-Hansen, 1950), is an introduction to Roman art. P. MacKendrick, *The Mute Stones Speak* (1960), is a fine study of the architectural achievements of the emperors, and the magnificent Skira edition of *Roman Painting* (edited A. Maiuri, 1953) traces the development of Roman painting through the period of the Empire. A. Grenier, *The Roman Spirit in Religion, Thought and Art* (1926), shows the influence of the Roman character on artistic achievements. There is information on Roman art in A. Hauser, *Social History of Art,* * Vol. I (1957), presented from a Marxist point of view. J. Finegan, *Light from the Ancient Past* (1951), is a scholarly study of the archeological background of the Hebrew-Christian religion. The sections on the catacombs and the early Christian churches are particularly interesting.

The achievements of the Roman poets, philosophers, and historians are available in many editions, often in paperback. Most of them are translated in the *Loeb Classical Library.* J. W. Duff, *A Literary History of Rome in the Golden Age* (1953), and *A Literary History of Rome in the Silver Age* (1959), are excellent studies of Latin literature. Duff emphasizes the national character imprinted on the literature of the Romans and re-creates the environment in which each author wrote. Both volumes have good bibliographies.

R. W. Buckland, *A Manual of Roman Private Law* (1925), which sets forth the main principles of Roman Law, is a readable introduction. Buckland's *A Textbook of Roman Law* (1932) is a technical and scholarly study of the chief aspects of public and private law. The same author's *Roman Law and Common Law* (1936) compares some of the main rules and institutions of the two systems. *The Legacy of Rome* (edited C. Bailey, 1923) traces the inheritance the modern world owes to the Romans.

3. The Anarchy of the Third Century

F. Lot, *The End of the Ancient World* (1951), gives considerable attention to the political and economic disorder of the third century. M. Rostovtzeff, *Social and Eco-*

* Available in paperback edition.

nomic History of the Roman Empire * (1926), is an invaluable reference work for the economic conditions of this period. The titles by Lewis and Reinhold, Cary, and Parker, and the *Cambridge Ancient History,* Vols. X–XII, mentioned in Section 1 above all have material on this subject.

4. Oriental Religions

Probably the best study of the eastern mystery religions in the Empire is F. Cumont, *Oriental Religions in Roman Paganism* * (1956). The New Testament is essential for an understanding of this period. W. M. Ramsay, *The Church in the Roman Empire* (1893), studies the history and thought of the Church down to 170 A.D., while C. Bigg, *The Origins of Christianity* (1909), carries the account down to the age of Constantine. Both are old but still valuable works. J. Lebreton, *History of the Primitive Church,* 4 vols. (1942–49), is a scholarly but readable study of the early Church from the birth of Christ to 313.

* Available in paperback edition.

5

The Late Empire

Even after the crisis of the third century, the Roman Empire still had two great assets: a formidable army and a well-organized bureaucracy. These two institutions proved strong enough to restore order and unity to the Roman world and to give the Empire, which had seemed mortally wounded, another century of tranquillity and power. The revival of the Roman state had a profound effect on the history of civilization, for it was during the fourth century that Christianity became the official religion of the reunited Roman

Empire, thereby winning for itself a firm foothold in the western world.

The Restoration of Order

There had already been signs of revival in the fifteen years preceding the accession of Diocletian in 284. The emperors of this period were almost all generals of unusual ability who took seriously their task of defending the frontiers. The work of restoration was begun by Aurelian (270–75), one of the ablest of all Roman commanders, who put an end to the independence of Gaul and Palmyra and started to drive the Germans and the Persians back to their old frontiers. Aurelian's work was carried on by his successors, and by 284 most of the invaders had been expelled from the Empire and the frontiers had been made reasonably secure. But the army was still making and unmaking emperors at its usual rate; between 275 and 284 six rulers were elevated and then put to death by their troops. It was Diocletian (284–305) who restored internal stability to the Empire.

Diocletian's Reorganization of the Empire

Diocletian's success was due first of all to his character. Shrewd, tough, and determined, he dominated rival generals as no emperor had been able to do for a century. He was able to keep most of the army on his side, and he put down the few commanders who did try to rebel. But Diocletian supplemented his personal prestige with a number of institutional reforms designed to discourage rebellion. By divorcing military authority from civil authority, and by increasing the number of provinces, he was able to cut back the power of the pro-

Diocletian, 284–305.

vincial army commanders. Since each province was now smaller, each general had fewer troops under his control; and since he now shared power with a civilian, his control of his province was never absolute. Moreover, the civilian and military authorities kept a jealous eye on each other and reported to the emperor any act of insubordination.

With the provincial troops split up under many commanders, Diocletian realized that he would have to have some mobile striking force to handle emergencies. The old legions had become little more than frontier guards, capable of turning back small raids but helpless before a determined attack by large forces. To take the place of the legions, the emperor organized under his own immediate command a large body of picked troops who could be rushed to any threatened area. This meant that he would have to abandon Rome as his imperial residence and live nearer the frontiers and the troops, in such places as Trier in Gaul or Nicomedia in western Asia Minor. It also meant that, so long as the emperor commanded his own elite troops in person, no ordinary general could organize a force capable of staging a successful revolt.

Just as ingenious, but in the end less suc-

Arch of Constantine, built in 315 to commemorate Constantine's liberation of Rome from the "tyrant" Maxentius.

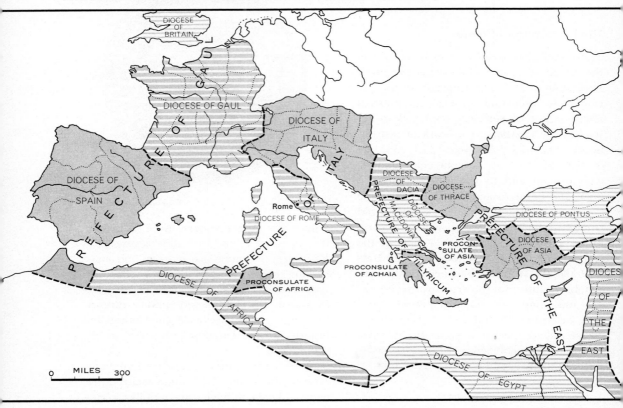

cessful, were Diocletian's attempts to solve the problem of succession. He realized that the troubled Empire needed more than one top commander, and he realized too that a general who shared imperial power would be less likely to revolt. Almost as soon as he was established in authority he named a fellow officer, Maximian, as coemperor, and assigned him the duty of defending the West. Later, each emperor selected a successor and gave him the title of Caesar and a share of the Empire. Eventually the Caesars were to become emperors in their own right and designate new successors in turn.

This scheme proved very effective in solving the problem of defense. During the troubled third century uprooted Germanic tribes were wandering about in search of new territories, and the Empire, even in its decline, was irresistibly attractive to them. All during the fourth century they pressed hard on its frontiers. Now one emperor could stand ready to meet them on the Rhine while the other guarded the Danube. This sharing of imperial authority also made it easier to keep rebellion within the armies from spreading. For example, when the army in Britain tried to establish its own line of emperors, Maximian was able to contain them until Diocletian came to his assistance and put down the revolt.

Diocletian's system also improved the administration of the Empire. Roman territories were divided into four parts, or prefectures, one for each emperor and one for each of the designated successors. The prefectures were in turn divided into dioceses, each of which included a number of provinces. Thus the administrative workload was shared among the emperors and their assistants, and no one man had to take responsibility for all final decisions. It was easier for a ruler to have exact knowledge of the affairs of one region than to worry about the administrative details of the whole Empire; decisions could now be made more rapidly and more intelligently. Diocletian, however, did not give his co-rulers a free hand; he made the policy decisions which applied to the whole Empire.

With all these advantages, Diocletian's system demanded too much of human nature. There were often two or more emperors in the years after his death, but they seldom cooperated as well as he and Maximian had. Even brothers eyed each other with suspicion, and strained relations between coemperors frequently led to civil war. Another problem was that descendants of a deceased emperor, avid for the throne, made it impossible to choose successors purely on the grounds of merit. The armies were often devoted to the son of their old commanders, and if he was set aside he usually had an even chance of staging a successful revolt. The hereditary principle continued to operate during the fourth century, as it had in the past.

Diocletian's reforms did reduce the frequency of civil war, however. Usurpations were less common than in the third century and both the emperors and their armies showed a somewhat greater sense of responsibility. On several occasions a ruler fighting on a sensitive frontier chose to recognize a rival as coemperor rather than leave his sector unprotected while he marched off to fight a civil war. Thus there was considerably more internal stability in the fourth century than in the third, and some of the damage caused by the earlier anarchy was repaired.

Economic Policy

Diocletian stabilized the Roman economy as well as Roman politics. Here again the first step had been taken by Aurelian, who had put an end to the debased currency introduced by his predecessors by restoring a sound coinage. Diocletian took the next step in reform by making the tax system more regular and predictable. All property was to be assessed at regular intervals, and taxes were to be collected throughout the Empire at uniform rates. Diocletian also tried to end inflation by freezing prices and wages, but his bureaucracy had neither the information it needed to adjust the fixed scale to local conditions nor the personnel to enforce the regulations. In spite of severe penalties, going as far as the execution of persistent offenders, Diocletian's edict soon became a dead letter.

This attempt to stabilize the economy by means of an elaborate set of regulations illustrates an essential weakness of Diocletian's program. One of the last great innovators in Roman government, Diocletian did more than anyone else to keep the Empire relatively strong and united during the fourth century. But above all he was a soldier, and he believed that a state could be organized and administered like an army. All authority was to be concentrated in the emperor; all decisions were to be made by him; all orders were to be carried out without question by subordinates. He was convinced that an unhealthy economy could be cured by edict, that men could be commanded to produce goods at fixed prices just as troops could be commanded to charge the enemy. Since most of Diocletian's successors were military men with this same military approach, almost all private activities came under state control during the fourth century.

Mithra sacrificing a bull in a sacred grotto, bas-relief of 2nd century A.D.

To reinforce his authority, Diocletian also stressed the divine and autocratic nature of the imperial office, thereby completing a process which had been going on for several generations. During the third century all pretense that the emperor was merely the First Citizen of the state had been abandoned. Diocletian was *dominus et deus,* lord and god; everything which pertained to his household or administration was "sacred"; he adopted many of the symbols and ceremonies of the oriental monarchies. By the fourth century, the emperor stood immeasurably above, and far removed from, the mass of his subjects.

The Triumph of Christianity

During the first three centuries of the Empire many people in the Roman world had been seeking a faith by which to live. The old religions of Greece and Rome had lost all vitality; the rituals were still performed but no one really believed in Jupiter and his fellow gods. The attempt to build a religion of the state, centering around the emperor and Rome, had failed (see p. 113). The patriotism and devotion to the Empire which would have given the cult real meaning were lacking. Most citizens were systematically excluded from any participation in political activity, even from service as minor officials and soldiers, and they could scarcely be expected to worship a governmental machine which went on its way regardless of their wishes and interests. The upper classes turned to Stoicism in the first and second centuries, but to the ordinary man Stoicism offered cold comfort. It was too intellectual and too impersonal; it valued eternal law, human brotherhood, and devotion to duty, but it elicited no strong emotional response. There was no individual salvation, no divine intervention, no promise of a better life for the poor and the oppressed. Although the Stoics would have denied it, their main motivation was probably pride: pride in not being deceived by appearances, pride in doing duty for duty's sake, pride in remaining unbroken by adversity. Most men cannot afford this kind of pride, and during the troubled third century even the upper classes began to abandon Stoicism. By the end of the century the great majority of Roman citizens who had any religion at all had become adherents of one of the eastern mystery cults, such as Mithraism or the worship of Isis and Osiris.

The Eastern Mystery Religions

Though based on earlier beliefs, these religions took on their characteristic form only during the Hellenistic and early imperial periods. Their gods were not the carefree deities of Greece and Rome who took little interest in human affairs, but heroes who had suffered as men suffer in the age-long struggle against darkness and evil.

Most of them had been killed in the conflict but had risen again, thus prefiguring a resurrection for their followers. An individual could secure salvation by worshiping one of these hero-gods and by taking part in rituals which wiped out the stains of sin and mortality. In the religion of Mithra, for example, the convert stood beneath a platform on which a bull was sacrificed and was regenerated by bathing in the blood which dripped down on him.

For many Roman citizens these religions satisfied a deeply felt need. The individual felt helpless and insecure in a society over which he had no control, in which his economic and political welfare was determined by remote and unapproachable authorities. He often felt a deep sense of sin, not so much because of personal misconduct but rather from a conviction that the misery of the human condition could be explained only by a fundamental blemish on the soul of each man. He had nothing to look forward to except an endless repetition of routine activities. To such a man the oriental religions promised forgiveness of sin and a happy future life. They assured him that he was important as an individual; they

Bronze statuette of *Magna Mater* (the goddess Cybele) in a lion-drawn chariot, late 3rd century B.C.

gave meaning and significance to his life. It is not surprising that they won adherents in every part of the Roman world.

Worship of the Great Mother and of Isis and Osiris spread from Asia Minor and Egypt to many parts of the Roman Empire. Even more widespread was Mithraism, which became almost the official religion of the army. A more popular form of the old Zoroastrian religion of Persia (see p. 34), it preserved the Persian doctrine of an unending struggle between the forces of light and the forces of darkness. Mithra was a warrior-god; he was also identified with the sun-god who was worshiped by many emperors in the third century. Though he was killed by the god of evil, he rose again; his death and resurrection were symbolized in the slaying of the bull, whose blood bestowed immortality on converts. The militancy of this faith, its explanation of all the troubles of the world as the result of a war between gods of good and gods of evil, made it particularly attractive to the army. It remained a strong competitor of Christianity all through the fourth century and was one of the sources of the Manichean heresy which troubled medieval Christendom (see p. 335). The Manicheans, like the followers of Mithra, believed in the existence of two almost equally powerful gods: a god of good and a god of evil. This belief seduced many Christians who could not understand how an omnipotent and benevolent god could permit the existence of evil.

Early Christianity

Christianity appeared later than most of the other oriental religions and for some time seemed to be the least successful of them. It was considered at first as merely a variant of Judaism, and the Jews were not very popular among the ruling classes of the Empire. They had revolted repeatedly, and both Titus and Hadrian had fought bitter wars against them, destroying Jerusalem and dispersing the Jewish people throughout the Empire. But at least the Jews belonged to an old and recognized religion, and the government was willing to tolerate some of their peculiarities, such as their refusal to participate in the official state religion. The Christians had no such status; they were disowned by the Jews and their religious exclusivism and pacifist beliefs gradually brought them into disfavor with the government. Moreover, Christianity lacked the prestige of religions descended from the ancient mysteries of the East, and it had no use for magical tricks and resounding incantations. Altogether, during the first two centuries of the Empire, Christianity made few converts among the ruling, or even the wealthy, classes. The fact that its primary appeal was to the lower and lower-middle classes may have saved it from destruction during these early centuries. The emperors disliked Christianity because it seemed unpatriotic and un-Roman. They persecuted Christians from time to time, but they could not take the religion seriously enough to make a systematic effort to destroy it. Refusing to believe that a handful of undistinguished subjects could be a real danger to the state, they persecuted Christians only when they needed a scapegoat, as Nero did, or when zealous subordinates complained that the Christians would not take part in the state religion. As a result, Christians were persecuted just enough to call attention to their courage and steadfast faith, but not enough to check their growth.

It was during these first two centuries that Christianity developed some of the characteristics which enabled it to triumph eventually over other religions. From the very beginning it was a missionary faith, as the Acts of the Apostles makes clear. Other religions were rather casual in their attempts to spread their doctrines, but the Christians

Early Christian tomb painting, from the Catacomb of Callixtus, Rome.

made a deliberate and sustained effort to win converts in every part of the Empire. Moreover, at a very early date the Christians began to build a religious organization to keep scattered groups in touch with each other and to assure uniformity in faith and morals. Each early Christian community was organized as a church under a group of bishops and elders, and the churches kept up a constant correspondence with one another. During the second century this organization became tighter. In each church the group of bishops and elders was replaced by a single bishop with full authority over his church, and the bishops of the greater cities, such as Rome, began to exert authority over the others. This organization seems so natural that we often fail to realize that it was an innovation as far as the ancient world was concerned. No administrative system existed for the pagan cults; the priests of Jupiter in one city were entirely independent of those in other municipalities. Neither Greek nor Latin had a word for "church"; the early Christians had to use the word "ecclesia," which meant a secular public assembly, to describe their new organization.

During the first two centuries the Christians worked to make their religion intellectually respectable. The simple ideas of the Gospels seemed fragmentary and unsophisticated to the educated classes in the Empire, who wanted a complete philosophical and theological system. Paul, the first great missionary of the Church, was also its first great theologian; it is significant that he came not from Judaea as the first Apostles did, but from the Greek-speaking city of Tarsus. His work was carried on by other Christians who had had a Greek education, and at the end of the second century the first theological writings in Latin began to appear. Tertullian (*ca.* 155–*ca.* 225), though he ended his career as a heretic, was the first Latin writer to discuss Christian theology, and from his time on the Latin Fathers were as important as the Greek.

These early Christians had two main purposes: first, to make a coherent and consistent theological system out of basic Christian doctrines; second, to express this system in language which could be understood by educated pagans. The development of the doctrine of the Trinity illustrates both points. The basic ideas about the Father, Son, and Holy Spirit are found in the Gospels, but the exact relationship among the Three Persons had to be worked out by generations of theologians. At the same time, theologians found that they could resort to Greek philosophy in their efforts to explain some of these ideas. For example, they often identified the Holy Spirit with the *Logos,* which in Neoplatonic philosophy was the guiding and formative principle which emanated directly from God.

Once this solid foundation had been laid, Christianity began to expand rapidly. Some of its earlier weaknesses now became strengths. For example, the exclusiveness of Christianity, its unwillingness to admit that there might be truth in other religions, had irritated tolerant Romans. But in an age in which everything seemed insecure, the certainty of the Christians, their conviction that they possessed the complete and unshakable truth, had a strong appeal. Adherents of other faiths often felt that they had to hedge their bets; devotees of the Great Mother would also become followers of Isis just to play safe. The Christians had no such doubts, and potential converts must have found their sureness very comforting. Again, because Christianity had grown out of Judaism, an austere and highly spiritual religion, it was freer from the superstition and grossness which marred other faiths. The Christians did not practice magic or try to predict the future; they were baptized, not with the blood of a sacrificed animal, but with water and the Word. Finally, the extreme other-worldliness of the early Christians, which had seemed mere foolishness to the prosperous second century, made more sense in the troubled years of the third century. If there was little to be hoped for in this world, then it was wise to concentrate on the next, and this the Christians did more wholeheartedly than any other group.

In any event, Christians became so numerous during the second century that the emperors began to grow alarmed. With the Empire falling to pieces around them, it seemed intolerable that a large number of citizens should refuse all outward signs of patriotism and place their own peculiar ideas above the welfare of the state. Also, the emperors, in their search for someone to blame for recurring disasters, found Christians an obvious choice. There were several waves of persecution, the first in 202, the last under Diocletian. The Church suffered severe losses under this oppression, but the number of Christians in the Empire was never permanently reduced. Either the persecuting emperor was killed and replaced by a more tolerant ruler, or his attention was distracted by a war, or else his officials failed to carry out his orders. The organization of the Church and the faith of most Christians were strong enough to withstand these intermittent blows. There were some apostates, but there were more martyrs, and the courage with which many Christians met their deaths brought in thousands of new converts. At the end of Diocletian's reign, in 305, the Christians were one of the largest religious groups in the Empire. Either a supreme effort would have to be made to exterminate them, or else they would have to be granted official recognition.

The Conversion of Constantine

This problem became inextricably involved in the quarrels over the imperial succession. Diocletian, an innovator to the end, abdicated in 305 and was one of the few Roman emperors to die peacefully in bed. But his elaborate provisions for an orderly succession were soon disregarded, and a series of civil wars left five different emperors in control of parts of the state. Perhaps, they reasoned, they could gain some advantage in their struggle for supremacy by extending protection to the large Christian communities in many parts of the Empire. At the very least, there was no sense in wasting energy persecuting a group of pacifists when each emperor was threatened by the armies of his rivals. As a result, three of the emperors issued an edict of toleration in 311.

Almost immediately a new civil war broke out between two of the most powerful emperors, Constantine and Maxentius. Constantine was one of the promulgators of the edict of toleration; his mother, Helena, had been a Christian, and his father had failed to carry out Diocletian's orders to persecute the Christians in Gaul. Maxentius, on the other hand, had not joined in the edict of toleration of 311. Constantine could thus be considered as sympathetic toward the Christians, and in his own contact with leaders of the Church he had been impressed by their claims for the power of the Christian God. In a great battle with Maxentius at the Milvian Bridge near Rome in 312, Constantine is said to have seen a vision of a cross in the sky, surrounded by the words: *"in hoc signo vinces"* ("in this sign thou shalt conquer"). Convinced that the Christian God had helped him to victory, he ordered his troops to carry Christian insignia from this time on.

The victory of the Milvian Bridge gave Constantine full control of the western part of the Empire. Another civil war established Licinius as sole ruler in the East. Meeting in 313, the two surviving emperors issued a new edict of toleration which ended persecution throughout the Empire. But Constantine, in the West, interpreted the edict in such a way that the Christians received special privileges, while Licinius in the East looked on them with suspicion and tried to inhibit their growth. The two emperors differed on other matters of policy, and each suspected the other of coveting his territories. They came to blows in 324. Licinius was defeated, deposed, and executed the next year on a charge of treason. Constantine then extended his permissive policy to the whole Empire, and by his death in 337 Christianity was well on its way to becoming the official religion.

Constantine received baptism only on his deathbed, and it is difficult to estimate

❖❖❖❖❖❖❖❖❖❖❖❖❖❖❖❖❖❖❖❖❖❖❖❖❖❖❖❖❖❖

Constantine's Religious Beliefs

The official policy of the Empire after 312 was toleration, as shown in a letter sent in the name of both emperors to the governor of Bithynia in 313.

. . . we resolved to make such decrees as should secure respect and reverence for the Deity; namely, to grant both to the Christians and to all the free choice of following whatever form of worship they pleased, to the intent that all the divine and heavenly powers that be might be favorable to us and all those living under our authority.

But Constantine showed stronger personal convictions in a letter written only a year later to the governor of Africa, dealing with the problem of heresy in that province.

Since I am assured that you are also a worshipper of the supreme God, I confess to your Excellency that I consider it absolutely wrong that we should pass over in insincerity quarrels and altercations of this kind, whereby perhaps the supreme divinity may be moved not only against the human race, but even against me myself, to whose care He has entrusted rule over all earthly affairs. . . . For then, and only then, shall I be able truly and most fully to feel secure . . . when I shall see all men, in the proper cult of the Catholic religion, venerate the most holy God with hearts joined together like brothers in their worship.

From *Great Problems in European Civilization,* ed. by K. M. Setton and H. R. Winkler (Englewood Cliffs, N.J.: Prentice-Hall, 1954), pp. 75, 79.

❖❖❖❖❖❖❖❖❖❖❖❖❖❖❖❖❖❖❖❖❖❖❖❖❖❖❖❖❖❖

the extent of his understanding and acceptance of Christianity. On the one hand, it seems likely that his favors toward the Christians were not inspired by purely political motives. The extreme western provinces, where he ruled at first, probably had the lowest percentage of Christians in the Empire, and in any case he had no reason to court the mass of Roman subjects. Real power lay with the armies, where there were few Christians to be wooed. On the other hand, Constantine probably did expect rewards from the Christian God. He was sure that the Christian God had power, and he wanted that power to be on his side. His long string of victories strengthened that conviction, and his association with Christian leaders gradually gave him a better understanding of their faith. Toward the end of his reign he had advanced beyond the stage of looking on Christianity only as an especially potent form of magic. He probably postponed his baptism not because of any lack of conviction, but because he reasoned, like many of his contemporaries, that if the rite washed away all sin, then it was better to receive it at the point of death when further sinning was unlikely.

During Constantine's reign, Church scholars were still trying to define the Christian theology. They had fallen into several disputes, the gravest of which concerned the doctrine of the Trinity. One writer, named Arius, taught that the Son and the Holy Spirit had been created by and were therefore subordinate to God the Father. While this solution ended some difficulties, it produced others; for example, if Christ was not fully equal to and of the same nature as God the Father, was His death a full atonement for men's sins? Many bishops attacked the teachings of Arius, and the quarrels that sprang up became so bitter that Constantine intervened. He wanted Christianity to promote the unity of the Empire, not to divide it into quarreling factions, and like a good Roman he was sure that there was one single legal formula which would be acceptable to all reasonable men. He had already ended a serious dispute in the western provinces by calling a council of bishops, and now he applied this formula to the whole Empire. By his orders, the first general council of the Church met at Nicaea in Asia Minor in 325. After some argument, the Council produced a confession of faith which completely rejected the teachings of Arius. Constantine had not tried to decide the issue by his own authority, but he had made it clear that he expected agreement and he did his best to make the whole Church accept the creed of Nicaea. Arius and his supporters were exiled and their places were filled by orthodox clergymen, but Arianism remained strong in many parts of the Empire and plagued the Church until well into the sixth century.

One of Constantine's last acts, in 330, was to found a new capital on the Bosporus for the eastern part of the Empire. This city, on the site of ancient Byzantium, was officially called New Rome, but ever since the death of its founder it has been known as Constantinople.* Constantine was anxious to establish a capital that would be free from the pagan associations and traditions of Old Rome, and from the very beginning Constantinople was a thoroughly Christian city. But Constantine had good military and administrative reasons as well. For centuries Constantinople, which occupied a position of immense strength, resisted all attacks. It was close to the most threatened part of the Danube frontier; it was also near the rich eastern provinces from which the Empire derived much of its wealth. Constantine did everything possible to make his new city prosper: he gave it

---

* The Turks now insist on calling it Istanbul, a corruption of a Greek phrase which simply means "The City."

prestige by creating a senate of New Rome to match that of Old Rome; he ordered his wealthiest subjects to build homes there; he transferred many administrative offices to the shores of the Bosporus. Few artificially created capitals have been as successful; Constantinople became immediately, and has remained, one of the great cities of the world.

The Empire and the Church in the Fourth Century

So towering was Constantine's prestige that for a generation after his death his family retained the imperial throne. They quarreled bitterly among themselves, but they managed to put down all attempts by other leaders to obtain a share of imperial power. They agreed no better in religion than in politics. Though they made Christianity the official religion of the Empire in 346, they soon quarreled over doctrine. It was during this period that caesaropapism, the control of the Church by secular authorities, first became an issue, and prepared the way for all the later conflicts between Church and state. One of Constantine's sons, Constantius, favored the Arians and exiled orthodox bishops when he became sole emperor in 350. The last ruler of the dynasty, Julian (361–63), withdrew all privileges from the Christians and tried to bring about a revival of paganism. Yet Constantine's successors were all men of considerable military ability, a quality which was badly needed in the fourth-century Empire, and they succeeded in holding the Empire together and protecting its frontiers.

The Barbarian Threat

Trouble was brewing almost everywhere along the eastern and northern frontiers. The Persians, the oldest and most dangerous enemies of the Empire, once more moved to attack the eastern provinces, and the best Roman troops and the most capable generals had to be used to repel them. Along the Danube and the Rhine the Germanic tribes were in a state of turmoil. Large groups were migrating in search of better lands or more secure homes, and each move touched off a series of tribal wars. The victors usually pushed on to the Roman frontier; the vanquished, in desperation, often tried to cross over the frontier and establish themselves in Roman territory. Moreover, individual tribes banded together in defensive confederations with such huge reserves of man power that they could challenge entire Roman armies. Julian, for example, who was charged with defending the Rhine frontier before he became emperor, had to use all his troops to repel the federations of the Franks and the Alamanni. Even in far-off Britain the Saxons were raiding the eastern coast and the Picts and the Scots (non-Germanic peoples) made a determined attack on Hadrian's Wall, which protected the northern boundary of the province.

The growing pressure on the frontiers was not due entirely to upheavals among the barbarians. True, the barbarians, harassed by external and internal enemies, were willing to run great risks and were organizing in larger groups. Moreover, they had learned a great deal about the art of war from their long conflicts with Rome. But Rome itself was weaker than ever before, and the barbarians realized that they had a golden opportunity, not merely to raid, but actually to occupy Roman territory. If such weak and scattered peoples as the Picts had the temerity to attack first-rate Roman fortifications, how much stronger must have been the hopes of the well-organized Germanic peoples.

The Roman army, unable to draw on the available man power of the Empire, was languishing. There was never a time when the inhabitants of the Empire did not

The Late Roman Empire *ca.* 395 A.D.

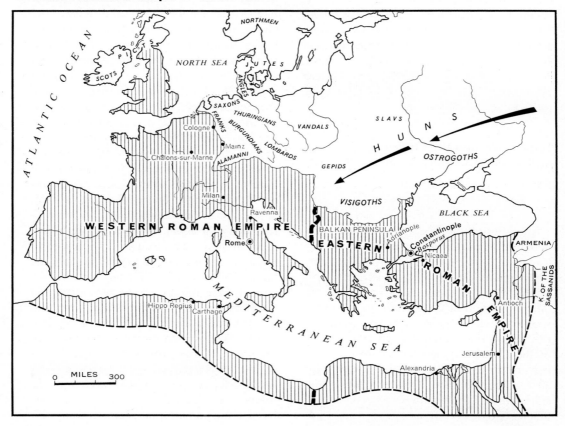

greatly outnumber all their barbarian enemies added together. But more and more men had been excluded from public rights and duties—a tendency that had especially evil consequences for the army. Senators were barred from army posts because they were not trusted, members of the middle class because they were needed for local administration. The peasants could not be spared from the land, and the city proletariat was useless for military purposes. The frontier provinces still supplied troops, but, since they were used almost entirely as border guards, they had little military value. To overcome this lack of officers and men for its field armies, by the fourth century the Empire was drawing recruits from among the barbarians themselves. Some enlisted as volunteers in the Roman army; others served in allied troops under their own commanders. These barbarian soldiers acted as the shock troops of the Empire. For the first time in the long history of Rome, armies composed of foreigners were valued more highly than armies composed of Roman citizens. But these barbarian troops lacked the discipline and the military skills of the old Roman legions. They were very like the enemies they were opposing, and they used the same weapons and tactics. They had a better service of supply and a more highly organized top command than their foes, but in a battle between armies of equal size it was by no means certain that the barbarized Roman army would prevail. And the process which had created this dangerous situation was irreversible, for by the fourth century it was too late to rebuild the army with Roman citizens. They had lost almost all their old military virtues and they felt only apathy toward the state. If barbarian armies could not defend the Empire, then there was no one left to defend it.

Economic and Social Problems

This growing apathy of the people of the Empire was even more dangerous than the barbarizing of the army. Few people seemed to care whether the Empire survived or not. Citizens obeyed orders and paid taxes when they could not evade them, but they showed no willingness to close the ranks in the face of danger, no readiness to sacrifice life or property to preserve the state. Politics and war? That was the emperor's concern; if he could not deal with these problems competently, no one was going to help him.

As if to reinforce this political apathy, the Roman economy continued to slump. Some parts of the Empire were reasonably prosperous in the fourth century, but in many other regions the depression which had begun in the third century persisted without relief. Population declined in both town and countryside. The towns were no longer able to discharge their old economic functions, and large amounts of arable land were permitted to slip out of cultivation. Many peasants, finding it impossible to make a living on their small holdings, became tenants or laborers on the estates of the wealthy. Those who were least affected by the depression were the great landholders, but they did nothing to strengthen either the

government or the economy. Instead, they retreated from the troubles of the world around them by getting themselves exempted from the authority of local officials and by making their estates self-sufficient economic units. Now the lower classes found it even harder to make a decent living, for the landlords could oppress peasants with impunity and the self-sufficient estates bought very little from the artisans of neighboring towns. Most citizens of the Empire had long ago given up hope for their political future. Now they gave up hope for their economic future as well. They had no prospect of rising in the world, and no assurance that they would be able to hold on to what little they had. Understandably, few people in these bleak years showed any great devotion to the Roman state or to the principles of Roman civilization.

A State-Controlled Economy

From the time of Diocletian, the emperors had been aware of these dangers. But they had neither the time nor the knowledge to trace back through five centuries of Roman history to the roots of the people's apathy. Busy men, they could deal only with symptoms; military men, they tried to run the Empire like an army. If the people failed to do their duty voluntarily, they would have to do it under compulsion; if ordinary economic motivations were not enough to get essential work done, then it must be done under state control.

The emperors' treatment of municipal governments offers a good example of their attitude. The chief function of city officials was to collect taxes for the imperial government. These taxes were not high by our standards; the imperial government was not extravagant and many of its activities cost less then than they would now. Wars, the most expensive item in any governmental budget, could be fought quite cheaply in the fourth century. Soldiers were poorly paid

groundwork for feudalism

and were equipped with relatively inexpensive and durable weapons such as spears, swords, and shields—a Roman legion could have been armed, fed, and paid for several months for the cost of a single high-explosive shell. But, with economic activity on the decline, even low taxes imposed a heavy burden on many communities. The local officials were responsible for all the taxes assessed against their community; if some inhabitants failed to pay, then the local officials either had to squeeze the missing money out of other taxpayers or else dig down into their own pockets for it. Predictably, well-to-do town-dwellers tried to avoid municipal office. But the central government, instead of trying to remove the cause of their unwillingness to serve, simply prohibited the effect. It ruled that the sons of town officials had to serve as officials in their turn; nor could they escape this burden by changing their status or occupation. They were forbidden, for example, to enlist in the army or to join the Christian clergy. Thus the government kept the municipal governments going through sheer compulsion, but it did nothing to halt the decline of the middle class and the ruin of cities.

The government also used compulsion to check the decline of cultivated land. It required owners of large estates to take over and cultivate a fair share of any abandoned lands near their holdings. At the same time, the government passed laws binding the peasants to the soil. The number of slaves had been declining through manumission and the ending of the wars of conquest, but the number of poor freemen had been increasing. When burdensome taxes or failure to make a decent living forced these men to give up their own little farms, the owners of great estates often took them on as tenant-farmers. Known as *coloni,* these tenant-farmers received a small piece of land whose produce they were obliged to share with the owner. Some of the *coloni* grew dissatisfied

with this unprofitable arrangement and tried to leave the great estates for other employment. But the central government, worried lest a decrease in the amount of land in cultivation might lead to a decrease in taxes, forbade the *coloni* to seek any other kind of employment. Successive enactments bound them more and more closely to the land as the years passed. In the end the *colonus* became something more than a slave and something less than a freeman; to use the later medieval expression, he became a serf. Though not bound to personal service, he was tied to a particular piece of land, and he and his heirs were bound to cultivate that land forever.

Some groups of artisans suffered a similar fate. Bakers were bound to remain in their trade and to furnish a son to succeed them; boatmen had the same obligation. In fact, by the middle of the fourth century much more than half the population of the Empire must have been frozen in permanent, hereditary occupations.

This is one reason why the gradual spread of Christianity throughout the Roman world had so little impact on the social and political structure of the Empire. The Romans had long needed a faith to live by, but by the time Christianity came to them their institutions had already begun to ossify. They could not combine the new religious enthusiasm with their weary old institutions; though the state was now a Christian state, it elicited no greater loyalty from the people than before. For the great majority of the inhabitants of the Empire, with no hope for improvement in their lot here on earth, it was largely irrelevant that the emperor was now a Christian. They were not going to sacrifice themselves to preserve a system that condemned them to unending drudgery, even if it was run by Christians.

It is also true that we are apt to exaggerate the number of Christians in the

Empire during the fourth century. There were many shallow converts who accepted baptism because it was fashionable at court but who never gave their new religion another thought. More important, there were wide areas, especially in the West, where Christianity had scarcely penetrated. Christianity was at first a city religion, and it had barely begun to develop the parish organization which was to make it effective in rural areas. But the West was predominantly rural; its cities were smaller, fewer, and weaker than those of the East. Thus hundreds of thousands of country-dwellers had little contact with the new religion; as late as the early sixth century missionaries could still make numerous converts in Italy and southern Gaul. The Christians called these people "pagans," a word which had something of the derisive meaning of our "hayseed," even though it officially meant nothing more than "countryman." * But there were a great many of these "hayseeds," and for a long time most of them clung stubbornly to their old beliefs.

Religious Controversies

The most ardent and active Christians were more concerned with defining their faith than with saving the Empire. They engaged in politics only to win imperial support for their particular creeds, and the resulting quarrels weakened rather than strengthened the state. The Arian heresy, which was aided by the emperor Constantius (see p. 149), continued to make trouble throughout the century. The Arians lost ground after Constantius and finally survived only outside the Empire among certain Germanic tribes. But the dispute over the Trinity gave way to a dispute over the relationship between the divine and the human elements in Christ Jesus, the God-Man. Did Christ have both a divine and a

* A rural district was called a *pagus*. People who lived in a *pagus* were *pagani*.

human nature, and if so, did one or the other predominate? The same questions were asked about His will. These were not just idle theological speculations, for they touched on the essentials of Christian doctrine. If Christ was predominantly divine, then He did not suffer as a human and there was little merit in the Atonement. If He was predominantly human, then it was not God who died on the Cross and there was doubt about the efficacy of the Redemption. If the separateness of the two natures was stressed, then God did not really become man; if the union of the two natures was emphasized, then the human was absorbed by the divine. Unfortunately, it was easier to accuse an opponent of taking one of these extreme positions than it was to find a formula which gave proper weight to both the human and the divine in Christ, and which was acceptable to all Christians. The argument became more and more bitter during the fourth century and was officially decided only in 451 at another great church council, at Chalcedon. Even then certain groups in the East refused to accept the rulings of the council and founded schismatic churches. Some of these, such as the Coptic Church of Egypt and the Jacobite Church of Syria, have endured to the present day.

These theological controversies absorbed the energies of the best thinkers and ablest writers of the fourth-century Empire, to the detriment of both literature and politics. The lack of interest in secular literature could be tolerated, but it was a serious loss to the state when no first-rate minds took an interest in law and administration. The ill-conceived and badly drafted laws of this period seldom solved the problem at hand. Roman administration was routine and unimaginative, achieving at best a preservation of an unsatisfactory *status quo*. Very little intellectual energy was going into the service of the state.

Good Christians might, and did, say that this was only right; it was better to study the things of God than the problems of this world. But concentration on theological disputes stirred up passions which injured both the Church and the Empire. This was especially true in the East, where there was strong rivalry among the religious leaders of Constantinople, Antioch, and Alexandria. The people of these cities supported their own clergy and fought in the streets over disputed doctrines. Religion became a means of expressing suppressed political desires; the Syrians and the Egyptians voiced their resentment against centuries of Greek domination by adopting theologies that infuriated the Greeks. Religious separatism and local patriotism went hand in hand, and during the next two centuries the loyalty of the eastern provinces to Constantinople diminished steadily.

The West was less shaken by religious controversy. Beginning with Tertullian in the second century, Latin theologians had shown a tendency to lay down the law rather than to speculate on fine points of doctrine, and fortunately the law they laid down proved acceptable to Church councils. The bishop of Rome, now regularly called the pope, was the heir to this Latin theological tradition, and was therefore always on the side of orthodoxy. Since no other bishop in the West had anything like the pope's authority, his interpretation of doctrine was usually accepted without question in the Latin-speaking provinces.

But while the Christians of the West were more united than those of the East, they did not entirely escape the troubles caused by religious controversy. Their bishops had to take part in Church councils in which there were vigorous debates about doctrine, and they were sometimes exiled or imprisoned by an imperial government bent on compromising disputes. Moreover, the West had its own heresies, though typically they dealt with problems of conduct rather than with the doctrine of the Trinity. Were the sacraments valid even if conferred by a sinful priest? How could free will be reconciled with divine omnipotence? These were the questions which stirred the West. They did not lead to rebellions, but they kept Christians from devoting very much of their time to politics.

The End of the Empire in the West

In the last quarter of the fourth century the threat to the Rhine and Danube frontiers of the Empire reached a new intensity. To the usual German thrusts and raids was added a fresh menace, the advance of the Huns from central Asia. The Huns are worth

Hunnish ornaments. Peacock heads, gold set with red glass, 3rd or 4th century.

5 / The Late Empire

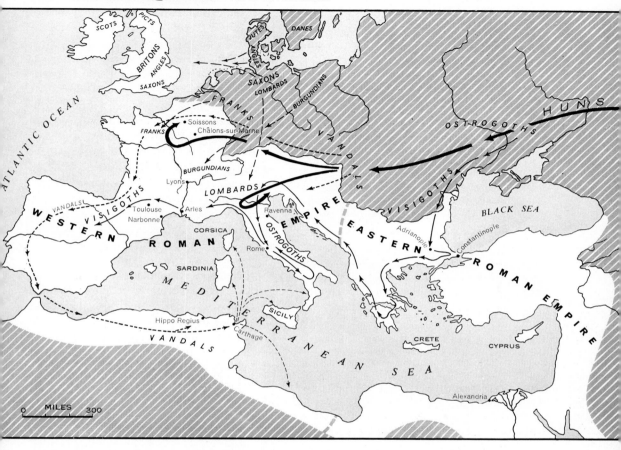

discussing in some detail, for they were the first of a long series of Asian nomads who drove across the Russian steppes toward the Danube.

The Huns

Central Asia is a harsh land with scanty vegetation, little rainfall, and great extremes of temperature. The people who lived in this region were by necessity nomads, but nomads on a grand scale. Some of them covered well over a thousand miles in their wanderings between summer and winter pasture. The best horsemen in the ancient world, they spent their days in the saddle and invented most of the equipment which transformed cavalry into an effective fighting force. For example, they used horseshoes and stirrups long before they were known in the West. If one imagines riding a horse into battle without stirrups one can see why early Roman commanders, including Caesar, had a low opinion of cavalry. But even after these devices were adopted by other peoples, the Asian nomads were still supreme as horse soldiers; they were wiry, tough, unafraid of death, and as pitiless as the land in which they lived.

Fortunately for their neighbors, they usually lived in scattered bands of a few hundred, or at most a few thousand, and hence had no great striking force. But every now and then bands threatened by a common danger would join together, or a leader of genius would arise and unite several groups. Once this process had started, it was almost irreversible. A commander of ten thousand nomads could force all the groups in an area of thousands of square miles either to join him or to move on into unknown hostile territories. They usually joined the victorious leader, building up great human avalanches which thundered down from the high plateaus of Central Asia onto the coastal civilizations of China, India, and Europe.

The western Huns who attacked Europe were a backwash from one of these avalanches. They had missed an opportunity to join a large coalition of nomads attacking China and had turned west instead. As they headed west, picking up fragments of other bands along the way, their army snowballed in the usual fashion. By the time it broke out into the Russian plain in the second half of the fourth century no Germanic tribe could withstand it. The impact of the Huns explains much of the restlessness of the Germanic peoples in the fourth century. The Huns conquered the East Goths (Ostrogoths) who lived exposed to attack north of the Black Sea; they drove the West Goths (Visigoths) in terror toward the Roman frontier; and they quickly built up an empire in Central Europe with many German tribes as satellites.

The Goths

The Goths, among the most advanced of the Germanic peoples, had come down from the north in search of better lands during the second century. Settling around the Black Sea, they had entered a region of fairly active trade, which led to contacts with more civilized peoples. They had had some dealings with the Romans, to whom they had been less hostile than had some of the western Germanic groups. So when the West Goths asked permission to seek refuge in the Empire from the Huns, the emperor Valens (364–78) granted it, with the proviso that the Goths surrender their weapons as they crossed the frontier. Unfortunately, some imperial officials seem to have regarded the West Goths as a new source of forced labor, and mistreatment soon led to revolt. Valens hurried to crush the uprising without waiting for reinforcements which were being sent from the West. He was defeated and killed in the battle of Adrianople in 378, and the Goths occupied a large part of the Balkan Peninsula.

This was not the first time that Germans had defeated a Roman army, nor was it the first time that a Germanic people had settled in Roman territory. True, both the defeat and the settlement were on a larger scale than usual. But if Rome had had its old powers of recuperation and assimilation, it could have isolated and then absorbed the West Goths. This, in fact, was the policy of the emperor Theodosius (378–95), and it very nearly succeeded. He checked the plundering of the Goths and herded them into a small strip of uncultivated land south of the Danube. There they lived as allies of Rome under their own kings and sent their most promising young men to Constantinople for education. For the rest of Theodosius' reign they remained quiet.

Theodosius was the last emperor to control the whole of the Roman world, and the last to keep the frontiers reasonably intact. But he achieved this success only by drawing more barbarians into the army. His highest-ranking general was Arbogast the Frank, and men of Germanic origin held other key posts as well. Theodosius was strong enough to control these men, but his weak successors were puppets of their

The Emperor Theodosius I and his two sons, ca. 388.
Silver plate, cut in half by the peasants who found it, to
give each a fair share.

after Theodosius

generals. For the next century all political power lay in the hands of military commanders, many of whom were barbarians.

Theodosius supported the orthodox interpretation of Christian doctrine as laid down by Church councils and tried to preserve religious as well as political unity in the Empire. But here again he ran into the barbarian problem. Around the middle of the century, when the Arians were enjoying imperial favor, some Goths had been converted by Arian bishops. These Goths became ardent missionaries and one of them, Ulfila, translated the Scriptures into Gothic. As a result, by Theodosius' time, most of the Goths, and many of the other eastern Germans, had accepted the Arian form of

Christianity, and the first Germans to enter the Empire in large numbers were all heretics. Theodosius could suppress Arianism among his own subjects, but he could not interfere with the religious beliefs of his allies; the majority of the Germans remained Arian for more than a century after his death. This pocket of heresy within the Empire offended the Romans and delayed the merging of the two peoples.

Theodosius was also the first European ruler to be forced to do public penance for offending the Church. His sin lay in ordering a massacre of the people of Thessalonica because they had killed one of his officers during a riot. St. Ambrose, bishop of Milan, refused to give Theodosius communion until he had done penance, and, in spite of threats, maintained this position until the emperor admitted his fault. Theodosius' submission proved the growing power of the Church, and medieval popes were to cite it as a precedent again and again in their struggles with lay rulers.

The Division of the Empire

When Theodosius died in 395, he was succeeded by his two sons, Arcadius in the East and Honorius in the West. This division of the Empire was not meant to be permanent. For the last century there had usually been more than one emperor, with each ruler primarily responsible for one part of the Empire. But the coemperors had always cooperated to some extent, and the more capable of them had never felt confined to one area. Thus while Theodosius had usually had a coruler in the West, he did not hesitate to interfere in Italy and in Gaul when he thought it necessary, and when his last colleague died he automatically took over the entire Empire. But the division of the realm between Arcadius and Honorius proved to be rather different. To begin with, the army commanders who held the real power under the two young emperors were jealous of one another and refused to cooperate. Moreover, the Germans grew so strong in the West that the eastern ruler could not reunite the two halves when his western colleague died. Theoretically, the Empire remained one state, but in fact it was permanently divided after 395, and each half had a different fate. The West fell completely under the power of the Germans and for centuries it remained backward both in political organization and in economic activity. In the East the Empire persisted, and, though it was gradually transformed into something quite un-Roman, it was far more prosperous and better organized than the barbarian kingdoms of the West.

The Visigoths and the Sack of Rome

At Theodosius' death the Visigoths broke out of their Balkan preserve and began raiding the nearby provinces. They might have been crushed had the government at Constantinople been willing to work with the western army commander, but there was already too much distrust between East and West to permit a common policy. As a result, the Visigoths went on plundering almost at will. When they had exhausted the loot of the Balkans they moved west, much to the relief and probably at the instigation of the eastern government. As they approached Italy they were checked for a while by Stilicho, a German general in the service of the western emperor. But when Stilicho was killed through a palace intrigue, the Visigoths stormed down into the peninsula. The emperor Honorius shut himself up in the fortified city of Ravenna and made no move to stop the invasion. The Goths occupied Rome in 410—a catastrophe that sent a last feeble impulse of patriotism through the Empire.

It was true that Rome had not been the real capital for many years, for the emperors had preferred to live in cities nearer the frontiers, such as Milan. But Rome was still the symbol of the Empire; no enemy had touched it for almost eight hundred years, and its fall shocked men who otherwise cared little about imperial affairs. The adherents of the old religions said bitterly that this disaster occurred only after the Empire had become officially Christian, an argument that the ablest Christian writer of the period, St. Augustine, tried to refute in his great work, *City of God* (see p. 164). St. Augustine insisted that the eternal City of God inhabited by the saints was far more important than any earthly city built and ruled by sinners. Yet even St. Augustine admitted that the Romans had created the best purely secular government which had ever existed, and less devout Christians must have been worried by signs that this government was collapsing.

The Visigoths soon exhausted the food supply in Italy and moved on to southwestern Gaul. Here they settled permanently, gradually adding most of Spain to their territories. For many years they remained allies of the Empire; they helped the Romans to repel the great Hun invasion of 451. But as the western Empire weakened they grew more independent, and by the end of the fifth century they were entirely free from Roman control. The Visigothic king ruled a state of his own, and the authority of Rome was only a distant memory.

Other Germanic Migrations

Shortly after the Visigoths started their long march toward the West, other Germanic groups pushed across the frontiers. There were not enough troops in the Roman army, nor was there enough determination in the Roman people, to throw them back. The best that could be done was to steer them toward remote provinces, weaken them by encouraging other Germans to attack them, and, as a last resort, give them the status of allies and allow them to set up their kingdoms on Roman territory. This last measure was not as useless as it seemed, for by regularizing the occupation a great deal of violence was avoided. The Germans had no grudge against the Romans and they were quite willing to take only part of the land as allies instead of all of it as conquerors. The Romans had no feeling of racial superiority toward the Germans, and, provided they could keep some of their property, they were willing to accept barbarian rulers. Thus in most of the western Empire there was relatively little loss of life or property as the Germans moved in. The great exception was Britain, the one province in which it had proved impossible to admit the Germans as allies.

The first large group after the Visigoths to establish themselves in the Empire was a coalition of peoples from North Germany, led by the Vandals. These tribes moved across Gaul into Spain, but the imperial government persuaded the Visigoths to attack them there. The Vandals were so weakened by this war that they abandoned Spain and occupied most of North Africa as far as the ancient site of Carthage. Here they built a fleet with which they controlled the waters of the western Mediterranean for half a century, even managing to seize Rome briefly in 455. Though they plundered the city systematically, they were not guilty of the wanton destruction which has become associated with their name. Their capture of Rome was only an incident and the Vandals did not try to establish themselves in Italy. The center of Vandal power remained in North Africa until it was crushed by the East Roman Empire in the sixth century.

Meanwhile the Burgundians and the Franks were advancing in Gaul. Both peoples had settled west of the Rhine in the fourth century but had been quarantined in border territories until the death of Theodosius. The Franks then began to occupy northeastern France, while the Burgundians settled in the Rhone Valley. At about the same time the Angles and the Saxons began to raid Britain from their homes along the North Sea. This Anglo-Saxon attack on Britain is one of the most obscure episodes in the history of the Germanic migrations. Britain had an unduly large number of ambitious generals in the late fourth and early fifth centuries, and these men repeatedly took their troops across the channel to bid for the imperial title. As a result, Britain had few Roman officials and almost no army in the early fifth century when the invasions began. The island had never been as thoroughly Romanized as Gaul, and the natives seem to have reverted to their old Celtic way of life. Joining together in small kingdoms, they fought the Angles and Saxons desperately but were unable to make treaties that might have permitted peaceful settlement. In the almost complete absence of contemporary historical records, all we can say is that by 500 the Angles and Saxons held a large strip of territory in the eastern part of the island.

By the middle of the fifth century all that was left of the Empire in the West was Italy and a fragment of Gaul. Even this remnant was threatened by a new advance of the Huns, who had kept a strong position in central Europe since their defeat of the Goths in the fourth century. Under their famous king Attila, "the Scourge of God," the Huns, supported by many German tribes, launched a great invasion of Gaul in 451. The last great general of the Empire, Aëtius, was able to repel this attack by calling on the German allies of Rome, such as the Visigoths and the Franks. Attila was repulsed in a bloody battle near Troyes, but he was still strong enough to invade Italy the next year. Like many of his predecessors, he found the peninsula too barren to support his army. He was persuaded to withdraw by an embassy led by Pope Leo I, an episode which gave great prestige to the papacy. With Attila's death in 453 his empire disintegrated and the Huns no longer menaced the Empire.

Aëtius' victory was the last success for the Empire in the West. The general himself was put to death by a suspicious emperor, who in turn was assassinated by Aëtius' followers. German generals and their troops now took over control of Italy. For a while they maintained puppet emperors, but in 476 Odovacar, the leader of a mixed band of German mercenaries, deposed the last emperor and sent the imperial insignia to Constantinople. Odovacar be-

came king of Italy, and other barbarian rulers took over the last Roman territories west of the Adriatic.

"The Fall of the Roman Empire"

Zeno, the emperor in Constantinople, promptly regularized the situation by making Odovacar his representative in Italy. Thus the fiction of imperial unity was preserved, even though the eastern emperor had no real authority in the West. A few years later the imperial government tried to regain control by authorizing a new group of Germans to attack Odovacar. These new invaders of Italy were the Ostrogoths, who had long been subject to the Huns, but who had regained their independence after Attila's death. They had settled in the Balkans as Roman allies, but they were dangerous neighbors, and the eastern emperor was delighted to speed them on their way to Italy. After several years of fighting, the Ostrogoths defeated and killed Odovacar and took over full control of Italy in 493. Their king, Theodoric, one of the ablest and best educated of the Germanic rulers, had lived several years at the court of Constantinople. He was more careful than Odovacar in preserving Roman forms of government and he was punctilious in acknowledging the formal suzerainty of the emperor. But his politeness did not disguise the fact that Theodoric was even more independent than Odovacar had been. The Ostrogoths had no intention of restoring imperial rule in the West.

The deposition of the last emperor in 476 is often referred to as the "Fall of the Roman Empire." Taken literally, this is a meaningless phrase. The Empire had long been so weak in the West that the absence of an emperor was hardly noticed. No one felt that a sudden catastrophe had occurred, and no one was particularly resentful that a German had taken over Italy. Moreover, the Empire survived in the East and even gained new vigor during the next century. No inhabitant of the Roman world felt that the Empire had "fallen" in 476, though many were aware that their government was decrepit.

Still, the passing of almost the entire Latin-speaking part of the Empire under German rule was a historical event of great significance. The Empire's basic ideas of government and law had sprung from the Latin West; an Empire which was largely Greek could not remain a Roman Empire, even though it kept the name. The Latins became barbarized under their Germanic rulers; the Greeks became orientalized as their contacts with the West decreased. Thus the two halves of the Roman world drifted apart, preparing the way for the later split between eastern and western Europe.

This divergence between the two parts of the Empire also makes it difficult to answer a question which has been puzzling historians for hundreds of years. Why did the Empire and the civilization of which it was the political expression collapse in the West and survive in the East? Most of the reasons which can be given apply almost as well to the East, and yet in the East the political organization survived and the civilization was gradually adapted to new conditions without going through a serious decline. About all that can be said is that the East was favored by geography and that it had a little more economic and spiritual vitality than the West. The barbarians never reached the richest provinces of the East; they regularly entered the Balkans, where they speedily exhausted all possibilities of loot and were easily persuaded to move westward. In the West, on the other hand, they slipped easily into the rich farmlands of Gaul and the Po Valley and established permanent settlements there. The commerce and industry of the Empire were concentrated in the East, and eastern cities were far more prosperous than those of the West. But while economic interests bound the East together, there were almost no economic ties among the western provinces.

Finally, in the East Christianity had cut deeper and spread more widely than in the West, and zeal for the orthodox faith sometimes became identified with patriotic support of the state which protected it. This identification of religion with patriotism was not universal, nor was it always advantageous to the imperial government. As we have seen, definitions of orthodoxy differed, and dissenters often bitterly opposed the authorities. But at least in the East some people felt strongly enough about their beliefs to fight for them; in the West there was almost universal apathy among Christians and pagans alike. During the fifth century the eastern emperor was able to recruit soldiers from among his own subjects, while in the West the Roman population hardly lifted a finger to protect itself.

But these were differences in degree and not in kind. The civilization of the entire Mediterranean world was in a very shaky condition; the eastern part of the Empire barely saved itself from the Germans, and might well have collapsed if it had had to face the same kind of blows that struck the West. The basic trouble was that very few inhabitants of the Empire believed that the old civilization was worth saving. The barbarians, after all, were not very numerous; they did well to raise armies of fifteen to twenty thousand men. The entire Vandal people, when it crossed into Africa, numbered about eighty thousand, including women, children, and other noncombatants. And yet this small group overran all North Africa. There never was a time when the Romans could not have driven out all the invaders if they had been able and willing to make a united effort. But they never made the effort. As we have seen, the overwhelming majority of the population had

Capella on Geographic Zones

Martianus Capella's *Satyricon,* from which the following was taken, was written in the early fifth century. It was one of the typical encyclopedic digests of the late empire.

The round world may be divided into five zones or bands of different characteristics. Of these, great excesses of heat or cold force three to be abandoned. The two zones which touch either end of the earth's axis, dominated by terrible cold, are deserted because of frost and snow, while the middle zone, baked by flames and breath-taking heat, scorches all living things that come near. The two other zones, tempered by the breath of life-sustaining air, offer a habitation to living things. These zones, curving around the sphere of the earth, go around both the upper and the lower hemisphere. . . . Those who live opposite us are called "antipodes.". . . For when we roast in summer, they shiver with cold; when spring here begins to cover the fields with flowers, there worn-out summer is passing into sleepy autumn.

From Martianus Capella, *De nuptiis philologiae et Mercurii* (Leipzig: Teubner, 1866), book VI (on Geometry), p. 252.

been systematically excluded from political rights and political responsibilities. They could not organize to protect themselves; they could not serve in the army even if they had so desired. Their economic plight was hopeless. Most of them were serfs bound eternally to the soil, and the small urban group saw their cities slipping into uninterrupted decline.

Art and Literature During the Migrations

For most of these people the Empire offered nothing to compensate for their political impotence and economic stagnation. Education, poor as it was, was open only to the well-to-do. The blight of imitation lay heavily on all secular thought and literature; the classics were studied and reproduced with appropriate variations; the most admired style was ornate, involved, and often deliberately obscure. Greek was seldom studied in the West—another sign of the drawing apart of the two halves of the Empire—and the Greek scientific tradition was scarcely known to men of Latin speech. Even in the East science was neglected for literature and law. A final sign of the degeneration of secular studies was the making of epitomes—handy collections of familiar quotations, summaries of all existing knowledge in a single book, little treatises of only a few pages on grammar and rhetoric. As time went on, these digests were studied more than the original works from which they were drawn, and they became the basic textbooks of the Middle Ages.

Official art, like secular literature, was heavy and imitative. Few new buildings or monuments were constructed, and those that were were often decorated with mate-

Tiberius, 14–37 A.D.

rials taken from earlier works. For example, on the Arch of Constantine there is a striking difference between the crude work of the fourth century and the more elegant sculptures which were borrowed from a second-century monument. The same decline is evident in the coins of the period. The Romans had been masters of realism, if not of the higher forms of art, and the coins of the emperors of the first and second centuries form a striking set of portraits. By the end of the fourth century the coins are less well made and the portrait is becoming only a symbol—the emperor as a type and not as an individual.

Thus wherever we turn in the late fourth and early fifth centuries we see apathy on the part of the multitude and a lack of creativeness and originality among the upper classes. The strong framework of imperial administration held the Roman world together long after Roman civilization was actually dead, but it could not support a corpse indefinitely. New forms of organization and new beliefs were needed before civilization could revive.

The new beliefs and many of the new forms of organization were to be supplied

Honorius, 395–423. Contrast the work on this 5th-century coin with the fine modeling on the coin at left.

by the Christian Church. Most of the vitality and originality which existed in the late Empire was concentrated in the Church; Christian literature and Christian art of the fourth century stand at the beginning of a long process of development rather than at the end, as late classical art and literature do. But, as we have already seen, it was impossible to transfuse this new vitality into the vein of a dying civilization. Christians could no more preserve classical literary and artistic forms than they could preserve the old political organization of the Empire.

The career of St. Augustine, the greatest Christian theologian of the period, illustrates this point. Augustine (354–430) was born in what is now Tunisia, the only son of a moderately well-to-do family. He received a good classical education and could easily have had a profitable career as a lawyer or as a member of the imperial bureaucracy. But Augustine had long been worried about problems of religion and ethics. He was not at first a Christian—one more proof of the slow spread of the faith in the West—and he examined both neoplatonism and Manichaeanism carefully before he accepted Christianity. But once he was converted he abandoned public life entirely and dedicated his great intellectual ability to the service of the Church. He was not greatly concerned by the troubles of the Empire, though the Goths seized Rome during his lifetime and the Vandals were besieging Hippo, the city of which he was bishop, at the time of his death. He was concerned with God's ways toward man, especially with the problems of free will and predestination, of evil and sin. Does man really have free will if God is all-powerful and all-wise? Why does God allow man to sin and condemn himself to endless suffering? How can a loving and merciful God countenance the existence of evil and suffering? These were the questions Augus-

St. Augustine
on the City of God

Accordingly, two cities have been formed by two loves: the earthly by the love of self, even to the contempt of God; the heavenly by the love of God, even to contempt of self. The former glories in itself, the latter in the Lord. For the one seeks glory from men, but the greatest glory of the other is God, the witness of conscience. . . . In the one, the princes and the nations it subdues are ruled by the love of ruling; in the other, the princes and the subjects serve one another in love, the latter obeying, while the former take thought for all. The one delights in its own strength, represented in the persons of its rulers; the other says to its God: "I will love Thee, O Lord, my strength." And therefore the wise men of the one city, living according to man, have sought for profit to their own bodies or souls, or both, and those who have known God "glorified him not as God, neither were thankful, but became vain in their imaginations, and their foolish heart was darkened. . . ." For they were either leaders or followers of the people in adoring images, "and worshipped and served the creature more than the Creator." But in the other city there is no human wisdom, but only godliness, which offers due worship to the true God, and looks for its reward in the society of the saints, of holy angels as well as holy men, that God may be all in all.

From St. Augustine, *City of God,* in *Basic Writings of St. Augustine,* ed. by Whitney J. Oates, Vol. II, p. 274. Copyright 1948 by Random House, Inc. Reprinted by permission.

tine wrestled with in his *Confessions,* a spiritual and intellectual autobiography which is one of the most remarkable documents of the period. He dealt with them again in the *City of God,* and in the many technical treatises which made him the most influential theologian in the West.

By avoiding extreme or oversimplified answers, Augustine worked his way through to solutions which have influenced Christian scholars of all sects. Thus he argued that evil is not an independent power (as the Manichaeans taught) nor yet the creation of God; it is merely the absence of good. Man has free will, but this free will is ineffective without the assistance of divine grace. Augustine used all the resources of a trained rhetorician. His style is emphatic, at times almost too vehement, and he loved striking phrases and sharp antitheses. But while the Latin of St. Augustine is based on classical models, it is far more vigorous and expressive than the language used by contemporary secular writers.

The other chief Latin Christian authors of the end of the fourth century were St. Jerome and St. Ambrose. Jerome (335–420), a better scholar than Augustine, knew both Greek and Hebrew. He spent much of his life translating the Bible into Latin—a translation that served as the basis of the Vulgate, the official text used in the Roman Church. Jerome also wrote some rather bitter letters about the behavior of nominal Christians at the imperial court and in high society. Ambrose (d. 397) was an administrator and popular preacher rather than a scholar. His father had been a high official in the imperial bureaucracy and Ambrose himself had a successful career as a civil servant before he was named bishop of Milan. He was involved in a long quarrel with Arian heretics, and, as we have seen (pp. 157–58), he forced the emperor Theodosius to do public penance for his sins. During these disputes he encouraged his flock by his sermons, and even more by writing hymns for them to sing. This was a rather new idea; Ambrose did much to popularize it in the West and his hymns are still sung in the Catholic Church.

Christian art in the fourth and fifth cen-

Fresco showing the cross section of a basilica church.

turies showed the same vigor as Christian literature. The trend away from realism toward symbolism was entirely appropriate for religious art, and during this period some of the basic formulas for representing Christian ideas were developed, such as the dove to represent the Holy Spirit. On the whole, painting and mosaic work were more successful than sculpture, which tended to be squat and clumsy. Even more important was the development of the basic patterns for church buildings. In the West the favorite plan was borrowed from the Roman law court or basilica, a long, rectangular room with two sets of pillars dividing it into a central hall, or nave, flanked by two side aisles. The roof over the nave was elevated to admit light through windows set above the aisle pillars. The far end of the nave was often rounded into an apse, which held the altar and seats for the bishop and his clergy. Later a transept was added between the nave and the apse. This was a hall which crossed the nave at right angles and protruded beyond the aisle walls, thus giving the church the form of a cross. There were basilicas in the East as well, but the most typical form of eastern church was a round or polygonal structure with a high dome over the central portion. This pattern, which was favored by the emperors of the fifth century, has remained typical of Greek churches ever since.

Both Christian art and Christian literature were to have their fullest development in the centuries after the collapse of the Empire in the West. But even before 500, Christian artistic and literary achievement was great enough to demonstrate two things: first, that new styles were at last arising to replace those which had dominated the Mediterranean world for a thousand years; second, that in spite of political collapse and economic decline, the peoples of the Greco-Roman world were still capable of creative activity.

Suggestions for Further Reading

1. Diocletian's Reform

There are many fine histories of the late Roman Empire. Perhaps the best one-volume study is the masterly synthesis by F. Lot, *The End of the Ancient World* (1951), which shows the causes of the political ruin, economic weakness, and intellectual and moral decadence that Diocletian attempted to check. Both S. Dill, *Roman Society in the Last Century of the Empire* (1910), and M. Rostovtzeff, *Social and Economic History of the Roman Empire* (1926), discuss the reforms of Diocletian. Rostovtzeff is more thorough and is useful as a reference, but Dill is more readable.

2. The Spread of Christianity

One of the great problems in European history is that of the conversion of the Emperor Constantine. The Swiss historian J. Burckhardt, in his great book *The Age of Constantine the Great* * (trans. M. Hadas, 1952), sees Constantine's conversion as completely an act of political expediency. A. H. M. Jones, *Constantine and the Conversion of Europe* (1948), interprets the conversion as religious in motivation. Both scholars base their arguments on the writings of the court bishop Eusebius and the scholar Lactantius, significant parts of which are in K. Setton and H. R. Winkler, eds., *Great Problems in European Civilization* (1954). This book has excellent source material on the spread of Christianity. L. Duchesne, *Early History of the Church*, 2 vols. (1902–15), discusses the spread of Christianity, the heresies, and the early Church Fathers. The short monograph of E. R. Goodenough, *The Church in the Roman Empire* (1931), presents Christianity as a summation of various religious ideas of the Roman environment. Goodenough is a useful introduction to the study of Christianity in this period.

3. Art and Literature

From its beginnings Christianity has inspired art in the pictorial form. C. R. Morey, *Early Christian Art* * (1942), is an interesting introduction. W. Lowrie, *Art in the Early Church* (1947), is an excellent study of early Christian art, with fine reproductions and a critical bibliography. The broad survey of W. R. Lethaby, *Medieval Art from the Peace of the Church to the Eve of the Renaissance, 313–1350* (revised D. Talbot-Rice, 1947), covers all art forms and has considerable material on the early Church.

Perhaps the greatest thinker the Western Church produced in the Middle Ages was St. Augustine of Hippo. *The Confessions of St. Augustine* * (many editions) is one of the greatest accounts of a spiritual pilgrimage ever written. St. Augustine's *City of God* * (many editions), which deals with such basic theological questions as the nature of God, the will, sin, and salvation, played a large part in the evolution of Roman Catholic and Protestant thinking. H. Marrou, *St. Augustine et la Fin de la Culture Antique* (1938), is a comprehensive study of Augustine's thought and of the intellectual climate of the late fourth century. The writings of most of the early Church Fathers have been collected and translated in *The Fathers of the Church* series (edited R. J. Deferrari, 1947 ff.).

H. Marrou, *History of Education in Antiquity* (1948), which carries the reader down to 700 A.D., has good material on Christian literature. B. Smalley, *The Study of the Bible in the Middle Ages* (1941), investigates the medieval conception of Bible studies in those circles where Bible study was a vocation. One of the greatest achievements in historical

* Available in paperback edition.

scholarship in our time, C. N. Cochrane, *Christianity and Classical Culture* (1939), is a brilliant study of the intellectual revolution which came about through the impact of Christianity upon the Greco-Roman world.

4. The Goths and the Huns

Tacitus on Britain and Germany * (edited H. Mattingly, 1952), is a mine of information about the political, social, and economic conditions of the Germanic peoples at the time when they first came in contact with the Roman Empire. There is a good picture of the Germanic migrations and warlike spirit in Jordanes, *Origins and Deeds of the Goths* (trans. C. C. Mierow, 1908). J. B. Bury's *The Invasions of Europe by the Barbarians* (1928) has valuable material on the barbarian impact on Europe, while L. Halphen, *Les Barbares* (1930), traces the beginnings and spread of the Germanic peoples down to the eleventh century. Halphen has good bibliographic material. The old study of P. Villari, *The Barbarian Invasions of Italy,* 2 vols. (1902) is still valuable.

5. The Fall of the Empire in the West

E. Gibbon's monumental work, *The History of the Decline and Fall of the Roman Empire* (edited J. B. Bury, 1896–1900), presents an answer to this problem in a book that has stood as a classic in English literature since 1776. A leading French medievalist, F. Lot, in *The End of the Ancient World* (1951), attributes the decline largely to economic causes, while H. L. B. Moss, *Birth of the Middle Ages* (1935), interprets the problem from a more political and military point of view. J. B. Bury, *History of the Later Roman Empire* (1923), analyzes the causes of the decline of the Empire in the West.

* Available in paperback edition.

6

Ancient India
and China

The civilizations we have discussed so far were all interconnected. The peoples of the ancient Middle East had exchanged techniques and ideas from the second millennium B.C.; Greece had drawn heavily on these older civilizations, and Rome had not only received the Greek heritage but had had direct contacts with all the peoples of the ancient world from the Celts in the West to the Persians in the East. The Romans were perfectly familiar with the religions, the social and political organization, the agricultural and industrial techniques, the science, the literature, and the art of all these peoples. They were more interested in some of these ideas than in others; for example, they accepted oriental religions but tended to neglect Hellenistic science. Neglect was not the same thing as total ignorance, however; the works of Archimedes were always available even if few inhabitants of the Roman world studied them.

It was far different with the civilizations which arose in East Asia. India and China were cut off from each other by jungles and mountains, and from the rest of the Eurasian continent by vast deserts and thousands of miles of semiarid steppes. There was some trade through these forbidding regions, even in the third millennium B.C. But

on the whole, the two great civilizations of East Asia for a long time had little influence on each other, and even less on the peoples of West Asia, North Africa, and Europe. After 500 B.C. teachers, missionaries, and conquering armies gradually ended this almost complete isolation. India and China came to know something of each other through trade, and one of the great Indian religions, Buddhism, penetrated the region north of the Himalayas. Chinese ideas about mathematics and science reached both India and the Near East. Greek soldiers of fortune, following Alexander's footsteps, built states in central Asia from which Greek ideas and artistic concepts were disseminated to both China and India. At the height of the Empire the Romans traded directly by sea with India and Ceylon, and indirectly with China through middlemen who carried silk across Asia to the Black Sea and the Mediterranean. The many Roman coins found in India testify to the extent of the trade.

These contacts, however, were tenuous and easily interrupted by political or economic disasters. Even in the second century A.D., the period of their closest contact with East Asia, the Romans knew little of the civilizations of China and India, and were scarcely influenced by them. The Romans borrowed religious ideas from Egypt, Asia Minor, and Persia, but neither Buddhism nor Confucianism had any impact on

A Buddhist figure from the frescoes of the Ajanta caves, ca. 600–642.

the Mediterranean world. The Romans understood the temple-states of Syria and the semidivine monarchies of Asia Minor but not the caste system of India or the imperial institutions of China. Even in the field of technology, where innovations spread most rapidly because they have no ideological flavor, the Romans ignored such significant Asian innovations as the stirrup and the horse collar. And if East Asia had little influence on the West, the West had even less influence on East Asia. Greek art had a considerable impact on India and, through Buddhism, some influence on China. Otherwise, neither the literature, the learning, nor the institutions of the West made any impression on East Asia. Limited as contacts between India and the civilizations of the Near East and Europe were, however, they were probably more frequent than between India and China. As a result, there was no wholesale borrowing between the two countries. Each developed its own way of life, very different from the other and equally different from the world the Romans knew.

This relative isolation of India and China from the West makes it hard to describe their civilizations in terms understandable to a western reader. There is bound to be some distortion when English words are used to describe Asian ideas and institutions, for there are no exact parallels in western experience to the intellectual and social patterns which developed in India and China. But it is well worth making an effort to understand the early civilizations of East Asia. From time to time events and discoveries in this region exerted a powerful influence on the peoples of the West. Some of the basic differences between East and West which still cause difficulties in our relationships with East Asian peoples were determined by the early history of India and China. Finally, and most important, it is well to remind ourselves that

Clay figurine of a goddess, from Mohenjo-Daro, ca. 2500 B.C.

there are other solutions to the perennial problems of mankind than those devised by the peoples of the West, and that the most enduring and successful of these alternative solutions have been formulated by the Indians and the Chinese.

India

India, like the ancient Middle East, had a very early river-valley civilization, centered in the basin of the Indus. This civilization, like those of Mesopotamia and Egypt, was flourishing about 3000 B.C. and in its early stages seems to have been at about the same level. There were large towns, notably at Mohenjo-Daro on the

Indus, which carried on a considerable amount of industry and commerce. In fact, contacts with the Middle East may have been closer in this period than in many later centuries. This Indus Valley civilization, however, was ruined by some great disaster —perhaps a series of floods—about 2500 B.C., and we know little about conditions in India for the next thousand years. When the darkness lifts there has been a great change. The early inhabitants of India—the Dravidians—have been enslaved or driven south by a conquering group from the north who speak an Indo-European language and seem to be related to the Greeks and even more closely to the Aryans of Persia. These Indo-Aryans are far less advanced than the builders of Mohenjo-Daro. They have no cities; they are herdsmen and farmers living in scattered villages. But they are excellent fighters and they gradually occupy first the Indus Valley, then the Ganges Valley, and finally the central part of the Indian Peninsula. As the dominant race they establish the religious concepts and the social institutions which have persisted in India down to the present day.

Early Indo-Aryan Society

The language of the Indo-Aryan invaders, Sanskrit, resembled Greek in many ways, and there were other parallels between the two peoples. They worshiped similar gods; they gave special honor to the warrior class; and they were organized in many small states instead of one unified kingdom. There was a Heroic Age in northern India, commemorated in their epics, which seems to have been very much like the period in Greek history described by Homer. But there were also significant differences between the Greeks and the Indo-Aryans. In the first place, the Indo-Aryans created a literature earlier than the Greeks; their oldest works, the Vedas, go back at least to 1400 B.C. The Vedas are religious

rituals or hymns to the gods, not accounts of worldly adventures. This illustrates the second great difference between the two peoples: religion and an organized priesthood were far more important among the Indo-Aryans than among the Greeks. Finally, race and class distinctions were sharper among the Indo-Aryans than among the Greeks, and eventually crystallized into a rigid caste system.

These characteristics of early Indian society tended to reinforce each other. The Indo-Aryans preserved their early literature because it had religious significance. As the language changed over the centuries, the only people who could still understand and interpret the early hymns were the priests, who thereby assumed added au-

Statuette of a man, perhaps a priest, wearing an ornamental robe, from Mohenjo-Daro, ca. 2500 B.C.

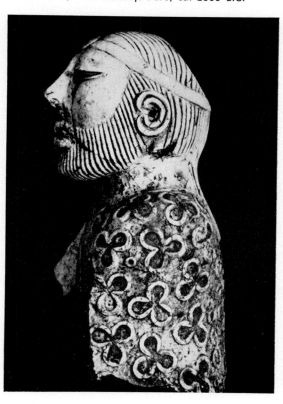

✣✣✣✣✣✣✣✣✣✣✣✣✣✣✣✣✣✣✣✣✣✣✣✣✣✣✣

Vedic Hymns

ORIGINS OF CASTE

When they [the gods] divided the Man,
  into how many parts did they divide him?
What were his mouth, what were his arms,
  what were his thighs and feet called?

The brahman [priest] was his mouth,
  of his arms were made the warrior.
His thighs became the vaisya [merchants and
    cultivators],
  of his feet the sudra [servants] was born.

The moon arose from his mind,
  from his eye was born the sun,
from his mouth Indra and Agni [the war god
    and the fire god],
  from his breath the wind was born. . . .

HYMN OF CREATION

Then even nothingness was not, nor existence,
There was no air then, nor the heavens beyond
  it.
What covered it? Where was it? In whose
  keeping?
Was there then cosmic water, in depths
  unfathomed?

Then there was neither death nor immortality,
nor was there then the torch of night and
  day.
The One breathed windlessly and self-sustaining.
There was that One then, and there was no
  other. . . .

But, after all, who knows and who can say
whence it all came, and how creation
  happened?
The gods themselves are later than creation,
so who knows truly whence it has arisen?

Quoted in A. L. Basham, *The Wonder That Was
India* (London: Sidgwick and Jackson, 1954;
New York: Macmillan, 1954), pp. 241, 247–48.

✣✣✣✣✣✣✣✣✣✣✣✣✣✣✣✣✣✣✣✣✣✣✣✣✣✣✣

thority. The caste system perhaps started as a means of preserving the distinction between the conquering Aryans and the subjugated Dravidians. The Dravidians were shorter and darker than the Aryans, so they could at first be easily distinguished from the ruling group. They were given the dirtiest jobs, so the conquerors had good reason to remain aloof from them. Although differences between conqueror and conquered were eventually forgotten in other societies, such as the Roman Empire, in India they were given a religious sanction and so became permanent. And if the barrier between conquerors and conquered could be justified by religion, then social distinctions among the ruling group itself might be intensified by the same means. Each principal occupation formed a caste, and marriage between men and women of different castes was frowned on by the priests.

Ultimately a society emerged in which religion played a far greater role than it did in ancient Greece or Rome. Thus philosophical speculation, which in Greece became completely divorced from religion, in India always remained closely associated with religious beliefs. The strongest tendency was toward pantheism, a feeling that all living things were part of a world-soul (Brahma) from which they emanated and to which they returned. A natural result of this doctrine was belief in the transmigration of souls. Before the final absorption in the world-soul, each individual soul might inhabit many bodies. But these individual existences, and the world of the senses, were mere illusion; the one reality was the world-soul. Thus death was not to be feared and worldly misfortune could be endured in the hope that the next reincarnation would be happier.

The first great expression of these ideas was in the Upanishads, a series of religious treatises written in the eighth and seventh centuries B.C. The same doctrine pervades the epic of the Mahabarata, which may have been first written down in the fifth century B.C., but which was re-edited and expanded until it reached its final form about 200 A.D. The Mahabarata is the story of wars among kingdoms and the creation of a great empire under the hero Krishna, but the narrative is frequently interrupted by discussions of right conduct and proper belief. And the best-known section of the epic is a religious poem called the Bhagavadgita, which closes with a strong affirmation of belief in the immortality of the soul through transmigration. "Never was there a time when I was not, nor thou . . . and never will there be a time when we shall cease to be. . . . Just as a person casts off worn-out garments and puts on new, so does the soul cast off worn-out bodies and put on others. . . ." The other great Indian epic, the Ramayana, was written about 200 A.D. It also discusses the relation between religious belief and right conduct, but its principal theme is the devotion of a faithful wife to the hero Rama, who is trying to regain his rightful position as a ruler.

During the Heroic Age (ca. 1000–ca. 500 B.C.), Indian religion gradually hardened and coarsened. The ideals of the leading thinkers remained high, but practice fell short of their teachings. The number of gods increased, and ceremonies and offerings replaced the inner enlightenment which the great religious leaders had sought. Caste lines became increasingly rigid; social mobility and intermarriage among castes were sternly discouraged. The priests, or Brahmans, profited from the increasing formalism of religion; since they alone knew what was pleasing to the gods, they became the dominant caste. Next to them were the kings and warriors, while farmers and artisans were lower down in the scale. Almost at the bottom were the laborers—Dravidians and others who performed humble tasks and whose very shadow would defile a Brahman. Most miserable of all were the outcastes—men who had lost their caste position by breaking caste rules and who could receive neither spiritual nor physical help. These became the untouchables of modern India. Every man was supposed to stay in his caste and to perform the duties appropriate to it, since this was the will of the gods. This belief often slowed down economic development, because the great majority of the people could not change their occupations. This waste of human resources explains, to some extent, India's economic backwardness.

The Buddha

Before the sixth century B.C. there were brief periods in which conquering kings united most of northern India under a single ruler. But these empires never included the whole peninsula and never lasted very long. The real genius of India lay not in politics but in religion. And about 580 B.C. India produced one of the great religious leaders of all time, Gautama Buddha. The Buddha, son of a petty Indian king, at first led the normal life of a wealthy aristocrat. He became convinced of the futility of worldly pleasures, but he was repelled by the formalism and superstition which had crept into the official religion. He renounced the world and spent many years seeking enlightenment through fasting and self-discipline. Finally he saw the true path. All man's troubles spring from his attachment to the things of this earth. So long as a man craves pleasure, or even merely existence, he is condemned to be reborn again and again, in higher or lower form, depending on his behavior in his last reincarnation. The only escape from this dreary repetition of sorrow and pain is to renounce all worldly desires. Then the individual soul will be freed from the Wheel of Things and can achieve *nirvana*. *Nirvana* is hard to define; it means a complete cessation of worldly cares, an end to the cycle of birth and rebirth, and complete absorption into the Universal Soul which is God.

The Basic Doctrines of Buddhism

The following is part of a sermon of the Buddha.

There are two ends not to be served. . . . The pursuit of desires and of the pleasure which springs from desires . . . leading to rebirth, ignoble and unprofitable; and the pursuit of pain and hardship, which is grievous, ignoble and unprofitable. The Middle Way . . . avoids both these ends; it is enlightened, it brings clear vision, it makes for wisdom, and leads to peace, insight, full wisdom and Nirvana. . . .

This is the Noble Truth of Sorrow. Birth is sorrow, age is sorrow, disease is sorrow, death is sorrow, contact with the unpleasant is sorrow, separation from the pleasant is sorrow, every wish unfulfilled is sorrow.

This is the Noble Truth of the Arising of Sorrow. [It arises from] thirst, which leads to rebirth, which brings delight and passion, and seeks pleasure now here—now there—the thirst for sensual pleasure, the thirst for continued life, the thirst for power.

This is the Noble Truth of the Stopping of Sorrow. It is the complete stopping of that being emancipated from it, being released from it, giving no place to it.

This is the Noble Truth of the [Middle] Way that Leads to the Stopping of Sorrow. It is the Noble Eightfold Path—Right Views, Right Resolve, Right Speech, Right Conduct, Right Livelihood, Right Effort, Right Recollection and Right Meditation.

Quoted in A. L. Basham, *The Wonder That Was India* (London: Sidgwick and Jackson, 1954; New York: Macmillan, 1954), p. 269.

Though the final goal of Buddhism meant the loss of individual consciousness, it was an intensely individualistic religion as far as life in this world went. No ritual or priesthood could save the seeker after enlightenment; everything depended on the individual's thoughts and actions. He must follow the Eightfold Path of right views, thought, and action; he must observe a strict moral code; above all else, he must never relax in his own personal quest for salvation. The need for concentration on salvation was so great that the first followers of Buddha lived grouped together in monastic communities; only gradually did it become possible to be a Buddhist and still follow ordinary occupations.

Buddhism was a reformation rather than a renunciation of the basic principles of Indian religion. The Buddha disdained the elaborate rites and rituals of the Brahmans and the worship of a multiplicity of gods. He also opposed the rigidities of the caste system; legend recounts that he died after eating with a poor laborer. But while Buddha wanted to purify Indian religion he accepted its basic ideas of the one world-soul, the notion that the world of the senses is illusory, and the transmigration of souls. His ideas spread rapidly during his lifetime, because he enlisted a devoted group of disciples who helped in turn to convert others. But at his death only the northern part of the peninsula had large blocs of Buddhists.

After the death of the Buddha the monasteries developed by his followers became great centers of learning. The new religion grew rapidly under this stimulus, and for a while it seemed that the whole subcontinent might become Buddhist. This was especially true under the Mauryan Empire, which lasted from 322 to about 184 B.C. The first great king of this dynasty, Chandragupta Maurya (322–298 B.C.), came closer to uniting India than any previous ruler; only

The Spread of Buddhism   6th century B.C. to 17th century A.D.

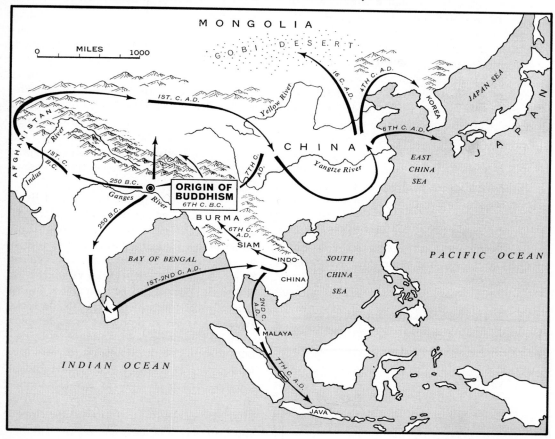

the extreme south escaped his domination. The unification of India under Chandragupta may have been in part a reaction to Greek pressure. Alexander had invaded the Indus Valley in 326 B.C., and one of Chandragupta's problems was to drive Alexander's successors out of the region. The third Mauryan king, Asoka (*ca. 273–ca.* 232 B.C.), became a Buddhist, and with his support Buddhism became the first great missionary religion. The only other faiths which have spread as widely are Christianity and Islam. With Asoka's support, Buddhism was accepted in most parts of India and throughout Ceylon. It began to influ-

ence the countries of Southeast Asia and to cross the mountains into China. And with Buddhism went Indian art, literature, and philosophy. The tremendous influence which India still exercises in eastern Asia began with this cultural conquest under Asoka.

The Mauryan Empire

The Mauryan Empire was well administered; it had a reasonably advanced civil service and an adequate financial system. Asoka was a more benevolent ruler than most of his predecessors, and he tried to soften the harsh penalties of earlier laws and

175

to improve the lot of the poor through extensive charities. Though a Buddhist himself, he was tolerant of other faiths and never tried to convert his people by force. Yet there were two serious weaknesses in the empire, even at the height of its powers. The first was economic; though India traded extensively with the Hellenistic states of Egypt and Syria, its economy remained based on agricultural villages rather than on cities. The government owned most of the land and took a large share of the peasants' income. Thus India never developed enough wealth to support an elaborate political superstructure for very long at a time.

The second weakness was that the Mauryan government was a despotism, enlightened at times, but always arbitrary. The *Arthasastra,* a manual of statecraft written under the Mauryans, shows the real nature of this government. It reads very like an Indian version of Machiavelli:

> With increasing strength, make war; when you have a clear advantage over a neighbor, march against him; do not disturb the customs of a newly conquered people.

But the most revealing sentence is this: "Government is the science of punishment." Even the kindly Asoka inflicted the death penalty freely, and the other kings of his house devised frightful tortures for rebels and traitors. There was no great loyalty to such a dynasty, as future events demonstrated.

Asoka, in encouraging the work of Buddhist monks, became a great builder and patron of the arts. During his reign and those of his immediate successors, Indian art developed some of its most typical forms. Stupas, or great burial mounds with elaborate carved stone gateways, were erected over relics of Buddhist leaders. At Ajanta a series of immense cave temples were built, with gigantic columns and carvings that imitated woodwork. It was also in the cave temples of Ajanta that Indian painting began, though the finest examples there come from a period a few centuries after Asoka. But already it had developed some of its chief characteristics—emphasis on rhythmic, curving lines, and an absence of a light-shadow pattern. Finally, some of the earliest Indian sculptures came from Asoka's time—mainly animal figures, though a few representations of the human figure also survive.

Soon after Asoka's death the Mauryan Empire fell to pieces, and for several centuries no ruler held more than a fraction of the territories Asoka had ruled. It is curious that India should have split into small states just at the time when Rome was uniting the Mediterranean world and the Han emperors were building an empire in China (see pp. 188–91). But separatist tendencies were always strong in In-

The Mauryan Empire   *ca.* 250 B.C.

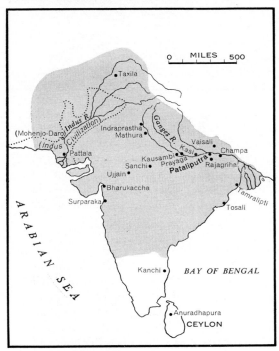

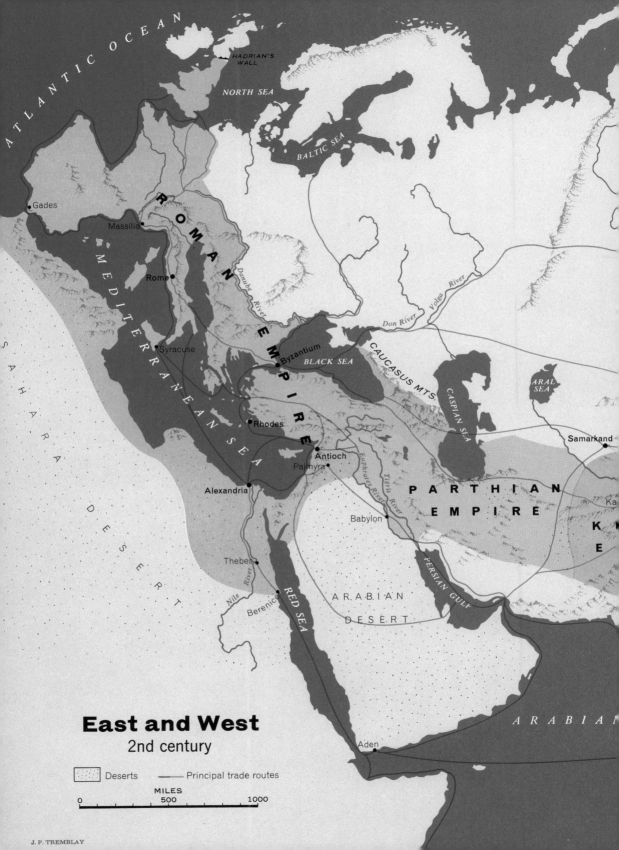

ATLANTIC OCEAN

HADRIAN'S WALL

NORTH SEA

BALTIC SEA

Gades

Massilia

ROMAN

Danube River

Rome

Don River

Volga River

MEDITERRANEAN SEA

E M P I R E

Syracuse

Byzantium

BLACK SEA

CAUCASUS MTS.

CASPIAN SEA

ARAL SEA

Rhodes

Samarkand

Antioch

Palmyra

Euphrates River

Tigris River

PARTHIAN

Alexandria

EMPIRE

Ka

Babylon

K

E

S A H A R A

D E S E R T

Thebes

Nile River

PERSIAN GULF

Berenice

RED SEA

A R A B I A N

D E S E R T

Aden

A R A B I A N

East and West
2nd century

Deserts   —— Principal trade routes

MILES

0   500   1000

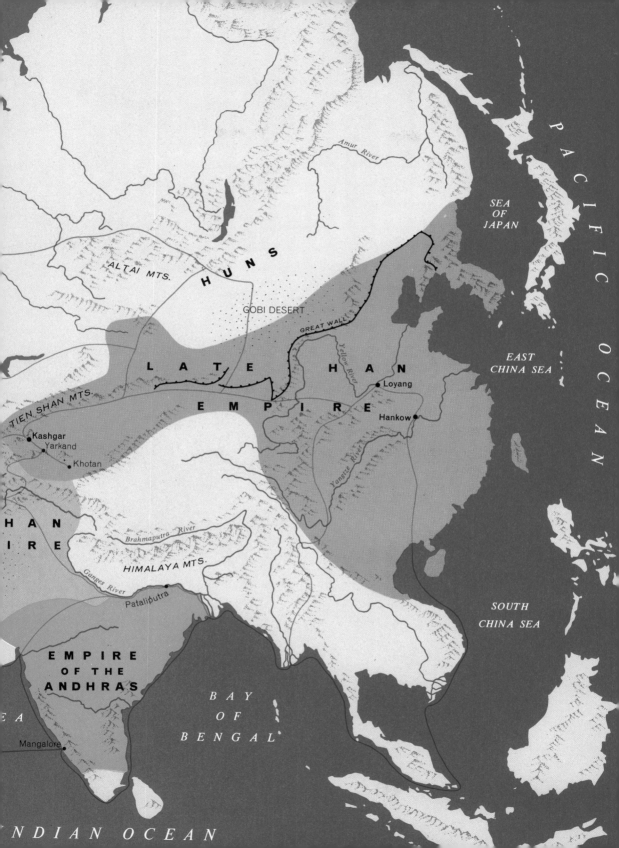

PACIFIC OCEAN

SEA
OF
JAPAN

EAST
CHINA
SEA

SOUTH
CHINA
SEA

Amur River

HUNS

ALTAI MTS.

GOBI DESERT

GREAT WALL

LATE HAN

Yellow River

● Loyang

EMPIRE

Hankow ●

TIEN SHAN MTS.

● Kashgar
Yarkand
● Khotan

Yangtze River

HAN
IRE

Brahmaputra River

HIMALAYA MTS.

Ganges River

Pataliputra ●

EMPIRE
OF THE
ANDHRAS

BAY
OF
BENGAL

EA

Mangalore ●

NDIAN OCEAN

Sarnath lion capital, 242–232 B.C., from a column erected by Asoka to commemorate the Buddha's preaching of the First Sermon in Sarnath.

dia, and outlying provinces may have felt oppressed by governors who threw off the control of Asoka's weaker successors. It is also possible that the Buddhist doctrine of nonviolence weakened the military strength of the Mauryans. Asoka renounced war as an instrument of policy, and his successors, though not going so far, were not military-minded. In any case, with the collapse of the Mauryan state, Buddhism began to decline and eventually almost disappeared from India. But the great missionary work of the Mauryan period enabled it to survive elsewhere in Asia.

In the second century A.D. Buddhism split into two branches, Mahayana Buddhism in the north and Hinayana Buddhism in the south. The Hinayana version is still the principal religion of Ceylon, Burma, Cambodia, and Laos, and in these areas it has remained fairly close to the ideals of its founder. The northern version of Buddhism dominates Tibet and is an important influence in China and Japan. This form of Buddhism has become more like other religions; in it Buddha is a savior who renounced nirvana in order to redeem mankind, and ritual and ceremony have become important.

It was during and just after the Mauryan period that contacts between India and the West were closest. Some of these contacts were by land, for the Seleucid kingdom and some of its successor states bordered on the realms of northern India. It was by this route that Greek sculpture entered India and modified, for a time, the native tradition, and by this route also that Indian philosophy and science reached the West. There was also a large amount of sea-borne commerce between the two regions, but this was less important as a cross-cultural influence. The chief Indian ports for this trade were in the extreme south, a region which lay outside the main centers of Indian culture. And this trade by sea declined rapidly as the Roman Empire weakened after 200 A.D.

The Kushan and Andhra Dynasties

The spread of Buddhism to the north was aided by the establishment of the Kushan Empire in the first century A.D. The Kushans, a nomadic people of central Asia probably allied to the Turks, gradually occupied the northwestern corner of India. Since they also held a large part of central Asia, their empire provided a

177

A stupa, or ceremonial mound, with gate, erected in honor of the Buddha, 1st century A.D.

channel through which Indian ideas and Indian goods could flow northeast toward China and northwest toward Rome. The greatest Kushan ruler, Kanishka, was converted to Buddhism soon after 120 A.D. and called a great council of Buddhist teachers to clarify and spread their doctrine. This

Scenes from the life of the Buddha, 1st century A.D. His life as a prince is represented in the upper relief. In the lower one, he preaches to a group of nobles (note that the Buddha was not yet represented in human form: the tree is a symbol of his presence). Detail from the gate above.

was the origin of the northern school of Buddhism, the version which spread to China and Japan.

At the same time that the Kushans ruled the northwest, the Andhra dynasty of central India (*ca.* 225 B.C.–*ca.* 225 A.D.) was expanding into the Ganges Valley. Though tolerant, the Andhras favored the Brahmans, and Buddhism lost ground under their rule. But the Andhra state declined and began to break up soon after it reached its greatest extent.

The Gupta Period

The Kushan Empire also fell apart during the first years of the third century. A period of disorder followed, but northern

178

6 / Ancient India and China

India was finally reunited under the Gupta dynasty, which began in 320. The Guptas never held as much of India as the Mauryans had, but the region which they ruled was prosperous and reached a high level in literature, science, and the arts.

On the other hand, during the Gupta period (*ca.* 320–*ca.* 500) Buddhism almost vanished from India proper. The religion had been weakened by disorder in the northwest, a region in which it had been particularly strong. It probably also suffered from the fact that some of its most important centers were now outside India. The Indians disliked people who did not follow the Indian way of life, and a religion taught by outer barbarians seemed un-Indian and unacceptable. The Guptas gave Buddhism little chance to recover lost ground. Though they were tolerant, their personal preference was clearly for the old, unreformed Indian religion, which was now taking on its final form of Hinduism. Buddhism gradually withered away and Hinduism, backed by the Gupta kings, became the religion of most of the inhabitants of India. Under the Guptas the basic ideas of Hinduism took on more or less permanent form.

The central beliefs of Hinduism—the unity of all life and the need to recognize and feel this unity as the highest good—had come down unchanged from earlier periods. The great Indian philosophers and religious leaders taught the necessity for meditation, renunciation, and union with the world-soul. But the mass of the population could not reach these heights; it needed images to worship and rules to obey. It needed gods who watched over each form of human activity and who could be placated by sacrifices. The most important gods were a trinity—Brahma the creator, Vishnu the preserver, and Shiva the destroyer. But there were innumerable other divinities, each with his own special

Statue of the Buddha from Gandhara, 2nd or 3rd century A.D., showing Greek influence.

temples and forms of worship. At the same time caste rules were becoming more rigid and complex; the large, original castes were divided into many subcastes. With this development went a deterioration in the position of women. Most well-to-do men had many wives, a practice that had been rare in earlier times. It was in the Gupta period that suttee, the practice of burning widows on their husbands' funeral pyres, became common.

Indian mathematics and astronomy probably reached their height under the Guptas. The Indians had long been interested in these subjects and surpassed even the Greeks of the Hellenistic period in some of their work. Unlike the Greeks, who preferred to think in terms of geometry, the Indians were more inclined toward algebra. While the Greeks independently discovered some algebraic principles, the In-

The Gupta Empire *ca.* 400 A.D.

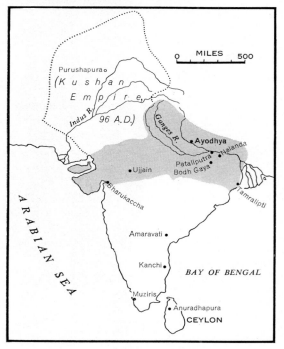

MILES 0 — 500

Purushapura

(K u s h a n E m p i r e,

Indus R.

96 A.D.)

Ganges R.

Ayodhya

Nalanda

Ujjain

Pataliputra

Bodh Gaya

Bharukaccha

Tamralipti

A R A B I A N   S E A

Amaravati

Kanchi

BAY OF BENGAL

Muziris

Anuradhapura

CEYLON

dians were far more advanced in this field. They invented the concept of negative quantities, solved quadratic equations, and found the square root of 2. They knew that the earth was round and that it rotated, and they had some idea of a theory of gravitation. Their most famous invention, however, was the system of so-called Arabic numerals, which first appeared in India in the third century B.C. By the time of the Guptas they had been perfected to the point where Indian mathematicians were using a sort of decimal system. The final and most important innovation, the zero, may or may not have come from Indian mathematicians. At least it is significant that the zero first appears in the works of scholars who were familiar with Indian numerals. It is also significant that Christian Europe did not know of Indian-Arabic numerals until the twelfth century and did

not use them extensively until the sixteenth. The two civilizations were too far apart and contacts were too infrequent for even important ideas to travel quickly from one region to the other.

Gupta literature influenced the West somewhat more rapidly than Gupta science. The great poets and playwrights, like Kalidasa (*ca.* 395–450), remained unknown outside India; their work was too thoroughly Hindu to be understood elsewhere. But the Gupta age was also an age of short stories, fables, and fairy tales, and some of these reached the Near East, and then Europe, in a relatively short time. The Indians had remarkably fertile imaginations, and invented situations and plots which have been borrowed by writers in all other languages. The story of Sinbad the Sailor, for example, is drawn from Indian sources. The most important collection of Hindu tales is the *Panchatantra*. It has been translated into English and even a casual glance at its contents will reveal the influence which it has had on other literatures. For example, the basic pattern of many fables—stories of animals acting like human beings—comes from the *Panchatantra*.

The Gupta period probably marks the high point of early Indian art. There had been considerable Greek influence on Indian art before the Guptas, but this influence declined after 300. Gupta art reverted to basic Indian patterns; it was essentially religious in purpose and symbolic in form. Restrained and dignified, it tried to express eternal truths. The finest paintings at Ajanta are from this period, as are some of the last great Indian sculptures representing scenes from the life of Buddha.

The Gupta state, which never included more than half of India, comprised only the Ganges Valley, the Punjab, and north-central India. Other rulers held the middle and south, and there were always dangerous enemies on the northwest frontier. The Gupta administrative system, which does not seem to have been very well developed, was certainly less bureaucratic than that of either of the great contemporary empires—the Roman and the Chinese. This may have made life easier for its subjects, but it made the kingdom less strong. With the death of Chandragupta II about 412, the Gupta state began to decline. The Huns, who so greatly weakened Han China (see pp. 189–90) and imperial Rome, also had a share in the fall of the Guptas. They invaded the Punjab late in the fifth century, and held northwest

An epiphany of Buddhas, 600–42. Detail of a fresco from Ajanta.

India for a time. But the Huns were driven out after a few decades, and the rise of quarreling local princes was probably a more important cause of the end of Gupta rule. By the sixth century the Gupta kingdom had collapsed, and it was many years before any large state emerged again in India. There was a temporary revival under Harsha (606–47), who reunited most of the north, but Harsha left no heir to carry on his work. For the next six centuries India suffered from internal wars and foreign invasions. Unlike the Chinese, who always rebuilt a new empire quickly on the ruins of the old, the Indians seemed unable or unwilling to make an effort to rise above the level of small, warring states. They were more interested in religion than in politics, and the fact that the Brahman priests always had the last word made it difficult for secular rulers to establish effective political institutions.

China

If Indian civilization became predominantly religious, Chinese civilization showed an equally strong tendency toward secularism. In the earliest phases of Chinese history, this secularism is less noticeable than later on, but it still can be observed. Thus while the early Chinese worshiped a god of Heaven, an Earth-god, and lesser divinities, while they made sacrifices and consulted oracles, they never brooded over religious problems as did the Indians, nor did they develop a powerful priesthood. The ruler held his power through the Mandate of Heaven, but the proof that he had lost divine favor was usually a rebellion led by some political subordinate and not a pronouncement by a group of religious leaders. The great problems for the Chinese were good crops and good government, not salvation and immortality.

Some of the oldest human fossils have been found near Peking in North China, but we know very little about the first stages of Chinese civilization. There were certainly agricultural settlements in the Yellow River Valley at an early date, but it is difficult to tell when they began to develop more elaborate forms of organization and specialization. It seems likely that the building of cities came somewhat later in this region than in Egypt or Mesopotamia—considerably after, rather than before, 3000 B.C.

At any rate, with the Shang dynasty (*ca.* 1500–*ca.* 1100 B.C.) we begin to reach firmer ground. Early Chinese historians preserved stories about the Shang which were once thought legendary, but which now seem to have a solid basis in fact. It was under the Shang that the Chinese apparently began to use bronze, and this new technique may have helped found the power and splendor of the dynasty. The Chinese rapidly acquired great skill in casting bronze; some of the sacrificial vessels of this period show remarkably fine workmanship. It is also from this time that we begin to find the first specimens of Chinese writing—pictographs which are not unlike early Egyptian hieroglyphs. Finally, while most of the people were still peasant farmers, there were walled cities with many artisans and traders, and palaces in which the Shang rulers led a luxurious existence.

The Shang dynasty was succeeded by the Chou soon after 1100 B.C. The Chou Empire stretched from the Gulf of Chili (southern Manchuria) to the lower Yangtze, but the heart of the state was the lower valley of the Yellow River. Since the Chinese people were predominantly agricultural, there were few economic ties to hold the country together, and the Chou king was really only the head of a confederation of local rulers. The relationship between the Chou ruler and the local lords was somewhat like the feudal relationship which later developed in western Europe (see pp. 260–62); the lord was supposed to aid the king in his wars, but was almost independent in his own region. Eventually these local rulers became less and less submissive to the orders of the central authority and began to contend with one another for land and power. The Chou rulers lost all authority and the dynasty came to an end about 250 B.C.

Confucius

It was during the later years of the Chou dynasty that China's great philosopher, Confucius (Kung Fu-tze, 551–479 B.C.), was born. A scholar, and for a while an official of one of the local rulers, he eventually retired from public life to devote himself to the development and propagation of an ethical system. The Chinese, as we have seen, had never been particularly concerned about religion, and had not developed an organized theology. Nor had they been especially concerned about political problems; everyone simply accepted the fact that there always had been, and always would be, rulers and subjects. But

Early Chinese bronzes: ceremonial vessel, late Shang dynasty, 13th century B.C. Another ceremonial vessel, Shang dynasty, 1766–1122 B.C. A ritual vessel in the shape of an elephant, early Chou dynasty, before 300 B.C.

6 / Ancient India and China

they were greatly concerned with human conduct, with the problems of how a man should adjust to the world in which he lived and the society of which he was a part. These problems were especially acute during the disorders of the late Chou period. Confucius taught respect for authority, for tradition, for custom, and for law. He was rather skeptical about religion—"If you do not know about the living," he said, "how can you know about the dead?" But he believed that at all levels there was a guiding force which should be honored and obeyed: the father guided the family, the ruler the state, and Heaven the universe. By accepting the guidance of these authorities, man could achieve both inner harmony and harmony with his environment.

This doctrine, with its emphasis on self-control, conformity, and obedience, in the end became a great conservative force in Chinese society. It strengthened existing tendencies toward ancestor worship, veneration of ancient customs, and acceptance of authority. This was not wholly contrary to Confucius' own desires, but it should be pointed out that in his own day he was a

Confucius on Government

Duke Ting [d. 495 B.C.] asked if there were any one phrase that sufficed to save a country. Master K'ung [Confucius] replied, saying, No phrase could ever be like that. But here is one that comes near it. There is a saying among men: "It is hard to be a prince and not easy to be a minister." A ruler who really understood that it was "hard to be a prince" would have come fairly near to saving his country by a single phrase.

Duke Ting said, Is there any one phrase that could ruin a country? Master K'ung said, No phrase could ever be like that. But here is one that comes near to it. There is a saying among men: "What pleasure is there in being a prince, unless one can say whatever one chooses, and no one dares to disagree?"

From *The Analects of Confucius,* trans. by Arthur Waley (London: Allen and Unwin, 1938), p. 175.

reformer who was trying to bring stability to a turbulent society, and that his teachings were opposed by many of the petty

The Chinese States at the Time of Confucius *ca.* 500 B.C.

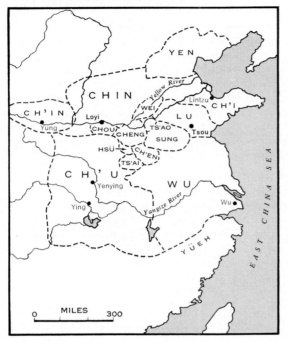

rulers of his own time. He taught that his ethical principles applied to nobles and kings as well as to commoners, and one of his successors, Mencius (*ca.* 372–288 B.C.), logically concluded from this that a bad ruler could be deposed by the people.

Moreover, the conservatism which flowed from Confucius' teaching was neither arrogant nor obscurantist. It was softened by punctilious respect for good manners, which Confucius felt were as important as good laws. This emphasis on courteous behavior proved a priceless lubricant as the Chinese population grew. It enabled millions of people with limited resources to live closely together without undue friction. And with good manners went a highly developed ethical code. The "superior man . . . in anger thinks of consequences, in the face of gain, of righteousness. . . . He repays evil with uprightness and kindness with kindness." He treats others as he himself would be treated.* Confucius also stressed the importance of education in developing men worthy to rule, and the Chinese upper classes never wholly abandoned this principle. It is true that education in China became formalistic and traditional and that the scholar who could quote extensively from ancient texts—such as Confucius' own sayings—was more honored than the one who developed a new idea. Nevertheless, Chinese education did produce men who had disciplined minds, and who had been trained to think clearly. And during most of China's history this educated class had great influence; periods of purely military domination were exceptional and brief.

Confucius never claimed divine inspiration, and he had little influence on Chinese society during his life. But his ideas survived and gradually, through the efforts of several generations of disciples, became dominant in the ruling classes. Eventually, sacrifices were offered to the spirit of Confucius and he was venerated as the great religious teacher of China. More than any other man, he gave permanent form to the basic ideas which the Chinese people held for centuries. The fact that Chinese ideas and customs were codified at such an early date gave enduring strength to Chinese society. For centuries the Chinese were able to maintain their own way of life in spite of the impact of foreign ideas and the rule of barbarian conquerors, because they had standards to which they could make both the foreign ideas and the foreign rulers conform.

Taoism

Yet while Confucius represented the rational principles on which Chinese society

---

* See Charles A. Moore, *Philosophy East and West* (Princeton: Princeton U. Press, 1946), p. 28.

Taoist Teaching

The following is ascribed to Chuang Tzu (*ca.* 320 B.C.).

I first learned to consider myself as an external object, then I no longer knew if I were dead or living. . . . After having seen the One [*tao*] he [the disciple] is able to attain a state where there is neither past nor present, and then a further state where he is neither dead nor living. . . . Were the thunder to bring down the mountains or the hurricane to spill the ocean, he would not care. He is borne up by the air and the clouds; he rides on the sun and moon and frolics beyond the limits of space.

How can we know if the self is what we call the self? Once I dreamed that I was a butterfly . . . and I felt happy. I did not know that I was Chuang Tzu. Suddenly I awoke and was myself, the real Chuang Tzu. Then I no longer knew if I were Chuang Tzu dreaming that he was a butterfly or a butterfly dreaming that he was Chuang Tzu.

From René Grousset, *The Rise and Splendour of the Chinese Empire* (London: Bles, 1952; Berkeley: U. of California Press, 1953), pp. 32–35.

was organized, there was always another side to Chinese thought. This side was represented by Lao-Tzu, who probably lived at about the same time as Confucius. His doctrine was intuitive and mystical, and even Chinese scholars are not in full agreement on what he was trying to say. At least this much is clear: that while Confucius believed that man could achieve harmony with his world by making an effort to think rightly, act rightly, and organize his society properly, Lao-Tzu believed that harmony came from renunciation and passivity. Man should allow the forces of nature to work on him as they do on all other material things; feeling is more important than thinking; harmony with the guiding world-principle is more important than action. This philosophy was called Taoism—the Way—and there are obvious resemblances between it and the Way of Buddha. Taoism, in fact, made it easier for Buddhist doctrines to spread in China, and Chinese Buddhism was colored by Taoist thought.

Taoism never became dominant in China, but it retained great influence for centuries. Politicians and scholars tended to be Confucianists, while painters and poets were more likely to have Taoist leanings. By following the Taoist principle of seeking complete harmony with nature, by passively allowing the inner essence of things to penetrate their minds, Chinese artists and writers were able to achieve remarkable results with great economy of effort. They avoided direct and literal representations of reality; instead, with a few strokes of the brush, or in a short poem, they evoked the mood caused by some event or some natural object.

Chinese Literature

The Chou dynasty was a period of great importance in the development of Chinese art and literature. Bronze works of high quality continued to be made, and some of the earliest and finest jade carvings were done in this era. The peculiarly Chinese art of calligraphy also became important at this time. The Chinese had developed a written language very early, long before the Chou period, but it had never gone much beyond the level of ideographs, with a separate symbol for each word or idea. By Chou times there were about four thousand of these symbols, many of them very intricate. It was difficult enough to draw these characters accurately, especially as a soft brush was the most common implement; it was even harder to draw them with style and elegance. A man who could do this well has

A rubbing from one of the ten "Stone Drums." The "Stone Drum Inscriptions" are the most admired examples of the Great Seal style of writing, which evolved in the latter part of the Chou dynasty, 1111–221 B.C.

studied thoroughly before anything else was attempted.

The First Emperor

The anarchy of the late Chou period was checked about the middle of the third century B.C., when the rulers of Ch'in, one of the petty kingdoms, began to unify all China. They were tough, cruel frontiersmen, who measured their victories by the number of enemy heads cut off, but they created a strong, disciplined army. King Sheng of Ch'in completed the task of conquering the rival kingdoms about 221 B.C. and took the title of First Emperor. He deserved this name, for he was the first real emperor in Chinese history. He ruled directly through provincial governors instead of depending on the doubtful cooperation of semi-independent local dynasties, and

always been admired by the Chinese; through the centuries fine calligraphy, to them, has been as satisfying as a beautiful painting.

It was also during the Chou period that the Five Classics of Chinese literature were compiled from earlier writings. These books include history, philosophy, poetry, and religious ceremonial. Tradition has always given Confucius credit for these compilations, but he almost certainly did not do the actual editorial work. The books are in harmony with his philosophy, however, and must have been put together under strong Confucian influence. For centuries the Five Classics were the foundation of Chinese education; they had to be

A rubbing from a stone inscription made in the later Han dynasty, 1st century A.D. These characters are inscribed in the Official Style which developed in the period from Ch'in to Han. They were so well made that they have been copied by thousands of later calligraphers.

6 / Ancient India and China

The Great Wall of China, completed in 204 B.C.

he imposed uniform laws and weights and measures throughout the empire. His authority and income must have been great, for he was able to build the Great Wall, stretching 1400 miles across North China, to protect his country from barbarian invaders. This work was done at the cost of great human suffering; whole families were uprooted to work on the wall, and food was scarce in the barren regions through which it was built. He also tried to wipe out the Confucian classics, because they were cited by opponents of his absolutism. This harshness may explain why the First Emperor's heir was quickly overthrown. He was succeeded by one of his generals, who founded the Han dynasty, which ruled China from 202 B.C. to 220 A.D.

The Han Period

The Han emperors extended the boundaries of their realm as far as Turkestan on the west and Canton in the south. They also made a real effort to learn about foreign peoples and to make treaties with them. Thus China was much less isolated under Han rule than it had been before, and trade, especially in silk, was developed with Persia and the Roman Empire. Since this trade was carried on through middlemen, the Chinese and Romans seldom came into direct contact, though each people knew a little about the other's country. Far more direct and influential were Chinese contacts with India. Buddhism, as we have already seen, began to enter China in the Han period, and with Buddhism came a host of intellectual and artistic concepts. To give only one example, the pagoda is modeled on Indian Buddhist shrines.

The Han emperors preserved and expanded the centralized administrative system of their predecessor. China and nearby lands were relatively peaceful and prosperous under their rule, and the doctrines of Confucius were nationally honored. From the emperor down, all important men paid reverence to the spirit of the philosopher, and an official Confucian cult was supported by the state. The Han emperors tried to recover and copy all the Confucian texts which could be found, a task which became much easier with the invention of paper-making early in the first century A.D. They honored scholars and

187

made scholarship a means of access to high official positions. The Hans also encouraged the writing of history, both of the ancient past and of the Han period itself. This emphasis on history tended to reinforce the Confucian emphasis on tradition and continuity.

It was during the Han dynasty that great water-control projects became important in building up the economic resources of China. The North China plain is easily flooded in times of heavy rainfall and is also subject to disastrous droughts. The petty princes of the period of warring states had made some efforts both to control floods and to irrigate dry lands, but none of them controlled enough territory to be very successful. The Han rulers could work on a large scale and their water-control projects greatly added to the productivity of Chinese agriculture. They also helped to break the power of local lords and to increase the authority of the imperial government, since water control could be carried out effectively only by a strong centralized state.

While the Chinese were probably more interested in trade than the Romans, and while Chinese cities played a more impor-tant economic role than those of the Western Roman Empire, in both empires an elaborate political structure was being supported on a rather narrow economic base. The Chinese peasant had to support the governing classes, the priests, the scholars, the writers, and the artists. It is not surprising that he became discontented at times and that toward the end of the Han period there were peasant revolts. Moreover, localism, which is usually strong in a predominantly agricultural society, began to weaken the unity of the Han Empire in the second century A.D. The third century, as in Rome, was a period of civil war and divided loyalties. The Han dynasty was overthrown in 220 A.D., and for generations no one was able to reunite the country.

Moreover, China, like Rome, had a long, vulnerable northern frontier to defend. Rainfall is scanty enough in North China; as one goes inland it dwindles to a point where agriculture becomes impossible. Here the domains of the central Asian nomads begin, the most dangerous barbarians the civilized states of the world have ever known. In their longer raids the nomads shook Europe and India, but they

Hsi Wang-Mu (upper right), Queen Mother of the West. Rubbing in the style of Wu Liang Tzu, an artist of the Han dynasty.

The Han Empire 100 B.C.

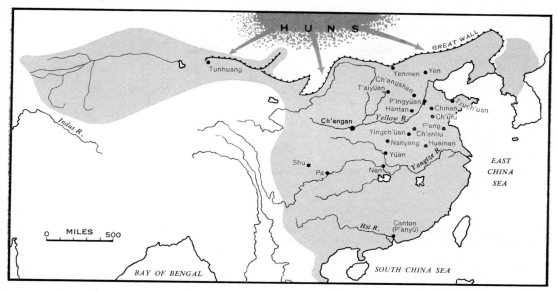

were always a danger to China. It was in order to protect the border zone where the nomads pressed on Chinese outposts that the First Emperor built the Great Wall, and that the early Han rulers conquered Turkestan. When China was strong, the nomads traded peacefully with the Chi- nese, but they were always ready to take advantage of Chinese weakness. Such a period of weakness came, as we have seen, at the end of the Han dynasty. In the fourth century the Huns and related tribes overran all North China, and for almost three centuries the original home of the

A Han dynasty silk.

The Attacks of the Huns 4th century

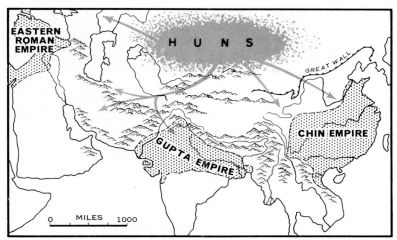

Chinese was ruled by barbarian dynasties.

These nomad rulers gradually took on the Chinese civilization. In the end they became far more Chinese than their contemporaries, the Germanic kings of western Europe, became Roman. But it took some centuries before they were fully assimilated. Meanwhile, just as a remnant of the Roman Empire survived in the East around Constantinople, so a Chinese state survived and preserved the old traditions in the Yangtze Valley in South China. Even in religion there is a parallel development. Christianity spread most rapidly in Europe at the end of the Roman Empire and in the period of the early Germanic kingdoms. Buddhism spread most rapidly and acquired its greatest influence in China during the collapse of the Han Empire and the period of confusion and division which followed. However, Buddhism never gained the overwhelmingly strong position of Christianity. Though it was favored by many rulers, other religions were tolerated, and in the end only a minority of the Chinese remained Buddhists.

Suggestions for Further Reading

1. India

There are a number of valuable works on the early history of India. P. Masson-Oursel, *Ancient India and Indian Civilization* (1934), in the *History of Civilization* series, treats all facets of early Indian history and culture and is a good starting point for study. Another fine survey is that of the great Indian authority R. C. Majumdar, *Ancient India* (1952), which devotes considerable space to religion and culture and has bibliographic material. A. L. Basham, *The Wonder That Was India* (1954), is particularly good on early Indian art and literature. Majumdar, *An Advanced History of India* (1946) is a more scholarly work with special attention to political history. The same author's *The Military System in Ancient India* (1955) traces the evolution of the military system up through the Moslem conquest of Hindustan. M. Wheeler, *Early India and Pakistan* (1959), is a very readable study based largely on archeological evidence. For an essentially political account, H. Raychaudhuri, *Political History of Ancient India* (1952), is interesting but technical, and P. Mookerjee, *Local Government in Ancient India* (1919), stresses that India's elaborate system of local government preserved the independence and integrity of Hindu culture. H. G. Rawlinson, *India and the Western World* (1916), studies the relations between India and the West up through the fall of the Roman Empire.

2. China

Probably the best introduction to the early history of China is H. G. Creel, *The Birth of China* (1937), which deals with the political, social, and cultural life of China in early times. L. C. Goodrich, *A Short History of the Chinese People* (1943), has very good material on the political history of China through 600 A.D., and W. Eberhard, *A History of China* (1955), is an excellent account of Chinese history with concentration on sociological development. Eberhard includes a good critical bibliography. C. P. Fitzgerald, *China: A Short Cultural History* (1938), a standard work on the subject, stresses the vitality of Chinese culture throughout her history. R. Grousset, *The Rise and Splendor of the Chinese Empire* (1952), is impressionistic but stimulating.

For the economic history of China, see the valuable monograph of E. S. Kirby, *Introduction to the Economic History of China* (1954), which has material on the period before 600 A.D. L. Wu-chi, *A Short History of Confucian Philosophy* * (1955), is a good starting point for the study of Chinese philosophy and the Chinese moral system, and H. G. Creel, *Confucius: The Man and the Myth* (1949), is valuable on the influence of Confucius. Both Wu-chi and Creel are great authorities.

For bibliography on Chinese history, L. C. Goodrich, *A Syllabus of the History of Chinese Civilization and Culture* (1941), is invaluable.

* Available in paperback edition.

7

The Germanic Kingdoms
in the West

The great empires of the Eurasian continent had all been destroyed by internal struggles and foreign invasions during the third, fourth, and fifth centuries. Rome, China, and India had disintegrated into small, quarreling states; they had all suffered a decline in economic and cultural activity. Each area faced the problem of adapting the remains of an old civilization to new conditions, of rebuilding political organization and stimulating economic growth. It is always easier to destroy than to restore, and everywhere it took centuries to put the pieces of civilization back together again. The people of western Europe had perhaps the most difficult task of all, for disintegration and barbarization had gone farther there than in most other areas. The period during which western Europe slowly rebuilt its civilization is known as the Middle Ages, and it is to the early centuries of the medieval period that we must now turn.

During the fifth century all the Roman territories of the West fell under the control of Germanic peoples. The Vandals ruled North Africa; the Visigoths held the Iberian Peninsula; Italy itself was occupied by the Ostrogoths. Gaul was split among the Visigoths in the southwest, the Burgundians in the southeast, and the Franks in the north and center. The eastern and southeastern coasts of Britain were conquered by the Angles and Saxons, although the rest of the island was still held by native Celts ruled by a group of petty kings. Only during the sixth century did the Germanic invaders take over the major part of the island, and even then the stubborn Celts preserved fiercely independent kingdoms in Scotland and Wales.

The Northern and Southern Kingdoms

The Germanic kingdoms which emerged from this welter of migration and conquest had very different fates. The Mediterranean group—the Vandals, Visigoths, Ostrogoths, and Burgundians—who had gained land easily and absorbed Roman civilization readily, preserved much of the Roman way of life. But though they seemed to be far more advanced than their northern rivals, the Germanic kingdoms of the Mediterranean had no staying power. During the sixth century the Vandals and Ostrogoths were crushed by the Eastern Roman Empire, and the Burgundians fell to the Franks. The Visigoths were weakened by Eastern Roman and Frankish attacks and finally, in the eighth century, came under the rule of Moslem invaders. In contrast, the northern invaders—the Franks and the Anglo-Saxons—conquered their territories slowly over several generations, learned much less from the Romans, and at first had a lower level of civilization. But their kingdoms endured and became the ancestors of most of the important states of western Europe.

This difference in the history of the northern and southern kingdoms can be explained largely by geographic and demographic factors. The Germanic groups which reached the Mediterranean were cut off entirely from their old homes and could not be reinforced by new migrants. They found themselves in the most densely populated and thoroughly Latinized area of the Empire, and they were vulnerable to attack from the strong states of the eastern Mediterranean, first the Eastern Roman Empire and then the Moslem caliphate. The Goths, Vandals, and Burgundians

The helmet of a 7th-century Anglian king. From the Sutton Hoo treasure, one of the great archeological discoveries of this century, found under the untouched funeral mound of an early Anglian king (see also the illustration on page 206).

also suffered from having been converted to the heretical Arian form of Christianity. This caused open clashes between them and the orthodox residents, and made it extremely difficult for their rulers to win the loyalty of the old Roman population. Thus the Germanic kingdoms which had the greatest need for strength were actually the weakest. The ranks of their fighting men were thinned by war, old age, and assimilation into the Roman population, never to be replaced. Their apathetic Roman subjects might not resist the new rulers, but neither would they fight for them.

The northern invaders, on the other hand, remained in constant contact with their homelands, and for several genera-tions their ranks were freshened by new bands of migrants. In the sparsely settled, slightly civilized lands they had entered, they had an ideal opportunity to preserve their old customs and to transform the native population into an effective fighting force. Since they were eventually converted to orthodox Christianity, they gained the valuable support of the Church. The Eastern Roman Empire never touched Gaul, and the Moslems, even at the height of their power, could only send raiding parties toward the Loire. So it was that the northern invaders had time to develop new institutions strong enough to enable them to survive during the troubled centuries of the early Middle Ages.

A glance at a modern map will illustrate

The Germanic Kingdoms ca. 550

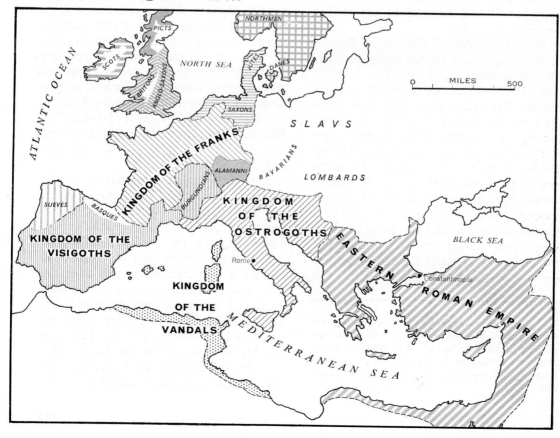

this difference between the northern and southern Germanic kingdoms. Italy and Spain have retained their old Roman names; they did not become East Gothia and West Gothia. But the Franks imposed their name on Gaul, which became France, just as the Angles imposed theirs on the largest part of Britain, which became known as England.

And yet the southern kingdoms, even though they were politically short-lived, helped preserve the culture of Rome by making a conscious effort to adapt Roman learning and law to the needs of their simpler, semibarbaric society. The Burgundian and Visigothic kings, for example, issued brief codes of Roman law for the use of their Roman subjects. These codes would have seemed crude and incomplete to the great lawyers of the Empire, but they covered most of the cases which were likely to arise and they preserved some of the basic principles of Roman law. Moreover, the fact that the written Roman law received official sanction encouraged the Germanic kings to record some of their own legal customs. They believed in the principle of personality of law—that is, every man was to be judged by the laws of his own people, no matter where he lived. Thus the Germanic subjects of the king of Burgundy were judged by Burgundian law, while his far more numerous Latin-speaking subjects were judged by Roman law. In mixed cases the plaintiff usually had to sue according to the rules of the defendant's law. Since the two laws existed side by side, a written Roman code was a powerful stimulant toward writing down the barbarian customs, which had hitherto been preserved only by means of oral tradition.

The Ostrogothic Kingdom of Italy

The most important work in assimilating Roman culture was done in Ostrogothic

A coin of Theodoric, king of the Ostrogoths, 474–526. An imitation of a Byzantine type.

Italy. The barbarian kings, who had been drawn in the first place by the comforts and pleasures of the Empire, had no desire to destroy that way of life now that it was in their grasp. But most of them did not understand Roman civilization, and through ignorance or weakness they did much to tear it down. Theodoric, king of the Ostrogoths, however, had been closely associated with the court at Constantinople and understood Roman ways very well. During his reign in Italy (493–526) he jealously safeguarded the elements of Roman civilization and ensured that the Roman administrative system continued to work in its usual way. The fact that the Ostrogothic army followed a special law meant no more to the ordinary citizen than does the existence of military law in a modern army. Theodoric also named eminent Roman scholars to the highest official posts. Two of these men, Boethius and Cassiodorus, anxious to preserve the learning of the past, made a deliberate effort to put it into a form which could be used by the semibarbaric generations of the future.

Boethius (*ca.* 480–524) was especially disturbed by the gap which had opened between Greek and Latin learning. Since the fourth century few inhabitants of the West had studied Greek, and even so eminent a writer as St. Augustine was not able to read it easily. This ignorance of Greek was particularly serious in mathematics, science, logic, and philosophy, where Latin scholars had done little original work and where all the advanced texts were in Greek. Boethius set about preserving this precious heritage by writing elementary treatises on mathematics and translating all the major works of Aristotle and Plato. Unfortunately, Boethius did not live to complete his ambitious project, and some of the translations he did make were neglected by later scholars. But his basic mathematical texts and his translations of two of Aristotle's elementary treatises on logic were used throughout the Middle Ages. Until the twelfth century these treatises supplied medieval scholars with most of their philosophical vocabulary and with most of their ideas about logic. By showing, in his theological *Tractates,* how logic could be applied to problems of Christian theology, Boethius ensured its survival as a branch of medieval learning.

Boethius' career was cut short when he fell into political difficulties. Theodoric, in spite of his admiration for Roman culture, was always a little uneasy about the loyalty of the upper-class Romans. There was religious friction between his own people and his new subjects, for the Ostrogoths were Arian heretics while the Italian population was orthodox. Moreover, he was harassed by political intrigues inspired by the emperor at Constantinople, who had never given up his claim to the western lands of the Empire. It is possible that Boethius may have entered into these plots against his king; at any rate he was accused of treason, jailed for a year, and then executed. While he was still in prison he wrote the work for which he is best remembered, the *Consolation of Philosophy,* a long dialogue, partly in prose and partly in verse, between the prisoner and Philosophy. Philosophy uses the language of a Stoic rather than that of a Christian, but her basic argument, that all worldly honors and pleasures are vain, and that external misfortunes are unimportant, is one that a Christian could easily accept. The only thing worth striving for is the good of the soul, expressed in virtue and in reason. This idea was at least as old as Plato, but the conviction with which Boethius stated it made his work a real consolation to many troubled men in years to come.

Cassiodorus (*ca.* 490–580) was more skillful in riding out political storms. Though he had been secretary to Theodoric, he survived both court intrigues and the long wars between the Eastern Romans and the Goths and died peacefully at the age of ninety in his ancestral home in southern Italy. He was something of a pedant; the letters he wrote for Theodoric are tricked out with many unnecessary allusions to classical literature and philosophy. But he saw, perhaps more clearly than Boethius, that ancient learning could be saved only with the aid of the Church. In his last years he founded a monastery to preserve the secular learning which he felt was necessary for true understanding of Christian writings. Cassiodorus preserved as much of classical literature as he could and set down rules for others to follow in copying and correcting ancient texts. His most important work was his *Introduction to Divine and Secular Literature,* in the first part of which he outlined the basic reading he felt necessary for educated churchmen and suggested books in which essential materials could be found. In the second part he gave a brief and uneven summary of the liberal arts.

An Ostrogothic gilt bronze buckle, with jewels, 6th century. The style is Germanic, in contrast to that of the Ostrogothic coin on p. 195.

gil might make a reader anxious to ferret out the whole *Aeneid;* a reference to Aristotle might encourage a scholar to seek the original work. It was a long time before any large-scale efforts were made to recover and study the basic works of the classical period, but at least the men of the early Middle Ages were aware that their knowledge was incomplete. The great intellectual revival of the eleventh and twelfth centuries (see pp. 303–09) would not have come as soon as it did or have taken the form it did if generations of medieval scholars had not studied the compilations ground out during the fourth and fifth centuries.

Digests such as that of Cassiodorus, and elementary treatises such as those of Boethius, made up the basic educational materials of the early Middle Ages. Many of the scholarly and literary works of the great period of Greek and Roman civilization had been lost, and those that survived were seldom studied because they were too long or too difficult. The digests and handbooks were no real substitute for the originals, for they stressed what was obvious and omitted or oversimplified what was complicated. Nevertheless, they preserved useful knowledge, and, even more important, they suggested that better sources might be available. A quotation from Ver-

Germanic Society

The early Germanic kingdoms were not very successful in preserving and assimilating the intellectual heritage of Rome. They were even less successful in preserving the Roman political and administrative system. Here they ran into a double difficulty: the native population was weary of the old imperial forms of government; the Germans themselves had no concept of the state and no experience in administration. Consequently, there was a drastic simplification of political institutions in all the countries of the West.

Since the early Germans had lived in rather small groups given over to agriculture and cattle-raising, they had felt no need to create elaborate political institutions. The family was their basic social unit—not the small family of father, mother, and children which we know today, but the large family which included grandparents, uncles, and cousins out to the second or third degree. The family protected the lives and property of its members, sometimes waging blood-feuds with other families. Above the family was the neighborhood, a group of family heads who cooperated in local defense, in settling disputes, and in performing difficult agricultural tasks. The folk, or people, which was made up of many neighborhoods, was supposedly a blood-group descended from a few common ancestors. It had almost no function except to make war on or defend itself against neighboring peoples.

Early Germanic society was not democratic; it was very conscious of differences in class and rank. Certain families, which claimed descent from the gods, had great wealth and supplied leaders in time of war. But these leaders—the kings and nobles— had little to do in time of peace. Their wealth and ancestry won them respect, and their bands of armed retainers commanded fear. Their advice was often sought when trouble arose, but they did not administer a state or govern a people. Most of the ordinary business of the people was conducted by the family and neighborhood groups.

Germanic Courts

The difference between Germanic and Roman political organization is seen most clearly in the administration of justice. A Roman who had a grievance against a neighbor went to a court established by imperial authority. His case was judged according to laws promulgated by the emperors, and the court's decision was enforced by local administrative officials.

A German who felt that he had been wronged, however, had to rely first and foremost on his own strength and that of his family. The most common remedy was reprisal, which easily developed into the blood-feud. Only if the injured family felt that reprisal and feud were unnecessary or dangerous would the case go to a court. The usual court was an assembly of neighbors which, lacking coercive power, relied largely on public opinion and religious sanctions. If the defendant was willing to take his chances with a feud, there was no public authority which could force him to come to court. If he did appear and denied his deed, the court had no means of establishing the facts in the case. If the defendant had a bad reputation, the court might summarily order him to make satisfaction to the plaintiff, or, more commonly, might send him to the ordeal. This meant that he was obliged to expose himself to a test and let the gods indicate whether or not he was lying. He might, for example, have to carry a hot iron three paces, or pluck a stone out of a kettle of boiling water. If his hand showed no infection after three days, he was judged innocent. Or he might be thrown into a pond to see if he would float or sink. Floating was a sign of guilt, for it meant that the pure element of water had rejected the accused. But a man of good reputation could clear himself by compurgation—that is, he would swear that the charge against him was baseless, and a fixed number of friends and relatives would swear that his oath was "clean." These oath-helpers were not giving testimony, in our modern understanding of the term, in behalf of the accused, for they might know nothing at all about the facts in the case. They were simply swearing that the accused was not a perjurer, and by so doing they automatically cleared him of the charges against him. The plaintiff might not be convinced by this demonstration; his only consolation was the thought that his adversaries had exposed themselves to divine vengeance by taking false oaths.

If the plaintiff won his case, he received compensation from the defendant, either in money or in kind. This was true even for crimes of violence, such as homicide or mayhem. There was no idea in this sort of justice that crime was an offense to the community as a whole, and no attempt was made to inflict physical punishment on the wrongdoer. Tables of compensation made up the largest part of the laws of every Germanic people. It cost more to kill a man of high birth than an ordinary freeman, more to kill a woman of childbearing age than a grandmother. The loss of a forefinger required a larger payment than the loss of a little finger; a rear tooth was more valuable than a front tooth. The penalties were substantial; the compensation for killing a man of high birth would ruin a poor family. But no provision was made for collecting the penalties, other than the threats of the injured family and the pressure of public opinion. If the man who owed compensation ran away, his family remained liable for the payment. If he delayed or refused payment, he would run the risk of starting a feud.

These courts were probably more effective than we would think in dispensing a rough kind of justice. The most common offenses among the early Germans were acts of physical violence of which no one was ashamed and which no one sought to conceal. To quarrel, fight, wound, and kill was the natural behavior of a self-respecting man; it led to no social stigma. Thus in many cases the facts were not denied and the sole function of the court was to prevent a feud by determining the compensation to be offered to the injured party. When the facts were in dispute and the defendant was a man of poor reputation, the court could simply make it more difficult for him to clear himself of the alleged offense. Moreover, while ordeal and compurgation might not reveal the truth, they at least provided quarreling families with an excuse not to launch a feud. Once the gods had spoken, it was unnecessary to prove one's manhood by fighting. Like many other legal systems, the system dictated by Germanic custom was more concerned with stopping fights than with administering abstract justice. Any solution, so long as it was peaceful, was better than a grievous outbreak of blood-feuds.

Nevertheless, this Germanic legal system had serious defects, and no civilized life was possible until they had been remedied. It gave no place to public authority, for no one had to accept the jurisdiction of a court unless he so desired. It set loyalty to the family far above loyalty to any larger group. It accepted as natural a state of violence in which no man's life was secure. It was effective only in dealing with open wrongdoing; it could not, for example, be applied to commercial transactions of any kind. From the fifth to the twelfth century western European rulers struggled to create effective courts of justice, and it

✣✣✣✣✣✣✣✣✣✣✣✣✣✣✣✣✣✣✣✣✣✣✣✣✣✣✣✣✣✣

Archbishop Hincmar on the Ordeal by Cold Water

9th century

Now the one about to be tested is bound by a rope and cast into the water, because, as it is written, each one shall be holden with the cords of his iniquity. And it is evident that he is bound for two reasons; to wit, that he may not be able to practice any fraud in connection with the judgment, and that he may be drawn out at the right time if the water should receive him as innocent, so that he perish not. . . . And in this ordeal of cold water whoever, after the invocation of God, who is the Truth, seeks to hide the truth by a lie, cannot be submerged in the waters above which the voice of the Lord God has thundered; for the pure nature of the water recognizes as impure and therefore rejects . . . such human nature as has once been regenerated by the waters of baptism and is again infected by falsehood.

From Archbishop Hincmar, trans. by A. C. Howland, *Translations and Reprints* (Philadelphia: U. of Pennsylvania Press, 1897), Vol. IV, No. 4, p. 11.

✣✣✣✣✣✣✣✣✣✣✣✣✣✣✣✣✣✣✣✣✣✣✣✣✣✣✣✣✣✣

was only when they had succeeded in this difficult task that the people they ruled could advance very far beyond the stage of small, self-sufficient agricultural communities.

Germanic Kingship

As we have seen, the loyalties of a German were personal. He was loyal first of all to his family—and understandably so, for he could scarcely hope to exist without family backing. Men who had no families or whose families were weak had to become dependents or even slaves of some strong man. Next, the German showed loyalty to a leading man in the local community who took responsibility for its defense. Finally, he might show some loyalty to the king, if that king was known and respected for his prowess in war. But the king could not count on spontaneous support from his people; his real strength lay in his bands of armed retainers. These retainers lived with the king, were bound to him by personal oaths of loyalty, shared in the spoils of conquest, and were usually faithful to him unto death. But the king seldom had more than a few hundred devoted retainers; the rest of his subjects owed him no particular obedience or service. So long as there was a king to lead them in times of emergency, they cared little who he was. Few of the early Germanic kings died in bed; they were either assassinated by rivals for the throne or else killed in battle with neighboring rulers.

It was difficult enough for the kings to exercise authority when they ruled small groups in limited territories and when they were personally acquainted with most of the fighting men of the folk. The task became far more difficult when they tried to rule large populations, composed of different races, scattered over wide areas of the old Empire. The king could not be present in person in all parts of his realm, nor could he know more than a few of the leading men in each district. He could not preserve the old Roman administrative system because he lacked financial resources and did not entirely trust the old Roman ruling class. He could not create a Germanic civil service to take the place of the Roman one that was collapsing, for there was no precedent for it in Germanic custom and the Germans did not know how to delegate authority. Either they ignored the king's delegate and tried to deal directly with the king, or else they transferred their loyalty to the delegate himself and enabled him to become an almost independent ruler in his administrative district. Until kings were able to delegate authority without losing control—and it took them centuries to find out how—the European kingdoms remained loose federations of local communities.

Given the primitive state of the Germanic economy and the structure of Germanic society, the local community was almost self-sufficient. The ordinary German was not particularly interested in anything that happened more than a day's journey from his home. He drew almost everything he required from his own land and he produced nothing to sell in distant markets. He relied on the great men of his community for local defense and he followed them to war without worrying about causes or objectives. Thus the division of a large kingdom into little principalities did not hurt the ordinary German's standard of living or upset his ideas of proper political arrangements, nor would the creation of a large kingdom aid him economically or satisfy his political aspirations.

There were two groups with somewhat wider horizons, the merchants and the heads of the great noble families. But the merchants were very independent of the king, giving him little support and receiving little protection from him in return.

They carried on no internal trade which would bind a kingdom together, trading as they did chiefly in luxuries brought from distant places. As for the men of noble rank, their chief objective was to win as much power as they could in their own region. If they supported a king, it was usually for selfish reasons, and the larger the kingdom the more local independence they thought they could get.

Although settlement in the Western Empire posed puzzling new problems for the Germanic kings, it also gave them some idea of how to solve those problems. Royal authority was always greatest in time of war, and the period of migration was a period of almost constant war. And, though they did not fully understand the Roman concept of the state and of public authority, they learned enough from contact with Romans to make them eager to be more than mere tribal war leaders. Most important, the Church, which had taken over many of the Roman traditions of government, sooner or later gained great influence over all the Germanic kingdoms. Not all churchmen were skillful lawyers or enlightened political theorists; in fact, many were only one degree less barbarous than the flocks they tended. But most of them realized that Christianity could not flourish in an area broken up into isolated small communities and that, bad as the kings might be, there was more to be hoped for from them than from the even more unenlightened lords of petty provinces. Many bishops served as advisers to the kings and helped them to preserve the rudiments of a centralized administrative system. Others helped preserve a certain degree of unity by meeting together in local church councils, which sometimes went beyond ecclesiastical business to matters of more secular concern. In fact, in the simplified society of the time it was almost impossible to draw a sharp line between religious

Gold Visigothic votive crown of King Receswinthe. With jewels, 7th century.

and secular affairs. Prominent laymen often attended church councils, and the councils often dealt with such matters as the suppression of violence.

The Church in the Germanic Kingdoms

Even though the Church had preserved much of the learning and many of the administrative techniques of the late Empire, it suffered severely during the chaotic years following the Germanic ascendancy. The West was far from being completely Christian in the fifth century, and the Germanic groups that had flooded the area were either pagans or heretical Arians. Even when they had been converted to Catholic Christianity after long, intensive missionary activity, they often tried to use the Church for their own purposes. A good many bishops of doubtful character, for example, were foisted on the Church by kings anxious to reward their friends and supporters.

And the Church at this time was not yet the self-sufficient, highly organized Church it was to become in later centuries. Formerly it had relied on the imperial government for support and protection, and it had not yet perfected its own administrative system or established clear lines of authority. Theoretically, each of the old Roman city-states should have formed the territory (diocese) controlled by a single bishop. North of the Alps this division was far from complete; many bishops had dioceses which were too large or whose boundaries had not been defined. The division of the dioceses into parishes had gone even less far. This meant that there were no churches at all in many rural areas, and that the few town churches were often overcrowded. Many nominal Christians had little opportunity to attend divine service. Finally, while the pope's authority to determine questions of faith and morals was generally acknowledged, his power to remove inefficient or corrupt bishops was not yet fully established. Thus the influence of the Church varied from diocese to diocese with the character of the bishop and the amount of support he could get from his king.

Fortunately for the Church, the development of monasticism presented a new, disciplined force at a time when it was badly needed. Even under the Empire many Christians, feeling that they could not live a truly religious life while absorbed in secular activities, had withdrawn from the world to desert or wilderness and had passed their lives in contemplation and prayer. But it was not easy for the hermit to endure the rigors of an isolated existence; his devotion might falter or he might be unable to provide himself with food and clothing. Thus there was a tendency for hermits to come together in communities in order to obtain spiritual and physical assistance from their fellows. By the end of the third century, some of these communities had become formally organized as monasteries under an elected head, the abbot, with a set of rules regulating the daily activities of the members.

Monasteries and monastic rules had existed in the East for several generations and were spreading to the West at the time of the Germanic migrations. But the eastern rules were not entirely suitable for western conditions; they were both too harsh and too soft. They were too harsh in physical matters, for the scanty food and clothing which would support life in the Egyptian desert were completely inadequate in the colder northern countries. They were too soft in matters of authority, for many eastern monks were completely undisciplined and wandered about from place to place as they saw fit. Yet the monastic life was becoming steadily more attractive to men in the West; it offered both spiritual and physical security in an age of increasing violence and instability.

St. Benedict and Monasticism

It was St. Benedict of Nursia (480–543) who adapted monasticism to the needs of the Western Church. He was born of a wealthy and distinguished Roman family, but, like many other men of his time, he had fled in disgust from a world which seemed hopelessly corrupt. At first he lived as a hermit in the hills near Rome, but as his reputation for holiness attracted others to him he found himself forced to organize a regular monastic community.

He built a monastery on the commanding height of Monte Cassino,* near the main route from Naples to Rome, and established a rule which gradually became the basic constitution for all western monks.

The great strength of the Benedictine Rule lay in its combination of firmness and reasonableness. The abbot's authority was absolute. A monk might humbly request the abbot to reconsider an order which seemed to demand the impossible, but if the abbot persisted, the monk had to obey. Monks were not to leave their monastery or transfer to another monastery without permission. They were to keep themselves occupied all day. Their first and most important duty was to do the "work of God" —that is, to take part in religious services which filled many hours of the day. But they were also to perform any manual labor that was necessary for the welfare of the house, including such activities as copying manuscripts or making religious works of art. The primary purpose of the Rule, however, was not to make the monastery an intellectual or artistic center, but to keep the monks from extremes of idleness or asceticism. Most monks were neither artists nor scholars, and most monasteries never distinguished themselves by their literary or artistic productions. They did, however, distinguish themselves as centers of prayer and worship, as dramatic examples of the Christian way of life. Most monasteries also performed certain social services, such as extending hospitality to travelers or giving food to the poor, and a few operated important schools. But many could do no more than preserve discipline among the monks and the daily order of worship in the monastery church.

* A great battle of World War II was fought for the strategic position of Monte Cassino. The mountain had been continuously occupied by a Benedictine monastery ever since the time of St. Benedict, though the buildings destroyed in the battle were not the original ones.

A Benedictine monastery in a Germanic kingdom exerted a powerful influence in both religious and secular affairs. It offered pure Christian doctrine to people who were pagans, heretics, or at best only nominal Catholics. Very early the monasteries became centers of missionary activity and reform. At the same time the Benedictine emphasis on obedience and the close connection between the early Benedictines and the pope helped to hold the

Page from a Gothic Bible, ca. 500. This translation, by the Arian bishop Ulfila, is one of the earliest specimens of a Germanic dialect that we possess. Notice that some new letters, not in the Latin alphabet, had to be devised to accommodate unusual sounds in the Gothic language.

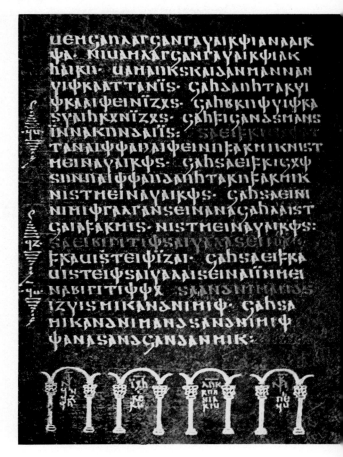

St. Benedict giving his Rule to his monks. This 8th-century drawing is the oldest known representation of St. Benedict.

Church together at a time when any sort of centralization was hard to achieve. The Benedictines emphasized papal authority and a well-organized Church; they opposed local autonomy and lack of discipline. Finally, in many parts of Europe the Benedictines introduced valuable new techniques, such as building in stone and organizing agriculture around the large estate. Benedictine monasteries often served as nuclei for the growth of towns, for they were almost always more prosperous than the neighboring countryside.

In view of these benefits, many kings and wealthy landowners decided that founding a monastery was a good investment. The founder and his family gained both spiritual rewards and material benefits. They did not always draw a very clear line between the two; for example, it was obviously good for the donor's soul to have holy men praying for him, but the mere presence of monks in a province was thought to ensure divine favor, good crops, and general prosperity. The monastery

might furnish grain in time of famine and lend its gold and silver ornaments when its benefactor ran short of money. By attracting settlers to waste lands, it might increase productivity and enhance the ruler's authority in remote areas. Thus monasteries spread rapidly throughout most of the Germanic kingdoms, often far more rapidly than organized dioceses and parishes.

The Conversion of the Anglo-Saxons

England offers a good example of the importance of monasteries under the Germanic kingdoms. The Anglo-Saxon conquest of Britain was slow, piecemeal, and bloody. The Britons put up a stiffer resistance than any other group in the western part of the Empire, and during this long resistance they abandoned many of their Roman ways. Faced with a stubborn enemy, the Angles and Saxons had to be more destructive than, for example, the Franks were in the Seine Valley; they burned towns and great country houses and killed or exiled most of the leading men in the east and south of the island. Very little of Latin civilization remained in Britain: the language was abandoned, the towns were deserted, and much of the cultivated area sank back into wilderness. Christianity survived among the natives who were being driven back into Wales, and from Wales it spread into Ireland. But the Anglo-Saxons were hardly prepared to be converted by their enemies, and in any case the Christians of Wales and Ireland, cut off from the rest of the western world, were developing peculiar ideas and usages. They celebrated Easter at a different time; they gave abbots authority over bishops; they did not follow the Roman ritual. In short, in Anglo-Saxon England the basic ingredients which were to produce early medieval civilization—the Latin, Germanic, and Christian traditions —had not yet begun to fuse.

But the picture began to change during the pontificate of Gregory the Great (590–604). Gregory had been a monk and then an abbot; in fact, he had been most unwilling to leave his monastic life to take on the responsibility of governing the Church. He realized more fully than his predecessors the value of the monks as a disciplined force obedient to the orders of Rome. Gregory also realized how hard it was to maintain unity and decent conduct among the clergy of the Western Church. His correspondence shows how diligently he worked at this task and how difficult it was to make any impression on bishops and priests protected by Germanic kings. Gregory kept some measure of control in Italy, but beyond the Alps he could do little more than register his complaints. The Frankish kings, who ruled both Gaul and parts of what is now Germany, were exploiting the Church for their own profit, and naming bishops from among court favorites, younger sons of wealthy families, and bribe-givers. A large part of the popu-

lation in Gaul and Germany had no regular contact with the clergy, for there were neither village churches nor parish priests. And beyond this area, where at least a form of Christianity existed, though corrupt and unsatisfactory, stretched a great expanse of heathen territory, from the North Cape down to the middle Danube, from England across Frisia and North Germany into the limitless lands of the Slavs.

Gregory, a practical man but no theorist, probably prepared no master plan for the reform and conversion of the West. But he was quite ready to tackle the specific problems of reform and conversion,

The Anglo-Saxon Kingdoms of England 7th century

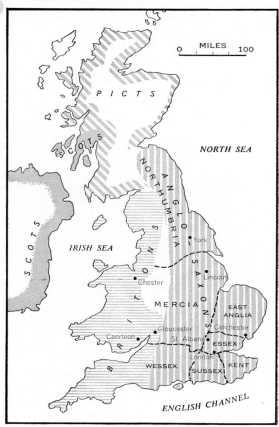

Anglian purse cover with gold and glass mosaic, 7th century. Like the helmet shown on page 192, this decorative cover was part of the Sutton Hoo treasure. In the same funeral mound were found Byzantine and Near Eastern silver bowls and Merovingian coins, showing evidence of trade.

and he turned to the monks for help. For several reasons, Britain seemed to be a promising field for conversion: Irish Christian missionaries were having some success in Scotland and northern England, and the king of Kent in southern England had married a Christian Frankish princess. So in 597 Gregory sent a group of monks to Kent, led by an abbot named Augustine.*

Augustine converted the king of Kent without much difficulty and established the first English bishopric, at Canterbury. But after this promising start the Roman version of Christianity spread only slowly through the island, partly because Augustine was not a very good organizer, partly because Irish missionaries were influ-

_____
* This Augustine also became a saint, but he should not be confused with the great theologian, St. Augustine of Hippo, who died more than a century and a half before the mission to England (see p. 163).

ential in the North, and partly because the Anglo-Saxons were divided and quarrelsome. It was only in the second half of the seventh century that these obstacles were overcome. Most of the North abandoned Irish forms after a council at Whitby in 664, and in 669 a great organizer, Theodore of Tarsus, became archbishop of Canterbury. Theodore gave the Anglo-Saxon Church a firm institutional base by restoring discipline and dividing the country into regular dioceses. Paganism disappeared and the influence of the Church on Anglo-Saxon society grew steadily.

From this time on the Anglo-Saxons were the most loyal and energetic supporters of the Roman Church. The most successful missionaries of the eighth century, Anglo-Saxon monks, converted the remaining pockets of heathen Germans on the Continent; they helped build regular church organizations among the nominal

Christians of the transalpine countries; and they even succeeded in reforming and making obedient to the pope the corrupt and anarchical churches of the Frankish kingdom. Gregory's decision to support monasticism and missionary activities produced remarkable results, for the missionary monks both increased the number of Christians and greatly strengthened papal authority throughout western Europe.

The Rise of the Franks

While the Germanic kingdoms were absorbing Christianity and a modicum of Roman learning, the Franks were rising to political dominance in western Europe. As we have seen, they occupied a favored position. They had penetrated deep enough into the Empire to profit from its wealth but not deep enough to jeopardize the sources of their military power. They held northern Gaul, which was Roman, but they also held the solidly Germanic regions of the middle and lower Rhine. Their first great king, Clovis, a member of the Merovingian * family, came to power about 470. He was king of only one group of Franks, and at first he held only a small corner of Gaul. But Clovis was both a good fighter and a skillful intriguer, and he rapidly increased the size of his realm. He defeated the last Roman official with any authority in Gaul, and got rid of the other Frankish kings by assassination or subversion. A pagan himself, Clovis had married a Catholic Burgundian princess, and through her he gained the idea that the Christian God could be a powerful help in war. He put this idea to the test in a battle with the Alamanni in 496 and gained a hard-fought victory. Convinced

* This family was named for an early and almost unknown Frankish king, Meroweg.

by this demonstration, Clovis and his warriors sought baptism from St. Remigius, bishop of Reims. The fact that Clovis received Catholic, and not Arian, baptism gave him a great advantage in dealing with the Roman population.

The conversion of Clovis, even more than that of Constantine which it resembled so closely, was based on expediency. Clovis remained a bloody and treacherous barbarian; all he wanted was to exploit the power of the Christian God and gain the support of the bishops and the old Roman population against Arian Germans. He used his newly acquired orthodoxy as an excuse to attack the Visigoths, who still held southwestern Gaul as well as Spain. Proclaiming that he could not endure the presence of heretics in Gaul, Clovis drove the Visigoths back across the

Chalice, copper gilded, with silver inlay, 8th century. Made for a Frankish priest, Grimfridus, part of whose name can be seen on the rim.

207

The Morals and Faith
of the Early Franks

Ragnachar was then king at Cambrai, a man so unrestrained in his wantonness that he scarcely had mercy for his own near relatives. . . . Clovis came and made war on him, and he saw that his army was beaten and prepared to slip away in flight, but was seized by his army, and with his hands tied behind his back, he was taken with Ricchar his brother before Clovis. And Clovis said to him: "Why have you humiliated our family in permitting yourself to be bound? It would have been better for you to die." And raising his ax he dashed it against his head, and he turned to the brother and said: "If you had aided your brother he would not have been bound." And in the same way he smote him with his ax and killed him. . . . These kings were kinsmen of Clovis, and their brother, Rignomer by name, was slain by Clovis's order at the city of Mans. When they were dead Clovis received all their kingdom and treasures. And having killed many other kings and his nearest relatives, of whom he was jealous lest they take the kingdom away from him, he extended his rule over all the Gauls. . . . For God was laying low his enemies every day under his hand, and was increasing his kingdom, because he walked with an upright heart before Him, and did what was pleasing in his eyes.

From Bishop Gregory of Tours, *History of the Franks, ca.* 575, trans. and annot. by E. Brehaut (New York: Columbia U. Press, 1916), pp. 48–50.

Pyrenees and annexed their territories on the French side of the mountains. This victory almost completed the task of unifying Gaul. Only the Burgundian kingdom in the Rhone Valley escaped Clovis' domination, thanks to the aid it received from the Ostrogoths of Italy.

The Frankish kingdom remained strong for a century after Clovis' death in 511.

His sons finally succeeded in conquering the Burgundians and added their territories to the Frankish realm. They also began to extend their authority over the Bavarians and other Germanic peoples east of the Rhine. Though they and their successors quarreled bitterly among themselves, the Franks still had the best army in the West, and none of their neighbors could profit from their disunity.

The Frankish kings also profited from the fact that their orthodoxy was seldom questioned, whatever might be said of their morals. Orthodoxy gained them the steady support of the bishops, who had great influence with both Frankish warriors and Gallo-Roman landholders. The bishops had the habit of command; moreover, they came from aristocratic families, were at least partially educated, and possessed religious authority. They could be very useful to the kings, especially as they did not insist on impossibly high standards of conduct. Thus Gregory of Tours (538–94), who wrote a famous *History of the Franks,* was rather gentle in his judgment of the Frankish kings. Gregory admits that Clovis was treacherous, and that on one occasion Clovis bewailed his lack of relatives "not because he grieved at their death but with the cunning thought that he might perhaps find one still alive whom he could kill." But Gregory could still sum up Clovis' career by saying: "The Lord cast his enemies under his power day after day, and increased his kingdom, because he walked with a right heart before him and did that which was pleasing in His sight." Gregory was equally favorable to King Guntram (561–93), of whom the best that could be said was that he murdered somewhat fewer people than his rivals did. "One would have taken him," says Gregory, "not only for a king, but for a priest of the Lord."

Nevertheless, the bishops did make an

effort to mitigate the cruelty and selfishness of their rulers. They protected men unjustly accused; they excommunicated one king for attacking a bishop and another for carrying off a nun; they did their best to prevent civil wars among members of the royal family. They were aided by the monasteries, which were just beginning to appear in the Frankish realm. Monks who had already abandoned the world were not easily terrified by the threats of kings. St. Columban, the founder of Luxeuil, denounced King Thierry (595–613) to his face as a sinner and predicted that his sons would never be kings. The saint was exiled, but he soon returned and saw Thierry's family wiped out in a civil war.

The efforts of bishops and monks to soften the savage behavior of the Franks were not always successful. Sometimes they could frighten kings and great men with threats of coming catastrophes, but they could not keep them frightened all the time. Few Franks who were not members of the clergy accepted the basic rules of Christian morality. They looked on religion as a particularly potent form of magic, not as a guide to conduct. And it must be said that many half-educated and politically ambitious bishops scarcely rose above this level themselves. Most of the Franks were Christians only in externals; it took a long time for the faith to sink into their hearts.

The Collapse of the Gothic Kingdoms

While the Franks were gaining control of Gaul and western Germany, their only possible rivals were being eliminated. After Theodoric's death, Justinian, the Roman emperor at Constantinople (see pp. 215–24), determined to conquer the Ostrogothic kingdom in Italy. It took him years of hard fighting, but by 552 the last resistance of the Ostrogoths had been snuffed out and a devastated Italy was re-

A page of a Merovingian book of the 8th century, from Reims. Note that the letters are not so legible as those of the Carolingian period (p. 247).

stored to imperial control. But Italy was too poor to contribute much to the emperor's treasury, and was so resentful of the restored bureaucracy and tax system that it proved a military liability rather than an asset. As a result, when, in the latter part of the sixth century, a new Germanic people, the Lombards, began to push into Italy from the Danube, a large part of the peninsula lay open to conquest. The imperial forces held on to the south and some outposts in the north, such as Ravenna and Venice; the Lombards took the rest. They extended their conquest somewhat during the next century, but they never subdued the whole peninsula; in fact, no one was able to unite Italy again until 1870. The Lombard kingdom, weak, divided, and far less influenced by Roman civilization than the Ostrogothic kingdom had been, posed no threat to the Franks and was eventually conquered by them in the eighth century.

The Visigothic kingdom of Spain lasted a little longer than the Ostrogothic. The Visigothic kings strengthened themselves by abandoning their Arian heresy and accepting Catholic Christianity. Justinian struck them only a glancing blow; he regained some of the southeast coast of Spain but never had enough resources to reconquer the whole peninsula. But for over a hundred and fifty years the Visigoths suffered all the usual troubles of Germanic kingdoms—disputed successions, weak control by the central government, and the rise of semi-independent local magnates. The Spanish terrain, with the many mountain ranges running across the country, encouraged these tendencies toward disunity. As a result, when a Moslem army crossed the Straits of Gibraltar in 711 (see p. 236) there was no effective resistance, and the Visigothic kingdom collapsed at once. A few Christians took refuge in the northern hills of Galicia and established a petty kingdom there. But the rest of the peninsula was drawn into an Arab empire and remained under Moslem control for centuries.

The Decline of the Merovingian Kings

Thus after the sixth century only one powerful state was left in western Europe —the Frankish kingdom. The Anglo-Saxons were divided into petty kingdoms; the Scandinavian monarchies were just beginning to take form; the Germans of the north and east, such as the Frisians and the Old Saxons, had almost no organization; and the Visigoths and the Lombards were weak and divided. But the apparent strength and solidity of the Frankish kingdom were deceptive. The Franks soon began to suffer from the same political ills as the other Germanic peoples;

their kingdom survived only because it was not seriously threatened by outside enemies. In Frankland, as elsewhere, the kings had found it difficult to establish any sort of central control, and political power was passing rapidly into the hands of the great landlords.

The landlords were also the local representatives of royal authority. The Frankish kingdom was divided into counties, each ruled by a count who collected the revenues, presided over the courts, and controlled the military forces of his district. The king supposedly could name counts as he saw fit, and in the sixth century men of poor families sometimes achieved the position. But once a man was a count he had many opportunities to amass wealth and to found a local dynasty. Moreover, other Frankish families became wealthy and powerful and began to push their claims to office. As the kings weakened, they lost more and more control over local government. By the eighth century counts could be selected only from a small group of well-to-do landowners, and many countships were in fact, if not in theory, hereditary.

The great landowners' virtual control over local government made them indispensable in the civil wars which regularly broke out in the Frankish realm. The Frankish kings treated their state as private property and regularly divided the kingdom among their sons. Just as regularly, one or more of the rival kings tried to eliminate his brothers and cousins and acquire their territories and treasuries. To gain support, he rewarded his own men, and bribed the retainers of his rivals, with grants of land and concessions of governmental power. These grants still further weakened royal authority. At the same time, assassination and civil war, inbreeding and vice, so shortened the lives of the kings that few of them reached middle age. Whatever powers they had left passed more and more into the hands of an official known as the mayor of the palace.

The Mayors of the Palace

Originally the mayor was merely the head of the royal household, the man who managed the king's private affairs. But the Germans made little distinction between public and private affairs and used any official for any business. Thus the mayor of the palace, who was always at court, gradually became a viceroy who acted for the king in all important matters. The mayor was usually a member of one of the great Frankish families and the head of a coalition of local magnates. In order to keep his place, he had to grant favors to his supporters just as the king had done.

Left. A Frankish brooch of the 7th century. Gold filigree with glass.

Center. Plaque in the shape of a cross. Frankish, 6th or 7th century.

Right. A Frankish fibula, or pin. Gold with garnets and red and blue paste, 7th century. Imaginary animals of this sort are typical of Germanic art of this period.

211

As a result, by 700 the Frankish kingdom was tottering. The last kings of the old Merovingian dynasty were puppets with little prestige and no authority. The Frankish lands had been split into an eastern, largely Germanic, kingdom called Austrasia, a western, more Latinized, kingdom named Neustria, and a much weaker southern kingdom of Burgundy. Southwest Gaul (Aquitaine) and southeast Germany (Bavaria) were practically autonomous. In each of the major kingdoms there was a mayor of the palace who was constantly threatened by rebellion among his own supporters and who constantly threatened his rival mayors with direct attacks and underhanded intrigues. There seemed to be little hope that the Frankish kingdom would avoid collapse.

Yet by 700 a remarkable family had appeared which was to reunite the Frankish kingdom and strengthen it so that within its shelter a new western European civilization could begin to take shape. This family, called Carolingian from its most famous member, Charlemagne, or Charles the Great (Carolus Magnus), came from the eastern Frankish kingdom of Austrasia. It gave strong support to the Church and especially to missionary and reform activities. It also showed remarkable skill in gaining and keeping the loyalty of the great landowners. With their support the head of the family, Pippin, made himself mayor of the palace in both Neustria and Austrasia late in the seventh century. A rebellion broke out when Pippin died, but after a few years of civil war his illegitimate son, Charles Martel (714–41), was accepted as mayor of all the Frankish kingdoms. With Charles Martel the old Frankish kingdom ended and all power was caught up by the Carolingian family. Although the Merovingian kings kept their empty title a few more years, they had no further influence on the course of events.

Suggestions for Further Reading

1. Theodoric, Boethius, and Cassiodorus

The life of one of the striking figures of the early Middle Ages is portrayed by T. Hodgkin, *Theodoric the Goth* (1891). Hodgkin writes in the "grand manner" of the nineteenth-century historian, and the book is still fresh. His *The Letters of Cassiodorus* (1886) contains the extensive correspondence of Cassiodorus and good biographical sketches of Cassiodorus and Boethius. A superior study of Cassiodorus and his monastic writings is *Introduction to Divine and Human Readings* (trans. L. W. Jones, 1946). Boethius' works are available in numerous translations. The most scholarly is in the *Loeb Classical Library* (trans. E. K. Rand and H. F. Stewart, 1918), but the Modern Library edition of Boethius' most famous work, *The Consolation of Philosophy* * (trans. W. V. Cooper, 1942), is more readable. Both E. R. Rand, *Founders of the Middle Ages* * (1928), and H. O. Taylor, *The Emergence of Christian Culture in the West* * (1901), discuss Cassiodorus and Boethius as "transmitters" of the Greco-Roman legacy. M. L. W. Laistner, *Thought and Letters in Western Europe, 500–900* (1931), combines fine scholarship with good style. Paul the Deacon's *History of the Langobards* (trans. D. Foulke, 1907) is our chief source for the Lombard kingdom of northern Italy.

* Available in paperback edition.

2. St. Benedict and the Monasteries

The cornerstone of monasticism in the West is the short *Rule of St. Benedict* (trans. J. McCann, 1952). The best scholarly study of the Rule is P. Delatte, *Commentary on the Rule of St. Benedict* (1908), but the more recent study by H. van Zeller, *The Holy Rule* (1958), is more interesting and more understandable to the modern student. C. Butler, *Benedictine Monachism* (1923), is valuable for an understanding of the spirit and meaning of the monastic life, and J. McCann, *St. Benedict* * (1952), gives a good account of St. Benedict and Benedictines through the centuries. A fascinating and provocative picture of monastic life today, in the form of a diary, is T. Merton, *The Sign of Jonas* * (1956). The classic work of William James, *Varieties of Religious Experience* * (1902), does a great deal to explain the "phenomenon" of monasticism in the perspective of modern civilization.

3. The Franks—Gregory of Tours

A shockingly vivid picture of the chaotic society of sixth-century Gaul is presented by the contemporary Gregory of Tours, *History of the Franks* (trans. E. Brehaut, 1916). This is our best evidence for the political and social condition of Merovingian Gaul. There is an excellent study of Gregory's language and its reflection of the decline of learning in the West in E. Auerbach, *Mimesis* * (1946). *The Life of St. Columban* (trans. D. C. Munro, 1921), reinforces Gregory of Tour's picture of moral decadence. F. Lot, *The End of the Ancient World* (1951), contains a scholarly study of Gaul under the Merovingians, with emphasis on political conditions. Lot includes a good recent bibliography. The older work of S. Dill, *Roman Society in Gaul in the Merovingian Age* (1926), concentrates on economic and social aspects.

4. The Conversion of the Anglo-Saxons

The Venerable Bede of Jarrow's *The Ecclesiastical History of the English Nation* * is incomparably the greatest authority we have for the early centuries of the English settlements. The best study of the life and works of Bede is the scholarly collection of essays edited by A. H. Thompson, *Bede: His Life, Times, and Writings* (1935). The classic poem *Beowulf* * (trans. D. Wright, 1957) is a mine of information about Anglo-Saxon society in the seventh and eighth centuries. D. Whitelock, *The Beginnings of English Society* * (1952), is a very good introductory treatment of the period, and G. O. Sayles, *The Medieval Foundations of England,* Chapters 1–3 (1948), is a "history of ideas in action" with an excellent and detailed critical bibliography. Much light has been shed on the Anglo-Saxon Church by S. J. Crawford, *Anglo-Saxon Influence on Western Christendom* (1933).

5. Gregory the Great

F. H. Dudden, *Gregory the Great,* 2 vols. (1905), the standard study of Gregory's pontificate, gives a good account of conditions in Italy at the time. Dudden pays special attention to the conversion of England. The increasing activities of the papacy under Gregory are shown in his letters in *Library of Nicene and Post Nicene Fathers,* Vols. XII and XIII (1895). *The Dialogues of St. Gregory the Great* (trans. E. G. Gardner, 1911), a collection of edifying stories of miracles and saints, illustrates the religious and intellectual climate of the times. *The Dialogues* is our chief source for the life of St. Benedict.

* Available in paperback edition.

8

Byzantium and Islam

The triumphant emperor, a large gold medallion of Justinian, struck after his early victories, ca. 534. Note the halo, which shows the emperor as a semisacred personage.

The first part of the Empire to be seriously threatened by the barbarian inroads of the fourth and fifth centuries was the East. The Visigoths crushed the army of the East Roman emperor at Adrianople as early as 378, and the Ostrogoths occupied the Balkans long before they moved on Italy. But the barbarian migrations, which profoundly altered the political and social pattern of the West, were only a passing episode in the history of the East. By 500 the Roman Empire in the West had vanished, while the Empire in the East was beginning a great revival which was to give it once more a strong government, a highly developed economy, and an active intellectual and artistic life.

The Eastern Roman Empire

This contrast shows once more that internal weaknesses rather than external attacks were the real cause of the collapse of the Roman Empire. In the West, where the internal weaknesses were greater and more pervasive, nothing could be done to save the Empire. But in the East there were strengths as well as weaknesses. The eastern cities were economic assets rather than parasites as they were in the West, for the active commerce they carried on reinforced the political bonds between the provinces. Christianity was both more widespread and more deeply felt in the East than in the West, and it served as a substitute for patriotism. The excellent defensive positions of the East made it possible for relatively small imperial forces to ward off dangerous attacks. Constantinople was impregnable, and the Germans were never able to touch the provinces of Asia Minor, Syria, and Egypt. Moreover, the eastern emperors and their advisers were somewhat more skillful—or at least more successful—politicians than their colleagues in the West. They prevented the Germans from making any permanent settlement in the Balkan Peninsula, and they freed themselves from dependence on barbarian soldiers by recruiting troops in the highlands of Asia Minor. Because they retained control of their richest provinces and because the great trading cities of Constantinople, Antioch, and Alexandria continued to flourish, the eastern emperors could always collect enough taxes to pay both their civilian officials and their soldiers. With the departure of the Ostrogoths for Italy and the weakening of the Huns, the Eastern Empire was freed from immediate danger. During the sixth century it was able to start the difficult task of readjusting its institutions and its way of life to the new situation that had arisen in the Mediterranean world.

Justinian

The leader of this first great revival of the Eastern Empire was the emperor Justinian (527–65), a man of ambition, energy, and imagination. In spite of his virtues, however, his stubborn determination in pursuing mistaken policies led him to waste resources, miss opportunities, and plunge the Empire into useless wars. He was successful in most of his projects, but a less successful ruler might have done less harm. Every success encouraged him to extend his commitments, so that by his death both the loyalty and the resources of his subjects had been nearly exhausted.

Justinian was not the sort of ruler one would expect to find in a state composed largely of Greeks, Syrians, and Egyptians. His uncle, the emperor Justin I, was a semiliterate soldier who had gained the throne more or less by accident after a disputed succession. The family came from the extreme west of what was left of the Empire, from a district near the Adriatic where Latin was still spoken. This Latin background may explain some of Jus-

tinian's policies. Fascinated by the idea of recovering the West, he was willing to sacrifice the people of the East in order to regain the old heart of the Empire. Justinian understood—though he did not always execute—what was necessary to conciliate the West, but he was far less understanding of his oriental subjects. In many ways he was the last of the Roman emperors. After his death the Latin tradition died out, Greek became the official language of the Empire, and the ties between East and West slackened.

Justinian was lucky in his immediate predecessors, for they had rebuilt the army, set the Empire's finances in order, and repaired its administrative system. He was even luckier in what seemed at the time to be a disastrous marriage. While he was still a young man, Justinian had fallen in love with a woman named Theodora, who had been the sixth-century equivalent of a strip-teaser in burlesque. She had had many lovers and apparently had no higher ambition than to gain wealth by seducing men of high rank. Marriage with such a woman was not only socially impossible; it was forbidden by law. But Justinian already controlled the government, since his uncle depended entirely on him in all matters of policy. So Justinian received permission to marry his mistress, and he never had cause to regret it. Theodora was a courageous woman who kept Justinian from fleeing early in his reign when he was threatened by a rebellion of the people of Constantinople. She was also an intelligent woman who understood the people of the East far better than her husband did; after her death he found it hard to retain their loyalty. Theodora, virtually a co-emperor, participated in making appointments to high office and in deciding policy.

Nevertheless, the basic pattern of the reign was set by Justinian. He was determined to restore the Empire, to regain its lost territories, to strengthen and reform its administrative system, and to rebuild its roads and cities. He always aimed high; he reached for the utmost in power and magnificence. Unfortunately, however, his resources were not always equal to his schemes, and his objectives had a regrettable tendency to conflict with one another.

Early in his reign Justinian set his mind on reconquering the West. The Germanic kingdoms on the Mediterranean, torn by quarrels among their ruling families and weakened by conflict between Arian Germans and Catholic Romans, seemed ready to collapse. Justinian's first campaigns were encouragingly successful. The Vandal kingdom of Africa fell after a short war in 533, and the Ostrogoths in Italy, left without a capable leader after the death of Theodoric, offered little resistance to the imperial army. In the end the tide of reconquest even reached far-off Spain, where Justinian seized a strip of the southeastern coast with little difficulty.

But these easy successes were deceptive; once Justinian had won control of the lands of the western Mediterranean he was beset by the same insoluble problems on which the Empire in the West had foundered in the fifth century. The Roman population of Italy, Spain, and Africa experienced no patriotic thrill on being reunited with the Empire; in fact, the reintroduction of the imperial tax system made many people long for the easier rule of the barbarians. Justinian tried to gain their loyalty

by accepting Roman religious dogmas and rejecting the views of a large part of the clergy of Syria and Egypt. But he succeeded only in alienating many of his eastern subjects without gaining solid support in Italy. Soon the West lapsed into its old

✺✺✺✺✺✺✺✺✺✺✺✺✺✺✺✺✺✺✺✺✺✺✺✺✺✺✺✺

A Byzantine Official Criticizes Justinian's Personal Rule

Procopius had served Justinian for many years and wrote a semi-official history of his wars in which he praised the emperor. But he was very conservative and was shocked by Justinian's innovations, his religious policies, and his heavy taxes. He took revenge by writing the *Secret History,* in which he accused Justinian and Theodora of injustice, extortion, maladministration and scandalous personal vices.

For in the administration of affairs it was a time of the greatest confusion and none of the customary procedures was maintained. . . . He [Justinian] neither himself possessed any quality appropriate to the imperial dignity, nor cared to foster any such quality in others, but in speech and in dress and in thinking he played the barbarian. And as to all the rescripts which he wished to have written from himself, he would not send them, as was the custom, to the . . . Quaestor to promulgate, but instead would generally insist on reading them out himself. . . . And the confidential secretaries . . . were not assigned the function of writing the Emperor's confidential matters . . . for he not only wrote practically everything himself, but also, whenever it became necessary to give instructions to the public arbitrators in the city, he would tell them in writing what course they must take. . . . For he would not allow anyone within the Roman Empire to give decisions on independent judgment. . . .

From Procopius, *Secret History,* trans. by H. B. Dewing (Cambridge, Mass.: Harvard U. Press, 1935), pp. 167–68.

✺✺✺✺✺✺✺✺✺✺✺✺✺✺✺✺✺✺✺✺✺✺✺✺✺✺✺✺

predicament. Justinian's rule was based on a small group of soldiers and bureaucrats; the bulk of the population was passive and took no part either in politics or in war.

The barbarians were quick to take advantage of the situation. The Vandals had been thoroughly crushed, but the Berbers, fierce tribesmen living on the fringes of the civilized area, took up the fight for Roman Africa. They pressed the imperial army hard, often bottling it up in fortified towns. After many years of fighting, the Berbers were pushed back, but they were not conquered. They continued to hold most of what is now Morocco and western Algeria, and remained a constant threat to the regions the Empire still ruled.

Justinian had even more trouble in holding Italy. There the Ostrogoths, who had been defeated but not broken, soon elected a new king who came very near to driving the imperial forces from the peninsula. Justinian never gave his Italian commanders enough troops, partly because so many other demands were being made on his resources and partly because he feared, like many a Roman emperor before him, that too successful a general might seek the throne for himself. As a result, the imperial army in Italy seldom numbered as many as twenty thousand men, and the war dragged on for eighteen years, from 535 to 553. In the end the Goths were almost exterminated, but Italy had been very nearly ruined. The two armies had driven each other up and down the peninsula, Rome had suffered a long and exhausting siege, and a large part of the population was destitute. Justinian retained Italy for the rest of his reign, but it added nothing to the strength or wealth of the Empire.

The same judgment could be passed on the whole policy of reconquest. None of the western provinces regained by Justinian was secure, either in a political or a military sense; most of them were lost within a generation or two after his death. Justinian had had to allow the Lombards to occupy the area between the Danube and the

The Mediterranean after Justinian's Reconquest *ca.* 560

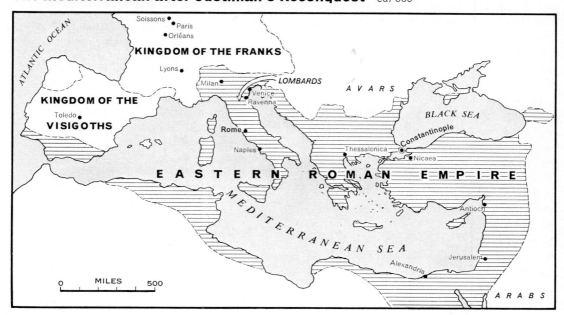

Alps, and shortly after his death they pushed through the mountain passes and settled in the Po Valley, to which they gave their name, Lombardy. Then they drove south until they had occupied most of the peninsula. Venice in its lagoons, Ravenna in its marshes, and Rome behind its walls held out for the emperor; otherwise all that was left of Justinian's conquest was the island of Sicily and the poverty-stricken provinces of the extreme south. The Spanish reconquest was just as ephemeral; by 624 the Visigoths had regained all the coastal territories they had lost. As for Africa, it stayed with the Empire a little longer, but fell to the Moslems at the very end of the seventh century.

Though Justinian took the offensive in the West, he was kept on the defensive in the East. The Persian kingdom, the ancient enemy of Rome, was once more growing in strength and was pressing hard on the eastern frontiers. On several occasions the Persians broke through the Roman defenses and plundered much of Syria and Asia Minor. Persian troops sacked the great commercial city of Antioch and pushed on to the Mediterranean and the Black Sea. With a large part of his army tied up in the West, Justinian was never able to defeat the Persians decisively, but through force of arms, diplomacy, and bribery he did manage to hold them in check. He had to cede a few outlying protectorates, but he retained all of Syria and western Asia Minor. The same pattern was repeated in the Balkans, where Hunnic groups staged one raid after another. The Slavs, an Indo-European language group, first became important at this time. Originating in western Russia, they spread out into territories abandoned by migrating Germans and frequently served the Huns as auxiliary troops. On some of these raids the Huns and their Slavic allies came very close to Constantinople, but none of the interior provinces were lost. Justinian was an expert at stirring up feuds within a tribe or between two tribes, and any group which threatened him soon found itself attacked by enemies at the rear. Thus he held on to most of the Balkan Peninsula, though he had to allow some of the Slavs to settle there. This was the beginning of Slavic predominance in the Balkans.

Justinian's policy in the East was not only cautious, which may have been sensible; it was also expensive. Diplomacy, bribes, and occasional payments of tribute to exceptionally dangerous enemies cost huge sums of money, but they did not end the necessity for maintaining an army and building fortifications. At the same time, many eastern provinces were devastated by raids and invasions and thus failed to pay their share of taxes.

Yet, burdened though he was by wars of conquest in the West and wars of defense in the East, Justinian did not spend the Empire's entire income on military operations. Restoration of the Empire meant more to him than territorial expansion; he was determined to restore the magnificence of Rome at the height of her power. The New Rome of Constantinople was to be even more splendid than Old Rome; provincial capitals were to reflect this splendor on a smaller scale; ports were to be improved and the great network of Roman roads restored. Justinian put as much energy into this program as he did into his wars, and the results were somewhat more lasting.

They were more lasting because he accepted eastern standards instead of trying to impose his own western, Latin prejudices. Classical Roman art and architecture had simply decayed in the West, but in the East they had been transformed under the joint impact of Christianity and the revival of oriental cultures. A new style

Justinian's church of St. Sophia, built between 537 and 562. Compare with St. Mark's and note how the windows in the dome here give a lighter effect. (The Turks covered the original mosaics with whitewash and hung up texts from the Koran.)

was already emerging when Justinian gained the throne, and he gave it a chance to express itself through his great building program. All through the Empire, from Mount Sinai in the Egyptian desert to Ravenna in reconquered Italy, magnificent churches rose, rich with mosaics, goldsmiths' work, and many-colored marble.

The architects of these churches, so far as we know their names, came from the Asiatic provinces, and the decoration was largely inspired by oriental examples. The important thing in the new churches was the interior, which blazed with light and color, rather than the exterior, which was often left rough and unadorned. In the famous church of St. Sophia in Constantinople, Justinian's architects built a great dome pierced with many windows high over the central part of the building. By solving the problem of setting a circular dome firmly atop a rectangular opening, they made the dome far more effective than before, both aesthetically and as a source of light. Earlier Roman architects had bolstered their domes with high walls which concealed it from view and blocked out the light. Even when Justinian's architects did not use the dome, they raised the walls of their churches and enlarged the window spaces in order to admit more light. And everywhere there was color— brilliant mosaics, gold and silver ornaments, richly woven textiles, polished stone of every hue. The decoration was stylized, symbolical, not at all realistic, but for this very reason it had a greater impact on the beholder. The endless ranks of saints and angels along the walls were clearly not human beings; rigid, solemn, and intense, these figures were unmistakably inhabitants of another world. And again and again, leading these lines of angels, appeared the figures of Justinian and Theodora, humble before their God, but haloed like saints and immeasurably superior to all other human beings. One of the emperor's most cherished titles was "Equal of the Apostles," and his churches gave visible support to this claim.

Religious Disputes

Justinian was certainly a sincere and pious Christian. But he was also something of a scholar with a dangerous taste for theology, and he ruled over subjects who would fight for a religious dogma when they would fight for nothing else. There had already been serious quarrels over basic articles of the faith before Justinian became emperor, and he probably could not have avoided interfering in religious matters even if he had so desired. But he did not so desire; instead, he wanted to use religion to unify the restored Empire, and he wanted to impose some of his own theological ideas on it. This was the old Roman tradition of caesaropapism; the emperor felt responsible for guiding and controlling the Church. His efforts failed, though he bullied popes, deposed patriarchs, and imprisoned monks and priests. At his death the Empire was still badly divided in its religious beliefs.

The basis of the controversy was the old argument about the union of the human

Interior of St. Mark's, Venice, 11th century. Compare this with the view of St. Sophia, which the Venetians copied but modified. Some of the lightness and spaciousness of the original was lost.

and divine in Jesus Christ. If Jesus was not fully divine, they reasoned, then the Redemption was impossible; if Christ was not fully human, then He did not suffer for us, and so the Crucifixion lost its meaning. Few people any longer took the extreme positions of "fully divine" or "fully human," but in trying to describe the way in which divine and human were joined together it was easy to overstress one or the other, and thus fall into heresy.

When Justinian took over the imperial government, the most dangerous heresy was that of the Monophysites. The name of this sect implies that the Monophysites believed in only one nature—that is, that Jesus was wholly and exclusively divine. But the name is somewhat unfair: Monophysite theologians recognized the existence of a human nature in Christ, but they subordinated it to the divine nature to such an extent that it became meaningless. In any case, those who supported and those who opposed the Monophysites were stirred by something more than a desire for precise theological definitions. Monophysitism had become the national religion of Egypt, and in Syria it probably had more adherents than any other sect. It gave the inhabitants of these lands a chance to voice their long-suppressed desire for cultural and spiritual independ-

Sant' Apollinare Nuovo, Ravenna, 6th century. Decorated under Theodoric the Ostrogoth, who employed Byzantine artists and imitated Byzantine style. The procession of saints and martyrs moves from Theodoric's palace (on the right) up the nave to the sanctuary. This is a good example of an early basilica, the type of church that was most common in western Europe during the early Middle Ages.

ence. It was anti-Greek, anti-Roman, anti-classical, and anti-West. The pope regarded the Monophysites as rebels against the truth which had been entrusted to Rome, and many officials of the imperial government regarded them as rebels against the authority of the emperor, God's lieutenant on earth.

Justinian's own personal beliefs were opposed to Monophysitism, and his political aims intensified his opposition. As we have seen, he wanted to recover the West, and the West, led by the pope, was almost unanimous in its rejection of Monophysite doctrine. Justinian's one source of strength in the West was his support of orthodox Catholicism against the Arian heresy, and he did not want to forfeit that strength by tolerating an equally dangerous eastern heresy. Early in his reign, therefore, Justinian persecuted the Monophysites and tried to suppress their teachings.

But in religion as in war, Justinian found that he could not concentrate exclusively on the West. Theodora, always far more understanding of eastern viewpoints than her husband, realized that his flat opposition to Monophysitism was endangering imperial control of Egypt and Syria. She probably had some personal inclinations toward the doctrine as well. Under her influence Justinian became somewhat more tolerant, but by so doing he stirred up protests among the orthodox in Rome and Constantinople. Finally, Justinian settled for an interpretation which was technically orthodox, but which leaned somewhat toward the Monophysite position.

No one was pleased with this solution. Pope Vigilius, who had come to Constantinople against his better judgment to confer with the emperor, refused at first to accept the compromise formula. He yielded only after a long period of house arrest and threats. The orthodox clergy of Constantinople were equally indignant, though

easier to deal with; Justinian simply dismissed them from their posts. And the Monophysites themselves, whom Justinian was trying to conciliate, found the new orthodox doctrine just as unacceptable as the old. They seceded from the official Church and formed their own religious organization, which was bitterly hostile to the government and to the orthodox, Greek-speaking clergy. Almost all Egyptians, and many Syrians, became members of this new Monophysite Church. This sharp division in religion helps explain the ease with which the Arabs took over most of the East in the next century (see p. 233). Syrians and Egyptians had no loyalty to an imperial government which denied their cultural identity by opposing their religious beliefs. They preferred to be ruled by tolerant Moslems rather than by intolerant and orthodox Greeks.

Justinian's Summary of Roman Law

Justinian's love of precise definition and exact scholarship, which led him into dangerous religious policies, found happier expression in the field of law. Perhaps his only two completely successful achievements were the building of St. Sophia and the codification of Roman law. The most impressive intellectual achievement of the Romans had been in law, and the keenest minds of the Empire had worked on legal problems. But this was the very reason that a codification was so badly needed; Roman law had developed over so many centuries that its basic rules had to be sought in voluminous official legislation, imperial edicts, and the opinions and commentaries of countless generations of lawyers. Even in the fourth century there had been several attempts to codify and digest Roman law. But no one had had the energy and the determination to survey the entire mass of legal literature and reduce it to manageable proportions.

Justinian attacked the problem of codifying the law with the same energy and the same ruthlessness with which he planned the reconquest of the West. At the very beginning of his reign he picked a group of capable men, of whom the most eminent was the great jurist Tribonian, and gave them a free hand to produce a statement of the law which would be brief, clear, and consistent. He must have put heavy pressure on them, for they completed the task with incredible speed. All the essential work was done between 528 and 534, and most of the significant amendments had been made by 546, the year of Tribonian's death.

The books produced by this effort came to be known collectively as the *Corpus Juris*. The first and most important unit was the *Digest,* a collection of extracts from the works of the leading Roman lawyers. By far the largest number of extracts came from the second century, the golden age of Roman law. They dealt with basic problems of jurisprudence, such as the nature of law and justice, and the relation between law and custom. But they also included brief statements on the guiding principles of Roman law in, for example, such matters as property, contract, and inheritance. The next book of the *Corpus Juris* was the *Code,* a restatement of statute law with the repetitious, contradictory, and obsolete provisions omitted. These two major works were followed by the *Institutes*, a textbook of Roman law for students, and the *Novels,* laws promulgated after 534 to amend or supplement the *Code.*

The speed with which the *Corpus Juris* was compiled led to some unfortunate results. Important material was omitted while insignificant, and even contradictory, statements were allowed to remain. Moreover, because the *Corpus Juris* was the only authorized version of Roman law, earlier works on the subject were neglected and lost. We have today only a handful of the thousands of volumes on Roman law written under the Empire. On the other hand, judging by what happened to Latin literary works, most of the legal writings would have been lost in any case, and the *Digest* did preserve much of the work of the ablest Roman lawyers.

Curiously, though the *Corpus Juris* was never applied as actual law in the West, it had a far greater effect on western countries than it did on the East. In the East the emperors continued to revise the laws, treating Justinian's work not as a final summary of legal thinking but only as a foundation for their own efforts. In the West the *Corpus Juris* was the last expression of Roman law, followed only by the incomplete and unsophisticated compilations of barbarian customs. For many generations the *Corpus Juris* was neglected; it survived only in a few rare manuscripts. But when the great expansion of medieval civilization began in the late eleventh century (see Chapter 10), Justinian's work seemed a treasure beyond price. It gave men who were struggling with primitive and confused notions of social relationships the precise concepts of a highly developed legal system. It had a tremendous impact on both state and Church, on both private and public institutions. The *Corpus Juris* became an essential part of the western intellectual tradition and affected the law of every western European country. Justinian's real reconquest of the West came many centuries after his death, not through his armies but through his law.

From Eastern Roman to Byzantine Empire

It is well to remember this ultimate triumph of Justinian, for the immediate results of his reign were disastrous. His successors ranged from mediocre to despicable, but even an able emperor would have found it difficult to cope with the legacy of bankruptcy, internal discontent, and external enmity which Justinian had left. Repeated rebellions made it impossible to guard the frontiers. The western conquests, as we have seen, were gradually eaten away by Lombards, Berbers, and Visigoths. In the East the Persians again started a great assault on the Asian provinces of the Empire. And a new danger arose in the North: the Avars, a nomad people akin to the Huns, crossed the lower Danube, pillaged the Balkan provinces, and threatened Constantinople itself. With the Avars came the Slavs, who took advantage of the weakened imperial government to occupy permanently large areas of the Balkans. They even penetrated Greece, though scholars still disagree about the size and the importance of the Slavic settlements there.

Early in the seventh century the plight of the Eastern Empire seemed hopeless. The Persians had taken Syria and Egypt and had occupied large areas of Asia Minor. The Avars were moving freely through the Balkans and had set up permanent camps close to Constantinople. Most of the land and most of the man power of the Empire were under foreign domination. But the Eastern Empire clung to life with amazing tenacity and showed marvelous powers of recuperation. Under the appearance of luxury and decadence, behind the intrigues and the factional quarrels, was a very hard core of administrative competence, diplomatic skill, military capacity, and a passionate loyalty among the people of Constantinople to their state and their religion. In the seventh century, as it would again and again in the future, the Empire rallied and beat off its enemies.

Heraclius, who became emperor in 610, slowly worked out a policy of keeping the Avars quiet by diplomatic means while throwing the bulk of his army against the Persians. He had little success at first, and some of the greatest Persian victories were won early in his reign. Fortunately for him, however, there was little cooperation between Persians and Avars. By the time they made a coordinated attack on Constantinople in 626, the Persians had become so weakened that their army in Asia Minor was of little help to the Avars. Heraclius held off the Avars, and resumed his campaigns against the Persians. He finally ended the war with a great raid deep into Persian territory and forced the Persians to make peace in 628.

The half-century of civil and foreign war which followed the death of Justinian wrought profound changes in the character of the Eastern Roman Empire. In the first place, the Latin element in the Empire, which had long been weakening, almost vanished. The Latin-speaking regions of the Empire were the first to be lost to the new waves of invaders; by 600 there were almost no important groups in the administration or the army who spoke or even wrote the language. Early in his reign Justinian had used Latin for the *Corpus Juris,* but by the time of his death Greek was the only language which could be used for administrative and legal purposes. In the second place, Justinian's successors were unable either to conciliate or to protect the inhabitants of Syria and Egypt. The religious split grew even deeper, and the long period of Persian occupation and raiding did nothing to strengthen the loyalty of Syrians and Egyptians to Constantinople.

The heart of the Empire was now the Greek-speaking, religiously orthodox region centering around Constantinople. The city itself supplied the wealth, the educated classes supplied the administrative personnel, and the poorer part of the population supplied the politico-religious fervor which kept the Empire going. But one more thing was needed, an army, and the best recruiting ground for soldiers was Asia Minor. Therefore a successful emperor had to hold Constantinople, the region around the Bosporus and the Dardanelles, and enough of Asia Minor to maintain his military strength. If he could manage all this, the Empire would stand virtually unbeatable. Heraclius seems to have had some understanding of this principle; at least he made little effort to hold the northern and western Balkans and postponed the reconquest of Syria until he had gained access to the old recruiting grounds in eastern Asia Minor.

But an empire based on Constantinople and Asia Minor was no longer a Roman Empire, even though the name continued in official use. To mark the change, most historians have called the continuation of the Roman Empire in the East the Byzantine Empire. This term, derived from the old Greek name for Constantinople (Byzantium), emphasizes the importance of the capital city and the Greek-speaking element in the Empire. It should not be used, therefore, for the fifth-century Empire, which was still Mediterranean in outlook and largely non-Greek in population. It becomes increasingly appropriate during the seventh century, however, when Syria, Egypt, and North Africa were lost, and when the Empire was restricted to the eastern Balkans, Asia Minor, and a few districts in Italy.

The Byzantine Empire gradually developed patterns of behavior and organization which made it very different from the countries of western Europe. In religion, for example, slight differences in creed, organization, and ritual between the Christians of the West and those of Constantinople were magnified by quarreling theologians, ambitious rulers, and subjects who feared everything foreign. The Roman Catholic Church and the Greek Orthodox Church slowly drifted apart, a divergence that encouraged divergences in other fields.

But religion alone does not account for all the profound differences between the Byzantine Empire and its neighbors. More than any other state, it preserved the cultural traditions of Greece and the political techniques of the old Roman Empire. Not that the Byzantine Empire was a stag-

Page from the Rossano Gospel, Byzantine, 6th century, gold letters on purple vellum. Above are drawings of the Last Supper and Jesus washing the feet of the Apostles; below are the four Evangelists.

nant society. It showed marvelous skill and flexibility in adapting itself to new conditions, and this is precisely why it was able to preserve so much of its heritage. The Byzantine Empire never had to make an entirely fresh start, for it was always able to modify and thus retain its old ideas and institutions. It always possessed a highly trained bureaucracy, an effective tax system, and a sophisticated and flexible legal system. Its diplomacy, its military organization, and its administrative hierarchy were carefully planned and consciously directed toward long-range objectives. The government regulated economic activity and exercised considerable control over the Church. Since the Byzantine emperors, like their Roman predecessors, encouraged art, literature, and scholarship, there was no break of any kind in the Greek literary and artistic tradition.

In short, the Byzantine Empire stood forth as a highly centralized and autocratic state at a time when the very concept of the state had almost been forgotten in western Europe. It was a state with a great urban center, an active commercial life, and a sophisticated literary and artistic tradition at a time when the society of western Europe was largely agricultural and illiterate. Either Augustus or Louis XIV would have understood and sympathized with many of the ideas and practices of the Byzantine Empire, but few western Europeans between 700 and 1400 could fathom the Byzantine way of life.

The breach between Byzantium and the Caliphate, which took over Syria, Egypt, Armenia, and Palestine (see p. 233), was not so great, for the Arabs inherited many of the political and intellectual traditions of the old Eastern Empire. But the difference in religion prevented close and enduring intellectual contacts, for the Arabs had accepted the new religion of Mohammed. Moreover, Arabic scholars were more interested in Aristotle and the Greek scientific tradition, while Byzantine scholars emphasized Plato and the Greek literary tradition. There were interesting similarities between the Arab Empire and the Byzantine Empire, but the Arab Empire soon broke up into warring and short-lived states. No Mohammedan state endured as long as Byzantium or created such a permanent bureaucracy. Thus the Byzantine Empire gradually became unique, and it soon began to glory in its uniqueness. Like their remote ancestors of the fifth century B.C., the Greeks of Constantinople believed that they were the only civilized people and that their neighbors—especially their European neighbors—were barbarians. Caught between the barbarous West and the infidel East, the Byzantines clung with increasing tenacity to their government, their culture, and their religion.

Mohammed and the Rise of the Arab Empire

A few years after the death of Justinian in 565 a child was born in Arabia who was to found a religion which spread more rapidly than Christianity and an empire which was larger than that of Rome at the height of its power. Few men have had a greater impact on history than Mohammed; his religion changed the civilizations of the Mediterranean, the Middle East, and South Asia, and his influence is felt today in a broad belt of territory stretching from West Africa to the East Indies. Mohammedanism was the last of the three great world religions to emerge, and for many centuries it was more vigorous than either of its rivals—Christianity in the West and Buddhism in the East.

The Early Arabs

Arabia had played no important role in history before the time of Mohammed.

The huge peninsula, about one-third the size of the United States, was a great, arid wedge driven into the fertile lands of the Middle East. The only moisture was in a small belt of land in the extreme south, which was touched by the monsoon rains, and a few oases which tapped underground water channels. Elsewhere a little land could be cultivated by means of elaborate systems of dams and irrigation ditches. Many of these irrigation systems had broken down by the time of Mohammed, largely as a result of the political and social instability caused by constant warfare. Most Arabs were nomads, driving their herds from one scanty patch of vegetation to another. A much smaller, but very influential, group was made up of traders who dealt in products of the southern part of the peninsula, notably frankincense, which was in great demand in the Mediterranean world, and in goods imported from East Africa, India, and the Far East. These merchants, regarding the Red Sea as very dangerous, customarily sent their goods overland through Arabia to Egypt and Syria. This overland trade had declined during the Roman period, when goods were often landed on the Egyptian rather than the Arabian side of the Red Sea. Enough of it persisted, however, to support a few small towns along the southern and western sides of the peninsula.

The early Arabs were thus in touch with all the great eastern civilizations and had learned something from all of them. Semites themselves, they had been most influenced by the Semitic peoples who lived in the fertile crescent north of the peninsula. They had a system of writing, related, at least indirectly, to the Phoenician alphabet. They had the usual Semitic interest in religion, though in their case it was expressed in almost indiscriminate polytheism. They had invented or borrowed hundreds of gods; they knew many Jewish legends and some elements of the Christian story. They gave great honor to poets, and the ideal Arab leader was as ready to make verses as he was to make war. They knew a good deal about astronomy, for knowledge of the stars was as helpful in crossing the desert as it was in navigating the seas. At their best, the Arabs were imaginative, eager to learn, and quick to absorb new knowledge. They were far more ready to profit from Greco-Roman civilization than the Germans were when they entered the Empire.

And yet there were grave defects in the social and political organization of the early Arabs. The nature of the country forced them to live in small scattered tribes, and each tribe was almost constantly at war with its neighbors. Occasionally they formed coalitions in order to plunder the frontier areas of the Roman Empire or the Persian kingdom, but these coalitions seldom lasted more than a generation. The leading families within each tribe were often jealous of each other, and blood-feuds were frequent and persistent. Although these feuds were sometimes settled by arbitration, there was no regularly organized judicial system. Weaker members of each tribe, and indeed of each family, were harshly treated by their stronger relatives. Sickly or superfluous children, especially girls, were often killed, and orphans had little hope of receiving their parents' property. Women had almost no rights; their fathers or their husbands controlled their lives and their property. Men who could afford it had many wives and could divorce any of them whenever they wished. The divorced woman was usually left without any property or regular income.

But even with all this disunity and bickering, there were certain strong ties which bound the Arabs together. They were great genealogists, and the leaders of many tribes could trace their ancestry back to the same ancient families—families that were known and respected throughout Arabia. The Arabs' admiration for brave fighters and capable military leaders sometimes meant that the reputation of a particularly outstanding man would spread far beyond his own tribe. Finally, most of the tribes accepted a few common religious observances. There was a sacred period in each year, for example, when fighting was suspended and when many Arabs made a pilgrimage to the religious center of Mecca, a trading town near the west coast. In Mecca was the Kaaba, an ancient building full of images, including one of Christ. Here almost every god known to the Arabs could be worshiped. Here, too, was the sacred Black Stone which came from heaven, the most venerated object in the Arab world. This habit of worshiping together at Mecca was the strongest unifying force in Arabia, and one that was carefully preserved by Mohammed.

Mohammed's Teaching

Mohammed was born about 570 in Mecca. We know little about his early years, except that he was a poor orphan. When he reached adolescence he began to work for his cousin, a rich widow named Khadija. In her service he made many caravan trips, during which he may have accumulated his information about the Jewish and Christian religions and his knowledge of the legends and traditions of other Arab tribes. He eventually married his employer, though she was considerably older, and the marriage gave him the wealth and leisure to meditate on religious problems.

Like many other Arabs, Mohammed had a sensitive mind, a deep appreciation of the wonders of nature, and a strong interest in religion. These qualities were enhanced by mysterious seizures, to which he had been subject since childhood. Dur-

The Kaaba of Mecca, the building which houses the sacred Black Stone. It is covered with a black drapery which is renewed every year. The lighter band across the drapery is made up of texts from the Koran.

ing these attacks he showed some of the symptoms of a man in a violent fever. He was completely unconscious of what he said and seemed to be struggling to express ideas which were not yet fully formed in his own mind. He gradually came to believe that this was God's way of trying to communicate with him, but until he was about forty he had no clear idea of what he was meant to do. Then he had his first definite revelation: a vision of the angel Gabriel who commanded him to speak "in the name of the Lord, the Creator . . . the Lord who taught man what he did not know."

Mohammed was still doubtful about his mission, but as revelation succeeded revelation he became filled with the vision of the one, eternal God, the Lord of the world. He began to appeal to his fellow citizens of Mecca to abandon their host of false deities and to worship the one, true God. These early revelations bear some resemblance to the Psalms, both in their poetic quality and in their appeal to the wonders of nature as proofs of God's greatness and mercy. The stars in the heavens, sunshine and rain, the fruits of the earth—"all are signs of God's power if you would only understand."

By now Mohammed was convinced that he was a prophet, the last and greatest in the succession of prophets whom God had sent to enlighten and save mankind. He never claimed to be more than a prophet, asserting repeatedly, "I am nothing more than a man." He even denied that he could work miracles, though he admitted that some of his predecessors had had this gift. He also admitted the divine mission of the Jewish prophets and of Jesus, though he claimed that their teachings had been distorted or misinterpreted. But he was quite certain that the revelations that he

✥✥✥✥✥✥✥✥✥✥✥✥✥✥✥✥✥✥✥✥✥✥✥✥✥✥✥✥✥✥✥

An Early Revelation to Mohammed

By the brightness of the morning, and by the night when it groweth dark, thy Lord hath not forsaken thee, neither does he hate thee. Verily, the life to come shall be better for thee than this present life, and thy Lord shall give thee a reward wherewith thou shalt be well pleased. Did he not find thee an orphan, and hath he not sheltered thee? Did he not find thee in error and hath he not guided thee to the truth? And did he not find thee needy and hath he not enriched thee? Wherefore, oppress not the orphan nor repulse the beggar, but declare the goodness of thy Lord.

From *The Koran*, Ch. 93, trans. by G. Sale (Philadelphia: Lippincott, 1874).

✥✥✥✥✥✥✥✥✥✥✥✥✥✥✥✥✥✥✥✥✥✥✥✥✥✥✥✥✥✥✥

himself received superseded everything which had come before. The earlier prophets had had glimpses of the true religion, but he alone had received the complete message. Their teachings were to be accepted only when they agreed with the final word of God which had been revealed to him.

Mohammed at first made little progress in converting his countrymen. His wife, Khadija, believed in him and comforted him when he was despondent, and his cousin Ali was one of his first converts. But the other Meccans of good family were hostile; except for Abu-Bekr, Othman, and Omar, most of his early followers were poor men or slaves. Mohammed's attacks on idols angered the prosperous citizens of Mecca, who believed that the prosperity of their city depended on the fact that it was the center of worship of all the known gods. Mohammed's followers were persecuted and his own life was threatened. Finally he fled with his supporters to the city of Yatrib, some distance north of Mecca. The Mohammedan era begins with this flight, or Hegira, which took place in 622 A.D.*

Mohammed was welcomed in Yatrib, which was renamed Medinet-en-Nabi (Medina), the City of the Prophet. Jewish influence was strong there, and the Arabs of Medina found nothing strange in Mohammed's doctrine of a single, all-powerful God. Mohammed hoped to persuade the Jews and their followers that he was the successor of the Jewish prophets. The attempt failed, and caused a good deal of bad feeling between the Jews and the exiles from Mecca. But Mohammed soon gained so many converts among the pagan and

* This does not mean that dates of the Mohammedan era can be converted to our reckoning simply by adding 622 years. The Moslem year is based on a lunar calendar, and so does not coincide with ours. 1960 A.D. is 1379 A.H.

half-Jewish Arabs that Jewish opposition became ineffectual.

Mohammed, now virtually the ruler of a large community, became involved in all sorts of political problems, and the revelations he received during this period dealt largely with law and government. For example, it was at Medina that the rules about marriage, inheritance, and punishment of criminals were laid down.

During the stay at Medina, Mohammed's reputation and power increased steadily. He led a simple, frugal life; he fed the poor and comforted the afflicted; he inspired fanatical devotion among his followers. A desultory war between Medina and Mecca gradually became more serious, and by 630 Mohammed had gained so many supporters that he was able to capture Mecca with little difficulty. He immediately destroyed the idols in the Kaaba, except for the Black Stone, and made the temple the center of his religion. He had long asserted that the Kaaba had been built by Abraham and that Abraham had placed the heavenly Stone there as a sign of God's power. Thus he was able to preserve Mecca as the religious center of Arabia.

The fall of Mecca convinced many Arabs that Mohammed really was a prophet, or at least that he was too strong to oppose. During his last years, most of the tribes of the peninsula acknowledged his spiritual and political leadership. Nevertheless, when Mohammed died in 632 Arabia was far from being a unified state, and many Arabs had only vague ideas about the religion they had accepted.

The Koran

Mohammed, however, had left behind the Koran, a collection of his revelations. He taught that the Koran was God's guide for the human race, that it had always existed in heaven, but that no one had been worthy of receiving it before his own appearance on earth. Though he had received it piece by piece, as circumstances made it applicable, it formed a consistent and coherent whole. It contained all that man needed to know, and it was to be followed without question. Mohammed said: "Let the Koran always be your guide. Do what it commands or permits; shun what it forbids."

From the very start of his mission Mohammed's followers had carefully preserved his revelations. They had written down his words on anything that was avail-

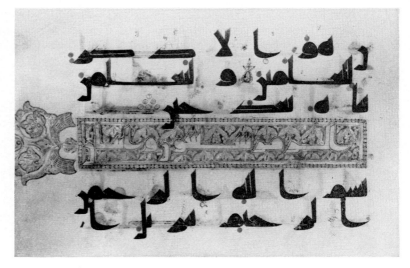

Page of a Koran, Egypt, 8th or 9th century. The chapter heading (in the middle) is white on gold; the text is brown with red diacritical marks. A fine specimen of an ornamental Arabic script.

able—parchment, palm leaves, bones, even stones. The task of sorting out and arranging this confused and scattered mass of sayings was begun soon after Mohammed's death by Abu-Bekr, but his version was not universally accepted. Othman, who ruled the Mohammedans from 644 to 656, ended the disputes by compiling an authoritative version and ordering all other collections destroyed. Othman's version has remained almost unchanged down to the present day.

In no other major religion was there such early agreement on the official version of the founder's teachings. In fact, the Koran was put together so hurriedly that it seems somewhat confused and illogical to a non-Mohammedan. The first revelation, in which Mohammed was ordered to begin his mission, comes in Chapter 96, only after many of the long, prosaic Medina passages. Seemingly repetitious and even contradictory statements were never harmonized, and many trivial remarks were preserved. But these faults are not admitted by orthodox Moslems, who consider the Koran a masterpiece of Arabic literature as well as the ultimate word of God to man.

The religion taught in the Koran was easy to understand and easy to follow. The basic creed was simple: "There is no God but Allah and Mohammed is his prophet." The faithful must also believe in the resurrection and the day of judgment, when every man will be rewarded according to his merits. The Mohammedan hell was very like the Christian one, but the Mohammedan paradise was unmistakably Arabian—a green garden full of running water and fruit trees with beautiful damsels to wait on the souls in bliss. Finally, the Koran emphasized predestination. "Every man's fate have We bound around his neck"—that is, all human events have been determined, once and for all, by the will of God. Mohammed's own name for his religion was Islam—"submission to the will of God"—and his followers were called Moslems—"those who submit."

The principal religious practices of Islam were as simple as its theology. Every Moslem was to pray five times a day and to fast during the daylight hours of the month of Ramadan. Alms-giving was a religious duty. As one of Mohammed's successors said: "Prayer carries us halfway to God, fasting brings us to his palace, and alms gain us admission." Finally, every believer was to make a pilgrimage, if possible, to Mecca. But "only he shall visit the Mosque of God who believes in God and the Last Day, and is constant in prayer, and gives alms and fears God alone."

The Koran forbade wine-drinking and gambling, and a dietary law, somewhat like that of the Jews, banned certain foods, especially pork. There was also a rudimentary code of law designed to check the selfishness and violence which had prevailed among the Arabs. Arbitration was to take the place of the blood-feud, infanticide was condemned, and elaborate rules of inheritance safeguarded the rights of orphans and widows. Mohammed also made an effort to improve the position of women, ruling that no man might have more than four wives. Though divorce was still easy, the divorced wife could no longer be sent away penniless. These and other provisions were enough to furnish a framework for the early Mohammedan judicial system. Later, however, as Mohammedan society became more complex, the Koran proved inadequate and additional laws had to be devised by Moslem rulers.

There were obvious resemblances between Mohammedanism and Christianity, especially between Mohammedanism and the Christian heresies which denied or minimized the divinity of Christ. Since

Abu-Bekr — unified
Omar → began conquests
Othman — assassinated
Ali — was
Ommiad
dynasty

Mohammed admitted that Jesus was a major prophet, many of these heretics could accept Islam without feeling that they had greatly changed their beliefs. Other unorthodox Christians in Asia and Africa were so angered by their persecution by the Greek Church that they turned to Mohammedanism as a lesser evil. In the long run, many of these people were converted to Islam. And in the competition for the loyalty of outlying groups who had little knowledge of either religion, Mohammedanism had a great advantage. It needed no organized church, for it had neither a priesthood nor a sacramental system. Each individual had to assure his salvation by his own right belief and good conduct. Every essential act of the religion could be accomplished by a man living quite by himself. It was customary for the faithful to meet together for prayers, especially on Friday, and from the earliest period certain men devoted themselves to explaining the Koran. But neither the assembly nor the theologian was essential; anyone could accept Islam without waiting for the organization of a religious community, and any believer could preach the faith without waiting for the coming of an ordained priest. Simple and uncomplicated monotheism was easier to explain than the doctrines of the Trinity.

These advantages often gave Mohammedanism the victory in competition with Christianity. On several occasions in the Middle Ages the Mohammedans were able to move in and convert a kingdom while the Christians were still trying to recruit a troop of missionary priests. And even today Mohammedanism is spreading more rapidly among the peoples of Asia and Africa than is Christianity.

The Caliphate

Since Mohammed had left no very clear instructions about the choice of a successor, at his death there was confusion in the ranks of his followers and rebellion on the part of recently converted tribes. The faithful finally decided to choose a caliph, or successor to the prophet, who would act as both spiritual and political leader of Islam. The first caliph was Abu-Bekr, one of the earliest and most pious of Mohammed's converts. Though he ruled only two years (632–34), he succeeded in suppressing the revolts and in completing the unification of Arabia. Under his successor, Omar (634–44), the great conquests of Islam began. The Arabs had long been in the habit of raiding their wealthier neighbors to the north. Now they found themselves united for the first time, while both the Byzantine and Persian states had been weakened by the disastrous wars which had begun under Justinian and had continued into the reign of Heraclius. Moreover, the non-Greek subjects of Byzantium were disgusted by the religious policy of the government and gave it little support. The first probing attacks of the Arabs met such slight resistance that they soon turned to wars of conquest. Their defeat of a Byzantine army at the Yarmuk River in 636 determined the fate of all the eastern provinces. Some fortified towns held out for a few years, but by 649 the Arabs had conquered Syria, Armenia, Palestine, and Egypt. Persia gave even less trouble and was completely in Arab hands by 642. At the same time the Arabs built a fleet with which they won control of the eastern Mediterranean. Only the outbreak of civil war in Arabia slowed this first wave of conquest.

The civil war was caused by bad feeling between the early converts and some of the leading Arab families who had accepted Islam only after Mohammed's triumph was assured. The trouble began under the caliph Othman (644–656), who was an early convert himself, but who was

The Growth of the Islamic Caliphate 632-750

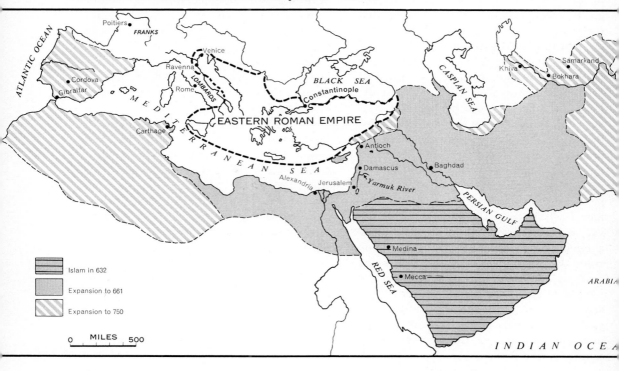

Islam in 632

Expansion to 661

Expansion to 750

MILES
0   500

not as fanatically opposed to the latecomers as were some of the prophet's other companions. He was accused of favoring recent converts in filling political positions, and especially of pushing forward his kinsmen, the Ommiads, who had at one time led the Meccan opposition to Mohammed. The accusation was largely true, but it is hard to see what else Othman could have done. He now had an empire to govern, and he needed the help of every man who displayed qualities of leadership, whatever his past religious behavior had been. Many of the early converts were more distinguished for their faith than for their political ability, and in any case there were not enough of them to do the work that had to be done.

Bad feeling between the two factions led to the assassination of Othman in 656. He was succeeded by the old believer, Ali, the son-in-law and adopted son of Mohammed. But, since Ali did nothing to punish his predecessor's murderers, he was suspected of having been an accomplice. The Ommiads soon revolted and secured the nomination of one of their family as caliph. Ali held Persia and Mesopotamia for a while but was assassinated in 661 by a member of a small, fanatical sect which believed that the office of caliph was unnecessary. After Ali's death the Ommiad caliph, who had not been involved in the assassination, was accepted as ruler by the entire Mohammedan world.

The Ommiad Dynasty

The first Ommiad caliph transferred the capital of the Arab Empire from Mecca to Damascus. This act was typical of the family, which put far more emphasis on politics than on religion. Damascus was not the prophet's city, but it had public buildings, a large group of educated and experienced civil servants, and a central location. It was far more satisfactory as a capital than Mecca, and it had the additional advantage of containing few of the prophet's early companions. The Ommiads bestowed key positions on members of the Arab aristocracy rather than on the old believers, and they filled the government bureaus with Christian Syrians and Egyptians. Thus the Arab Empire began to change from a loosely organized theocracy into a centralized state employing many of the Byzantine administrative techniques. Finally, the office of caliph ceased to be elective and was made hereditary in the Ommiad family.

The policy of the Ommiads toward the religion of conquered peoples was also based on purely political considerations. The Arabs had never paid taxes, and they had no intention of doing so now that they were lords of a large part of the civilized world. The government was financed by tribute exacted from unbelievers, which meant that mass conversions were a threat to its financial stability. So, instead of forcing Islam on their subjects, the Ommiad caliphs adopted a harsh policy toward new converts, imposing on them a heavy land tax from which Arabs were exempt and seldom granting them responsible positions in the government. In fact, men who remained Christian had a better chance of attaining high office than did those who accepted Islam.

This policy pleased the Arab aristocracy, which was enabled to retain its special privileges, and caused little trouble in Syria, where the Christians were numerous and relatively well treated. It was several centuries before Islam became the dominant religion in this area, and even

then large Christian groups continued to exist along the Mediterranean coast. But in Persia and Mesopotamia, where Ommiad control was less secure, most of the population became converted to Islam. They resented their inferior position and often revolted against the rule of the Ommiad officials. They were encouraged in this resistance by the more pious Arabs, who felt that the Ommiads were far too worldly, and by survivors of the faction which had supported Ali.

Most of the people of Syria and Egypt, however, welcomed Ommiad rule. They had never really accepted Greek domination, even though it had lasted almost a thousand years. During the centuries of Hellenistic and Roman rule they had preserved many of their old habits of life and thought, and they found that they had much more in common with the Arabs than with their former rulers. Ommiad justice was at least as good as that of the Byzantine Empire, and taxes were probably lower. Constantinople no longer meddled with the Syrian and Coptic (Egyptian) churches, and the leaders of these communities had a better opportunity to obtain government positions than they had ever had before. The Ommiads, who showed little religious prejudice, were perfectly willing to profit from the skills of all their subjects.

Cooperation between conqueror and conquered was greater in the Arab Empire than in the Germanic kingdoms of the West. The Arabs showed more understanding of the civilization they had taken over than did the Germans, and they made a greater effort to put it to good use. And the civilization of the East was far more useful than that of the West. Syria, the heart of the Ommiad state, had always been more advanced intellectually and economically than Gaul, the heart of the Frankish state. Making the most of their opportunities, the Ommiads began to draw on their heritage from the older civilizations of the East almost as soon as they gained power. They organized their administrative services on Roman and Persian models. They welcomed scholars of all nationalities to their court, and urged them to undertake the great task of translating philosophical, scientific, and medical works into Arabic. They built impressive mosques at Damascus and Jerusalem, adapting Syrian architecture to the needs of the Mohammedan religion. A new civilization began to grow up around the Ommiad court, a civilization based on Greek, Syrian, Egyptian, and Persian traditions, and yet with a style and a spirit of its own. This new civilization reached its peak only after the Ommiads had lost the throne and the capital had been moved from Damascus to Baghdad. Much of the work of the Ommiads was either absorbed in or surpassed by the accomplishments of their successors. But the Ommiads laid the foundations, and they did so at a time when western kings had almost no administrative services, when western scholars had almost no tools but compendia and epitomes, and when western architects showed almost no skill in designing monumental buildings.

New Conquests

The efficiency and energy of the Ommiad government soon made it possible to undertake further conquests. In the East they took Khiva, Bokhara, and Samarkand, thus gaining control of one of the oldest and most important trade routes in Eurasia—the silk road from China. They also occupied Afghanistan and the valley of the Indus, thereby creating a threat to India—a threat that was realized in invasion after invasion during the next thousand years.

In the West the Arabs advanced steadily along the southern shore of the Mediter-

ranean. North Africa was their first objective, and here, as often before, the invaders profited from the hatred of the native population for Byzantine government. Justinian's reconquest of the Vandal kingdom had been followed by heavy taxation and by persecution of heretics, and many of the Romanized Africans had either lost all influence or had fled the country. The Berbers, natives who were only superficially Romanized, became more and more independent and paid little attention to the orders of Byzantine officials. When the Arab attack came, both the Roman cities and the Berber countryside resisted bravely, but there was little cooperation between them. The hard-fighting Arabs triumphed over their divided enemies, taking Carthage in 697 and winning control of the entire North African coast by 708.

Although the Berbers had fought fiercely to preserve their independence, they had no particular antipathy to Islam. Many of them became converts and joined the victorious army in the hope of sharing in the spoils of the next conquest. This addition to their strength enabled the Arabs to pass over into Spain. The Visigothic rulers of Spain, only slightly more capable than the last Merovingians in Gaul, had never managed to control their powerful nobles and had never won the loyalty of the common people. A single victory in 711 was enough to open the whole country to Tarik, who commanded the invading forces, and from whom Gibraltar takes its name.* The largest part of his army was probably composed of Berbers, and now many Visigothic nobles joined the victors —an illustration of the Arabs' ability to gain the cooperation of conquered peoples in a remarkably short time. There were never enough Arabs to fill the armies of Islam, and the great conquests of the

---

* *Gebel Tarik*—Tarik's hill.

Mohammedans would have been impossible had it not been for the support of thousands of non-Arabs.

The Mohammedan army rapidly overran the entire Iberian Peninsula except for the extreme northwest, where a few Christians maintained their independence. The Mohammedans then pushed on across the Pyrenees into the Frankish kingdom, which was not quite so helpless as Spain. The Franks could not defend the south, but when the raiders pushed north Charles Martel, the mayor of the palace, assembled an effective army with which he stopped the Mohammedans. Charles' victory at Poitiers in 732 was not very decisive, for the Mohammedans withdrew in good order and held towns in southern Gaul for another thirty years. But they made no more raids on the north. The Mohammedan failure to advance farther into Gaul was due chiefly to a shortage of man power caused by a Berber revolt in North Africa. By the time they had replenished their forces, Charles Martel and his son Pippin had so strengthened the Frankish state that the Mohammedans could not renew their attack.

The early years of the eighth century saw the high-water mark of Ommiad power. They had created the largest Moslem state which ever existed and in less than a hundred years they had built an empire greater than that of Rome. But they had reached their limit; their setback at Poitiers in 732 matched their earlier failure to take Constantinople in the great siege of 716–17. Though the Byzantine Empire had lost almost all its outlying provinces, it had preserved the most vital part of its territories. Like the Frankish kingdom, Byzantium grew stronger after the early eighth century, and the Moslems were unable for a long time to make any headway against these two bulwarks of Europe.

Mosque at Cordoba, Spain, 9th century. An example of western Islamic architecture.

The Rise of the Abbasids

The Ommiad state had also begun to weaken internally. As is true of many dynasties, the later Ommiads were less able than the first rulers of the line. Even if they had been men of extraordinary ability, they would have found it difficult to rule effectively a vast empire stretching from Spain to India and including dozens of different nationalities. Moreover, many Moslems continued to distrust and oppose the Ommiads. There was still a party which honored the memory of Ali and considered the Ommiads usurpers; there were puritanical Moslems who loathed Ommiad luxury and worldliness; and there were recent converts, especially in Mesopotamia and Persia, who resented the domination of the Arab aristocracy.

All these groups were united by Abu'l Abbas, who was to found the great Abbasid dynasty. By claiming one of Mohammed's uncles as an ancestor, he satisfied most of the legitimists; by making himself appear more devout than the Ommiads, he gained the support of most of the inhabitants of Mesopotamia and Persia. By 750 Abu'l Abbas was strong enough to risk rebellion. He decisively defeated the Ommiad caliph, and almost exterminated the family. One Ommiad escaped to Spain, where he founded an independent state in 756, but the rest of the Mohammedan world accepted Abu'l Abbas as caliph.

Since the Abbasid caliph's chief strength was in Mesopotamia and Persia, he moved his capital to Baghdad, a new city built on the banks of the Tigris. This move symbolized a great turning point in the history of civilization. The old unity of the Mediterranean world, shaken by earlier events, was now forever destroyed. Whereas the Ommiad caliphs at Damascus had drawn heavily on the experience of the Greco-Roman civilization, the Abbasids at Baghdad were increasingly influenced by the ancient traditions of Mesopotamia and Persia. This tendency was reinforced by the deep-seated, long-smoldering resentment of the peoples of North Africa and West Asia against Greek and Roman domination. The Mohammedan world on the southern and eastern shores of the Mediterranean became more and more unlike the Christian world on the northern shores. At the same time, Mohammedan pressure was forcing Byzantium in on itself and accentuating the peculiarities of the Byzantine way of life.

A citizen of the Roman Empire had been equally at home in Rome and Constantinople, in Alexandria and Antioch. Now these centers of civilization were drifting apart and becoming more and more strange to each other. By the tenth century a westerner, merely by crossing the Mediterranean, entered a completely different world. Egypt was as strange as China, and even Christian Byzantium seemed remote and oriental.

Thus the world of the Romans had broken into three fragments of unequal size and wealth. The largest and richest area was held by the Mohammedans, who also controlled the most important trade routes and all but one of the great cities of the Middle East. Next came the Byzantine Empire, anchored on impregnable Constantinople, rich from its own industry and from the trade which flowed through its lands to the west and the north. Far behind was western Europe, poverty-stricken and ill-governed, no match for the great civilizations which centered in Constantinople and Baghdad. For centuries western Europe had depended on the East in trade and industry, in art and religion. It remained to be seen what it could do now that it was on its own.

Suggestions for Further Reading

1. Byzantium

A wealth of literature is available on the life and thought of Byzantine civilization. P. N. Ure, *Justinian and His Age* * (1951), which discusses many facets of Byzantine history and civilization, is a good starting point. S. Runciman, *Byzantine Civilization* * (1933), combines deep knowledge of the subject with a superb prose style in a very sympathetic treatment. The old theory that the Byzantine Empire was perpetually

* Available in paperback edition.

moribund is severely attacked in N. H. Baynes, *The Byzantine Empire* (1926), which stresses the vitality of the Empire's history. N. H. Baynes and H. L. B. Moss, *Byzantium* (1948), is a collection of essays on Byzantine history and culture written by leading scholars in the field. The most thorough and scholarly treatment of Byzantine history is G. Ostrogorsky, *History of the Byzantine State* (trans. J. M. Hussey, 1956). The older work of A. A. Vasiliev, *History of the Byzantine Empire*, 2 vols. (1928), is more readable than Ostrogorsky but lacks recent bibliographic material. Two works by the French scholar, C. Diehl, *History of the Byzantine Empire* (1901) and *Byzantium: Greatness and Decline* (1957), are valuable for the facts but are considerably dated in historical interpretation.

The beauty of Byzantine art has fascinated many who have come in contact with it. C. R. Morey, *Early Christian Art* (1942), which has good plates, describes the influence of Byzantine iconography on western art in the early Middle Ages. But for the magnificence of its reproductions and the general excellence of its text, no survey of Byzantine art can compare with the fine Skira edition, *Byzantine Painting* (ed. A. Grabar, 1953). The brief study of D. T. Rice, *Byzantine Art* * (1935), is worth while and perhaps more accessible.

2. Islam

The best introduction to the world of Islam is the Koran,* of which there are many translations. Perhaps the best is that of G. Lamsa, *The Koran* (1949). H. A. R. Gibb, *Mohammedanism* (1949), is a good historical survey of the Moslem religion, while B. Lewis, *The Arabs in History* (1950), emphasizes the political and social aspects of Moslem history. Both books have good critical bibliographies. The foremost American historian of Islam, P. K. Hitti, has written a number of fine studies. His *The Arabs* * (many editions) is a scholarly treatment of the rise and spread of Mohammedanism; his translation of *The Origins of the Islamic State* (1916) traces the growth of Islam and is excellent for an understanding of the Moslem world-view. The now classic study by H. Pirenne, *Mohammed and Charlemagne* * (1936), advances a significant theory about the impact of Islam on western Europe in the early Middle Ages. H. A. R. Gibb and H. Bowen, *Islamic Society and the West*, 2 vols. (1950), explores the impact of the West on Islam in later times. G. von Grunebaum, *Medieval Islam* (1946), traces the temper and flavor of the Moslem Middle Ages and gives a fine account of the Moslem influence on western Europe in the Middle Ages. Both R. P. A. Dozy, *Spanish Islam* (1913), and S. Lane-Poole, *The Story of the Moors in Spain* (1886), give exciting accounts of the Arabs in Spain. Washington Irving's *The Alhambra* gives a vivid and unforgettable picture of Moslem culture in Spain. There is interesting material on the Ommiads in W. Muir, *The Caliphate: Its Rise, Decline and Fall* (1915), and in T. W. Arnold, *The Caliphate* (1912), but neither is so thorough in historical interpretation as is the research of Hitti.

H. A. R. Gibb, *Arabic Literature* (1926), is a brief survey of Arabic literature with an appendix of Arabic works in English and other modern languages. T. W. Arnold, *Painting in Islam* (1928), is a readable study of the place of art in Moslem culture, with very good reproductions. T. W. Arnold and A. Guillaume, *The Legacy of Islam* (1931), an account of the elements in European culture which are derived from the Islamic world, is the best one-volume study of Moslem culture and thought.

* Available in paperback edition.

9

The Emergence

of a Western European

Civilization

The Roman Empire at its height had caught up most of western Europe in its civilization. The Roman genius had touched even the peoples outside the Empire—the Celts in Ireland and Scotland, and the Germans in Scandinavia and Germany. But after the collapse of the Empire's political unity in the fifth century, the Mediterranean world broke into three distinct cultural units—a German-Latin bloc in the West, a Greek-Slavic bloc in the East, and an Arab-Syrian-Persian bloc in the South. These three units had many things in common, and they continued to influence one another in many ways. Merchants still traveled back and forth across the Mediterranean; ideas and artistic techniques passed from the Byzantine Empire and the Mohammedan Caliphate to Italy, France, and Germany.

And yet contacts among the West, the East, and the South of the Mediterranean world were less frequent and less intimate than they once had been. This was due in part to the endless wars between Byzantium and Islam, in which the Byzantines tried to discourage any commerce that might strengthen their enemy. It was due even more to the poverty and backwardness of western Europe, whose stocks of precious metals had been seriously depleted, making it difficult for westerners to purchase eastern goods. The western commodities most useful to the Greeks and Arabs were timber, iron, and slaves—all of which could be considered contraband of war in times of political or religious conflict. As a result, the West could not earn enough foreign exchange to trade extensively with either Byzantines or Arabs. Nor did the West have adequate intellectual capital for a rewarding exchange of ideas with Greek or Arab scholars. There were relatively few educated men in western Europe, and most of them were at work painfully trying to understand the writings of the Latin Church Fathers and fragments of the Latin classics.

Until the West had fully assimilated its Latin heritage it had little interest in the learning of the East.

Western Europe, though by no means cut off from the peoples of the East and the South, was more dependent on its own resources than it had been for centuries. It had to work out its own destiny and create its own civilization. That it was able to do so was due to several favorable factors. Although it seemed poor and backward in comparison with the East, it actually possessed a great potential for growth. It had plenty of good agricultural land and virtually untouched resources of raw materials. Though trade in the Mediterranean had fallen off, trade in the northern seas was flourishing. The whole Atlantic coastline, from northern Spain to Denmark and Sweden, was bound together by merchants of various nationalities. The Scandinavians were beginning to import eastern goods through the Russian river system. The Church had preserved the rudiments of an educational system and some ideas about political and social organization. Most important of all, at the crucial moment when western Europe seemed weakest and most backward, a new line of Frankish rulers emerged to bring unity and stability and lay the foundations for a new civilization.

King Pippin and the Church

This new line of rulers was descended from Pippin and Charles Martel, the mayors of the palace who had already begun to put an end to the disorders of the seventh century (see p. 212). These men had been the real rulers of the Frankish state, even though they had found it expedient to govern in the name of a puppet Merovingian king. The son of Charles Martel, another Pippin, chose to aim higher. After ruling for ten years as mayor (741–51), he decided he was strong enough to make a bid for the kingship itself. He won over most of the nobles, and to overcome the scruples of those who were still attached to the old dynasty Pippin asked the pope for an opinion on the legitimacy of his bid. Pope Zacharias declared that the man who bore the responsibilities of the king deserved the title, and his successor actually journeyed to France and anointed Pippin in the manner of the Old Testament kings. This was probably the first example of the practice of anointment in the West, and it is hard for us to realize the impression it must have made on public opinion. As God's anointed, Pippin became a semisacred personage, far above all ordinary lay dignitaries. He and his family were firmly established on the throne and nothing more was heard of the Merovingian claims.

This collaboration of the papacy in Pippin's ascension to the throne was to have important consequences for all future European kings. The pope had certainly not been the prime mover in the shift of dynasty, but the very fact that he had been consulted enabled later pontiffs to claim that Zacharias had deposed an unworthy king and had chosen a suitable successor. They found this a useful precedent in dealing with recalcitrant rulers. Equally significant was Pippin's consecration, for it was soon believed that a king did not have full authority until he had been anointed by the Church. This precedent enabled ecclesiastical authorities to assert their superiority over lay rulers. No layman could consecrate a bishop, but a bishop could consecrate a king. The obvious conclusion was that the bishop had a higher authority and that royal power, in some fashion, was dependent on the sanction of the Church.

The Alliance of the Papacy with the Franks

Probably none of this had been foreseen by either Pippin or Zacharias. Their co-operation was based rather on the realization that each could gain some practical advantage by supporting the other. As we have seen, the pope in the eighth century was far from being the unquestioned and invulnerable head of the Church. In Italy he was harassed by the Lombards and annoyed by the Byzantine emperor, who quarreled with him about theology but gave him no help against his barbarian enemies. To the north, beyond the Alps, the pope had little direct authority, except in the recently converted Anglo-Saxon kingdoms. He was especially distressed by the condition of the Church in the Frankish realm, for many of the Frankish clergy were ill-educated and corrupt, and a large part of the population, only half-converted, had little contact with the Church. A strong Frankish king might be willing to protect the pope against the Lombards and might also aid in the administrative and moral reform of the Church.

As for Pippin, he had inherited a family tradition of cooperating with the Church. One of his ancestors had been a bishop and a saint, and his father, Charles Martel, had had the support of the Church in his struggle with the Frankish aristocracy. In return, Charles had supported the work of missionaries and reformers in the Frankish kingdoms. Pippin's brother, Carloman, had entered the monastery of Monte Cassino after sharing the mayorship with Pippin for several years. Pippin, in addition to his religious convictions, also had worldly reasons for aiding the Church. Educated and reformed bishops were likely to support strong government and resist aristocratic factionalism, and they would probably make useful advisers and administrative agents for the king. Moreover, a reformed Church that emphasized the principles of Christian morality might make the king's task of preserving public order a little easier.

The alliance between Pippin and the pope changed the political fate of western Europe. First, and perhaps most important of all, it removed Italy from the Byzantine sphere of influence and attached it to the Germanic North. The pope had long found the Byzantine emperors unsatisfactory suzerains. It was bad enough when they failed to push back the Lombards; it was even worse when they stirred up an unnecessary theological controversy. The Christians of the East had begun to pay such extravagant respect to sacred images that the emperors feared it might degenerate into idolatry. They may have been influenced by the taunts of the Moslems, who were strictly forbidden to have any images and who were quick to accuse Christians of worshiping idols. The emperors were certainly concerned about the political influence that was being exerted by monasteries with wonder-working images. In 725 the emperor Leo III forbade sculptured images, and his policy was followed by most of his immediate successors. Excessive devotion to images had not been particularly troublesome in the West, and the popes felt that to resort to the remedy of iconoclasm (the destruction of images) was as bad as the disease itself. The largely illiterate western population needed images as illustrations of Christian doctrine and the popes had no intention of giving up this resource.

Coolness over the problem of iconoclasm, combined with concern over the Lombard threat, made the pope look to the Franks for support. Charles Martel had already been asked to intervene in Italy, but he had refused. Pippin was more willing to act, at least against the Lombards. He invaded Italy in 753 and forced the Lombards to withdraw from the environs of Rome. The campaign closed with two significant acts. Pippin gave Pope Stephen II a large belt of territory, stretching across central Italy from Rome to the Adriatic, which had formerly been held by the Byzantine Empire. The pope gave Pippin the title of "patricius Romanorum," which had formerly been held by the chief Byzantine representative in Italy.

To ignore Byzantium's centuries-old claim to Italy was a bold act. This is probably why an unknown churchman (probably a Frank) forged the famous *Donation of Constantine* about this time. This document, supposedly an act of gratitude by Constantine after his conversion, purported

❖❖❖❖❖❖❖❖❖❖❖❖❖❖❖❖❖❖❖❖❖❖❖❖❖❖❖❖❖❖

The Donation of Constantine

Constantine tells how pope Sylvester I cured him of leprosy. In gratitude Constantine accepts baptism and decrees

that the sacred see of blessed Peter shall be gloriously exalted above our empire and earthly throne. . . . And the pontiff who presides over the most holy Roman Church shall be the highest and chief of all priests . . . and according to his decision shall all matters be settled . . . for the worship of God or the confirmation of the faith.

We convey to the most blessed pontiff, our father Silvester, universal pope, both our palace [the Lateran] and likewise all provinces, places and districts of the City of Rome and Italy and of the regions of the West, . . bequeathing them to the power and sway of him and his successors.

Wherefore we have perceived that our empire and the power of our government should be transferred to the regions of the East . . . for it is not right that an earthly emperor should have authority . . . where the head of the Christian religion has been established by the Emperor of heaven.

From the Donation of Constantine, as quoted in *Select Documents of European History*, ed. by R. G. D. Laffan (London: Methuen, 1930), Vol. I, pp. 4–5.

❖❖❖❖❖❖❖❖❖❖❖❖❖❖❖❖❖❖❖❖❖❖❖❖❖❖❖❖❖❖

to give all Italy and the western part of the Empire to the pope. After withdrawing to the East, the emperor was supposed to have left the pope as the supreme authority in the West. This was a clumsy falsehood, but no one challenged its authenticity for seven hundred years. Meanwhile it enabled the pope to claim lordship over a large part of central Italy and to intervene in all political affairs in the West.

North of the Alps the alliance of Pippin and the pope was equally important. There were two problems in the Frankish kingdoms: first, Pippin had only nominal control over outlying districts such as Bavaria and Aquitaine; second, the Church had little contact with, and less influence over, most of Pippin's subjects. To solve the first problem, Pippin, with the backing of the Church, attacked the semi-independent rulers of Aquitaine and Bavaria and gained some measure of obedience from them. The second problem was solved by one of the greatest missionaries and organizers the Church has ever known, an Anglo-Saxon monk named Boniface.

St. Boniface

Boniface came to Frankland as a young man with the hope of converting the still-heathen Germans of Frisia and Saxony. Though he had some success in his missionary work, he soon realized that an even graver problem was posed by the corruption of the Frankish Church and the low level of Christianity among the Frankish people, many of whom were called Christians only because they had no other faith. They seldom saw an orthodox priest, and the visits of wandering Irish monks did little to strengthen their beliefs. Boniface realized that a thorough reform and reorganization of the Frankish Church was essential, and he spent most of his life in this great task.

With the steady support of both Charles Martel and Pippin, he did much to strengthen the organization of the Church in Germany, especially after he became archbishop in 748 with full powers over the German clergy. In Gaul he summoned local councils to improve the morality of Frankish churchmen and to make them more obedient to the pope. As the years passed, the Church north of the Alps became a far more effective force in the lives of the people, and its increased centralization and better administration raised the standards of the clergy and gave the Church strength enough to resist the selfish demands of local aristocrats. At the end of his life Boniface returned to missionary work and found the martyrdom he had long desired. He was killed by heathen Frisians in 754.

The Establishment of Parishes and Tithes

Boniface was neither the first Anglo-Saxon missionary on the Continent nor the only leader of reform. He succeeded only because he had the support of a band of devoted disciples and the backing of the better members of the Frankish clergy. Moreover, his reform was made more effective by the development of rural parishes in the Frankish kingdom—a development which had begun long before, but which received its greatest impetus from the descendants of Charles Martel. So long as churches existed only in the cities, as they did at first, country-dwellers found it impossible to maintain regular contact with the clergy. As we have seen, this was one reason for Christianity's lack of influence on the mass of the population during the Merovingian period. A rural parish with a resident priest was the obvious solution to this problem, but priests were not likely to stay resident, or to be very useful if they did, until local churches had an adequate income. North of the Alps the landlords and counts were the only men wealthy enough to build and endow rural churches.

They began to do so on a large scale only in the eighth century, prompted by Boniface's reforms and by the example and persuasion of the ruling family.

The final step in giving parish churches an adequate income was taken when Pippin's son Charles made tithes compulsory. The clergy had long taught that the faithful should give 10 per cent of their produce to the Church, but they had permitted tithing to remain a purely voluntary act. By ruling that all Christians had to tithe, the king assured the Church sufficient income to support an extensive network of rural parishes. Not all tithes went to parish priests, and their share tended to diminish as time went on. Nevertheless, they always received enough to keep the rural churches in existence.

The character and organization of the Church were undergoing revolutionary changes in the eighth century. For the first time the ordinary inhabitant of the Frankish realm was in regular and frequent contact with Christianity. The priests were more numerous and better qualified than ever before, and the rapid growth of the parish system gave them more opportunities to impress Christian doctrine and morality on the people. There had always been sincere believers, but in the Merovingian period many men had acted as if Christianity were only a superior form of magic. They venerated relics which were alleged to bring good luck, but they had no strong convictions about either faith or morals. Now the religion really began to get under their skins and affect their daily behavior. The eighth century is the first period in which one can be sure that all western Europe was hearing and beginning to understand the Christian message.

This improvement in the position of the Church had begun before Pippin and continued under his descendants. But Pippin's reign was the crucial period. He accelerated the pace of the reform movement, and he made the binding alliance with the papacy which ensured the cooperation of religious and secular authorities in building a new civilization. Pippin's work has been overshadowed by that of his son Charles, but Charles built on the solid foundation left by his father.

Pippin was right in his conviction that by aiding the Church he would enhance royal authority. The work of Boniface in Germany made it easier to bring outlying districts, such as Bavaria, under the king's control. The growing centralization of the Frankish Church was paralleled by a growing centralization of the royal administration. Bishops were used as administrative agents of the king, and local magnates became less independent and more responsive to the king's wishes. Pippin left his heirs a strong kingdom in which there was no longer any real opposition to the ruling family.

Charles the Great

Pippin died in 768 and was succeeded by his two sons, Charles and Carloman. Once again fate saved the Franks from the dangerous consequences of divided authority. Carloman died after three years, and Charles, ignoring the claims of a nephew, retained sole control of the government.

Charles' reign was so successful that even in his own lifetime he was known as Charles the Great, or Charlemagne. To his contemporaries he was great first and foremost because he was a persistent and victorious warrior. He ended the Lombard problem by defeating the Lombard king and annexing the Lombard lands in northern and central Italy. He eased the Moslem threat by crossing the Pyrenees and pushing the Mohammedans back toward the Ebro, thereby adding a small strip of Spanish territory to the Frankish kingdom. When

Charlemagne's Conquests and Empire 814

the nomadic Avars, who had established themselves on the middle Danube (see p. 225), became troublesome, he almost annihilated them in a single campaign. He sacked their main camp and seized the enormous plunder that they had amassed over the years from the Byzantines and other peoples of eastern and central Europe. His longest and hardest war was with the Saxons of northeastern Germany, the last great group of German heathens. They resisted Frankish domination and Christianity with equal bitterness, and only after thirty years did Charlemagne manage to conquer and convert them.

Charles' Educational Reforms

But Charlemagne was more than a successful general, as again many of his con-

temporaries realized. He wanted a strong kingdom, but he also wanted it to be a Christian kingdom, and his efforts to make it so left an indelible impression on western civilization. Even more than his father, Charlemagne realized that an uneducated clergy was an unorganized and uninfluential clergy. Both by decree and by his own example he tried to raise the level of learning in the Frankish realm. He imported scholars from every country of western Europe, and either kept them with him in his Palace Academy or gave them high positions in the Frankish Church. The most famous of these scholars was the Anglo-Saxon Alcuin, abbot of St. Martin's of Tours, but there were also Franks, Lombards, and even Saxons among them.

The work of these scholars was not very

original or imaginative, but originality and imagination were not what was needed most in the eighth century. The great need was for men who could preserve and assimilate the intellectual heritage left by Rome and the early Church. Even to preserve it was no easy task, for much of Latin literature had already been lost and there were few copies of the works which had survived. The Scriptures and the works of the Church Fathers were in less danger of being lost, but Charlemagne complained that even copies of the Bible were so full of errors that people were being led astray. By encouraging the making of new and accurate copies of ancient texts, Charlemagne saved many classical works from oblivion; we have almost no manuscripts of Latin authors from before his time. The acceleration of manuscript production in turn led to a reform in handwriting, a reform in which Alcuin and his monastery at Tours played a leading role. These monks developed a beautiful, clear script which was a great improvement on earlier handwriting. The Romans had used only capital letters, which were hard to read when they filled a solid line. Later writers developed small letters, but they were badly shaped and easily confused. It was the Carolingians who gave small letters almost the form they have today.

Moreover, Charlemagne's educational revival gave Europe a common cultural

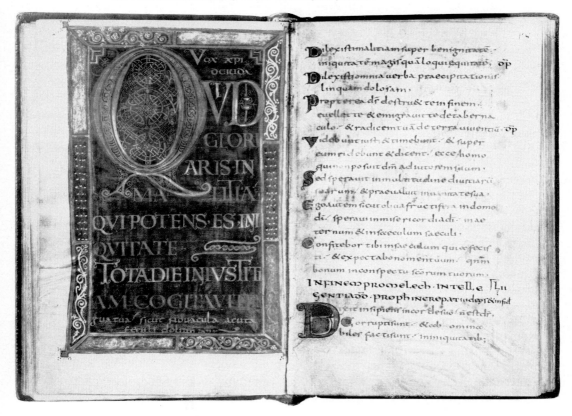

Psalter given by Charlemagne to Pope Adrian I. The small letters are a good example of the reformed handwriting of the Carolingian period.

Detail of a page from the Book of Kells, ca. 800 A.D. The script is Irish uncial.

heritage. As we have seen, scholars of all nations mingled at the Frankish court, and men of Germanic origin were, if anything, more prominent there than those of Latin stock. All these scholars worked with the same materials—the Bible, the Church Fathers, the encyclopedias of the Late Empire, and some of the Latin classics. When they were sent out to various parts of the realm as bishops or abbots, they carried this common stock of learning with them and taught it to their own students. All scholars used Latin, so there was no problem of translation once the basic knowledge of Latin had been acquired. This saved a great deal of time and effort, for neither the Romance languages which were developing out of Latin nor the early Germanic tongues had yet progressed far enough to allow abstract thinking or adequate generalization. Thus scholars everywhere were reading the same books and commenting on them in the same language, and so western Europe developed a common stock of ideas and a common vocabulary in which to express them. If western Europe has any unity at all today, it is in its ideas, in its way of looking at the world, and for this unity it owes much to the work of Charles the Great.

Revival of the Empire in the West

By wiping out the Lombard kingdom, Charlemagne had made himself directly responsible for the security of the pope and the government of Rome. Taking this responsibility seriously, he intervened repeatedly to protect the pope from his enemies and thus made the pope politically dependent on the Frankish king. Charles also felt responsible for the behavior of the clergy throughout his realm, and his laws dealt as often with ecclesiastical matters as with secular affairs. He laid down rules of proper conduct for monks and priests; he ordered schools to be established for the training of the clergy; he intervened in theological disputes. And, as we have seen, he gave the Church a solid financial basis by making the payment of tithes compulsory. He respected the divine mission of the Church and honored the pope, but he felt it his personal duty to make Christianity a more effective force in his kingdom. He was the head of a Christian people and he expected clergy as well as laity to follow his leadership.

This close relationship between king and Church reached its climax in the year 800. Pope Leo III, driven from Rome by his enemies, had appealed to Charlemagne for aid. Charlemagne reinstated the pope and spent several weeks in Rome to make sure there would be no further trouble. On Christmas Day, 800, the pope placed the imperial crown on Charlemagne's head and hailed him as Augustus. The West once more had an emperor.

In one sense, the coronation merely symbolized existing facts. As ruler of France, Germany, and most of Italy, Charlemagne already had more power than the last West-

Left: First page of the Gospel of St. Matthew, with Matthew's symbol, a man. From the Book of Durrow, Iona. 7th century A.D. This Irish book shows fewer traces of foreign ornamental ideas than does the Book of Kells (see p. 248).
Right: A so-called carpet page from the Book of Durrow.

Interior of Charlemagne's Chapel at Aix-la-Chapelle. Charlemagne at one time thought of making Aix a capital city rivaling Rome. Compare this with the next picture, San Vitale.

The church of San Vitale at Ravenna. Built under Byzantine influence in the 6th century, it furnished a model for Charlemagne's Chapel at Aix-la-Chapelle.

Panel from the shrine at Aix-la-Chapelle. Charlemagne presents a model of his church to the Virgin.

ern Roman emperors. The emperor had been the traditional protector of the Church, and now that the Byzantine ruler could no longer fulfill this function it was logical for a western king to take his place. Charlemagne's rule over non-Frankish peoples and his use of the Church to support that rule were both legitimized by his assumption of the imperial title. There seems to be no doubt that Charlemagne wanted to be emperor, for the pope was in no position to impose undesired titles on his powerful protector.

Nevertheless, a man who knew Charlemagne well said that the king grumbled that he never would have gone to church that Christmas Day had he known what the pope had in mind. This was probably false modesty; if the report has any substance it may reflect Charlemagne's dislike of receiving his title from the pope. And such misgivings would have been well founded. Later popes claimed that Leo III, by his

own authority, had transferred imperial power from the Greeks to the Franks, and that Charlemagne's coronation was one more proof of the superiority of ecclesiastical rulers over secular rulers. But whatever doubts Charlemagne had were soon quieted. He worked hard to persuade the Byzantine emperor to recognize his title; he referred to himself as emperor in public documents; and, before his death, he was careful to see that his son was crowned emperor. The pope took no part in the coronation of Charlemagne's son, which suggests that by the end of his life Charlemagne did not want his subjects to believe that the pope could make an emperor.

Armed with the prestige of the imperial title, Charlemagne ordered all his subjects to take a new oath of allegiance to him, an oath which emphasized their duties as Christians as well as the emperor's role as protector of the Church. But added prestige and new oaths of allegiance were highly

The Coronation of Charlemagne

Now when the king upon the most holy day of the Lord's birth was rising to the mass after praying before the tomb of the blessed Peter the Apostle, Leo the Pope, with the consent of all the bishops and priests and of the senate of the Franks and likewise of the Romans, set a golden crown upon his head, the Roman people also shouting aloud. And when the people had made an end of chanting praises, he was adored by the pope after the manner of the emperors of old. For this was also done by the will of God. For while the said Emperor abode at Rome certain men were brought to him who said that the name of Emperor had ceased among the Greeks, and that there the Empire was held by a woman called Irene, who had by guile laid hold on her son the Emperor and put out his eyes and taken the Empire to herself. . . . Which when Leo the Pope and all the assembly of the bishops and priests and abbots heard, and the senate of the Franks and all the elders of the Romans, they took counsel with the rest of the Christian people, that they should name Charles king of the Franks to be Emperor, seeing that he held Rome the mother of empire where the Caesars and Emperors always used to sit.

From *Chronicle of Moissac,* trans. by J. Bryce, *The Holy Roman Empire* (New York: Macmillan and St Martin's Press, 1911), p. 54.

personal things, and they died with the ruler who possessed them. Charlemagne never quite succeeded in transforming his own great personal authority into institutions which would hold his empire together under weaker successors.

Charlemagne's Government

The essential unit of government under Charlemagne, as under his Merovingian predecessors, was the county. Each county was headed by a count, who was almost al-ways a member of a wealthy and well-established family of the region. The count was assisted by various subordinates and deputies; he was checked by the heads of the other great families of his county and by neighboring bishops and abbots. Nevertheless, an energetic count could build up a great deal of local power. He presided over the local courts and kept a third of the fines collected there. He led the freemen of his district to war. He collected tolls and other scattered survivals of the old Roman system of taxation. He built and garrisoned forts. Clearly, the king's chief problem was to keep his counts under control.

Charlemagne tried to meet this problem by two devices. First, he tried to keep the counts from abusing their judicial power by creating independent groups of local judges to decide cases. Second, he sent out royal envoys—called *missi dominici*—to see that the counts obeyed his orders and observed reasonable standards of justice and honesty. The *missi,* who usually traveled in pairs made up of a layman and a cleric, were chosen from men of the highest standing at court and had the full support of the emperor. Their admonitions and reports helped immeasurably to improve the conduct of local government. Nevertheless, even the *missi* did not give the emperor full control over his counts. Abuses of power continued, and there were cases of flat disobedience to Charlemagne's orders.

In directing and coordinating the work of local authorities, the central government managed to get along with a remarkably small group of functionaries. First, there was a small secretarial staff to handle correspondence and keep records. It is worth noting that under Charlemagne these men were all members of the clergy,* whereas

---

* This is reflected in the similarity of our English words *clerk* and *cleric*. From the time of Charlemagne to the end of the Middle Ages all "clerks" were members of the clergy.

the Merovingians had had no difficulty in finding laymen who were capable of doing the job. This change suggests both the decline of education among laymen and the fact that an educated clergy was essential to Charlemagne's system of government. In addition to the secretaries there were a few lay judges to hear the rare cases which were brought to the emperor's court, and a large and undifferentiated group of household officials and counselors. Charlemagne, guided more by his estimate of a man's ability and loyalty than by the title he possessed, used any of these men for any task.

In directing and controlling local officials Charlemagne issued a series of capitularies, which were simply ordinances made up of many *capitula,* or chapters. These were largely administrative directives which told the local officials what to do. For example, one capitulary contained rules for the education of the clergy, and another listed detailed regulations for the administration of royal estates. Charlemagne seldom attempted to make law, since he, like most men of his age, believed that law consisted of eternal and unchanging principles reflected in the customs of the people. Never-

A gold and jeweled book cover for the Lindau gospels, late Carolingian, ca. 870.

theless, by issuing capitularies which interpreted the law, Charles in effect changed the law. And by laying down rules which were applicable to all subjects, Charles did a good deal to wipe out earlier distinctions between Roman and German, or Frank and Burgundian. There was never complete uniformity among his subjects, but his administrative and judicial system was accepted throughout the Empire and persisted after the Empire broke up.

Thus in government, as in religion and education, Charlemagne gave western Europe a common tradition which overrode differences of language and nationality. The county remained the basic unit of local government in all European countries for many centuries, and most of the royal courts of the Middle Ages were organized much as Charlemagne's had been. Even his system of reckoning money in pounds, shillings, and pence was followed by almost every European country down to the time of the French Revolution.

Charlemagne had accomplished a great feat in uniting the West and helping it to attain common ideals and common institutions. But he had succeeded only because he was a man of boundless energy, unusual perseverance, and strong personality who had impressed himself on his contemporaries. It was too much to expect his descendants to be men of equal stature, and the Carolingian Empire was too large and too imperfectly unified for lesser men to hold it together. There were few economic ties among the far-flung regions; Bavarians, for example, had no reason to care about what happened in Aquitaine. Western Europeans could satisfy their common ideals simply by sharing in the life of the Church; their common institutions, which were most effective at the county level, seemed to work equally well whether there was one empire or many kingdoms. Charlemagne himself apparently was not particularly concerned about preserving the unity of the Empire, for he followed the old Frankish tradition and divided his holdings among his sons. It was only the premature death of two of his heirs which gave an undivided realm to his son Louis.

The Division of Charlemagne's Empire

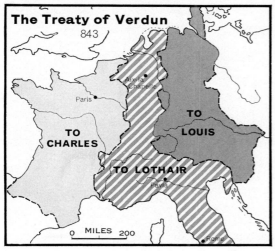

The Treaty of Verdun
843

Aix-la-Chapelle

Paris

TO CHARLES

TO LOUIS

TO LOTHAIR

Pavia

0   MILES   200

Rome

The Treaty of Mersen
870

Aix-la-Chapelle

Paris

WEST FRANKISH KINGDOM

EAST FRANKISH KINGDOM

KINGDOM OF ITALY

Pavia

MEDITERRANEAN SEA

Rome

The Collapse
of the Carolingian Empire

Louis had increasing difficulty in holding the Frankish state together. He was a well-meaning but weak man, easily swayed by his family and friends. In order to gain the aid of the Church, the only institution which was really concerned with western unity, he humbled himself as Charles never would have done. Thus Louis allowed himself to be crowned emperor a second time by ecclesiastical authority, and so undid his father's effort to free the imperial title from church control. He did public penance for mutilating a nephew who had rebelled against him, and he was always responsive to the wishes of his bishops. Most dangerous of all to the Empire were the jealousies among his three sons, Lothair, the younger Louis, and Charles. Louis drew up several plans for partitioning the Empire, but none of them satisfied all his heirs. They fought with him and they fought with one another. When Louis died in 840, he left the Empire in a state of civil war.

Louis' sons finally settled their quarrels by dividing the Empire in the Treaty of Verdun (843)—a division that had a lasting effect on European history. Charles received the western part of the Empire, a

Section from the Strasburg Oaths, the earliest examples of the dialects which eventually became French and German. The oath reproduced here was taken by Louis the German and Charles the Bald, sons of the Emperor Louis I, in 842, when they agreed to oppose their brother Lothair. The first paragraph gives the oath in French, taken by Louis, the second the same oath in German with the names changed, taken by Charles. Oaths were also taken by the followers of the two kings, in French for Charles' men and in German for Louis's.

The oath of Louis: "For the love of God and the salvation of the Christian people and our common salvation, from this day forward, in so far as God gives me knowledge and power, I will succour this my brother Charles in aid and in everything, as one ought by right to succour one's brother, provided that he does likewise by me, and I will never undertake any engagement with Lothair which, by my consent, may be of harm to his my brother Charles."

Pro dõ amur & pxpian poblo & nrõ común
saluament. dift di fn auant. inquantdí
sauir & podir medunat. sisaluaraieo.
cift meon fradre Karlo. & in adiudha.
& in cad huna cosa. sicū om p dreit son
fradra saluar dift.] no quid il miatre
si faze&. Et ab ludher nul plaid nūqua
prindrai qui meon uol cift. meon fradre
Karle in damno fit | Quod cū lodhuuī
epleff&. Karolus teu disca lingua sic'ex
eadē uerba teftatus eft.

Ingo des minna in dumhes xpanes folches
indunser bedhero gealtnissi. fonthese
moda ge frammor desso framsó mirgot
gewuzci indimadh fur gibit sohaldihtes
au minan bruodher soso man mit rehtu
sinan bruher scal inthi intha zermig sóso
maduo. in dumit luheren in nóhein jut
hung nege ganga. zheminan uuillon imo
ces cadhen uuerhen.

kingdom which corresponded roughly to modern France. Louis took eastern Frankland, including Saxony, Bavaria, and the counties along the Rhine. The eldest son, Lothair, became emperor and held a long, narrow strip of territory between the eastern and western kingdoms embracing the Low Countries, Alsace-Lorraine, Switzerland, Savoy, Provence, and North Italy. Lothair's kingdom was meant to be a buffer state, but like many buffers it was ground to pieces in conflicts between its neighbors. On Lothair's death in 855 his kingdom was divided into three smaller realms, and the kings of West Frankland and East Frankland soon began to contend for possession of these fragments of the Middle Kingdom. In the end, the king of East Frankland secured the parts which lay north of the Alps, but the dispute has continued even to our own day. In 1870, 1914, and 1939 France and Germany were still fighting for Alsace and Lorraine, fragments of the old kingdom of Lothair.*

---

* *Lorraine* is simply a French form of *Lotharingia*—Lothair's kingdom. The German, *Lothringen,* shows the connection even more clearly.

Invasions of the Northmen, the Moslems, and the Magyars 8th to 10th centuries

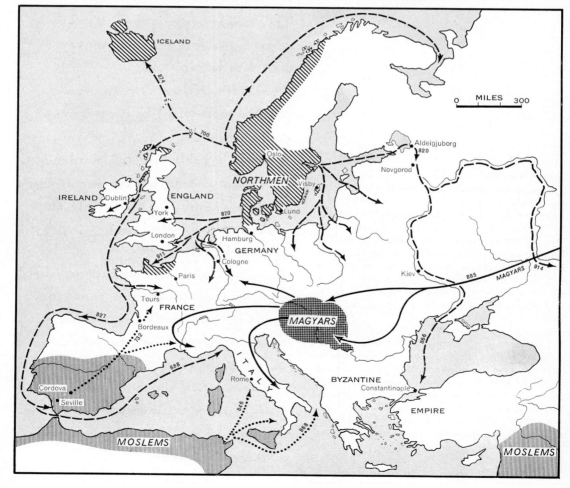

The New Invasions: The Northmen

The Frankish state, gravely weakened by the civil wars among Charlemagne's descendants, now was threatened by a series of new invasions with which the later Carolingians simply could not cope. Attacks from the north, east, and south strained the resources of the three central governments beyond their limits and threw the burden of defense on local leaders.

The most dangerous and persistent of these new invaders were the Scandinavians of the north. Though related to the Germans and with the same love of fighting, the Scandinavians had taken no part in the early migrations. By the ninth century, however, many of them had begun to seek new lands overseas. They were great seamen and traders, and they had already visited most of the shores of northern Europe in their long, shallow-draft ships. These vessels used a sail when the wind was astern, but most of the time they were propelled by oars. So well designed were they that they could ascend the rivers of western Europe and cross the North Atlantic with equal ease. The Scandinavians, equipped with such craft, could swoop down from the sea and loot a whole river valley before the local troops, moving slowly over bad roads, could be mobilized to repel them.

No one knows why the Scandinavians became so aggressive during the ninth century. It may be that improved metallurgical techniques enabled them to construct better weapons, such as their famous war axes. It may be that the frequent civil wars between ambitious kings and local leaders striving for independence forced defeated bands of warriors to flee the country. It may be that the increasing population of the homeland had convinced enterprising young men that there was little opportunity for them at home. In any case, the political weakness of Europe must certainly have lured them to dreams of conquest. The

Frankish Empire was disintegrating; the British Isles were split up into small, warring kingdoms; and the Slavs who now held eastern Europe were politically disorganized. The Continent lay open to any group

A viking animal head found at Oseberg, Norway, 9th century.

of determined men bent on marauding, on looting, and even, perhaps, on founding a new state.

Though the Scandinavian raiders called themselves vikings, the rest of Europe usually referred to them as Northmen. In their first serious raids, against Ireland early in the ninth century, they rapidly occupied the east coast and plundered the rest of the island. They met somewhat stiffer resistance from the Anglo-Saxons in England, but by 870 they had subdued all their kingdoms except the southern state of Wessex. Next they turned to the Frankish lands; though they never conquered these kingdoms, year after year the Northmen pushed their long ships up the Rhine, the Seine, and the Loire to collect tribute and loot from the towns and monasteries. The Northmen held the counties at the mouth of the Rhine for several decades, but they failed to build a permanent state there. Another band forced the West Frankish king to cede them the land at the mouth of the Seine. This outpost, founded about 911, became the nucleus of Normandy, the most famous and long-lived of the viking states.

In a show of bravado, the Northmen even sailed their ships down into the Mediterranean. Though never a real threat to this area, they did plunder a few coastal cities in Spain, southern France, and Italy. Their move west across the Atlantic had more permanent results, for they had settled Iceland by the year 1000 and from Iceland a few adventurous leaders moved on to Greenland. There they established colonies along the west coast of the island which endured to the fourteenth century, when they were wiped out because the climate became colder. And from Greenland some ships reached the North American continent, although we are still not sure just where the Northmen landed or how long they stayed.

The viking raids and settlements in the West were largely the work of Danes and Norwegians. In the East the Swedes began to push down the Russian river valleys toward Constantinople. They had known this route for a long time, and eastern goods and eastern coins had been common in Scandinavia long before the great raids began. In the late ninth and tenth centuries, however, the Swedes began to settle in Russia and to bring the scattered Slavic population under their control. The fortified trading posts where the vikings settled soon burgeoned into towns; the most famous of them was Kiev, which became the capital of a large principality. Once they had gained a footing in Russia, the vikings, with typical boldness, soon turned their eyes south to Constantinople. Their attacks on the great city were unsuccessful, but they did manage to wrest a very favorable commercial treaty from the emperor. These early viking princes and warriors gave the eastern Slavs their first effective political organization; in fact, the word *Russia* itself probably comes from *Rus,* the name of a Swedish tribe.

The New Invasions: The Moslems and the Magyars

Compared to the Northmen, who settled from Greenland to the Ukraine and raided from the Orkneys to the Straits of Gibraltar, the other invaders of the ninth and tenth centuries seem almost provincial. But they covered enough ground to cause suffering and poverty in many parts of southern and central Europe. The Moslems, coming up from the south, seized Sicily and the other islands of the western Mediterranean, thus endangering navigation in that part of the sea. They also established fortified outposts near Rome, and on the coastal road from France to Italy, from which they molested land travelers as well. Even worse were the Hungarians, or Magyars, who belonged to the great nomadic stock of central Asia which, century after century, had launched raids against the coastal civilizations of China, India, and Europe. The Magyars were as great horsemen as the vikings were seamen, and their skill gave them the same advantages of surprise and mobility. They drove into the Danube Valley in the ninth century and established headquarters in what is now Hungary. From this base they raided Germany and Italy regularly and eastern France occasionally. At least twice they rode around the Alps, striking from southern Germany into Burgundy, moving down the Rhone to the sea, then crossing into the Po Valley and returning home through northern Italy. The Magyar occupation of the middle Danube basin split the western Slavs into two groups. The Slavs were politically backward in any case, but this division made it even harder for them to form kingdoms strong enough to resist subjugation. And the weakness of the states of the western Slavs has in its turn been a source of war with and quarrels among their neighbors, as the history of Czechoslovakia demonstrates.

The End of the New Invasions

The people of western Europe suffered grievously at the hands of the new invaders. Large areas were either depopulated or impoverished. The plundering of monasteries and the disruption of communications dissipated many of the benefits of the Carolingian reforms. Yet western Europe resisted the new invasions far more successfully than Rome had resisted the earlier invasions of the Germans and Huns. Instead of a whole continent, only a few small territories, such as Normandy and Hungary, were permanently relinquished to the invaders. The Northmen and Magyars were converted to Christianity and assimilated the western tradition fairly quickly; the

Moslems were pushed back from their advanced positions.

How was it that western Europe managed to weather these disastrous new invasions? There were several reasons. First, the new invaders were probably not as numerous as the Germanic and Hunnic groups which had overrun Europe at the end of the Roman Empire. Second, the Church was more effective in inspiring resistance and in converting the invaders. Finally, and most important, there was effective local resistance. The people of the Roman Empire had depended almost entirely on the imperial government for protection; when its armies failed they accepted barbarian rule without protest. But when the Carolingian kings failed to defend Europe during the ninth-century invasions, local leaders arose to rally their people against the threat.

This growth of new leadership was especially noticeable in England, Germany, and France. In England, the collapse of all the other Anglo-Saxon kingdoms had left Wessex alone to face the Danish invaders. The king of Wessex, Alfred the Great (870–99), proved to be a brave and stubborn fighter. Though he was defeated again and again, he never gave up and eventually forced the Danes to accept a peace which gave him control of about half of England. His son and grandson carried on the fight until they had seized the rest of the Danish-occupied territories. By 950 all England was united under the Wessex dynasty. In Germany, one of the last Carolingian kings dislodged the Northmen from their hold on Frisia, and they were never again a serious menace to the country. The Carolingians never managed to hold the Magyars in check, but the new Saxon dynasty (see p. 264) which replaced the Carolingians brought them under control and thoroughly defeated them in 955.

France is the most instructive example

of the development of new leadership. As long as the Carolingian kings were able to raise armies to fight the Northmen, they kept the loyalty of most of the country. But when, at the end of the ninth century, they failed completely in their efforts to defend northern France, their subjects turned to other leaders. Odo, count of Paris, who had made a heroic defense of his city against the vikings in 885, founded a rival dynasty which contested the throne with the Carolingians for half a century. During these years local leaders took over most of the responsibility for defense. At last the viking danger diminished and the Carolingians were restored. But they had little real power, and the rival Capetian family, descended from the count of Paris, took permanent possession of the throne in 987, when Hugh Capet became king.

In short, the inhabitants of western Europe showed a will to resist which had been lacking in the fourth and fifth centuries. This will was strongest at the local level, among the counts who governed local districts and among the professional fighting men whom they controlled. When the kings proved that they could handle the job of governing, as they did in England and eventually in Germany, the local nobles supported them and a certain degree of unity was preserved. But when the kings failed, as they did in France, the counts became virtually independent rulers and gained the loyalty of most of the people in their districts.

Feudalism

Out of the ninth-century invasions emerged a new type of government, which we call feudalism. The invasions were only a contributing factor, however, for the civil wars among the last Carolingians and the lack of strong economic ties between districts also played a part in this development. Never-

theless, the fact that feudalism first appeared in northern France and only gradually spread to other countries suggests that the invasions gave the final push toward the development of this new form of political organization. France had suffered more severely from the invasions than any other country, and her kings had been less successful than other monarchs in coping with the danger.

The Ingredients of Feudalism

Feudalism may be characterized by three factors: localism, public power in private hands, and the lord-vassal relationship. The typical feudal state was a county, and the typical feudal lord was a count who had turned his office into a private, hereditary possession which he exploited for his own benefit. He kept control over his county through his vassals, or retainers, many of whom lived with him in his fortified dwelling. Other vassals lived on their own estates, which the lord had granted them as a reward for faithful service. The lands and rights held by a vassal from a lord were at first called benefices; later, fiefs.* All vassals were bound to help their lord in war and government. Though their chief duty was to fight for their lord, they might also be asked to attend law courts or to administer small areas within the county. This was feudalism in its simplest form: a small area ruled by a lord with the aid of a band of military retainers.

Some of the ingredients of feudalism had come into existence during the last years of the Merovingian kingdom, but it was almost two centuries before these ingredients were combined into a consistent pattern. The lord-vassal relationship, for example,

---

* Our word "feudalism" comes from the medieval Latin "feudum," which meant fief. No medieval writer ever spoke of "feudalism"; he was more apt to say "vassalage," which stressed the personal relationship.

first emerged clearly in the eighth century, when the Carolingian monarchy was still strong. It probably became important at this time because of a change in military techniques. During the long wars with the Moslem invaders (see p. 237) Charles Martel and Pippin had discovered that heavy-armed cavalrymen gave them the greatest striking power. They wanted large numbers of these soldiers, but they found that the ordinary freeman, with at best a small farm, could not afford to provide himself with a specially bred horse, a mail shirt, and a sword and spear. No ordinary horse could carry a fully armed soldier, nor could an ordinary village blacksmith make armor or forge a sword. Only the king or a wealthy lord could afford to provide this equipment, and they naturally expected the men who received it to accord them special loyalty in return. The new type of fighting men became vassals of the king or the lords and before long were the most important element in the army.

The Frankish kings soon sensed that the bond between lord and retainer was far more compelling than the loose tie between king and subject. So they began to use vassalage to strengthen their political authority as well as their military position. Pippin, Charlemagne, and Louis all encouraged fighting men to become vassals of lords, and lords to become vassals of the king. They began the practice of granting public offices, such as countships, as benefices to lords, just as the lords granted estates as benefices to some of their soldiers. But there was a great difference between an ordinary mounted soldier who was completely dependent on his lord for his livelihood, and a powerful count who needed no help from the king. The lesser vassals were almost always obedient to their lords and gave them good service. But the great vassals of the king became more and more disobedient during the ninth century and gave

****

Duties of Vassals and Lords

He who swears fealty to his lord ought always to have these six things in memory: what is harmless, safe, honorable, useful, easy, practicable. Harmless, that is to say that he should not be injurious to his lord in his body; safe, that he should not be injurious to him in his secrets or in the defenses through which he is able to be secure; honorable, that he should not be injurious to him in his justice or in other matters which pertain to his honor; useful, that he should not be injurious to him in his possessions; easy or practicable, that that good which his lord is able to do easily, he make not difficult, nor that which is practicable he make impossible to him.

However, that the faithful vassal should avoid these injuries is proper, but not for this does he deserve his holding; for it is not sufficient to abstain from evil, unless what is good is done also. It remains, therefore, that in the same six things mentioned above he should faithfully counsel and aid his lord, if he wishes to be looked upon as worthy of his benefice and to be safe concerning the fealty which he has sworn.

The lord also ought to act toward his faithful vassal reciprocally in all these things. And if he does not do this he will justly be considered guilty of bad faith.

From Letter of Bishop Fulbert of Chartres to Duke William of Aquitaine, 1020, trans. by E. P. Cheyney, *Translations and Reprints* (Philadelphia: U. of Pennsylvania Press, 1900), Vol. IV, No. 3, p. 23.

****

him service only when they felt like it. The king received a certain amount of deference and exercised a good bit of influence in the region in which he was actually residing. But by the tenth century the real rulers of France were the feudal lords who held the counties into which the country was divided.

Nevertheless, the theoretical subordination of the great lords to the king had important consequences in the long run. They were vassals, even if they seldom gave service; they held their counties from the king, even if he could not intervene in local affairs. The idea of a kingdom of France was preserved, even though the kingdom in fact was an amorphous confederation in which the lords only occasionally cooperated with the king. And, after several centuries, a new line of kings finally succeeded in transforming their theoretical supremacy over the lords into genuine control.

A Changing Institution

During the centuries when feudalism was at its height—from about 900 to about 1100—the institution underwent several important changes. First, some lords succeeded in subduing their neighbors and building up relatively large and powerful states. This was especially true of the count of Flanders and the duke of Normandy, who added many counties to their original holdings and kept them under fairly effective control. Nine or ten other lords were almost as successful, and their wars and alliances determined the political history of France for two centuries. Second, since these new states were too large to be governed through the informal and personal decisions of their rulers, various new legal and financial institutions were created. And these institutions in turn produced a body of feudal law and custom. Third, the benefice, or fief, became more important. In the early years, only the great men had received lands and offices, when they became vassals of the king; lesser vassals had been primarily household retainers, and only occasionally were they granted small amounts of land. Even then they spent most of their time in the personal presence of their lord or else garrisoning his forts. They enjoyed little financial security and the lord was obliged to keep them supplied with arms, horses, clothing, and food. Clearly it would be more convenient for both if the lord assigned all vassals estates, or fiefs, large enough for them to support themselves. This arrangement was adopted only gradually—even in 1100 many of the lesser vassals had no fiefs—but in time it became customary. It also became customary for the vassal to spend most of his time on his fief and to serve his lord only on special occasions or in time of war. Moreover, the fief, which originally had been only a loan to the vassal, gradually became hereditary, to be held by the vassal and his heirs as long as they gave service. In short, the relationship between vassal and lord was changing, with the vassal becoming more of a country gentleman and less of an armed retainer. He began to begrudge the time spent in his lord's service and tried to reduce it as much as he could. The lord countered by defining the service owed by vassals more and more precisely, and by developing legal procedures for confiscating the fiefs of defaulting vassals. Thus what had at first been a close personal relationship began to assume the form of a contractual obligation.

Feudalism was an inadequate and limited form of government. Designed primarily for military purposes, it did little for the great mass of the people except to protect them against external and internal enemies. And even this protection was not always very effective. In the endemic wars between neighboring lords, the favorite tactic was to ravage the peasants' fields and drive off their animals. Pitched battles between feudal armies were rare, and noncombatants usually suffered more severly than the fighting men themselves. The lord and his retainers conducted local courts from time to time, but they were more interested in pocketing fines than in administering justice. They knew little about law or administration, nor could they even manage to maintain the roads and other public facilities. At its best, feudal government was inefficient paternalism; at its worst, it was pure exploitation of the peasants.

Yet with all its disadvantages, feudalism showed a real vitality and a genuine capability for growth. It spread from France throughout most of western Europe, and the countries which were most thoroughly feudalized, France and England, were the first medieval states to develop effective political institutions. Moreover, feudal rulers managed to gain the loyalty of their subjects, something which neither the late Roman emperors nor the Germanic kings had achieved. With this loyalty it was possible to build stronger states and to give more protection and better justice to the people.

Feudalism was almost perfectly adapted to conditions in early medieval Europe. The working political unit, the county, matched the working economic unit, the local neighborhood. The struggle to base a large political organization on what was essentially a local economy—a struggle which had weakened both the Roman and the Carolingian empires—was abandoned. The exploitation of the peasants by an aristocracy was nothing new, and at least the feudal aristocracy had duties as well as privileges. Lords and vassals had to defend and govern their lands in person—no one else would do it for them—and if they did their job badly they would lose their lands to more efficient neighbors.

It is true that at best feudal government was only rudimentary, but even this was an advantage. Europe at this time did not need and could not support a complicated government; it had to concentrate on essentials. And precisely because early feudalism was highly informal and personal, it was little bound by obsolete laws and traditions.

Change was easy and experimentation common. In the end the ablest feudal lords devised more effective forms of government than Europe had had for many centuries, and their methods were copied by their less imaginative colleagues.

Germany

It took several centuries for feudalism to reveal all its possibilities. At first it seemed only a desperate improvisation, which did as much harm in encouraging local wars as it did good in warding off outside raiders. Feudal France was weak and divided. Germany and England, still unfeudalized and united under their kings, were far stronger. Germany, in fact, was the dominant country in Europe from the early tenth down to the end of the eleventh century.

In the period after the break-up of the Carolingian Empire, Germany had been less hard hit by invasion and civil war than France. Its kings had been more successful in war and the kingdom remained more united. The transition to a new dynasty was made more quickly, which meant fewer civil wars and fewer opportunities for the lords to usurp power while rival kings fought for the throne. In France it took over a century of war and intrigue to displace the Carolingians, while in Germany it took less than a generation. The last able German Carolingian died in 899; by 919 King Henry I had established the new Saxon dynasty firmly on the throne.

In spite of these advantages, however, the German king had lost much of his authority by 919. During the troubles of the ninth century most of the country had come under the control of five great men, the dukes of Saxony, Franconia, Swabia, Bavaria, and, after its annexation to Germany in 925, Lorraine. Each of these dukes ruled a wider territory than that of any French feudal lord, and each exercised reasonably effective control over the counts and other great men of his duchy. The dukes were willing to have a king as a sort of a president of their club, but they expected to be virtually independent within their own duchy. Henry I, for example, was duke of Saxony, and was really strong only there; elsewhere he had to negotiate with the other dukes to carry out his policies. Both the dukes and their counts were making their offices hereditary, and sons had begun to succeed their fathers as a matter of course.

Nevertheless, Germany was not yet feudalized, though feudal ideas were creeping in through Lorraine, the duchy which lay closest to France and which was most affected by conditions there. Counts and dukes were not completely independent of the king; they were public officers who could be removed if they failed to show obedience. Lords and their vassals had not yet gained a monopoly of military power, since ordinary freemen, especially in Saxony, still served in the armies. Strong regional loyalties acted to hold the duchies together, especially among the Saxons and Bavarians, who were determined to preserve their customs and their identity. Germany had not disintegrated as France had, and the dukes and counts of Germany did not have the monopoly of power which their French counterparts enjoyed. The king had supporters throughout the realm and exercised firm control over one great duchy. He had a chance to make a real kingdom out of Germany.

Otto the Great and the German-Roman Empire

Otto the Great (936–73) made the most of this opportunity. He held Saxony in his own right, and he gradually brought the other duchies under control by forcing out disobedient dukes and by bestowing their offices on members of his own family. This policy was not wholly successful, for Otto's own sons rebelled against him. But there was still the Church, which had great wealth and cherished the idea of unity. Otto, as an anointed king, had the right to ask the Church for aid. Moreover, the popes at this time were weak and most of the bishops and abbots owed their positions to Otto. They supplied him with money and troops from their estates; they furnished him with administrative officers and even army commanders. The support of the Church made Otto supreme in central Europe; he was able to put down all rebellions and inflict a crushing defeat on the Magyars in 955.

Otto's position was so strong that he was able to intervene repeatedly in Italian affairs and eventually to annex northern Italy. He has often been blamed for this, since in the long run the involvement in Italian politics weakened the German monarchy. But, given the situation in the tenth century, it would have been difficult for

Germany and Italy at the Time of Otto the Great 962

9 / The Emergence of a Western European Civilization

Ivory from the altar of Magdeburg Cathedral, ca. 970. The Emperor Otto I, holding the model, dedicates the newly built cathedral to Christ.

Otto to avoid involvement. The Italian kingdom, one of the weakest states to emerge from the break-up of the Carolingian Empire, included only the northern half of the peninsula, and even in this half the kings had little power. The title passed from one adventurer to another, and often there were two claimants to the throne. Tempted by this chaotic state of affairs, French feudal lords had already tried to establish themselves as kings of Italy, and the duke of Bavaria also had thoughts of crossing the Alps and trying his luck. Otto, anxious to preserve his position as the strongest ruler in western Europe, could hardly allow Italy to pass to a potential rival, much less to one of his own subjects.

Otto's close relations with the Church in Germany also impelled him to intervene in Italy. He was not a mere exploiter of the Church; he felt, as Charlemagne had, that it was his duty to preserve and strengthen ecclesiastical institutions. The papacy was in a miserable condition; deprived of the support of the Carolingians, it had fallen under the control of corrupt and self-seeking Roman nobles. So little authority and prestige did it enjoy that a tenth-century German archbishop actually refused to become pope. Otto reasoned that intervention in Italy would free the papacy from domination by Roman nobles and would also reduce the possibility that a pope might some day try to drive a wedge between the German king and the German bishops. Too dependent on the resources of the Church to risk losing them, Otto resolved to forestall his enemies from gaining control of the papacy.

Otto at least had a romantic excuse for his first invasion of Italy. Adelaide, widow of an Italian king, was being annoyed by her husband's successor. Otto came to the rescue of the queen, married her, and then claimed the Italian throne. His conquest of Italy was interrupted by rebellions and wars in Germany, but he eventually established his authority over the kingdom. The union of Germany and Italy made Otto the dominant ruler in Europe, and the pope recognized this position by crowning him emperor in 962.

Since there had been no emperor with real power since Louis, Charlemagne's son, and not even a nominal emperor since 924, Otto's coronation was a refounding of the medieval Empire. After Otto there was no break; the imperial title and the German kingship were to remain indissolubly united for the rest of the Middle Ages. This Roman Empire of the German nation, as it was called by some contemporaries, was the strongest state in Europe until about 1100 and an important force in European politics for 200 years after that. Especially significant were the relations between the German-Roman Empire and the popes. Otto, as successor to Charlemagne, thought of himself as leader of the Christian West and protector of the papacy. He took this second responsibility so seriously that he soon irritated the pope, who had sought an ally, not a master. But Otto persisted, and by the end of his life he dominated papal elections. This proved to be a dangerous precedent, since the Church eventually reacted violently against imperial control, but for almost a hundred years the emperors named and deposed popes whenever they were in Italy. And on the whole they strengthened the Church; popes chosen by the emperors were abler and better men than those selected by Roman nobles.

Gerbert

Having revived the Carolingian tradition of an alliance between emperor and Church, an alliance in which the emperor was unquestionably the dominant partner, Otto proceeded to revive the Carolingian interest in scholarship. He gathered scholars from all over Europe to reassemble and reinterpret classical and ecclesiastical texts. One of the most famous of these scholars was Gerbert, who was born in southwestern France about the middle of the tenth century, but who spent most of his life in the service of Otto's son and grandson. Gerbert had studied in Spain, where contact with the Moslems had revived interest in mathematics and astronomy. He learned what he could of these subjects—very little by later standards but enough to give him a reputation for profound, even magical, knowledge in his own day. He also tried to teach elementary ideas about astronomy and devised some simple apparatus to demonstrate his points.

These scientific interests were not unprecedented, though few westerners had paid much attention to mathematics or astronomy during the ninth and tenth centuries. What made them important was the fact that Gerbert was more than a secluded scholar; he was one of the most influential churchmen of his time. The emperors he served made him first the abbot of a great monastery, then archbishop of Reims, and eventually pope. As Sylvester II (999–1003) he was the chief adviser of the emperor Otto III (983–1002), whose tutor he had been. The two men dreamed of an empire which would be much more like the old Roman Empire than Charlemagne's had been, an empire in which emperor and pope would act as the joint heads of a unified western state.

This was a hopeless dream, though both pope and emperor died before they realized quite how hopeless it was. But the fact that they could conceive of such a plan shows how strong Roman ideas were in the Ottonian court. And Gerbert might be excused for overestimating imperial power. After all, he had been imposed as archbishop on Reims, a province which was largely French, and had been made pope simply because the emperor wished it.

Gerbert's political program was a failure, but his scholarly work marked a turning point in European intellectual history. The fact that such an influential man had made an effort to master mathematics and science was long remembered. Western Europe was never again quite so indifferent to these subjects. Other scholars took the road to Spain and prepared the way for a great intellectual revival in the twelfth century, a revival in which western Europeans, for the first time, took a real interest in science.

Gerbert had also become absorbed in the study of logic, partly because logic and science were closely related in the Greek scientific tradition he was trying to revive,

partly because he felt that he needed this tool in order to comprehend the new knowledge he had acquired. He was the first student for many generations to use and understand the elementary treatises of Aristotelian logic which Boethius had translated. Logic, like Latin, was a great aid in assimilating ancient knowledge, and Gerbert's use of logic, simple as it was, greatly impressed his contemporaries. Here again his example was not forgotten. The study of logic continued throughout the eleventh century and was one of the most important forces in the intellectual revival which came at the end of that century.

The direct line of Otto I ended in 1002 with the death of Otto III, but collateral branches of the family retained the throne and kept the Ottonian system of government going. Compared with France, which was splitting up into feudal states, Germany seemed to be flourishing. The German emperors stood unrivaled in their

The four provinces of Slavinia, Germania, Gallia, and Roma (left) paying homage to Otto III (right) with the clergy and the nobility, from the Reichenau Gospels, 10th century. Note that Otto is wearing a Roman imperial costume, not a Germanic one.

France Before William the Conqueror   early 11th century

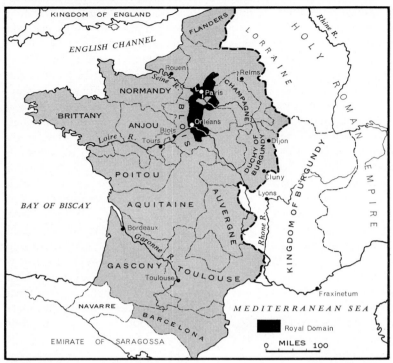

realm, in full control of both the Church and the great lords. They had wealth and prestige, and the greatest scholars of Europe came flocking to their courts. But the German state had serious weaknesses, weaknesses which had been masked by the remarkable ability of the emperors and the relatively slow development of feudal elements in German society. Imperial power depended on the support of the Church, and it was by no means certain that the Church would always be willing to remain subordinate to a secular ruler. The power of the local lord was growing in Germany as it had earlier in France, and there was no assurance that local lords would not some day seek independence. The emperor had to rely on churchmen and nobles to carry out his plans, for he had no bureaucracy. In short, the Ottonian Empire was lit-

tle more than a slightly modified Carolingian Empire, and the Carolingian Empire had long been out of date. The emperor's position rested on a precarious balance of forces—clergy versus laymen, one group of lords versus other lords—and the crises that arose in the last half of the eleventh century were to show just how precarious that balance was.

Anglo-Saxon England

England, like Germany and unlike France, was not feudalized in the tenth century. Like Germany again, it developed a relatively strong monarchy and an active intellectual life during that century. As the descendants of Alfred drove back the Danes, they had had to develop new institutions with which to hold and govern the territo-

9 / The Emergence of a Western European Civilization

England at the Time of the Norman Conquest late 11th century

ries they reconquered. These institutions were especially effective at the local level, so effective that they survived the Anglo-Saxon monarchy for centuries and even formed the basic pattern of local government in the United States.

New Institutions

The Anglo-Saxon kings of the tenth century divided the country into shires, or counties, and then subdivided the shires into smaller units called hundreds. Shires and hundreds were judicial as well as ad-ministrative units; there was a shire court which met twice a year and a hundred court which met about once a month. Fortified towns, important as military and trading centers, were called boroughs; the borough also had a court of its own.

This system was not unlike that of the Carolingian Empire and the states which succeeded it. But there was one important difference: in England the great men never had complete control of shire, hundred, and borough government, whereas in France the count was the ultimate author-

269

ity within his county. In England the highest royal official was the alderman, later called the earl. But the alderman usually was responsible for many shires stretching across the country, and he could not handle all the administrative details that demanded attention. Some local official was needed in each shire to collect revenue, muster troops, and preside over the courts. After a long period of experimentation the Anglo-Saxon kings eventually developed a very effective local official, the shire-reeve, or sheriff.

The shire-reeve at first was only one of a group of reeves, or agents, who managed the king's estates. It was logical to ask one of these men in each shire to supervise the others, and to see that all the king's revenue in that district was brought together in one place. Soon the chief reeve was asked to look after other royal interests as well, and eventually he became the king's representative in all affairs, with wide administrative and executive powers. Just as the sheriff of a western county in the United States in the nineteenth century was the key official in his district, so the Anglo-Saxon sheriff by the eleventh century was the most important official in his shire.

Silver penny of Alfred the Great, 870–99.

Powerful as the sheriff was, he never became independent of the king. He ranked beneath the really great men, the aldermen, or earls, and he could always be replaced if he failed to do his job loyally and efficiently. Though there were a few exceptions, on the whole the office of sheriff never became hereditary. From 1000 on, the king of England always had a local official in every part of his realm who would carry out his orders with reasonable efficiency and collect his revenues with reasonable honesty. Kings on the Continent grew weak and poor because they had lost control of local government and revenues. But the king of England grew strong and rich, even though his country was small and thinly populated, because he could use the resources of all his counties.

Law and Literature

The Anglo-Saxon kings of the tenth and eleventh centuries also improved internal security by discouraging blood-feuds and by forcing their subjects to take their quarrels to local courts. Certain serious crimes, such as murder, arson, and rape, were considered offenses against the king, and, since he received a substantial fine when a defendant was convicted of such crimes, he had an added incentive to strengthen and support the local courts in which these cases were tried. Much of the legislation of the Anglo-Saxon kings deals with the arrest and punishment of criminals. And it is a sign of their power that they could issue general laws; the great period of Anglo-Saxon legislation was between 950 and 1050, a time when the king of France could hardly make rules even for his own private estates.

Like the German kings, the Anglo-Saxon rulers encouraged ecclesiastical reform and sponsored literature and scholarship. But they were interested in writings in the vernacular as well as in Latin. Alfred the

Great had translated Latin works into Anglo-Saxon, and under his successors Anglo-Saxon literature reached its peak. The epic of *Beowulf* was put into its final form about 1000; the two great battle poems *Maldon* and *Brunanbuhr* came about the same time. Even more important for the historian is the *Anglo-Saxon Chronicle,* which was probably begun in the days of Alfred and was continued until the end of the eleventh century. It is mainly a history of kings and bishops, of wars and rebellions, but it tells us much about Anglo-Saxon customs and beliefs. The *Chronicle* survives in several different versions, a fact which indicates both official support and wide interest in history among the educated class. It is one of the most useful chronicles of the early Middle Ages, and the only important one to be written in a native language.

Military Weakness

With all its achievements, the Anglo-Saxon monarchy was not exempt from the difficulties which had weakened the continental kingdoms. The free warriors of the heroic age of the Anglo-Saxon conquest of Britain had lost both their fighting ability and their independence. They were now, for the most part, peasants who were coming increasingly under the domination of the landlords. Most of the peasants had put themselves under the protection of lords, and most of the lesser landlords had placed themselves under the patronage of some great man. Everywhere the bond between lord and follower was becoming stronger than the old ties of kinship and community. But, though the followers of the king and the great men had honorable status and were entrusted with important missions, they did not become a class of specialized military retainers. Thus, while the lords interposed themselves more and more between the king and the people, they did not

Page from the earliest manuscript of *Beowulf,* 10th century.

develop the bands of heavy-armed cavalrymen that were proving so effective on the Continent. England could no longer produce a strong folk-army, and it was not yet able to produce an army of mounted vassals.

This military weakness became evident soon after 1000 when the Danes renewed their attacks on England. King Ethelred the Ill-Counseled, after failing to defeat the Danes in battle, resorted to the hopeless expedient of buying them off with the proceeds of a national tax, the Danegeld. This gesture of weakness only encouraged the

Danes, and by 1016 their king Canute (or Knut) had completed the conquest of England.

England did not suffer greatly under Danish rule (1016–42), though some Anglo-Saxon lords lost their lands and official positions to Danes. Canute preserved, and even strengthened, Anglo-Saxon institutions; in fact, the last Anglo-Saxon laws were promulgated during his reign. But he did not solve England's military problem. He dominated the country through his bodyguard of housecarls, or retainers, but they were warriors of the old Germanic type, not mounted knights. England still had no army which could match the new type of forces which were developing in France.

Edward the Confessor

Canute's sons died without leaving direct heirs, and the Anglo-Saxons had no trouble in restoring the old line of kings descended from the House of Wessex. But the first restored king, Edward the Confessor (1042–66), was strong only in his piety; in all other things he was easily swayed by his relatives and advisers. He had spent long years of exile in Normandy and wanted to bring Norman ways into England and give Normans high positions in both ecclesiastical and secular administration. At the same time he was influenced by the earl Godwin, who was half Danish and wholly anti-French. Edward married Godwin's daughter and gave earldoms to Godwin's sons. These favors, in turn, made other Anglo-Saxon leaders jealous of Godwin and his family. So England suffered from quarrels between pro-French and anti-French, pro-Godwin and anti-Godwin factions—quarrels which at times reached the level of civil war.

The quarrels that surged around Edward were not unlike those endured by France a century before, when the last Carolingians

Silver penny of Edward the Confessor, 1042–66.

were trying to preserve a precarious balance among aristocratic factions. As in France, there was a notable transfer of political power into private hands during Edward's reign. Bishops, abbots, and great lay lords assumed control of the courts of many hundreds, and even lesser lords acquired police court jurisdiction over their men. Moreover, many of the powerful lords built up bodyguards large enough to constitute private armies.

Here we have some of the ingredients of feudalism, and it is possible that if Anglo-Saxon institutions had developed without interference they might eventually have produced a feudal system of an unusual type. Actually, however, the Anglo-Saxons had not advanced very far along the road to feudalism. The followers of the great lords did not have the specific duties or the special military training of the French vassals. Many of them were not even permanently bound to their lord; as the records say, they "could go with their land" to any lord they chose. This meant in turn that there were no fiefs, that the followers of a lord did not hold land and offices in return for service. And this was even more true of the earls and other great men than it was of ordinary retainers. They were not vassals of the king, and they owed him no service for the lands they possessed. Because they were rich and powerful they expected, as a matter of course, to be consulted by the king, and they also expected to receive the chief offices of government, such as the earldoms. On his side, the king expected the great men to assist him in the work of governing and defending the realm. But there were no permanent and binding obligations on either king or lord. The king could take an earldom from one lord and give it to another, and a lord who failed to serve the king in an emergency did not thereby forfeit his land.

Under Edward the Confessor, this absence of specific obligations worked to the advantage of the lords. Some of the great men, notably the earls of Godwin's family, were challenging the king's right to redistribute the earldoms at will. With private armies and strong local support they were able to hold on to their offices even when Edward sought to withdraw them. At the same time, the king was finding it difficult to raise an effective army to enforce his orders. A general levy of peasants was of little use, and he had no way of forcing the lords to come to his aid with their retainers. The earls were growing increasingly independent of the king, especially in the north, and there was some danger that the kingdom of England would break up into separate states.

England, in fact, was facing the same problem that Germany was facing in the eleventh century. In both countries the king still acted on the theory that the great men were his obedient subjects, that he could use them as public officials and dismiss them at will. But in both countries this theory was becoming unrealistic; the great men had acquired independent strength and it was increasingly difficult for the king to control them. But while in Germany the tendency toward disintegration proved irreversible, in England it was checked at the end of the eleventh century. The military weakness of the Anglo-Saxon kingdom, especially its lack of heavy-armed cavalry, laid it open to conquest by a French feudal army. And the leader of this army, William the Conqueror, introduced into England the most rigorous type of feudalism which Europe had yet seen. He imposed heavy and precise obligations on the lords and seized their lands if they failed to fulfill them. Thus William corrected the chief weakness of the old Anglo-Saxon state. At the same time, he preserved all the really effective Anglo-Saxon institutions, especially the remarkable Anglo-Saxon system of local government. The work of the Anglo-Saxon kings had not been wasted; the combination of their institutions with Norman feudalism was to make England for many generations the strongest state in Europe.

Suggestions for Further Reading

1. Pippin and St. Boniface

"The evolution of monarchical institutions and the idea of kingship during the Dark Ages from 400 to 1000 provides one of the most instructive examples of the complex process by which different social and religious elements became interwoven in a culture," writes C. Dawson in *Religion and the Rise of Western Culture* * (1950), a very good introduction to this period. C. H. Talbot, *Anglo-Saxon Missionaries in Germany* (1954), gives the correspondence of Pippin and St. Boniface and provides a cross section of the religious life of the eighth century difficult to parallel elsewhere.

2. Charlemagne and the Revival of the Empire

The best biography that we have of the man who was at the center of this epoch is the contemporary Einhard's *Life of Charlemagne* * (Foreword by S. Painter, 1960). J. H. Robinson, ed., *Readings in European History,* Vol. I (1904), has excellent source material on the administration of the Carolingian Empire. There are several good studies of the man and the age: H. Kleinclausz, *Charlemagne* (1934), is a scholarly work which concentrates on political conditions, while the recent and very readable study by H. Fichtenau, *The Carolingian Empire* (1957), gives greater attention to social conditions. F. L. Ganshof, *The Imperial Coronation of Charlemagne* (1949), focuses on a problem which has interested many historians. The best study of the rise and decline of the Carolingian Empire is L. Halphen, *Charlemagne et l'Empire Carolingien* (1949). Halphen, however, is not such interesting reading as Fichtenau.

3. The Carolingian Renaissance

Most of the general works cited above have material on the Carolingian Renaissance. M. L. W. Laistner, *Thought and Letters in Western Europe, 500–900* (1951), devotes considerable attention to the prose and poetry of the period. E. S. Duckett, *Alcuin, Friend of Charlemagne* (1951), gives a somewhat romantic picture of the Frankish court and the palace school. The influence of political and social factors on Carolingian art is brought out in A. Hauser, *Social History of Art,* * Vol. I (1957). W. Levison, *England and the Continent in the Eighth Century* (1948), combines great knowledge of the literature of the age with a fine prose style.

4. Collapse of the Empire and the New Invasions

Both T. F. Tout, *The Empire and the Papacy* (1903), and J. Bryce, *The Holy Roman Empire* (many editions), are broad surveys with valuable material on the decline of the Carolingian Empire. The work of Halphen cited above presents a fresher historical explanation and has a more up-to-date bibliography.

The best introduction to the age of the vikings is J. Brønsted, *The Vikings* * (1960), a fascinating account of viking art and civilization by a distinguished Danish scholar. T. D. Kendrick, *A History of the Vikings* (1930), shows the impact of the viking invasions on Britain, western Europe, Russia, and even America. A. Olrik, *Viking Civilization* (1930), and G. Turville-Petre, *The Heroic Age of Scandinavia* (1951), interpret the age of the vikings from the legends and sagas of individual Norsemen; of the two, Turville-Petre is the more readable. The great poem *Beowulf* * (trans. D. Wright, 1957) provides information about viking civilization which has been documented by archeological findings. C. A. Macartney, *The Magyars in the Ninth Century* (1930), is a scholarly study of the origins and wanderings of the Magyars.

5. Feudalism

Both *Raoul de Cambrai* (trans. J. Crosland, 1926) and *The Song of Roland* * (trans. D. L. Sayers, 1957) present excellent pictures of the ideals and attitudes of the feudal caste in the first age of western feudalism. F. L. Ganshof, *Feudalism* (1952),

* Available in paperback edition.

shows the development of "classical feudalism" from its Carolingian origins. M. Bloch, *La Sociétié Féodale*, 2 vols. (1929–40), is an outstanding study from a more social and economic point of view, while a more political interpretation is offered by the constitutional historian, C. Stephenson, *Feudalism* (1942). A. Boutrouche, *Seigneurie et Féodalité* (1959), studies the first age of the feudal and manorial systems and compares European feudalism with eastern forms. Boutrouche has a thorough recent bibliography. F. Kern, *Kingship and Law in the Middle Ages* (1939), is a historical essay which is invaluable for an understanding of the nature and development of the idea of kingship in early medieval Europe.

6. Otto I and the Saxon Dynasty

Medieval Germany, Vol. I (trans. G. Barraclough, 1938), has as its theme the internal development of the German state in the obscure period from the tenth to the thirteenth century. There is information on Otto I and the Saxon dynasty in H. A. L. Fisher, *The Medieval Empire*, Vol. I (1898). Luitprand of Cremona, *Chronicle of the Reign of Otto I, Embassy to Constantinople* (trans. F. A. Wright, 1930), presents a picture of Church-state cooperation under the Saxons and an insight into the western attitude toward Byzantium in the eleventh century.

7. The Anglo-Saxon Monarchy to 1066; Anglo-Saxon Art

The Anglo-Saxon Chronicle (Everyman's Library) is the indispensable framework for developments in England before 1066. There is interesting source material in *Six Old English Chronicles* (trans. J. Giles, 1875) and *English Historical Documents, 1042–1189* (edited D. C. Douglas and G. W. Greenaway, 1953–55). F. Barlow, *The Feudal Kingdom of England, 1042–1216* (1953), has a good account of the reign of Edward the Confessor. The best scholarly treatment of the entire period is F. M. Stenton, *Anglo-Saxon England* (1943), but G. O. Sayles, *Medieval Foundations of England*, Chapters 5–16 (1948), is much more readable and has a good critical bibliography.

Most of the works cited above have information on the artistic achievements of the period. T. D. Kendrick, *Anglo-Saxon Art* (1938), is a good survey. D. Talbot-Rice, *English Art, 950–1100* (1952), traces the development of architecture, sculpture, and manuscript illumination. It has good plates and an excellent bibliography.

10

Revival

and Reform

in Western Europe

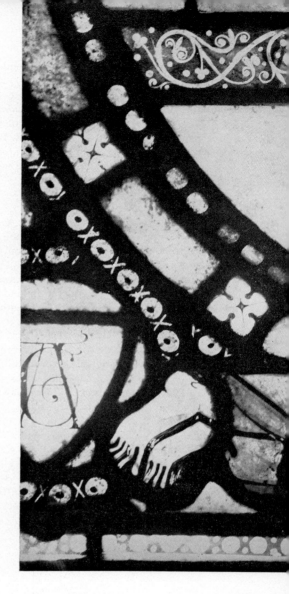

Battered and torn by invasions and civil wars during the tenth century, western Europe began to recover after 1000. The worst of the invasions were over: the Moslems were no longer very aggressive, the Magyars had been confined to Hungary, and the Northmen were a threat only to England. France was achieving some degree of stability under its feudal lords, while England and Germany were relatively peaceful under their kings. Italy was more turbulent, but even there the inter-

vention of the emperor and the rise of great trading cities had led to some decrease in disorder and violence. There were troubles on the periphery: Spain was still being devastated by wars between Christians and Moslems; the Scandinavian countries were still torn by blood-feuds among viking leaders and rebellions against the kings; and much of central Europe was held by loosely organized Slavic tribes. But the heart of western Europe, the great stretch of land running from Rome to London

Abbot Suger, detail from a stained-glass window in the apse of his church of St. Denis, first half of 12th century. The window shows the Annunciation, with Suger prostrate at the feet of the Virgin.

and from Bremen to Venice, had survived its worst difficulties.

The increase in security had been slight, almost imperceptible, but western Europe had the resources and the vitality to profit from even slight improvement. Beginning in the last half of the eleventh century and

277

continuing throughout the twelfth, there was a great surge forward in all forms of human activity. Production and trade increased; political, legal, and religious institutions grew stronger; religious feeling became deeper and more meaningful; more and better work was done in art and in scholarship.

The Economic Revival

The first and most obvious result of this greater stability was a rise in population. The evidence for this rise—indirect, but convincing—is simply that during the late eleventh and twelfth centuries men could always be found to undertake new occupations and activities. There were enough men to clear forests and drain swamps, to enlarge old towns and build new ones, to establish new farms and villages in the half-deserted Slavic lands beyond the Elbe. There were enough men for conquests and crusades, for William's seizure of England, for the expansion of Christian holdings in Spain, for repeated expeditions overseas to regain the Holy Land. And there were enough men, too, to furnish a striking increase in the number of students and teachers, of writers and artists, of clergymen, lawyers, and doctors.

Agriculture

The increase in population, however, would have been a burden on society, rather than a stimulus, if production had not increased at the same time. The most important, and most difficult, increase to achieve was in the production of food. Clearing new land helped, since soil which had lain uncultivated for centuries was often very fertile. But the new land came into production very slowly, not nearly fast enough to keep up with the growing population. Production from old land had to be increased by better organization of labor and by better farming techniques.

The two developments—better organization and improved techniques—must have gone hand in hand, but we can see the relationship only in broad outline. Briefly, what seems to have happened was that the peasants, simply in order to survive during the years of invasion and warfare, were forced to find more effective ways of working together. At the same time the lords, who drew almost all their income from the land, encouraged only those changes that would increase production.

The result was a tightly integrated village community which used its resources with considerable efficiency. The arable land was divided into large fields, each of which was in turn divided into long, narrow strips. Each peasant held strips in each field, and some strips were cultivated for the benefit of the lord. Thus everyone had an equal share of good and bad land. All the heavy work was done in common; the peasants pooled their work animals to form plow teams and all joined together to harvest the big fields when the grain was ripe. Since farm animals were few and scrawny and tools were dull-edged and heavy, this was the best way to handle a hard job in a reasonable length of time.

One of the most bothersome problems was to find enough feed for the work animals. The yield of grain per acre was low, probably not more than eight to ten bushels, and almost all of it had to be saved for human consumption. Since grass grew only in small meadows along the streams, few villages produced enough hay to feed their animals during the winter months. To solve this problem, the poorer lands were reserved exclusively for pasture, and animals were allowed to graze on the big cultivated fields after the crops were harvested and on arable land that was lying fallow. Here again, through community organization the peasants saved themselves trouble

Plowing with oxen and harrowing with a horse, two scenes from the Luttrill Psalter, ca. 1340.

and time, for a few herdsmen could take care of all the animals of the village.

Finally, the village needed a common woodland. Wood was needed for fuel, for the frames of peasant huts, and for tools, which were made with as much wood and as little iron as possible. Forests were also used for pasturing great herds of half-wild pigs, very like the razorback hogs of our southern states. These pigs supplied the peasants with most of their meat, since other animals were too scarce to serve as a regular source of food. The wild game of the forests was reserved for the lords, though there was a good deal of poaching. This agricultural system, though it had

obvious advantages, had equally obvious drawbacks. It left little room for individual initiative, for everyone had to follow customary routines of planting and harvesting, and the work pace was set by the slowest oxen driven by the most stupid villager. Moreover, it provided no chance to improve the breed of animals or the stock of seed, since the animals ran together in common pastures and the seed on one strip was inevitably mixed with that of neighboring strips. Little could be done to increase the fertility of the soil, since the animals were not kept in barns where manure could be collected.

And yet the medieval village proved re-

Peasants reaping, from Queen Mary's Psalter, 14th century.

markably tough, surviving invasion and war, flood and drought. It not only survived; it even furnished a surplus to support the ruling class of lords and knights, the educated class of priests and monks, and the trading and industrial class of townsmen. Though these nonagricultural groups grew steadily from the eleventh through the thirteenth century, food production more than kept up with their needs.

Moreover, the medieval village was much less hostile to innovation than is sometimes believed. In the obscure years between the breakup of the Carolingian Empire and the end of the eleventh century, improved agricultural techniques spread widely throughout much of Europe. The heavy wheeled plow with a moldboard to turn the soil had been used from a very early date in a few districts in Germany. It was far more effective than the light Mediterranean plow in cultivating the heavy, wet clay soils of northern Europe, but it required a large team, usually eight oxen, to draw it. The ordinary peasant never had eight oxen; the only way to form such a plow-team was for neighbors to pool their animals. Understandably, the area in which the heavy plow was used corresponds fairly closely to the area in which integrated villages were common. By 1100 the heavy plow had been adopted in Germany, north-

ern France, and southern and central England. It led to a great increase in food production, for it enabled the peasants to cultivate lands the Romans had never touched.

Another innovation, also closely connected with the integrated village, was the three-field system. Since artificial fertilizers were unknown and manure was scarce, the usual method of preserving the fertility of the soil was to let half the land lie fallow each year. In northern Europe farmers discovered that they could get equally good results by keeping only a third of the land out of cultivation. So they divided the land into three large blocks (hence the term three-field system) and rotated their crops. During the first year of the cycle, they planted one of these blocks in winter wheat, which they harvested in July; then they let the winter-wheat field rest until the following spring, when they sowed it with spring grains. This crop they harvested in the fall, and then let the land rest once more until the following fall, when it was sown with winter wheat. In the other blocks, they followed the same cycle, but one year and two years, respectively, behind the first block. Thus in any year, one-third of the land produced winter wheat, one-third produced spring grain, and one-third was left uncultivated. And yet, over the three-year cycle, each field could lie fallow for at least a year and a half. This system could not be used in the Mediterranean basin, where there is not enough summer rain for spring grain to mature. And it was hard to use in regions where there were no well-organized villages. But where it was used, it increased production by a third.

Only about half of western Europe was organized in integrated villages. Where the soil was thin and rainfall scant, or where strong local tradition resisted innovation, there were only small, loosely organized hamlets and individual farms, as in northern England, Brittany, and Mediterranean France. On the whole, these districts produced less per acre and per man than did districts marked by integrated villages. The wine-growing districts, which required individual rather than group effort, were an exception to this rule, though they were not very prosperous until trade increased enough to open an outside market for their produce. But even the more backward areas were normally self-sufficient in food. It is true that, until transportation became better organized, there might be severe local famines even during a time of general surplus. But, by and large, western Europe had solved the problem of food production by the middle of the twelfth century.

by 1150 — food problem o.k.

Commerce and Industry

During these same years the towns of western Europe were experiencing a striking increase in size and number. They absorbed some of the surplus population and furnished a steadily growing market for agricultural products. In return, they intensified trade among all parts of Europe and increased the production of textiles and goods made of iron, copper, and other metals. The growth of towns was especially conspicuous in Italy and Flanders.

The Italian towns depended almost entirely on international trade, particularly in oriental goods such as silk and spices. During the eleventh century Italian merchants began to find it a little easier and safer to send their ships to the eastern Mediterranean. With the Byzantine Empire weakening and the Mohammedan caliphate breaking up, neither of these ancient rivals could interfere with Mediterranean trade as they had during the height of their struggle. The Italians still had to contend with piracy, but the larger cities had strong enough fleets to beat off any pirate attack. Pisa went even further; its fleet captured and wiped out the pirate stronghold of Mehdia on the North African coast. As if to aid the Italian merchants in their newfound prosperity, nomadic invaders were strangling the alternate trade route from the East along the Russian rivers to the Baltic. Thus the Italians almost monopolized the trade in oriental goods for western markets. And these markets were becoming steadily more profitable, thanks to the general increase in prosperity and security throughout the West. The great seaports of Venice, Pisa, and Genoa flourished most brilliantly, but the towns of the Po Valley, especially Milan, were not far behind. And as the Italian merchants carried their wares north through France and Germany they stimulated the growth of trading centers along their routes.

The towns of Flanders found their nourishment in industry rather than trade. The flat, marshy lands along the sea seemed to be good only for sheep-raising, so that Flanders had a surplus of wool from a very early date. Moreover, since Flanders was one of the first feudal states to achieve a relatively high level of stability and internal security, there was soon a surplus population which could be used to process the surplus wool. Wool was almost the only material used for clothing in western Europe, for cotton was unknown and both linen and silk were terribly expensive. But to transform raw wool into good cloth took a great deal of time and energy. The wool had to be cleaned and carded, spun into thread, woven, smoothed by shearing off the knots and rough places, and finally dyed. All these tasks could be performed after a fashion by village workers, but the rough homespun cloth they turned out was neither comfortable nor attractive. Anyone who had an income above the subsistence level wanted better cloth produced by skilled craftsmen. For many people, a good suit of clothes was the only luxury they possessed. This is why, from the early Middle Ages clear into the nineteenth century, the textile industry was the most important industry in western Europe.

Perhaps as early as the time of Charlemagne, and certainly by the eleventh century, Flanders had become the textile center of Europe. It had the wool, it had the labor, and soon Flemish cloth was famous near and far. It was bought by well-to-do people throughout Europe and even found a market outside Europe in the Mohammedan world. The first European manufactured product with much appeal for non-Europeans, it helped to balance European trade with the Orient. By the twelfth century the Flemish textile towns of Ghent, Bruges, and Ypres rivaled the flourishing seaports of Italy in wealth and population.

Outside Italy and Flanders the towns were smaller and the growth of commerce and industry was less spectacular. But everywhere new towns were springing up and old ones expanding in wealth and population. Some served as distribution centers along the trade routes between great commercial and industrial centers. Others specialized in manufacturing goods for local consumption. Even a small town could usually make better cloth, tools, and utensils than a peasant village could, and there was a steady demand for whatever it produced. Thus western Europe began to enjoy a more rational division of labor and a better use of human resources. Peasants and landlords began to specialize in producing food for the market while skilled craftsmen in the towns concentrated on manufacturing. This development may seem so elementary that it is hardly worth mentioning, but it was precisely this division of labor between town and country which had been lacking in the late Roman Empire and the early Germanic kingdoms.

The growth of towns stimulated the economy of Europe, but it put serious strains on the social and economic system. The ruling classes, feudal lords and churchmen, knew how to control and exploit peasants, but they were not so sure of themselves in dealing with merchants and artisans. Obviously, townspeople needed personal freedom and some local self-government. A serf could not function as a merchant and a feudal court designed to settle disputes among serfs and landowners was poorly equipped to deal with lawsuits among businessmen. But if the townsmen became too free they might escape completely from the control of the ruling classes. The ideal solution for the lords was to grant the towns enough freedom to become prosperous but retain enough control to share in that prosperity, through taxes, tolls, and payments for market rights. It was not easy to strike this balance, however, and all through the eleventh and twelfth centuries the lords and the towns were engaged in a long series of disputes, which sometimes led to violence. The Church had an especially difficult time in dealing with the towns. Like all landlords, it hated to surrender any of its rights, and it found the morals of the townspeople deplorable. At best, the townspeople's concentration on profits and money distracted their attention from the teachings of the

Church; at worst, some of them became so critical of the clergy that they fell into heresy. There were bloody conflicts between the rulers of ecclesiastical towns and their subjects in eastern France, and Rome itself staged frequent rebellions against the pope during the twelfth century.

In the end, the towns of every country of the West gained personal freedom for their people and a separate system of municipal government. But the extent of their self-government varied with the strength of the country's kings and nobles. In England and in the feudal states of France, for example, the towns never became independent. In Spain, though they enjoyed considerable liberty at first, it was gradually whittled away as the kings became stronger. In Germany, the process went the other way: So long as the emperors were strong, the towns had little independence; but after the collapse of the Empire in the thirteenth century (see p. 355), many, though not all, of the cities became free. In Italy no medieval ruler managed to hold the towns under control for any length of time, and most of them became independent city-states. These differences in the autonomy of towns from one country to another were to have a significant effect on the political structure of Europe. Rulers who could not tap the wealth of their towns found it difficult to build strong centralized states; this is one reason why Italy and Germany remained disunited for so long. Conversely, rulers who could draw on the resources of their towns were able to build powerful administrative and military organizations; this is one reason why France and England were united at such an early date.

The Political Revival

The economic revival of Europe was accompanied by a political revival. The period of invasions had ended by 1000, and by the middle of the eleventh century the chronic disease of local warfare was being mitigated in many districts. As we have already seen, a new line of emperors, beginning with Otto I, succeeded in keeping Germany peaceful and united. The emperors were less successful in Italy—no one, for many centuries, could keep the Italians from quarreling—but at least they ended the wars for possession of the Italian crown. Now the Italian towns had an opportunity to develop, but in the process they tried to dominate weak neighbors and check dangerous competitors and so launched the bitter intercity feuds which lasted until the sixteenth century. But the regions where the political revival was most noticeable, and where it produced the most enduring results, were northern France and England.

Flanders and Normandy

In northern France the feudal lords had restored a certain degree of order by the middle of the eleventh century. Two of them, the count of Flanders and the duke of Normandy, had gone even further and had built up relatively well-governed states. The counts of Flanders were fortunate in having neither dangerous neighbors nor powerful vassals. They enlarged the boundaries of their original holdings without ever losing personal control over the county. They named their own men to occupy the fortified castles; they suppressed private wars; and they kept the most important law courts firmly in their own hands. Warfare often broke out along the borders, but the heart of Flanders was relatively peaceful and Flemish industry grew apace.

The vikings had received eastern Normandy in 911, but they carried on their policy of conquest and settlement for another generation. Only after 950 had the duchy reached its permanent boundaries, and only then could the dukes begin to organize their government. This late start gave them a real advantage, for they could profit by the experience of their neighbors. Given the environment, Norman government had to be a feudal government, but the dukes could stress those elements in the feudal relationship that kept them strong and could minimize those that reduced their power. Proceeding with great intelligence, they imposed heavy and carefully specified duties on their vassals and meted out swift punishment to anyone who failed to meet his obligations. The duke of Normandy could raise a larger army in proportion to the size of his holdings than any other French feudal lord. At the same time, to ensure that no vassal became too powerful, he discouraged private war, ordered that no new castle could be built except by special license, and reserved to himself important rights of justice throughout Normandy. His firm control over most of the towns assured him a good income from their flourishing commerce. And, since he named all the bishops and most of the important abbots, he had absolute control over the Norman church. In order to keep their lands, churchmen had to become vassals of the duke, supplying him with a large part of his army and much of his administrative staff. Normandy, like Flanders, was a relatively peaceful and prosperous state, and its population soon began to expand.

The energies of Normandy and Flanders were directed into different channels, however. The Flemish concentrated almost exclusively on industry and agriculture. Many of them settled in the towns and be-

Castle of the counts of Flanders, Ghent, late 12th century. The square inner tower was the keep, or donjon, the center of resistance if the outer walls were broken.

10 / Revival and Reform in Western Europe

came textile-workers; others began the centuries-long struggle to reclaim from the sea the flooded land of the coast. They became so skillful in the arts of diking and draining that they were sought by rulers of other provinces. In the twelfth century thousands of Flemish peasants moved across Germany to clear and drain the lands which German lords had won from the Slavs. In Normandy, on the other hand, though some new land was cleared, there was none of the intensive agricultural and industrial activity which marked Flanders. Instead, the Normans channeled their energies into military and political expansion.

The Normans in Italy

The first Norman Conquest was in southern Italy, where only the wreckage of earlier political systems survived. The Byzantine Empire held the mainland coasts; the mainland interior was divided among Lombard princes; and the island of Sicily was ruled by rapidly shifting Moslem dynasties. After 1000, when the Normans began drifting in as mercenary soldiers, they realized that the chaotic condition of southern Italy offered a fine opportunity to bold and courageous men. Soon they were fighting for themselves instead of for their employers. By 1071, under Robert Guiscard, the Normans had conquered almost all of the mainland and were even trying to seize Byzantine provinces in Greece and Albania. Meanwhile Robert's younger brother, Roger, had launched the conquest of Sicily. In this slow and bloody operation, the Moslem strongholds had to be reduced one by one, but by 1091 Sicily was firmly in Roger's possession. His son, Roger II, eventually inherited the mainland conquests as well and in 1130 took the title of king of Sicily.

This conquest of southern Italy and Sicily was in many ways a more remarkable feat than the Norman conquest of England.

The Norman Conquest of Southern Italy 1130

There were fewer Normans in southern Italy than there were in England, and their first leaders had far less authority. But in Italy, as in Normandy earlier and in England later, the Normans showed an uncanny ability to build a strong government out of whatever institutions they found ready at hand. They introduced Norman feudalism in order to guarantee the ruler a strong army, but they preserved much of the Byzantine and Moslem bureaucratic apparatus. The Norman kingdom of Sicily, when it finally took shape in the twelfth century, was one of the wonders of the medieval world. Norman barons and knights, Greek secretaries, and Moslem financial experts—all worked together to make the king strong. He had full control over justice and administration; he regulated the commerce of the entire kingdom; he enjoyed a steady income collected by a centralized financial bureau. Only the king of England

could rival him in these matters, and during most of the twelfth century even the king of England probably had less authority.

The Norman Conquest of England

In the long run, however, it was the Norman conquest of England that had the more important consequences. The brilliant Sicilian state fell on evil days in the thirteenth century, and its remarkable institutions were eroded away by successive waves of conquest. Only in England did the Norman genius for government have an opportunity to produce lasting results.

In the years just before 1066, Anglo-Saxon England was torn by dissension. King Edward the Confessor was a pious Christian but an ineffective ruler, and he left no direct heir. Earl Godwin and his sons stood forth as the most powerful men in the kingdom, much to the disgust of the other earls, who tried on several occasions to pull them down. As Edward grew older, the question of the succession became more acute. At one time he had thought of naming his cousin William, duke of Normandy, to succeed him. But the relationship was only through marriage; William was not descended from the Anglo-Saxon kings; and the English disliked the Normans. Later Edward seemed to turn his favor toward Earl Harold, the son of God-

win; at least he allowed him the dominant voice in the government. And when Edward finally died in 1065, Harold was in such a strong position that the bishops and earls accepted him as king.

But William was determined not to lose the inheritance which had once been promised to him. As duke of Normandy he already had the best army in western Europe, and he reinforced it by recruiting knights from all the neighboring feudal states. The pope, who was annoyed with the Anglo-Saxons because they had driven out a French archbishop of Canterbury during one of their anti-Norman demonstrations, gave his blessing to William's enterprise. Helped in his recruiting campaign by papal support and the promise of English wealth and land, William had assembled an army of over five thousand men by the summer of 1066.

Harold, aware that the attack was coming, massed his forces in southern England. But just as William was ready to sail, Harold was called away by the last great invasion of the Northmen, along the east coast of England. Harold defeated the Northmen in a hard battle and hurried back to the south in time to take up a strong position on a hill near Hastings. But forced marches had exhausted his army, and heavy battle casualties had thinned its

S.ADMA...RE = ...STI ...PORTANT:ARMAS: ADNAVES: ETB
TRAbVNT: CARR
CVM VINO:ETARM

William preparing to attack England, scenes from the Bayeux tapestry, late 11th century. From left to right trees are felled, planks shaped, and ships built and dragged to the water; then mail shirts, swords, spears, and wine are carried to the ships.

ranks; moreover, expected support from the northern earls failed to materialize. Harold, with forces composed entirely of infantry, could not take the offensive against William's heavy cavalry. He made a heroic defensive stand, but in the end he was killed and the English shield-wall broke. William marched on London and was accepted as king.

William's victory owed much to chance, but his subsequent consolidation of power in England demonstrated both his own ability and the strength of Norman feudal institutions. He had to deal with a bewildered and disoriented native population and with an overconfident group of conquerors, more than half of whom were not Normans. There were some Anglo-Saxon risings; there were even more cases of disobedience and rebellion on the part of his French barons. But he rode them all down: "The rich complained and the poor murmured," says the *Anglo-Saxon Chronicle,* "but he was so sturdy that he recked naught of them; they must will all that the king willed, if they would live or would keep their lands."

William's power rested on two basic principles. First, he insisted that he was the lawful heir of Edward the Confessor and so had inherited all the rights of the Anglo-Saxon kings. The Anglo-Saxon aristoc-racy, by opposing their rightful ruler, had forfeited their lands and rights. This led to the second principle: the new Norman aristocracy now held all lands and rights as fiefs of the king. No lord *owned* anything; he merely had a right to hold it so long as he obeyed and rendered service to the king. This arrangement overcame the chief weakness of the Anglo-Saxon monarchy—namely, its failure to control or discipline the earls and great landlords. A Norman baron who failed to meet his feudal obligations knew that he would lose all or part of his land.

William gave his barons and knights extensive powers in local government. He transferred most of the hundred courts (see p. 268) to private hands and named Norman barons as sheriffs. The peasants were now completely at the mercy of the foreign aristocracy; many free peasants became serfs, and many serfs were obliged to surrender more money and service to their new lords. But the lords could not ignore the rights of the king as cavalierly as they ignored the rights of the peasants. The

287

county courts were still the king's courts, and any baronial sheriff who showed signs of trying to build up independent power could be summarily removed. The king was obeyed throughout the land and drew large revenues from every county in England. He forbade private war and the building of castles without license; he kept the peace so well that, to quote the *Chronicle* again, "a man might travel through the kingdom unmolested with a bosomful of gold."

Norman Government in England

The most striking result of the Norman Conquest was the steady growth of the

❖❖❖❖❖❖❖❖❖❖❖❖❖❖❖❖❖❖❖❖❖❖❖❖❖❖❖❖❖

The Domesday Survey

1086

The monks of Ely added this note to their copy of Domesday returns for their lands.

Here is written down the inquest of the lands [of Ely] as the king's barons inquired about them: namely, by the oaths of the sheriff of the shire and of all the barons and their French soldiers, and of the whole hundred [court], and of the priest, the reeve and six villeins of each vill. Then, how the manor is called, who held it in the time of King Edward [the Confessor] and who holds it now, how many hides,* how many plows on the demesne, how many men, how many villeins, how many serfs, how much woods, how much meadow, how much pasture, how many mills . . . how much it was worth altogether and how much now. . . . All this three times over, once for the time of King Edward, once for the time when King William gave it out, and once as it now is—and whether more can be had from it than is now being given.

Trans. from W. Stubbs, *Select Charters* (Oxford: Clarendon Press, 1921), p. 101.

* **hide:** 120 acres.

❖❖❖❖❖❖❖❖❖❖❖❖❖❖❖❖❖❖❖❖❖❖❖❖❖❖❖❖❖

power of the king's central court. This court had a solid core of household officials and clerks, and a fluctuating population of bishops and barons who happened to be with the king at any given moment. The court assisted the king in any business which he laid before it; it could advise on policy, audit accounts, or try cases involving great barons. William kept it very busy, and he himself traveled incessantly up and down England visiting his estates and settling local quarrels. When he could not be present himself, he sometimes sent a delegation from his court to represent him. These delegations, with the full authority of the king, could try suits involving land disputes between great vassals. They often used a new and very effective procedure which William had imported from Normandy: trial by inquest. In an inquest neighbors of the litigants were sworn in and instructed to give true answers to questions concerning the matters in dispute. Only the king could order an inquest, and this monopoly gave his court a great advantage. Procedure by inquest was a much better way of getting at the facts than trial by battle (which was the favorite procedure of the Norman barons), and it enabled the king to settle disputes peacefully and to protect both his own rights and those of his vassals.

The most famous example of the inquest was the Domesday Survey. Faced with the confusion caused by the rapid redistribution of land after the Conquest, William wanted to know what each district owed him and what estates were held by his vassals; he probably also wanted to settle a number of boundary disputes among his barons. In 1086 he sent delegations from his court to every county in England with orders to swear in an inquest from each village. The village inquests told the king's men how much land there was in the village, how many men, who had held the

William the Conqueror, William Rufus, Henry I, and Stephen as benefactors of Westminster Abbey. From the *Historia* of Matthew Paris, 13th century.

land before the Conquest, who held it now, and what it owed the king. The results of all these inquests were summarized by the king's clerks in Domesday Book, a nearly complete survey (London and the northern counties are missing) of the kingdom of England. This amazing feat shows both William's power and his administrative skill. No other eleventh-century king could have done it; no later medieval king had vision enough to attempt it. Domesday stands alone between the tax surveys of the Roman Empire and the censuses of the modern period.

William died in 1087 and was followed by his sons William Rufus (1087–1100) and Henry I (1100–35). Rufus exploited his rights over bishops and barons until he had brought them to the point of rebellion, but he made no permanent innovations in government. Henry, on the other hand, made the central government much more efficient. Under him the financial work of the king's court was segregated in a separate department, the Exchequer, to which the sheriffs had to give an accounting twice a year for every penny of income and expenditure. All these reports were copied out each year in a great document called a Pipe Roll. By consulting the Pipe Rolls the Exchequer could make sure that the sheriffs had not overlooked or embezzled royal revenues and that they were paying their arrears. Though England was still thinly inhabited—Domesday figures suggest a population of not much over a million—Henry's efficient administration gave him an income greater than that of the king of France, who nominally ruled a much larger country.

Henry also improved the administration of justice. In fact, he sent out delegates from his court so often that they came to be more like circuit judges than special commissioners. Few important cases were any longer heard by the sheriffs—a precaution which, added to the strict financial accounting imposed on them, removed any danger of their becoming too independent. Henry also used inquests frequently and kept the peace as his father had done. At his death in 1135 England was a unified kingdom, far more peaceful than most of western Europe, far more powerful than its size and population seemed to warrant.

The Religious Revival

The economic growth and improved government that we have been discussing were essential ingredients in the great European revival of the eleventh and twelfth centuries. But neither would have been possible if Europeans had not grown less violent, less suspicious of one another, and more willing to cooperate. The creation of this new atmosphere was largely the work of the Church.

The perfecting of the parish system and the elimination of paganism west of the Elbe during the Carolingian period (see pp. 244–45) meant that for generations everyone in western Europe had been exposed to Christianity. By the eleventh cen-

tury the cumulative effects of this exposure began to make themselves felt. True, the strength of Christian ideals was diluted by the corruption of many members of the clergy in the early days of feudalism, but the ideals were powerful enough to survive. The most ignorant priest still proclaimed the basic doctrines of the faith; the most corrupt bishop preached, if he did not practice, the Christian virtues. And not all the clergy were ignorant or corrupt; there were good pastors and saintly bishops even in the darkest days of the tenth century. Slowly Christianity became less and less a matter of external observance, more and more a matter of strong internal conviction. A great wave of popular piety swept through Europe in the eleventh and twelfth centuries and changed the whole character of European society.

The Peace Movement

This so-called Peace Movement was one of the earliest manifestations of the growing influence of Christian ideals. As we have seen, feudal warfare was waged largely at the expense of noncombatants; the usual tactic was a raid on enemy lands in which crops were destroyed, cattle driven off, and churches plundered. During the tenth century the suffering populations turned to the Church for protection against the horrors of war. The movement began in central France, the most divided and therefore the most war-ridden section of the country. Under the leadership of local bishops, peace associations were formed in which each member swore not to attack peasants, merchants, or churchmen. These associations raised armies to punish violators and often levied an annual assessment to support their operations. The various measures devised for the protection of noncombatants and the punishment of plunderers were known as the Peace of God. The leaders of the Peace Movement also tried to forbid fighting on certain holy days, such as Sunday and the Christmas and Easter seasons. This attempt, known as the Truce of God, was far less effective than the Peace of God and did little to curb feudal warfare.

So long as the Peace of God depended on diocesan armies led by churchmen, it had only limited success. But in the eleventh century the idea was taken up by powerful lords in northern France and western Germany as a means of restraining unruly vassals. With no hope of plunder, feudal war seemed less enticing; and with no chance to make war on his neighbors, a minor lord could seldom become strong enough to challenge his lord. The count of Flanders and the duke of Normandy, along with many other rulers, enforced the Peace of God in their lands. Thus the Peace Movement served as yet another source of security for peasants and merchants and therefore helped increase agricultural production and trade.

Monastic Reform

Another sign of the growing strength of Christian ideals was the movement toward monastic reform. This movement began in Germany and in France in the tenth century and reached its peak in the eleventh. Reforming abbots, after they had improved the discipline and the administration of their own monastery, were often asked to help reorganize neighboring establishments. Thus groups of monasteries, inspired by the same ideals and governed by the same methods, were formed. The most famous of these groups was the one headed by Cluny, a monastery in eastern France, and the abbot of Cluny was often as influential as the pope.

Many people were attracted by the opportunity to enter one of the reformed monasteries, and by the end of the eleventh century there were more monasteries and more monks than ever before. The reformed monks, who seemed to be adhering more closely to Christian ideals than other members of the clergy, had great influence on laymen. Respect for the monastic way of life was so widespread that semimonastic communities were established in cathedrals and large urban churches. As a result, the ideas of the reforming abbots spread throughout the Church as a whole.

The Problem of Secular Control

The most dramatic manifestation of popular piety and the desire for reform was a struggle, in the late eleventh century, to free the Church from secular control. The monastic reformers had worried little about this problem. So long as kings and lords let them restore discipline within their orders they were quite willing to give service to the ruler and even to accept his candidates as abbots. But so long as laymen controlled the appointment of bishops, there was no hope of restoring discipline outside the monasteries. It was bad enough when a ruler gave a bishopric to one of his clerks as a reward for faithful service, for such a bishop would spend most of his time in secular administration, diplomacy, and war, and would pay little attention to supervising his clergy. But it was downright scandalous when bishoprics were sold to the highest bidder or awarded as a sort of pension to junior members of the ruling family. Such men made poor administrators and they often led such vicious lives that they demoralized their subordinates. Some reformers were reluctant to break entirely with the kings, who after all were semi-sacred personages, but as the eleventh century went on more and more of them came to believe that a reformed Church must be independent of lay authority.

They also came to believe that the only way to gain independence for the Church and complete the reform of the clergy was to strengthen the position of the pope. An isolated bishop or group of clergymen could not resist the pressure of secular rul-

❋❋❋❋❋❋❋❋❋❋❋❋❋❋❋❋❋❋❋❋❋❋❋❋❋❋❋❋❋

Principles of Gregory VII

ca. 1075

This document was certainly drawn up in Gregory's circle, and probably by the pope himself. It expresses the views of those who were trying to increase papal power in both Church and state.

1. That the Roman church was founded by the Lord alone.
2. That only the Roman pontiff is rightly called universal.
3. That he alone can depose or reestablish bishops.
4. That his legate, even if of inferior rank, is above all bishops in council; and he can give sentence of deposition against them. . . .
12. That it is permitted to him to depose emperors. . . .
18. That his decision ought to be reviewed by no one, and that he alone can review the decisions of everyone.
19. That he ought to be judged by no one.
20. That no one may dare condemn a man who is appealing to the apostolic see.
21. That the greater cases of every church ought to be referred to him.
22. That the Roman church has never erred nor will ever err, as the Scripture bears witness.
23. That the Roman pontiff, if he has been canonically ordained, is indubitably made holy by the merits of the blessed Peter. . . .
24. That by his precept and license subjects are permitted to accuse their lords. . . .
27. That he can absolve the subjects of the unjust from their fealty.

From *Dictatus Papae Gregorii VII,* trans. by E. Lewis, *Medieval Political Ideas* (New York: Knopf, 1954), Vol. II, pp. 380–81.

❋❋❋❋❋❋❋❋❋❋❋❋❋❋❋❋❋❋❋❋❋❋❋❋❋❋❋❋❋

ers. But if the Church were tightly organized under the pope's leadership, then the moral influence of the entire Church could be brought to bear on specific local problems. It took some time, however, to lift papal authority from the depths to which it had fallen in the tenth century. While the German emperors had freed the popes from the Roman nobles, they had merely substituted their own control over the papacy for that of the local aristocracy. Only after 1050, however, were the reformers ready to break with the emperor. They began to proclaim that the pope should be completely independent of all laymen, even the emperor, and that he should have complete administrative jurisdiction over all churchmen, even those who were officials and vassals of kings.

The man who did most to formulate and execute this program was the monk Hildebrand, who later became Pope Gregory VII. He had served in the papal court since the 1040's, and he inspired the famous decree of 1059 which placed the election of the pope in the hands of the cardinals. The cardinals were the leading clergymen of the Roman region, priests of the major Roman churches and bishops of the dioceses around the city. This decree, designed to eliminate the influence of both the Roman nobility and the emperor, proved remarkably successful; after 1059 no pope ever again owed his position to direct lay appointment.

The Investiture Conflict

Now the pope, himself liberated from lay control, set about trying to win equal independence for the bishops. He concentrated his attack on lay investiture, the practice by which a secular ruler bestowed the symbols of spiritual authority, such as the ring and staff, on the bishops he had appointed. The target was well chosen. A king might legitimately claim that he should have some influence in the choice of bishops, since they had secular as well as religious duties. But he could hardly justify a ceremony which suggested that he was bestowing spiritual authority on officials of the Church. In attacking lay investiture the pope was seeking much more than just the abolition of an obnoxious ceremony. He was trying to end all forms of lay control over ecclesiastical appointments, and striving to bring the nomination and approval of all officials of the Church under his own authority.

There had been some opposition to lay investiture in the middle years of the eleventh century, but the issue grew acute only after Hildebrand became pope. As Gregory VII (1073–85) he issued a decree flatly forbidding lay investiture. This move plunged him into a bitter struggle with the emperor Henry IV (1056–1106), a struggle which had repercussions throughout western Europe.

Henry had succeeded to the German throne as a child, and royal power had been seriously weakened during the troubled years of his minority. But when he came of age he moved swiftly, and often tactlessly, to restore his authority. His efforts stirred up revolts which he was able to suppress only because he controlled the resources of most of the bishoprics and abbeys of Germany. Thus Gregory, by forbidding lay investiture, was in effect depriving Henry of the only means he had to preserve the unity and strengthen the central government of Germany.

Henry's reaction was violent and ill-advised. He had just defeated a dangerous group of rebels in Saxony and felt both belligerent and overconfident. He denounced Gregory as a false monk and an illegally elected pope, and summoned a council of German bishops to depose him from the papal see. In a bitter letter announcing this decision to Gregory, Henry ended with

Henry IV before Canossa, a miniature from an early-12th-century manuscript of the life of Countess Matilda of Tuscany. Henry, kneeling, asks Abbot Hugh of Cluny and Countess Matilda to intercede for him with Pope Gregory VII.

the curse: "Down, down, to be damned through all the ages!" Gregory countered by excommunicating Henry and freeing his subjects from their oath of allegiance to him. "It is right," said Gregory, "that he who attempts to diminish the honor of the Church, shall himself lose the honor which he seems to have."

The issue was fairly joined. Now everything depended on the reaction of the bishops and princes of the Empire. Most of the German princes were delighted to have an excuse to resist Henry, and some of them were honestly impressed by the arguments of the church reformers. The bishops, who owed their jobs to Henry, were more loyal to him than the lay lords, but enough of them were shaken by the religious issue to weaken his position. In a great assembly of bishops and princes at Oppenheim in 1076 it was decided to depose Henry unless he was absolved by the pope.

Henry, headstrong but no fool, saw that he must make his peace with the pope. Evading his enemies, he journeyed to Italy by a roundabout route and came to Gregory at the castle of Canossa in 1077. He stood as a penitent outside the castle for three days while Gregory wrestled with the conflict between his political aims and his spiritual duties. If he absolved Henry he would wreck the coalition supporting his

Portal of the church of Notre-Dame-du-Port, Clermont-Ferrand, early Romanesque. This church existed when the First Crusade was preached and many of the crusaders must have worshiped here.

German policies, but the head of the Church could scarcely reject a repentant sinner. In the end Gregory admitted Henry, accepted his promise to obey papal orders, and granted him absolution.

In the short run Henry gained a great political victory by his act of submission. As both he and Gregory had foreseen, the German princes felt that the pope had failed them, and they could no longer oppose a king who had been reconciled with the Church. Henry regained much of his authority; he even became strong enough to invade Italy and force Gregory to take refuge with the Normans in the South. But in the long run the victory went to the papacy. The pope had demonstrated that he could force the most powerful ruler in the West to yield, and that he could stir up rebellion against an anointed king. The lesson was not lost on western rulers; for two hundred years after Canossa few of them were willing to risk outright defiance of the pope.

The struggle over lay investiture persisted for a generation after Gregory's death in 1085. Henry was never entirely secure in Germany, and rebellion after rebellion broke out against him. Trouble continued under his son, Henry V (1106–25). At last a compromise was reached at the Concordat of Worms, 1122, by which lay investiture in the strict sense was abandoned and the pope received full control over appointments to ecclesiastical offices in Italy. In Germany the emperor could still nominate candidates, but they had to be formally elected by the clergy of their cathedrals. Moreover, the pope could refuse approval to men who were clearly unqualified, and he could suspend or even remove bishops who proved unworthy. In practice, this meant that the German bishops had to show a certain amount of obedience to the pope if they wanted to keep their jobs. The German ruler, deprived of full control over the Church in his own country, lost his chief source of power. The independence of the German princes increased accordingly.

Similar but less acute struggles took place in France and England. The king of neither country was dependent on control over the Church as the German emperor had been, so it was easier to reach a settlement. The outcome was about the same: the pope admitted royal influence over appointments, but he remained the final judge of the qualifications of bishops. No one who offended the pope could hope to become or remain a bishop. Assured of administrative control of the Church, the pope could now insist that his policies be accepted throughout Europe. Acceptance was slow and grudging in some places, but it could never be entirely denied. The Church, far stronger and more independent than it had ever been before, had an unprecedented opportunity to influence European society.

The First Crusade

The victory of the Church in the Investiture Conflict was due largely to the support of the barons and knights, whose rebellions had forced the kings to yield to the pope. The influence of the Church over the military class was further demonstrated by the First Crusade. A crusade was a military expedition organized by the pope to attack enemies of the Church. There had been earlier expeditions against the Moslems of Spain and Sicily which were encouraged by some churchmen, notably the abbot of Cluny, but these campaigns included only small groups of knights and were not fully under Church control. By the end of the eleventh century, however, the military class was looking for new conquests and was eager to prove its devotion to the Church.

The First Crusade was proclaimed by

****

Urban's Speech at Clermont

I exhort you . . . to strive to expel that wicked race [the Turks] from our Christian lands. . . . Christ commands it. Remission of sins will be granted for those going thither. . . . Let those who are accustomed to wage private war wastefully even against believers go forth against the infidels. . . . Let those who have lived by plundering be soldiers of Christ; let those who formerly contended against brothers and relations rightly fight barbarians; let those who were recently hired for a few pieces of silver win their eternal reward. . . . The sorrowful here will be glad there, the poor here will be rich there, and the enemies of the Lord here will be His friends there. Let no delay postpone the journey . . . when winter has ended and spring has come . . . enter the highways courageously with the Lord going on before.

Adapted from Fulcher of Chartres, *History of Jerusalem*, trans. by M. E. McGinty (Philadelphia: U. of Pennsylvania Press, 1941), p. 16. Fulcher was at Clermont and went on the crusade.

****

Pope Urban II at the Council of Clermont in 1095. He had many reasons for this decision, and it is impossible to decide which was dominant. Clermont is in south-central France, the region where feudal war had been most vicious, and at Clermont Urban reaffirmed the principles of the Peace of God in addition to preaching a crusade. Urban certainly believed that Europe would be more tranquil if the military classes turned their weapons against an outside foe rather than against one another. Moreover, the investiture struggle was still going on and partisans of Henry IV held Rome; if the pope could enlist large numbers of fighting men under his banner, it would demonstrate that he and not the emperor was the real leader of the West. Finally, the situation in the Near East seemed ripe for intervention. The Turks, who had come into Mesopotamia as mercenary soldiers, had managed to seize most of the lands of the caliphs. They had crushed the Byzantine army at Manzikert (1071) and had occupied most of Asia Minor. The Byzantine Empire, in mortal peril, turned to the West for aid. At the same time Jerusalem had fallen to a fanatical Moslem dynasty which ruled from Cairo. Pilgrimage to the Holy City was now more difficult than it had been when Jerusalem was held by the tolerant Abbasid caliphs. A western army could strengthen Byzantium; gratitude for its assistance might close the breach which had grown between the Roman and Greek Churches since the controversy over iconoclasm (see pp. 243–44). The capture of Jerusalem would make it easier for Christians to accomplish the most salutary of all pilgrimages, the visit to the Holy Sepulchre.

Urban's appeal for an army to fight the Turks and regain Jerusalem met with an astonishing response. The count of Toulouse was the first to take the Cross, and he was soon joined by the duke of Lorraine, four great lords from northern France, two Norman princes from southern Italy, and an innumerable horde of lesser men. The largest number of crusaders came from France and the German provinces near France, but all the countries of western Europe were represented in the undertaking. Nothing shows more clearly the strength of religious conviction and the effectiveness of the leadership of the Church. Some of the greater nobles may have thought of the crusade as an opportunity to acquire new lands; some knights may have merely sought adventure. But the thousands of lesser men who took the Cross had purely religious motives. Urban had promised them full absolution for their

sins and immediate entrance to Heaven if they died fighting the infidel. And that was all they asked. So numerous were the volunteers that it took a year to organize the main armies; meanwhile thousands of non-combatants, escorted by a few knights, set off for the East. Most of them were massacred by the Turks, and the few that survived joined the western armies when they arrived.

The crusaders' slogan was "God wills it!" Certainly it was a near miracle that they succeeded. Almost everything was against them: they knew nothing of the geography or politics of the East; they had little money and no supply services; they had no single commanding officer and bitter feuds broke out among their leaders. The Byzantine emperor, as soon as he found that he could not use them as mercenaries, grew suspicious of them; he wanted to reconquer Asia Minor, not go off on a hare-brained raid on Jerusalem. That they overcame all these obstacles was due partly to their enthusiasm, and partly to the fact that the Turks were divided into many small principalities and were disliked by other Moslems. Moreover, in spite of bad leadership, the heavy-armed western cavalry was one of the best fighting forces in the Eurasian continent. The crusaders suffered severely from disease and starvation; they were battered in two hard-fought battles; they were weakened by dissension among their leaders. But somehow they kept going. In 1099 they took Jerusalem and set up a series of crusading states stretching from Antioch in the north down through Tripoli and Jerusalem to the Dead Sea.

The dramatic success of the First Crusade reinforced the influence of the Church and strengthened the self-confidence of the peoples of western Europe. The many chronicles which describe the great campaign, though ascribing victory to God's

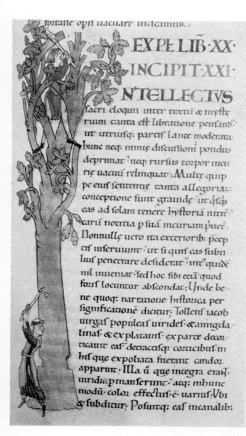

Page of a manuscript of St. Gregory's *Moralia in Job*, written at Cîteaux in the 12th century. This page illustrates both the beautifully clear handwriting of the 12th century and the emphasis on manual labor at Cîteaux—the man felling a tree is a monk.

protection, nevertheless show obvious pride in the crusaders' heroic deeds. But it would be a mistake to overemphasize the effects of the crusade; it was a result, not a cause, of the great medieval revival.

The "Renaissance of the Twelfth Century"

That revival continued without break into the twelfth century. Few periods in the history of the West have shown as much energy and originality; the men of the twelfth

century not only continued the reform of ecclesiastical and secular government but also laid the foundations for a new architecture, a new literature, and a new system of education. All these activities drew on the Church for intellectual inspiration and material support, and in many of them churchmen played a leading role.

Probably the most influential men in the first half of the twelfth century were the monks of the great reformed monasteries. More than half the popes and many of the leading bishops of this period began their careers as monks. And one abbot, St. Bernard of Clairvaux, was more powerful than any bishop and in some respects more powerful than the pope himself.

St. Bernard

St. Bernard was a member of the Cistercian Order, one of the very strict monastic groups which had been founded toward the end of the eleventh century. Earlier reformers, such as the monks of Cluny, had aimed only at honest observance of the Benedictine Rule (see p. 203), but this was not enough for the new generation of religious leaders. The strong religious feeling which made possible the First Crusade also found expression in extreme forms of asceticism. The Cistercians interpreted the Rule as strictly as possible, especially the sections prescribing poverty and manual labor. Refusing to own serfs or revenue-producing properties, they insisted on living in the wilderness by the labor of their own hands. In the end, this uncompromising attitude gained them considerable wealth, for they had to develop new agricultural techniques, such as large-scale sheep-raising, to make up for their lack of serfs and manorial rights. But in the early heroic days of the order the Cistercians suffered great physical hardships. As they attracted able and zealous men by the example of their rigorous life, the order grew rapidly and founded many new monasteries. But its strength was always greatest in eastern France, where its original home was, and it preserved its unity under the leadership of the abbot of Cîteaux.

St. Bernard, who entered the Cistercian Order as a young man, was soon sent to found a new monastery at Clairvaux. Under his direction this early offshoot of Cîteaux became as famous as the motherhouse itself. Clairvaux was a center of piety and asceticism, and St. Bernard aspired to nothing more than to serve as a worthy abbot of this model monastery. But though he had no ambitions for himself he had great zeal for the Church. Whenever he saw its unity threatened by schism or heresy, or its ideals menaced by worldly pressures and interests, he could not sit still. Therefore this abbot, who quite honestly believed that all he wanted was a narrow cell in a secluded monastery, spent most of his life in public business, advising popes, lecturing kings, preaching to crowds, and writing letters to every prominent man in Europe.

From 1125 to the year of his death in 1153, St. Bernard dominated the West through his eloquence, his piety, and his boundless energy. His support saved causes that were tottering to failure; his opposition damned men who seemed born for success. In the dispute over the papal election of 1130, St. Bernard convinced the rulers of Europe that Innocent II was the rightful pope, even though he had received fewer votes in the College of Cardinals than an opposing candidate. Innocent II was naturally influenced by St. Bernard, as was Pope Eugenius III (1145–53), who had been a Cistercian monk himself. When Eugenius inaugurated the Second Crusade in 1147 to regain some lost territories in Syria, he turned to St. Bernard for help in recruiting leaders for the campaign. St. Bernard did not disappoint the pope; he persuaded both the king of France and the emperor of Germany to take the Cross. The armies were cut to pieces crossing Asia Minor and failed to take Damascus, their main objective. The failure was due to bad leadership and not to the advice of St. Bernard, but he wrote an official apology ascribing the debacle to the sins of the Christians.

St. Bernard was in many ways a conservative man. He disliked the new architecture of the twelfth century; worldly splendor seemed to him unnecessary for the worship of God and a waste of money which might better be given to the poor. He disliked the new learning, which exalted human reason and led men to think that they could approach God through logic rather than through faith. He worried about the growing bureaucracy at the papal court, even though he realized it was essential to the unity of the Church and the authority of the pope. His most bitter letters are attacks on the sumptuous buildings of Cluny and on the writings of the great scholar Abelard (see pp. 303–05).

But, conservative though he was, St. Bernard was essentially an innovator, not a reactionary. He was a leader of the new piety, the movement to humanize Christianity and Christianize human life. He emphasized devotion to the Virgin and dwelt on the life of Jesus on earth among men. As Dante was to point out, the central theme in St. Bernard's teaching was love, the love of God for man and the love which man in turn should have for God. He talked much more of the joys of Paradise than of the pains of Hell. He was saddened and angered by those who rejected the love and mercy of God, but he always hoped to save the sinners whom he denounced. In all this he gave a lead to his contemporaries. The number of churches dedicated to the Virgin increased sharply, more emphasis was placed on the Nativity and the childhood of Jesus, and hope of salvation began to outweigh fears of damnation. In many ways the twelfth century was an age of optimism, an optimism reflected in its religion as well as in its secular activities.

Abbot Suger and Gothic Architecture

Another great abbot, second only to St. Bernard in his influence, was Suger of St. Denis (*ca.* 1091–1152). The son of poor peasants, he had been given to the monastery by his parents when only a child. Sheer ability carried him to the position of abbot, in an outstanding example of the opportunities the Church offered to men of low birth. St. Denis was one of the wealth-

❖❖❖❖❖❖❖❖❖❖❖❖❖❖❖❖❖❖❖❖❖❖❖❖❖❖❖❖❖

St. Bernard on Love

Let not our hearts rest from meditating day
and night on the law of the Lord,
which is the law of love. . . .
Let us love and be loved,
striving to benefit ourselves in the other
and the other in ourselves.
For those whom we love, on those do we rely,
as those who love us rely in turn on us.
Thus to love in God is to love charity,
and therefore it is to labor for charity,
to strive to be loved for the sake of God.

From St. Bernard, Letter 28, *Some Letters of St. Bernard,* ed. by S. J. Eales (London: J. Hodges, 1904).

❖❖❖❖❖❖❖❖❖❖❖❖❖❖❖❖❖❖❖❖❖❖❖❖❖❖❖❖❖

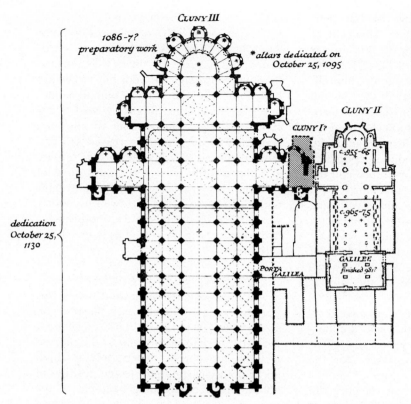

CLUNY III

1086-7?
preparatory work

*altars dedicated on
October 25, 1095

CLUNY II

CLUNY I?

c.955-68

c.965-75

dedication
October 25,
1130

GALILEE
finished 981?

PORTA
GALILEA

Plan of the great church of the monastery of Cluny, showing nave, side aisles, transepts, and apse with radiating chapels. The choir and the apse are especially large to give room for the elaborate religious ceremonies which were typical of Cluny.

iest monasteries in France, and it was also the burial place of the French kings. Suger was thus closely associated with the royal house, and his great administrative ability soon made him a close adviser of two kings, Louis VI and Louis VII. During the absence of Louis VII on the Second Crusade, Suger acted as regent of France; he was remarkably successful in preserving both the stability and the solvency of the realm.

Suger was more than a successful administrator, however. He wrote several books, flamboyant in style, but full of solid information. His biography of King Louis VI is one of our most important sources for French history of the early twelfth century. But Suger's overwhelming interest was the rebuilding of the church of St. Denis, which he was determined to make the most beautiful church in France, the "crown of the kingdom." St. Bernard was suspicious of this desire for magnificence, as he was of Suger's involvement in worldly business, but the abbot of St. Denis had tact as well as energy. By giving his full support to the Cistercians' reform policy, he conciliated St. Bernard and gained a free hand for his own activities.

Suger wanted his church to be full of light and color. He had great wealth at his disposal and a remarkable willingness to experiment with new ideas. Workmen flocked to St. Denis from all over France, bringing with them all the solutions to problems of church architecture which had been worked out in the last half-century. The result was a church which, for the first time, incorporated all the essential elements of the Gothic style.

From 1000 on there had been a great wave of church-building in western Europe. The basic plan was still that of the old basilica, a long nave with lower side aisles and a transept crossing the nave before the altar. This basic plan was elaborated, especially by the monks of Cluny, by enlarging and rounding the apse (the end of the church behind the altar), and by adding subsidiary chapels. For example, the east end of some Cluniac churches looked like the plan on page 300. At the same time there was an attempt to make the churches lighter by raising the walls and enlarging the windows. Soon architects discovered that a pointed arch over a window increased the area that could be glazed. Some experiments were also made in the use of stained glass.

But the most important innovations had to do with the vaulting (that is, the interior roof) of churches. The flat, wooden roofs of the early Roman churches were not very satisfactory in the wet, cold climate of the North. A stone vault covered by a steep-sloped roof would be far more satisfactory in keeping out the weather and reducing the danger of fire. But it took generations for architects to devise the best way of covering the great open spaces of a church with a stone vault. The first and easiest solution was the barrel vault (see below), a continuous semicircular arch extending the entire length of the church. But this scheme was not particularly safe when used for very wide areas. Moreover, it put an equal strain on every part of the side walls, making it impossible to weaken them by cutting

Barrel vault, church of St. Savin, 11th century. This was a very large church for that period. Notice that no light can be admitted in the upper part of the nave. On the other hand, the vault is covered with fine Romanesque paintings, a practice which had to be abandoned in the new Gothic style.

in large windows. Then architects hit on the idea of designing a roof as if it were the intersection of two barrel vaults (see below), in that way concentrating the downward and outward thrust of the roof at a few points along the wall, which in turn could be strengthened by pillars and buttresses. Now the walls could be pierced with large, high windows, flooding the church with light. The final refinement was to mark the lines of the intersecting vaults with stone ribs, thus both strengthening and improving the appearance of the roof.

The churches of the eleventh and early twelfth centuries were larger and more beautiful than any that had been built before in the North, but no one of them embodied all the innovations we have just mentioned. They all adhered more or less to the Romanesque style, which was massive and solid with strong emphasis on horizontal lines. Romanesque in many ways is a very satisfactory style for church architecture—it has been revived in our own day—but it did not satisfy the desires of many churchmen of the twelfth century. They wanted a style that reflected their new aspirations, something less practical and earthbound, something that symbolized the mystery and splendor of heaven.

Suger felt these longings with particular keenness; even his writings are marked by a play of light and color. And it was under his direction in the church of St. Denis that the decisive step was taken in the evolution of the new style. Suger used almost all the new

ideas: pointed arches, rib vaults, larger and higher windows, stained glass, an elaborate apse. He described the result perfectly in one of his verses: "Bright is the noble building which is pervaded by the new light." Churches were built around Paris along the same principles, and the new Gothic style soon became the standard for church architecture. Southern France, Germany, and Italy clung for some time to Romanesque, but by the early years of the thirteenth century Gothic was triumphing even in these countries.

Abelard

A third great figure of the early twelfth-century revival, Abelard (*ca.* 1079–1142), was also an abbot, but an unwilling and unhappy one. Never wanting to be anything more than a scholar and teacher, he was forced into monastic life by misfortune rather than conviction. The son of a minor vassal in Brittany, he had somehow, like many other men of the twelfth century, become inflamed with the love of learning. About 1100, he abandoned the career of knighthood and went to study at Paris.

Paris was full of famous teachers, though there was as yet no formal curriculum. The growing horde of students had overflowed the old cathedral school on the Île de la Cité and lectures were already being given on the Left Bank in what was to become the Latin Quarter. This new enthusiasm for learning resembled in some ways the new piety; men were examining old materials

Far left: Groin vault, formed by the intersection of two barrel vaults. Mont-Saint-Michel, Romanesque, 12th century.

Left: Rib vault, Mont-Saint-Michel, late Romanesque. The groin vault is reinforced by ribs along the intersections, but the effect is still low and heavy.

Right: Gothic rib vault, Mont-Saint-Michel, early Gothic. The possibilities of using this vaulting to gain greater height and light are now being exploited.

which had been taken for granted for centuries and were discovering in them new meanings and personal applications. The students were using the same books that had been known for centuries, but they found them far more stimulating than most of their predecessors had.

Abelard was one of the young men who were excited by learning and eager to use their minds. His first love, like that of many of his contemporaries, was logic. He mastered all the available material in a remark-

Rib vaulting on a large scale, the nave of Chartres Cathedral, 1194–1220. Notice how the ribs carry down to the base of the piers. Great height and light have now been achieved; the upper (clerestory) windows are larger and more useful than those at floor level.

ably short time, and immediately set himself up as a teacher, much to the annoyance of some of his former professors. Abelard thoroughly enjoyed teaching logic, but, again like many of his contemporaries, he saw in it more than a formal intellectual exercise. He was convinced that it was a universal tool (somewhat like mathematics today) which could be used to solve old problems and acquire new knowledge. And since, to a man of his age, the most important problems were theological, he decided to become a master of theology as well as logic. Again he completed his studies in record time and began to steal students from, and contradict, his old teachers.

Abelard was a great teacher and scholar; he was also a very brash young man. He began to irritate the conservatives around him by advancing a new solution to an old problem in logic. His solution showed remarkable insight and eventually became perfectly respectable, but at the moment it ran contrary to the general trend of thinking. Next he produced an exercise book for his students called *Sic et Non* (*Yes and No*), in which he marshaled opinions from the Bible and the Church Fathers on both sides of controversial questions. It took considerable ingenuity to find support for some of his statements—e.g., that God is threefold and the contrary; that sin is pleasing to God and the contrary—and his cleverness added to the suspicions of his contemporaries. The prologue to the book made it seem even more dangerous, for here Abelard announced: "The first key to wisdom is this—constant and frequent questioning. . . . For by doubting we are led to question and by questioning we arrive at the truth." Finally, Abelard wrote a treatise on the Trinity in which he tried to define the attributes of each Person by a rigorous use of logic. This meddling with the central mystery of the faith annoyed St. Bernard, who in one of his angriest letters denounced Abelard as a writer who sought to "place degrees in the Trinity, modes in the Majesty, numbers in the Eternity." St. Bernard felt that God was too great to be defined by the human mind and that all the virtue went out of faith when it was made too rational.

Abelard's personal life increased his reputation for vanity and presumption. His downfall began when he seduced Héloïse, the niece of a canon of the cathedral of Paris. The affair could not be hushed up, for his love-poems had been circulated throughout the city, and Héloïse had had a child. So Abelard was forced to marry the girl, which blocked his chances for advancement in the Church. Héloïse was ready to remove this obstacle by taking refuge in a nunnery, but this self-sacrifice only irritated her uncle the more. Fearing that Abelard was seeking to repudiate his niece, he hired a gang of thugs to castrate the scholar. The scandal was so great that Abelard temporarily retired from teaching and took refuge as a monk in St. Denis.

Abelard, finding neither intellectual nor religious stimulation in St. Denis (this was just before Suger became abbot), tried to stir things up by criticizing some of the legends about the monastery's patron saint. He was right, as he often was, but the monks became so hostile that Abelard was obliged to flee. When Suger became abbot, he permitted Abelard to live outside the monastery, but this merely led to new trouble. First Abelard was chosen as abbot of a remote Breton monastery, but he found the monks brutal and ignorant and soon abandoned the post. Then he returned to the neighborhood of Paris and began teaching once more with great success. His return proved unendurable to his enemies. Led by St. Bernard, they succeeded in having his work on the Trinity condemned by a council of bishops. Abelard was forced to renounce his errors and then retired to Cluny, where he lived out the rest of his life in peace.

Abelard's real fault was vanity, not impiety; he had sought to make Christian doctrine more precise, but not to contradict it. He was only the most conspicuous of many scholars who were trying to combine logic, philosophy, and theology in order to give Christian doctrine a more rigorous intellectual structure. St. Bernard, who was a mystic rather than a scholar, was perhaps right in feeling that excessive rationality would weaken the appeal of religion. But he was fighting a losing battle; the future belonged to men who followed Abelard's methods, though with somewhat more restraint. For the rest of the Middle Ages theology was studied according to the rules of formal logic, which demanded that problems be carefully defined and elaborately divided into topics and subtopics. Authorities were cited on both sides of every question, though most scholars, unlike Abelard, were careful to give a final, and orthodox, answer. But the most popular theological book of the twelfth century, Peter Lombard's *Sentences,* resembled Abelard's work far more than it did that of St. Bernard. The system used by Abelard, Peter Lombard, and others eventually became known as scholasticism, and scholastic methods dominated European thought for the next three centuries.

The Beginnings of Universities

Exciting as theology was, it was far from monopolizing the attention of twelfth-century scholars. A revival of interest in the Latin classics, especially noticeable in the cathedral school of Chartres, led to a marked improvement in Latin style. A growing interest in medicine, centered at Salerno in southern Italy, prompted the study of old Roman textbooks and of the new observations of Arab doctors which

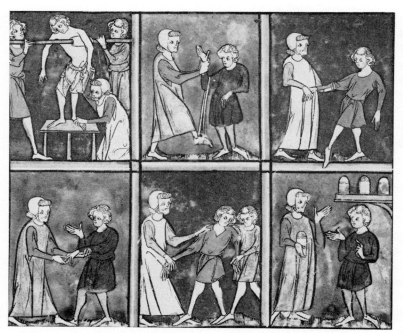

Detail of a page from Roger of Parma, *Treatise on Surgery*, a 12th-century French manuscript. The surgeon is treating dislocations.

The Revival of Roman Law

❖❖❖❖❖❖❖❖❖❖❖❖❖❖❖❖❖❖❖❖❖❖❖❖❖❖❖❖

Three times has Rome given her laws to the world, three times has she bound different peoples together: first, by the unity of the state, when the Roman people stood at the height of their strength, second, by the unity of the Church after the Empire had fallen, and third, by the unity of law when Roman Law was accepted during the Middle Ages. The first victory was won by force of arms, but the other two by the power of the mind. . . . Roman Law, like Christianity, has become an essential element of modern civilization.

From Rudolph von Jhering, *Geist des römischen Rechts* (Leipzig: 1907), Vol. I, p. 1.

❖❖❖❖❖❖❖❖❖❖❖❖❖❖❖❖❖❖❖❖❖❖❖❖❖❖❖❖

came in through North Africa. But theology's real rival was law, and in the long run students of law became far more numerous than students of theology.

Although Roman law had not been completely forgotten during the early Middle Ages, it had been little studied, and most of the copies of Justinian's *Corpus Juris* had disappeared. But at the end of the eleventh century there was a great revival of interest in Roman law, especially in Italy and southern France. The first great teacher, Irnerius, attracted so many students to his school at Bologna that the city became, and remained for centuries, the chief center of legal studies in Europe. Roman law appealed to students for many reasons: it was a fine example of logical and precise reasoning; it was part of the greatly respected intellectual legacy of Rome; it gave intelligent answers to problems of human relations which the unsophisticated customary law of medieval Europe had scarcely considered. The Romans had been the most legal-minded people of antiquity and western Europe had inherited their fondness for law. The *Corpus Juris,* which summed up the work of generations of Roman lawyers in fairly compact form, could be mastered by students within a reasonable length of time. And a young man soundly trained in Roman law could look forward to a brilliant career; by the middle of the century legal training had become the surest route to promotion in the service of popes and kings. The number of law students who flocked to Bologna from the most distant parts of Europe increased steadily over the century.

A special branch of legal studies was canon law, the law of the Church. The Church, of course, had relied heavily on Roman law in formulating its basic rules and procedures, but it had to cope with many problems which Roman law had never touched—for example, the forms to be followed in choosing a bishop, or the requirements for a valid Christian marriage. In deciding these questions the Church relied on the writings of the Fathers, decrees of councils, and administrative and judicial rulings of the popes. Some imperfect collections of this scattered material had been made, but none of them enjoyed unquestioned authority. Then about 1140 the monk Gratian produced his *Decretum,* or *Concordance of Discordant Canons,* which was rapidly accepted as the definitive treatise on canon law. Gratian, following the pattern already set by Abelard and other theologians, divided his book into topics and subtopics, quoted the authorities on both sides of each question, and then gave what seemed to him the approved solution. Since Gratian too taught at Bologna, students came there to study canon

A Problem
from Gratian's Decretum
ca. 1140

The twelfth-century revival of learning raised again the question of whether Christian clergymen should study books written by Greek and Roman pagans.

But the question is asked whether these men [priests] should be made acquainted with profane literature. Here is what is written upon the matter in the fourth Carthaginian Council: A bishop should not read the books of the heathen. . . . So Jerome to Pope Damasus: Priests are blameworthy who, to the neglect of the Gospels, read comedies. . . . And the same: They walk in the darkness and vanity of the sense who occupy themselves with profane learning. . . .

But on the other hand, one reads that Moses and Daniel were learned in all the wisdom of the Egyptians and Chaldeans. One reads also that God ordered the sons of Israel to spoil the Egyptians of their gold and silver; the moral interpretation of this is that should we find in the poets either the gold of wisdom or the silver of eloquence, we should turn it to the profit of useful learning. . . . And Pope Clement says: For the understanding of Sacred Scriptures knowledge of profane writings is shown to be necessary. . . .

As therefore is evident from the authorities already quoted ignorance ought to be odious to priests.

From A. O. Norton, ed., *Readings in the History of Education* (Cambridge, Mass.: Harvard U. Press, 1909), pp. 60 ff.

law as well as Roman law, and soon there was a large group of experts in the subject. Canon law, even more than Roman law, opened the road to high office, in this case high office in the Church. Many bishops and almost all the popes from 1159 to the

Medieval Schools and Universities 1100-1250

end of the fourteenth century were students of canon law.

These groupings of students and teachers at centers like Paris and Bologna eventually coalesced into universities, one of the great institutional legacies of the Middle Ages. We can hardly speak of universities before 1150, but even then there were signs that some sort of academic organization was needed. The many foreign students at Bologna, for example, felt that they were being cheated by the Italian boardinghouse keepers, and sometimes by their professors as well. They formed a union to keep down the price of food and lodging and to make sure that teachers covered an adequate amount of material in their lecture courses. At Paris the chief problem, illustrated by Abelard's career, was to determine at what point a student was entitled to set himself up as a teacher. The bishops, or their chancellors, who were supposed to license

teachers, had neither the knowledge nor the time to deal with the growing number of applicants. So in Paris the teachers themselves formed a union, to which they admitted only students who had passed a rigorous examination. It was out of these unions of students and teachers that the university was to emerge.

The intellectual interests which created the first universities were the most striking manifestations of the new vigor of western European society. The people of western Europe had not yet equaled the Romans in the arts of government, and possibly they still fell behind the Romans in total economic production. But they had an intellectual curiosity, an urge to acquire new ideas, which the Romans of the Empire had never possessed. And in the long run this curiosity and drive were to lead to the revival of science and the transformation of European society.

Suggestions for Further Reading

1. Economic Revival

There is excellent source material on the revival of medieval trade in R. S. Lopez and I. W. Raymond, *Medieval Trade in the Mediterranean World* (1955). H. Heaton, *Economic History of Europe,* Chapters 5–11 (1936), is a good introductory survey, and E. Lipson, *Economic History of England,* Vol. I (1936), traces the growth of English economy through the Middle Ages and includes a good bibliography. The effect of the Moslem control of the Mediterranean on European economy is discussed by H. Pirenne, *Economic and Social History of Medieval Europe* * (1937), with special attention on the economic activity of Italy and the Low Countries. H. F. Brown, *Venice: An Historical Sketch of the Republic* (1895), is the best one-volume study in English of that important commercial center. E. Power, *Medieval People* * (1954), gives a vivid picture of social and manorial life from the point of view of individuals.

H. Pirenne, *Medieval Cities* * (1925), is a fine general study of the beginnings of urban civilization and the part played by the middle class in the development of a modern economic system and modern culture. Both C. Stephenson, *Borough and Town* (1933), and J. Tait, *The Medieval English Borough* (1936), are scholarly studies of town development in England with opposing interpretations on the origins of towns.

2. Political Revival

There are many valuable works on the political history of this period. C. Petit-Dutaillis, *Feudal Monarchy in France and England* (1936), discusses the preservation and development of the monarchy in France and England from the tenth to the thirteenth century. An excellent brief study of the growth of royal power in France is R. Fawtier, *The Capetian Kings of France* (trans. L. Butler, 1960). The older study of E. Lavisse, *Histoire de France,* Vol. II, Part II (1901), which reviews economic, social, and cultural phenomena as well as political, has not been surpassed for comprehensiveness.

Medieval Germany, Vol. I (trans. G. Barraclough, 1938), has good material on Germany in this period, and G. Barraclough, *The Origins of Modern Germany* (1952), analyzes the reasons Germany lagged behind the rest of Europe in the development of political institutions.

We have interesting evidence on England at this time in the contemporary Ordericus Vitalis, *History of England and Normandy,* 3 vols. (trans. T. Forester, 1854), which concentrates on religious events, and in William of Malmesbury, *Chronicle* (trans. J. A. Giles, 1847), which gives attention to both political and religious developments. Both histories go up to 1154. F. W. Maitland, *Domesday Book and Beyond* (1897), is a monument in historical prose writing. The best scholarly treatment of the establishment of Norman feudalism in England is F. M. Stenton, *First Century of English Feudalism* (1932). The titles cited under Chapter 9, Section 7, also have material on this subject.

C. H. Haskins, *The Normans in European History* (1915), shows the Normans as founders and organizers of states. Political developments in Italy are discussed by P. Villari, *Medieval Italy from Charlemagne to Henry VII* (1910), a broad, readable survey. C. Cahen, *Le Régime Féodal de l'Italie Normande* (1940), is a critical study of Norman institutions in Italy.

* Available in paperback edition.

3. Religious Revival

Since the impetus for the religious revival of the eleventh century was the monastery at Cluny, J. Evans, *Monastic Life at Cluny* (1931), is a good starting point for study. L. M. Smith, *Cluny in the Eleventh and Twelfth Centuries* (1930), is a valuable if somewhat disjointed study of the influence of Cluny on the religious life of Europe, while D. Knowles, *The Monastic Order in England* (1951), is a thorough and readable study of almost every facet of English monastic life from 900 to 1215.

There is interesting source material on the Investiture Controversy in E. F. Henderson, *Select Historical Documents* (1903). A. J. Macdonald, *Hildebrand: A Life of Gregory VII* (1932), is a good brief biography, and the *Correspondence of Gregory VII* (trans. E. Emerton, 1932), contains information not only on the problem of investiture but on the increase in papal activities under Gregory. The excellent book of G. Tellenbach, *Church, State, and Christian Society at the Time of the Investiture Controversy* (1940), shows the conflict as a papal attempt to revalue Christian society in the light of canon law. The consequences for the Church and the state are carefully analyzed by N. F. Cantor, *Church, Kingship and Lay Investiture in England, 1089–1135* (1959), a very scholarly study. W. Ullmann, *Growth of Papal Power in the Middle Ages* (1955), treats the effect of the controversy on the growth of the papal government.

4. The First Crusade

A. C. Krey, *The First Crusade* (1921), gives a very good picture of the crusade from the accounts of eyewitnesses and participants. There is good evidence in F. Duncalf and A. C. Krey, *Parallel Source Problems* (1912), and in *Fulcher of Chartres: Chronicle of the First Crusade* (trans. M. E. McGinty; *Translations and Reprints,* Vol. I, 3rd Series, 1941). *The Alexiad of Anna Comnena* (trans. E. A. S. Dawes, 1928) contains the Byzantine attitude toward the crusade, and Usāmah ibn Murshid, *An Arab-Syrian Gentleman and Warrior in the Period of the Crusades* (trans. P. K. Hitti, 1929), gives the Moslem point of view. The best recent book on the crusade is the fascinating account of S. Runciman, *A History of the Crusades,* Vol. I (1954). Runciman includes a thorough bibliography. M. L. W. Baldwin, ed., *The First Hundred Years* (1955) (Vol. I of *A History of the Crusades,* edited K. M. Setton), is a collection of essays by leading historians of the crusades. The establishment of feudalism in the conquered East is treated by J. La Monte, *Feudal Monarchy in the Latin Kingdom of Jerusalem* (1932).

5. The Renaissance of the Twelfth Century

The best general study of the revival of learning in the West is C. H. Haskins, *The Renaissance of the Twelfth Century* * (1927), which discusses scholarship, Roman law, and philosophy, and has a good critical bibliography. H. O. Taylor, *The Medieval Mind,* Vol. I (1953), has good material on intellectual developments in the twelfth century, and R. W. Southern, *The Making of the Middle Ages* (1953), presents an excellent account of the influence of the new piety on cultural growth. There is a good cross section of the poetry of the period from 900 to 1160 in H. Waddell, *Medieval Latin Lyrics* * (1929).

6. St. Bernard, Abelard, Suger

There is a wealth of material on these three men, who to a great extent dominated the intellectual life of the first half of the twelfth century. *St. Bernard of Clairvaux* (trans. G. Webb and A. Walker, 1960) is an interesting biography written by Bernard's friend,

* Available in paperback edition.

William of St. Thierry. Bernard's relations with political and intellectual leaders of his time are presented in *The Letters of St. Bernard* (trans. S. J. Eales, 1904). The best scholarly study is E. Vacandard, *Vie de St. Bernard*, 2 vols. (1910), a history of Bernard and his times; the recent work of B. S. James, *St. Bernard of Clairvaux* (1957), focuses attention on Bernard the man.

Suger on the Abbey of St. Denis (trans. E. Panofsky, 1946) is a mine of information about the beginnings of Gothic architecture and about monastic government and life. Panofsky's introduction has a good brief biography of Suger.

The best serious study of Abelard is E. Gilson, *Eloise and Abelard* * (1948). H. Waddell's novel *Peter Abelard* * gives a good picture of twelfth-century intellectual activity based on sound scholarship. *Abelard's Letters* (trans. C. K. Scott-Moncrieff, 1926) shows the influence of the man on the life of the times.

* Available in paperback edition.

11

Medieval Civilization

at Its Height

After 1150 western Europe began to cash in on the pioneer work of the tenth and eleventh centuries. It became prosperous, almost complacent. The boom in population, production, and trade continued. The peasants embarked on a great migration to new lands, comparable only to the movement to the New World in the nineteenth century. Forests were cleared in England, France, and West Germany; marshes were drained and walled off from the sea in the Netherlands. In the biggest shift of all, a huge migration toward the East, the Germans filled up the land between the Elbe and the Oder and settled large areas of western Poland, East Prussia, and Bohemia. This drive to the East almost doubled the size of medieval Germany. It also set the stage for contending nationalisms of modern times, for the Slavs retained most of Bohemia and much of the land beyond the Oder, which meant that many German settlements were surrounded by Slavic territory.

Towns and Trade

Trade increased and towns became even more important than they had been before. In the north, German merchants almost monopolized the commerce of the Baltic and pushed their outposts to Reval, Riga, and even to Novgorod in Russia. They dealt in furs, timber, and grain—bulky commodities that returned only a small profit per ton of freight. But by making their ships bigger, and by building more of them, the northern German towns, notably Lübeck, managed to achieve a modest prosperity. Atlantic trade—in wool from England and in salt and wine from the ports of the Bay of Biscay—was also only moderately profitable. Most of these goods were carried by German and French ships; the English still did little shipping and could not even move their own wool overseas without the aid of foreigners.

The most profitable trade, still the trade in oriental goods, followed the old route across the Mediterranean, through Italy, and into the transalpine lands. Though Marseilles and Barcelona had a small share of this trade, it was dominated by the Italians, especially by the merchants of Venice, Genoa, and Pisa. Great Italian fleets made regular voyages every year to Constantinople, Alexandria, and Acre, carrying pilgrims and woolen goods to the East and bringing back incense, spices, and silk. After 1150 the Italian fleets of the Mediterranean were large enough to move whole armies in a single operation. The crusaders no longer had to take the long and dangerous overland route; they simply hired ships

Rose window from the north transept of Notre Dame of Paris, ca. 1270, depicting subjects from the Old Testament. Notice that Gothic design is becoming more elaborate and intricate.

313

German Expansion to the East 800-1400

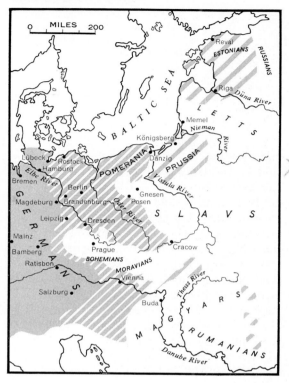

from the Italian towns. Some of their expeditions may have included as many as twenty-five thousand men.

It was not until the second half of the thirteenth century that the Genoese and the Venetians began to make regular voyages through the Strait of Gibraltar and around Spain to England and the Netherlands. Even then, by far the largest part of their trade was still across the Alps by packtrain to Germany and France. The steady stream of merchants along this route helped make the fortune of the towns of the Po Valley, southern France, and southern Germany. It also stimulated the development of the fairs of Champagne, which became the central market for all western Europe. Champagne lay across the

river valleys leading south to the Mediterranean and north to Paris, the English Channel, and western Germany. The counts who ruled it were wise enough to encourage commerce and strong enough to protect the wandering merchants. At the fairs of Champagne textiles and wool from the north were exchanged for oriental goods from the south. So well attended were they that merchants gradually developed the practice of settling their yearly accounts when they met in Champagne, thus making the fairs the money market as well as the commodity market of the West.

By the end of the twelfth century the bloody conflicts between lords and towns had almost ceased, and no one could any longer deny that businessmen were entitled to special status. Personal freedom and some degree of local autonomy made the townsmen a privileged class—not as privileged as the clergy and nobles, but still well above the peasants. As a privileged class they began to be given a special name —*bürgers* in Germany, *burgesses* in England, *bourgeois* in France, whence the collective term, *bourgeoisie.** Most towns were satisfied with this special status; only the greatest cities could dream of full independence, and only in Italy did they have much hope of getting it. But the old hostilities still ran deep. The bourgeoisie still distrusted the nobility and criticized the clergy, who in turn still suspected the bourgeoisie of harboring dangerous ideas about religion and the social order. A twelfth-century clergyman could still speak of free towns as *tumor plebis, timor regis*—a cancer of the people and a threat to kings.

Bankers and Moneylenders

The growth of banking and of moneylending strengthened this hostility. The

---

* All these terms are derived from the German word *burg,* which meant first a fort and then a walled town. Walls were the symbol of a town's autonomy.

great international merchants, and the money-changers who served them, had become expert at transferring funds from one region to another and had also accumulated surplus capital which they were perfectly willing to lend. They gradually began to act as bankers, receiving deposits, paying out money on order, making loans, and helping to collect taxes. Kings and popes called on the bankers when, for example, they wanted to transfer money to the East to pay for one of their crusades. And bishops and abbots, lords and knights, all borrowed money from the bankers to meet the demands of their steadily rising living standards. But as a result of all these transactions the bourgeoisie seemed to be profiting at the expense of the clergy and nobility. A pope who could draw on the facilities of a far-flung banking house found it easier to tax the clergy of distant provinces, and a king trying to raise money to put down a baronial rebellion could simply borrow what he needed from his banker. Even kings, however, had to pay a high rate of interest on their loans—8 to 10 per cent for a ruler with as good a reputation as Saint Louis (see pp. 347–50)—and lesser folk paid more. When the day of reckoning came, the borrowers often had a hard time repaying their loans: kings had to impose new taxes on their subjects; barons had to

Medieval Commerce   ca. 1200

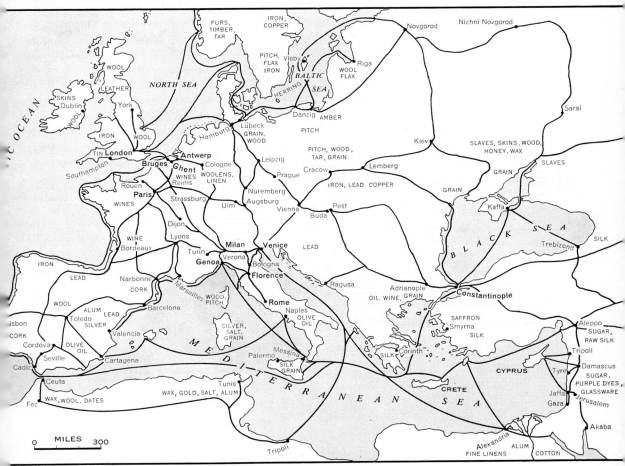

sell their lands; churches had to melt down their altar vessels. Bankers were generally unpopular, for they seemed to be thriving on the misfortunes of their fellow Christians. And their unpopularity often extended to the towns and cities of which they were the most conspicuous representatives.

Artisans, Gilds, and the Proletariat

Most of the inhabitants of the towns were not bankers or international merchants, but small shopkeepers with purely local trade. Butchers, bakers, and the like profited little from the growth of international commerce. The same was true of many of the artisans in the metal and textile industries. And even artisans who produced goods for a wider market had to rely on international merchants who kept most of the profits in return for their services. A Flemish weaver in Ghent, for example, could not import his raw wool from England directly; he had to obtain it from a merchant. And when his cloth was finished, he himself could not carry it to the fairs of Champagne or the ports of Italy; he had to sell it at a low price to a merchant who knew the markets and the trade routes and was willing to assume the risks of distributing it. Many skilled artisans were thus no more than subcontractors who could work only when the merchants supplied them with raw materials, and whose income was determined by distant markets beyond their control. Less-skilled men, whose position was even more precarious, often suffered long periods of unemployment. For the first time since the fall of the Roman Empire an urban proletariat began to appear in the countries of western Europe.

It was during the twelfth century that the urban population began to organize itself into occupational groups. Before this, towns had often had a general association of all merchants, but there were obvious reasons, both social and economic, for organization along trade lines. The men within each trade or craft naturally saw a good deal of each other and felt that they had common interests to defend against outsiders. They usually had a patron saint, whose feast day they celebrated together. Moreover, they often had a code prescribing standards of good workmanship, and they were determined to see that these standards were maintained. And so they formed their own associations, called gilds in England, to pursue their common objectives. The gild contributed to the local church that honored its patron saint, and acted as a mutual benefit society for the families of its members. It also tried to enforce regulations barring strangers and untrained men from the craft and forbidding careless or dishonest production. The gild was usually dominated by its most experienced members, the master workman, who owned their own shops and equipment. Under them were the journeymen, who worked for daily wages, and under them the apprentices, who were boys learning the trade. In the thirteenth century, when most journeymen could still hope to become masters themselves one day, there was relatively little friction among these groups.

There was considerably more friction among the gilds themselves, including all the jurisdictional disputes that we find among trade unions today. For example, the harness of a horse contains both metal and leather: should it be made by leather-workers, metal-workers, or both? There was also a good deal of jockeying for political advantage. Strong gilds tended to take over the control of town governments, and often the larger gilds would line up against the smaller ones, or the wealthy gilds against the poor.

To escape such controversies, and to protect themselves from the excessive power of the gilds, many lords refused to allow gilds to be established in their towns. But the advantages of some sort of trade organization were so obvious that the lords usually created similar, but looser, associations under their own control, thus ensuring the regular collection of dues and the enforcement of high standards of workmanship. And everywhere, in the nongild towns as well as the gild towns, urban workers came to be divided into the three classes of masters, journeymen, and apprentices. Only the first of these classes had much property, so the line between the moderately well-to-do and the very poor became as sharply drawn as the line between the very rich and the small artisans or tradesmen.

In the long run the division between the urban rich and the urban poor sharpened into political conflict and even armed rebellion. But during the first part of the thirteenth century, in spite of growing tensions, the people of most towns remained fairly well united. Still rather insecure in a society which originally had had no place for them, they feared outside oppressors more than internal exploiters. Only when the bourgeoisie began to feel reasonably secure, only when their ideas had begun to permeate other strata of society, did their internal differences break out into open feuds.

Literature and Art

The general prosperity of the period was reflected in a burst of artistic and literary activity. Wealth does not necessarily produce great art, but it certainly increases the opportunities open to artists. Very large sums of money were needed to build a Gothic cathedral, and more cathedrals were built in the late twelfth and early thirteenth centuries than at any other time in European history. This money did not all come from the Church; kings and feudal lords made large contributions, as did the people

of cathedral cities. In fact, there seems to have been a good deal of civic rivalry; if one town erected a handsome new cathedral, its neighbors strove to surpass it. The classic example is Beauvais, whose residents decided that they would build the loftiest cathedral in France. The technical difficulties were great—the vaults collapsed twice—and by the time they were overcome money and enthusiasm were running out. So the cathedral of Beauvais stands today still unfinished, with choir and tran-

Notre-Dame de la Belle-Verrière, window from the choir of Chartres Cathedral, 12th century.

Three different styles of French sculpture. The first picture, from the abbey church of St. Pierre at Moissac, is Romanesque sculpture of the 12th century. It shows the Annunciation to the Virgin, and the visit of Elizabeth (mother of John the Baptist) to the Virgin. The work is linear and heavily stylized, reminiscent of a manuscript drawing. The second picture shows the same subjects from

septs and almost no nave. But it does have the greatest interior height of any church built during the period.

Gothic Art

As the example of Beauvais shows, the architects of the day were trying to exploit all the possibilities of the new Gothic style. They strove for greater height and more light; they emphasized vertical lines and made their windows larger and larger. In a small church like the Sainte-Chapelle in Paris they were able to reduce the walls to a few slender pillars, constructing all the

rest of magnificent stained glass. Even in the larger churches there is far more glass than stone at the upper (clerestory) level. At the same time architects were solving the problems of proportion and balance; for example, they learned to fit great round windows into the long rectangle of the west front of their churches.

The great age of cathedral-building also brought about a rapid development of sculpture and glass work. The portals of churches were embellished with hundreds of statues of Christ and the Virgin, of apostles and saints; the windows were filled

the west façade of Reims Cathedral, late 13th century. The Annunciation here is done in an earlier style than the Visitation: in the Annunciation the drapery reveals the bodies beneath it; in the Visitation it hides them. But both later groups are more naturalistic than the Romanesque, and this tendency toward naturalism becomes even more marked after about 1275.

with scenes from the Scriptures and from the stories of saints' lives. There was a strong tendency toward allegory and symbolism; thus at Chartres the continuity between the Old and New Testaments is illustrated by windows in which a prophet carries an evangelist on his shoulders. Since the figures were meant to convey a religious truth, not to portray real men and women, the Virgin appears as the Queen of Heaven and not (as in later art) merely as a pretty girl. But there was always a strong tendency toward realism in Gothic art, a tendency that appears even in the twelfth century in

some of the floral decorations. This tendency strengthened during the thirteenth century, preparing the way for the very realistic art of northern Europe in the fifteenth century. But it destroyed much of the religious feeling which had characterized the greatest works of Gothic art.

Technically, Amiens is perhaps the most perfect Gothic cathedral of all—the cathedral in which all the problems were solved most successfully. But many critics prefer the massive solidity of Notre Dame of Paris or the less uniform but more interesting cathedral of Chartres, with its glorious

Two of the great Gothic cathedrals of France, both begun in the 12th century and completed in the 13th.

Notre Dame of Chartres

Notre Dame of Paris

stained glass. And as the Gothic style spread to England, Germany, and other countries, it produced remarkable buildings, not entirely like the French, but beautiful in their own right. Only in Italy was the Gothic less likely to succeed. The commercially minded Italians were less willing to spend money on their churches, and also were so imbued with Roman traditions that they never really understood the basic principles of the Gothic style.

Histories and Vernacular Literature

The great period of cathedral-building was also a great period of literary activity. We shall return to the work of scholars writing in Latin (see p. 336) and mention only one of their activities here—the writing of history. Western Europeans had always been interested in history, partly because they had inherited this tradition from Rome, partly because the Christian religion puts strong emphasis on the way in which God's plans are worked out through history. There had always been chronicles, but never before had they been as numerous or as well written as they were after 1150. English historians were the most prolific, with the Germans running them a close second. But important historians were at work almost everywhere. Kings began to patronize writers who would glorify their deeds and justify their policies—men like Otto of Freising in Germany, Guillaume le Breton in France, and the St. Albans group of historians in England. Counts and bishops also sought to have their acts remembered in local histories. Western Europeans were proud of their recent achievements and wanted to put them on record.

An even more striking change was the rapid development of vernacular literature. Minstrels had been composing songs and epic poems long before 1100, but very few of their early compositions had been written down. During the twelfth century the practice arose of recording their poems in more or less permanent form, and by the early years of the thirteenth century there was a respectable body of literature in French, German, and Provençal (a southern French dialect). Italy lagged somewhat, perhaps because the Italian dialects were still so close to Latin that they were scarcely recognized as separate languages. The habit of writing in vernacular English was delayed even longer, mainly because of the Norman Conquest. The upper classes in England spoke French and patronized French poets well into the thirteenth century, and without their support the Anglo-Saxon literary tradition could not survive. Left to the peasants, Anglo-Saxon gradually became what we call Middle English, and it was only toward the end of the thirteenth century that the ruling classes began to use this language and to take an interest in English poetry.

Works in the vernacular were largely written for the feudal class. The *chansons de geste,* for example, are long narrative poems celebrating the courage and fortitude of feudal warriors. The most famous, the *Song of Roland,* tells of the heroic death of

The oldest extant manuscript of The Song of Roland, 1130–1140.

a handful of Charlemagne's knights ambushed by a Moslem army; others describe conflicts between unreasonable lords and long-suffering vassals. Lays, based on Celtic legends about King Arthur and his

✤✤✤✤✤✤✤✤✤✤✤✤✤✤✤✤✤✤✤✤✤✤✤✤✤✤✤✤✤✤✤

The Death of Roland

This passage comes from the *Song of Roland*. Roland, commander of the rear guard of Charlemagne's army, has been cut off by a greatly superior Moslem force. He beats off their attacks repeatedly, but finally all his men are killed and he himself is mortally wounded. He hears the horns of Charlemagne's army as it advances to avenge him, and prepares for death.

Then Roland feels that death is seizing him;
Down from the head upon the heart it falls.
Beneath a pine he staggers, lays him down
On the green grass, and hides beneath his heart
His famous sword and his great ivory horn.
He turns his face toward the infidel
For greatly he desires that Charles should say,
With all his men: "Roland, the noble count,
Roland the brave has died a conqueror."

Then Roland feels that his last hour has come.
Facing toward Spain he lies upon the hill. . . .
And many memories flood into his mind
Of all the conquests he, the brave, had made.
Of gentle France, of heroes of his House,
Of Charlemagne, his lord, who fostered
        him. . . .
He cries his Culpe, he prays to God for grace:
"O God the Father who has never lied,
Who called the holy Lazarus back to life,
And Daniel from the lions' jaws preserved,
Protect my soul, and pardon all my sins!"

His right-hand glove he proffered unto God;
Saint Gabriel took it from his faltering
        hand. . . .
God sent to him his angel cherubim
And the count's soul they bore to Paradise.

Translated from *La Chanson de Roland*, ed. by T. A. Jenkins (Boston: Heath, 1924), ll. 2355–95.

✤✤✤✤✤✤✤✤✤✤✤✤✤✤✤✤✤✤✤✤✤✤✤✤✤✤✤✤✤✤✤

court, appear a little later. They introduced an element of the marvelous—Merlin and his magic—and also the theme of romantic love. Finally, there appeared the short lyric poems, which seem to have originated in southern France but quickly spread to Germany and Italy. Some of these lyrics describe the joys of battle, others are political satires, but many are love poems. They show a high degree of skill in versification; the sonnet, for example, was to develop out of this type of poem.

The rise of vernacular literature is important for three reasons. First, it introduced themes, such as the legends of the Grail and the story of Tristan and Isolde, which are still common in our literature, and in expressing these themes the poets of the day developed most of our traditional poetic forms. Second, it helped destroy Latin as the universal language and contributed to the collapse of the idea of the unity of Christendom. Not all of the early vernacular literature was written for amusement, for portions of the Bible were translated into French in the twelfth century, and several histories had been written in French by the early thirteenth century. If French could be used for these purposes, it could also be used for official documents, and during the thirteenth century we find an increasing number of royal letters and government records written in French. This same pattern developed in other countries, and the growing use of the vernacular language was one, though only one, of the forces which gave each kingdom a sense of its own identity and contributed to the rise of nationalism.

Finally, the new literature was one of the forces which helped to soften the manners of the upper classes. Even the poems about warfare were often a substitute for violence. Just as people who read "westerns" today seldom spend their time chasing outlaws, so the lords and knights who listened to the

A tournament from a manuscript illustration of one of the Arthurian stories, *ca.* 1310, with armor and weapons typical of that time. Notice that the knights are fighting in groups; in early tournaments individual combats were rare.

Song of Roland were likely to be less belligerent than the heroes they admired. Love poems and religious works were even farther removed from the old tradition of violence. Courtly life was taking on a style of its own, and a man who wished to shine at one of the great courts had to be able to recite stories and poems and even to turn out a few verses himself. It is easy to exaggerate this development; many members of the feudal class were still ignorant and brutal. But in some circles and at some levels ignorance and brutality were being softened by the desire for a little learning and for rudimentary good manners. Vernacular literature both reflected and helped to spread this new pattern of courtly life.

The Western Monarchies

It is in this context of a more prosperous and peaceful western Europe that political developments must be placed. There was a general desire for more government and better government to help preserve the gains of the last hundred years—a desire that eased the task of the political leaders who were reorganizing ecclesiastical and secular government during the late twelfth and early thirteenth centuries. The greatest progress was made in England and France, but everywhere there was a tendency to create new institutions and new officials and to make law more exact and more inclusive.

England under Henry II

Royal government in England had been weakened by a dispute over who was to be Henry I's successor. But in 1154 Henry II, the grandson of Henry I, came to the throne with a clear title. He was already lord of all western France, for he had inherited Anjou and Normandy from his parents and had acquired Aquitaine by marrying Eleanor, the only child of the last duke. Henry spent more than two-thirds of his reign in France, but he made a greater impression on England than many kings who spent their entire lives there. He needed a strong government in England both to keep the country quiet while he was abroad and to obtain men and money to protect his French possessions against jealous neighbors. In his attempts to strengthen the English government, he enlarged the activities of the royal courts and created the English common law.

Henry invented no new procedures; he simply used old devices, such as the circuit

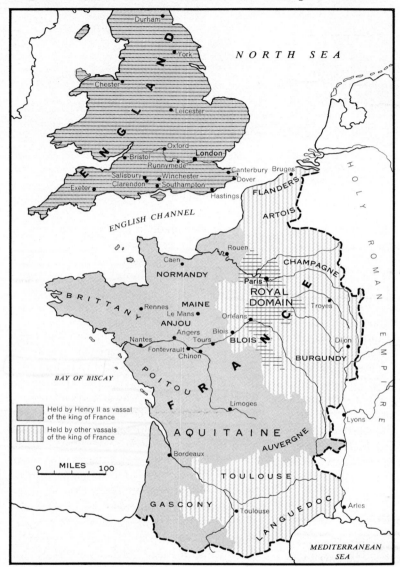

judge and the jury, more intensively. But by making regular and habitual the procedures which his predecessors had employed only on exceptional occasions Henry changed the whole nature of royal government. Whereas William the Conqueror had used inquests or juries on a large scale only once in his reign, to obtain the information recorded in Domesday Book, Henry's circuit judges summoned juries in county after county, year after year. These juries were something like our grand juries today, but they not only indicted criminals; they also had to respond to questions about the state of the royal domain and the behavior of local officials. Again, William the Conqueror and Henry I had, at long intervals, allowed a few great men to use juries to determine the possession of contested land. Henry II made this procedure available to every free man and threw open his courts to all cases involving land.

The early jury was by no means an ideal instrument of justice, for it based its decisions on common knowledge and neighborhood gossip rather than on the carefully tested evidence of sworn witnesses. But imperfect as it was, it was far better than trial by ordeal or combat. Litigants began to flock to the king's courts, and by the end of Henry's reign all disputes over land were being settled by juries in royal courts. By the middle of the thirteenth century all cases of any importance, both criminal and civil, were decided by juries.

This great increase in the amount of work done by the king's courts naturally strengthened the royal government and weakened the control of feudal lords over their vassals. Important cases no longer came to the courts of the lords, and if they tried to resort to extralegal means their vassals could always turn to the king's courts for protection. The circuit judges rode regularly through the counties, executing the king's orders, settling local disputes, and collecting information. Henry also established a permanent court at Westminster to hear cases that came up when circuit judges were not available. Everyone in the country was subject to the king's justice and most men, sooner or later, appeared in royal courts as jurors or litigants.

This constant exposure to royal justice enhanced the people's respect for royal power and indoctrinated generation after generation in the principles of English law. By applying the same rules in all parts of the country, the king's judges gradually created a common law for the whole realm. At the end of Henry's reign the first great textbook on the English common law was written, and others followed in the thirteenth and fourteenth centuries. A great unifying force, the common law eventually stood as a symbol of English nationalism. Englishmen took great pride in it, regarding it as a guarantee of their liberties rather than as a manifestation of royal power. And this pride is one reason why English common law survived when all the other countries of Europe were abandoning their medieval legal systems in favor of codes based on Roman law.

Henry II also increased royal revenue.

The murder of Archbishop Thomas Becket in his cathedral at Canterbury. This is an almost contemporary representation; it was made shortly before 1200. The knights are wearing mail shirts of the type shown in the Bayeux tapestry (see pp. 286–87).

Above, Richard Lionheart, returning in disguise from his crusade, is captured by men of the duke of Austria. Below he makes submission to the Emperor Henry VI. He was released after paying ransom, a new excuse to tax England.

Following the precedent of his grandfather, he regularly accepted money from his vassals in lieu of the military service they owed him. He also imposed a general tax on the country in 1188 in order to pay for a crusade he had promised to join. A tax of this sort was not easy to make stick, for medieval opinion was strongly set against taxation, even for a worthy cause. But, while the king of France had to abandon his efforts to impose a tax for the same crusade, Henry's tax was collected and set a precedent for additional taxes in the years ahead.

Although the English barons offered no effective opposition to Henry's reforms, he did have one dangerous opponent: Thomas Becket, archbishop of Canterbury, who resisted Henry's efforts to subject offending clergymen to the jurisdiction of royal courts. The quarrel grew bitter, and at last the archbishop was murdered in his own cathedral by four of Henry's knights, who thought they would please their king by ridding him of a troublesome foe. Henry swore, probably quite truthfully, that he had played no role in the assassination, and he abandoned his attempts to bring clergymen under the jurisdiction of royal courts. For the rest of the Middle Ages English clergymen accused of crime were tried by church courts; they lost their exemption from secular justice only after the Reformation.

Magna Carta

Henry's sons, Richard (1189–99) and John (1199–1216), lacked his political ability. Richard was a good general and nothing more; he spent his entire reign either on the Third Crusade or in fighting Philip Augustus of France. Richard was feared for his strength and admired for his bravery, but he gave little attention to the government of England. He spent less time than ten months of a reign of ten years in his island kingdom; all he wanted from England was men and money. It says much for the political institutions built up by Henry II that the government continued to function in spite of Richard's neglect and his repeated demands for taxes.

John was not even a good general. Richard had been winning the war with the king of France, but John lost it. He was intelligent but neurotic; he suspected his most loyal supporters of treason and thus forced them into neutrality or opposition. William Marshal, Earl of Pembroke, was famous throughout Europe as a model of knightly behavior; John exiled him to Ireland because he did not trust him. This kind of behavior ruined John's military position; in the long war with Philip Augustus of France, John's vassals either deserted or fought with little enthusiasm. As a result John lost Normandy, Anjou, and the northern part of Aquitaine to the French king. He also suffered a serious defeat by the Church; after resisting for five years, he had to accept an archbishop of Canterbury he did not want, but who had been chosen by the pope.

John had taken large sums of money from his vassals for his wars in France; he had also punished without trial many of the men whom he did not trust. These actions might have been tolerated if he had been successful, but his repeated failures made him very vulnerable. The lords or barons of England were outraged by the loss of Normandy, where many of them had extensive holdings. They were irritated by the heavy fines that John imposed on them, and resentful of his confiscation of many of their lands at home. In 1215 a large group of barons revolted, aided by the advice of the archbishop of Canterbury and the backing of the merchants of London. This coalition was too powerful for John to resist, and on June 15 at Runnymede he put his seal to a document which embodied all the barons' demands for reform.

This document, which soon became known as Magna Carta—the Great Charter of Liberties—was a remarkable document for the period. It shows how well John's predecessors had done their work of unifying England and instilling a respect for law even among the feudal lords. The barons made no attempt to break England into autonomous feudal states or to preserve local laws and institutions. The new legal system and the institutions of central government created by Henry II were accepted almost without question. The barons simply wanted to restrain the abuses of the central government, not to destroy it. They insisted that the king, like everyone else, was bound by law, and that he was not to use feudal relationships as a means of raising money or tax his barons without their consent. They demanded that he observe due process of law and forego punishing an alleged offender before he had been convicted in the king's courts. And if the king broke these promises, the barons warned, his subjects were free to rebel against him.

The purpose of Magna Carta was to protect the rights of the barons, not to establish parliamentary government. But the English barons were more advanced politically than the feudal lords of other countries, for powerful kings had forced them to work together and to think in terms

William Marshal, earl of Pembroke and regent of England 1216–19, in armor, from a 13th-century manuscript of Matthew Paris' *Historia Major*. William was one of the few loyal supporters of King John.

****

Excerpts from Magna Carta

1215

We [John] have conceded to all free men of
our kingdom, for us and our heirs forever, all
the liberties written below, to be held by them
and their heirs from us and our heirs: . . .

12. No scutage [redemption of military service]
or aid [grant to the king] shall be taken
in our kingdom except by the common
counsel of our kingdom. . . .

14. And for obtaining the common counsel of
the kingdom, for assessing an aid . . . or
a scutage, we will cause to be summoned
by our sealed letters the archbishops,
bishops, abbots, earls and greater barons,
moreover we will cause to be summoned
generally by the sheriffs . . . all those who
hold of us in chief [the other vassals] for
a certain day . . . and place . . . and
once the summons has been made the business shall proceed on the assigned day according to the advice of those who are
present, even if all those summoned have
not come. . . .

39. No free man may be seized, or imprisoned,
or dispossessed, or outlawed, or exiled . . .
nor will we go against him or send against
him except by the legal judgment of his
peers and by the law of the land.

40. To no one will we sell, to no one will we
deny or delay right and justice.

Trans. from W. Stubbs, *Select Charters* (Oxford:
Clarendon Press, 1921), pp. 294 ff.

****

of laws which affected the whole kingdom.
Consequently, they stated the liberties they
claimed for themselves in such a way that
those liberties could easily be extended to
other classes. Thus the right to consent to
taxes, originally restricted to the barons, was
gained by lesser landholders and merchants
before the end of the century, and the right
to a fair trial was appropriated even by un-
propertied classes. Magna Carta symbolized the supremacy of law, the conviction
that even the king was bound by law and
must respect the limits it set on his power.
Since it was invoked again and again in
protests against the arbitrary use of royal
power, it served as a foundation stone in
the English system of constitutional government.

The Growth of Royal Power in France

In England, which had achieved unity
at a very early date, the chief political problem was how to restrain an over-powerful
sovereign. In France, which had been divided into autonomous feudal states since
the tenth century, the chief political problem was how to build larger and more effective units of government. The first tentative
solutions to this problem had been reached
in the feudal states themselves, and by the
end of the twelfth century provinces such
as Normandy, Flanders, and Champagne
had well-developed legal, financial, and administrative systems. There were as yet no
similar institutions for the kingdom as a
whole, however. Even in the region stretching from Paris to Orléans, which the king
ruled directly, political institutions were
less advanced and less specialized than
in some of the great feudal states.

But, as the king of France gained power
and prestige during the twelfth century, he
gradually became master of his own domain; no longer could petty lords defy him
from castles only a few miles from Paris.
With the resourceful collaboration of the
Church he built up a series of legends
which transformed him into a semisacred
personage far above any ordinary feudal
lord—in the end, far above any other European king. At his coronation he was
anointed with holy oil which had miraculously descended from heaven; he healed
the sick; he carried the sword and banner
of Charlemagne. This increased prestige
was reinforced by the growing desire for

law and order which appeared everywhere in the twelfth century. More men sought the judgment of the royal law courts, and the king was occasionally able to impose his decisions even on lords outside his own domains. In short, a remarkable opportunity existed for a great expansion of royal power. And at the end of the twelfth century a king appeared who made the most of that opportunity.

This king was Philip Augustus (1180–1223), the first really able ruler of the Capetian dynasty. Philip's great rivals were the kings of England, who held all of western France, and he spent much of his reign in trying to pull them down. Richard withstood his attacks, but John was more vulnerable. John had made himself even more unpopular in France than in England by murdering one of his nephews, who was heir to the county of Brittany. He exposed himself even more by marrying an heiress who was engaged to one of his own most powerful vassals in Aquitaine. This was a clear breach of feudal law. John had dishonored his vassal, and the aggrieved man promptly appealed to the king of France, from whom John held all his French lands. Philip Augustus seized on this excuse joyfully. He was already planning to attack John; now he could do so in a way that would give him the support of many feudal lords. Philip summoned John to his court, and when John failed to appear to answer

The Expansion of the Royal Domain in France 1180-1314

Royal Domain at the death of Louis VII 1180

Acquisitions to the death of Philip Augustus, 1223

Acquisitions to the death of Philip III, 1285

Acquisitions to the death of Philip IV, 1314

the charges against him, he was again clearly in the wrong. Philip then ordered all John's French fiefs confiscated for default and carried out the sentence by force of arms. John's English vassals fought badly, and most of his French vassals refused to fight at all. So Philip annexed Normandy, Anjou, and Poitou with little difficulty.

By this conquest of northwestern France Philip more than tripled the royal domain. For the first time in centuries the king of France was stronger than any of his vassals. And in order to hold and exploit the territory he had gained, Philip went on to devise new institutions which set a pattern for all his successors. Because he created a territorial base from which the king could dominate the rest of the country and provided an institutional base with which to control the enlarged domain, Philip was the real founder of the French monarchy.

He seems to have been guided by two principles. One was to use local institutions whenever he could, thus preserving the earlier work of the feudal lords and at the same time conciliating his new subjects. The other was to divide the new provinces into small administrative districts and to give full powers in each district to men sent out from his own court. Thus Normandy, for example, retained its Norman law and its Norman court system and was never subjected to the law and customs of Paris. But it was divided into thirteen districts, in each of which a bailiff appointed by the king presided over the courts, collected the king's revenues, and commanded the castles and the military forces. No Norman was named as bailiff until much later in the century, and even then most of the bailiffs still came from the old royal domain around Paris.

Philip's principles of government served him well. His respect for local institutions and customs induced the new provinces to accept his control with little protest. The bailiffs, who depended on him for their very position, did their best to enforce his orders and increase his revenues. Philip made sure that his bailiffs were always strangers to the district they ruled, and he moved them frequently from one district to another to keep them from forming local attachments. He paid them well and made it clear that they could expect better jobs if they gave him faithful service. Some of them were unnecessarily harsh and some were dishonest. But on the whole their behavior convinced Philip's new subjects that royal government was better than the government of most of the feudal lords had been.

All Philip's successors followed his practice of permitting local diversity within a centralized bureaucratic framework. They enlarged the administrative districts, reducing the thirteen original districts in Normandy to five, for example, and they sent out more and more officials to help the bailiffs in their work. But they did not alter Philip's basic system. In the end, France became a very different sort of country from England. With no common law, most Frenchmen remained attached to their local rights and customs. This meant, in turn, that local leaders could seldom be trusted with much responsibility in the central government, because their loyalties were primarily to their provinces. France was held together by the king and his officials; it was a much more bureaucratic state than England. Moreover, as France grew into the most powerful state in Europe, its example was followed by others. The bureaucracies of the continental countries today are all descended from the model set by Philip Augustus.

Germany and Italy under the Hohenstaufen

Germany and Italy, meanwhile, were still nominally united under the emperor.

But the emperor's power, which had been based on his control of the Church, had been seriously weakened by the struggle over lay investitures (see p. 293). The German princes, profiting from the emperor's predicament, had seized local rights for themselves and had begun to insist on their right to elect the emperor. Moreover, feudalism, which had produced effective governments in England and many of the French provinces, was much less fully developed in Germany and was overshadowed in Italy by the growing power of the towns. Thus the old institutions of the Empire were falling into decline, and there were no new institutions to replace them.

In spite of these difficulties, Frederick Barbarossa of the new Hohenstaufen dynasty * (1152–90) made a heroic and almost successful effort to unify the Empire once again. Apparently impressed by the

* The Hohenstaufen descended, in the female line, from Henry V. They took their name from their ancestral castle in Swabia.

achievements of the kings of France and England, he modeled much of his program on their example. Imitating the king of France, he tried to build a secure royal domain in the Hohenstaufen lands in the southwest corner of Germany. Imitating the king of England, he tried to make all vassals take an oath of allegiance directly to the king, no matter who their immediate lord was. Most important, however, was his attempt to transform German feudalism into a coherent and all-embracing system of government. Many of the most powerful men in Germany owed him no allegiance, and many of those who did held part of their lands as private property exempt from feudal obligations. Frederick seems to have hoped that by bringing all men and all lands into a feudal system he could check the disintegration of the Empire. Thus by making the leading churchmen vassals of the king, as they were in England, he could regain his control over the resources of the Church, and by making

The battle of Bouvines, 1214, from a 13th-century manuscript of Matthew Paris' *Historia Major*. King Philip Augustus has been unhorsed; his men come to aid him. Others drive off an enemy knight, Hugo de Boves.

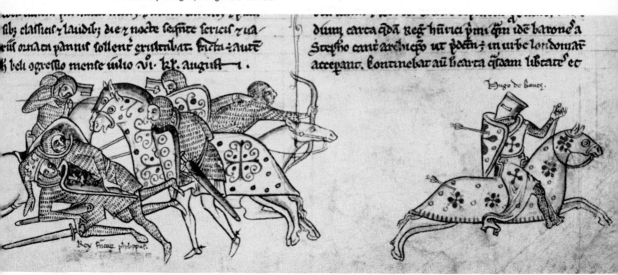

Frederick Barbarossa as a crusader, from a contemporary manuscript, 1188–89. The small figure is Provost Henry of Schäftlarn, who is giving Frederick a copy of Robert of St. Rémy's *History of the First Crusade*.

the princes of the Empire his vassals, he could curtail their growing independence and punish them for disobedience by confiscating their fiefs.

Frederick had some success in these attempts, but his own personal version of feudalism proved inadequate. It was too theoretical, possibly because it was too imitative. Both points are illustrated by his conflict with Henry the Lion, duke of Saxony and Bavaria. Henry was the head of the Welf family, which had long had hopes of gaining the imperial throne, and his two duchies made him the most powerful man in Germany. When Henry failed to give Frederick the military support he owed

during an imperial war, Frederick decided to eliminate this dangerous enemy once and for all. He had Henry condemned by a feudal court in 1180, just as Philip Augustus of France was to have John of England condemned by a feudal court some twenty years later. But while Philip was able to seize John's lands and incorporate them into the royal domain, Frederick was immediately obliged to regrant Henry's duchies to other princes. Frederick seems to have become seduced by the idea of a perfect feudal pyramid, in which all lesser lords held their lands and powers from the princes, who in turn held them from the emperor. Thus when one prince was dispossessed, his place had to be filled by another, or else the pyramid would lose its symmetry. For obvious reasons the princes were delighted with this rule, and for reasons of his own the emperor seems to have accepted it as well. In the long run this peculiar form of feudalism tended to build up the power of the princes rather than that of the emperor.

Frederick also tried to reassert his imperial rights in Italy, for he knew that if he could gain control of the Italian towns he would be the richest ruler in western Europe, and very probably the strongest. And the incessant quarrels among the Italian towns did enable him to establish himself in the Lombard plain and take over control of many of its cities. But the Italians, frightened by his success, soon called a halt to their feuds and formed a coalition—the Lombard League—to oppose him. The pope, Alexander III, who feared that any increase in imperial power in Italy would threaten his independence, supported the League. Frederick tried to overcome this opposition by supporting a series of antipopes and destroying Milan, the chief Lombard town. But the combination proved too strong for him. In the end the army of the Lombard League defeated

Frederick at Legnano in 1176 and with the pope's backing forced him to accept a peace which assured them virtual independence. But Frederick, still hoping to make something of his Italian claims, moved his base of operations farther south to Tuscany, where the towns were weaker and less hostile. Though he had some success in Tuscany, his advance there created new problems for himself and his successors. Tuscany was even farther from Germany and closer to Rome than Lombardy, and the imperial base there frightened the pope and involved Frederick more and more deeply in Italian affairs, to the detriment of his position in Germany.

The problem was still further complicated by the marriage of Frederick's son to the heiress of the Norman kingdom of Sicily. When Frederick was drowned in 1190 while leading a crusading army through Asia Minor, his son, Henry VI (1190–97), was accepted as emperor by the German princes. But Henry spent almost all his time in Italy, first making good his claim to Sicily and then opening a corridor along the east coast of Italy to connect his south Italian kingdom with Germany. Henry secured his corridor by taking lands claimed by the papacy, by virtue of the donations of Pippin and Charlemagne. Rome was now encircled by lands held by the emperor—Tuscany, Sicily, Naples, and the east coast—and this revived the popes' old fears of imperial domination.

The Church at the Height of Its Power

The late twelfth century was a bad time in which to alarm popes, for they were at the height of their power. They had full administrative control of the Church, and in a fervently Christian Europe this meant that they could control public opinion. The bishops were no longer chosen by kings, lords, or the local clergy; the pope now approved all appointments and quashed those which he felt to be irregular. In the event of a dispute over the choice of a bishop, the pope frequently set aside both candidates and imposed a man of his own choice, as he did at Canterbury in 1207 (see p. 327). At the same time he kept a close watch over the bishops by sending out legates to enforce papal orders and encouraging appeals from bishops to the papal court. Thus no bishop could have an independent policy, for his acts would be reversed by legates or the papal court. The bishops in turn increased their control over the clergy of their dioceses by making frequent tours of inspection and appointing men trained in canon law to preside over the ecclesiastical courts. Thus the Church became a highly centralized organization, with the bishops responsible to the pope and all lesser clergy responsible to the bishops.

This centralization brought with it new problems. With the popes and bishops spending more and more of their time on administrative and judicial details, they were in danger of abdicating their role as spiritual leaders. St. Bernard was already worried about this problem in the middle of the twelfth century, and generation after generation of reformers shared his concern. Moreover, the new administrative system was expensive to operate, and the papal and episcopal courts had to demand heavy fees from those who did business with them. But even these fees were not enough to cover expenses, and in 1199 Pope Innocent III imposed an income tax on the clergy, an example which was followed by all his successors. The higher clergy shifted these expenses to the parish priests, who in turn began to exact fixed fees for services such as marriage and burial. Soon the complaint arose that the Church was selling its spiritual benefits.

Moreover, though the pope legally had full administrative control of the Church, he found it politically expedient to accept some of the lay rulers' nominations to bishoprics in order to enjoy support for his own candidates elsewhere. Thus many royal officials were rewarded by high positions in the Church, and they seldom surrendered their early interest in secular politics.

Innocent III

And yet the Church reached the height of its power at the end of the twelfth century, during the pontificate of Innocent III (1198–1216). Innocent, who felt responsible for the moral and spiritual welfare of all western Europe, once said, "Nothing in the world should escape the attention and control of the Sovereign Pontiff." The Vicar of Christ, "less than God but more than man," he could reprove and punish kings who broke the divine law. A man of remarkable energy (he was only thirty-seven years old when he became pope), he came very close to making the papal court a supreme court for all of Europe. He kept the clergy under tight control and intervened repeatedly in secular affairs whenever he felt a moral issue was involved. Thus he threatened to support a French invasion of England in order to make John accept his own choice as archbishop of Canterbury. As soon as John yielded, however, Innocent granted him papal protection and forbade the French to carry out their planned attack.

Innocent III and the Empire

Innocent's most striking intervention, however, was in the affairs of the Empire. The premature death of Henry VI in 1197 created a complicated problem of succession. Henry's heir, Frederick II, was only three years old, and, though Frederick's claim to Sicily was undeniable, the princes of the Empire had never accepted the rule of strict hereditary succession. They split into two factions, one supporting Philip of Hohenstaufen, the brother of Henry VI, the other supporting Otto, the son of Henry the Lion and head of the Welf family. Innocent took advantage of this dissension by driving the German troops and governors out of central Italy and regaining control of all the Papal States, including the territory on the east coast. Alleging that since the pope crowned the emperor he had a right to reject unworthy candidates, he postponed the solution of the German problem for ten years. Finally, in 1208, after Philip had been assassinated, Innocent recognized Otto as emperor on condition that Otto renounce all claims to the lands in central Italy which had been seized by Frederick Barbarossa and Henry VI. When Otto broke his agreement, Innocent turned against him and persuaded the German princes to accept Frederick II as their ruler. By 1215 the young Frederick was in full control of Germany, and Innocent felt that he could trust the new emperor to be a dutiful subordinate of the Church instead of a dangerous rival.

Actually, Innocent had made a series of disastrous mistakes. By prolonging the dispute over the succession in Germany, he had given the German princes a chance to increase their power at home; after 1215 the position of the emperor north of the Alps was very shaky indeed. Frederick II, soon deciding that he could make nothing of Germany, turned his eyes toward Italy, thus reviving the danger of encirclement, which Innocent thought he had ended by putting Frederick on the German throne. Instead of showing gratitude for the pope's support, Frederick renewed the old attempt to annex a corridor along the east coast and to assert imperial power in Tuscany and Lombardy. But Innocent was determined that the Papal States must stretch from coast to coast and had no intention of

334

11 / Medieval Civilization at Its Height

permitting the emperor to gain control of central and northern Italy. The result was a long struggle which badly damaged the prestige of the Church. It also destroyed the last chance of unifying Germany, or of bringing Italy under a single government, thus leaving two dangerous problems for the nineteenth century.

Innocent III and Heresy

Innocent was also beset by problems spawned by the economic and intellectual revival of the twelfth century. For the first time since the end of the Roman Empire the Church was seriously threatened by heresy. Dangerous ideas were creeping in from the East along the busy trade routes; others were being formulated by the leaders of towns in Italy and southern France. Many people were attacking the ignorance of the priests and the greed and immorality of the prelates. Some of these critics remained Christian but felt that they were as capable as the clergy of interpreting the Bible. Laymen organized themselves into groups to read the Scriptures together and to try to apply Christian standards in their daily life. The Waldensians, who still exist, were typical of these groups; they had adherents throughout the Rhone Valley and in many northern Italian towns. Other anticlerical groups accepted a new version of the old Manichaean faith (see p. 144) which had been imported from Bulgaria. Like the Manichaeans they believed that the world was the scene of a constant struggle between a God of good, whom they identified with the God of the New Testament, and a God of evil, whom they identified with the God of the Old Testament. They organized a church of their own and were especially numerous in the region of Albi in southern France, whence they took the name Albigensians.

By 1200 these heresies had the support of thousands of people and dominated whole communities. Innocent tried at first to convert the heretics by peaceful means, but he soon became convinced that force was needed. He proclaimed a crusade against the Albigensians in 1207 and enlisted an army of knights from northern France to invade the south. The conflict was as much a civil war as a religious war; since the northerners aimed at the conquest of the south, many Catholic nobles of the region aided the Albigensians. At the sack of Béziers the exasperated northerners cried: "Kill them all, God will know his own!" In spite of stubborn resistance, the southerners were crushed and the lords of northern France now ruled the entire land.

The victory over heresy was still not complete. There were repeated revolts against northern domination, which could be suppressed only by a new crusade led by the king of France himself. He took over all the conquests of the northern lords; thus one unforeseen result of the Albigensian war was a great increase in the power of the French king. The king's victory ended open manifestations of heresy, but many heretics, while ostensibly accepting the orthodox faith, practiced their rites in secret. In order to unearth them the Church had to develop a new court, the Inquisition. This court accepted neighborhood rumors as a basis for accusations and used torture to secure confessions. The Church justified this procedure on the grounds that the heretic, who caused the loss of an immortal soul, was far worse than the murderer, who merely killed the body. In the end the Inquisition wiped out the Albigensian heresy, but it had an evil effect on European society. It often corrupted communities by encouraging fanatics and talebearers, and it provided a regrettable example for secular courts to follow. The only major areas to escape the Inquisition were England and Scandinavia, where there were not enough heretics to bother about.

The Revival of Science

Along with the popular heresies there were intellectual heresies which had developed out of the twelfth-century revival of learning. By the middle of the twelfth century the scholars of the West had absorbed all the Latin learning they could come by —the literary classics, the works of the Church Fathers, and the Roman law. Searching about for new materials, they seized on the rich store of learning in the East which never had been translated into Latin. Though Aristotelean logic had greatly stimulated the revival of scholarship, the West had only a few of Aristotle's elementary treatises on logic. Though scholars were deeply interested in astronomy and astrology, they had only a few brief texts on these subjects, while the Greeks

Pythagoras, sculpture on the west façade of Chartres Cathedral, 12th century. Pythagoras symbolizes arithmetic, one of the seven liberal arts, all of which are represented on this portal. Their appearance on a cathedral shows the revived interest in learning of the 12th century and the close connection between religion and scholarship. Notice that Pythagoras, though a pagan, can be shown on a Christian cathedral; the Church has appropriated the learning of the ancients.

and Arabs had scores of volumes. The same poverty of materials prevailed in medicine and biology, in mathematics and physics. All the really advanced works were in the eastern languages; in Latin there was nothing but elementary textbooks and tantalizing references in the encyclopedias of the late Roman Empire.

To correct this deficiency, the scholars of the West turned to the great task of translating into Latin the works of Aristotle and the scientific writings of the Greeks and Arabs. The difficulties were formidable—there were no grammars, no lexicons, none of the scholarly apparatus which we take for granted in learning foreign languages. The Romans had never been particularly interested in science and had never developed a scientific vocabulary; consequently, even when a translator knew the meaning of a Greek or Arabic word he had trouble finding a Latin equivalent. Moreover, many of the important texts had been corrupted by repeated translation— for example, a work originally written in Greek might have been translated into Syriac at the Ommiad court, then into Arabic at Baghdad, then into Hebrew in Spain, and finally into Latin by a western scholar.

Nevertheless, western scholars completed the task they had set for themselves. By the middle of the thirteenth century they had translated into Latin almost all the works of Aristotle and a great mass of other material. The West had acquired the philosophy and the science of the East— and just in the nick of time, for during the thirteenth century both Byzantium and the Arab world were ruined by civil wars and foreign invasions. Though they made a partial recovery later on, they were never again the intellectual centers they had been in the early Middle Ages. The scientific tradition which the Greeks had originated and the Arabs had preserved would have van-

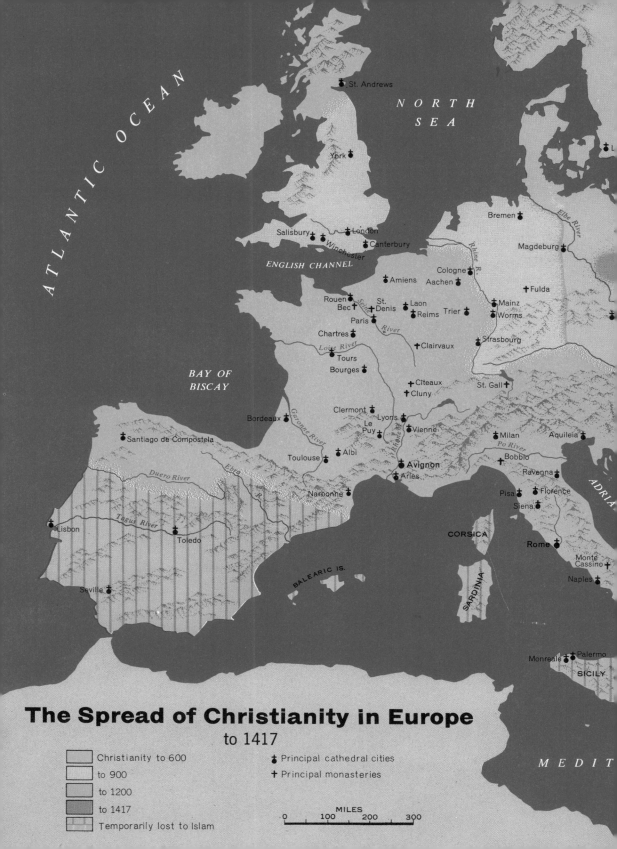

The Spread of Christianity in Europe

to 1417

ATLANTIC OCEAN

NORTH SEA

⚓ St. Andrews

York ⚓

Bremen ⚓

Magdeburg ⚓

Elbe River

+ Fulda

Salisbury ⚓ ⚓ London
Winchester ⚓ Canterbury

ENGLISH CHANNEL

Cologne ⚓
Aachen ⚓
Amiens ⚓

Rhine R.

⚓ Mainz
Trier ⚓ ⚓ Worms

Rouen ⚓
Bec +
St. + Denis
Laon ⚓ Reims
Seine

Paris ⚓
Chartres ⚓
+ Clairvaux
Strasbourg ⚓

Loire River

Tours ⚓
Bourges ⚓

+ Cîteaux
+ Cluny
St. Gall +

BAY OF BISCAY

Clermont ⚓
Lyons ⚓
Le Puy ⚓ Vienne
Milan ⚓
Aquileia ⚓

Bordeaux ⚓
Garonne River

Po River

Bobbio +

ADRIA

Santiago de Compostela ⚓

Duero River

Ebro

Toulouse ⚓ ⚓ Albi

+ Avignon
+ Arles

Ravenna ⚓
Pisa ⚓ + Florence
Siena ⚓

Narbonne ⚓

Tagus River

Lisbon ⚓

Toledo ⚓

BALEARIC IS.

CORSICA

Rome

SARDINIA

Monte + Cassino

Naples ⚓

Seville ⚓

Monreale + ⚓ Palermo

SICILY

MEDIT

MILES

0   100   200   300

Christianity to 600

to 900

to 1200

to 1417

Temporarily lost to Islam

⚓ Principal cathedral cities

+ Principal monasteries

sala ✝

BALTIC SEA

✝ Novgorod

+ Moscow

Volga River

Gnesen ✝

Vistula River

ROMAN CHURCH
GREEK CHURCH

Kiev ✝

Dnieper River

Don River

Cracow ✝

River

Gran ✝

Danube River

BLACK SEA

Constantinople ✝

Tigris R

Thessalonica ✝

AEGEAN
SEA

Euphrates River

ANEAN SEA

CYPRUS

CRETE

Nile R.

J. P. TREMBLAY

ished had it not been for the efforts of the translators of the twelfth and thirteenth centuries.

Medieval science was not the science of our own day. It was based on authority rather than direct observation, though the Arabs had made some very accurate tables of star positions and had done original work in optics and medicine. In general, medieval science developed its ideas through formal logic rather than through experimentation, and it was contaminated by the wishful thinking of philosophers and magicians. But at least it was an attempt to explain the physical world, to find ways of summing up seemingly unrelated phenomena in general laws. The important thing was not the accuracy of the results, but the fact that the effort was being made to ask meaningful questions about the nature of the universe. The questioning, once it began in the twelfth century, has never stopped, and from the questioning our modern science has developed.

Understandably, the Church was suspicious of this new learning, which was derived at best from schismatic Greeks and at worst from Moslems, Jews, and agnostics. It carried with it many dangerous ideas— remnants of old religions disguised as magic, philosophies which were older than either Christianity or Mohammedanism, materialistic doctrines which denied the validity of all religions. For example, some of the Arabic commentators on Aristotle had advanced the idea that the world was eternal, and by so doing denied the Creation and the Last Judgment. By 1200 western scholars were teaching these ideas to eager young students, especially in the great center of learning at Paris.

The First Organized Universities

It seemed clear that the Church must take vigorous measures to check the spread of such insidious ideas. The need became

✾✾✾✾✾✾✾✾✾✾✾✾✾✾✾✾✾✾✾✾✾✾✾✾✾✾✾✾✾✾✾✾✾

Church Regulation
of the University of Paris
1215

Robert [de Courçon] by the divine mercy cardinal priest . . . and legate of the apostolic see, to all the masters and scholars at Paris, eternal safety in the Lord.

Let all know, that having been especially commanded by the lord pope . . . to better the condition of the students at Paris, and wishing . . . to provide for the tranquility of the students in the future, we have prescribed the following rules:

No one is to lecture at Paris in arts before he is twenty years old. He is to study in arts at least six years before he begins to lecture. . . . He must not be smirched with any infamy. When he is ready to lecture, each one is to be examined according to the form contained in the letter of the bishop of Paris. . . .

The treatises of Aristotle on logic, both the old and the new, are to be read in the schools in the regular and not in the extraordinary courses. The two Priscians [on grammar] . . . are also to be read in the schools in the regular courses. On the feastdays [there were nearly one hundred of these] nothing is to be read except philosophy, rhetoric, books on the *quadrivium* (arithmetic, geometry, music, and astronomy), the Ethics [of Aristotle] and the fourth book of the Topics [of Boethius on logic]. The book of Aristotle on Metaphysics or Natural Philosophy, or the abridgements of these works, are not to be read, nor the doctrines of [certain contemporary teachers accused of heresy].

From Robert de Courçon, Statutes, trans. by D. C. Munro, *Translations and Reprints* (Philadelphia: U. of Pennsylvania Press, 1899), Vol. II, No. 3, p. 12.

✾✾✾✾✾✾✾✾✾✾✾✾✾✾✾✾✾✾✾✾✾✾✾✾✾✾✾✾✾✾✾

particularly urgent during the second half of the twelfth century, when several other forces were leading toward a more highly organized system of education. As we have seen, professors and students were already forming associations to protect their interests. Both groups found it to their advantage to insist on prescribed courses of study and examinations as prerequisites to obtaining a license to teach or, as we would say, a degree. This system enabled the students to know what their obligations were and permitted teachers to bar unqualified men from their profession. It was not unlike the system that prevailed in the gilds, where a journeyman had to demonstrate his knowledge of his craft to a board of masters before he could become a master himself. In fact, the word "university" originally meant a gild of any sort, and not just an association of scholars.

But gilds of any sort had to be recognized by some higher authority, and the natural authority to sanction a gild of scholars was the Church. The Church saw obvious advantages in patronizing associations of scholars; it could more easily control the new learning, and it could use the professors as experts to examine suspect doctrines. The University of Paris, for example, began to denounce dangerous ideas derived from Aristotle and the Arabs almost as soon as it received official recognition from the pope.

Innocent III, who had been a student at both Paris and Bologna, favored university organization and bestowed valuable privileges on both his old schools. His patronage was matched by secular rulers, who needed educated men to staff their rapidly growing bureaucracies. By the end of the thirteenth century there were universities at Oxford and Cambridge in England, at Paris, Montpellier, and Orléans in France, at Coïmbra and Salamanca in the Iberian Peninsula, and at Bologna and Padua in Italy. There was no university in Germany until the fourteenth century. Paris remained the unquestioned leader in theology and liberal arts, and Bologna in law, but many men studied at more than one university. All the famous scholars of the thirteenth century were university professors, and university graduates filled most of the high offices in the Church and many important positions in secular governments. In short, during the thirteenth century the universities took over the intellectual leadership of western Europe.

The idea of the university was one of the great medieval contributions to modern civilization. Most civilized peoples have had schools of one kind or another, but they have usually consisted of private instruction of novices by priests, or the private tutoring of wealthy young men by individual teachers. True, the Roman Empire established professorships for scholars to lecture to anyone who cared to listen, but it never developed the university or an examination system. China, during the European Middle Ages, developed a more or less prescribed course of study, with an examination system and something very like our system of scholarly degrees, but it lacked an autonomous, self-perpetuating faculty. Only in medieval Europe do we find all the elements that make a modern university—a faculty constituting an organized and privileged community of scholars, a regular course of study, and final examinations leading to the degree as a certificate of scholarly competence. This type of educational organization has its disadvantages—it tends to become overly conservative and tradition-bound—but by and large it has proved the most successful form of higher education ever devised, and it has spread throughout the world.

The Mendicant Orders: Franciscans and Dominicans

The popular and intellectual heresies that we have mentioned were only the most

St. Francis strips off the garments he wore as a well-to-do young man and renounces all worldly goods. Painting by Giotto (1266?–1337), in the church of St. Francis at Assisi.

obvious manifestations of a slow weakening of the Church's influence over the population of western Europe. Townspeople, feudal landholders, and lay officials complained that the ordinary parish priests were ignorant and unsophisticated and that the higher clergy were preoccupied with perfecting their administrative systems and increasing their incomes. They accused monks of being greedy and questioned the value of the monastic ideal of withdrawal from the world. The men who made these criticisms were not heretics; they simply felt that the Church was not doing its job, that it was failing to meet the challenge of changing times. They feared that the Church was yielding to the temptations created by a more prosperous and better-organized society—the love of wealth and the love of power—instead of finding ways to combat them.

It was in response to these criticisms that the medieval Church embarked on its last great wave of reform, with the establishment of the Franciscan and Dominican Orders. St. Francis (*ca.* 1182–1226), the son of a well-to-do Italian merchant, was particularly sensitive to the problem of wealth. His own conversion began with his renunciation of all claim to his family's property, and throughout his career he insisted on absolute poverty for himself and his followers. He also demanded literal and unquestioning observance of the precepts *of Christ* given in the Gospels to the disciples of Christ. Probably no other group of Christians has ever come closer to imitating the life of Jesus and the Apostles than did St. Francis and the early Franciscans. Their example of holy living impressed laymen who had become weary of routine religious services and encouraged them to make a new effort to apply Christian principles in their daily life.

The other leader of the new religious movement was St. Dominic (ca. 1170–

✤✤✤✤✤✤✤✤✤✤✤✤✤✤✤✤✤✤✤✤✤✤✤✤✤✤✤✤✤

St. Francis
Gives a Lesson in Poverty

Once when the blessed Francis had visited the Cardinal of Ostia [who was afterward Pope Gregory IX] at the hour of dinner he went as if by stealth from door to door begging food. And when he had returned, the Cardinal had already sat down at table, with many knights and nobles. But blessed Francis placed those alms which he had received on the table beside him. . . . And the Cardinal was a little ashamed . . . but he said nothing. . . . And when blessed Francis had eaten a little he took of his alms and sent a little to each of his knights and chaplains of the Cardinal on behalf of the Lord God. And they all received them with great joy and devotion. . . . [The Cardinal later rebuked him gently, but Francis answered:] "I will not be ashamed to beg alms, nay, I hold this a very great nobility and royal dignity before God and a means of honoring Him Who, when He was Lord of all, wished for our sakes to become servant of all, and when He was rich and glorious in His majesty became poor and despised in our humility."

From Anonymous, "The Mirror of Perfection," *Little Flowers of St. Francis* (New York and London: Everyman, 1910), Ch. 23, p. 203.

✤✤✤✤✤✤✤✤✤✤✤✤✤✤✤✤✤✤✤✤✤✤✤✤✤✤✤✤✤

1221), a Spanish priest who had begun his career by trying to convert the heretics of southern France. He was primarily concerned with the instruction of the faithful through preaching and teaching. He accepted the principle of absolute poverty, but his order was to be above all an order of preachers. Realizing that perfunctory sermons and routine services were scorned by the more sophisticated groups of western Europe, he spent his life training men who would be subject to the rigorous discipline of a religious order but would also be well enough educated to hold their own in arguments with scholars, townsmen, and secular officials. The Dominicans established excellent schools to train members of the order, and the graduates of these schools soon dominated the faculties of theology of European universities.

Both the Franciscan and Dominican Orders met with immediate success. Thousands of men joined their ranks during the thirteenth century, and these friars, as they were called, became the most influential group among the clergy. Unlike the monks, who secluded themselves in their cloisters, the friars wandered about as missionaries, preaching and talking to laymen. They brought religion to the very centers of thirteenth-century society—to the courts, the universities, and the towns. At first there was some tendency for the Franciscans to appeal more to emotion and the Dominicans to reason, but by the middle of the century this difference had almost vanished. Each order produced a great teacher of theology—the Dominicans, St. Thomas Aquinas; the Franciscans, St. Bonaventura. And each order carried on revivals among the people of the towns. The fact that the leadership of the Church was preserved during most of the thirteenth century, in spite of growing prosperity and worldliness, was due largely to the work of the friars.

Suggestions for Further Reading

1. Towns and Trade

The evolution of inventions in industry and agriculture and the elaboration of international commerce is traced by P. Boissonade, *Life and Work in Medieval Europe* (1927). W. Cunningham, *The Growth of English Industry and Commerce* (1910), reviews the same material for England in a more interesting fashion. The best study of the organization of the gild system is probably C. Gross, *The Gild Merchant*, 2 vols. (1890). R. de Roover, *Money, Banking and Credit in Medieval Bruges* (1948), is a readable study of the Italian merchant-bankers and their operations in Flanders from the early thirteenth through the fifteenth century. The books by Heaton, Lipson, and Pirenne cited for Chapter 10, Section 2, also contain material on this subject.

2. Gothic Art

There are many beautiful and exciting books on Gothic art. A. Temko, *Notre-Dame of Paris* * (1955), is a charming study of this cathedral written as a biography. A. E. M. Katzenellenbogen, *The Sculptural Program of Chartres Cathedral* (1959), is a detailed study of Chartres, with the latest and most plausible historical interpretation. The best treatment of Gothic art in the High Middle Ages is P. Frankl, *Gothic Architecture* * (in preparation), which traces the development of this architecture in all regions of Europe and stresses the slow perfection of the art. Frankl includes the most up-to-date bibliography. The old work of T. J. Jackson, *Gothic Architecture* (1915), is sound and still valuable. Every student of medieval art, in fact every student of medieval history, should become familiar with one of the great monuments of American scholarship, Henry Adams' *Mont-Saint-Michel and Chartres* * (1905). This is a great appreciation not only of the art but of the entirety of medieval civilization. In the same way, E. Mâle, *Religious Art in France in the Thirteenth Century* (1913) (published in paperback as *The Gothic Image* *), is a study of the thought of the thirteenth century as expressed in art.

3. Vernacular Literature

Both C. C. Abbott, *Early Medieval French Lyrics* (1932), and J. A. Symonds, *Wine, Women and Song* (1899), have selections of typical lyric poetry of the twelfth century; the translation of Symonds, although somewhat more romantic, is superior. *French Medieval Romances* (trans. E. Mason, 1911) is a collection of short novels probably dating from the reign of Henry II. The best critical study of the vernacular literature of the twelfth and thirteenth centuries is E. Curtius, *European Literature and the Latin Middle Ages* (1953), which has excellent bibliographic material.

4. Scholarship and the Rise of the Universities

Perhaps the central figure of the Christian humanism of the twelfth century was John of Salisbury, most of whose works have now been translated. *The Statesman's Book* (trans. J. Dickinson, 1927), a work of political theory, had a great influence on the development of twelfth-century humanism. John of Salisbury's *Historia Pontificalis* (trans. M. Chibnall, 1956) describes western Europe during and after the Second Crusade as seen through the eyes of an Englishman in the papal Curia. An excellent penetration into

---

* Available in paperback edition.

John's thought and personality and his close association with Canterbury and Rome is given in *Letters of John of Salisbury*, 2 vols. (edited W. J. Millor and H. E. Butler, 1955). C. J. Webb, *John of Salisbury* (1932), presents him as a great medieval churchman and plays down his role as scholar and humanist.

There is very good source material on university life in L. Thorndike, *University Records and Life in the Middle Ages* (1944). L. Thorndike, *History of Magic and Experimental Science*, Vol. 11 (1923), traces the origins of modern science in the medieval universities. C. H. Haskins, *The Rise of the Universities* * (1923), is a good general survey of the beginnings of the universities; the standard scholarly study is H. Rashdall, *The Universities of Europe in the Middle Ages*, 3 vols. (revised and edited F. M. Powicke and A. B. Emden, 1936). H. Waddell, *The Wandering Scholars* (1927), gives an amusing picture of student life.

5. Henry II, Richard, and John

The English practice of preserving records has provided us with a vast amount of evidence for this period. Both Roger of Hoveden, *The Annals*, 2 vols. (trans. H. T. Riley, 1853), and Roger of Wendover, *Chronicle*, 2 vols. (trans. J. A. Giles, 1849), are interesting contemporary histories. There is valuable material in *English Historical Documents*, Vols. II and III (edited D. C. Douglas and G. W. Greenaway, 1953–55). For the study of the growth of English law there are representative documents in C. Stephenson and F. G. Marcham, *Sources of English Constitutional History* (1937). J. E. A. Jolliffe's *Constitutional History of Medieval England* (1937) is a readable and scholarly study with a good critical bibliography, and F. Pollock and F. W. Maitland, *History of English Law*, Vol. I (1923), is fundamental. J. E. A. Jolliffe's *Angevin Kingship* (1955) traces the character and growth of royal power and the development of the organs of government through the twelfth century. The old work of L. F. Salzmann, *Henry II* (1914), is interesting but weak in historical explanation, while the recent study of J. Boussard, *Le Gouvernement d'Henri II Plantagenet* (1956), is more scholarly but suffers from a number of factual errors. S. Painter, *The Reign of King John* (1949), gives an excellent account of the political and administrative history of this reign. Painter's *William Marshal: Knight-Errant, Baron, and Regent of England* (1933) is an exciting biography that presents a vivid picture of the thoughts and attitudes of the English feudal class. The most thorough treatment of Magna Carta is that of W. S. McKechnie, *Magna Carta* (1914), a chapter-by-chapter analysis. A. L. Poole, *Domesday Book to Magna Carta* (1951), is the most comprehensive one-volume history of this period; although it is sometimes dull reading (on a fascinating period), there is an excellent critical bibliography.

6. Philip Augustus

Both J. Evans, *Life in Medieval France* (1925), and A. Tilley, *Medieval France* (1922), are very good surveys arranged in topical fashion. There is a good account of French society in A. Luchaire, *Social France at the Time of Philip Augustus* (trans. E. B. Krehbiel, 1912). The works by Petit-Dutaillis, Fawtier, and Lavisse listed under Chapter 10, Section 2, also contain material on this subject.

7. Innocent III

The best study of this important pope is that of the great French historian, A. Luchaire, *Innocent III*, 6 vols. (1904–08). *Selected Letters of Innocent III Concerning England* (edited C. R. Cheney and W. H. Semple, 1953) provides us with con-

---

* Available in paperback edition.

siderable information on English-papal relations in the stormy period from 1198 to 1216. There is a very readable interpretation of Innocent's remarkable ascendancy in S. R. Packard, *Europe and the Church under Innocent III* (1927).

8. Heresy and the Friars

H. C. Lea, *A History of the Inquisition of the Middle Ages,* 3 vols. (1888), has considerable material on the Albigensian heresy, but the reader would do well to take Lea's judgments with some reservations and to read in conjunction with it E. Vacandard, *The Inquisition* (1908), which sees this terrible institution more in the light of its time. S. Runciman, *The Medieval Manichee* (1947), follows the history of the Dualist tradition in Christianity. This is a sound and urbane book.

The best one-volume collection of the lives and writings of St. Francis is in *The Little Flowers of St. Francis* (Everyman's Library). P. Sabatier, *The Life of St. Francis of Assisi* (1894), is a scholarly book with good bibliographic material, but J. Jorgensen, *St. Francis* * (trans. T. O. Sloane, 1955), is more interesting. B. Jarrett's *Life of St. Dominic* (1924) gives a good if adulatory picture of the man, and P. Mandonnet, *St. Dominic and His Work* (1944), emphasizes the spirit and work of the Order.

* Available in paperback edition.

ct ce qui or l'an en est
e lacite de paris nest
p lus q̃ de nule autre cite
Cele en a la nobilite
Des · iij · manieres degens que
Li philosofe poserent au mon̄

cleigie
regno
oze a
paris
Ensi q
ele fu
ra dis
a ath
nes q̃
liet en
grece

b ne cite de g̃nt noblece
a philosofe q̃ loez furen̄
Or les autres euesq̃ durent

12

The Rise

of the Secular State

The strong rule of Innocent III and the great popularity of the new orders of friars enabled the Church to overcome many of the dangers which threatened it at the end of the twelfth century. Popular heresy ceased to be a threat for several centuries, thanks to the Albigensian Crusades and the Inquisition (which was staffed largely by Dominicans). Intellectual heresy became less common, partly because orthodox faculties of theology were quick to detect the first signs of error, partly because a series of great theologians succeeded in reconciling the new Greco-Arabic learning with the Christian faith. By the middle of the thirteenth century there was almost no open dissent from orthodox doctrine in western Europe. Most people were honestly and sincerely Catholic in belief; the few who were not found it expedient to pretend that they were.

The Impact of Economic Change

Yet the situation of the Church was not as secure as it seemed. It could deal with the heretic who was an open enemy; it found it much harder to handle the problem of the lukewarm friend. Men had to make a

Representatives of the three estates—a clergyman, a knight, and a laborer—from a late-13th-century manuscript. The chapter heading over the picture says: "Of the three sorts of people whom the philosophers place in the world."

living and support their government. But at what point did a normal desire to make a decent living turn into an immoderate lust for wealth; at what point did obedience to authority turn into a loyalty which subordinated the interests of the Church to those of the state? It was easier to sense this gradual growth of worldliness than to do anything about it in specific cases, and the task was made no easier by the fact that the Church itself was infected by the very disease it sought to cure. Some clergymen gave themselves over to the business of accumulating offices and increasing their income. Even more of them spent most of their time working in the administrative offices of secular rulers. The first group exposed the Church to criticism; the second often failed to defend its interests.

It has always been hard for a religion to deal with the problem of prosperity. Wealth creates pride and self-assurance, neither of which is entirely compatible with devotion. The thirteenth-century Church strove, with some success, to give the wealthy a sense of social responsibility. It condemned flagrant profiteering and callous neglect of the poor. It accepted the idea that a man who invested in a commercial enterprise was entitled to interest on the money he risked, but it frowned on financiers who charged high rates for personal loans. It was easier to make this

Corruptness in church

distinction in theory than to enforce it in practice, but the loan-sharks were made uncomfortable. Many moneylenders, prompted by some vague sense of guilt, bequeathed large sums of money to charities to atone for the profits they had made from usury. But while the Church could mitigate some of the consequences, it could not alter the fact that western Europe was gradually shifting to an economic system in which money was more important than inherited status. Men whose life centered on making money were not particularly receptive to the teachings of the Church. They might repent their sins during revival meetings held by the friars, and they almost always repented on their deathbeds, but their daily conduct was marked by a pursuit of the profits of this world rather than the rewards of the next.

The growth of a money economy also imperiled the status of the old ruling classes, though for different reasons. Prices rose, slowly but steadily, but income from landed estates remained almost constant. What the landowners received from their peasants was determined by custom or by special agreements; on many estates the lords had commuted all labor services and payments in kind for rents of a few pennies an acre. It was not easy to change either customary payments or contractual agreements, for if the peasants were pushed too hard they simply walked away and found employment in the towns or on the new lands which were still being cleared. Thus the real income of landlords tended to decrease during the thirteenth century.

The more capable landlords saved themselves by abandoning the idea of the highly integrated, almost self-sufficient estate. By leasing their domain lands and other holdings for short terms, they enjoyed an income that was related to the market value of their property rather than an income tied to a customary rent. And in

some regions they found it more profitable to use most of their land for sheep rather than grain crops. But these devices worked better for men with moderate holdings who could concentrate on financial details than for great landlords who had to rely on agents of dubious competence and honesty. In general, neither kings nor great feudal lords could derive enough income from their land to meet rising prices and new expenses. Sooner or later they all had to impose taxes on their subjects. But in so doing they incurred the resentment of the taxpayers and stirred up bitter conflicts among overlapping authorities over who had the right to levy the taxes.

The Church was especially hard hit by the relative decline in income from land. Large gifts to the Church fell off markedly after 1250, for landlords who were barely making ends meet were not likely to be very generous. Except for the Cistercians (see p. 297), who had never maintained great agricultural estates and had always concentrated on sheep-raising, most of the ecclesiastical foundations proved inept in adjusting to the new economic situation. Yet the Church needed more money than ever, both to pay for its growing administrative costs and to support its political aims. Thus, like every other thirteenth-century government, the Church was forced to resort to taxes. The income tax on the clergy, first imposed by Innocent III, was levied more and more frequently and at higher and higher rates. By the end of the century it was regularly 10, and often 20, per cent, and was being levied for three- or four-year periods.

The Church supplemented its income from taxes by charging fees for papal letters, legal documents, and appointments to bishoprics. And both taxes and fees depended, in the last analysis, on contributions from laymen. As a result the Church was criticized for being too interested in raising money, too ready to give spiritual benefits in return for cash payments. The more zealous wing of the Franciscans urged that clergymen abandon all their property and lead lives of apostolic poverty, but this solution was hardly realistic. The Franciscan Order itself was acquiring property, held for its use by trustees, and when Franciscans became bishops and popes they found they could do little to alter the Church's financial system. Given the economic situation, it was probably true that no changes could be made, but the result was a loss of respect for the Church as an organization, even among men who were entirely orthodox in doctrine.

The French and English Monarchies

At the very time respect for the Church was declining, the prestige of secular governments was increasing. Most of these governments were not enemies of the Church, but they were competing with the Church for the loyalty of the people. And just as the Church was becoming more worldly and more like a secular government, so secular governments were beginning to surround themselves with an aura of sanctity and to take on responsibilities hitherto reserved for the Church. Kings claimed to be protectors of the common welfare, agents of divine justice, defenders of the faith. No thirteenth-century pope became a saint, but several kings were canonized. And one of these saintly kings, Louis IX of France, probably exercised greater moral authority over the Europe of his day than did any churchman.

St. Louis

Louis IX (1226–70) was the grandson of Philip Augustus, the first really strong French king. Philip had conquered the northwestern part of France in his war with John (see p. 327), and Philip's son, Louis VIII, had acquired large holdings in the south by his timely participation in the crusade against the Albigensians. As a result, Louis IX was far more powerful than any possible combination of hostile French lords. He put down a few half-hearted rebellions early in his reign, and for the rest of his life his authority was never challenged again. He could preserve his rights merely by asserting them, and he could keep peace among his vassals simply by ordering them to refrain from war. An arrogant man might have abused this power, but Louis was determined to follow the ideals of a Christian ruler. He settled the long-standing dispute with England by a very generous treaty which gave the English king many border districts in Aquitaine. He kept faith with all men, even with Moslems. In France he submitted all disputed questions to the decisions of his courts and did his best to restrain the zeal of his administrative agents, who tended to exaggerate the extent of royal rights. No other medieval king had such a reputation for honesty and fair dealing.

Louis was pious and generous, but he was not soft. His loyalty to the faith did not keep him from exercising independent judgment about the policies of the Church. He refused to join Pope Innocent IV in the attack on the emperor Frederick II; he rejected demands of the French bishops that he punish all men who remained excommunicated for more than a year. With an exalted idea of his position as a Christian king, he felt it his duty to secure the spiritual and material welfare of everyone in France. His recognition of the rights of individual men was always tempered by concern for the common welfare.

Moreover, Louis' concern for law and justice led, naturally enough, to a great

St. Louis as Described by Joinville

Jean de Joinville, a noble of Champagne, was a friend of St. Louis and went with him on his crusade of 1248.

This holy man loved God with all his heart, and imitated his works. For example, just as God died because he loved his people, so the king risked his life many times for the love of his people. . . . He said once to his eldest son: . . . "I beg you that you make yourself loved by the people of your realm, for truly, I would rather that a Scot came from Scotland and governed the people of the kingdom justly and well than that you should govern them badly. . . ." The holy king loved the truth so much that he kept his promises even to the Saracens.

A friar told the king . . . that he had never read that a kingdom was destroyed or changed rulers except through lack of justice. . . . The king did not forget this lesson but governed his land justly and well, according to the will of God. . . . Often in summer he went to sit down under an oak-tree in the wood of Vincennes, after hearing mass, and made us sit around him. And all those who had suits to bring him came up, without being hindered by ushers or other people. And he would ask them: "Does anyone here have a suit?" And those who had requests would get up. . . . And then he would call Lord Pierre de Fontaines and Lord Geoffroi de Villette (two of his legal experts) and say to one of them: "Settle this affair for me." And if he saw anything to correct in what they said on his behalf, he would do so.

From Jean de Joinville, *Histoire de Saint Louis,* ed. by N. de Wailly (Paris: Firmin Didot, 1874), pp. 11, 34.

strengthening of the royal judicial system. During his reign one of the great institutions of the French monarchy was created—the Parlement of Paris. This was the king's own court, staffed with his closest advisers. It heard appeals from the decisions of his local administrative agents, and, even more important, it heard appeals from the courts of the great feudal lords. By reviewing, and often reversing, the decisions of feudal courts, it clearly established the king's supremacy over his most powerful subjects. It gradually developed a set of rules which gave legal support to Louis' claim that he was responsible for preserving peace and order throughout his realm.

The king's local courts, headed by the bailiffs and other administrative agents, were even more zealous than the Parlement in upholding royal rights. Since earlier kings had been too weak to enforce their theoretical claims to supremacy, no exact boundary between the privileges of local lords and the rights of the monarch had ever been drawn. Thus in the many issues that arose for the first time during the reign of Louis IX—issues for which there were no clear precedents—it was only natural that the bailiffs should rule in favor of the king. Louis did not take undue advantage of this situation; in fact, he and his Parlement often modified the more extreme claims of the bailiffs. But the net result was a great increase in royal power, an increase which was cheerfully accepted by most of the people in the country. After all, Louis had suppressed disorder, and his courts, though not perfect, dispensed a better brand of justice than those of most feudal lords.

A just and powerful king, Louis was also a zealous crusader. Jerusalem had been lost to the Moslems in 1187, and the first great effort to recover it—the Third Crusade of 1189—had failed. The Fourth

Scenes from *The Book of Hours* of Jeanne d'Evereux, queen of France, drawn by Jean Pucelle ca. 1325. The first picture shows the canonization of St. Louis in 1297; his relics are being carried by his grandson, Philip the Fair. In the second picture St. Louis is helping to bury the bones of Christians killed by a Saracen attack on Sidon while he was crusading in Palestine.

Crusade (1202–04) had been perverted into an attack on Constantinople, and the Fifth Crusade of 1218, after a promising start, had been unsuccessful. These successive failures had somewhat dampened enthusiasm for overseas expeditions, and the popes made matters worse by using the crusade as a weapon against their enemies in Europe. But Louis, who felt that his responsibilities as a Christian ruler extended beyond the limits of his realm, made two great efforts to recover Jerusalem, one in 1248 and one in 1270. The earlier expedition had some chance of suc-

cess, but, after a first victory, Louis' army was cut off from its supplies and was forced to surrender. The second expedition was hopeless from the beginning, for Louis let himself be talked into attacking the outlying Moslem state of Tunis. Even if he had conquered the country, it would have done his cause little good; as it was, he and many of his followers died of fever soon after they had landed.

Louis IX was made a saint within a generation of his death. His canonization was more than a personal tribute to a pious crusader; it completed the work of sanctifying the French monarchy. Louis' long search for justice and order had created an almost inexhaustible reservoir of support for his dynasty. Some of his successors were evil and some were weak, but for centuries loyalty to the king was the strongest political force in France. The king stood as the symbol of unity and good government, and he alone could override provincial differences and selfish local ambitions. France remained Catholic, but loyalty to the Church now took second place to loyalty to the state.

Henry III of England

France was united only through her king and his bureaucracy. The provinces retained their own customs and privileges; no one could have spoken of a French common law, or the "rights of Frenchmen." But in England the monarchy, in its long years of ascendancy, had created a common law and common institutions. The propertied classes in England had become attached to these common institutions and were already proud of the English way of government. The law of England, as stated in Magna Carta, protected their rights. Thus the growing loyalty to the English state was loyalty to a system of government as much as it was loyalty to a dynasty. The king could not claim that he alone was working for the common welfare, for his opponents could assert that they too were seeking the good of the "community of the realm." Thus in England even bitter struggles between king and aristocracy could not destroy the unity of the country.

This unusual political situation in England explains the apparent contradictions in the reign of Henry III (1216–72). On the one hand, royal officials strengthened the administrative and judicial institutions of the country. They created new types of general taxation, and improved the procedures of the Exchequer. The judges devised new schemes for bringing more cases into royal courts. Most important of all, trial by jury, already used to settle most land disputes, became the normal procedure in criminal cases. These changes completed the task of bringing all lawsuits of any significance into the royal courts. Many private courts simply ceased to exist, and those that survived had only police court jurisdiction. All these legal developments were summed up in a great treatise on English law written about 1250 by Henry de Bracton, a royal judge. Bracton gave a clear, logical, and thorough explanation of the common law, citing precedents and stating general principles. He made the common law so coherent and self-sufficient that it was able to ward off all outside influences for many centuries, and his book became the basic text for the training of English lawyers.

On the other hand, during Henry's reign there was constant friction between the king and his barons. The barons were not trying to destroy the growing power of the central government or safeguard their rights of local government. Rather, they were trying to protect their property and influence the policies of the king. And they often found it expedient to claim that they were defending the community of the realm against a foolish and spendthrift monarch.

When Henry came of age in 1225, the barons persuaded him to confirm Magna Carta by granting him a tax. This time there was no question of a forced promise as there had been in 1215. John had been coerced by a rebellion, but Henry III had given his free consent, and the 1225 version of the Charter was accepted by everyone as the law of the land. What is more, the king made his officials enforce it, and this satisfied the barons for some time. But by the 1240's they were once more in open opposition to the king. They could not hate him as they had John—Henry was a likable, honest man, almost as pious as St. Louis—but they did dislike his policies. He had spent a great deal of money in vain attempts to reconquer some of the land that John had lost in France. He seemed to favor foreigners, for he filled bishoprics and administrative posts with men from France and Savoy. Moreover, he was too much under papal influence; he allowed the pope to draw large sums of money from England, and he was becoming involved in the papal war against the Hohenstaufen rulers of Italy. We cannot speak of fully developed nationalities in the thirteenth century, but we can detect at least a beginning of nationalism in the attitude of the barons. They were not interested in Henry's French lands; they resented his French friends; they saw no reason for England to help the pope. They wanted English jobs to be filled by Englishmen, and they wanted English money to be spent in England. The barons' opposition to foreign intruders and foreign entanglements was supported by large numbers of lesser landholders and by a surprising number of English clergymen.

Henry III's chronic shortage of money enhanced the power of the barons. His ordinary income from the royal domain was barely adequate for peacetime needs, and Magna Carta prevented him from increasing his revenue without the consent of the barons. If Henry wanted to wage war in France or aid the pope, he had to levy taxes. But the barons steadily refused to grant any taxes after 1240. Henry nevertheless went ahead with an ambitious project to help the pope in a scheme to conquer Sicily. The English clergy, under papal pressure, gave him some money, but not enough. By 1258 Henry was hopelessly in debt, and his foreign policy was in a state of collapse. In desperation, he appointed a committee of barons to reform the government.

The baronial committee made some useful reforms—notably in the administration of justice—but it was primarily interested in formulating policy and controlling appointments to high office. Moreover, as soon as the barons started running the government they began to split into factions. It had been easy for them to agree in opposing Henry's policies; it was much more difficult to agree on a positive policy of their own. Few of the barons were willing to spend their time on administrative details, and they were suspicious of anyone who did. Though they clearly needed someone to act as leader, they felt that they were all equal, and they were jealous of the ablest man in their group, Simon de Montfort. In the end Simon took over most of the power, but he lost most of his baronial support in doing so. Henry's eldest son at last managed to raise an army with which he defeated and killed Simon in 1265, and Henry's authority was fully restored.

This episode is extremely significant, for two reasons. First, it set a pattern which was to be repeated in England many times during the next two centuries. Again and again the barons, annoyed by royal policy, took over the central government, and again and again laziness, factionalism, and jealousy kept them from maintaining their position. Second, the long struggle between Henry and the barons for control of the central government speeded up the development of a representative assembly in England. The two sides were so evenly matched that they both sought support from men of lesser rank—namely, the knights and other free landholders in the rural areas, and the burgesses of the towns. The easiest way to win the support of these men was to invite them to send representatives to the full meetings of the king's court, which, from the 1240's on, were beginning to be called Parliaments.

Early Parliaments

A Parliament, in the middle years of the thirteenth century, was a meeting of the king with his chief officials, his bishops, and his barons. *Parliament* was a slang term at first; it meant *talk-fest* and could be used for any sort of discussion. Its first precise meaning was a meeting to hear difficult cases which could not be decided by ordinary law courts. The English Parliament, like the French *parlement,* was a high court of justice. Even today the House of Lords is the highest court in England, though cases are actually heard only by lords who have served as judges. But the English Parliament also became a Great Council which advised the king on matters of policy and granted taxes. It was in Parliament, for example, that the English barons criticized Henry III's plans and refused to give him money. A meeting of Parliament, with all the great men of the realm assembled to deliberate and make important decisions, was an impressive occasion.

Representatives from the countryside and the towns who were summoned before Parliament were naturally influenced by its authority and prestige, and they in turn influenced their constituents when they went back home to report what had taken place. It was important to impress these people because local government in England was still largely controlled by local notables. The king of England, unlike the king of France, had never had to establish a provincial bureaucracy. With no conquered provinces to hold down and no strong loyalty to provincial institutions to fear, it was perfectly safe, and much cheaper, for the central government to pass on its orders to local notables, who served without pay. Thus in the counties

the sheriffs, the tax collectors, and the custodians of royal property were usually knights—that is, country gentlemen. And in the towns the mayors and aldermen were well-to-do businessmen. These local officials proved reasonably loyal, but they found their government jobs burdensome and annoyingly unprofitable. When they did not like government orders they could drag their feet with no fear of reprisal. It was no great punishment to remove them from office, and if they were removed they could only be replaced with men of the same sort. Thus, when the king or his barons wanted to introduce any innovation in government, such as a new law or a new tax, it was clearly advisable to gain the goodwill of the knights and burgesses. And a good way of doing so was to invite them to send representatives to Parliament, where they could hear and discuss the reasons for the shift in policy.

Several times during the troubled years from 1254 to 1265 both Henry III and the baronial leader, Simon de Montfort, asked the counties to send knights to Parliament to hear justifications of their policies. And in 1265 Simon de Montfort, in an effort to compensate for his loss of baronial support, took the additional step of asking the towns to send representatives. Simon may have acted out of desperation, but the precedent he set was not to be forgotten. In 1268 Henry III summoned both knights and burgesses to Parliament, and Edward I (see p. 364) called the same groups to the first great assembly of his reign in 1275. These early representatives had little power and always accepted the propositions laid before them by king and barons, but the very fact that they were being summoned at frequent intervals was to have great importance in the future.

England certainly did not invent the idea of a representative assembly. Both the Greeks and the Romans had experimented

Germany and Italy at the Time of Frederick II *ca.* 1250

Legend:
- Germany and Italy in 1138
- Acquisitions to 1250
- Area claimed by the Pope

MILES 0 — 150

with it, though they had never carried it very far. But in medieval Europe local communities were so strong and so closely knit that it was easy to believe that a small number of men could speak for a town or a county. At the same time the relatively weak central governments found it highly expedient to explain their policies and to try to win the backing of local leaders. Thus representative assemblies developed almost automatically; no one deliberately tried to create them. Innocent III, for example, had called representatives of the towns when he was establishing his government in the Papal States, and the Spanish kings held similar assemblies during the reconquest of the peninsula from the Moslems. In the end, the English Parliament was to prove unique, but there was nothing unusual in the experiments conducted by Simon de Montfort and Henry III.

The Papal-Hohenstaufen Feud

In Germany and Italy the central government was far weaker than in England and

The condemnation of Frederick II, from a 13th-century manuscript of Matthew Paris' *Historia Major*. At the left, Innocent IV pronounces sentence before the Fathers of the Council of Lyons. At the right, Frederick's agent, Thaddeus of Suessa, sorrowfully leaves the Council.

France—a situation that Frederick II, whom Innocent III had made emperor, spent his life trying to correct. Though he failed in this effort, he came close enough to success in Italy to precipitate the last great struggle between Empire and papacy.

Frederick II was by birth and education an Italian, though descended from the Hohenstaufen of Germany. He spent a few years in Germany after becoming emperor, but he never felt at home there and never had much power over the Germans. Apparently deciding that he could do nothing with Germany, at least until he had brought Italy fully under control, he abandoned almost all authority to the princes of the Empire. All he expected from Germany was a steady support of soldiers to help him in his Italian wars.

In Italy he followed exactly the opposite course. First he eliminated all opposition in his hereditary kingdom of Sicily, transforming it into a nearly absolute monarchy,

and then he began to revive the old imperial claims to central and northern Italy. Thanks to the factional quarrels within the Italian towns and the bitter rivalries among the larger cities for provincial leadership, he was able to build up fairly strong support for himself. In fact, some of the northern Italians became so frightened that they revived the Lombard League, but Frederick completely defeated them at Cortenuova in 1237. For the moment he seemed to be master of the entire Italian peninsula.

The papacy, however, was still determined to keep Italy from falling into the hands of one master. The independence of the Church seemed bound up with the independence of the Papal States, and Frederick's victories were threatening that independence. No pope could believe that an emperor who ruled all Italy except the region around Rome would long respect the independence of Rome itself. Innocent III had kept the Empire in turmoil for years rather than risk this danger, and the precedents he laid down were hard to forget.

Moreover, Frederick II's orthodoxy was somewhat doubtful. A brilliant and inquisitive man, no one was ever sure what he really believed. He exchanged friendly letters with Moslem rulers; he dabbled in science and magic; he was accused of writing a book called *The Three Impostors: Moses, Jesus, and Mohammed.* This last charge was completely false, but the fact that it could be made tells something of Frederick's reputation. He tried hard to convince people that he was an orthodox ruler, even going on a crusade and persecuting heretics, but these actions raised more doubts than they settled. He succeeded in regaining Jerusalem for a few years, not by fighting the Moslems, but by making a treaty with the sultan of Egypt, and his persecution of heretics seemed largely prompted by a desire to destroy their political power.

Frederick had been excommunicated several times before his victory over the Lombard League at Cortenuova. When it became apparent that he was going to insist on full control of both northern and southern Italy, the pope decided that more drastic measures were necessary. Innocent IV, just as determined and almost as able as his great namesake Innocent III, called a council at Lyons in 1245. The council declared that Frederick had forfeited all his possessions, and that neither he nor any member of his family should ever be allowed to rule in Germany or Italy. Innocent IV proclaimed a crusade against Frederick and imposed a tax on the clergy to pay for armies to carry it out.

The papal attack destroyed the last few remnants of imperial power in Germany. Turning the conflict to their own advantage, the princes refused to obey either Frederick or the opposition line of rulers who were elected by a propapal faction of nobles. Germany became a loose confederation of states under the control of princes who were free to accept or reject the policies suggested by the nominal ruler. After the dust of the papal-Hohenstaufen wars had settled, they were usually able to agree on a single emperor, but the title bestowed no real authority on the incumbent. The emperor became only the presiding officer of a club of princes.

In Italy the issue was not decided so quickly. Frederick held on to most of the territory he had gained, but he never managed to build up a strong government in the North. After his death in 1250 the towns of northern and central Italy became completely independent, though the Kingdom of Sicily remained loyal to his sons. The papacy might have been satisfied with this state of affairs—after all, the danger of encirclement had been dispelled forever—but it had been too badly frightened by Frederick to take any chances. So the popes carried on the war against the "viper brood" of the Hohenstaufen, refusing to rest until the hated family had been ejected from Sicily and Naples. They preached crusades, collected taxes from the clergy to cover their expenses, and sent cardinals out with armies to do battle with Frederick's heirs. And when all these efforts proved ineffectual, they turned for help to the royal families of England and France. The attempt to involve England led only to the rebellion of the English barons against Henry III (see p. 351), but the approach to France met with greater success. St. Louis reluctantly permitted his brother, Charles of Anjou, to attempt the conquest of the Kingdom of Sicily. Charles, aided by crusade privileges (including remission of sins for his soldiers) and crusade taxes, defeated the last Hohenstaufen ruler of Sicily in a lightning campaign in 1266. A grandson of Frederick II made a desperate attempt to regain the kingdom, but his forces were crushed in 1268 and the young Hohenstaufen was executed in cold blood. The papacy, aided by the French, had won a complete victory over its enemies.

Loss of Prestige by the Church

But in winning this political victory, the papacy had lost moral prestige. There had been some doubts about Innocent IV's deposition of Frederick II—St. Louis had preserved a careful neutrality in this struggle—but the Church clearly had a case against him. Frederick was, as we have seen, threatening the independence of the Papal States, and he was an odd, unpredictable person, certainly unconventional and possibly unorthodox in his ideas. But Frederick's heirs were much less powerful and much less dangerous to the Church, and it seemed pure vindictiveness to harry them for two decades. Using all its spiritual authority to gain a political end, the Church was directing crusades against Catholic Europeans and raising money for a European war by threats of excommunication. The pope was acting very much like a secular prince, assembling armies, making alliances, carrying on political intrigues. The distinction between ecclesiastical government and secular government was being eroded away, and loyalty to a king who was striving for the common welfare seemed just as respectable as loyalty to a politically minded pope. This state of mind was already producing a dangerous doctrine: if it was proper for the pope to tax the clergy to carry on a war in Italy, why was it not proper for a king to tax the clergy to defend his kingdom? This doctrine was to cause the next great conflict between the papacy and secular rulers.

Moreover, the popes had won their victory over the Hohenstaufen only by creating political instability in both Germany and Italy, and this instability in the long run weakened the Church. Germany was torn by petty wars among the princes, and the German bishops, who were also princes, could not avoid being drawn into these conflicts. By fighting and intriguing they managed to keep most of their possessions, but their involvement in such secular matters did nothing to increase their spiritual authority. In northern and central Italy almost every town was rent with factionalism and at war with its neighbors, and their feuds spread into the Papal States themselves. Many towns were developing a new type of government in which they handed over all power to a tyrant in order to put an end to civil war. But the tyrants, as soon as they had consolidated their power in one town, tried to conquer others. Most of them were unscrupulous opportunists who fought bishops and popes almost as cheerfully as they did laymen. The pope fell deep into the morass of secular politics in his efforts to preserve the Papal States and to keep any Italian ruler from becoming too strong.

In short, the weakening of the Empire did not strengthen the Church, nor did the defeat of the emperor free the pope from political entanglements. He now had to deal with a host of petty rulers instead of one great opponent, but this was no real gain. The princes of Germany and the tyrants of Italy were just as annoying as any emperor, and the issues they raised were harder to dramatize. There was no great principle involved—such as lay investiture, or the ambitions of Frederick II—only a mass of local problems. And in playing petty politics, the papacy itself came to look petty.

Scholarship and the Arts

It took a generation for the Church to feel the full consequences of the new political situation, and in the meanwhile it en-

Scribes at work, ca. 1226–34, from the Bible of Blanche of Castile, mother of St. Louis. The monk at the left is dictating to a scribe who holds a pen and a knife for scratching out mistakes.

joyed its last years of unquestioned leadership in Europe. The kings of the West were at peace with one another and obedient to the pope; Gregory X (1271–76) could even dream for a moment of uniting them all in a great crusade to regain Jerusalem. Both the education and the behavior of the clergy had steadily improved; careful administration might not produce saints, but at least it helped weed out the incompetent and the unworthy. Most important of all, the years from 1250 to 1275 saw the building of the last great Gothic cathedrals and the culmination of medieval Christian philosophy in the work of Thomas Aquinas (1225–74).

It was probably no accident that these two forms of expression reached their peak at about the same time. There was a strong logical element in the perfected Gothic cathedral, just as there was a strong architectonic quality in Thomas Aquinas' thought. In both, the basic structural plan is clearly revealed, uncluttered by architectural or literary decorations. Just as the cross section of a pillar of a Gothic church shows exactly what the superstructure will be, so the first paragraph of a chapter of Thomas Aquinas reveals exactly how his argument will proceed. But while we still appreciate the qualities of Gothic architecture—the emphasis on height and light, the clean expression of the function of each architectural member—we are less at home with the methods and ideas of medieval scholastic philosophy.

St. Thomas Aquinas

Thomas Aquinas, unlike some other Christian thinkers, feared neither the world nor the new knowledge about the world which scholars had acquired from the Greeks and the Arabs. God had made the world and had given man the gift of reason; He had put man in the world not to punish him but to enlighten his feeble understanding. Man could rely on his reason, properly used; the truths discovered by the ancient philosophers were perfectly valid truths, though they might be incomplete. Thus a pagan philosopher could give a completely acceptable proof of

357

the existence of God, even though he knew nothing of the doctrine of the Trinity. Reason needed to be enlightened by faith, but there was no conflict between the two;

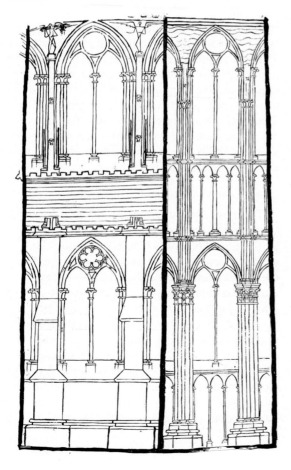

Exterior and interior elevations of the nave of Reims Cathedral, drawn by Villard de Honnecourt, a French architect of the first half of the 13th century. This is not an accurate drawing of the nave as it now is; Villard probably prepared it from working drawings which he saw before actual construction started in the 1240's. Notice the proportion and balance between upper and lower windows and the way in which the whole structure of the nave could be inferred from the study of a single pillar. Villard's notebook, from which these drawings are taken, is one of the most fascinating books of the 13th century. He drew everything that interested him—floor plans and elevations of churches, people and animals (including a lion "drawn from life"), and machinery. He even has a sketch of a perpetual-motion machine.

reason rightly used would never contradict faith.

In the same way, there should be no conflict between the Church and secular governments. Secular government was necessary and good in itself, for it gave men an opportunity to manifest social virtues. Even among the pagans, secular governments were divinely established and should be obeyed. Thomas admitted that it was proper to resist a king who was openly violating the law of God, but he felt that resistance to a secular ruler should be resorted to only after everything else had failed.

As for the new wealth, here again there was no danger if men used their reason properly. God had given man dominion over the world, and in exploiting its natural resources man was fulfilling the divine plan. Land did not fulfill its function unless it was cultivated; a tree was of no use unless it was used for construction. Men should remember their Christian duty to the poor, and they should never allow the desire for wealth to become immoderate. But there was nothing wrong in an honest effort to earn a decent living for one's self and one's family.

Thomas Aquinas believed that in the light of true reason everything made sense, that the world was a harmonious whole. Wisdom was the greatest earthly good, and the felicity of the afterlife consisted in the contemplation of the eternal Wisdom which is God. It was this serene conviction of the unity and rationality of all experience which made Thomas Aquinas' work so persuasive, which led to his early canonization and to his present reputation as the leading Catholic philosopher.

Even in his own day, not all scholars shared the views of Thomas Aquinas. Doubtless there was some professional jealousy involved; Aquinas was a Dominican, and scholars in other orders resented

358

the influence which the Dominicans had acquired in theological studies. But there was honest worry, both about the extreme rationalism of his approach, and about the reliance he placed on Aristotle and other Greek philosophers. The great Franciscan theologian, St. Bonaventura, emphasized will rather than reason. And a group of Franciscan scholars at Oxford helped to show that Aquinas was wrong by proving that his chief authority, Aristotle, had made certain mistakes about natural phenomena. In correcting these mistakes they made some experiments, notably in the field of optics, and helped start a new trend in physics, which, working through obscure scholars of the fourteenth and fifteenth centuries, culminated in the work of Galileo. Roger Bacon was a member of this Oxford group, but he has received more credit than he deserves; his vague predictions about automotive vehicles and the like had no scientific basis. The really great scholar was Bacon's teacher, Robert Grosseteste.

Scholarly disputes about the theology of Thomas Aquinas had no immediate significance. More important was the fact that his point of view made little impression on laymen. Thomas' arguments were too rational to have much influence on the behavior of most of his contemporaries. He might see no conflict between reason and faith, no opposition between secular interests and those of the Church, but for most people these contradictions did exist and could not be exorcised by words. They were faced with hard choices between the teachings of the Church and the demands of secular life, and when they chose they did not always come down on the side of the Church.

Dante

The greatest medieval poet—one of the great poets of all time—was Dante

Science in the 13th century, from the Psalter of St. Louis and Blanche of Castile. Three scholars are at work: the one in the middle is using an astrolabe to find the elevation of a heavenly body: the one on the left consults an astronomical table written in Arabic; the one on the right takes notes.

(1265–1321). One of the first men to write in the vernacular in Italy, he helped to establish the Tuscan dialect as the standard form of the Italian language. He wrote graceful lyrics in Italian and two notable treatises in Latin, one defending his use of the vernacular, the other a strong plea for strengthening and preserving the Empire. But the work for which Dante will always be remembered is the *Divine Comedy,* a vision of Hell, Purgatory, and Heaven written in magnificent Italian verse.

Dante had a troubled and unhappy life. He was deeply involved in Florentine politics, and because he belonged to the discredited pro-imperial faction he was permanently exiled from the city he loved in 1302. In spite of these troubles Dante, like Thomas Aquinas, remained convinced of the unity and meaningfulness of all human experience. He did not sink into pessimism or seek out partial truths like so many of his contemporaries. He was almost the last representative of the confident, optimistic, all-embracing spirit of the great period of medieval civilization.

Dante was well-read in both secular and religious literature. His guide through Hell and Purgatory was the Roman poet Vergil, and this part of his poem is full of allusions to classical mythology. But he also knew his scholastic philosophy; the *Paradise* in many places reads like a verse translation of Thomas Aquinas. Like Thomas Aquinas, he saw no contradiction between the truths worked out by human

Portrait of Dante by the first great Italian painter, Giotto (1266?–1337).

Dante's Divine Comedy

THE INSCRIPTION ON THE ENTRANCE TO HELL

Through me you pass into the woeful city
Through me you pass into eternal pain
Through me you go amid those lost forever.
Justice it was that moved my Great Creator;
Power divine and highest wisdom made me
Together with God's own primeval love.
Before me there was nothing save those things
Eternal, and eternal I endure.
All hope abandon, ye who enter here.

THE ATTACK AT ANAGNI

Dante disliked Boniface VIII, whom he consigned to Hell, but still felt the attack at Anagni, which he describes below through the lips of Hugh Capet, was an outrage.

O avarice, what worse canst thou now do
Since thou dost so completely rule my race
That they care nothing for their flesh and blood?
Past wrongs and future they will now compound.
Into Anagni storms the lilied flag;
Christ is a captive in his Vicar's form,
And the old mockery again renewed
With vinegar and gall. I see him bleed
Amid the living robbers; Pilate too,
I see, so cruel that even this dreadful deed,
Is not enough.

THE FINAL VISION

O grace abundant, through which I presumed
To fix my gaze on the eternal light
Which near consumes who dares to look thereon.
And in those depths I saw, bound up by love
Into one volume, all the universe. . . .
Here vigor failed the lofty vision, but
The will moved ever onward, like a wheel
In even motion, by the love impelled
Which moves the sun in heaven and all the stars.

From Dante, *Inferno*, canto 3; *Purgatory*, canto 20; *Paradise*, canto 33, trans. by H. F. Cary (London: G. Bell, 1877).

Scene from a manuscript of the *Romance of the Rose*. The lover enters the garden in which he will catch his first glimpse of the Rose.

reason and the truths revealed to the Church; all knowledge led to God if it were rightly used.

But to him knowledge was not enough; even good conduct was not enough. Faith in God and love of God and of one's fellow man were the essentials. In Hell the most lightly punished sins were those against oneself, such as gluttony. The lower depths were reserved for those who hurt others, and the worst sinners of all were Judas who betrayed Christ and Brutus and Cassius who betrayed Caesar. In Purgatory sins were purged through suffering and angels sang Beatitudes at each step of the ascent. In Paradise Dante came closer and closer to the eternal Light until he finally had his great vision of God— "the love which moves the sun and all the stars."

The *Divine Comedy* was recognized as a classic almost as soon as it was written, but admiration for the poem did not mean wide acceptance of its point of view. Few of Dante's contemporaries had his serenity or his breadth of vision; few could accept any longer his dream of a harmonious world in which men could seek both happiness on earth and eternal rewards in heaven. By the end of the thirteenth century secular and religious goals were coming into conflict, and more and more attention was being given to secular interests.

Secularism in Art and Literature

The gradual growth of secular interests may be seen clearly in art and literature. For example, after 1270 there is a striking change in statues of the Virgin. In early Gothic sculpture she is the Queen of Heaven, majestic and dignified. In late Gothic sculpture she is graceful and human, with none of the semidivine characteristics of the earlier period. In literature the break is shown by the difference between the two parts of a famous poem, the *Romance of the Rose*. The first part, written by Guillaume de Lorris in the 1230's, is an allegory of courtly love; the second part,

****

The Courtly Lover

But be thou careful to possess
Thy soul in gentleness and grace
Kindly of heart and bright of face
Towards all men, be they great or small. . . .
Watch well thy lips, that they may be
Ne'er stained with ill-timed ribaldry. . . .

Have special care
To honor dames as thou dost fare
Thy worldly ways, and shouldst thou hear
Calumnious speech of them, no fear
Have thou to bid men hold their peace. . . .
Above all else beware of pride. . . .
Let him who would in love succeed
To courteous word wed noble deed.

And next remember that, above
All else, gay heart inspireth love.
If thou shouldst know some cheerful play
Or game to wile dull hours away
My counsel is, neglect it not. . . .
And much with ladies 'twill advance
Thy suit, if well thou break a lance
For who in arms his own doth hold
Winneth acceptance manifold.
And if a voice strong, sweet and clear
Thou hast, and dames desire to hear
Thee sing, seek not to make excuse.

From Guillaume de Lorris, *Romance of the Rose,* Part I, ca. 1237, trans. by F. S. Ellis (London: Dent, 1900), Vol. I, 11. 2184–291.

****

written forty years later by Jean de Meung, is a satiric encyclopedia. The first part respects the ethics and conventions of upper-class society; the second part attacks the fickleness of women and the greed of the clergy, and gives brief summaries of the knowledge that every educated man was supposed to possess. The discrepancy between the two parts is obvious to us, but apparently it was not obvious to men of the late thirteenth century. No other poem was so popular during the later Middle Ages. It was copied and recopied in hundreds of manuscripts, and at the end of the fourteenth century Chaucer began an English translation of it. Nothing illustrates better the rise of a class of educated laymen, eager for worldly knowledge, suspicious of the clergy, and a little cynical about ideals of any kind.

Not everyone was affected by these new attitudes, and even those who were did not abandon their religion. They fulfilled all the external obligations of the faith and they would have been shocked if they had been told they were not good Christians. But they tended more and more to put their religion in a separate compartment where it would have little influence on their daily life. They could no longer be counted on to support the policies of the Church if those policies interfered with their interests, or even with their convenience. This loss of the support of a large group of influential laymen was to prove fatal to the pope in his next great conflict with secular rulers.

England, France, and the Papacy

In England and France the central government grew stronger than ever in the last quarter of the thirteenth century. Edward I of England (1272–1307), an able and ambitious politician, was determined to increase his power but clever enough to retain the support of most of the propertied classes. He seems to have had two main objectives: first, to restore royal authority after the weak reign of his father, and second, to make himself supreme ruler of the British Isles. He achieved his first goal through sheer force of personality, hard work, and intelligent selection of officials. Edward's royal rages were terrifying —the dean of St. Paul's dropped dead of fright during a dispute with him—and few men dared to contradict him openly. And there was less reason to contradict him than there had been to oppose Henry III, his father. Edward's policies were on the whole successful, especially during the first part of his reign. His avoidance of continental entanglements and his concentration on the conquest of Wales and Scotland harmonized with the desires of the aristocracy. As a result, Edward had complete control of his administration at all times and was never dominated by a baronial council as his father had been (see p. 353).

He was less successful in attaining his second objective. He did complete the conquest of Wales, which had been begun long ago by the barons of William the Conqueror. He deposed the last native prince of Wales and in his place set his own infant son, thereby creating a precedent which has endured to the present day. But Scotland proved more troublesome. Edward had vague claims to suzerainty over Scotland, and he found an occasion to enforce them when the direct heir to the Scottish throne died, leaving a disputed succession. Edward selected a new king, but when his candidate proved less subservient than he had hoped he deposed him and tried to rule the country directly. But Edward could not keep a big enough army in Scotland to suppress all dissent, and the Scots rebelled, first under William Wallace and then under Robert Bruce. The rebellion was still raging when Edward died, and the Scots soon won complete independence in the battle of Bannockburn (1314).

Edward I and Parliament

Outside his own island, Edward had to resist an attempt by the king of France to take over the duchy of Aquitaine, the last remnant of the French holdings of the English royal family. These conflicts cost huge sums of money and they kept

***

Jean de Meung on Women

To Virgil I the case refer,
Who well knew woman's character.
A woman's heart is nowise stable,
Saith he, but ever variable,
Capricious, and by anger led.
And Solomon declares her head
Is than an angry serpent's worse,
Which merited God's primal curse.
Nought else, saith he, is so with spite
Possessed, and ne'er hath man aright
Described in old or later times
Her evil ways in prose or rhymes.
And Titus Livius (who well knew
The modes and manners through and through
Of women and their minds perverse)
In language vigorous and terse
Declares, he best succeeds who tries
To warp their minds with japes and lies.
So foolish are they and unstable,
That truth they hate, but cling to fable.

From Jean de Meung, *Romance of the Rose*, Part II, *ca.* 1277, trans. by F. S. Ellis (London: Dent, 1900), Vol. III, 11. 17,117–36.

***

Edward very busy—two reasons why he made greater use of Parliament than any of his predecessors. With all the important men in the kingdom present at meetings of Parliament, Edward could get their advice on policy, settle difficult legal cases, make statutes, and obtain grants of taxes. He could probably have done all this outside Parliament, but it was more efficient to take care of everything at one time and in one place. Moreover, Parliament had great prestige; it was the highest court in the kingdom and it spoke for the community of the realm. England, unlike other countries, was so thoroughly united that decisions made in a single central assembly were accepted as binding on all men. Thus it was clearly advantageous to obtain the sanction of Parliament for as

many decisions as possible. Edward saw no danger in this situation, for he controlled Parliament as effectively as he did every other branch of government. He could not have foreseen that he was building up a powerful institution which might some day develop a will of its own.

Representatives of counties and towns attended a meeting in 1275, but for the next twenty years Edward seldom summoned these representatives. The essential part of Parliament was still the Council, composed of high officials, bishops, and barons. But in 1295 Edward summoned representatives to a very full meeting (the "Model Parliament"), and from that time on they were frequently present. Again, Edward's decision seems to have been prompted by the desire to save time and trouble. Legally, baronial approval was probably enough to validate his new laws and new taxes, but in practice it was necessary to win the support of the knights and burgesses as well. They were the men who, as sheriffs and mayors, would have to enforce the new laws, and they were the men from whose ranks tax-collectors would have to be appointed. Edward could, and did on some occasions, secure their goodwill by sending emissaries to each county and town or by calling regional meetings to explain his policies. But it was easier, and even more effective, to bring representatives of all the counties and towns together at a meeting of Parliament, where they could listen to the great men of the realm discuss the king's needs.

These representatives had not yet joined together in an organized body, and their role seems to have been largely passive: "to hear and to obey," as some of the early summonses put it. Such opposition as there was in Parliament came from the barons.

King Edward I of England (1272–1307) consults his bishops. From a 14th-century manuscript.

Edward I in Parliament with Alexander, king of Scots, and Llewellyn, prince of Wales. The bishops are seated on the benches at the left and in the foreground, the barons on the right. The commons, as was true in most early Parliaments, are not present.

Alexander Rex Scotore.

lewellin princeps wallie

On one notable occasion in 1297, when Edward had pushed a new tax through at a very small meeting of the Council, the barons protested and forced the king to promise that in the future he would levy taxes only "with the common assent of the whole kingdom." This was not quite an admission that only Parliament could grant taxes, but it certainly implied that the assent of a large number of people was needed, and clearly the easiest way to obtain such assent was in Parliament. The barons, like their ancestors under Henry III, hesitated to grant taxes on their own responsibility and were usually anxious to get the endorsement of at least the county representatives. And when, in the last years of the reign, the barons sent petitions to Edward asking for government reform, they invited the represent-atives of both counties and towns to join them. In these ways the representatives gradually became caught up in the more important work of Parliament, though their position was still greatly inferior to that of the barons.

France under Philip the Fair

In France, which was less unified politically than England, the growth of royal power followed a different course. The French barons were still struggling to preserve their local rights of government and their exemptions from the authority of royal officials. Not particularly interested in controlling the central government in Paris, they simply wanted to keep it from interfering with their lands and their subjects. The chief problem of the French king was not to keep the barons from dominat-

Siege of a city, from a French manuscript, ca. 1250. The defenders are making a sortie from a gate in the wall to break up the attack. A soldier is pulling down the arm of a catapult; when it is released it will hurl a stone against the wall.

ing his council but to enforce his orders in their lands.

This problem came to a head in the reign of Philip the Fair (Philip IV, 1285–1314), the grandson of St. Louis. Like his grandfather, Philip was pious, upright in his private life, and imbued with a sense of the divine mission of the French monarchy. But he was narrow-minded where St. Louis had been magnanimous, and grasping where St. Louis had been merely firm. The number of bureaucrats grew enormously during his reign, and Philip encouraged them in their efforts to expand royal authority. He was willing to condone any expedient—legal chicanery, bribery, or blackmail—to break the power of any local ruler who tried to retain a semi-independent status. Lesser vassals could not resist, but the more powerful men were in-

dignant. It is not surprising that Philip spent a large part of his reign warring with his greatest vassals, including the king of England (as duke of Aquitaine) and the count of Flanders. He gained some land from both, but he never took the rich textile cities of Bruges and Ghent from Flanders, or the flourishing port of Bordeaux from Aquitaine.

Philip the Fair had a harder time than Edward I in raising money to pay for his wars. The French had never been subjected to a general tax, whereas the English had been afflicted with national taxes off and on ever since the end of the twelfth century. Moreover, France was so divided that no central assembly like the English Parliament could impose a uniform tax on the whole country. Instead, royal agents had to negotiate with each region, and often with each lord or each town within each region. This cumbersome system consumed a great deal of time and reduced the yield. France was at least four times larger than England in both area and population, but it is doubtful whether Philip enjoyed any greater tax revenue than did Edward I.

These difficulties in collecting taxes explain some of the weaknesses of the French army during the next hundred years. They also explain why the French representative assembly, the Estates General, never became as important as the English Parliament. Philip, as we shall see, was the first French king to call representatives to meetings at Paris. But he never asked them for a grant of taxes, for he knew that the country at large would pay little attention to the decision of a central assembly.

This lack of any real power over taxation remained one of the great weaknesses of the Estates General. Conversely, tax negotiations with local leaders and assemblies, though tedious, gave the ruler a free hand in imposing levies. It was easy to play one region off against another, or to threaten isolated areas which could not count on outside support. The steadily growing royal bureaucracy was persistent and skillful in conducting these negotiations, and sooner or later it succeeded in breaking down most of the resistance to taxation.

Thus England was a strongly united country in which the king and the propertied classes were cooperating in policies of which they both approved. France was united more by the royal bureaucracy than by common interests, but there was

King Philip IV of France in the center with his daughter-in-law, Margaret of Burgundy, on the left, his son Louis, the king of Navarre (later Louis X), on his right, and three other members of the royal family. From Raymond de Byterris, *Livre de Dina et Kalila*, 1313.

Pope Boniface VIII receives St. Louis of Toulouse, a great-nephew of St. Louis of France and son of King Charles II of Naples. The portrait of the pope seems to be an accurate one; it corresponds to other representations of him. Fresco by Ambrogio Lorenzetti, Siena, ca. 1330.

no real opposition to the policies of the king and his ministers. The propertied classes in France, concerned mainly with local issues, were on the whole ready to trust the king in general on policy matters. And in both England and France some of the ideas which distinguish the modern sovereign state were beginning to appear. The welfare of the state was the greatest good; the defense of the realm was the greatest necessity; opposition to duly constituted authority was the greatest evil. As one of Philip's lawyers put it: "All men, clergy and laity alike, are bound to contribute to the defense of the realm." People who were beginning to think in these terms were not likely to be particularly impressed by papal appeals and exhortations.

The Struggle with Boniface VIII

The pope at this time was Boniface VIII (1294–1303), a veteran of the political conflicts endemic to Italy and an able canon lawyer. Sensing that the new type of secular authority developing in the West would be more dangerous to the Church than the medieval Empire had ever been, he tried to reassert the superiority of ecclesiastical interests and the independence of the Church. He made no claim that had not already been made by his predecessors,

12 / The Rise of the Secular State

but the climate of opinion had changed since the days of Gregory VII and Innocent III. With the shift in basic loyalties from the Church to the state, many people now believed that it was more important to support their king than to obey the pope. As a result, Boniface was defeated in a head-on clash with the kings of England and France—a blow from which the medieval Church never recovered.

The issue was clear-cut. Were the clergy to be treated as ordinary subjects of secular rulers, or were they, in the last analysis, responsible only to the pope? Specifically, could they be taxed for defense of the realm without the pope's consent? As we have seen, thirteenth-century rulers could not run their governments without taxes, expecially in time of war. Their lay subjects gave money grudgingly, and it was always a temptation to tap the resources of the Church. By granting taxes on the Church to kings and princes who supported political crusades, the popes had suggested that the clergy might also be taxed for purely secular conflicts. And so, when Edward I and Philip the Fair drifted into a war over Aquitaine in 1294, they both asked their clergy for a grant of taxes. They were outraged when Boniface prohibited these grants in 1296. Both Edward and Philip put heavy pressure on their clergy and succeeded in stirring up public opinion against them as unpatriotic members of the community. Both kings seized ecclesiastical property and forbade the transfer of money to Rome. Edward went further and virtually outlawed the English clergy. In the end, the harassed churchmen of both countries begged the pope to remove his ban. Boniface did so, grudgingly but effectively, in 1298.

This was bad enough, but worse was to follow. In 1301 Philip the Fair imprisoned a French bishop on a flimsy charge of treason and refused to obey a papal order to

❖❖❖❖❖❖❖❖❖❖❖❖❖❖❖❖❖❖❖❖❖❖❖❖❖❖❖❖❖❖

The Issue Between State and Church

Boniface VIII says in the Bull Unam Sanctam (1302):

Both the spiritual sword and the material sword are in the power of the Church. But the latter is to be used for the Church, the former by her; the former by the priest, the latter by kings and captains, but by the assent and permission of the priest. The one sword, then, should be under the other, and temporal authority subject to spiritual power. . . . If, therefore, the earthly power err, it shall be judged by the spiritual power. . . . Finally, we declare, state, define and pronounce that it is altogether necessary to salvation for every human creature to be subject to the Roman pontiff.

One of Philip's ministers, speaking for the king, says (1302):

The pope pretends that we are subject to him in the temporal government of our states and that we hold the crown from the Apostolic See. Yes, this kingdom of France which, with the help of God, our ancestors . . . created—this kingdom which they have until now so wisely governed—it appears that it is not from God alone, as everyone has always believed, that we hold it, but from the pope!

From *Select Documents of European History,* ed. by R. G. D. Laffan (London: Methuen, 1930), p. 117; C. V. Langlois, *St. Louis, Philippe le Bel, et les derniers Capetiens directs* (Paris: Hachette, 1911), pp. 149–50.

❖❖❖❖❖❖❖❖❖❖❖❖❖❖❖❖❖❖❖❖❖❖❖❖❖❖❖❖❖❖

free him. When Boniface threatened to punish the king and his agents, Philip countered by calling a great assembly at Paris in 1302. This assembly contained representatives of the three estates, or classes, of clergy, nobility, and bourgeoisie; it was the first French Estates General. Philip, through his minister, Guillaume de

Nogaret, accused Boniface of immorality and heresy, and appealed to a general council to condemn the pope. The Paris assembly endorsed his plan—the nobility and townsmen enthusiastically, the clergy reluctantly but almost unanimously. Philip undoubtedly resorted to pressure to ensure this response, but he clearly had the backing of his people, as subsequent events were to show. They may not have believed all the accusations, but they felt that a worldly Church was very probably corrupt and that the pope should not interfere with French internal affairs.

Assured of support at home, Philip now launched a very risky venture. He sent Nogaret with a small force to Italy in 1303, where Nogaret joined some of the pope's Italian enemies. Together they staged a surprise attack on Boniface's summer home at Anagni and succeeded in capturing the pope. They probably hoped to bring him back to France as a prisoner to await trial by a Church council, but they had no chance to put their plan into effect. The Italians had no great love for the pope, but they cared even less for the French. A counterattack by the people of Anagni and neighboring regions freed Boniface from his captors. He took refuge in Rome and began to prepare bulls of excommunication against the French. But Boniface was in his eighties, and the shock of capture had proved too much for him. He died before he could act.

Force had been used against a pope before, but for the last two centuries the Church had always been able to retaliate and put the aggressor in a worse position than before. After the assault at Anagni, however, the Church did not dare to react strongly. No one, either inside or outside France, seemed disturbed by what had happened, and Nogaret remained one of Philip's favored ministers. The cardinals chose a man of compromise to succeed Boniface rather than a strong pope who would seek revenge, and when he died within a year of his election they backed down even further. They picked a French archbishop, a man who was not even a member of their group and a man who was clearly agreeable to Philip, if not suggested by him. This new pope, Clement V, yield-

The palace of the popes at Avignon, built during the 14th century. Notice the fortresslike character of the palace; the popes of this period needed a residence which could be defended against roving bands of mercenaries.

ed at every turn to the king of France. He absolved Nogaret and declared that Philip had been prompted by laudable motives in his attack on Boniface. By failing to defend itself—indeed, by praising the aggressor—the papacy revealed that it had surrendered its leadership and its control over public opinion. From this time on the papacy could influence and advise, but it could no longer command as Innocent III had done.

The Popes at Avignon

The pliability of Clement V soon led him to an even more momentous decision. After he was elected pope, he set off for Rome, but, dismayed by the disorder in Italy, he paused in the Rhone Valley. The papacy was now paying for its stubborn opposition to the establishment of a strong Italian kingdom; the warring city-states, led by their tyrants, had made even the Papal States unsafe. Somehow Clement never got started again. France was pleasant and Italy was dangerous; moreover, the French king and the French cardinals were urging him to stay on. And so Clement settled down at Avignon on the Rhone, where he and his successors were to reside for over seventy years.

This long period of exile in France (1305–78) is known in church history as the Babylonian Captivity.* The papacy did not lose its independence, for Avignon was papal territory and the surrounding country was technically part of the Empire and not of France. No subsequent Avignonese pope was as subservient to the French king as Clement V had been; most of them, in fact, were able, even forceful, administrators of the affairs of the Church. And yet, though the papacy did not lose

---

* This is an allusion to the exile of the Jews to Babylon under Nebuchadnezzar in the sixth century B.C. The original Babylonian Captivity lasted only fifty years.

The first Avignonese pope, Clement V (1305–14), consecrates Baldwin of Luxembourg as archbishop of Trier, 1307. Baldwin was brother of the count of Luxembourg, who was soon to be the Emperor Henry VII. From the *Codex Baldwineus*, a 14th-century manuscript.

its independence, it lost its reputation. Many people, especially the English, were convinced that the pope was a servant of the French king, in spite of evidence to the contrary. Many more believed that no true successor of Peter would abandon Rome for the "sinful city of Avignon." They could see no good reason for the pope's refusal to return to his sacred city; a spiritual leader was not supposed to be swayed by motives of expediency or fear of discomfort. This conviction made them more willing than ever to accept the charges of worldliness and corruption which reform leaders were leveling against the Church.

Actually, the Avignonese popes were not especially corrupt, but they were primarily administrators rather than religious leaders. Their chief accomplishments were to perfect the Church's legal system and its financial organization. To men who were already critical, this looked like a proliferation of red tape and a perfection of methods of extortion. No one could obtain anything from the papacy without engaging in long and expensive lawsuits or paying heavy fees to everyone from door-keeper to cardinal. So drastically did papal prestige sink that the Church was defied by even the weakest secular rulers. One story, told in England, illustrates the contempt in which many people held the pope.

A company of mercenary soldiers besieged the pope and demanded a large sum of money. The pope offered them ten thousand pounds with his blessing, or twenty thousand with his curse. The soldiers took the larger sum. Leadership in Europe had clearly passed from the papacy to secular rulers; what they would do with it remained to be seen.

Suggestions for Further Reading

1. St. Louis

The royal councilor Joinville's *Life of St. Louis* * (Everyman's and other editions) is one of our chief sources for the life of King Louis IX of France and for an understanding of the spirit of the thirteenth century. F. Perry, *St. Louis, the Most Christian King* (1901), is an interesting account but not much concerned with historical interpretation. There is excellent material on the growth of monarchical power and the development of institutions under St. Louis in C. Petit-Dutaillis, *Feudal Monarchy in France and England* (1936), and in E. Lavisse, ed., *Histoire de France,* Vol. III, Part 2 (1911). J. R. Strayer, *The Administration of Normandy under St. Louis* (1932), is a study of one of the most important provinces of the French monarchy and the Norman influence on that monarchy.

2. Henry III and England

There is a vast amount of significant detail in the contemporary Matthew of Paris, *Chronicle* (trans. J. A. Giles, 1852), a valuable framework for events in the period from 1235 to 1273. F. M. Powicke, *King Henry III and the Lord Edward,* 2 vols. (1947), is an excellent study of the political and social history of England at the time and the best biography of a medieval king. There is documentary material on early representative assemblies in C. Stephenson and F. M. Marcham, *Sources in English Constitutional History* (1937); the best commentary is F. Pollock and F. W. Maitland, *History of English Law,* Vol. II (1923). R. F. Treharne, *The Baronial Plan of Reform, 1258–1263* (1932), has a good account of the aristocratic reaction to royal rule presented as a great constitutional revolution. F. M. Powicke, *The Thirteenth Century* (1953), is a fine study of the entire period, with a thorough critical bibliography.

3. The Papal-Hohenstaufen War

Philippe of Novara's *The Wars of Frederick II Against the Ibelins* (trans. J. L. La Monte, 1936), has primary material on the career and imperialism of Frederick II and presents a vivid picture of the life and ideas of the thirteenth-century knights who settled

* Available in paperback edition.

in the Latin Orient. E. Kantorowicz, *Frederick II* (1931), encompassing the broad and complex field of papal-Hohenstaufen relations, is a classic study in historical biography. There is a broad survey of politics, religion, literature, and art in H. D. Sedgwick, *Italy in the Thirteenth Century*, 2 vols. (1912). W. F. Butler, *The Lombard Communes* (1906), has information on the Lombard Communes in the Hohenstaufen wars.

4. Scholasticism: St. Thomas Aquinas

The most useful edition of St. Thomas' writings is *Basic Writings of St. Thomas Aquinas* (edited A. C. Pegis, 1944), which contains a good selection of the most significant and widely read treatises. F. C. Copleston, *Aquinas* * (1955), is a very good introduction to Aquinas' ideas, and G. Leff, *Medieval Thought* * (1958), shows the influence of Aquinas' thought on the thirteenth century. M. De Wulf, *Philosophy and Civilization in the Middle Ages* * (1922), describes how the thought of the period was intimately connected with the whole of medieval civilization. The best scholarly treatment of scholastic philosophy is in E. Gilson, *History of Christian Philosophy in the Middle Ages* (1954), which has valuable bibliographic material. E. Panofsky brilliantly shows the parallel development of art and philosophy in the thirteenth century in *Gothic Architecture and Scholasticism* * (1954).

5. Edward I and Parliament

T. F. Tout, *Edward the First* (1893), is an old but sound biography of Edward with a good account of the beginnings of legislation and the English Parliament. A good introduction to the development of Parliament is G. L. Haskins, *Growth of English Representative Government* (1948). D. Pasquet, *Essay on the Origins of the House of Commons* (1925), is an excellent study of the evolution of Parliament from the king's court. See also the titles by Stephenson and Marcham, and Pollock and Maitland mentioned above.

6. Philip the Fair and Boniface VIII

There is valuable material on the reign of Philip the Fair in E. Lavisse, ed., *Histoire de France*, Vol. III, Part 2 (1911). J. R. Strayer and C. H. Taylor, *Studies in Early French Taxation* (1939), explores the relationship between finances and early representative assemblies under Philip the Fair and Philip V. There is material on the reign of Philip the Fair in the books by Fawtier and Petit-Dutaillis cited above.

H. K. Mann, *Lives of the Popes in the Middle Ages*, Vol. XVIII (1932), is a lengthy study of Boniface VIII and his pontificate from a Catholic point of view. A. C. Flick, *The Decline of the Medieval Church*, Vol. I (1930), has material on Boniface from a Protestant point of view. Though interesting reading, both are rather provincial in interpretation. The best study of this pope is T. S. R. Boase, *Boniface VIII* (1933), which is a sympathetic but far more critical treatment.

7. Clement V and the Babylonian Captivity

W. E. Lunt, *Papal Revenues in the Middle Ages,* 2 vols. (1930), contains considerable source material on the bureaucracy and finances of the papal Curia. An amusing if infuriating study of the period of the Babylonian Captivity is L. E. Binns, *The Decline and Fall of the Medieval Papacy* (1934), which was written as a supplement to the great history of E. Gibbon. A serious introduction to this period, M. Creighton, *A History of the Papacy,* Vol. I (1904), traces the reasons for the decline of papal power.

* Available in paperback edition.

13

The End of the Middle Ages

The fourteenth and early fifteenth centuries were a time of confusion and chaos in the history of the West. Decade after decade everything seemed to go wrong: economic depression, war, rebellion, and plague harried the people, and neither ecclesiastical nor secular governments seemed capable of easing their distress. At times the whole structure of European society seemed to be crumbling, as it had at the end of the Roman Empire. Yet the Europe that emerged from this period of decay went on to conquer the world. The science and technology, the navies and the armies, the governments and the business organizations which were to give Europe unquestioned supremacy for four centuries—all were taking shape in the fourteenth and fifteenth centuries. The dire stretch of history marked by the Hundred Years' War, the Black Death, and the Great Schism seems an unlikely seedbed for these great accomplishments. We are struck by the decay of the medieval way of life rather than by the almost imperceptible emergence of new ideas and new forms of organization. But we should never forget that the new ideas were there, that the people of western Europe never quite lost faith in their destiny, never quite gave up striving for a more orderly and prosperous society.

Economic Weakness and Political Failure

The most obvious cause of the troubles of the last medieval centuries was economic depression. Given the techniques then

The Madonna of Chancellor Rollin, by Jan van Eyck (ca. 1385–1441). The Chancellor, who served the duke of Burgundy, is shown in adoration before the Virgin and Child. The realistic portrait, the elaborate detail of robes and floor, and the interest in perspective are all typical of Flemish painting of the 15th century.

prevalent, by 1300 western Europe had about reached the limit of its capacity to produce food and manufactured goods. There were no more reserves of fertile land to bring into cultivation; in fact, a good deal of the land which was already being cultivated was marginal or submarginal in quality. There is some evidence that the climate was unfavorable during much of the period, with many cold and rainy years: food production fell accordingly, especially in the north. For many years there was no significant increase in industrial output; production might shift from one center to another, but the total remained about the same. Population ceased to grow; most towns barely held their own and some, especially in southern France, declined sharply. The Italian towns fared better than those of the North, for they took over much of the trade of the southern French ports and some of the production of luxury textiles which had once been a Flemish monopoly. But even Italy had economic difficulties during the middle years of the fourteenth century. Italian bankers had lent large sums of money to northern rulers, who, burdened by economic stagnation and futile and expensive wars, repudiated most of their debts. Florence in particular was badly shaken by the bankruptcy of Edward III of England, which ruined most of its banking houses and caused widespread unemployment.

Economic stagnation created a climate of opinion hostile to innovation and to efforts to cooperate for the common welfare. Each individual, each community, each class was eager to preserve the monopolies and privileges which guaranteed them some share of the limited wealth available. With little opportunity to increase their share, they concentrated on holding on to what they had; it was during these years that the towns and gilds adopted their most

Left, miniature painting of a pewterer of the 14th century driving a lathe, from the Guild Book of the Twelve Brothers' Foundation in Nuremberg. Two people were still needed to execute turning operations—one to operate the wheel and the other to give shape to the material. Later a lathe with a foot treadle and a balance wheel was invented so that no special operator for the power wheel was required. Though originally introduced for woodworking, the lathe was applied at an early date for the shaping of other materials like stone, ebony, and metal.

restrictive regulations. Ordinary laborers found it difficult to become master workmen; master workmen were discouraged from devising new methods of production. Towns sent out raiding parties to destroy unregulated workshops in the open country which were competing with their own businessmen. Fortunately the attempt to preserve the status quo was thwarted by the weakness of government and by the ingenuity of a few enterprising businessmen. Some new techniques were introduced and some new industries were established. But, outside Italy, which remained wealthier than the rest of Europe, capital was limited, and businessmen had to work long and hard to build up new centers and new methods of production.

Economic weakness helps explain the weakness of most governments. Rulers were always short of money, for the old taxes brought in less and less and it was very difficult for them to establish new ones. Salaries of government officials were low, and were often years in arrears. Most officials supported themselves by taking fees, gifts, and bribes from private citizens. Many of them bought their jobs, in the hope of obtaining a steady income. This practice was convenient for the rulers, but it produced dishonest and listless administrators. And the vested interest of many officials in their jobs made them resist attempts to reorganize and reform the governments.

Above, miniature painting of a locksmith from the Guild Book of the Twelve Brothers' Foundation in Nuremberg.

13 / The End of the Middle Ages

But financial difficulties were not the only cause of weakness in government. The assertion of sovereignty by secular rulers at the end of the thirteenth century had been somewhat premature. They had neither the ability to plan realistic goals for their society nor the authority to impose the plans they did devise. Most secular rulers could think only of annexing more and more land by intrigue or war. Such a policy solved no problems; it merely postponed them for the victor and aggravated them for the vanquished. And the methods used by many rulers to advance their policy of aggrandizement did nothing to raise their prestige. The pattern had already been set by Edward I in his attempt to annex Scotland and by Philip the Fair in his attempt to annex Flanders—trumped-up claims, legal blackmail, and unprovoked attacks. In the thirteenth century most men had been willing to cooperate or at least to acquiesce in the building of stronger and more stable governments. In the fourteenth century they lost faith in their political leaders and turned to rebellion and civil war.

The leaders of revolt, however, showed no more ability than the kings and princes against whom they were rebelling. Usually they were members of the landed nobility, who still had great wealth and influence even though they had lost their old rights of feudal government. But though they found it easy enough to gain power, they did not know how to exercise it. Their main purpose was to preserve their own privileges and those of the groups that supported them, a policy which again solved no basic problems. Impatient with the routine tasks of administration, they usually split into quarreling factions. They often used parliamentary assemblies to voice their opposition to those in authority, and to give their acts an appearance of legality. This practice stimulated the growth of rep-

A money-changer exchanging currency, perhaps for travelers going from Europe to the Near East, from *Book of Marvels,* mid-15th century.

resentative institutions, but led, in the long run, to suspicion of the very ideas on which they were based. Parliaments could be no wiser than the cliques which led them, and that was not very wise. When the desire for stronger government finally arose once again, parliaments were discredited as vehicles of factionalism and disorder. Consequently, the kings found it easy to abolish or suspend them; only in England did they retain any vitality.

Other classes performed no better than the nobles. The bourgeoisie seldom had any influence on the nation as a whole, and they were inept in running their own municipal governments. The townsmen split into factions—old families against new families, international traders against local merchants, rich against poor—and the faction in power tried to ruin its opponents by unequal taxation, discriminatory economic legislation, and oppressive lawsuits. As a result, local self-government collapsed in town after town. Venice remained powerful and independent under a merchant oligarchy, as did some of the German trading towns. But more often a tyrant seized power, as in Italy, or else the officials of a king or a powerful noble took over control.

As for the peasants, they were far more restive and unhappy than they had been in the thirteenth century. With no new lands to clear and no new jobs to be had in the towns, they had little hope of improving their lot. They grew more and more conscious of the burden of payments and services to landlords, for if they had to remain tillers of the soil they wanted to retain the profits of their labor. Some of them managed to renegotiate their leases or move from one estate to another, but for most of them this road to advancement was too tedious and uncertain. The peasants rebelled in country after country, killing landlords, burning records, and demanding that payments for their land be lowered or abolished altogether. These rebellions were hopeless; untrained and poorly armed peasants were no match for an aristocracy with a strong military tradition. But the fact that the peasants did rebel reveals the despair and the tendency to violence which marked the end of the Middle Ages.

The Troubles of the Church

The failure of secular government would not have been so serious if the Church had been able to regain its old leadership. The people of western Europe were still Christians, and they knew that they were not living up to the precepts of their faith. They multiplied religious ceremonies and appeals for the intercession of the saints; they flocked to revival meetings to repent of their sins with tears and trembling. But the Church failed to remedy the disorders of western society; in fact, the Church was infected with the same evils which beset secular government. Repentant sinners returned to their careers of violence and fraud, because no one could show them any other way to survive.

The Great Schism

The weakness of the Church was made worse by the circumstances in which the Babylonian Captivity (see p. 371) came to an end. The popes at Avignon, who had realized for some time that their exile was impairing their authority, had made several half-hearted efforts to return to Rome. Finally, in 1377 Gregory XI actually moved back to Italy, but he was appalled by the disorder in Rome and the Papal States. He was about to return to Avignon when he died in 1378. The Romans, with the papacy once more within their grasp, had no intention of surrendering it again, for they lived on the income from pilgrims and visitors to the papal court. When the cardinals met to elect Gregory's successor, they were besieged by a howling mob demanding that they choose a Roman, or at least an Italian, pope. It is hard to estimate how effective this pressure was; certainly it had some influence. In the end the cardinals elected an Italian archbishop who took the title of Urban VI.

The cardinals may have hoped that Urban would be a pliant and cooperative pope; instead he bullied them unmercifully. He rejected their advice, denounced their behavior, and even threw some of them into prison. The majority of the cardinals were French, but even the non-French ones were outraged by Urban's behavior. The whole group soon fled to Avignon, where they declared that Urban's election was void because it had taken place under duress. They proceeded to choose a new pope, a French-speaking cardinal of the family of the counts of Geneva. He took the title of Clement VII and denounced Urban as a usurper.

There had been schisms in the Church before, but usually it had been easy enough to identify the true pope. Religious and secular leaders had never been deceived, for example, by the efforts of

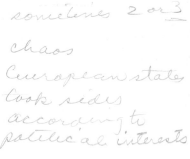

sometimes 2 or 3

chaos

European state

took sides

according to

political interests

The Great Schism 1378-1417

Land giving allegiance to Rome

Land giving allegiance to Avignon

Shifting and divided

Henry IV to depose Gregory VII (see pp. 293–94) or by Frederick Barbarossa's attack on Alexander III (see pp. 331–33). But this time there was no such consensus, and most of Europe was honestly bewildered. Both popes had been elected by a majority of duly appointed cardinals; if Urban had the advantage of being the first named, he also had the disadvantage of being chosen in the midst of a riot. The result was that political expediency, rather than honest judgment, determined the decisions of rulers. France, and her ally Scotland, naturally accepted the Avignonese pope; England just as naturally supported Urban at Rome. The Spanish kingdoms backed Clement, while most of Germany and Italy held to the Roman pontiff. Both popes intrigued to gain support in hostile areas, and both created new cardinals. When Urban and Clement died, in 1389 and 1394, respectively, the rival groups of cardinals each elected a new pope, thus prolonging the Great Schism into the fifteenth century.

Though the people of western Europe were greatly distressed by the schism, they could see no way out of their troubles. Their hopes of salvation were threatened by the scandalous division in the Church. Some fanatics claimed that no one had entered heaven since the Great Schism began, and certainly adherence to a false pope was perilous to the soul. But who could be sure which was the false pope and which was the true one? This uncertainty weakened both the organization and the moral influence of the Church. The popes of the Captivity had at least been good administrators, but the schism made

379

effective administration impossible. Reform in the Church's financial system was more desperately needed than ever before, but a pope who controlled only half the Church could hardly afford to lose revenues or alienate supporters by abolishing profitable abuses. A divided and unreformed Church had little hope of guiding European society.

Reformers and Heretics

The state of the Church during the Captivity and the Great Schism seemed so hopeless that many men began to seek salvation by their own efforts. The mildest, and probably the most numerous, group did not break openly with the Church; they simply ceased to rely on it. They formed little associations, such as the Brethren of the Common Life, to encourage one another to lead devout Christian lives, and to seek direct contact with God through mystical experiences. These groups, which were especially numerous in the Rhineland and the Low Countries, produced some remarkable works of devotion, such as the *Theologia Germanica,* which influenced later reformers. They also founded schools which were to play a great role in the educational revival of the fifteenth and sixteenth centuries; Erasmus (see pp. 519–20) was educated in such a school. They were looked on with some suspicion by conservative churchmen, but most of them remained within the bounds of orthodoxy and some were even canonized.

There was also a more radical element which was not content simply to withdraw into devout groups. These men wanted a thoroughgoing reform of the Church, and their demands often led them into open heresy. They stressed anticlerical views and renewed the old demand for apostolic poverty. One of the most persuasive attacks on the organization of the Church

was the *Defensor pacis,* written by Marsilius of Padua about 1324. Marsilius, who, like many Italians, had a thoroughly secular point of view, believed that the state should control all forms of organized social activity. He admitted that religion was necessary, but insisted that churchmen should be treated like any other group of professional men. If the state could regulate the behavior of doctors, it could also regulate the behavior of priests. Marsilius' book was condemned, but his ideas inspired criticism of the Church throughout the fourteenth and fifteenth centuries.

Another dangerous critic of the Church was an Oxford professor, John Wiclif (*ca.* 1320–84). At first merely a student of the problem of private property, including the property of the Church, Wiclif ended by declaring that the Church was being corrupted by wealth and that it would be better for everyone if most church lands were taken over by kings and nobles. This position naturally made him popular with members of the English aristocracy and explains why he was never punished for his unorthodox doctrines. Wiclif went on to cast doubt on the Catholic doctrine that the bread and wine in the communion service are transformed into the Body and Blood of Christ. He wound up by attacking the whole administrative structure of the Church as corrupt and largely unauthorized by the Bible. He taught that the pope could err, that the hierarchy had no absolute authority, and that kings should assume responsibility for the welfare of the Church in their realms.

Though Wiclif had no intention of launching a popular movement, his ideas spread rapidly beyond the scholarly circles for which he had written. By emphasizing scriptural authority, he had given radical leaders a weapon with which to attack the institutions of the Church. He had encouraged an English translation of the Bible which could be used very effectively by wandering preachers. These preachers, taking advantage of social discontent, popularized Wiclif's most radical views and added revolutionary ideas of their own. They had considerable following among the lower and middle classes in England during the last two decades of the fourteenth century. Some of them became social as well as religious reformers: if the Church had no right to property because it misused it, did the barons and knights have any more right? Ideas such as this may have helped to touch off the English Peasants' Rebellion of 1381 (see below, p. 386). And fear of economic radicalism may have induced the English upper classes to join with the king in suppressing the religious radicals—or Lollards, as they were called—after 1400. But the suppression was not wholly effective; copies of the Wiclifite translation of the Bible, together with vague memories of Lollard doctrines, survived until the time of the English Reformation. And Wiclif's writings reached as far as Bohemia, where they had considerable influence on John Hus, the great fifteenth-century opponent of the Church (see pp. 493–94).

The Black Death

The effects of economic depression, political confusion, and religious uncertainty were intensified by terrible outbursts of plague in the middle years of the fourteenth century. The Black Death (probably bubonic plague) first appeared in Italy in the 1340's and then swept through Europe during the next two decades. The worst was over by 1360, but there were minor outbreaks through the rest of the century. No accurate estimate can be made of the mortality, but it was especially severe in thickly populated areas. Some towns lost at least two-fifths of their inhabitants, and some

****

The Black Death in England

Then that most grievous pestilence penetrated the coastal regions by way of Southampton and came to Bristol, and people died as if the whole strength of the city were seized by sudden death. For there were few who lay in their beds more than three days or two and a half days; then that savage death snatched them about the second day. In Leicester, in the little parish of St. Leonard, more than three hundred and eighty died; in the parish of the Holy Cross, more than four hundred, and in the parish of St. Margaret, more than seven hundred. . . .

And the price of everything was cheap, because of the fear of death, there were very few who took any care for their wealth, or for anything else. For a man could buy a horse for half a mark [about 7 shillings] which before was worth forty shillings, a large fat ox for four shillings, a cow for twelve pence, a heifer for sixpence, a large fat sheep for four pence. . . . And the sheep and cattle wandered about through the fields and among the crops, and there was no one to go after them or collect them. They perished in countless numbers everywhere, for lack of watching . . . since there was such a lack of serfs and servants, that no one knew what he should do. For there is no memory of a mortality so severe and so savage. . . . In the following autumn, one could not hire a reaper for less than eight pence [per day] with food, or a mower at less than twelve pence with food.

From Henry Knighton, *Chronicle*, in *The Portable Medieval Reader*, ed. by J. B. Ross and M. M. McLaughlin (New York: Viking, 1949), pp. 218–19.

****

monasteries almost ceased to function. Since doctors were helpless, the only way to avoid the plague was to take refuge in isolated country towns.

The panic caused by the Black Death drove the sorely tried people of western Europe into emotional instability. It is no accident that the bloodiest peasant rebellions and the most senseless civil wars took place after the plague, and that the witchcraft delusion, unknown in the early Middle Ages, reached its height. It is important to note that this was a double delusion. Innocent men and women were falsely accused of practicing black magic, but there were people who genuinely believed that they could gain their desires by making a compact with the devil. Men of high position participated in obscene rituals; there were even a few cases in which children were sacrificed to the powers of evil. More than anything else, the witchcraft delusion demonstrated the state of shock in which western Europe found itself at the end of the fourteenth century. The rationalism and confidence in the future which had been so apparent at the height of medieval civilization were gone. There was little hope and less certainty; men were willing to believe any devilish rumor and try any desperate remedy.

England in the Later Middle Ages

Even France and England, the two strongest states in the West, were shaken by the events of the fourteenth century. They had

A procession of supplicants against the plague, a miniature from *Les Très Riches Heures* of the duke of Berri.

enough momentum to survive as political units, but there were times when neither country had a government capable of preserving law and order. In both countries the nobles regained much of the power they had lost in the thirteenth century. In England they used this power to harass and depose kings; in France they reverted to their old objective of creating autonomous provincial governments.

The expansionist policies of Edward I (see pp. 362–63) had greatly strained English resources. A reaction would have taken place in any case; it was made more severe by the character of Edward II (1307–27). Edward was so incompetent that no one respected him, and he turned over the business of government to a series of favorites who were hated by the great lords. The barons tried the old expedient of setting up a committee to act as the king's council, but it worked no better than it had under Henry III. Edward, however, showed no improvement when he regained power. He lost Scotland in the battle of Bannockburn (1314), and he gave more and more authority to an able but greedy favorite, Hugh le Despenser. One rebellion against him failed, but the next, led by his own wife and her lover Mortimer, one of the lords of the turbulent lands of the Welsh frontier, succeeded. Edward was deposed in 1327 and quietly murdered a few weeks later; his young son, Edward III (1327–77), became king.

The Hundred Years' War: The First Phase

Edward III shared the fondness of his barons for courtly magnificence and chivalric warfare. This fondness made him more popular with the aristocracy than his father had been, but it also kept him from doing all that he might have done to restore royal authority. Never quite willing to risk his popularity by forcing a

✤✤✤✤✤✤✤✤✤✤✤✤✤✤✤✤✤✤✤✤✤✤✤✤✤✤✤✤✤✤✤✤

The Later Middle Ages

So violent and motley was life, that it bore the mixed smell of blood and of roses. The men of that time always oscillated between the fear of hell and the most naïve joy, between cruelty and tenderness, between harsh asceticism and insane attachment to the delights of this world . . . always running to extremes. . . .

Bad government, the cupidity and violence of the great, wars and brigandage, scarcity, misery, and pestilence—to this is contemporary history nearly reduced in the eyes of the people. The feeling of general insecurity . . . was further aggravated by the fear of hell, of sorcerers and of devils. Everywhere the flames of hatred arise and injustice reigns. Satan covers a gloomy earth with his sombre wings.

From J. Huizinga, *The Waning of the Middle Ages* (London: Arnold, 1927), pp. 18, 21.

✤✤✤✤✤✤✤✤✤✤✤✤✤✤✤✤✤✤✤✤✤✤✤✤✤✤✤✤✤✤✤✤

showdown with the barons, he always compromised or postponed making decisions. As a result, though he regained some of the authority his father had lost, he allowed the barons to retain a strong position in his Council. This is probably one of the reasons why he drifted into the Hundred Years' War with France. War was one policy on which he and his barons could agree, and so long as the war was successful he could avoid domestic controversies.

There were, of course, other reasons for the war. France was still trying to annex the English holdings in Aquitaine and gain full control of Flanders, which was the best market for English wool. France was aiding Scotland, which was now in a state of almost permanent hostility with England, and French and English sailors were intermittently plundering each other's ships. All this might have logically resulted in a brief war, or even in several short conflicts,

The Hundred Years' War *ca.* 1358-1453

but it does not quite explain a war that lasted for generations. The war was prolonged largely because neither Edward nor his barons could think of anything else to do.

After floundering about for a while, trying to cope with financial difficulties, Edward came up with an amazing string of victories. He gained control of the Channel in a naval battle at Sluys, and nearly annihilated the French army at Crécy (1346). Then he went on to take Calais, which remained a port of entry for Eng-

lish armies for two centuries. Ten years later Edward's son, the Black Prince, crushed another French army at Poitiers and took the French king prisoner. In the treaty which followed this victory the French agreed to pay a huge ransom for their king and to cede about two-fifths of their country to the English.

Edward had succeeded because his country was more united than France and thus gave him better financial support, and also because he had developed new tactics for his army. He mixed companies of archers, armed with the famous English longbow, with companies of dismounted cavalry in heavy armor. The most effective French fighting units were still heavy-armed cavalry, but they were helpless against this formation. When they attacked they were thrown into confusion by showers of arrows, and if they broke through to the lines of armored soldiers the archers fired at their flanks. This was the beginning of the end of the long dominance of cavalry, but only the beginning. Edward's formation was essentially defensive; it could not be used for a charge. Only when portable firearms were invented at the end of the fifteenth century did infantry gain the attacking power which made it the dominant force in military engagements.

Like many other generals, Edward found it easier to win victories than to profit from them. The French, with no intention of fulfilling the terms of the treaty they had signed, launched a war of attrition which gradually exhausted their enemies. England simply did not have enough men or enough resources to garrison territories which were larger than Edward's whole kingdom. The French learned to avoid headlong rushes at large English armies and concentrated instead on picking off isolated garrisons and small detachments. As a result, the English had lost a large part of their conquests by the time of Edward III's death in 1377.

Rebellion and Revolution

Military misfortunes abroad led to bickering at home. There was a complete failure of leadership during Edward's last years. The king was sinking into senility and the Black Prince, stricken with an incurable disease, died a year before his father. One of Edward's younger sons, John of Gaunt, duke of Lancaster, had more authority than anyone else, but he was disliked and distrusted by many members of the aristocracy. He was accused, with some justice, of associating with a group of corrupt officeholders, and, with less justice, of coveting the throne. The duke's taste in art and literature was excellent—he gave a government job and a pension to Geoffrey Chaucer—but interest in the arts has seldom endeared a politician to English public opinion.

Two battles in the Hundred Years' War, from Jean Froissart's *Chronicles. Above,* the battle of Sluys, with the English ships on the right, the Norman on the left. *Below,* the battle of Crécy, with the king of France on the left, the king of England on the right.

385

The new king, Richard II (1377–99), the son of the Black Prince, was only a child when he inherited the throne. During the first part of his reign, England was governed by successive groups of barons. These men did nothing to distinguish themselves, for they were more interested in driving one another out of power than in prosecuting the French war or establishing an efficient government at home. Their inefficiency and bad judgment led directly to the Peasants' Rebellion of 1381. The war in France was still costing a great deal of money, even though the English were now almost entirely on the defensive. Casting about for a new source of revenue, the government hit on the idea of a poll tax, a levy of a few pennies on each English subject. This sort of tax was harder on the poorer classes than the traditional tax on personal property, but it failed to produce as much revenue as the government had hoped for. To make up the deficit, the government sent out commissioners to re-examine the tax rolls and to catch evaders. This brought to a peak all the smoldering resentment of the peasants and the poorer inhabitants of the towns. They were already suffering from economic stagnation and loss of opportunity; now they felt that they were being asked to carry an unfair share of the tax burden. All southern England exploded in rebellion. Peasants and artisans burned tax rolls and manorial records, killed unpopular officials and lords, and finally marched on London. The barons were taken off guard and had to scurry about trying to raise forces to put down the peasants. Meanwhile Richard had to stand by and watch the rebels occupy London, burn the palace of the duke of Lancaster, and murder the Chancellor and Treasurer of England. Forced into humiliating negotiations with the rebel leaders, he was obliged to promise complete forgiveness for all past offenses, the end of serfdom, and the remission of almost all manorial dues.

The rebellion was suppressed as soon as the barons could get their troops together, for the poorly armed peasants were no match for professional soldiers. The king repudiated his promises and apparently all was as before. Actually, the rebellion had two important results. First, serfdom declined steadily after 1381. It hardly seemed worth the trouble it caused, and by 1500 there were almost no serfs left in England. Second, Richard had seen a convincing demonstration of the inefficiency and clumsiness of baronial government. It is not surprising that when he came of age in 1386 he tried to increase royal authority and to concentrate all power in his own hands.

Richard showed considerable skill in his efforts to strengthen the monarchy, but he made two fatal mistakes. The barons might have tolerated the loss of their political power, but Richard threatened their economic position as well by confiscating the property of anyone who opposed him. Moreover, Richard failed to build up a powerful army under his own control. Most of the armed forces in the country were private companies paid by the king but recruited and commanded by barons and knights. This system had developed during the Hundred Years' War, when it had seemed easier to order members of the aristocracy to raise troops than for the king to do so himself. It was to have dangerous consequences all during the fifteenth century, for it meant that any lord with a taste for fighting could maintain a little army of his own. The king's personal bodyguard was no match for the combined forces of several great barons. As a result, Richard was helpless when a rebellion broke out in 1399 under the leadership of Henry of Lancaster, son of John of Gaunt and cousin of the king. Henry himself had

The capture of Richard II by the earl of Northumberland near Conway, from Jehan Creton, *Account of the Fall of Richard II.*

been driven into exile and stripped of his lands, and he was supported by many members of the aristocracy who feared the same fate. Richard was deposed and died in prison, and Henry of Lancaster mounted the throne as Henry IV (1399–1413).

The Hundred Years' War: The Second Phase

The Lancastrian kings, who ruled from 1399 to 1461, never quite lived down the violence by which they had come to power. Their title was faulty—there were other descendants of Edward III with a better claim—and they seldom had the unanimous support of the great lords. Henry IV had difficulty suppressing two serious rebellions, and Henry V (1413–22) tried to unite the country by the dangerous expedient of reviving the Hundred Years' War. He was a brilliant general, as he revealed in his victory at Agincourt (1415), and he was the first commander of a European army to use siege artillery on a large scale. He rapidly overran most of northern France and forced the French

king, Charles VI, to accept a treaty in which Charles disinherited his son, married his daughter to Henry, and agreed that any son born of this union was to be king of France. The next year both Charles and Henry died, and a one-year-old baby, Henry VI, became king of England and of France.

Henry V, with all his ability, would have found it hard to control two kingdoms; Henry VI never had a chance. His long minority was disastrous. In England his uncles and cousins, each supported by a baronial faction, quarreled bitterly. In France, the disinherited son of Charles VI claimed the throne as Charles VII and carried on the war from the unconquered country south of the Loire. The English pressed him hard, but just as he was losing his courage he was saved by the appearance of Joan of Arc (see pp. 391–92). To the English Joan was "a limb of the devil." But she stirred the French to abandon their overcautious policy; she drove the English back from the Loire

River crossings at Orléans; she had Charles VII properly crowned at Reims. It hardly mattered to the French cause that she fell into English hands and was burned as a witch, for the courage and enthusiasm with which she had inspired the French survived her. The English, whose position in France was now hopeless, surrendered their forts and provinces one by one until by 1453 only Calais was left. And so, after twelve decades of fighting and plundering, the war at last came to an end.

The Wars of the Roses

When the English could no longer blame Joan of Arc for their defeats, they began to blame one another. Commanders were accused of treason and incompetence; some were executed and others exiled. Henry VI, even when he came of age, could do nothing to stop the feuds among the great lords. Humble in spirit and weak in mind, he was dominated by a French wife whom most of the aristocracy heartily disliked. The English barons had acquired the habit of violence, and within a decade after the end of the Hundred

Years' War they plunged England into the series of civil conflicts known as the Wars of the Roses. The ostensible reason for these wars was an attempt by some of the barons to replace the Lancastrian king by the duke of York, who represented the oldest line of descent from Edward III. The attempt succeeded, but the Yorkist kings, who ruled from 1461 to 1485, had almost as much trouble with the barons as their Lancastrian predecessors. In fact, the Wars of the Roses were the last uprising of the barons, the last attempt of a small clique to take over the central government and use it for their own purpose. The wars destroyed everyone who took part in them—the Houses of Lancaster and York and many of the great noble families. It was left for the half-alien Tudors, indirect and illegitimate descendants of John of Gaunt, to restore order in England.

England made some economic gains toward the end of this period in spite of the failure of political leadership. The kings of the fourteenth and fifteenth centuries were no economists, but they were able to grasp one simple fact: that so long as England was content merely to produce raw materials, she would never grow very rich. From Edward III on, they encouraged the migration of textile workers to England and protected the growing English textile industry. They also encouraged the development of English shipping. The results should not be exaggerated, for even at the end of the fifteenth century England could not rival Flanders in textiles or Italy in shipping. But a good start had been made; England had come a long way from being a country whose chief economic function was to raise raw wool which was carried in foreign ships to Flemish looms.

The Development of Parliament

There were also two important institutional developments: the rise of the justices of the peace and the continuing growth of Parliament. The justices of the peace were created by Edward III in the fourteenth century to take over some of the work of local law enforcement which had formerly been the duty of sheriffs and feudal lords. The justices were men of position and leisure, not great lords but well-to-do local landholders of the class which had long carried heavy responsibilities in local government. Like the sheriffs and the tax collectors, they served without pay; their reward was leadership in their own community. By the middle of the fifteenth century their powers had grown to a point where they controlled local government. They arrested criminals and tried minor offenses (major cases were reserved for the circuit judges). They were responsible for enforcing economic regulations and orders of the central government. They collected information for the Council and were supposed to inform it of plots against the government. In practice, the justices of the peace were often the creatures of a powerful baron in their region whose in-

terests they served rather than those of the king. But when the Tudors re-established royal authority, the justices of the peace, with their wide local knowledge and great local influence, became very useful agents of the crown.

The century and a half of political weakness, stretching from Edward II through Henry VI, gave Parliament a chance to make itself an indispensable part of the government. Weak rulers sought the appearance of public support, and revolutionary rulers sought the appearance of legitimacy. Both were eager for Parliamentary ratification of important acts, since Parliament represented all the important groups in the country. Thus Edward III and Henry IV called on Parliament to approve the deposition of their predecessors. Similarly, all taxes and most legislative acts were submitted to Parliament for approval. Indeed, by the fifteenth century the king had lost the initiative in legislation, for by then most laws were originated by influential groups in Parliament and were merely submitted to the king for approval. Finally, and most important, the county representatives (knights) and the town representatives (burgesses), who under Edward I had acted separately, joined together about 1340 to form the House of Commons, thus making Parliament a far more effective assembly. Now there were only two houses (Lords and Commons) instead of three, or, as in some other countries, even four. And the lower house included an element, the knights, who would have been considered noble in any other country. The knights were landlords, just as the barons were; they could intermarry with baronial families and some of them became barons themselves. Their presence gave the House of Commons much more influence than a mere assembly of burgesses (such as the French Third Estate) could have had. Through the leadership of the knights, cooperation with the Lords could be assured. This situation sometimes enabled Parliament to effect significant changes in government, for when both houses attacked a minister of the king they could usually force him out of office.

An English court in the later Middle Ages. This miniature is one of four vellum leaves surviving from a law treatise of the reign of Henry VI, early 15th century. At the top are the five judges of the Court of King's Bench; below them are the king's coroner and attorney. On the left are the jury and in front in the dock is a prisoner in fetters, with lawyers on either side of him. In the foreground more prisoners, chained to each other, wait their turn, watched over by jailers. On the center table stand the ushers, one of whom seems to be swearing in the jury.

By the fifteenth century Parliament had become an integral part of the machinery of government, and no important act was valid until it had received parliamentary approval. So well established had Parliament become that it survived even the period of strong kingship which began under the Tudors in 1485. But Parliament was still only part of the machinery of government, not the motivating force. Real power still lay with the king or the great lords, and Parliament merely approved what they determined. Edward II and Richard II were not deposed by the initiative of Parliament; Parliament was merely asked to ratify the results of a revolution engineered by a few great barons. Not until the seventeenth century did Parliament begin to formulate policies of its own.

France in the Later Middle Ages

The monarchy in France was also having its troubles during the fourteenth and fifteenth centuries. The sons of Philip the Fair (see pp. 365–68) died in rapid succession, leaving only daughters to succeed them. No woman had ever ruled France, and the barons, apprehensive about what might happen to the realm when a reigning queen married, invented a rule barring women from the succession, the so-called Salic Law. In 1328 they placed Philip of Valois, a cousin of the last king and a nephew of Philip the Fair, on the throne. But since Philip owed his position to a few great barons, his claim to the crown was not unanimously accepted. He had to spend most of his reign bestowing favors on his supporters and keeping peace among factions of nobles. With the disappearance of the widespread loyalty to the king that had marked the late thirteenth century, rebellions and acts of treason plagued the country. These internal disorders help to account for the French defeats in the first few decades of the Hundred Years' War.

Philip's son, John (1350–64), had no better fortune. His capture by the English at Poitiers, with the subsequent loss of territory and the heavy taxes needed to raise his ransom, caused widespread dissatisfaction. In 1358 the peasants rose in a revolt that was no more successful than the English rebellion but much more bloody and destructive. In the same year the Estates General, led by the Paris bourgeoisie, tried to take over the government. The attempt failed, both because the Estates had had little experience in government, and because their leaders had no support among the great nobles. John's son, Charles V (1364–80), regained much of the lost ground by suppressing his opponents at home and by driving the English from one stronghold after another. If his successor had been a more capable ruler, the French might have escaped the worst ills of the fourteenth century.

Unfortunately, most of the brains and determination in the French royal family went to uncles and cousins of the new king rather than to the king himself. Charles VI (1380–1422) was never strong either in mind or in character, and after 1390 he suffered intermittent spells of insanity. The government was conducted largely by princes of the blood royal who quarreled bitterly among themselves over offices, pensions, and gifts of land. When the duke of Burgundy was assassinated by the followers of the duke of Orléans, the quarrels turned into a civil war and the new duke of Burgundy eventually allied himself with the English. Since he had inherited Burgundy and had acquired Flanders and most of the other provinces of the Low Countries, he was almost as wealthy and powerful as the king. His defection proved disastrous for France. It was during this period of feuds and civil war that Henry V made his rapid conquests and

An illustration from Froissart's *Chronicles* showing a peasants' insurrection which was put down by the king of Navarre in 1358.

forced Charles VI to recognize Henry's son as heir to the French throne.

Joan of Arc

Charles VII (1422–61) faced an almost hopeless situation when his father died. He had been officially disinherited; the English held the largest and richest part of France; and many of the great nobles were either actively or tacitly supporting the Anglo-Burgundian alliance. Charles had little military strength, and he was not using what he did have very effectively. It was at this moment that Joan of Arc, a peasant girl from the extreme eastern frontier, appeared at court and announced that heavenly voices had ordered her to drive the English out of the country. Joan, self-confident and persuasive, shook Charles from his lethargy and talked him into the counteroffensive which turned the tide of the war. The fact that Joan was captured and burned at the stake by the English scarcely checked the reconquest, for Charles soon had another stroke of good fortune. England under Henry VI was as

A French court of the later Middle Ages. The king, seated above the others in the rear, presides over a special session of *Parlement,* the highest French court, called to judge the duke of Alençon, who has been accused of high treason. Miniature by Jean Fouquet, late 15th century.

torn by factional strife as France had been under Charles VI, and in a squabble over the spoils of government an uncle of the English king mortally offended the duke of Burgundy. The duke's return to the French cause made the English position hopeless, and in a few years Charles VII had regained all of France except Calais.

Joan of Arc was not unique in having visions, for in those troubled years many men and women were convinced that they had spoken to heavenly emissaries. But in the content of her visions we can see how deep were the roots that the religion of the French monarchy had struck among the people. Joan was absolutely convinced that only Charles VII was the rightful king of France and that it was her duty to restore him to his throne. Her beliefs were shared by people of all classes. In spite of all the misgovernment of the last century there was still a deep reservoir of loyalty to the French monarchy. And in spite of treachery and factionalism there was at least a beginning of national feeling among the French people. They could agree in their dislike for English rule if they could agree on nothing else. Under all the confusion and disorder of the early fifteenth century they clung to two basic beliefs: faith in the French monarchy and faith in the Christian religion. When the two beliefs were united, as they were in Joan of Arc, they were irresistible. Joan foreshadowed that union of religion and monarchy on which the absolute states of the early modern period were to be built.

Restoration of Royal Power

France suffered more severely than England during the Hundred Years' War, since all the fighting took place on French soil. Wide areas were devastated by raiding armies and wandering companies of mercenary soldiers who found indiscriminate plundering more profitable than loyal service. But, precisely because the French predicament was so much graver than the English, royal power was restored more rapidly and more completely in France. A king who showed any promise of putting an end to disorder could override all limitations on his power. This was especially true of restrictions on his power to levy taxes. Charles V began the work of freeing the monarchy from these restraints, and Charles VII finished the job. As soon as he had the English on the run he began to levy taxes at will, without asking consent from the Estates General. His task was made easier by the fact that provincial feeling was so strong in France that a central parliamentary assembly was seldom called, and when it was called it had little authority. Real influence lay with provincial and regional assemblies, with the local Estates of Normandy or of Languedoc rather than with the Estates General. And it was relatively easy for Charles to overcome the fragmented opposition of these local assemblies. The same overwhelming interest in provincial affairs kept the great French nobles from entrenching themselves in the central government, which remained the preserve of the king and his bureaucrats. Thus in the long run the Hundred Years' War reinforced tendencies which had been apparent in France before the end of the thirteenth century—tendencies toward a bureaucratic state in which the king was strong and all other political forces were weak and divided. This French pattern became a model for the rest of Europe during the early modern period.

Germany in the Later Middle Ages

The political history of the rest of western Europe during the later Middle Ages resembled that of France and England.

Germany in the Fourteenth Century

Hapsburg states

Luxemburg states

Held briefly by Luxemburg

MILES
0   100

BALTIC SEA

Konigsberg

DOMAIN OF
THE TEUTONIC ORDER

NORTH SEA

Hamburg

Bremen

BRANDENBURG

Vistula River

Utrecht

Rhine

Magdeburg

Berlin

POLAND

Antwerp

Ghent

Bruges

Brussels

BRABANT

Cologne

Aix-la-Chapelle

DUCHY OF
LUXEMBURG

Treves

Frankfort

Elbe River

S I L E S I A

Oder River

Prague

BOHEMIA

F
R
A
N
C
E

Reims

Luxemburg

Metz

Nuremberg

Ratisbon

H
U
N
G
A
R
Y

Troyes

Sens

Toul

Strasburg

Langres

Seine River

Ulm

Augsburg

Munich

BAVARIA

Salzburg

Vienna

AUSTRIA

STYRIA

Gran

Buda

Pest

Danube River

Loire River

Lyons

Rhone River

TYROL

LANDS OF THE
VISCONTI

Milan

CARINTHIA

Po River

Venice

VENETIAN REPUBLIC

BOSNIA

LANDS OF
C. OF SAVOY

Ravenna

ADRIATIC SEA

Everywhere there were rebellions, civil wars, and attempts to conquer neighboring territories. But all this furor produced surprisingly little change. A political map of Europe in 1450 looks very like a map of 1300, and the basic characteristics of most of the governments were similarly unchanged.

There were, however, certain developments in Germany that deserve attention.

First, during the early fifteenth century the dukes of Burgundy gradually gained control over all the provinces of the Low Countries, roughly the equivalent of modern Belgium and the Netherlands. This was one of the richest and most productive regions of Europe. The union of the Low Countries under the House of Burgundy separated their fate from that of the rest of Germany and gradually gave them a distinct national identity. At the same time their wealth made them the object of a long series of European wars which began in the fifteenth century and have continued to our own day.

Second, during the fourteenth century the peasants and townsmen of Switzerland gradually gained their independence from the Hapsburg family who had dominated this part of Germany. In defeating the Hapsburgs the Swiss developed well-disciplined infantry formations, armed with long pikes, which could beat off a charge of heavy cavalry. This was another step in the rise of the foot soldier; by the fifteenth century companies of Swiss infantry had acquired such a reputation that they were being hired by French kings and Italian princes. The Swiss were also demonstrating the possibility of republican government to a Europe which had had little recent experience with this system. Each district, or canton, of the very loosely knit Swiss Confederation had its own institutions, and no canton was under a feudal lord. The towns were ruled by the wealthier burgesses, but the peasant cantons, where the movement for independence had begun, were almost pure democracies.

The third important development in Germany was the rise of a new power center on the middle Danube as a result of the peculiar electoral habits of the German princes. By the end of the thirteenth century the number of princes taking part in imperial elections had been sharply restricted, and this practice was made official by an imperial decree, the Golden Bull of 1356. Seven men were designated as "electors": the archbishops of Mainz, Trier and Cologne, the king of Bohemia, the margrave of Brandenburg, the duke of Saxony, and the Count Palatine (the ruler of the Palatinate on the Rhine). These great men feared giving too much power to one of their own group, or to any other powerful prince, so for some time they regularly chose as emperors counts with small holdings. Though the title gave no real power, it did give enough social prestige to enable these counts to marry into powerful families. Thus the Hapsburgs, petty princes in West Germany who had served briefly as emperors around 1300, managed to acquire the duchy of Austria and nearby counties. A little later, the count of Luxembourg, an equally undistinguished prince, became emperor and arranged a marriage through which his son received the kingdom of Bohemia. Later Luxembourg emperors acquired Silesia and eventually Hungary. When the last male Luxembourger died in 1438, his nearest heir was the Hapsburg duke of Austria. The union of the two sets of holdings marked the beginning of the vast Hapsburg Empire which for five centuries was to be one of the great powers of Europe.

Art, Literature, and Science

At first glance the art and literature, the scholarship and technology, of western Europe during this period seem almost as futile as the politics. There was a great deal of sterile imitation and elaboration of familiar themes. Technical competence was high, but good taste and originality were rare. Thus many late Gothic churches were either cold and uninspired copies of earlier work, or gigantic wedding cakes in which spikes and gables, traceries and canopies, concealed the basic lines of the structure. It is no accident that one late Gothic style is known as the Flamboyant. In literature there was the same technical perfection and lack of content. The old narrative poems became fantastic romances; the lyrics became society verse. In scholarship there was much threshing of old straw and very little new intellectual grain. These were the aspects of late medieval culture which were to disgust the Italians of the Renaissance and led them to damn most medieval work as "gothic" and barbarous.

Literature

But there was still fire beneath the ashes of imitation and fussiness, and some men managed to breathe new life into the old forms. Thus the French prince, Charles of Orléans, composed lyrics which expressed genuine feeling rather than conventional sentiments. A better-known example is Chaucer (1340?–1400), who began as a mere translator and adapter of French works and developed into one of England's greatest poets. His most famous work, the Prologue to the *Canterbury Tales,* reveals his skill in describing individual character and his wit in depicting human foibles. His people range from the "perfect, gentle Knight" and the poor parson, who taught Christ's lore, "but first he followed it himself," through the earthy Wife of Bath, who had buried five husbands, down to scoundrels like the Miller and the Summoner. Perhaps his knowledge of all levels of Eng-

lish society is due to the fact that Chaucer worked for years in the customs service in the busy port of London. But his subtle portrayal of human behavior, shown not only in the *Canterbury Tales* but also in *Troilus and Criseyde,* comes only from his own genius. Chaucer was something of a psychologist as well as a poet, but while he saw through pretense and sham he never became bitter. He rose fast in English society under the patronage of John of Gaunt; he took the world as he found it and rather liked what he found.

François Villon (b. 1431), who lived in Paris during the worst years of the Hundred Years' War, was less fortunate. A friend of thieves and prostitutes, and a convicted criminal himself, he shows how closely French society came to breaking down under the strains of the early fifteenth century. He used the old poetic forms to describe with gusto life in taverns and thieves' dens. But his poems also express his bitterness over his wasted life and portray the hopes and fears of the poor and the outcast—the simple piety of an old woman, the last thoughts of men

A 15th-century portrait of Chaucer from the Ellesmere manuscript of *The Canterbury Tales.*

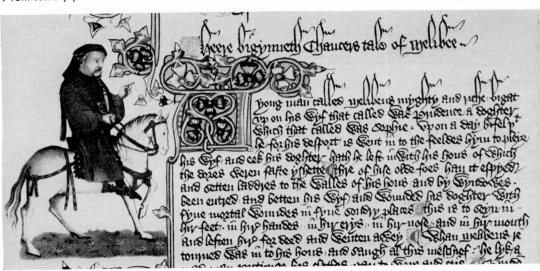

13 / The End of the Middle Ages

Villon: Ballad of the Hanged Men

This is Algernon Swinburne's translation. Villon wrote this ballad when he and some of his accomplices had been condemned to death for burglary. His sentence was later commuted to exile.

If we call on you, brothers, to forgive,
Ye should not hold our prayer in scorn,
   though we
Were slain by law; ye know that all alive
Have not wit always to walk righteously,
Make therefore intercession heartily
With him that of a virgin's womb was bred,
That his grace be not as a dry well-head
For us, nor let hell's thunder on us fall.
We are dead, let no man harry or vex us dead,
But pray to God that he forgive us all.

The rain has washed and laundered us all five,
And the sun dried and blackened; yea, perdie,
Ravens and pies with beaks that rend and rive
Have dug our eyes out, and plucked off for fee
Our beards and eyebrows, never are we free
Not once, to rest, but here and there still sped,
Driven at its wild will by the wind's change led,
More pecked of birds than fruits on garden-wall;
Men, for God's love, let no gibe here be said,
But pray to God that he forgive us all.

From François Villon, *Poems,* ed. by John Payne (New York: Modern Library, n.d.), p. 246.

condemned to hang. The tendency toward realism, already evident in Chaucer, became even stronger in Villon.

Devotional works written for laymen were far more numerous after 1300 than they had ever been before. There was a tremendous desire among all classes for more intense and personal religious experience to supplement the conventional observances. The fourteenth and fifteenth centuries produced innumerable meditations, visions, and moral tracts. Some of the greatest mystical writings of any period were composed at this time, including the *Theologia Germanica,* which influenced Luther (see pp. 520–27) and the *Imitation of Christ,* ascribed to Thomas a Kempis. In England there was *The Vision of Piers Plowman* by William Langland, one of the first important works written in English after the long eclipse following the Norman Conquest. We know little of Langland, except that he lived in the middle years of the fourteenth century and that he came of peasant stock. *Piers Plowman* is one of the last works to use the alliterative, unrhymed verses of the Anglo-Saxon poets, and one of the first to use the simplified grammar and spelling which had developed during the centuries when the language was spoken only by the lower classes. The English of *Piers Plowman* is archaic, but it is recognizably English and not, as Anglo-Saxon was, an early German dialect.

Piers Plowman also illustrates the widespread desire to transform religion into a strong social force. The poet criticizes every class for its worldliness and selfishness; only by a return to the pure principles of the Gospel can the world be saved. There was nothing anti-Catholic in Langland's program, but it did bear testimony to the continuing inability of ecclesiastical authorities to satisfy the aspirations expressed in the poem, and in many similar works.

Painting

The same tendency toward realism that we have noted in Chaucer and Villon is also evident in much of the sculpture and painting of the period. This tendency, which had already appeared in some of the details of thirteenth-century works, now began to be expressed in the principal figures. It sometimes took a macabre form: skeletons and corpses were depicted

Detail from the month of June, from *Les Très Riches Heures* of the duke of Berri, 15th century. Over the wall is a view of the royal buildings on the Île de la Cité in Paris, including the Sainte Chapelle and the Palais de Justice.

with loving care on funeral monuments and in the Dance of Death, a favorite subject of artists. But we also find at this time the first real portraits painted in western Europe and the first attempts to depict a

The Dance of Death, from a manuscript of about 1400. Death, playing a trumpet decked with the papal banner of the Keys of St. Peter, summons the pope.

landscape which is more than a conventional background. There were capable artists everywhere—English, French, and German sculptors, French and German painters. But the most interesting group were those who worked for the dukes of Burgundy. The Flemish school of painting, which developed in the late fourteenth and early fifteenth centuries, was a worthy rival of the Italians of the early Renaissance. In some techniques these painters were ahead of the Italians—the first painting in oils, for example, was done in Flanders. The great Flemish painters, such as the van Eycks, van der Weyden, and Memling, combined meticulous attention to detail with genuine religious feeling. And there is nothing in Italy which quite equals the Flemish portraits of this period, such as Jan van Eyck's picture of the Arnolfinis, or his *Léal Souvenir*.

Science

The scholarly work of the period is less well known, and a few years ago would

398

have been dismissed as unoriginal and unimportant. But even when it was unoriginal it was useful to men with ideas of their own. For example, Columbus drew most of his ideas about geography from books written in the fourteenth and early fifteenth centuries. And not all the work was unoriginal. In philosophy there was a sharp attack on the system of Thomas Aquinas which gradually led to a separation between secular learning and theology. Thomas' statement that no truth found by natural reason could contradict the faith was directly challenged. Several scholars asserted that it was possible for a proposition to be true in philosophy and false in theology. This position allowed wider speculation on scientific subjects and freed scholars, to some extent, from their adherence to the Aristotelian ideas which had been incorporated in Thomas' theology. This was especially true of studies of motion and acceleration. The problems through which Galileo revolutionized the science of physics were problems which had been raised by fourteenth-century scholars.

More important than any specific achievement was the very fact that interest in scientific problems persisted. Up to the end of the Middle Ages, western scholars, relying largely on the work of the Greeks and Arabs, had made no outstanding contributions to the general body of scientific

A 15th-century Flemish miniature. Philip the Good, duke of Burgundy (1422–67), receives a copy of *Les Chroniques de Hainaut* from the author, Jean Wauquelin, 1446.

knowledge. But they had been remarkably persistent and kept working at scientific problems over a longer span of centuries than any other people. The Greeks and Arabs eventually lost interest in science, as did the Chinese, who had had their own independent scientific tradition. But from the twelfth century on, there were always some scholars in the West who were interested in science, and this long devotion led, in the end, to the great discoveries of the early modern period. Men like Copernicus and Galileo were trained in universities which used the methods and the books of the later Middle Ages.

No one has ever given a completely satisfactory explanation of this continuing interest in science. Certainly westerners were paying more attention to the things of this world during the last half of the Middle Ages, and less attention to the aims of the Church. But Chinese society was far more secular, and the Chinese, after a promising start, lost their interest in science. Perhaps more important was the western tendency to be dissatisfied with the status quo, a tendency which was especially evident in the crucial years between 1300 and 1600. In China, a philosopher like Thomas Aquinas would have become an unchallenged authority; in Europe his system was questioned within a generation of his death. Europeans respected authority, but they always felt that authoritative treatises needed to be brought up to date and corrected. Finally, coupled with this impatience with general theories there was a curious patience with details, a willingness and an enthusiasm to work very hard for very small gains.

Technology

These qualities also explain some of the advances in technology which were made in the last medieval centuries. The most important was probably the development

of firearms. Here, as in many other cases, the Europeans capitalized on a technique that had already been discovered by other peoples. The Chinese, for example, were the first to discover gunpowder, and they had cannon about a century before the Europeans. But Chinese guns were never very efficient, and the Chinese never developed an army which was primarily dependent on firearms. The Europeans began experimenting with cannon only in the early decades of the fourteenth century, but they carried their experiments much further than the Chinese. While the first European guns were not very good —they were as apt to kill the men who fired them as those against whom they were aimed—they had become fairly reliable by the end of the fifteenth century. The military significance of this development is obvious. It reduced the power of local lords by making their castles untenable; conversely, it increased the power of kings and great princes like the duke of Burgundy, for they were the only ones who could afford the expensive new weapons.

The development of firearms caused a rapid growth in other branches of technology. In order to make gun barrels that would not burst under the shock of an explosion, a great deal had to be learned about metallurgy. And in order to make gun barrels which were truly round and hence could deliver the full effect of the charge, better metalworking tools and more precise measuring instruments had to be developed. Better techniques in using metal led to greater demands for metal, and this in turn stimulated the mining industry. The miners of Germany (including Bohemia and Austria), which was the great source of metals for Europe, learned to push their shafts deeper and to devise ways of draining off underground water. Greater use of metals and greater skill in mining in the long run transformed Euro-

An early gun, lighter and more portable than the first cannon. The gun is placed on a forked stand and is braced by its long tail against the ground. From a German manuscript, ca. 1405.

pean industry. To take only one example, the first steam engine was developed in order to pump water out of mines, and it could not have been built without the knowledge of metalworking gained in the fifteenth and sixteenth centuries.

The invention of printing in the fifteenth century (see pp. 452–53) also owed much to developments in metallurgy. The essential element in printing was the use of movable type, and good type in turn depended on finding a metal which would take the exact shape of the mold into which it was poured. Thanks to their knowledge of metallurgy, the Germans succeeded in developing an alloy which expanded as it cooled, so that it fitted the mold exactly and gave sharp, clear impressions.

The other great technical advance of western Europe in the later Middle Ages was in ocean shipping. Here it was more a matter of patient experimentation than of brilliant discoveries. By the end of the thirteenth century the sailors of western countries had ships which could tack against the wind and were seaworthy enough to brave the storms of the Atlantic. These navigators could find their latitude, though not their longitude, by star and sun sights; they knew that the earth was round, that there were rich countries in the East, and that the distance to them was not impossibly great. Very little more was needed for the great voyages of discovery except practice, and during the fourteenth and fifteenth centuries men of daring were mastering the art of oceanic navigation. French and Spanish seamen discovered the Canary Islands early in the fourteenth century, and the Portuguese by 1400 had pushed down to the great bend in the African coast, claiming Madeira and the Cape Verde Islands along the way.

These voyages illustrate the point which was made earlier: Europeans were no more skillful or intelligent than other peoples; they were simply more persistent or more aggressive. During the same years in which the Europeans were making their first sorties into the Atlantic, the Chinese were sending great expeditions into the Indian Ocean. There they found rich kingdoms, ancient civilizations, and profitable sources of trade. In contrast, the Europeans discovered only barren islands and the fever-stricken coast of Africa. Yet the Chinese abandoned their explorations because they, or at least their rulers, were satisfied with what they had at home. The Europeans persisted, though it was almost two centuries before they reached the thriving trading centers of the East or the treasures of Mexico and Peru.

During the fourteenth and fifteenth centuries western Europeans also made significant improvements in their measurements of both space and time. Mediterranean pilots produced the first really accurate maps by making charts of the coastlines. These charts, in turn, were possible because the compass had come into general use and the astrolabe, the instrument by which latitude was determined, had been improved. Optical experiments had long fascinated Europeans, and by the fourteenth century they had learned to grind lenses with sufficient accuracy to make the first spectacles. Finally, the first mechanical clocks appeared in the fourteenth century. They were not, at first, very accurate; in fact, the earliest clocks had only hour hands. But they were greatly improved with the discovery of the principle of escapement—that is, the system by which a train of gears is permitted to move only a precisely measured distance before it is checked, and is then released to move the same distance again.

These first improvements in measurements were crude compared to our ability to measure in millimeters and microseconds. But they laid the basis for modern science and industry. They also modified, in the long run, the mental outlook of the western peoples. For several centuries one of the sharpest differences between the West and the rest of the world lay in attitudes toward precise measurement, especially precise measurement of time. Western civilization has come to be dominated by the clock and the timetable, and westerners have had little sympathy with people who have escaped this domination.

Suggestions for Further Reading

1. Economic Weakness

J. W. Thompson's *Economic and Social History of Europe in the Later Middle Ages* (1931), which has excellent material on almost all aspects of European economic life in this period, is a good starting point for study. There is a very thorough treatment of the methods for the enforcement of early economic legislation in England in B. H. Putnam, *The Enforcement of the Statutes of Labourers* (1908). B. N. Nelson, *The Idea of Usury* (1949), studies the development of a universal morality conducive to systematic capitalist enterprise. The books on economic history listed for Chapters 11 and 12 also contain material on this problem.

2. Attacks on the Church: Marsilio, Wiclif, and Huss

There is a wealth of material available in English on these men who revolutionized the political and religious thinking of western Europe. A. Gewirth, *Marsilius of Padua*, Vol. I (1951), is a scholarly and readable treatment of the political philosophy of Marsilius. The great treatise of Marsilius, *The Defensor Pacis* (trans. A. Gewirth, 1956), brings out the premises by which Marsilius overthrew the doctrines of the papal plenitude of power and the Gelasian theory of the parallelism between the spiritual and temporal powers.

A good introduction to the political, social, and religious climate on which the thought of Wiclif fell is G. M. Trevelyan, *England in the Age of Wycliff* (1899). Trevelyan is one of the great social historians of this century and a very good writer. H. B. Workman, *John Wyclif,* 2 vols. (1926), is a study of the impact of Wiclif's thought on his times and on the English church. D. S. Schaff, *John Huss* (1915), is an interesting biography of this Czech nationalist and precursor of reformation. The short monograph of M. Spinka, *John Huss and the Czech Reform* (1941), is a study of the influence of Wiclif on the thought of Huss. There is valuable material on the influence of Marsilius and Wiclif on the evolution of political thought in C. H. McIlwain, *Growth of Political Thought in the West* (1932).

3. The Great Schism

The best background for understanding the Great Schism of the west is W. Ullmann, *Origins of the Great Schism* (1948). W. E. Lunt, *Papal Revenues in the Middle Ages,* 2 vols. (1934), has source material on the finances of the papacy at this time. There is a full account of the Great Schism in M. Creighton, *A History of the Papacy,* Vols. I and II (1905), and in L. Pastor, *History of the Popes,* Vol. I (1891), but the interpretation of Creighton is more balanced.

4. The Black Death

F. A. Gasquet, *The Black Death* (1893), is a good study of this terrible epidemic, with detailed material on the consequences of the plague for the social and economic life of England in the later Middle Ages. The more recent work of A. E. Levett, *The Black Death on the Estates of the See of Winchester* (1916), rejects the older view that the Black Death seriously disrupted the economic development of England. There is material on the Black Death in all political and economic histories of this period.

5. England from 1307 to 1485

A. R. Myers, *England in the Later Middle Ages* * (1952), a broad survey of this entire period, is a good introduction. There is valuable source material on the reign of Edward II in *The Life of Edward II* (trans. N. Denholm-Young, 1957), which goes into considerable detail on the revival of baronial powers and the civil wars under Edward. T. F. Tout, *The Place of the Reign of Edward II in History* (1936), sees this reign as the period of marked transition between court administration and national administration.

J. Froissart, *Chronicles* (many translations), presents a vivid picture of the life and spirit of fourteenth-century England. Froissart is an invaluable source for the reign of Edward III. There is a wealth of primary information on the reigns of Henry VI, Edward IV, and Richard III in *The Paston Letters,* 3 vols. (edited J. Gairdner, 1895). H. L. Gray, *The Influence of the Commons on Early Legislation* (1932), is a scholarly study of the development of the House of Commons and its power in the fourteenth and fifteenth centuries. S. Armitage-Smith, *John of Gaunt,* (1904); A. Steel, *Richard II* (1941); and P. M. Kendall, *Richard the Third* (1955), are all interesting reading and based on sound scholarship.

* Available in paperback edition.

For the study of the development of the English constitution, see also the titles by Stephenson and Marcham, Pasquet, and Pollock and Maitland cited for Chapters 11 and 12 above.

E. Perroy, *The Hundred Years' War* (trans. W. B. Wells, 1952), is an excellent account of the military history of this period, with a discussion of the implications of the war on the constitutional growth of England. R. B. Mowat, *The Wars of the Roses* (1914), is an interesting, if somewhat romantic, treatment of this confusing struggle.

6. France from 1314 to 1461

H. Pirenne and others, *La Fin du Moyen Age* (1931), is a thorough study of this period by outstanding French historians. The broad scholarly work of E. Lavisse, ed., *Histoire de France,* Vol. IV, Part II (1902), is invaluable for the political, economic, military, and cultural history of France in this period.

There is a full documentary account of the trials of Joan of Arc in *Jeanne d'Arc* (edited T. D. Murray, 1902), a very readable translation. L. Fabre, *Joan of Arc* (trans. G. Hopkins, 1954), is a fine biography of Joan and presents a fascinating picture of France in the period of the Hundred Years' War.

7. Germany in the Later Middle Ages

E. F. Henderson, *A Short History of Germany* (1901), is a survey of German history written in the late-Victorian grand manner. Both J. Bryce, *The Holy Roman Empire* (many editions), and G. Barraclough, *Origins of Modern Germany* (1946), contain information on Germany in the later Middle Ages. Barraclough presents a fresher historical interpretation. The old study of H. Zimmer, *The Hansa Towns* (1889), is still valuable.

The origins and development of Switzerland are carefully treated in W. D. McCracken, *Rise of the Swiss Republic* (1901).

The titles by Pirenne and Lavisse in Section 6 above contain information on the rise of the Hapsburg dynasty and the Burgundian take-over of the Low Countries.

There are two very readable studies of the last duke of Burgundy: J. F. Kirk, *Charles the Bold, Duke of Burgundy,* 3 vols. (1864–68), is a study of the man in relation to his times; R. Putnam, *Charles the Bold* (1908), concentrates on Charles the man. A good picture of the brilliant life of the Burgundian court is given in O. Cartellieri, *The Court of Burgundy* (1929). The outstanding achievement of J. Huizinga, *The Waning of the Middle Ages* * (1929), is a study of the forms of life and thought in France and the Netherlands in the last days of the brilliant court of Burgundy.

8. Art, Literature, Science, and Scholarship in the Later Middle Ages

E. Panofsky, *Early Netherlandish Painting* (1953), is a beautiful study of art in northern Europe at this time, and M. Meiss, *Painting in Florence and Siena after the Black Death* (1951), describes the impact the Black Death had on the art of southern Europe. Both volumes are by outstanding art historians and have good reproductions.

Some of the greatest literature of the western world was produced in the later Middle Ages. Chaucer's *Canterbury Tales* * (many editions), Villon's *Poems* (trans. H. D. Stacpoole, 1926), and Dante's *Divine Comedy* * (trans. D. L. Sayers, 1949–58) are all masterpieces. Each was written in the vernacular, each reflects the changing world-view, and each gives a superb picture of the spirit and thought of the times. The great English poem of Langland, *Piers the Ploughman* * (trans. J. E. Goodridge, 1959), is a fourteenth-century inquiry into the good life as judged by contemporary criteria. G. Lagarde, *Naissance de l'Esprit Laïque,* 2 vols. (1956–58), a brilliant treatment of late

* Available in paperback edition.

medieval thought and scholarship, traces the development in western Europe of a distinctly secular spirit. There is interesting material on late medieval science in H. Butterfield, *Origins of Modern Science* (1949), a broad survey. A. C. Crombie, *Medieval and Early Modern Science,** 2 vols. (1959), gives considerable attention to methods in physics in the late Middle Ages and stresses the continuity of the western scientific tradition from Greek times to the present. Crombie includes a good up-to-date bibliography. The thought of the fourteenth century is lucidly presented in G. Leff, *Medieval Thought* * (1958), which discusses Occam, science, and political theories. E. Gilson, *History of Christian Philosophy in the Middle Ages* (1954), has information on Occam and the later Schoolmen. There is a wealth of material on the intellectual and spiritual life of the period from 1216 to 1485 in D. Knowles, *Religious Orders in England,* 2 vols. (1954–55).

* Available in paperback edition.

14

Western Europe's Neighbors During the Middle Ages

As we saw in Chapter 8, both Byzantium and the Moslem world preserved and used more of the materials of Greco-Roman civilization than did western Europe. All through the early Middle Ages they had well-organized bureaucratic states, large cities humming with industry and commerce, and first-rate scholars and scientists. In contrast to these complex and sophisticated societies, the governments of western Europe were weak, its cities were almost nonexistent, and its scholarship was limited to the study of encyclopedias and digests. It is easy to see why western Europeans felt awkward in dealing with their more fortunate neighbors, and why this sense of inferiority often led them into suspicion and hostility. But neighbors they were, and contacts of some sort were inevitable.

The Byzantine Empire

The Byzantine Empire recovered only slowly from the external shock of the Arab conquests and the internal shock of the long religious controversy over the use of images (see p. 243). The Arabs remained a constant danger and new enemies appeared in the north. The Bulgars, an Asiatic people who gradually mixed with the southern Slavs, established a powerful state in the Balkans, and the Russians, under viking leaders, threat-

ened Constantinople on several occasions. But the Empire still had its wealth, its diplomatic skill, and its professional army, and with them it managed to limp through the eighth and early ninth centuries.

With the accession of Basil I (867–86), who founded the Macedonian dynasty, the Byzantine Empire began one of its marvelous recoveries. For almost a century and a half most of the emperors were above average in ability; many of them were also first-rate generals. They took advantage of dissensions among their enemies to drive back the Moslems in the south and the Bulgars in the north. They recovered all of Asia Minor, along with a small strip of northern Syria, including the great trading city of Antioch. They thinned the ranks of the Bulgars in a long series of wars. With the Byzantine navy they gained control of the eastern Mediterranean, making possible the reconquest of Crete and Cyprus. The Byzantine Empire was never richer or more powerful than it was about the year 1000.

Byzantine Art and Literature

An intellectual and artistic revival accompanied the political revival, and had a

A Byzantine icon of St. Michael, 10th century. This work, richly decorated with enamel, gold, and stones, was made for a church in Constantinople and is now in the treasury of St. Mark's, Venice.

longer life. The schools at Constantinople reached the peak of their activity soon after 1000 when a faculty of philosophy and a school of law were established. This was not quite a university of the western type, since standardized courses and degrees were lacking, but professors were paid regular salaries and often held important positions at the imperial court. Some men of high rank were actually more interested in scholarship than in politics—the emperor Constantine VII (912–58), for example, wrote several books, including a treatise on the administration of the Empire. In the next century the most important writer was Michael Psellus, a philosopher and historian, whose interest in the work of Plato reinforced a tradition which was already strong in Constantinople.

Byzantine scholars were almost too impressed by their inheritance from the past. They spent much of their energy copying and commenting on ancient texts and trying to write a classical Greek which was far removed from the popular language. This work was very useful, though not original, since it preserved many books which otherwise would have been lost. Especially important was Byzantine interest in Plato. The other great group of scholars of this period—those who wrote in Arabic—were much more concerned with Aristotle, and western Europe had inherited only a few fragments of Plato in Latin translation. When the Italians of the fifteenth century became interested in Plato, they had to obtain their texts, and scholars to expound them, from Constantinople.

Not all Byzantine writing, however, was based on ancient materials. Impelled by

Byzantine treatments of Persian motives: *upper left*, 8th–9th century; *left*, 7th–10th century. Fine fabric work was a Byzantine specialty, and such pieces were sold both to Moslems and to westerners.

their great respect for tradition, the Byzantines produced some notable works in history, for example. Byzantine histories were not impartial—they were usually written to justify the actions of a ruler or a faction—but they were far superior to contemporary western chronicles. Another important genre which flourished during this period was the popular epic. These stories of heroic deeds performed against the enemies of the Empire were written in the language used by the people, and for this reason they were far more widely known than the scholarly works written in correct classical Greek. The most famous of these poems, the epic of Digenis Akritas, was still remembered at the time of the Cypriote rebellion of 1957–58.

Under the Macedonian emperors and their immediate successors, Byzantine art entered into its golden age. As in scholarship, so in art there was a revival of classical influence, but the artists were far less imitative than the writers. What they took from ancient works was a certain dignity and sobriety, but they retained the Byzantine love of color and ornamentation. Unlike the scholars, they had something to say to the people; they portrayed the truths of the Christian faith, and the events of recent history. Every church and many private homes had their icons (paintings of sacred personages); every public building was decorated with paintings and mosaics; every important manuscript was illustrated with miniatures. With enough work to support hundreds of artists, it is not surprising that most of them were competent and a few great.

Byzantium and the West

Byzantine influence stretched far beyond the boundaries of the Empire. There were always contacts with the West, even when travel was most unsafe. Italian merchants came regularly to Constantinople and after 1100 took over most of the carrying trade of the Empire. There were also many Byzantine subjects in Italy; much of the south was held by Byzantium until 1071, and Venice was for a long time within the Byzantine sphere of influence. Popes and German kings exchanged embassies with the emperor at Constantinople, and thousands of western pilgrims passed through the great city on their way to the Holy Land. The commercial contacts were the most important, for the economic revival of the West would have been slower and would have taken a different form if the Italian cities had not had easy access to the markets of Constantinople. But there were also important artistic influences: Byzantine painters were hired to decorate Italian churches and Byzantine architects designed the Venetian cathedral of St. Mark's. The first native Italian painters were clearly influenced by Byzantine models.

Since western scholars disliked the theology of the Greeks and took little interest in their philosophy, the intellectual influence of Byzantium on the West was less marked. But after 1100 a few westerners journeyed to Constantinople to discover and translate ancient manuscripts. Their work was less appreciated than that of their contemporaries who were working on translations from the Arabic, and sometimes a very faulty version of Aristotle which had passed from Greek to Syriac to Arabic to Latin was preferred to a direct translation from the Greek. Because they were primarily interested in Aristotle, western translators overlooked their opportunity to increase the stock of Platonic works available in Latin. Nevertheless, some very important texts, such as the advanced works of Euclid, would have been unknown to western medieval scholars had it not been for the efforts of the translators at Constantinople.

During the eleventh century the Latin and Greek Churches gradually drifted apart. There had long been friction between them, since the patriarch at Constantinople disliked the pope's claims to universal authority and the pope resented the patriarch's claim to independence. There were theological disputes, such as the one over sacred images, or the question raised by Charlemagne about the relationship between the Holy Ghost and the other Two Persons of the Trinity. But the basic reason for the split was that the West and Byzantium were becoming so different in institutions and culture that each was suspicious of the other's motives. The result was that pope and patriarch excommunicated each other in 1054 and the two Churches broke off relations. The break was not taken too seriously at first; such splits had happened before and had always been repaired. But this time, in spite of repeated efforts, the breach could not be healed. Each Church went its own way and cooperation between them became more and more difficult.

Byzantium and the Slavs

Byzantium's greatest influence was on the peoples of the Balkans and Russia. In spite of frequent wars and rebellions, there were long periods in which the Serbs and Bulgars were either subject to, or allied with, the Eastern Empire. Byzantine rulers frequently married their daughters and nieces to Slavic princes in order to gain influence in neighboring courts. These ladies brought with them missionaries and teachers, artists and scholars, thus helping to spread the Greek Orthodox religion and Byzantine culture throughout the regions inhabited by the eastern Slavs. The conversion of the Bulgars began in the ninth century and that of the Russians in the tenth; both peoples were soon thoroughly Christianized. For a long time the leading clergymen in Bulgaria and Russia were appointed by the Greek Orthodox patriarch of Constantinople. Even with a growing tendency toward autonomy in the Slavic churches, Byzantine influence remained strong. Down to the fifteenth century all but two or three of the metropolitans (heads) of the Russian church were Greeks.

The fact that the eastern Slavs * received their religion and their culture from Constantinople had important consequences for the history of modern Europe. Byzantine civilization and western European civilization had a common origin, but, as we have seen, they drifted apart during the Middle Ages. Byzantium remembered much that the West forgot, and it was always more strongly influenced by eastern ideas and customs. The West absorbed Germanic and Celtic influences which scarcely touched Constantinople, and it was forced to develop new institutions for which there were no parallels in the East. As a result, the two civilizations, while recognizing that they were related, found it difficult to understand each other. These misunderstandings often led to bitterness, because each expected better things of a related Christian civilization, and because each felt that the other was betraying a common heritage. The eastern Slavs, and especially the Russians, absorbed this point of view. Thus the eastern Slavs never felt that they belonged entirely to the world of western Europe, and current Russian hostility to the West is a new and intensified form of an old suspicion.

---

* The Rumanians offer a complicated problem, which we cannot discuss in detail. They spoke a Latin dialect, and some of them were certainly descended from Roman soldiers and settlers in the Danubian provinces. But they were overrun repeatedly by invaders, and there is a large Slavic element in the population today. In any case, they were Greek Orthodox in religion, and largely Byzantine in culture.

The Caliphate

The Abbasid Caliphate, established in 750, had its golden age a little before the great tenth-century revival at Constantinople. For a century and a half all Moslem territories except Spain were ruled by the caliph of Baghdad. His empire stretched from Morocco to the Indus River, from the steppes of central Asia to the Sudan. After 900 the Caliphate began to break up into separate states, but the Mohammedan world remained an economic and cultural unit. This vast territory had great wealth of its own and was traversed by all the important east-west trade routes. Baghdad was probably the largest and richest city in the Eurasian continent, and there were dozens of other populous and prosperous cities in the Moslem world.

Arabic Scholarship

The city of Baghdad attracted books and scholars just as it did merchandise and traders. The Ommiads had already begun to assimilate the knowledge of the Greeks and the Persians, but the Abbasids did even more to transform their empire into a center of scholarship. Hundreds of Greek works, especially those dealing with philosophy, science, and mathematics, were translated into Arabic. A great deal was also learned from Persian and Jewish sources. Chinese scholarship had little influence, but the Abassids derived important ideas from the Indians, notably the

A Moslem pharmacist concocting a medicinal wine, from a 13th-century manuscript of Dioscorides' *Materia Medica*. The text reads: "The making of a drink (*shirab*) for catarrhs, coughs, swelling of the belly, and loosening of the stomach. Take myrrh, ¼ *uqiyya*; roots of *sussan*, ⅛ *uqiyya*; and white pepper, ⅛ *uqiyya*. Pound them together, tie them up in a rag, put in 3 *qusts* of good wine, and let stand 3 days. Then strain and put into a clean vessel. Drink after supper."

system of arithmetic notation which we call Arabic figures. Much of the early work of translation was done by non-Mohammedan writers, including a large number of Syrian Christians. But by the ninth century Moslem scholars had assimilated the work of their predecessors and were beginning to make original contributions of their own. From 900 to 1200 the most important work done anywhere in the world in the fields of mathematics, astronomy, physics, medicine, and geography was done in Moslem countries.

Many of the scholars writing in Arabic merely furnished new and useful observa-

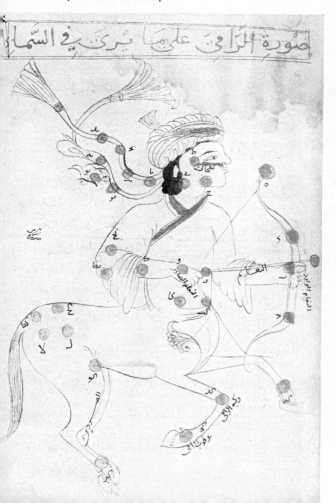

Astronomical chart of the constellation Sagittarius, the Archer, used to illustrate a book on the fixed stars by a 10th-century Moslem astronomer. From a 14th-century Persian manuscript.

tions to support already established scientific theories. Thus in astronomy they contributed many accurate observations of star positions, and in medicine they recorded excellent clinical descriptions of certain diseases. They went somewhat further in geography because they knew more of the world than the ancient writers. But their most remarkable contribution was in physics and mathematics. In physics they worked out new theories about light and performed interesting experiments in reflection and refraction. In mathematics, besides greatly simplifying arithmetical operations through the use of the new Arabic figures, they carried trigonometry far beyond the Greek accomplishment. And their performance in developing algebra was even more impressive, for they fashioned a whole mathematical discipline out of the few hints provided by their predecessors. Their contribution is recorded in the very word *algebra,* which is Arabic.

Two of the great Mohammedan mathematicians were al-Khwarizmi (d. *ca.* 840) and the poet Omar Khayyám (d. *ca.* 1120). Al-Khwarizmi recognized, more clearly than many of his contemporaries, the value of the new Hindu-Arabic figures, especially the zero. Use of the zero made it possible to reckon by position and simplified all work in arithmetic. Al-Khwarizmi did much to popularize this new arithmetic; he also wrote a text on algebra which was used in both Moslem and Christian countries for centuries. Omar Khayyám calculated the length of a solar year with great accuracy and devised methods of solving algebraic equations which had been too complicated for his predecessors.

Arabic Influence on the West

Mohammedan interest in mathematics and the natural sciences had a decisive influence on the course of western civilization. As we have seen, the Byzantines tended to neglect these subjects, and little was known about them in western Europe. The Chinese had great technical skill—for example, they discovered the principle of the compass very early—but they developed few general theories. And the Indians, after a promising start, lost their interest in mathematical and scientific problems. Thus the Mohammedan world was the only region in which the Greek scientific tradition survived, the only region which was both actively interested in science and close enough to western Europe to touch off a revival of scientific interests there. Western European scholars made their first attempts to recover ancient scientific texts by going to the Mohammedans of Spain and Sicily; only after the revival was well under way did they begin to seek manuscripts in Constantinople. And throughout the Middle Ages translations from the Arabic were more esteemed in the West than translations from the Greek. Certainly the West would not have developed a scientific tradition of its own as rapidly as it did without the assistance of Mohammedan scholarship, and quite possibly it never would have developed the tradition at all.

It is somewhat anachronistic, however, to separate science so sharply from other studies. For Moslem scholars, as for medieval Christians, science was merely one form of philosophy. Aristotle, the great authority on science for both peoples, was thought of primarily as a philosopher, and one of the great intellectual problems of the Middle Ages was to reconcile his philosophy with other sources of knowledge. Here again, Moslem scholars led the way. Avicenna (ibn-Sina, 980–1037), who wrote a famous book in Arabic on medicine, also prepared commentaries on Aristotle which had a great influence on western scholars during the twelfth and thirteenth centuries. Even more influential was the Spanish

Moslem, Averroës (ibn-Rushd, 1126–98), who held several beliefs which shocked Mohammedans and Christians alike—for example, that the world is eternal, and that there is no personal immortality. But Averroës was no freethinker; one of his strongest convictions was that there can be no real conflict between the truths of philosophy and truths of revealed religion. This doctrine, which was taken over by Christian scholars in the thirteenth century, made it easier for them to justify the assimilation of Greco-Arabic philosophy into the Christian tradition. Maimonides (Moses ben Maimon, 1135–1204), a Spanish Jew living under Moslem rule, was thoroughly familiar with the Arabic versions of Aristotelian philosophy and tried to reconcile them with the Jewish faith. His proofs of the existence of God are very like those advanced a half-century later by Thomas Aquinas (see pp. 357–59).

Although the Mohammedan world also produced some able historians, they were largely unknown to other peoples and so had less influence than the philosophers. More important to the West were the poets, especially those of Moslem Spain. Some of their songs of love and chivalry are very like those written in southern France in the twelfth century, and it is possible that the Moslems exerted some influence on the early troubadours. Finally, the central position of the Mohammedan world made it a great storehouse of marvelous stories. They flowed in from China and India, from Africa and Greece, were given a proper Mohammedan setting, and then were carried by merchants all over the world. The most famous collection of these stories is *A Thousand and One Nights,* or *The Arabian Nights.*

Until the Moslems broke away from the Koran's strict ban on representing living beings, they could do nothing with sculpture and painting. They were, however,

The Court of the Lions in the Alhambra, the palace of the Moorish rulers of Granada. The central part of the Alhambra was built in the 13th century; additions were made later. Notice the elaborate carving and the interplay of light and shade.

great builders and created a distinctive style out of such old forms as the dome, the arcade, and the tower. Moslem architectural styles made a deep impression on every country in which they appeared; their influence may still be seen in Spain and India. Moslem buildings were lavishly decorated with colored tiles and intricate geometric carvings, and these techniques were also appropriated by their neighbors.

The Decline of Byzantium and the Caliphate

The Byzantine Empire and the countries included in the Abbasid Caliphate re-

mained important centers of commerce and of intellectual and artistic activity throughout the European Middle Ages. But after the tenth century they had increasing difficulty in surviving as political units. Some problems were common to both states—for example, the lack of a fixed rule of succession to the throne. Neither the emperor nor the caliph was necessarily the eldest son of his predecessor; he might be anyone connected with the ruling family who had been able to win the support of the bureaucracy and the army. Theoretically this practice might have assured the selection of the ablest individual; actually it encouraged palace intrigues and civil wars. The western European custom of following the rule of primogeniture was not an ideal way of picking a ruler, but in practice it gave greater stability and continuity to political institutions. Another difficulty was that as the Byzantines and the Moslems of the caliphate grew wealthier and more sophisticated, they became more reluctant to serve in the armed forces. It was easier to hire soldiers from among the neighboring barbarians than to disrupt civilian life by forcing city workers and peasant farmers into the army. But mercenaries were never entirely reliable, and the better they were as fighting men the greater the danger that they might try to take over the government.

In addition, each state had its own problems. In Byzantium there was a growing hostility between the bureaucracy of the capital city and the great landlords of the rural districts. The bureaucrats, quite rightly, felt that the landlords were trying to reduce the peasants to a state of serfdom and to make themselves independent rulers of the outlying provinces. But when the bureaucrats tried to check these tendencies, the landlords resisted bitterly. The landlords felt, quite rightly in turn, that the bureaucracy was a nest of intrigue and corruption. But every time one of the landlords became emperor, he found that he had to rely on the very bureaucracy he had opposed. These disruptive tendencies were held in check during the tenth century, but after the death of the last great Macedonian emperor, Basil II, in 1025, they grew more virulent.

The problems peculiar to the Caliphate sprang from its size and from the widespread disrespect for law. It was almost impossible to establish a centralized administrative system for such widely separated regions, each with its own difficulties and traditions. A great deal of authority had to be turned over to regional viceroys, and there was always the danger that one of them would set himself up as an independent ruler. Moreover, though the caliphs had built up an elaborate bureaucracy on Roman and Persian models, and though they had developed a comprehensive legal system, the Moslem government was always rather arbitrary and unpredictable. No one wanted to be bound by rules, and both the caliph and his officials broke them whenever they saw advantage in doing so. Since everything depended on the whim of the man in power, it was better to catch his ear than it was to try to win a case at law. This lack of respect for constitutional and legal principles encouraged intrigue and disobedience. It was made worse by religious divisions among Moslems. Minority groups, which questioned the Abbasid ruler's claim to be the orthodox successor of Mohammed, naturally had little respect for his government.

The first crack in the Caliphate opened up in 756, when a member of the deposed Ommiad dynasty established an independent state in Spain. This did little damage, and the Abbasids went on to the height of their power and wealth during the reign of Harun al-Rashid (786–809), a contemporary of Charlemagne. The next secessions were more serious, for they cost the Caliphate all of North Africa. Local leaders set themselves up as independent rulers of petty states, which, in the tenth century, were united under the new Fatimid dynasty. This family claimed descent from Fatima, the daughter of Mohammed, which gave them the support of the Shiites, the largest group of dissenters in Islam. The Shi-ites believed that Islam must always be led by a lineal descendant of Mohammed; they had rejected the Ommiad caliphs and were now ready to turn against the Abbasids. By taking the title of caliph in 909, the founder of the new

A Byzantine galley of Michael II using Greek fire to destroy an enemy, 9th-century manuscript. Greek fire was a mixture of pitch, saltpeter and sulfur expelled from a tube, as shown here. It stuck to people and equipment, burning fiercely, with great smoke and cracklings. This weapon contributed to Byzantine success in naval warfare during the early struggles with the Moslems.

dynasty directly challenged the claim of the Abbasid ruler to be leader of all the Moslems. And by conquering Egypt in 969, the Fatimids gained one of the wealthiest Moslem provinces; they established their capital in the newly built city of Cairo in 973. The Fatimid domains now stretched from Morocco to the Red Sea and even included Palestine as far as Jerusalem. At the height of their power the Fatimid caliphs of Cairo were far stronger than the Abbasid caliphs of Bagdad.

The Coming of the Turks

By the end of the eleventh century the Fatimid Caliphate was beginning to weaken, but the Abbasids profited little from the decline of their rivals. In an effort to hold on to their remaining provinces, they had come to rely more and more on mercenary soldiers, especially the Seljuk Turks. A branch of the great nomadic stock of central Asia, the Turks had all the toughness, bravery, and love of conquest of their eastern relatives. They became devout Moslems and fought well for their new religion, but they also fought for themselves. Having become the dominant military power in the lands of the Abbasid Caliphate, they soon began to seek political power as well. By the eleventh century the Turkish sultans (kings) had become the real rulers of most of Syria and Mesopo-

tamia. They preserved the caliph as a religious leader, and they sometimes listened to him when he tried to arbitrate quarrels between members of the Turkish royal families. But they granted him no real power in government.

The rise of the Turks had serious consequences for the Byzantine emperors as well. Disputes over the succession to the imperial throne and quarrels between the bureaucrats of Constantinople and the great landlords of Asia Minor had seriously weakened the Eastern Empire. Suspecting that they would meet with little resistance, the Turks began to push into Asia Minor; when the emperor Romanus IV tried to drive them out he was defeated and captured at the battle of Manzikert in 1071.

The Byzantine Empire never fully recovered from this defeat. After Manzikert the Turks overran almost all of Asia Minor; they even took Nicaea, only fifty miles from Constantinople. Through heroic efforts a new Byzantine dynasty, the Comneni, regained some of the lost territory, but it could never eject the Turks from central and eastern Asia Minor. This was a serious loss to the Empire, for the provinces seized by the Turks had furnished large numbers of fighting men and had served as a buffer protecting the wealthy coastal regions. Skillful diplomacy and wise use of limited resources enabled Byzantium to survive, but the Eastern Empire under the Comneni never had the vigor it had displayed under the Macedonians.

Fortunately for the Byzantines, the Turkish Empire began to disintegrate almost as soon as it was established. As might have been expected in this part of the world, the lack of a fixed rule of succession did most of the damage. There were usually two sultans, one in the East and one in the West, and each sultan established little principalities, which often became independent, for junior members of the family. Military commanders also had a tendency to turn their governorships into independent principalities. All these petty rulers fought and intrigued to gain one another's territories. In the end the

old Abbasid Caliphate dissolved into a welter of petty states, only loosely associated by their theoretical allegiance to caliph and sultan.

The Early Crusades

It was this confused situation in the Near East which made possible the success of the First Crusade (see p. 296) and the establishment of the crusader Kingdom of Jerusalem in 1099. The Moslems were too divided to cooperate against the common enemy, and some of them even encouraged the Christians to attack their rivals. Only a part of the Turkish forces could be assembled to fight the crusaders at Dorylaeum and Antioch; once Antioch had been lost to the Christians, few of the

Crusade Routes 1096-1270

political boundaries are those of the middle of the twelfth century

—1— First Crusade, 1096-99 ····4 Fourth Crusade, 1202-04
—2—· Second Crusade, 1147-49 ··L·· First Crusade of Louis IX, 1248-54
— 3 — Third Crusade, 1189-92 ·LL· Second Crusade of Louis IX, 1270

MILES
0   300

417

A Byzantine View of the Crusaders

Anna Comnena, the author of this piece, was the daughter of the Emperor Alexius I.

Now he [the emperor] dreaded the arrival of the Crusaders, for he knew their irresistible manner of attack, their unstable and mobile character, and all the peculiar . . . characteristics which the Frank retains throughout; and he also knew that they were always agape for money, and seemed to disregard their truces readily for any reason that cropped up. . . . The simpler-minded Franks were urged on by the real desire of worshipping at our Lord's Sepulchre, but the more astute, especially men like Bohemund . . . had another secret reason, namely the hope that . . . they might by some means be able to seize the capital itself. . . . For the Frankish race . . . is always very hot-headed and eager, but when it has once espoused a cause, it is uncontrollable.

From Anna Comnena, *The Alexiad*, trans. by E. A. S. Dawes (London: Kegan Paul, 1928), pp. 248, 250.

✧✧✧✧✧✧✧✧✧✧✧✧✧✧✧✧✧✧✧✧✧✧✧✧✧✧✧

Syrian Moslems cared about the fate of Jerusalem. Jerusalem, after all, was held by the Fatimid heretics, who were little better than the Christian infidels. And the Fatimids themselves regarded Jerusalem as an outlying possession of little military or political value. They clung tenaciously to Ascalon and Gaza, which controlled the Palestinian end of the land route to Egypt, but they made no great effort to regain the Holy City. A dynasty of Christian kings, descended from the crusader Baldwin of Lorraine, held Jerusalem and most of Palestine from 1099 to 1187.

The emperor Alexius Comnenus (1081–1118) must have looked on the First Crusade as a very successful piece of Byzantine diplomacy. True, he had created

neither the religious revival in the West which caused the people to rally to the crusade appeal, nor the political situation which made the pope feel that a crusade was necessary. But his request for troops to defend his empire against the Turks had provided the catalytic agent which enabled religious aspirations and political desires to crystallize into the crusade. Moreover, Alexius had shown great skill in whisking unruly western armies through his lands with a minimum of friction and looting, and he had used the crusading forces to screen his reoccupation of much of Asia Minor. The establishment in 1099 of the Kingdom of Jerusalem and the northern crusading states of Tripoli, Antioch, and Edessa drove a wedge into the Near East and made cooperation among the Moslem lands even more difficult than before. Moreover, by posing a threat to Islam, the crusading states also distracted Moslem attention from Byzantium. The Kingdom of Jerusalem, in particular, harassed the Moslems of Syria during the first half of the twelfth century and thus aided the revival of Byzantine power.

The crusade was not all profit for the Byzantines, however, for it reinforced western suspicion of Byzantine morals and motives. The leaders of the crusade suspected Alexius of being much more interested in recovering his lost provinces than in freeing the Holy Places from the Moslems. They resented his failure to aid them in the siege of Antioch and his subsequent efforts to assert his lordship over the city. Western hostility to Byzantium was strengthened by the events of the Second and Third Crusades. The Byzantines were not really interested in fostering these movements; in fact, they twice retreated to a position of neutrality in return for advantageous treaties with the Turks. The westerners, dismayed by this subtle diplomacy, soon began to think that the

14 / Western Europe's Neighbors During the Middle Ages

Byzantines were almost as great a threat to Christendom as the Moslems. When a crusading army sacked Constantinople in 1204, the Byzantines paid dearly for arousing these suspicions.

The Moslems recovered only slowly from the shock of the Christian conquest of Jerusalem, and remained on the defensive for the first decades of the twelfth century. But gradually a series of able army commanders began to reunite the scattered Moslem states. The first of these generals, Zangi, took the outlying Christian county of Edessa in 1144 and held it against the badly mismanaged Second Crusade. Even more important was the work of Zangi's son, Nureddin (Nūr-al-Dīn), who put an end to the decaying Fatimid Caliphate of Egypt in 1171. Nureddin was already master of most of Syria; by adding Egypt to his domain he became far stronger than the Christian kings of Jerusalem. He was succeeded by his ablest general, Saladin (salāh-al-Dīn), who overran the Kingdom of Jerusalem and seized the Holy City itself in 1187. The Christians were left with only a few seacoast towns.

The loss of Jerusalem sent a shock of horror throughout Latin Christendom. The three greatest kings of the West—Frederick Barbarossa of Germany, Philip Augustus of France, and Richard Lionheart of England —agreed to unite their forces in an attack on Saladin. But the Third Crusade was only partially successful. Frederick was drowned while crossing Asia Minor with his army, and Philip Augustus, after helping to recapture Acre, rushed back to France to look after the affairs of his kingdom. Richard hung on, fighting so bravely that he became a legend among the Moslems, but he never had a large enough army to risk an attack on Jerusalem. He did reconquer a long strip of coastal territory, thus prolonging the life of the Kingdom of Jerusalem for a century. The

✦✦✦✦✦✦✦✦✦✦✦✦✦✦✦✦✦✦✦✦✦✦✦✦✦✦✦✦✦

A Crusader's View of Byzantium

Odo of Deuil, the author of this piece, was a historian of the Second Crusade.

And then the Greeks degenerated entirely into women; putting aside all manly vigor, both of words and of spirit, they lightly swore whatever they thought would please us, but they neither kept faith with us nor maintained respect for themselves. In general they really have the opinion that anything which is done for the holy empire cannot be considered perjury. . . . When the Greeks are afraid they become despicable in their excessive abasement, and when they have the upper hand they are arrogant. . . .

Constantinople itself is squalid and fetid. . . . People live lawlessly in this city, which has as many lords as rich men and almost as many thieves as poor men. . . . In every respect she exceeds moderation, for just as she surpasses other cities in wealth, so too does she surpass them in vice. . . .

[The bishop of Langres] added that Constantinople is Christian only in name and not in fact . . . and that her emperor had ventured a few years ago to attack the [Crusader] prince of Antioch. . . . "Though it was his [the emperor's] duty to ward off the near-by infidels by uniting the Christian forces, with the aid of the infidels he strove to destroy the Christians."

From Odo of Deuil, *De profectione Ludovici VII in orientem,* trans. by V. G. Berry (New York: Columbia U. Press, 1948), pp. 57, 65, 69.

✦✦✦✦✦✦✦✦✦✦✦✦✦✦✦✦✦✦✦✦✦✦✦✦✦✦✦✦✦

revived kingdom, however, was never very strong, and it played a far less important role in Near Eastern politics in the thirteenth century than it had in the twelfth.

The Later Crusades

Saladin's empire began to dissolve soon after his death in 1193. As so often hap-

Crusaders crossing the Mediterranean in a sailing ship, from a miniature of the late 13th century. The knights on board wear armor; a cleric is at the rudder. This is not a very accurate picture of a 13th-century ship, but it is interesting to see that it steers with a rudder, a device which was just coming into use, replacing the steering oar.

pened in the Moslem world, his states were divided among members of his family, who promptly began intriguing against one another. The heir who held Egypt had a certain pre-eminence over the others, but he was never sure of the loyalty of his relatives, and his control of Palestine was often threatened. The Christians could once more hope to regain Jerusalem, and they staged three major and several minor expeditions to the East in the first half of the thirteenth century. None of these crusades succeeded in re-establishing the power of the Kingdom of Jerusalem, though Frederick II did manage to regain Jerusalem itself briefly (1229–44) through a treaty with the sultan of Egypt. On the other hand, the thirteenth-century crusades, by weakening both Saladin's dynasty and the Byzantine Empire, aided the rise of new powers in the Near East.

The Byzantine Empire in 1200 was neither as rich nor as powerful as it once had been. Most of its commerce was in the hands of Italian merchants, though Constantinople still drew a large income from its port services and its manufacturing. The Byzantine navy had almost ceased to exist, and the army, composed largely of mercenaries, was too weak to guard all the frontiers. The Turks were threatening Asia Minor and a revived Bulgarian kingdom was attacking Thrace. Internal dissension had reached a dangerous point, with many of the great families lined up against the emperor. More or less by accident, the first people to take advantage of this inviting situation were a group of crusaders.

The Fourth Crusade started in 1202 as a routine expedition against the Moslems of the East. But it ran into bad luck; the army, which never achieved full strength, was heavily in debt to the Venetians, who had supplied the transports to carry it to the East. The Venetians, who cared little about crusades but a great deal about profit, made the army work off part of its debt by capturing Zara, a rival trading town across the Adriatic. Then a pretender to the Byzantine throne turned up with a very tempting proposition: he would pay

14 / Western Europe's Neighbors During the Middle Ages

all the army's debts and augment its forces if the crusaders would help him conquer the Eastern Empire. The Venetians saw a fine chance of acquiring a monopoly of trade with Byzantium, and under their urging most, though not all, of the crusaders agreed to attack Constantinople. Aided by Byzantine weakness and disunity, the small western force—probably not more than twenty thousand fighting men—managed to seize one of the most strongly fortified positions in the world (1203). The pretender was installed as emperor and the crusaders agreed to help him consolidate his position while waiting for the money and men he had promised.

But neither money nor men were forthcoming. The bargain had probably been extravagant in any case, and the Latin-supported emperor was too unpopular with his subjects to persuade them to make any great sacrifices for the westerners. A new revolution soon swept him off the throne and replaced him with a ruler who was strongly antiwestern. Once more the crusaders had to attack impregnable Constantinople and once more they succeeded in taking it (1204).

This time they resolved to take no chances. They first looted the city, sacking churches, stealing relics, and melting down ancient works of art. Then they installed one of their own leaders, Baldwin, count of Flanders, as emperor, and divided most of Greece and Thrace among the Venetians and western feudal lords. This Latin Empire of Constantinople lasted only a half-century (1204–61), but some of the feudal principalities in Greece survived into the fourteenth century, and Venice held some of the Greek islands and ports in the Peloponnesus until the seventeenth century.

Innocent III, who was pope at this time, at first severely condemned the diversion of the Fourth Crusade. After 1204, however, he was seduced by the prospect of ending the schism with the Greek Church and gave full support to the Latin Empire. His first reaction was the sounder one; the capture of Constantinople was an unmitigated disaster for western Christendom. Instead of healing the breach between the two Churches, it intensified Byzantine hatred of the Latins and convinced the Greeks that the independence of their Church was synonymous with national survival. Even when they were about to be conquered by the Turks, the Greeks refused to consider union with Rome; as one of them said: "Better the turban of the sultan than the tiara of the pope." Nor did the capture of Constantinople help the kingdom of Jerusalem; instead, it meant that western money and fighting men had to be diverted to support the Latin Empire and the feudal principalities of Greece. It did ruin the Byzantine Empire and expose all southeastern Europe to Turkish conquest. Even though the Latins were driven out of Constantinople in 1261, the revived Byzantine Empire was only a shadow of what it had been. It held only a fragment of the Balkans and a small strip of Asia Minor; it could not check the Turkish advance into Europe in the fourteenth century.

Saladin's dynasty would have lost power in any case, but the thirteenth-century crusades speeded up the process. The sultans of Egypt showed no great skill in warding off attacks; one sultan, as we have seen, surrendered Jerusalem to Frederick II. Louis IX of France precipitated a crisis by leading an army against Egypt in 1248 and taking Damietta. The sultan of Egypt by this time was almost entirely dependent on his household slaves, who formed the core of his army and held many high administrative posts. There were many able men among these slaves, or Mamelukes, as they were called, and they were weary of fighting to keep a decaying dynasty in power. They assassinated the sultan and replaced him with one of their own commanders. For centuries Egypt was to be ruled by Mameluke generals who rose from the ranks of a slave army. Only tough and brutal men could reach the top, and when one of them showed signs of softening he was apt to be replaced by a younger and more vigorous fighter. But in spite of their internal quarrels, the Mamelukes remained a first-rate military power, and they had none of Saladin's tolerance for Christians or his chivalrous admiration for a worthy opponent. They were determined to drive the westerners out of the Near East, and they rapidly accomplished their purpose. By 1271 they had occupied the entire area except for a few coastal towns, and in 1291 Acre, the last stronghold of the crusaders, was taken by the Mameluke sultan.

The fall of Acre did not end the crusades; there were some important expeditions against the Turks in the fourteenth century, and popes talked of crusades as late as 1464. But none of the later crusades gained a permanent foothold for Latin Christians in the East or did much to halt the Turkish advance. Whatever influence the crusades had on the civilizations of Islam and the West had been exerted by the end of the thirteenth century. And that influence was considerable: The crusades had reflected the vigor of western medieval civilization at its height. They had kept the Mohammedans on the defensive for several generations. They had helped to stimulate the growth of Italian naval power which was to make the Mediterranean a Christian lake for three centuries. The fact that thousands of westerners lived in, or visited, Syria and Palestine encouraged the demand for east-

The Fragmentation of the Byzantine Empire 1265

ern luxuries and thus changed western standards of living, although there would have been some increase in demand in any case.

On the other hand, the crusaders showed little evidence of intellectual or cultural interests. Armies of occupation are more likely to bring home material objects than ideas. Western scholars learned more from peaceful contacts with the Moors of Spain and the Greeks of Constantinople than they did from the inhabitants of the Kingdom of Jerusalem. In short, the importance of the crusades in East-West relationships was primarily political. They marked the first attempt of western Europe to expand into non-European areas, and they added to the difficulties of both the Byzantine Empire and the Moslem caliphates. They did little to promote understanding or intellectual contacts among the three civilizations which bordered on the Mediterranean.

The Mongol Empire

Far more important than the thirteenth-century struggle over the dying Kingdom of Jerusalem was the advance of the Mongols into Russia and the Near East. The Mongols were another of those nomadic peoples of central Asia who from time to time developed great military power and burst into the lands of their civilized neighbors. The pattern was a familiar one: an able leader would organize his own tribe into an effective striking force and then subjugate other tribes belonging to the same racial stock. Once he had established himself as the predominant power in the vast steppes of central Asia, other nomadic peoples would join him either out of fear or in the hope of sharing in the loot. Finally, the united forces would become strong enough to strike out at China, India, or Europe. This had been the story of the Huns, and it was to be the story of the Mongols. A small group originally, they became the dominant element in a great federation of nomadic tribes. But while the Mongols followed the old pattern, they expanded more widely and held their conquests longer than any of their predecessors. Their first great leader, Genghis Khan (ca. 1160–1227), was undoubtedly the ablest of all the nomad rulers, and his immediate descendants were almost as competent. The Mongol khans were not only first-rate generals; they also knew how to organize and administer an empire. As a result, the Mongols were to stand as the dominant power in Asia and eastern Europe for a century and a half, and they remained a force to be reckoned with well into the fifteenth century.

The first great effort of the Mongols was against China; they took Peking in 1215 and had occupied most of northern China by the death of Genghis in 1227. The Sung dynasty in the south held out longer, and the Mongols were not able to gain control of the whole country until the 1270's. Meanwhile they found easier conquests to the west. A strong army, under one of the ablest Mongol generals, set out against Persia and Mesopotamia. The Mongols overran Persia fairly quickly and in 1258 they took Baghdad, plundered the city, and put the caliph to death. This attack ended the Abbasid Caliphate, the last symbol of Moslem unity.

For a moment it looked as if the Mongols were going to conquer all the Mohammedan states of the Near East. But when the Mongols attempted to take Syria, they were completely defeated by the Mameluke sultan of Egypt (1260). Since no one else from the Mediterranean to the Yellow Sea could claim to have defeated a Mongol army, this victory gave the Mamelukes great prestige. The Mongols made little effort to advance further, and the Mame-

Russia ca. 1200

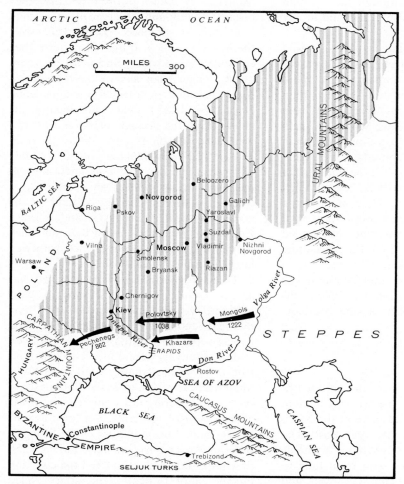

lukes in Egypt and the Turks in western Asia Minor remained independent.

Russia and the Mongols

Meanwhile another Mongol horde had attacked Russia, the chief outpost of Byzantine culture. The viking leaders, who had invaded Russia in the ninth century, had built a strong state around Kiev. This state controlled the trade route between the Black Sea and the Baltic, a route which in the early Middle Ages carried at least as many oriental wares as the route across the Mediterranean. The princes of Kiev grew rich from their trade, and were powerful enough to attack Constantinople itself on several occasions. But after the conversion of the Russians to Greek Orthodox Christianity at the end of the tenth century, relations between Kiev and Byzantium were generally friendly. The Russians accepted the civilization of the Eastern Empire along with its religion; their churches were built in the Byzantine style and their scholars worked on Byzantine texts, translating many of them

VIKINGS - orginally

into Russian. Although the Russians added ideas of their own, both in art and in literature, Kiev at the height of its power in the early eleventh century must have resembled Constantinople in many ways. It was certainly larger, wealthier, and much more of an intellectual center than either the Paris of the first Capetian kings or the London of William the Conqueror.

In the twelfth century Kiev began to decline. It lost some of its trade to the Italians, who not only exploited the Mediterranean route but even sent their ships into the Black Sea. It suffered even more from the Pechenegs, a nomadic people who pushed through the gap between the Urals and the Caspian and occupied the steppes of southern Russia. Raids by the Pechenegs reduced the flow of eastern goods through Kiev to a trickle. Meanwhile, other centers of power were growing up in the upper Volga basin. The princes of Kiev had given outlying towns to younger members of their family to be ruled as dependent principalities. This practice worked well enough at first, but as Kiev declined and family ties weakened, the junior princes became greedy for power. They made war on each other and on their nominal superior, the ruler of Kiev. They sacked Kiev itself in 1168, and this disaster, combined

with commercial difficulties, put an end to the unity and prosperity of early Russia. The strongest ruler was now the prince of Suzdal, a region which included the newly founded town of Moscow, but his territories were poor and backward compared to Kiev in its great days. Once a land of cities and merchants, Russia was now becoming a land of peasants scratching out a bare living from the thin soils of the north. Declining prosperity, however, did not improve the behavior of the princes. They continued their feuding and their custom of dividing their lands among their children. It was almost impossible for them to take combined action against a common enemy such as the Mongols.

It is not surprising, then, that the Mongols found it so easy to conquer Russia. Their first serious attack came in 1237; by 1241 they had overcome all resistance and were pushing across the Carpathians into Hungary. Hungarian resistance was no more effective than Russian—their armies were slaughtered near Budapest—but the death of the Great Khan ended the Mongol threat to central Europe. The commander of the Mongol army rushed back home to exert his influence in the choice of a new ruler, and he never resumed his attack. The Mongols were at last satiated.

Thirteenth-century Mongol attack on a town in Silesia, one of the Mongols' furthest penetrations of the West, from a miniature of 1353. One Mongol carries the head of a captured enemy on a pole to terrorize the defenders.

They had every right to be, for they had created one of the largest empires the world has ever known.

The Mongols at first were entirely destructive. They used terror as a means of conquest, wrecking cities and executing entire populations in cold blood in order to convince their neighbors of the dangers of resistance. But once they had established their empire they were willing to profit from the knowledge and skills of their subjects. In China and Persia, where they came in contact with relatively advanced civilizations, they soon became assimilated, and carried on the old artistic and literary traditions. In Russia, where they had less to learn, they held themselves apart and retained more of their original characteristics. They occupied only the steppes north of the Caspian and the Sea of Azov, a region in which there never had been very many Slavs. The great majority of Russians were allowed to live under their own princes and had little direct contact with the Mongols. So long as the princes paid tribute and sought confirmation of their authority from the khan, they could have whatever laws and religion they pleased.

Russia Loses Contact with the West

Nevertheless, the period of Mongol domination was a difficult one for Russia. Contacts with the West were greatly reduced, for both in commerce and in diplomacy the Russians had to deal primarily with the Mongols. The Russians were also blocked off from the West by the growing power of Poland and Lithuania.

The Mongol Empire and Its Successor States 13th century

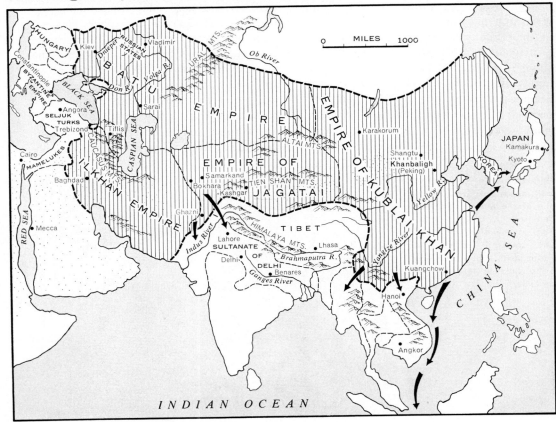

Poland had received its religion and much of its civilization from the West; down to 1200 it had often been a vassal state dependent on the German Empire. The Greek Church had had little influence on the Poles; they were converted to Christianity by Roman Catholic missionaries at the end of the tenth century and became zealous supporters of the Latin Church. Often weak and divided, the Poles gradually began to build a stronger state in the fourteenth century, as the German Empire fell apart. Their trade was largely with the West, their official language, for government as well as for religious affairs, was Latin, and they were rather inclined to look down on the Russians as a backward people. They disliked the Greek Orthodox Church of Russia and they had little respect for Russian political or military capabilities.

The Lithuanians were a very ancient people, of the Indo-European language group, who had struggled for centuries to maintain their independence in their original home on the south Baltic coast. Both Russians and Germans had tried to convert them, but the bulk of the population remained pagan until well into the fourteenth century. Just as the Poles profited from German weakness, so the Lithuanians gained by the collapse of Kievan Russia. They expanded south and east, acquiring some of the most fertile Russian lands in the process.

In 1386 the Poles and the Lithuanians united. The Poles accepted the Lithuanian grand duke as their king; in return the Lithuanians were supposed to become Latin Christians. Not all of them did so, especially in the eastern part of the realm where the Greek Church had been strong. Nevertheless, Poland-Lithuania was definitely oriented to the West, and it was usually hostile to the Russians. Down to the sixteenth century, Poland-Lithuania was larger and stronger than all the Russian principalities put together. It intervened again and again in Russian politics, and it acquired so much Russian land that Moscow, at times, was almost a frontier city. Russia was cut off from the Baltic and had few dealings with any western state.

Russia's loss of contact with the West was at first compensated for by increased contacts with the East. As long as the Mongols remained relatively united, the long land route across the Eurasian plain to China was heavily traveled—more heavily than it was to be again until the nineteenth century. But the Mongol state was too large to remain united, and the subordinate khans who governed outlying regions gradually became independent of the Great Khan, who had his headquarters in Mongolia. Thus the Russians had little to do with the relatively civilized Mongols of China and Persia. They dealt primarily with the so-called Golden Horde, the Mongols of the lower Volga region, who were the least advanced of all the Mongol groups.

Thrown back on themselves, the Russians took refuge in their religion. Their faith marked them off from the Mongols, but it separated them almost as sharply from the West. They became fiercely orthodox and even less willing than the Greeks to compromise with the Roman Church. This stubbornness, added to their fear of the Catholic Poles, made them suspicious of westerners and western influences which might change their way of life and endanger their faith.

The Rise of the Autocratic Russian State

Isolation and poverty, constant wars with Poles, Mongols, and Turks, were not ideal conditions for the growth of Russian society. Opportunities diminished for all classes, especially for the peasants. The most the peasants could hope for was to keep their freedom and a little piece of land, and often they found even these modest desires thwarted. Almost the only productive group in the country, the peasants had to support the Mongols, the princes, the nobles, and the Church. The easiest way for their overlords to make sure that they would meet all these obligations was to bind them to the soil; thus serfdom developed in Russia at the very time it was declining in the West. In order to escape serfdom, some peasants moved off into the desolate forest regions of the northeast, but even there the princes often caught up with them and assigned them as serfs to monasteries and nobles.

The government of the princes became increasingly arbitrary, though its arbitrariness was always tempered by administrative inefficiency. Economic pressure almost forced the princes into absolutism; their states were small and the burdens of Mongol tribute and war expenses were great. It is also true that the princes had inherited a tradition of autocracy from By-

The Church of the Savior at Novgorod, 12th century. This is an early example of what became a typical style of ecclesiastical architecture in Russia.

zantium, and that Mongol pressures encouraged this tendency. A prince who could not collect his tribute was sure to be in trouble; it did him no good to explain that he could not raise the money without violating the rights of his nobles and peasants. By the end of the fifteenth century there was almost no legal check on the power of Russian rulers.

During the fourteenth century the principality of Moscow became the strongest state in Russia. Its rise was due partly to chance; for several generations only one heir to the principality survived and thus it was not weakened by constant divisions. Moreover, the metropolitan of Russia moved his seat from Kiev to Moscow, thus bestowing on the Muscovite princes the support of the highest religious authority in the country. Many of the Muscovite princes were men of superior ability, both in diplomacy and in war. They managed to keep on relatively good terms with the Mongols and were given the title of grand prince, which meant that they were the chief tribute-collectors for the entire country. This position gave them an excuse to intervene in the incessant quarrels of other principalities and an opportunity to annex surrounding territory. As the Mongols weakened, the Grand Princes of Moscow became bolder and began to reduce the amount of tribute they were willing to pay to the Mongols; one of them actually defeated a Mongol army in 1378. Their assertion of independence was premature, however, for the Mongols still had a strong enough army to defeat the Grand Prince and threaten Moscow a few years later. Mongol suzerainty was re-established and continued into the fifteenth century. Nevertheless, the Grand Prince had established himself as leader of the Russians, and his victory over the Mongols was better remembered than his subsequent submission.

428

Early in the fifteenth century Moscow was temporarily weakened by a war among members of the ruling family. In the end, however, the war strengthened the principality, for the legitimate heir won the final victory and established the principle that Moscow was not to be divided as other Russian states had been. From this point on, the growth of the Muscovite state was phenomenal. It quickly absorbed neighboring principalities and, under Ivan the Great (Ivan III, 1462–1505), annexed the Republic of Novgorod, which held all northern Russia to the White Sea and the Arctic. Ivan also rejected, once and for all, Mongol suzerainty, and the Russians soon began to annex Mongol lands along the lower Volga. By the end of the

The Growth of the Grand Principality of Moscow   1300-1584

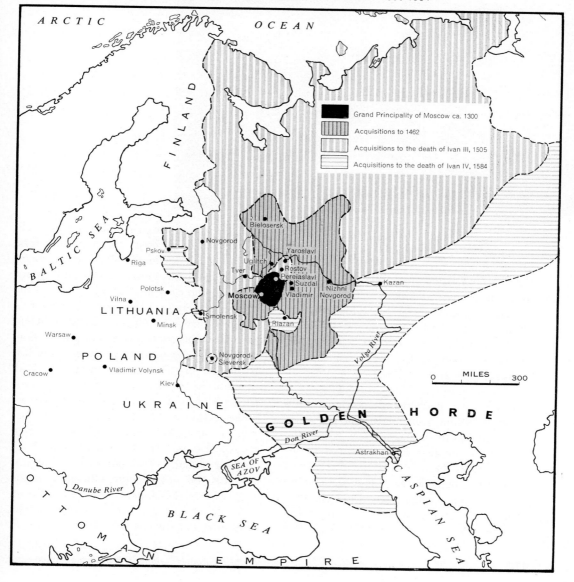

The Cathedral of St. Basil in Red Square, Moscow, built by Ivan the Dread in 1554–60. Notice how much more elaborate this is than the Novgorod church of the 12th century (p. 428).

sixteenth century the Muscovite state had expanded into a Russian Empire, with territories stretching from the White Sea to the Caspian and from the Lithuanian frontier well into western Siberia. The original principality of Moscow had covered only about five hundred square miles; the Russian Empire of the sixteenth century was the largest state in Europe.

Absolutism grew in almost exact proportion to the growth of the Muscovite state. The peasants had lost their rights long before; serfdom grew in Russia just as it was declining in the West. Now it was the turn of the nobles. They were not as independent as the nobles of the West; most of them had become servants of the princes and held their estates only so long as they performed various services for the ruler. Soon their very life and property depended on the whim of the prince. By the sixteenth century the greatest men in the land could be put to death on the mere suspicion of disloyalty, and bishops and metropolitans who contradicted the wishes of the sovereign were sent into exile. The old title of grand prince no longer seemed sufficient to express this concentration of power. Ivan the Great, who married a niece of the last Byzantine emperor, soon began to think of himself as successor to the Caesars. Moscow was to be the "Third Rome" which would endure forever, and Ivan began to call himself Autocrat and Sovereign of All Russia. He also occasionally used the title of tsar (a Russian form of *caesar*), but this did not become official until the reign of Ivan the Dread (Ivan IV, 1533–84). Ivan the Dread was a great conqueror; he was also one of the bloodiest tyrants in history. He massacred nobles and townsmen with little reason and killed his own son in a fit of rage.

In spite of its size and the authority of its ruler, sixteenth-century Muscovy was not yet a very powerful state. Still cut off from the main trade routes, its only outlet to the ocean was in the far north, on the White Sea. It was thinly settled; probably there were more people in France than in all the territories of the tsar. It was poor; it had almost no industry, and agriculture was backward. It was still militarily weak, open to attack by Poles on the west and Turks and Tatars in the southeast. The bulk of the peasants were still farming the poor soils of the north by primitive methods, and there were few settlers in the rich black-earth districts of the south. It was far behind its neighbors in all intellectual activities, in science and technology as well as in scholarship and literature. Only after 1600 did the Russians begin to overcome these handicaps.

Western Europe and the Mongols

The coming of the Mongols had changed the history of Russia. It might have changed the history of all Europe if western Europeans had been better informed and more alert in seizing the opportunities offered by the establishment of the Mongol Empire. For several decades the most dangerous opponents of the Mongols were Mamelukes and Turks, and the Mongols repeatedly suggested to Christian rulers that they form an alliance against the common Moslem enemy. None of these suggestions was ever followed up very seriously, although Louis IX of France did send an embassy to the Great Khan at the time of his crusade against Egypt. Perhaps an alliance was impossible; the arrogant Mongols were inclined to treat western rulers as tributary kings, and the westerners failed to realize the full extent of Mongol power. Nevertheless, a Mongol alliance probably could have saved the fragments of the Kingdom of Jerusalem and might have checked the rising power of the Turks.

Europe also missed the opportunity to convert the Mongols to Christianity. The Mongols were quite open-minded about religion; they were not greatly attached to their own primitive beliefs, and they were eager to learn something of other faiths. At times they seemed attracted by Christianity. None of the Chinese creeds were suitable for a warrior people, and Islam was the religion of their most dangerous enemies. The first Mongol viceroy of Persia had a Christian wife and favored her coreligionists, and the Mongol khan of China, Kublai, asked the pope several times to send him missionaries. Travel across the Mongol Empire was relatively easy and safe all through the thirteenth century, and a determined missionary effort might have resulted in the conversion of many Mongols. Unfortunately, the thirteenth-century popes were occupied with matters nearer at hand, such as their feud with the Hohenstaufen and their efforts to preserve the

Kublai Khan (1216–94), the descendant of Genghis Khan who ruled China at the time of Marco Polo's visit.

The Polos en route to China, from the *Catalan Atlas* of 1374. Cities through which they passed are represented by symbols below.

crusading states. They sent a few envoys, but no solid corps of permanent missionaries. The popes of the early fourteenth century made a greater effort, but by that time it was too late. The western Mongols had already been converted to Islam, one more example of the decided advantage which the simpler Moslem faith enjoyed in missionary competition. The Mongols of China were becoming submerged in the sea of Chinese culture and were soon to lose their power. The few missionaries who were sent from the West made thousands of converts, and a Catholic archbishop sat in Peking for a few years. But the whole effort was swept away when the Mongols were overthrown in 1368 and the strongly antiforeign Ming dynasty came to power.

European laymen took greater advantage of the opening of the overland route to China. We know that there were a number of European artisans at the court of the Great Khan, and that some Italian merchants made the long trip to the Far East. The most famous of these travelers was Marco Polo, who went to China in 1275 and spent many years in the country, part of the time as an official of the Mongol government. Marco wrote a long and fairly accurate account of his travels after he returned to Italy, and his description of the wealth and splendor of the Far East did much to encourage the great explorations of the fifteenth century. But Marco had less influence on the people of his own time. He was accused of wild exaggeration and nicknamed "Marco Millions"; few other merchants followed in his footsteps. Here was another lost opportunity. At the end of the thirteenth century the European economy was grinding toward stagnation; it desperately needed the stimulus of new markets. But fourteenth-century Europe lacked the capital, the energy, and the technical skill needed to open direct trade with the Far East. It was not until the late fifteenth century that western merchants could again dream of reaching China.

The Advance of the Turks

Meanwhile, the immediate problem for much of Europe was not the Mongols but the Turks. As we have seen, the Mongol advance left the Turks of Asia Minor relatively unharmed, and the old barrier of the Byzantine Empire had been fragmented by the Fourth Crusade. The Serbs and Bulgars dominated the back country, western feudal lords ruled most of Greece, and Venice held the islands. The Byzantine Empire, as revived in 1261, possessed only Constantinople and a narrow strip of land on each side of the Straits. The new Turkish dynasty of the Ottomans, which was founded by Osman I in Asia Minor in 1299, rapidly exploited the weakness of the Christians. The Ottomans were just as good warriors as their predecessors, the Seljuks, and showed far more ability in building a permanent state with a strong administrative system. They conquered most of western Asia Minor in the first third of the fourteenth century and in the 1350's they began to make permanent settlements on the European side of the Straits. The Christians offered no concerted resistance, for the Serbs and Bulgars, the Greeks of Byzantium, and the French and Italian rulers of Greece and the islands hated each other at least as much as they did the Turks. In fact, the Turks often were able to ally themselves with one Christian group against the others. By 1365 they had established their capital in Adrianople, only a few miles from Constantinople, and in 1389 they broke the power of the Serbs, who had the strongest state in the Balkans, at the battle of Kossovo. This victory brought the Turks to the borders of Hungary, and the West at last began to take alarm. The pope proclaimed a crusade, and a large army— mostly German and Hungarian with some French knights—advanced against the Turks. But bad generalship and poor discipline ruined whatever chance of success it had, and the crusaders were thoroughly defeated at the battle of Nicopolis in 1396.

The victory of the Turks might have ended all Christian power in the Balkans, but before it could be fully exploited the Turkish state was almost ruined by an attack from the east. Timur the Lame (Tamerlane), who claimed to be a descendant of Genghis Khan, had created a nomad army worthy of his supposed ancestor. The Mongols were once more on the march, and this time the Ottoman Turks were one of their chief enemies. The two armies met at Ankara in 1402 and Timur won a complete victory. The Mongols captured the Turkish sultan and occupied most of his lands in Asia Minor.

A Persian portrait of the great conqueror, Tamerlane (1336?–1405).

Timur died soon after his victory, and his successors made little effort to hold the remote regions he had taken from the Turks. Nevertheless, the defeat at Ankara nearly shattered the Turkish state. The sons of the captured sultan fought among themselves, while local leaders tried to set up independent emirates. This was the real test of the Ottoman political system, and the fact that in the end the state could be pulled together again showed that the early sultans had done their work well. They had created a corps of disciplined and capable administrators, and it was with their assistance that one of the Ottoman princes was able to re-establish himself as sole ruler. It took several decades to regain the lost territories and to repair the damage done by the Mongols, but by the 1440's the Turks were once more advancing in the Balkans. Their chief opponents this time were the Hungarians, commanded by John Hunyadi. Though Hunyadi was a first-rate general, he was defeated by the Turks in two major battles.

The End of the Byzantine Empire

Now the road lay open to Constantinople. The last Byzantine emperor, Constantine XI, made a desperate appeal to the West for aid. Over the strong opposition of his subjects, he agreed to reunite the Greek and Latin Churches and to accept papal supremacy. But the union was never effective and the popes of the fifteenth century lacked the prestige needed to rouse the West. Constantine received no real help and was left to fight the final battles alone. In 1453 the Turks made an all-out attack on the imperial city. The emperor was killed defending a breach in the walls and the Turks poured into Constantinople. This was the end of the Byzantine Empire, and of the emperors who claimed to be heirs of Caesar and Augustus. For many years there had been nothing Roman about them except their titles, but they were not unworthy of those titles in their last struggle.

Europe was shocked by the fall of an empire which had endured for fifteen hundred years, but, in spite of exhortations by the pope, it made no concerted effort to repel the Turks. The Hungarians, as before, carried the chief burden of defense, and the Hungarians could not do the job alone. They fought valiantly but were pushed back little by little until the Turkish tide of conquest reached its height at the siege of Vienna in 1529.

As the Turkish advance slowed down in Europe, it was speeding up in Asia and Africa. During the sixteenth century Syria, Mesopotamia, and Arabia were added to the Turkish Empire in Asia, and Egypt, Tunisia, and Algeria in North Africa. With this Turkish conquest of the southern and eastern coasts of the Mediterranean, Moslem naval power began to revive. The Turks never closed the Mediterranean to Christian shipping, but they and the semi-piratical fleets of their subjects did interfere seriously with commerce from time to time. It was not until the nineteenth century that the Mediterranean became as safe for western merchants as it had been in the thirteenth century.

The Decline of Moslem Civilization

The rise of the Turks coincided with a decline in the level of Moslem civilization, a decline which was especially noticeable in the fields of science and philosophy. Both the Turks and the Mongols have often been blamed for this decline, but neither people seems to have been entirely responsible. It is true that both Turks and Mongols were originally rough warriors from the steppes with little interest in intellectual matters, but both of them absorbed some aspects of Moslem civilization with great rapidity. Art and literature flourished un-

14 / Western Europe's Neighbors During the Middle Ages

der the Mongol rulers of Persia, while the Turks did some remarkable work in architecture and developed a highly literate corps of administrators. Moreover, one of the most eloquent laments over the decline of Moslem learning came from the historian ibn-Khaldun (1332–1406), who spent most of his life in North Africa, a region which was never touched by the Mongols and which fell under Turkish control only in the sixteenth century. There must have been more deep-seated causes, prevalent throughout the Moslem world, for the decline of Moslem civilization.

Ibn-Khaldun, probably the greatest of all Moslem historians, tried to work out a historical theory to explain the decline. His basic idea was that there had always been antagonism between the educated, open-minded, prosperous city-dwellers and the ignorant, narrow-minded, poverty-stricken inhabitants of the desert and the steppes. When the city people became soft and decadent, as they had in his time, power passed to the crude but warlike tribes of the open country. This political shift in turn caused a shift in the climate of opinion. Rigid orthodoxy was favored and science and philosophy were looked on with contempt and suspicion.

There is some truth in ibn-Khaldun's explanation. The dominant dynasties of the Moslem world in the fourteenth century were all nomad in origin, and some of them did emphasize strict Moslem orthodoxy. But this is only part of the story. Earlier nomadic conquerors, beginning with the Arabs themselves, had absorbed the entire intellectual heritage of the ancient world without difficulty, and fourteenth-century orthodoxy did not prevent the rise of mysticism in the Mohammedan world. Some leaders of the mystical movement, who had large followings, advanced ideas that went far beyond the early teachings of Islam, so that we cannot

say that a sort of Mohammedan fundamentalism blocked all forms of speculation. It seems rather that Mohammedan science and philosophy had reached a dead end, and that the educated classes had become disinterested in them.

Perhaps Moslem learning had reached its peak too early and too rapidly. Few new ideas entered the world of Islam after the tenth century, and all the changes on the old themes had been rung by the thirteenth century. With nothing new to be done, there was naturally a loss of interest in academic subjects. In comparison, western scholarship, which was far inferior to that of the Moslem world in the tenth

❋❋❋❋❋❋❋❋❋❋❋❋❋❋❋❋❋❋❋❋❋❋❋❋❋❋❋❋❋❋❋

Ibn Khaldun on Dynastic Decay

The term of life of a dynasty does not normally exceed three generations. For in the first generation are still preserved the characteristic features of rough, uncivilized rural life, such as hard conditions of life, courage, ferocity and partnership in authority. Therefore the strength of the common ideals is maintained and men submit to their domination. In the second generation their condition has changed under the influence of possession of political power from rural to city life, from a hard struggle to ease and abundance, from partnership in authority to autocracy, wherefore the strength of common ideals is partly broken. The third generation has forgotten the time of rural life as if it had never existed, unlike the second generation which lives on the memory of the first. . . . Ease reaches its peak under them [the third generation] because they become used to a pleasant and abundant life. Common ideals collapse completely and they forget about defence, attack and pursuit of the enemy.

From Ibn Khaldun as quoted in E. I. J. Rosenthal, *Political Thought in Medieval Islam* (Cambridge, Eng.: Cambridge U. Press, 1958), p. 88.

❋❋❋❋❋❋❋❋❋❋❋❋❋❋❋❋❋❋❋❋❋❋❋❋❋❋❋❋❋❋❋

century, received a fresh stimulus every time it was about to reach a dead end. There were the translations from the Arabic in the twelfth century, the revival of Greek studies in the fifteenth, and the great scientific discoveries of the early modern period. Moreover, theology, philosophy, and science were closely associated in Christian thought until fairly recent times, and activity in one of these fields necessarily involved activity in the others. Christian theology was so complicated and so controversial that it could never be entirely neglected. The fourteenth century was not a brilliant period in western thought, but the voluminous writings on theology were accompanied by some activity in philosophy and science. The theology of Islam, on the other hand, was much less complicated. Some Moslems took it for granted; others simply memorized the Koran, paying no attention to philosophy. Thus religious education in Moslem countries did not necessarily require corresponding activity in philosophy or science. Finally, as we have seen, western scholars were not quite so bound to authoritative, scholarly interpretations; more innovation was possible in fourteenth-century Paris than in fourteenth-century Cairo.

Whatever the value of these explanations, one basic fact is clear: For the first time in history, western Europe was to take the lead in certain types of scholarly investigation. Byzantine scholarship, never very original, was blighted by the Turkish conquest. Moslem scholarship was rapidly decaying in the fourteenth and fifteenth centuries. Of all the peoples who had inherited the great Greek tradition of philosophical and scientific inquiry, only the scholars of western Europe were still active. And their activity was to give the West an incalculable advantage in the next four centuries.

Suggestions for Further Reading

1. Byzantium, 750–1453

S. Runciman, *Byzantine Civilization* * (1933), gives a good general picture of Byzantine institutions and culture and is the best introduction. The most thorough and scholarly study is G. Ostrogorsky, *History of the Byzantine State* (trans. J. Hussey, 1956). The older work of A. A. Vasiliev, *History of the Byzantine Empire,* 2 vols. (1928), is more readable than Ostrogorsky but not as thorough nor as fresh in historical interpretation. There is valuable material on the commercial activities of the Italian city-states within the Byzantine Empire in E. H. Byrne, *Genoese Shipping in the Twelfth and Thirteenth Centuries* (1930), and in C. Diehl, *Une République Patricienne: Venise* (1916). G. Every, *The Byzantine Patriarchate* (1947), compares the liturgical and doctrinal differences between the Eastern and Western Churches; and J. M. Hussey, *Church and Learning in the Byzantine Empire* (1937), is useful for understanding Byzantine intellectual activity. See also the titles by Baynes, Diehl, Grabar, and Talbot-Rice mentioned after Chapter 8, in Section 1.

2. The Caliphate, 750–1258

B. Lewis, *The Arabs in History* (1956), a broad, quick survey, is a good starting point for study. B. Spuler, *The Muslim World,* Vol. I (trans. F. R. C. Bagley, 1960),

* Available in paperback edition.

is an authorative survey of the entire period and a useful handbook. The old account of T. W. Arnold, *The Caliphate* (1934), is still valuable for the theory and development of the Caliphate. There is considerable material in P. K. Hitti, *A History of the Arabs* (1956), the standard treatment of the subject, invaluable for the facts of the period but quite controversial in historical interpretation. For the Caliphate as an institution, see E. Tyan, *Le Califut* (1954), and E. I. J. Rosenthal, *Political Thought in Medieval Islam* (1958).

3. The Crusades

There are several accounts of the later crusades which give us real insight into the spirit and motivation of the crusaders. Both Geoffrey de Villhardouin, *The Conquest of Constantinople* * (Everyman's Library), and Robert of Clari, *The Conquest of Constantinople* (trans. E. H. McNeal, 1936), are fascinating eyewitness accounts of the Fourth Crusade. Philippe of Novara, *The Wars of Frederick II Against the Ibelins* (trans. J. L. La Monte, 1936), contributes a great deal to our knowledge of Frederick II and his crusades. The counselor Joinville's *Life of St. Louis* * (Everyman's Library) has exciting material on St. Louis' expeditions to Egypt and Tunis on the Sixth and Seventh Crusades.

E. Barker, *The Crusades* (1923), is old but still valuable. The best recent study is the beautifully written and highly urbane account by S. Runciman, *A History of the Crusades,* 3 vols. (1951–54). Runciman includes a thorough bibliography. There is good material on the crusades in the books by Setton, Hitti, and La Monte listed after Chapter 10, in Section 4.

4. The Mongols in the Arab World and Russia

B. Spuler, *The Muslim World,* Vol. II: *The Mongol Period* (trans. F. R. C. Bagley, 1960), is excellent. G. Le Strange, *The Lands of the Eastern Caliphate* (1905), a study of the historical geography of the Near East and central Asia in the Middle Ages, is an old treatment but very good reading. Juvaynī 'Alā' al-Din 'utā Malik, *The History of the World Conqueror* (trans. J. A. Bayle, 1952), is an important study, while V. V. Barthold, *Four Studies on the History of Central Asia* (1955), contains the authoritative history of central Asia and the Mongols. Probably the best treatment of the Mongol rule of Russia is G. Vernadsky, *The Monguls and Russia* (1953), a scholarly and readable work by a leading authority on Russian history.

5. Russia, 1100–1600

There are several very good studies of this period of Russian history. M. T. Florinsky, *Russia: A History and Interpretation,* Vol. I (1955), has valuable material on this formative period of the Russian state. The old work of V. O. Kluchevsky, *A History of Russia,* 2 vols. (1912), is very interesting reading and still important. Undoubtedly the best treatment of Russia from 1100 to 1600 is G. Vernadsky, *Russia at the Dawn of the Modern Age* (1959). Vernadsky includes excellent maps and genealogical tables and up-to-date bibliographic material. *A History of the U. S. S. R.* (edited A. M. Pankratova, 1947), is a modern Marxist interpretation of the evolution of the Russian state.

6. The Decline of Arabic Learning

Most of the titles mentioned in Section 2 above have information on Arabic learning. R. Landau, *Islam and the Arabs* (1958), devotes considerable attention to Moslem culture. T. Arnold and A. Guillaume, *The Legacy of Islam* (1947), is a good summary which traces those elements in European culture which have roots in the Islamic world.

* Available in paperback edition.

15

India, China, and Japan During the European Middle Ages

The fifth-century invasions of the Huns and other tribes were a disaster from which northern India never fully recovered. Its political system was shattered, and not until the establishment of the Moslem sultanate of Delhi in 1206 was a single state able to dominate northern Indian again. The Ganges Valley was divided into small warring kingdoms which were briefly united by the rajah Harsha (606–47). Northern India was fairly prosperous during his reign, and both scholarship and literature flourished. But Harsha failed in his attempt to conquer central India, and his success in the Ganges Valley must have been due more to his personal qualities than to his administrative institutions, for his kingdom collapsed after his death. During the next two and a half centuries northern India was dominated by the Rajputs, many of whom were descendants of warriors from central Asia who had entered India with the Huns or during the chaotic years following the Hunnic invasion. The Rajputs intermarried with Hindus and adopted Hindu religious beliefs and social practices with great enthusiasm. After a time they began to claim that they were members of the Hindu warrior caste—next to the Brahmans the highest group in Hindu society—

and therefore the rightful lords of the common people.

Indian Kingdoms

The Rajputs created a way of life not unlike that of the nobles of western Europe in the thirteenth and fourteenth century. They loved combat and developed a chivalric code which valued fair fighting and mercy to the weak and helpless. They had court poets who recited epics commemorating past heroes, and they showed more respect to women than was customary in other parts of India. The Rajput aristocracy led a brilliant and exciting life, but it showed little political capacity. It used up its qualities of courage, honor, and loyalty in endless internecine wars and left northern India so weak that it was easily overrun by Mohammedan invaders after the tenth century.

Farther south, dynasties were established which had a somewhat longer life. South-central India, the Deccan, was united for two centuries under the

Siva, god of destruction and creation, as Lord of the Dance. The equilibrium of the dancer expresses the balance between creation and destruction in the universe. Indian, 12th or 13th century.

Chalukya kings (*ca.* 550–*ca.* 750), who were strong enough to repel Harsha and other invaders from the north. Even after the fall of the Chalukyas, the Deccan was less fragmented than the northern kingdoms. It broke up into a few fairly large states, which preserved their independence until the fourteenth century. In the extreme south were the Tamils, remnants of the original Dravidian inhabitants of India (see p. 171). They too created large kingdoms, first Chola, which lasted from the

tenth to the fourteenth century, and then Vijayanagar, which fell to the Moslems only in 1565. At its height Vijayanagar held the whole southern third of the peninsula, carried on an active foreign commerce, and was fabulously wealthy.

The Spread of Indian Culture

The most important events of these centuries were not the rise and fall of dynasties, but the consolidation of Hindu culture and the spread of Indian influence overseas. As we have seen (p. 179), Buddhism was declining in India during the Gupta period, and it lost even more ground during the invasions and wars which followed the downfall of the Gupta dynasty. By the end of the tenth century Buddhism was almost extinct in India and the entire population followed some form of the old Hindu beliefs. There were many variants of this religion; each part of the country had its own special rituals and favorite gods. But each sect was usually tolerant of the others, since all divinities were considered manifestations of the same underlying spiritual forces. And the basic elements of the Hindu way of life—the power of the Brahmin priesthood, the caste system, and the intellectual and religious tradition—permeated the whole peninsula.

The real strength of Hindu civilization was in its social rather than its political structure. The great majority of the people lived in small agricultural villages which were administered by a council of elders and were advised—often dominated—by a Brahmin priest. These villages showed little interest in the changes of dynasties and the rise and fall of kingdoms; they paid tribute to the ruler of the moment and preserved their traditional way of life through all the storms of war and rebellion. Under the caste system every man had his place in society and his occupation clearly marked out, and it took more than a change of rulers to upset these well-established patterns. At a higher level the Brahmins, who served as intellectual and religious leaders, preserved the continuity of tradition. Some kings were more influenced by the Brahmins than others, but between the collapse of Buddhism and the Mohammedan conquest of northern India there was no rival religious or intellectual leadership. In the long run the ideas of the Brahmins influenced all governments and all classes and gave a basic unity to Indian life in spite of great local diversity.

During the centuries of the European Middle Ages the Indians were barred from the West by the growing power of Islam, but they found that the backward and unorganized peoples of Southeast Asia were easily influenced by their civilization. It is

✦✦✦✦✦✦✦✦✦✦✦✦✦✦✦✦✦✦✦✦✦✦✦✦✦✦✦✦✦✦✦✦✦

The Rajput Code

A widow speaks to the page who witnessed her husband's death:

"Boy, tell me, ere I go, how bore himself my lord?"

"As a reaper of the harvest of battle. I followed his steps as a humble gleaner of his sword. On the bed of honor he spread a carpet of the slain, whereon, a barbarian his pillow, he sleeps ringed by his foes."

"Yet once again, boy, tell me how my lord bore himself?"

"Oh mother, who can tell his deeds? He left no foe to dread or to admire him."

She smiled farewell to the boy, and adding, "My lord will chide my delay," sprang into the flames.

As quoted in H. G. Rawlinson, *India: A Short Cultural History* (New York: Appleton-Century, 1938), p. 202.

✦✦✦✦✦✦✦✦✦✦✦✦✦✦✦✦✦✦✦✦✦✦✦✦✦✦✦✦✦✦✦✦

One of the earliest Indian miniatures, painted on a palm-leaf manuscript of a Buddhist text. Eastern India, late 11th or early 12th century.

still not clear whether Indian emigrants conquered neighboring lands or whether they secured a dominant position by peaceful penetration. Certainly many of the ruling families of the kingdoms to the east of India bore Hindu names, and the art and literature of these countries show strong Indian influence. Great Buddhist and Hindu shrines were built, of which the most imposing was the enormous temple of Angkor Wat in Indochina. With its five great towers and its long walls covered with scenes from Hindu epics, Angkor Wat is one of the largest religious centers ever created by man. The complex of buildings covered more ground than most medieval European cities, and the individual structures were larger and more richly ornamented than most cathedrals.

Indian influence was strongest and most lasting in Burma, western Siam, and the Malay Peninsula. In Indochina it had to compete with Chinese influence from the north. Tongking and part of Annam (North Vietnam) were always closely connected with China, while South Vietnam, Cambodia, and Laos were more like India —a fact which may help to explain the present political situation in this region. Indonesia received Buddhism and much of its culture from India, and the Sailendra dynasty, which ruled the archipelago from the eighth to the eleventh century, built

some of the most magnificent Buddhist shrines the world has ever seen. The Sailendra kings were followed by Hindu rulers, who held the islands until the Moslem conquest of the sixteenth century. Java, the most populous of the islands, became thoroughly Mohammedanized at this time, but the smaller island of Bali to the east preserved a basically Hindu culture.

The Political Weakness of India

During this eastern expansion India was at its best—full of energy, imagination, and understanding in dealing with strange peoples. But by the end of the tenth century the period of greatest expansion was over and the qualities which had made it possible seem largely to have vanished. This decline was due partly to the Indians' failure to create permanent and stable governments. Every society needs constant rebuilding if it is not to stagnate or disintegrate, and it is very difficult to rebuild without effective political institutions. Individual Indian rulers often had excellent ideas, but their plans died with them and India failed to adapt itself to new conditions. In addition, the prevailing Hindu way of life became more and more conservative, and leaders of Hindu thought became complacent and self-satisfied. They had little to do with the Moslems on the west, and their contacts with China de-

A view of Ankor Wat showing the long wall surrounding the inner temples.

Detail from Ankor Wat. The battle of gods and demons as recounted in the Mahabharata.

creased; the people they knew best were those of Southeast Asia, and these people they considered inferior. As a result, there was a tendency for Indian civilization to freeze in a rigid pattern and to fall back on its past accomplishments rather than to advance to new ground. The caste system became both more complicated and more unchangeable; little new work was done in either science or philosophy. Even the art of war fell into a set pattern in which armies were maneuvered according to the teachings of ancient writers rather than according to the needs of a campaign.

The Moslem Conquest

All these weaknesses became critical when Mohammedan pressure on the northwest frontier increased. In the eighth century, during the first wars of expansion, the Mohammedans had taken over the southern Indus Valley, but this annexation neither influenced Indian culture nor caused much ill-will between the Islamic and Hindu religious communities. The situation changed sharply, as it did in so many other regions, with the coming of the Turks in the tenth century. The Turks renewed the conquering tradition of Islam and showed themselves far less tolerant of alien religions than the Arabs. It is true that Hinduism, with its images, its hundreds of gods, and its elaborate ceremonies, contradicted everything for which Mohammed had stood, and that it was far easier for Moslems to be tolerant of Christianity, with which they had some common traditions, than of Hinduism, which was completely alien to them. Nevertheless, the Arab rulers of the lower Indus Valley had not been implacably hostile to the Hindus; it was the Turks who transformed the two religious communities into bitter and persistent enemies.

The Turks, and related peoples, first established themselves in Afghanistan in the tenth century and immediately began to nibble away at the holdings of the Rajput princes in northwest India. This process was completed by Mahmud of Ghazni, who held most of the northwest by 1022 and pushed his daring raids deep into Hindu territory. Intermittent raiding and fighting continued for a century and a half, until the next great Moslem conqueror appeared. This was Mohammed Ghori, who pushed east toward the Ganges Valley and defeated the allied Hindu kings of the north in a decisive battle in 1192. This victory opened the entire region north of the Deccan to the Moslems. Mohammed Ghori was assassinated in 1206, but in the same year his chief minister made himself sultan of Delhi. The Delhi sultanate rapidly became the dominant state in India. It controlled all of the north by 1236 and had taken over most of the Deccan by 1320. Only Vijayanagar in the extreme south remained an independent kingdom where the Hindu tradition could flourish without Moslem interference.

The Moslem Impact on India

The Delhi sultanate lasted nominally until 1526, but it lost most of its power after 1398. Even with its decline the Hindus found no relief, however, for the sultan's provincial governors set themselves up as independent kings and continued to dominate the native population. The Delhi sultanate failed to create stable political institutions and never established a fixed rule of succession. Consequently, most sultans acquired the throne by murdering their predecessor, and the art of government consisted largely in collecting taxes from the Hindu peasants. Many of the sultans and their agents were fanatical Moslems who delighted in killing Hindus or in forcing them to accept Islam at the point of a sword. This policy of forced

The Moslem Conquest of India 1192-1320

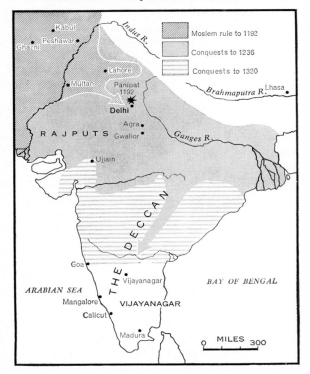

sian and Arabic literature and elements of Moslem architecture, such as the minaret and dome. The conquerors even developed a new language, Urdu,* based on Hindu rules of grammar but with a vocabulary which was largely Persian. This language is still spoken in West Pakistan and in parts of northwestern India. The Moslems also influenced Hindu social customs; the practice of keeping women in seclusion and discouraging them from appearing in public was due largely to the example of the Mohammedan ruling class.

The Delhi sultanate was almost annihi-

* Urdu, which means "camp language" or "army language," comes from the Turkish word for a camp of armed tribesmen which in English has become "horde."

❈❈❈❈❈❈❈❈❈❈❈❈❈❈❈❈❈❈❈❈❈❈❈❈❈❈

Moslem Persecution of the Hindus

The Hindu was to be so reduced as to be unable to keep a horse, wear fine clothes, or enjoy any of life's luxuries. No Hindu could hold up his head, and in their houses no sign of gold or silver or any superfluity was to be seen. These things, which nourish insubordination, were not to be found. . . . Ala-ud-din [sultan of Delhi, 1296–1316] was a king who had no acquaintance with learning and never associated with the learned. He considered that polity and government were one thing, and law another. "I am an unlettered man," he said, "but I have seen a great deal. Be assured that the Hindus will never become submissive and obedient until they are reduced to poverty. I have therefore given orders that just enough shall be left them of corn, milk, and curds from year to year, but that they must not accumulate hoards and property."

From the Moslem historian Barani, as quoted in H. G. Rawlinson, *India: A Short Cultural History* (New York: Appleton-Century, 1938), p. 228.

❈❈❈❈❈❈❈❈❈❈❈❈❈❈❈❈❈❈❈❈❈❈❈❈❈❈

conversion succeeded in making the northwest largely Moslem, and even in the Deccan some 10 to 15 per cent of the population was persuaded to adopt the faith of the conquerors. But it also created enduring hostility between Moslem and Hindu, hostility so great that when India gained its independence in 1947 the country had to be split into two states, Moslem Pakistan and Hindu India.

The Moslem conquerors—mostly Turks and Afghans—were the first invaders of India who did not merge fully with the Hindu population. But though they remained a separate community, they had some influence on Hindu civilization. Some of the most bloodthirsty sultans were also the patrons of scholars, writers, and artists. They introduced ideas from Per-

lated by an invasion by Tamerlane in 1398—the same Tamerlane who checked the advance of the Ottoman Turks in the West (see p. 433). Tamerlane, who wanted only booty from India, looted the northwest, sacked Delhi, and killed tens of thousands of noncombatants and prisoners. But he did not found a government in northern India, and the Delhi sultanate was eventually restored, though it held only a fraction of its former territory. Independent Moslem rulers controlled the rest of the country, except for some Rajput strongholds in the north and Vijayanagar in the extreme south. It was during this period that firearms and heavy artillery began to be used in India.

The Moguls

India finally gained some degree of unity and orderly government under the Mogul dynasty in the sixteenth century. The Moguls, who, like so many earlier conquerors, came from central Asia, had both Turkish and Mongol ancestry; the first strong Mogul ruler, Babur, claimed descent from both Genghis Khan and Tamerlane. He entered India in 1524 and defeated the sultan of Delhi in 1526, thus winning control of most of the north. Babur secured his position in 1527 by defeating a coalition of Rajput leaders who were trying to establish an independent Hindu state in the northwest.

Babur's son was unseated by a Mogul general, but the supremacy of the invaders remained unshaken. The usurper was an able administrator who established an effective government throughout the north. Eventually Babur's grandson, Akbar, regained the throne, and under him the Mogul Empire reached the height of its power. Akbar had completed the conquest of the north by 1576 and then turned to the Deccan, which he brought largely under control by 1600. A few more or less in-

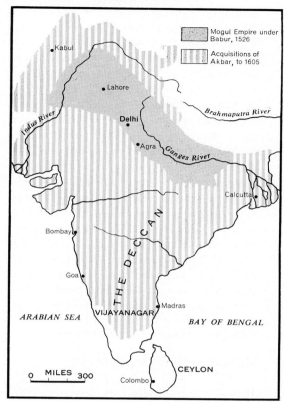

The Mogul Empire 1605

Legend:
- Mogul Empire under Babur, 1526
- Acquisitions of Akbar, to 1605

Kabul
Lahore
Delhi
Agra
Brahmaputra River
Ganges River
Indus River
Calcutta
Bombay
Goa
THE DECCAN
ARABIAN SEA
VIJAYANAGAR
Madras
BAY OF BENGAL
0 MILES 300
CEYLON
Colombo

dependent states survived in the south, but none of them had any importance. Vijayanagar had been destroyed by the Moslem kings of the Deccan shortly before Akbar's conquest, so that for all practical purposes Akbar was master of India.

Akbar

Akbar was a Moslem in religion and a Turko-Mongol in race, but he had far more regard for his Indian subjects than most earlier conquerors with this background. He set up an efficient administrative hierarchy and tried to keep his officials reasonably honest by paying them regular salaries and punishing them severely for accepting bribes. He was determined to see that justice was done and often acted as a judge himself. His more efficient and honest government made it possible to keep taxation at a moderate level. In fact, the assessment of the land tax under the Moguls was equitable enough to be used as the basis for later assessments under British rule.

Akbar realized that religious intolerance and racial quarrels were a threat to the permanence of his empire. He tried to conciliate the Rajputs, who were still resisting at the beginning of his reign, by honoring their bravery and marrying three Rajput princesses. He appointed Hindus to high government positions, though Moslems still held most of the important posts. Most important of all, he insisted on complete religious toleration. Scholars of all faiths were welcome at his court; he even extended hospitality to a Jesuit mission and allowed them to build a chapel. Toward the

****

Akbar's Religious Beliefs

O God, in every temple I see those who seek
    thee.
And in every tongue that is spoken Thou art
    praised.
Polytheism and Islam grope after Thee.
Each religion says, "Thou art One, without
    equal."
Be it mosque, men murmur holy prayers;
    or church,
The bells ring for the love of Thee.
Awhile I frequent the Christian cloister, anon
    the mosque,
But Thee only I seek from fane to fane.
Thine elect know naught of heresy or ortho-
    doxy, whereof
Neither stands behind the screen of Thy truth.

From a poem by Akbar's secretary, Abul Fazl, as quoted in H. G. Rawlinson, *India: A Short Cultural History* (New York: Appleton-Century, 1938), p. 310.

****

end of his life he became convinced that there was some merit in every religion and that claims to exclusive possession of the truth were unjustified. He tried to create a universal religion which would include all that was good in earlier faiths, and which would end religious controversy in India. But artificial universal religions, like artificial universal languages, have little appeal to most people. While Akbar lived he was able to win some support for his new faith, but on his death India fell back into its old religious disputes.

Akbar's court was a center of art and learning. He collected a large library and was eager to have his books illustrated by the best artists of the country. One of the most brilliant schools of manuscript illumination which has ever existed developed at his court. Akbar was also a great builder, and some of the finest Indian architecture comes from his period. Both manuscript illumination and architecture showed strong Persian influence, but the Hindu tradition continued and many works of art show an intermingling of the two styles.

The Collapse of the Mogul Empire

In spite of his great ability, Akbar did not succeed in ending the evils of misgovernment and religious controversy which had plagued India for so many centuries. Under his successors, who were less competent and less broad-minded than he, Islam was re-established as the official religion of the governing class, and Hindus were again persecuted. Civil wars among members of the ruling dynasty weakened the government, and provincial viceroys gradually became independent rulers. Now Hindu leaders began to organize resistance groups to throw off Mogul domination. India, as she had done so often in the past, was dissolving into a welter of conflicting states.

A seventeenth-century Mogul miniature showing Persian influence. Akbar, the man seated at the right, is visited by his son Jahangir.

This time, however, there was a new force to be reckoned with: the merchants and soldiers of western Europe. The first European settlements in India had been made by the Portuguese just before the founding of the Mogul Empire. The Portuguese never held more than a few seacoast towns, but they were followed by French and English merchants who were more ambitious and had more powerful governments to back them. The growing disunion of India gave these adventurers from overseas easy opportunities to establish themselves in key positions throughout the country. The battles which determined the fate of modern India were directed by French and English generals and were fought for the profit of their respective nations. The heirs of the Moguls were to be not the Hindu rajahs who struggled so hard to regain their independence, not the Mohammedan viceroys who tried to hold together fragments of the old empire, but the directors of the British East India Company.

China under the T'ang Dynasty

The old center of Chinese civilization, the valley of the Yellow River, fell to the Huns only about a century before they helped to destroy the Roman Empire in the West. For the next two and a half centuries, from about 317 to about 580, northern China was ruled by Huns or related nomadic peoples. There was little political stability; few dynasties lasted for as long as a century, and most of the time China was divided into several warring states.

Yet with all these political difficulties, Chinese civilization made a quicker recovery from the shock of the Hunnic conquest than did the civilization of the Roman Empire. The Chinese quickly assimilated the barbarians and showed themselves even more successful than the Indians in molding invaders to their own way of life. Southern China remained for the most part independent, and the fertile valley of the Yangtze was fully exploited, for the first time, by refugees from the north. These settlers in the Yangtze Valley preserved and developed all the essential elements of Chinese civilization and began to impress their ideas on the still barbarous peoples who lived even farther south. Most important of all, contact with all these strange peoples had a stimulating effect on the Chinese; they were more open to foreign influence at this time than they were to be again for centuries. It was during this period that Buddhism made its greatest gains in China. It was also during this period that Chinese Buddhists made frequent pilgrimages to India and other countries in Southeast Asia. They brought back a great deal of information about the history and geography of Asian lands, and some very useful mathematical and scientific lore from India. Thus instead of decaying, Chinese civilization spread beyond its original limits and was enriched by new ideas from abroad.

Nevertheless, these years of disunity and foreign invasion were hard for the masses, who suffered from war, famine, and exploitation by selfish rulers. There was a great burst of energy and optimism when the country was at last reunited under Chinese rulers. The Sui dynasty (580–618), which accomplished this feat, "ruled without benevolence," as one Chinese historian put it, but at least its harshness had some purpose other than exploitation. The Sui emperors built great granaries to help avert famine; even more important, they completed a canal system which united north and south and made it easier to move grain from surplus to deficit regions. Although the Chinese had been building canals before the Sui, and the work was continued under the next dynasty, the most important links seem to have been built under the Sui by forced labor. Each district had to supply thousands of men who were overworked, underfed, and neglected when they fell ill. Resentment grew, and a defeat by the Turks served as an excuse for open rebellion. The Sui dynasty was overthrown and replaced by the T'ang.

The T'ang period (618–906) was one of the most brilliant in Chinese history. The first emperor of the dynasty, an able general, drove the Turks and other nomads from the frontiers and eventually attacked the heart of Turkish power in central Asia. Most of the Turkish leaders acknowledged the suzerainty of the Chinese emperor and paid him tribute. This victory extended Chinese power into Turkestan and ended, for over a century, the threat of invasion from the northwest. Succeeding emperors made Korea a protectorate and, at the other extremity of the Empire, established their authority over some of the tribes of northern Indochina. Not until the time of the Manchus in the seventeenth century was China again to control such a vast territory.

Chinese Government and Society under the T'ang

Early T'ang government was efficient and, on the whole, benevolent. It revived the professional civil service, following precedents which had been established in the Han period (see p. 189). By recruiting civil servants through a system of competitive examinations, it again followed the precedent of the Han period, though the Han examinations had been neither as regular nor as uniform as those of the T'ang era. Under the T'ang emperors young men were examined at regular intervals on a fixed body of materials, mainly the classics of Chinese literature and philosophy. There were various levels of difficulty, ranging from the preliminary examination, which admitted a man to an official career, to the highest examination, which qualified him for the top posts in the imperial court. Theoretically the examinations were open to all subjects, regardless of birth and wealth. In practice, few men could take them unless they belonged to the family of an official or a landlord. It took years of study to qualify for even the preliminary examination, and more years to reach the highest level. No peasant family could have afforded to give its son this expensive training, especially since the examiners sometimes showed a tendency to favor candidates from well-connected families.

This flaw in the examination system illustrates one of the enduring characteristics of Chinese society. From at least the T'ang

period until the twentieth century, the most important class in China was the one that has been called the scholar-gentry. This was a landlord class, which owned and leased to the peasants most of the land in the country. It was also the class which furnished most of the officials to the government at both the local and higher levels. And since official position depended on education, it was the class of scholars. Thus a single family might own most of the land in a district, hold most of the government jobs there, and have one or two representatives in high positions at court.

These scholar-gentry families were almost indestructible. If they lost favor at court, they retired to their estates and waited until the ruler or the dynasty changed. If the central government collapsed, they kept local government going until central authority could be re-established. If nomad invaders conquered the country, they preserved classical learning and Confucian philosophy and taught them to the conquerors. More than any other group, they were responsible for the continuity of the Chinese way of life.

At the same time, the scholar-gentry class aggravated some of China's social problems. It was supported by the peasants and it often exploited them. If the central government made unreasonable demands, the gentry merely passed them on to the peasants, thus increasing their burden. If the central government was weak, the gentry used its official position to increase its land-holdings and to take illegal payments from peasants and artisans. No government could exist without using the services of the gentry, but it was often difficult to make them behave honestly and efficiently. And the oppression of the gentry often led to peasant discontent and even to rebellion.

Most Chinese dynasties, when they were strong, tried to protect the peasants against

the landlords, and the early T'ang rulers were no exception. They broke up some of the large estates and remitted taxes in years of crop failure. They were able to reduce the burden on the peasants because commerce was flourishing and taxes on merchants produced a substantial revenue. In addition, the government was profiting from its monopoly on sales of iron, salt, and other staples.

China seems to have been generally prosperous during the early T'ang period. There was a wide market for all manufactured goods; Chinese silk and porcelain were exported to Japan on the east, to India and Indochina on the south, and to the Arab Empire on the west. The population increased notably, an indication that the peasants and artisans were thriving. It was also during the T'ang period that tea became the national drink of China. Formerly tea had been a luxury, but now it could be purchased by all classes. Since it had to be shipped from the south, the only region where it could be grown, its use throughout the country suggests that transportation facilities were good and that even the poorest people had risen a little above a bare subsistence level.

Religion under the T'ang

The T'ang dynasty's revival of a national government and its emphasis on knowledge of the Chinese classics for admission to the civil service strengthened Confucianism and weakened other sects. Confucianism was the basis for the Chinese political and social system. It was also highly rational and secular in spirit. A good many T'ang officials looked with some suspicion on Buddhism, which did not seem so useful in inculcating respect for authority, and which, in some of its variants, led to mystical and emotional excesses, such as self-immolation. They were also worried by what seemed to them an excessive number of Buddhist priests, monks, and nuns. They used the same arguments against them which European politicians used against Christian monks in the sixteenth century—they were idle and unproductive; they held too much of the wealth of the country; they encouraged supersition. On several occasions the government seized Buddhist temples and monasteries and compelled the monks and nuns to return to secular life. These attacks were intermittent, and Buddhism continued to influence many inhabitants of China. But Buddhism was weakened by official disfavor and came to play a less important role in Chinese life than it had before.

T'ang Scholarship

The T'ang period was a great age of scholarship during which encyclopedias were compiled, a national academy was established, and dictionaries of foreign languages were prepared. The government established the practice of employing large groups of scholars to write histories of earlier dynasties, a practice that was faithfully followed by later rulers. As a result, China has hundreds of volumes of official histories which cover almost its entire past.

In spite of their troubles, Buddhist monks made important contributions to T'ang scholarship. In the first place, they wanted to translate large numbers of Sanskrit texts into Chinese. Since the two languages are very different, the monks were obliged to pay careful attention to problems of syntax, grammar, and vocabulary. Some of the first books on these subjects were the work of Buddhist monks. The famous traveler, Hsüan Tang, who made a pilgrimage to India in 629–44,

Polychrome clay figure of a bodhisattva. China, T'ang dynasty, 8th century.

was one of the leaders in this work. He not only wrote a notable account of his travels; he also succeeded in translating all the complexities of Buddhist thought into Chinese.

Chinese Printing

In the second place, the Buddhists were probably responsible for the invention of block printing. They wanted to make many

451

copies of their sacred writings, both because the act of multiplying prayers and sacred texts was meritorious in itself, and because they could reach more people by reproducing key passages of their scriptures. They had an ideal material on which to print, for paper had been invented in China in the first century A.D. The Chinese had probably already developed the custom of brushing engraved seals with ink and stamping them on paper, and block printing carried this idea one step further. The text of an entire page was carved out of a single block of wood; the wood was inked; and then a sheet of paper was pressed on it. The first block prints come from the eighth century; the first printed book (only six sheets of text) is dated 868.

Preparing these printing blocks involved a tremendous amount of labor, though once they were ready it was easy to make many copies of a text. Later, Chinese scholars began to experiment with individual, movable type, but this idea was never accepted by Chinese printers. Since there are thousands of Chinese characters, preparing and setting movable type seemed to offer little saving in time and expense. In Korea, however, individual, movable type was used with great success early in the fifteenth century.

The history of the diffusion of paper and printing shows how isolated China was, in spite of superficial commercial contacts, and how slowly ideas and techniques spread from East to West. Paper, invented in China a little before 100 A.D., as we have seen, began to be used in Arab countries only in the eighth and ninth centuries. Western Europeans learned about it from the Arabs, but it was seldom used in

Two styles of Chinese calligraphy. The example above was written by the painter Mi Fei (1051–1107 A.D.) in the Running Style (this remains the most popular style for daily use because it is quickly written). The stone rubbing on the right was made from an inscription in the Regular Style by Ou-Yang Hsün, a scholar and calligrapher of the T'ang dynasty.

The first portion of the oldest printed book, the *Diamond Sutra* of 868, printed on a scroll from wooden blocks. The *Diamond Sutra* gives discourses of the Buddha, who is shown on this page teaching.

Europe until the thirteenth century and did not become common until the fifteenth. Thus it took over a thousand years for a fairly simple and obviously useful technique to travel to Europe from China.

The history of printing is even more curious. Block printing spread rapidly throughout the Chinese cultural area and was used in Japan almost as soon as it was invented in China. But the Moslems, who sat in the middle of every trade route between China and the West, took no interest in block printing, and, except for a few early experiments, never used the invention. Eventually Europe obtained a few samples of Chinese printed work, such as playing cards and paper money, and these may have stimulated some early European experiments with block printing. But there is no evidence that Europeans knew that the Chinese had oc-

casionally used movable type. The typical European method of printing with independent, metal, movable type, locked in a form and mounted in a press, seems to have been an independent invention. It is an amazing coincidence that men at the two extremities of the Eurasian continent—Korea and Germany—discovered almost simultaneously how to put movable type to practical use.

T'ang Poetry

The T'ang period was an age of poets as well as an age of scholars. The Chinese believe that this was their greatest period of lyric poetry and have preserved thousands of poems of the T'ang era. Li Po (*ca.* 700–62) is probably the best known to the West of the T'ang poets, but some Chinese critics would place Tu Fu (712–70) higher. Chinese poetry tries to re-

453

create a mood, brief flashes of intense feeling caused by the sight of a mountain valley, a sudden rainstorm, an empty road, or piercing moments of clarity in which the unity of nature or the impermanence of all worldly beauties is realized. It is often indirect and allusive, and always highly subjective. At its best it is very great poetry, and it has been increasingly appreciated by the peoples of the rest of the world.

There is a gentle melancholy in much of this poetry; rain, loneliness, and autumnal scenes are favorite topics. Thus one of Tu Fu's poems ends:

> A few last leaves are falling, blown by
> the breeze;
> The sun sets behind the curving hill!
> How late the solitary crane returns!
> In the twilight the rooks are already
> flocking to the forest.

The same note of sadness appears in many of Li Po's verses:

> Before my bed a patch of moonlight
> shone;
> I thought there must be frost upon the
> ground,
> And raised my head and stared at the
> moon so bright,
> Sank back again and longed for my na-
> tive land.

And at times T'ang poetry becomes sardonic, as in this poem of Li Po:

> Life is a journey, death is a return to the
> earth.
> The universe is like an inn, the passing
> years are like dust.
> We complain when we think of the past.
> We would complain more if we thought
> of the future!

These poets also disliked the T'ang wars of conquest. As Tu Fu said:

> Snow is falling, the army makes its way
> through the high mountains;
> The track is dangerous; for fear of slip-
> ping they cling from rock to rock,
> Their frozen fingers slip on ice. . . .

> There they are far distant from the land
> of Han [China].
> When will men be satisfied with building
> a wall against the barbarians?
> When will the soldiers return to their
> native land? *

The Fall of the T'ang Empire

As we have already suggested, the T'ang period was one in which China had great influence on its eastern neighbors. Both Korea and Japan adopted some of the basic elements of Chinese civilization at this time—the Chinese system of writing, Chinese literary and artistic techniques, Chinese ideas about philosophy and religion. Buddhism came to Japan from China and struck even deeper roots in the islands than it had on the continent. Japanese students read the Chinese classics; in fact, the curriculum in Japanese schools was almost the same as that in Chinese schools. Even in government Korean kings and Japanese emperors borrowed many techniques from their Chinese contemporaries.

The T'ang dynasty prospered for over a century. Its first great setback came at the hands of the Turks. The Turks had been weakened by the first T'ang emperor, but in the eighth century the western Turkish tribes came into contact with Islam, and their subsequent conversion changed the history of the world. The Turks had been stout fighters before; now the fervor of their new religion, the backing of the Arabs, and the better organization which they learned from the Moslem Caliphate made them almost invincible. We have already seen the great impact they had on India, the Caliphate, and Byzantium. They had almost as decisive an influence on Chinese history. The T'ang emperor, trying to extend Chinese suzerainty in cen-

---

* All these excerpts are quoted from René Grousset, *The Rise and Splendour of the Chinese Empire* (London: Geoffrey Bles, 1952; Berkeley: U. of California Press, 1953), pp. 155, 152, 163.

tral Asia, sent his armies far to the west where they were caught by a combined Turko-Arab army and decisively defeated in 751. China thus lost its best chance to control the nomads of central Asia, and the Turks were free to expand in all directions.

The defeat of 751 ended the legend of T'ang invincibility. The subject peoples, one by one, regained their independence and the nomads again threatened the northern frontier. With hostile forces on the borders, trade declined and the expenses of war became more and more of a burden on the people. The later T'ang emperors were less able than their predecessors and could not keep their officials from growing corrupt and oppressive. Popular rebellions broke out in the ninth century, provincial governors began to throw off imperial authority, and the T'ang dynasty ended in 906.

The Sung Dynasty and the Mongols

The fall of the T'ang was followed, as usual, by a period of disunity and internal war. Order was eventually restored by the Sung dynasty, which began to reign in the north in 960 and had gained control of the independent southern states by 979. The Sung were never as strong militarily as the T'ang, and they were always threatened by nomads in the north, to whom they paid tribute. After 1126 they lost control of all territory north of the Yangtze to the Jurchen nomads, who established the Chin dynasty which ruled northern China until the Mongol invasion.

In spite of military weakness the Sung period saw some notable advances in Chinese civilization. Block printing was much more extensively used than under the T'ang, and the basic religious and scholarly texts were more widely distributed. A great

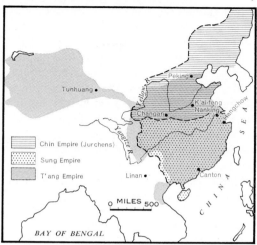

The Sung and Chin Empires 11th century

Chin Empire (Jurchens)

Sung Empire

T'ang Empire

history of China from 400 B.C. to the advent of the Sung was written by Ssu-ma Kuang. Confucianism was reinterpreted and strengthened by the addition of religious and philosophical ideas to what had been primarily a code of ethics. Thus the idea that there was a universal law governing the entire universe became prominent at this time. There was also a strong belief that human reason, pushed to its limits, could grasp the basic principles behind the workings of the universe. These ideas were brilliantly expressed by Chu Hsi in the twelfth century, and the revised version of Confucianism gradually became the dominant force in Chinese philosophy and religion.

Two important inventions were made in the Sung period. The exact date of the origin of the compass is uncertain, but it was certainly used by the end of the eleventh century. It is still not clear whether the compass came to Europe from China, or whether it was independently invented in the West. Gunpowder had long been known to the Chinese, but had been used only for fireworks. In the twelfth century it

455

began to be used in warfare in the form of bombs and grenades. It is not certain when cannon were invented, but they may have been developed during the great wars with the Mongols toward the end of the twelfth century. The Mongols had cannon by the middle of the thirteenth century, and it is most likely that they obtained them from the Chinese. However, as we have seen, gunpowder was not very useful until metallurgical techniques had reached a high level of development. Europeans learned of gunpowder later than the Chinese, but they soon surpassed them in the art of making firearms.

Sung Culture and Government

If the T'ang period was the great age of Chinese poetry, the Sung was the great age of Chinese art. Like T'ang poetry, Sung painting tried to recreate a mood—the beauty and vastness, the harmony and inner meaning, of nature. Like poetry again, the paintings are reduced to bare essentials; a few lines suggest the whole. The landscapes of the Sung painters are especially famous; perhaps no other people ever painted so many landscapes or painted them so well.

With all its achievements, the Sung period had serious limitations. Cut off from the rest of the world by the nomads who ringed the frontiers, the Chinese turned in on themselves and became rather self-satisfied. They resisted new ideas and clung stubbornly to their old ways. For example, one of the most interesting men in Chinese history, the statesman Wang An-shih (1021–86), failed utterly to make permanent reforms in Chinese government. He tried to reform the examination system so that less emphasis would be placed on

purely literary studies and more on practical knowledge. He hoped to save the small farmer by regulating and refinancing loans to peasants; he started vast projects of irrigation and flood control; he even wanted to control prices and wages. Not all his measures were practical, but he might have increased China's prosperity and he certainly would have improved the lot of the common people if he had been supported by other members of the ruling class. But the welfare state was no more popular with Chinese conservatives than it has been with some conservatives of our own day, and Wang An-shih's reforms were soon forgotten.

The upper classes in the Sung period probably had the most comfortable existence and the highest civilization of any group on the Eurasian continent. But luxury was at times carried to absurd lengths; it was at this time that the practice became common of binding the feet of girls so that they could only take mincing little steps. And the comfortable existence of the upper classes depended on the exploitation of the peasants.

The Mongols in China

In spite of these weaknesses, the Sung made a surprisingly strong resistance to the rising Mongol power. We have already seen how Genghis Khan united the nomads of the steppes and sent great armies west into Russia. At the same time he attacked the Jurchen kingdom of northern China and took its capital, Peking, in 1215. The successors of Genghis Khan rapidly completed the conquest of the north, but the south held out for almost two more generations. It was only in 1279 that the last Sung ruler was killed—curiously enough,

Detail from Clearing Autumn Skies over Mountains and Valleys, a Sung landscape scroll attributed to Kuo Hsi, ca. 1020–90.

Civil Service Examinations under the Sung Dynasty

The candidates had to get up in the middle of the night and come to the palace at dawn, bringing their cold meals with them, for they would not be able to leave until the examinations were over. During the examinations they were shut up in cubicles under the supervision of palace guards. There was a rigorous system to prevent bribery or favoritism. The candidates' papers were recopied by official clerks before they were submitted to the examiners, to avoid recognition of their identity by their handwriting. In the recopied papers the writers' names were taken out and kept on file. While the candidates were let out after the examinations, the judges themselves were shut up within the palace, usually from late January till early March, until the papers were properly graded and submitted to the emperor. The candidates were examined first on questions of history or principles of government. There was a second examination on the classics, and finally, after the successful ones had been graded, there was one —under the direct supervision of the emperor— on lyrics, descriptive poetry, and again, essays on politics.

From Lin Yu-t'ang, *The Gay Genius* (New York: Day, 1947), p. 38.

in an attempt to reach Formosa and set up a government-in-exile. All China was now ruled by the Mongols, the first time a foreign dynasty had held the entire country.

The great Mongol Empire was too large to remain unified, however. It was at first divided into subordinate khanates, ruled by members of the royal family under the suzerainty of the Great Khan. But in 1260 the khan of China, Kublai, became practically independent, and he and his successors ruled China as a separate empire until 1368. Korea was also under the control of this Mongol dynasty, and Kublai annexed Yunnan (now the southernmost Chinese province) and established his suzerainty over part of Indochina. He failed, however, in his efforts to conquer Japan. The Mongols knew little of naval matters and their Chinese subjects were not enthusiastic about an attack on the islands. Kublai finally succeeded in sending a fleet against Japan, but it was destroyed by a typhoon. This was the "Divine Wind" (Kamikaze) which the Japanese invoked during their struggle with the United States during World War II.

The Mongols rapidly accepted Chinese civilization and soon restored the prosperity of the country. They built great roads, with relays of horses every twenty-five or thirty miles to carry official messages. They repaired and extended the canal system and built granaries to store food against famine. Trade by both land and sea increased, and foreign travelers journeyed throughout the empire.

The Mongols and the West

In contrast to the Sung period, China was now in close contact with foreigners from many lands. While the Mongol supremacy lasted, it was easier to travel by land from Europe to China than it had ever been before, or than it was ever to be again until the nineteenth century. Ambassadors from the pope and the king of France visited the Mongol court, and dozens of Europeans who had no official position found employment there. Marco Polo's book shows how easy it was for a European to travel through the Mongol domains. His account, and those of other travelers, gave Europeans their first real information about China. Stories about the great wealth and strange customs of this distant land made a strong impression on Europe and did much to inspire the voyages of discovery of the fifteenth and sixteenth centuries.

The Mongol emperors were open-minded and ready to use good men and new ideas, whatever their origin. The Mongol court was full of officials of every race and religion—Persian Moslems, Russian Christians, Chinese Confucians. Marco Polo would probably have reached a high position in the Mongol government if he had chosen to remain in China. And with the men came the ideas, such as a new grain crop, sorghum, and a new way of handling problems in arithmetic, the abacus.

The Mongols had no very strong religious convictions and were willing to listen to missionaries of every faith. As we have seen, Kublai asked for Christian priests (p. 431), but the Church had too many problems in Europe to comply with his request. When missionaries were finally sent in the fourteenth century, it was too late. Although there was a Catholic archbishop of Peking in the 1340's, and some thousands of Chinese converts, the small Chinese Christian organization was not strong enough to survive the downfall of the Mongol dynasty.

❖❖❖❖❖❖❖❖❖❖❖❖❖❖❖❖❖❖❖❖❖❖❖❖❖❖❖

Marco Polo Describes Chinese Paper Money

ca. 1275

When ready for use, it [a specially prepared paper] is cut into pieces of money of different sizes, nearly square, but somewhat longer than they are wide. . . . The coinage of this paper money is authenticated with as much form and ceremony as if it were actually of pure gold or silver, for to each note a number of officers, specially appointed, not only subscribe their names, but affix their signets also; and when this has been done . . . the principal officer, deputed by his majesty, having dipped into vermilion the royal seal committed to his custody, stamps with it the piece of paper, so that the form of the seal remains impressed upon it, by which it receives full authenticity as current money, and the act of counterfeiting it is punished with death. When thus coined in large quantities, this paper currency is circulated in every part of the grand khan's domains, nor dares any person, at the peril of his life, refuse to accept it in payment. All his subjects receive it without hesitation, because, wherever their business may call them, they can dispose of it again in the purchase of merchandise they may have occasion for, such as pearls, jewels, gold, or silver.

From *The Travels of Marco Polo* (New York and London: Everyman's Library, 1950), p. 203.

❖❖❖❖❖❖❖❖❖❖❖❖❖❖❖❖❖❖❖❖❖❖❖❖❖❖❖

The Ming Dynasty

Like most other Chinese dynasties, the Mongol line of rulers degenerated after the first few generations. They allowed

The Ming Empire 14th-17th centuries

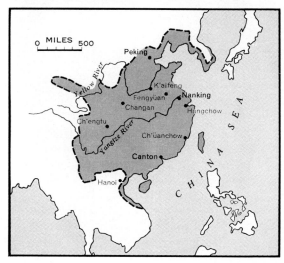

the people to be oppressed by corrupt officials and failed to maintain their military strength. Rebellion broke out in the south, and finally in 1368 an ex-Buddhist monk captured Peking. He founded the Ming dynasty which ruled China until the coming of the Manchus in the seventeenth century.

The Ming dynasty has had a bad reputation because, in its efforts to wipe out the memory of Mongol domination, it encouraged a rather imitative culture based on the great works of the T'ang and Sung period. Thus the civil service examinations became more difficult and more formalized, demanding an encyclopedic knowledge of Confucian works. The restatement of Confucian doctrine by the Sung philosopher

Porcelain jar of the Ming period.

Chu Hsi became the official dogma for all candidates for government posts. In fact, one Ming writer remarked that Chu had discovered everything worth knowing and that no more scholarly books were necessary. In art and in poetry there was the same tendency to imitate, or at most to add only a few minor refinements. It is perhaps significant that the most interesting literary works of the Ming period are novels, a form of writing which had not been greatly cultivated before and hence had fewer set standards to follow.

Perhaps the greatest contribution of the Ming rulers was their support of cotton growing. Cotton had been known in China much earlier, but had not been extensively used. The Ming government resorted to both persuasion and force to increase the size of the cotton crop, even insisting that the farmers in some districts pay their taxes in cotton. As a result, China became one of the great cotton-growing and cotton-using areas of the world.

Ming Explorations and Commerce

The early Ming emperors, who were intensely interested in exploration by sea, sent out great fleets which surveyed the Indian Ocean and even penetrated the Persian Gulf and the Red Sea. They forced distant rulers, including the king of Ceylon, to pay them tribute and brought back many novelties and luxuries. Chinese shipbuilding and navigation must have been flourishing to make these voyages possible. But they suddenly ceased after 1433, and an imperial edict restricted Chinese shipping to coastal voyages. This fatal decision was probably the result of Ming suspicion of foreign influences. It left the eastern seas open to the Portuguese invaders and their French and English successors.

The Ming dynasty was ruling China when the first Europeans reached the country by sea in the sixteenth century. This was unfortunate, for the Ming period, like several earlier periods, was marked by dislike of foreigners and strong belief in Chinese superiority. It is true that the first Portuguese traders were cruel and arrogant, but the Chinese were almost equally arrogant in their dealings with Europeans. They did not reject the obvious advantages of mutual trade, but they tried to minimize foreign influence on the Chinese way of life. They confined the traders to a few coastal towns and dealt with them through a handful of carefully selected officials. They were suspicious of European ideas and even of European technology. Thus the coming of the Europeans tended to reinforce Ming conservatism rather than to stimulate a re-examination and an enrichment of Chinese culture.

At the end of the dynasty the Ming emperors did begin to take an interest in European learning, thanks to the efforts of Jesuit missionaries such as Matteo Ricci. But by this time it was too late to shake off the effects of generations of hostility to foreign influences. China never assimilated European science and technology, and it became steadily weaker in relation to European powers.

Japan

The Japanese islands were inhabited at least as early as 3000 B.C., but very little is known about their early history. The first inhabitants were probably the Ainu, who still exist on the northernmost island, and who are very different physically from other Japanese. The Ainu were overrun by successive waves of Mongoloid invaders who entered the islands by way of the narrow Korean Straits. There is also evidence of invasions by Malay-like peoples coming up from the islands to the south of Japan. All these peoples except the Ainu gradually merged and formed a united kingdom.

The Early Japanese

Chinese records begin to mention Japan after 25 A.D., but these early accounts describe it as a very backward and primitive country. Only in the fifth century A.D. did writing become common in Japan, and then the Chinese script was used. Since the

Specimen of Japanese calligraphy, by Takuan, a late-16th-century Zen Buddhist teacher.

461

Wooden figure of the Buddha from the 8th-century temple of Muro-ji, Japan.

Chinese characters were not well suited to the Japanese word forms, the written language could not be very precise. Even today it is difficult to express certain legal and political concepts in Japanese.

Even more important than the beginning of writing was the introduction of Bud-

dhism, in 552 A.D. The old native religion, Shinto, was a rather undeveloped form of nature worship, and, though its supporters made some resistance, Buddhism spread rapidly throughout the islands. It was supported by members of the royal family, especially by the first great Japanese scholar, Prince Shotuku (d. 621). Dozens of temples with enormous statues of the Buddha were erected and Buddhist monasteries were founded in many parts of the country.

With Buddhism came a significant increase in Chinese influence. Priests and scholars came over from China, and Japanese Buddhists crossed to the mainland to study with the leaders of Chinese Buddhism. There was great and fully justified admiration in Japan for all aspects of Chinese culture. These close contacts began when China was at the height of the T'ang civilization, and the Japanese borrowed their administrative system, their ceremonial, their fashions, their art, and their literature from the Chinese.

At the same time, Japan was not a mere imitation of China. It developed its own verse forms, its own drama, and its own style of painting. Tea drinking was learned from China, but the elaborate tea ceremony was a Japanese development. On the other hand, while there were some notable Japanese scholars, learning was never honored in Japan as it was in China.

Japanese Political Development

The most conspicuous difference between the two countries, however, was in their political development. China had its periods of weak government and civil war, but in general the country remained unified. The emperor and his officials really ruled the country and military men seldom had much power. In Japan, on the other hand, the emperor was usually a figurehead, and real power lay in the hands of military leaders. Civil wars between the heads of great military families were frequent, especially in the period from 1200 to 1600. The most honored men in Japan were soldiers, not scholars.

At first the emperor had been theoreti-

cally all-powerful, owner of all the land and direct ruler of all the people. In practice, however, he had to grant great estates to powerful nobles, and he tended to lose

Drawing of Hideyoshi, with an inscription by Hideyoshi's son, early 17th century.

more and more control over actual government. The leading courtiers intrigued for power and often dominated the emperor by marrying him to ladies of their families.

Finally, even the appearance of power was transferred from the imperial court. There had long been a custom of appointing an official, known as the shogun (generalissimo), to take full charge of the defense of the country in times of emergency. About the middle of the twelfth century the general Yoritomo succeeded in making himself permanent and hereditary shogun. He established a new government under his control, leaving the emperor and his court with only religious and ceremonial duties.

Japanese Feudalism

With the establishment of a permanent shogunate went the establishment of a feudal system not unlike that of western Europe (see p. 260). Under the shogun were great lords, the daimyos, and under the daimyos were fighting men, or samurai. All these people were immeasurably superior to common peasants and artisans. who had to prostrate themselves whenever a member of the military caste passed by. The whole system was based on the labor of the peasants; a feudal lord was usually given a fief of so many measures of rice which the peasants had to produce.

The Tokugawa Shogunate

Like the European feudal system, Japanese feudalism produced frequent wars.

At times the shoguns themselves were displaced, or turned into puppets while a constable ruled in their name. These constant shifts in power went on for centuries, and at times Japan seemed ready to dissolve into a group of petty warring states. It was saved from this fate by two great soldiers of the sixteenth century, Hideyoshi and Iyeyasu. Hideyoshi united the country and brought most of the warring daimyos under his authority. When he died in 1598, Tokugawa Iyeyasu completed his work and re-established the shogunate. The Tokugawa shoguns ruled Japan from this time until 1867. The civil wars ended and Japan remained at peace for almost three centuries.

Hideyoshi and Iyeyasu were also responsible for the long isolation of Japan from the rest of the world. During the sixteenth century first the Portuguese and then the Dutch had begun to trade with Japan. With the traders came Jesuit missionaries, who converted thousands of Japanese. Hideyoshi felt that the new religion might cause renewed factional quarrels in Japan; he also feared that European soldiers and colonizers would follow the missionaries. He persecuted the Jesuits and the native Christians, and in 1614, soon after his death, Christianity was outlawed. The final step was taken in 1639 when foreign ships were forbidden to come to Japan. The Dutch were allowed to keep a small trading post at Nagasaki, but otherwise Japan was closed to foreign contacts until Perry forced the shogun to accept a commercial treaty in 1853.

Suggestions for Further Reading

1. The Rajputs

There is interesting source material on India in this period in *The History of India*, Vols. I and II (edited H. M. Elliott, 1867). R. C. Majumdar, *Ancient India* (1946), is probably the best general treatment of political history to 1200 A.D. Majumdar, a leading authority on Indian history, includes a good critical bibliography. The older study of S. Lane-Poole, *Medieval India* (1903), is less scholarly than Majumdar but presents a more exciting account of India under Moslem rule. V. A. Smith, *The Oxford History of India* (1923), is an excellent reference work. There is considerable material on the medieval period in J. C. Powell-Price, *A History of India* (1955), and in I. Prasad, *History of Medieval India* (1928), which stresses military and administrative achievements.

2. The Spread of Indian Culture

H. G. Rawlinson, *India: A Short Cultural History* (1938), is a thorough account of India's contribution to world culture and a good starting point for study. R. C. Majumdar, *Ancient Indian Colonies in the Far East,* 2 vols. (1955), is a scholarly treatment of the expansion of Indian culture, and F. W. Thomas, *Indianism and Its Expansion* (1917), treats the same subject in a somewhat more lucid fashion. The best recent work is R. Mukerjee, *The Culture and Art of India* (1959), which gives excellent selections of Indian literature and beautiful illustrations of Indian art. Mukerjee includes a good up-to-date bibliography. A. A. MacDonell, *India's Past* (1927), a survey of India's literatures and religions, traces the growth and spread of her culture. For a valuable summary of India's achievement, see *The Legacy of India* (edited G. T. Garratt, 1937).

3. The Moslem Conquest

Undoubtedly, the best account is given in the brief monograph of R. C. Majumdar, *The Arab Invasion of India* (1931). The impact of Moslem rule on the political, economic, and cultural life of India is carefully studied in *The Struggle for Empire* (edited R. C. Majumdar, 1957), a collection of essays by leading scholars of Indian history.
See also the general works cited above for material on the Moslem period.

4. European Contacts in the Sixteenth Century

There is an exciting eyewitness account of India in early modern times in F. Bernier, *Travels in the Mogul Empire* (trans. A. Constable, 1891). P. Spear, *India, Pakistan, and the West* (1949), traces the relations between India and the West in a good survey. *The Travels of Peter Mundy in Europe and Asia* (edited R. Temple, 1956–58), describes East-West relations in the sixteenth century.

5. China under the T'ang Dynasty

Most of the general works mentioned after Chapter 6, in Section 2, have material on the T'ang period. W. Bingham, *The Founding of the T'ang Dynasty* (1941), is probably the best study of the early history of the Dynasty. *The Veritable Record of the T'ang Emperor Shun-Tsung* (trans. B. Solomon, 1955) is a fascinating picture of China in the early ninth century and gives valuable insight into the old Chinese world-view. The standard study of Chinese history is K. S. Latourette, *The Chinese: Their History and Culture* (1946), a scholarly and readable work with excellent bibliographic material.

6. Buddhism in China

The Buddhist Scriptures * (trans. E. Conze, 1959) contains a good selection of Buddhist writings drawn from the central tradition of Buddhism. C. Humphreys, *Buddhism* * (1951), devotes considerable attention to Buddhism in China and is a very good introductory survey. There is material on the growth of Buddhism in China in both L. Wieger, *History of Religious Beliefs and of Philosophic Opinions in China* (trans.

E. T. C. Werner, 1927), and J. Edkins, *Chinese Buddhism* (1893). The most thorough treatment is that of C. Eliot, *Hinduism and Buddhism: An Historical Sketch,* 3 vols. (1921).

7. Printing and Scholarship

T. F. Carter, *The Invention of Printing in China and Its Spread Westward* (rev. ed., 1931), is very important. There is information on printing and scholarship in C. P. Fitzgerald, *China: A Short Cultural History* (1938), and in H. G. Creel, *Chinese Thought from Confucius to Mao Tsê-tung* (1953), a very interesting work by a leading American authority.

8. The Sung Dynasty

The first volume of the monumental study of K. A. Wittfogel and Fêng Chia-shêng, *History of Chinese Society, 907–1125* (1945), includes texts and translations from major Chinese sources on this period. Since the civil service system was the key feature of the Chinese state, E. A. Kracke, *The Civil Service in Early Sung China* (1953), is important for an understanding of the Chinese political system; this work also shows China as a classic example of the managerial state in practice. J. T. C. Liu, *Reform in Sung China* (1959), reveals the "modern" policies of an eleventh-century reformer.

9. The Mongols

Both R. Grousset, *L'Empire des Steppes* (1939), and H. H. Howarth, *History of the Monguls from the Ninth to the Nineteenth Century,* 4 parts (1876–1927), are reliable accounts which give special attention to political history. The famous thirteenth-century Venetian's trip to the Mongol court is presented in H. Yule, *The Book of Ser Marco Polo,* 2 vols. (rev. ed., H. Cordier, 1921). The best account of Christianity in China under the Mongols is A. C. Moule, *Christians in China Before the Year 1550* (1930).

10. The Ming Dynasty

The most trustworthy general treatment is in R. Grousset, *Histoire de l'Extreme-Orient,* 2 vols. (1929). There is material on the Ming period in two works of O. Lattimore, *China: A Short History* (1944) and *Inner Frontiers of Asia* (1940), which is more detailed but also more interesting. F. Michael, *The Origin of Manchu Rule* (1942), is excellent for the development of the Manchus.

11. China's First Contacts with Europe in the Sixteenth Century

The best picture that we have of Chinese-European intercourse is *China in the Sixteenth Century: The Journal of Matthew Ricci* (trans. L. J. Gallager, 1953), an account of missionary activity. K. S. Latourette, *A History of Christian Missions in China* (1932), is a most comprehensive treatment, while C. Cary-Elwes, *China and the Cross* (1957), though not so scholarly, is more readable than Latourette.

12. Japan from the Beginnings to the Tokugawa Period

K. S. Latourette, *The History of Japan* (1947), is a quick survey of Japanese history and a good introduction. Latourette is mainly concerned with Japanese influence on China. There is excellent material on political and social history in F. Brinkley, *A History of the Japanese People* (1915), an invaluable handbook. The standard treatment of the intellectual achievement of Japan is G. B. Sansom, *Japan: A Short Cultural History*

* Available in paperback edition.

(1943). For economic development, see Y. Takekoshi, *The Economic Aspects of the History of the Civilization of Japan,* Vol. I (1930), a scholarly and readable study. A fascinating picture of Japanese civilization in the twelfth century is offered in M. Shinoda, *The Founding of the Kamakura Shogunate* (1960).

The titles by Latourette, Brinkley, and Takekoshi above have information on Japanese feudalism and religion. There is excellent material also in *Feudalism in History* (edited R. Coulborn, 1956) and in R. Boutrouche, *Seigneurie et Féodalité* (1959). Probably the best study of antiforeignism in Japan is in J. Murdoch, *A History of Japan,* Vol. II (1925).

16

Italy's Golden Age

The fifteenth century was a period of rapidly accelerating change in the history of European civilization. At the start of the century, the institutions and ideas developed during the twelfth and thirteenth centuries were no longer growing, but they still dominated Europe. The Church's prestige had suffered badly through the pope's residence at Avignon and the ensuing election of two rival Vicars of Christ (see p. 378). Anticlericalism was increasing and heresy spreading. But for the vast majority of men there was still no salvation outside the Church, divided and corrupt as it was. The feudal nobility was losing much of its military and political power, but the trend toward stronger monarchy seemed to be arrested throughout western Europe in the

---

The hand of God (right) about to touch and give life to the hand of man (left), in Michelangelo's conception of *The Creation* (see p. 490): a high moment in the Renaissance portrayal of man's dignity.

general exhaustion and devastation that accompanied the Hundred Years' War. The violence and irresponsibility of feudal magnates whose families had governed Europe for centuries were becoming intolerable to the new middle classes, but no real alternative to the feudal organization of society was yet in sight. In spite of the growth of population and trade during the twelfth and thirteenth centuries, the custom-bound agricultural village and the tightly regulated urban gild were still the typical units of economic organization. A certain vague frustration and hopelessness pervaded the writings of the early fifteenth century in most of Europe. To stop the wars, to restore production and commerce, to establish stronger and more stable governments, to heal the papal schism, reform the clergy, and stem the tide of heresy—everyone knew that these were the tasks to be done. But no one knew how to begin.

By the end of the fifteenth century a startling change had taken place. Economic expansion amounting to a revolution was under way throughout most of the Continent. New careers open to talent were developing in urban centers everywhere. European ships had made direct contact with the ancient civilizations of the Orient and had discovered an utterly unknown new world in the Occident. Strong centralized monarchies had appeared in France, Spain, and England, and for the first time in over a century monarchs were powerful enough to challenge the independent power of feudal magnates. The papal schism was healed and Rome was once more the capital of Christendom. Ecclesiastical abuses were perhaps worse than ever, but at least no new heresy worthy of the name was spreading among the faithful. In the universities, scholasticism now had a competitor in Humanism, a scholarly enthusiasm for the literary forms and ethical ideals of ancient Greece and Rome. Melancholy was

still the fashionable mood, particularly among the upper classes, and other-worldliness was still the dominant ideal held before men in sermon and sacrament. But a new note was beginning to sound more and more clearly among the intellectuals and artists, particularly in Italy—a note of optimism and confidence, of excitement and enjoyment. There was occasional talk of a "new age" dawning, a "dark age" past, a rebirth of the political skill and literary genius of the ancient Greeks and Romans. By 1500 the major "medieval" institutions and ideas were in full retreat and the outlines of our "modern" world were beginning to take shadowy form: its dynamic competitive economy, fluid society, territorial states, and international anarchy, its secular ideals, its technology and science.

In most but not all of these developments, the Italian peninsula took the lead. The fifteenth century was Italy's golden age. During the two centuries between the death of Dante (1321) and the sack of Rome by mutinous imperial troops (1527), the Italian city-states made their most important contributions to the development of western civilization. Particularly during the fifteenth century, Italian cultural leadership was unchallenged. Italians devised the best methods of business accounting. They minted the best coins, made the finest cloth, and, until the late fifteenth century, built the best ships in Europe. Their craftsmanship and their art were unsurpassed. They recreated Greco-Roman architecture and brought sculpture and particularly painting to a height that some would insist has never been surpassed. They set the scholarly standards and dictated the literary taste that Europe was to follow for generations. They developed a genuinely new social ideal, that of "the gentleman," and gave us our educational ideal of a "liberal education." What Athens had been to the rest of

Greece in the fifth century B.C. Florence was to Europe in the fifteenth century A.D., a fashioner of ideals, both ethical and aesthetic, a center of economic enterprise and artistic creativity, a forum of social and political ideas—but unlike Athens a failure so far as political organization and leadership were concerned. Italy's leadership in the fifteenth century was technical, economic, aesthetic, and intellectual, not political. The failure of the petty Italian city-states to find a path to political union was to result in three centuries of domination of Italy by larger and stronger foreign states.

There are several obvious reasons for Italy's leadership in the fifteenth century. In the first place, much of Europe outside the Italian peninsula was devastated by civil and foreign wars through most of the century. There were the Hundred Years' War in France, the Hussite Wars in Bohemia, the Wars of the Roses in England, and continual struggles in Spain. Although Italy had her petty wars, she was untouched by these exhausting feudal and international struggles. Until the close of the fifteenth century she was safe from foreign invasion, and so was able to develop along lines peculiar to herself. In the second place, the cultural movements of the medieval north were losing their earlier vigor. Scholasticism, instead of developing new ways of finding and testing truth, was degenerating into finespun arguments about the meaning of terms. Gothic architecture was becoming so elaborate and complicated in its striving for more height and light that fifteenth-century churches sometimes seemed to be as dangerously suspended in mid-air as the arguments of the scholastic philosophers in their classrooms. Chivalry as a code of life and an inspiration for romance and poetry was becoming stilted and artificial, more and more divorced from the way real nobles and real knights lived. It

was the turn of the south to seize the initiative and create new ideals and patterns of living.

The City-States of Northern Italy

By 1400 the whole face of Europe was dotted with towns, but they were generally small and widely scattered across a countryside that was still predominantly agricultural. There were two striking concentrations of urban population, however: in the Netherlands and in northern Italy. Here the cities were larger and wealthier and closer together than anywhere else. Here the lines of the trade routes converged by land and sea in two thick knots. Here were concentrated the most advanced industries, the largest commercial enterprises, and the biggest banking houses in Europe. The population was more dense and the ratio of town-dwellers to country-dwellers was higher in these two areas than anywhere else in Europe.

There were important differences, however, between the Netherlands and northern Italy. There was more continuity with the past in the north, less in the south. The gilds still dominated the organization of industry and trade in the Netherlands, and feudalism was still strong outside the town walls. The duke of Burgundy was able to gain lordship over most of the Netherlands cities, and the burghers tended to accept the social ideals of the feudal nobility above them. By the end of the thirteenth century, however, the towns of northern Italy were developing in genuinely new directions, both in their internal characteristics and in their relation to the surrounding society.

Economic Basis

The northern Italian cities by now were dominated by international trade. A third of the population of Florence lived by importing wool from countries as far away as England and selling finished cloth all over Europe and the Levant. Almost the whole population of Venice was indirectly involved in importing spices and silks from the Orient via the Levant and distributing them throughout Europe. Obviously enterprises like these could not be organized by gilds, which were designed to monopolize and exploit purely local markets. Regulations designed to ensure that each master of a hatters' gild, for example, got his fair share of the raw materials and the local market could be enforced well enough in a single town, but they could not be enforced on the scale of far-flung international trade. Particularly in Italy this larger trade was organized by merchant capitalists outside the older gilds, which still dominated local industries and the distribution of food. The banker, the large-scale manufacturer, and the export merchant were the most important figures in the larger Italian towns.

Politics

These towns came to dominate the countryside in a way the towns of northern Europe did not. The Florentine townsmen broke the power of the nearby landed nobility in the thirteenth century and forced the defeated nobles to live in the city. As time went on, all the more powerful northern Italian cities extended their control over the immediate countryside, absorbing the feudal nobility into their urban communities. Merchants bought the land that nobles had to relinquish, and in the end a "city-state"—that is, a tight-knit territorial state controlled by a city at the center—was the typical result. The town thus dominated the countryside of northern Italy as nowhere else in Europe.

A new and sharper class division began to appear in these cities. At the top, displacing or absorbing the older nobility,

The Marriage of Giovanni Arnolfini and Giovanna Cenami, by Jan van Eyck. In painting the wedding of two of his friends, the artist suggests that he was a witness by noting on the wall above the mirror: "Jan van Eyck was here, 1434." Arnolfini was a merchant of Lucca who lived in Flanders. The details of the picture, chosen to symbolize the joys of marriage (the mirror, for instance, symbolizes purity; the dog, faithfulness), also reflect the comfortable bourgeois life of the fifteenth century.

were the wealthy merchants and bankers—the *popolo grasso,* or "fat people," as they were called. Beneath them were the older bourgeoisie, the *popolo minuto,* or "little people"—craftsmen, shopkeepers, and petty businessmen. And beneath them was a growing proletariat of workers. Outside the town walls was the peasantry, whose lot was changing very little. Conflict was constant between the *popolo grasso* and the *popolo minuto,* and occasionally the workers themselves rose in brief, short-lived rebellions, as they did in Florence in 1378.

471

Generally an oligarchy representing the big business interests managed to maintain political control. During the fourteenth century these class conflicts became so frequent and so bad for business that one or another of the factions in town after town called in an outsider and gave him absolute power to restore law and order. These men set up military dictatorships and held

Bartolommeo Colleoni, by Andrea del Verrocchio, 1488. Perhaps the finest equestrian statue of the Renaissance. Colleoni (1400–75) was a Venetian *condottiere* who tried unsuccessfully to carve out a state for himself between Milan and Florence. The arrogance and self-reliance of the typical professional soldier of the *quattrocento* is beautifully portrayed in this study.

adventurer commanded a bunch of thugs to impose order

on to their power through a combination of ruthlessness and shrewdness. They shed the blood of political opponents without hesitation or scruple, but they were generally careful at the same time to improve the city's public utilities, strengthen its defenses, devise an efficient system of taxation, provide police protection, and above all, foster business. Popular history remembers the crimes of these rulers, but economic and social historians see them as the natural result of irresolvable class struggles between groups of businessmen who could see no other way to maintain law and order. The broadly based republican governments of the twelfth century disappeared as the power of the medieval gilds declined, and in the social confusion accompanying the rise of big business northern Italy entered "the age of the despots."

War and Diplomacy

The merchant princes, industrialists, and shopkeepers often hired dictators because they were unwilling to assume the burdens of political office. They were also unwilling to bear arms, although their economic ambitions often led into war with neighboring city-states. The result was that city governments took to hiring mercenary troops, or *condottieri*. These troops changed sides whenever they were offered more money, preferred maneuvering to actual bloodshed, and often were as much of a threat as a protection to their employers. But attempts by city governments to restore a citizen militia were generally fruitless. The city-states drifted into a system in which they were often the helpless victims of unscrupulous men-on-horseback and of military *coups d'état*.

What distinguished northern Italy most sharply from the rest of Europe was the total independence of its city-states from any central government. The despots often

NOT

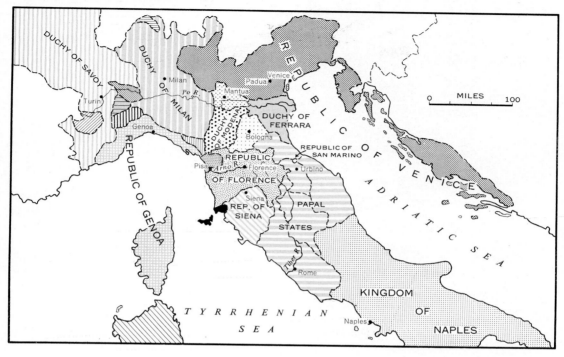

gained papal or imperial approval of their "lordships," but they and everyone else knew that neither pope nor emperor had any real power in northern Italy. From Venice, oldest and proudest of the city-states, on down to towns of a few thousand population, the city governments acted as if they had no earthly superior. The leagues of the twelfth century had served their purpose and had been dissolved. There remained only dozens of small city-states, each motivated by economic and political self-interest, fighting each other in constant wars, making and breaking alliances with each other, and jealously watching the most powerful state of the moment to make sure that it did not become strong enough to conquer the peninsula. It was in Italy about the middle of the fifteenth century that the modern practice of maintaining resident ambassadors at the courts of rival states began, to enable rulers to keep in constant touch with other governments which might become useful allies or dangerous enemies. It was here about the same time that a kind of "balance of power" began to operate among the five leading states in Italy—Venice, Milan, Florence, the Papal States, and the Kingdom of Naples—thanks to an unwritten understanding that no one of the five must be allowed to gain a preponderance of power. When France and Spain intervened in Italy at the close of the fifteenth century, both these practices—the basic machinery of modern diplomacy and the balancing of power among a group of sovereign states—spread to the larger stage of Europe. By the mid-sixteenth century, resident ambassadors were common throughout central and western Europe, and a

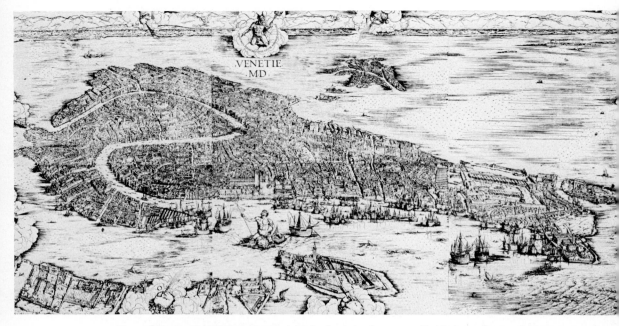

Map of Venice in 1500 by Jacopo de' Barbari. In the center, behind the figure of Neptune, god of the sea, are the Campanile, the Palazzo San Marco, and the Doges' Palace. The Grand Canal winds up and to the left. On the far right is the Arsenal with its shipyards and the fleet at anchor in the foreground. The dependence of Venice upon commerce for its very life is graphically illustrated by this picture.

rough balance of power had been established between the ruling dynasties of the two most powerful states, France and Spain.

Fifteenth-century Italy has been called "the laboratory of the modern world." Many of the problems of the twentieth century and many of the economic and political devices used to meet these problems appeared on a small scale in the Italian city-states: class struggle and unemployment, the income tax and public works programs, the problem of professional armies versus compulsory military service, the dilemmas of diplomacy in a world of independent states. For better or worse, Italians tried out one after another of the policies and practices that were later adopted by European governments in similar sit-

uations but on a larger scale, when the rest of Europe had become as relatively urbanized as northern Italy was in the fifteenth century.

Milan, Venice, and Florence

Not all these generalizations apply equally well to all the city-states of Italy. There was a striking variety and individuality about the Italian cities of this era. Each had its own unique character and tradition.

Milan, the most important city of the Po Valley, submitted early to a despot, as most of the other towns of the valley did. Around 1400 one of her rulers, Gian Galeazzo Visconti, came as close as any strong man of the time to knocking out his rivals and uniting northern Italy. He failed, but the fear he inspired remained, and no other Italian was later able to come so close as he.

Venice, the greatest commercial power of the peninsula, was absorbed in her widespread Mediterranean interests and relatively isolated from Italian politics until she began to acquire considerable territory on the mainland in the later fifteenth century. Her republican constitution was the oldest and her government the most stable in Italy. There was no despot in Venice— her doge, or duke, was a figurehead—but there was a tight-knit commercial aristocracy which ran the city, committing broad powers to a small and tough-minded committee, the Council of Ten. Perhaps because her commercial enterprises were so far-flung and the energies of her whole population so absorbed in commerce, there were no real revolutions and few conspiracies in Venetian history. Her constitution stood as a model of republican stability to other Italians.

Florence, like Venice, was proud of being a republic among the welter of despotisms, and especially proud of having helped to frustrate Gian Galeazzo Visconti's attempt to snuff out republican liberties in Italy. But in every other respect these two leading cities of the period were unlike. Venice lived primarily by her commerce, Florence primarily by her industry, especially her textiles and fine crafts. The energies of Venetians were directed outward toward the sea, the energies of Florentines were largely focused on industry and politics within the city walls. Venetian society and Venetian government exhibited a high degree of stability, whereas nothing seemed to be stable in Florence. Bitter party struggles of the thirteenth century became more purely economic conflicts during the next two centuries. It sometimes seemed as if revolution were the chief outdoor sport in Florence, and constitution-

making the chief indoor sport. During the fourteenth and early fifteenth centuries the Florentines tried everything from dictatorship to radical democracy, compromised on oligarchy, and finally ended in boss rule. In 1434 a new-rich party within the oligarchy, led by one of the city's wealthiest and shrewdest bankers, Cosimo de' Medici, gained power. For almost sixty years after 1434 Cosimo and his grandson, Lorenzo the Magnificent (d. 1492), ran the city by manipulating its republican constitution. Cosimo was a banker who had been drawn into politics by his financial interests and was forced to stay in to save his skin. Lorenzo was more a typical despot, only incidentally interested in the family banking business. But each devoted his energy, his money, and his taste to the job of pro-

Lorenzo de' Medici, by an unknown artist. The city of Florence is visible in the background, with Brunelleschi's dome (built 1420–34) visible over Lorenzo's left shoulder.

tecting, expanding, and beautifying the city. Historians are generally agreed that the most glittering example of Italy's golden age was Florence under the Medici.

Italian Urban Civilization

In these busy, crowded cities of northern Italy a new sort of society and a new set of social ideals grew up, quite unlike feudal society and chivalric ideals. Birth and status counted for almost nothing. The chivalric virtues of loyalty and honor seemed irrelevant. Here were urban communities built upon advanced industrial methods and a division of labor, dependent upon the continental market for their economic existence. Competition was keen at every level of life, from managing a shop or fashioning altar pieces to serving as banker to the pope or running a city government. Careers were open to talent everywhere. The cities needed stonecutters and artists, engineers and architects, lawyers and teachers, soldiers and civil servants. It was talent, education, and determination that counted, not birth or ownership of land, although these might still bring social prestige. The man who ended his life as a famous painter, a widely read author, a wealthy banker, or an infamous despot, often began life as a poor peasant or a penniless worker. Self-reliance, rational calculation, ingenuity in adapting means to ends, imagination and boldness—these were the qualities that carried men to the top. And there was always room at the top for creative and brilliant minds, if they had also the will to achieve fame. All these qualities were summed up in a word often on the lips of artists, writers, and statesmen: *virtù*. This was the quality that made a man a true man (Latin: *vir*). It did not mean "virtue" in the modern sense, but rather "virtuosity," that combination of genius and determination which makes for

greatness in artistic creation, statesmanship —or crime.

Individualism

The first mark of this society, at its upper levels at least, was individualism. For the typical Italian city-dweller, few of the old authorities carried the weight they once had carried. He owed no allegiance to a feudal lord. His gild could not regulate his business practices so closely as it might have done two centuries earlier. The city government demanded strict obedience, it is true, but he had a large say in how this government was run, laying down limits which even a despot could not overstep without facing trouble. He recognized no worldly power of king or emperor or pope within the boundaries of his city-state. And although the city-dweller professed himself a good Christian and a hater of heresy, he generally despised the clergy and tended to accept their authority only when it was backed by strong ecclesiastical sanctions. The older authorities were losing ground, and in the literature of the fifteenth century there emerged a startlingly new view of man as a private person, mainly concerned not with any cause beyond himself, whether of gild or of church or of state, but rather with himself, his family, his friends, his own self-development, his individual relation to nature, society, and God. Such an individualistic view of man could only emerge in the highly competitive and mobile society we have described. Sometimes it went to extremes, as it did in the case of Benvenuto Cellini (1500–71), the sixteenth-century sculptor who described his violent and colorful career in a famous *Autobiography*. Cellini assumed, with characteristic frankness, that the ordinary laws of morality were made for ordinary people and neither could nor should be enforced in the case of geniuses like himself. He also assumed that autobiography, a literary form practically unknown in the Middle Ages (except for Augustine's *Confessions*), was a natural form of expression and one that would find eager readers. He begins his book: "All men of whatsoever quality they be, who have done anything of excellence, or which may properly resemble excellence, ought, if they are persons of truth and honesty, to describe their life with their own hand." Later he remarks, "I make no profession of writing history. It is enough for me to occupy myself with my own affairs." Cellini was obviously interesting to himself, and, like many strongly developed individuals of his day, he was sure he was interesting to others as a man of genius.

Secularism

The second mark of this new society was its predominantly secular tone. This does not mean that it was pagan or anti-Christian. It means that the things of this world increasingly occupied the time and attention of the Italian townspeople—manufacturing processes, the balance of profit and loss, well-built houses and fine clothes, richer food and drink, the enjoyment of leisure—and that the ascetic and otherworldly ideals of the medieval Church seemed more and more remote to them. Their tastes and attitudes are evident in the marvelously realistic stories of Boccaccio's popular *Decameron* (ca. 1350). The heroes and heroines are not exactly irreligious or critical of Christian ideals, but they despise the hypocrisy of priests and monks, and they rejoice in the triumph of clever people of the world over clerical busybodies.

The secularism of Italian society can thus be broken down into two components: preoccupation with worldly pursuits, and contempt for those who professed the ascetic ideal but did not live up to it. Along with these attitudes sometimes went a de-

****

Petrarch
on Mortal and Immortal Ends

I do not think my way of looking at it is so unreasonable as you imagine. My principle is that, as concerning the glory which we may hope for here below, it is right for us to seek it while we are here below. One may expect to enjoy that other more radiant glory in heaven, when we shall have there arrived, and when one will have no more care or wish for the glory of earth. Therefore, as I think, it is in the true order that mortal men should first care for mortal things; and that to things transitory things eternal should succeed; because to pass from those to these is to go forward in most certain accordance with what is ordained for us, although no way is open for us to pass back again from eternity to time.

From Petrarch, as quoted in *Petrarch's Secret*, trans. by W. H. Draper (London: Chatto and Windus, 1911), p. 176.

****

mand for a simpler Church, with less emphasis on ceremonies and more emphasis on works of charity. There were a few scoffers and atheists. But most men simply thought more constantly of this world than of the next, without denying the ultimate importance of the next. Few of the writers and artists of the day were pagans. But many of them were deeply troubled by the conflict between this-worldly and otherworldly ideals, and tried to communicate their anxiety with brush or pen. This conflict or tension between older and newer ideals was more typical of the period than was the frank and untroubled enjoyment of temporal pleasures.

Humanism

The third mark of Italian urban society was its enthusiasm for classical antiquity. This enthusiasm came to be called Humanism, from the Latin *humanitas* as used by Cicero to describe the literary culture proper to a well-bred man. The Middle Ages had always lived in the shadow of Rome, and interest in Roman ruins or in Cicero's *Orations* was nothing new. John of Salisbury in the twelfth century had a first-rate knowledge of classical Latin literature, and the greatest medieval poet, Dante, made it his conscious concern to blend the best of both classical and Christian ideals throughout the *Divine Comedy,* as we have seen (p. 359). However, Francesco Petrarca, or Petrarch (1304–74), is rightly called the father of a new Humanism. His enthusiasm for Cicero, his love for Rome (he said he wished he had been born in the ancient world instead of his own), and his feel for the style of classical Latin were contagious. He started a movement. Within a generation or two after his death Petrarch's followers were busily digging out classical manuscripts from monasteries, writing letters to one another in impeccable Ciceronian Latin, pouring contempt on the Latin style of medieval scholastic philosophers, and, most important, getting jobs as civil servants, as secretaries at the papal Curia, as court poets at the palaces of despots, or as teachers to the children of the ruling classes in the cities. These professional Humanists were something new in European society. They were classical scholars who made a living by their learning. Generally they were laymen, not clerics or monks devoting spare time to classical study as medieval classical students had been. They were self-made men who were selling a new enthusiasm to their contemporaries—and who found the market very good. Before the end of the fourteenth century they had attracted many of the sons of ruling families to the study of Cicero, Vergil, Horace, and Livy. From 1395 on, refugee scholars from Constantinople began to teach Greek to

Petrarch, from a portrait in the Metropolitan Museum of Art. The poet is shown crowned with laurel.

eager students in Florence and elsewhere. And by the end of the fifteenth century a few Italians were even beginning to learn Hebrew and Arabic. Humanism was both a scholarly movement of considerable importance and a social fad. The Humanists revived the study of classical Latin, Greek, and Hebrew. And somehow they got the ruling classes of the Italian cities excited about what they were doing.

It is not hard to understand why the ruling circles supported Humanists and adopted Humanism as a kind of cult. The chivalric romances of the feudal nobility were not their kind of literature, nor were the difficult treatises of the medieval Schoolmen. But Plato and Aristotle, Cicero and Seneca, had belonged to societies much like their own. The civic and ethical interests of the ancient writers touched a respondent chord in fifteenth-century business and professional men. The historical analysis of Livy and the moral judgments of Plutarch made sense to burghers who felt that the *Song of Roland* was bombastic and Thomas' *Summa Theologiae* soporific. So a knowledge of classical Latin and an acceptance of the Greco-Roman world as the Golden Age of history became the hallmark of an educated man in fifteenth-century Italy.

The Humanists initiated a revolution in educational theory and practice. Formal education in the Middle Ages had been dominated by the clergy and directed mainly to the production of clerics. The nobility had their own program of training knights to hunt and fight and behave properly at court. But neither of these systems of education offered much to the sons of business and professional town-dwellers, and already there were town schools primarily for laymen which taught arithmetic and medieval Latin grammar. What the Humanists of the fifteenth century did was to rediscover what Greco-Roman writers had meant by the "liberal arts" as the basis of education: the liberating effect on mind and imagination of the study of great literature and philosophy, mathematics and science. To this they added the chivalric emphasis on outdoor activity and athletic skill as an integral part of education. The result was an educational program designed to produce well-rounded and well-read laymen, able to write classical Latin and perhaps Greek, well-mannered and at home in polite society, physically strong and well groomed, skillful in the art of war. "We call those studies liberal," wrote one Humanist educator, "which are worthy of a free man . . . that education which calls forth, trains, and develops those highest gifts of body and of mind which ennoble men." In practice this education too often degenerated into a narrowly literary training, floundering in the grammatical details of dead languages and consciously aristocratic in its ideals. But at its best it passed on to later generations, including our own, the ideal of turning out well-balanced human beings, devoted to the best in both classical and Christian ideals, and able to become better businessmen or lawyers or statesmen because of their liberal education in the arts and sciences.

Historical Self-consciousness

The fourth and final mark of this urban society was its historical self-consciousness. The historical sense of the Middle Ages was not highly developed. The crucial events of the Christian drama had already happened, it was thought, in Bethlehem and Jerusalem, and time now had only to run on and out to its conclusion in the Last Judgment. There had been no essential change since the days of Constantine: the emperor was still theoretically the temporal head of Christendom, and the pope, Christ's Vicar, was the spiritual head. The passage of time would not bring further significant change.

Petrarch and his Humanist successors in the fifteenth century revolutionized this conception of the past. They became more interested in this world and its history. Their enthusiasm for classical antiquity enabled them for the first time to see the ancient world as a civilization that had run its course. It had been born, it had flourished, and it had died. They talked of the "Fall of Rome" and of a "Dark Age" that had followed. Above all, they talked of a "rebirth"

479

or "revival" that was beginning in their own age. This revival was both material and spiritual. It meant the revival of free cities and civic life as well as the revival of arts and letters. Rome had flourished and fallen, darkness had succeeded, but now the light was beginning to dawn once more. For the first time since Greco-Roman civilization was in its prime, a generation had appeared that was highly conscious of its position in history and of its historical mission.

Italian urban society of this period, then, at least in its higher ranks, was a society marked by individualism, secular interests, enthusiasm for an earlier society (the Greco-Roman), and historical self-consciousness. In the minds of its own leading spokesmen, the fifteenth century was an age of rebirth.

The "Renaissance"

The Italian Humanists managed to persuade future generations that theirs was an age of light after darkness, an age of revolt against medieval ideals in which Italy led the way while the rest of Europe slumbered on in darkness until roused by the dawn streaming up from the south. This remained a vague and hazy historical conception, however, until it was elaborated and documented by the Swiss historian, Jacob Burckhardt, in a brilliant book called *The Civilization of the Renaissance in Italy* (1860). Thanks to Burckhardt and his contemporaries, our own generation has become used to the idea that there was a "Renaissance" or rebirth after the Middle Ages, that it marked a sharp break with medieval ideals and practices, and that it was centered in Italy. This idea has helped historians following in Burckhardt's footsteps to see the civilization of the period as a whole—its economic base, its society and politics, its art and literature—as parts of a unified civilization. But, when used to explain every aspect of a complex period, it has resulted in much confusion and positive misconception. Furthermore, enthusiasts have often made the concept ridiculous by insisting that the "Renaissance" was the abrupt end of all things medieval and the beginning of all things modern. There was much truth in Burckhardt's thesis, but he exaggerated both the sharpness of the breach with the medieval past and the uniqueness of Italy over against the rest of Europe.

The term "Renaissance" is most useful when it is applied to the revolutionary change in the arts, in literature, and in the conception of man which took place in Italy in the fourteenth, fifteenth, and early sixteenth centuries. It is less useful when applied to political and ecclesiastical history, because it is hard to say what "rebirth" means in these areas. And it is quite useless when applied to economic and social history, in which changes are always slow and in which the important developments began as far back as the eleventh century. Historians of art and literature are relatively sure of what "Renaissance" means; other historians are unsure in varying degrees to the point of total doubt. This does not mean that artistic and literary developments did not have their roots in economic and social change. It means simply that the word "Renaissance" is best used to describe the revolution in artistic and literary taste and skill that occurred at the close of the Middle Ages.

From the very beginning the idea of "Renaissance" was ambiguous. To fifteenth-century writers as well as to nineteenth-century historians it meant not only "rebirth" but also "new birth." From one point of view it was the revival of antiquity; from another it was an outburst of creative originality. Much in the Renaissance owed its inspiration directly or indirectly to re-

NORWAY

SW

ATLANTIC OCEAN

NORTH SEA

DENMARK

SCOTLAND

Edinburgh

IRELAND

Dublin

ENGLAND

Hamburg

Lübeck

Bremen

Brunswick

Magdeburg

Elbe River

Oxford   Cambridge

Leiden

Rotterdam

Antwerp

Rhine River

Leipzig

Cologne

Erfurt

HOLY   RO

London

ENGLISH CHANNEL

Bruges

Ghent

Brussels

Louvain

Noyon

Paris

Seine River

Trier

Mainz

Prague

BURGUNDY

Nuremberg

Regensburg

EMPIRE

Fontainebleau

Loire Ri

Tours

FRANCE

Dijon

Augsburg

BAY OF BISCAY

Angoulême

Bordeaux

Lyons

Basel

Zurich

Constance

Geneva

Milan

Trent

Venice

Po River

Rhône R.

Avignon

Genoa

Ferrara

Bologna

ADRIA

Marseilles

Pisa

Florence

Siena

PAPAL STATES

Perugia

NAVARRE

Ebro R.

ARAGON

Duero River

Ebro

PORTUGAL

CASTILE

Escorial

Tagus River

Madrid

Barcelona

CORSICA

N A

Rome

Lisbon

Seville

SARDINIA (ARAGON)

Napl

GRANADA

Palermo

SICILY (ARAGON)

European Civilization

15th century

MEDIT

TEST

N

Novgorod

Moscow

BALTIC SEA

Danzig

Königsberg

Thorn

Vistula River

Volga River

POLAND — LITHUANIA

Kiev

Dnieper River

Don River

Cracow

er River

ienna

Buda

HUNGARY

Danube River

OTTOMAN

BLACK SEA

Constantinople

Salonika

Tigris Riv

AEGEAN SEA

EMPIRE

Euphrates River

RHODES

CYPRUS

CRETE

RANEAN SEA

Nile R.

J. P. TREMBLAY

newed knowledge of ancient models in literature and art, but much was quite unconnected with such models. On the one hand, the word "Renaissance" describes the revival of classical architecture, classical sculpture, classical history, philosophy, and poetry. On the other, it describes original developments in the arts and letters which were the natural outgrowth of medieval creativity. These two main streams are often difficult for critics and historians to separate, but it was their simultaneous presence, their competition with each other, and their final blending in the art of the High Renaissance that gave the period its peculiar character.

Both "rebirth" and "new birth" were evident in the work of Petrarch. He wrote an epic poem in purely classical Latin on the career of Scipio, and he also wrote exquisite lyrics in Italian celebrating the loveliness of his Laura. In the first he was purely imitative, in the second he was developing a recent poetic tradition that had originated in Provence. So it was with Boccaccio (1313–75), who attempted a Latin epic himself but was more successful with his collection of stories in the vernacular, the *Decameron*. And so it was through the subsequent history of the Renaissance. The two streams sometimes diverged and one or the other might be predominant for the moment in one or another of the arts. But always revival and originality, criticism and creativity, tended to balance each other. While going back to classical antiquity, the artists and writers of the period also moved forward along paths unexplored by their predecessors.

Literature, Philosophy, and Scholarship

Wherever there were classical models to fall back on, the tendency at first was for both writers and artists to lose themselves in simple imitation, in the first flush of excited rediscovery. It was easy, for instance,

A Great Historian's Conception of the Renaissance

In the Middle Ages both sides of human consciousness—that which was turned within as that which was turned without—lay dreaming or half awake beneath a common veil. The veil was woven of faith, illusion, and childish prepossession, through which the world and history were seen clad in strange hues. Man was conscious of himself only as member of a race, people, party, family, or corporation—only through some general category. In Italy this veil first melted into air; an *objective* treatment and consideration of the state and of all the things of this world became possible. The *subjective* side at the same time asserted itself with corresponding emphasis; man became a spiritual *individual*, and recognised himself as such. In the same way the Greek had once distinguished himself from the barbarian, and the Arabian had felt himself an individual at a time when other Asiatics knew themselves only as members of a race. It will not be difficult to show that this result was owing above all to the political circumstances of Italy. . . . At the close of the thirteenth century Italy began to swarm with individuality; the charm laid upon human personality was dissolved; and a thousand figures meet us each in its own special shape and dress. Dante's great poem would have been impossible in any other country of Europe.

From Jacob Burckhardt, *The Civilization of the Renaissance in Italy*, 1860 (London: Allen & Unwin, 1878), Part II, Ch. 1, p. 129: "The Development of the Individual."

for Humanists to imitate the letter-writing, the orations, the moral essays, and even the poetry of the Romans—and they did, *ad nauseam,* in the early fifteenth century. It was fashionable for these same Humanists to pour contempt on Dante because he wrote in the vulgar tongue. When it became possible for educated Florentines to read Plato in the original Greek, it was perhaps natural for their enthusiasm to know no bounds. Cosimo de' Medici founded, and Lorenzo fostered, an informal group of scholars who became known as the Platonic Academy. Their leading members, Marsilio Ficino (1433–99) and Pico della Mirandola (1463–94), tried to reconcile Platonism and Christianity, as the Schoolmen had tried to reconcile Aristotelianism and Christianity (see p. 359). It was the one serious attempt at philosophical synthesis during the Renaissance, and it was a failure. But its authors' enthusiasm for Plato and Platonism was infectious and had widespread influence on poets and painters throughout Europe in the next century. In fact, Plato dominated the imagination of the Renaissance as Aristotle had dominated the thought of the Schoolmen.

All was not mere imitation in Italian thought and writing, however. Particularly in their scholarship and in their social and political thought, Italians broke new ground. Modern critical scholarship, in the sense of careful linguistic and historical analysis of the literary remains of the past, dates from the Renaissance, and particularly from one of the keenest minds of the age, Lorenzo Valla (*ca.* 1405–57). Valla analyzed the language and the historical background of the so-called Donation of Constantine (see p. 243), one of the main bulwarks of the popes' claims to temporal power, and proved for the first time beyond a shadow of a doubt that the document was a clumsy forgery of the Dark Ages. He further compared several Greek manuscripts of the New Testament with the accepted Latin translation, the Vulgate, and showed that the translation was full of errors and distortions. The critical spirit and scholarly technique which he inaugurated

influenced Erasmus, Pierre Bayle, and Voltaire, and resulted in the end in the "scientific" scholarship of the nineteenth century.

Social and Political Thought

Much of Renaissance thought about the relation of man to man simply paraphrased the ethics and political theory of the Greeks and Romans. But sometimes a man wrote freshly from his own experience, and although his book might owe much on the surface to the ancients, it revealed his own society and spoke directly to its members. Such a book was Leon Battista Alberti's (1404–72) *On the Family.* Its author was one of the incredibly versatile geniuses so much admired by the age. He was a thorough classical scholar, but he was much more: poet, musician, architect, inventor, mathematician, and athlete. In this book, written not in Latin for the learned but in Italian for the ordinary citizen, he described the interests and ideals of a well-to-do bourgeois family. The virtues and concerns are those of the Florentine families he knew: prudence and thrift, strong

A terra-cotta bust of Machiavelli which suggests both the clear-sightedness and the inscrutability of the man.

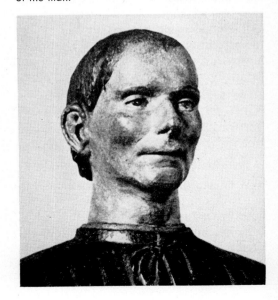

family feeling and little concern for larger causes outside, appreciation of comfort, planning and foresight, and pride in owning a house in the city and an estate in the country to produce all the family's food. It is one of the earliest idealized portraits we have of what will later be called the bourgeois virtues.

The social stratum just above that described by Alberti is sketched in Baldassare Castiglione's (1478–1529) widely read description, *The Courtier,* based on his memories of the court of the duke of Urbino. If Alberti painted the good householder for future generations, Castiglione painted the gentleman—graceful, attractive, courteous, liberally educated, noble in spirit if not now necessarily in birth, at home either on the field of battle or among cultivated ladies. Here the society of the despotic courts was presented at its best. The concept of "the gentleman" owed much to chivalry and other traditional sources, but as Castiglione presented it it was a genuinely fresh ideal in the history of European civilization.

The historical writing and political theory of the Renaissance were heavily indebted to classical models, but in the case of Niccolò Machiavelli (1469–1527) wide reading in the classics was added to years of practical political experience. Machiavelli believed that the classics could be useful. His experience as ambassador and secretary of the Florentine government helped him to understand the Roman historian Livy, and Livy helped him to understand the power politics of his own age. Exiled by the Medici from Florence in 1512, he began to read widely and to reflect on what makes states expand and grow, what are the causes of political breakdown, how political leaders get and hold power, what can be learned from the past.

Machiavelli set down his reflections in a

Machiavelli on the Policy of Princes

You must know, then, that there are two methods of fighting, the one by law, the other by force: the first method is that of men, the second of beasts; but as the first method is often insufficient, one must have recourse to the second. It is therefore necessary for a prince to know well how to use both the beast and the man.

A prince being thus obliged to know well how to act as a beast must imitate the fox and the lion, for the lion cannot protect himself from traps, and the fox cannot defend himself from wolves. One must therefore be a fox to recognise traps, and a lion to frighten wolves. Those that wish to be only lions do not understand this. Therefore, a prudent ruler ought not to keep faith when by so doing it would be against his interest, and when the reasons which made him bind himself no longer exist. If men were all good, this precept would not be a good one; but as they are bad, and would not observe their faith with you, so you are not bound to keep faith with them.

From Machiavelli, *The Prince,* in *The Prince and the Discourses,* ed. by Max Lerner (New York: Modern Library, 1940), Ch. 18, p. 64.

long rambling book, *Discourses on Livy,* and in a briefer and more famous essay, *The Prince.* He made it clear that he was describing things as they were, not as they ought to be. Ideal states he left to others to describe. In the world as it is, power is what counts. The Roman Republic, he thought, was the best example in history of successful state-building. Its constitution was a masterly blend of monarchy, aristocracy, and democracy; it had good laws and a good citizen army; its religion supported the civic virtues of justice, prudence, and courage, not those of patience and humility; its rulers knew that the good of the state came before the rules of individual morality. And so Rome, unlike any Italian city-state or despotism of Machiavelli's day, had been able to unite the whole of Italy, to preserve order, and to continue growing at its rivals' expense.

But Machiavelli realized that this ideal, real though it once had been, might be too difficult for a corrupt, divided, and powerless group of Italian city-states to revive. Perhaps a prince of real *virtù,* with the courage of a lion and the cunning of a fox, might be able to learn the laws of politics from history and experience and use them to seize power, hold it, and thus build a strong state in Italy. He would know that men in their collective relations with one another are bad, and therefore he would not be held back by any moral scruples. If others broke faith with him, as they certainly would, the prince must be prepared to break faith with them for the good of his state. Fortune might frustrate his work, but a man of *virtù* had at least an even chance of overcoming bad luck. If his generation had both the intelligence and the will, Machiavelli believed, something could be done about the helpless state of Italy, which was by now falling under the heels of France and Spain.

Machiavelli's *Prince* was to become a grammar of political and diplomatic practice to heads of state as remote as Mussolini and Hitler. In its origin it was a perfect example of the fruitful combination of classical "rebirth" and contemporary "new birth," of historical example and practical experience in Renaissance thought. Both his disillusioned analysis of things as they were and his passionate plea for reform were entirely characteristic of the age.

The Arts

The influence of classical examples was strong also in the visual arts, but here the creative element was even more prominent than in social and political thought. Roman buildings survived, of course, all over Italy. Brunelleschi (1377?–1446), the greatest architect of his generation, absorbed their spirit and designed new churches in purely classical style after 1420, thus inaugurating a return to the classical from the Gothic style in architecture. The late Roman sculpture which was dug up (hardly any of the great Greek works of the classical age were yet known) inspired sculptors to imitation. But there were no ancient paintings to look at (Pompeii was not unearthed until the eighteenth century), and so Italian painters had to depend on the inspiration of their medieval predecessors and their own genius in elaborating their art. It is generally agreed that they outdistanced all their competitors, and many think that they brought painting to the highest point it has ever reached.

Italian Renaissance painting developed mainly out of the late medieval tradition known as Gothic naturalism. The dominant interest of fourteenth-century writers, artists, and philosophers was in the concrete, individual thing as it actually existed, not so much in the general idea or eternal truth behind and in all things, which had been the typical concern of earlier medieval thinkers. Late medieval artists and writers tried to represent nature and man more and more realistically—to model a leaf as it actually appeared in nature, to chisel the features of a real man or woman, to sketch the character of a person in concrete detail, as both Boccaccio and Chaucer did with such success in their collections of tales. In fifteenth-century painting, particularly in the Netherlands, this effort resulted in the most astonishing skill in representing the smallest details of visual reality—the wrinkles of a man's face or the stubble on his chin, for instance (Van Eyck, p. 471, was of this school).

It was an Italian painter, however, who

first realized that photographic realism is not enough, that the artist must conceive the human figure as a whole, place it in three-dimensional perspective, and represent it through a more sophisticated realism that sacrifices minute details to organic unity. This painter was Masaccio (1401–ca. 1428), the founder of Renaissance painting and one of the great innovators in the history of the art.

Italian painting of the fifteenth and sixteenth centuries is far too rich in content and varied in technique for us to describe here in detail. Some of its general characteristics may be suggested, however. The first thing that strikes the historical observer is the separation of painting and sculpture from architecture. It was as if the sculptured prophets and many-colored saints had stepped down from their niches and stained-glass windows in the great medieval cathedrals to be reincarnated in bronze statues in Italian public squares or painted portraits in Italian palaces. Painting and sculpture were no longer arts subordinate to architecture. Painters began to adorn the walls of monasteries and houses with frescoes. After they had learned from Flemish artists the technique of painting with oils, the Italians went on to develop the easel painting, meant to be hung in a palace or house and enjoyed for its own sake. Donatello (1386?–1466), the great innovator in sculpture, was the first to model a free-standing nude figure in his *David*, and from then on to the great works of Michelangelo (1475–1564) sculptors developed their art with no thought but of its own perfection. The zest of solving fresh problems infected the architects as well as the painters and sculptors. Brunelleschi had no classical or medieval models to help him in designing and building his famous dome over the transept of the cathedral in Florence (1420–36). Architecture, sculpture, and painting each went its own way.

An individual artist might turn his hand to all three as many did, and a painter might borrow ideas from sculpture. But in each case the artist could create as he pleased without subjecting one art to another.

The second characteristic worth noting was the heightened individuality and social prestige of the artist. A famous passage in Cellini's *Autobiography* describes the unveiling of his great bronze statue of Perseus in the central square of Florence in 1554. "Now it pleased God," he wrote, "that on the instant of its exposure to view,

Benvenuto Cellini's bronze statue of Perseus with the head of Medusa, in Florence.

a shout of boundless enthusiasm went up in commendation of my work, which consoled me not a little." Such a shout might have greeted the proclamation of a crusade in the eleventh century or the triumphant conclusion of a world war in the twentieth. But the public appreciation of a work of art, the assumption that great art is the product of individual "genius," which is something to be nurtured—these were as characteristic of the Renaissance as they were atypical of ages before and after. The artist was to the age of the Renaissance what the saint was to the Middle Ages and what the scientist was to be to the modern world. Italy's Golden Age was the golden age of the artist and the writer.

As Italian industry and commerce reached maturity in the fourteenth and fifteenth centuries, more and more of the surplus capital which had been plowed back into business in earlier centuries was invested in civic building, public improvements, and luxury. Sometimes the result was simply display and bad taste. But particularly in Florence, later in Rome and Venice and elsewhere, public and private patrons developed the ability to distinguish between mere craftsmanship and real art. And artists who could communicate human emotion and timeless truth through their creations came forth to fulfill the commissions of the wealthy and to enter the competitions advertised by city govern-

Air view of St. Peter's Cathedral in Rome. In 1505 Pope Julius II commissioned the architect Bramante to tear down the older church, which was reputed to have been built in 326 A.D. over the grave of St. Peter, and to begin the construction of a vastly larger structure which would mirror the classical-Christian aspirations of the 16th century at their best. The plans were changed several times; the dome was designed by Michelangelo, and the church itself was completed in 1626. The colonnades framing the approach to the cathedral were designed by Bernini in the seventeenth century. The small rectangular building just to the right of the cathedral is the Sistine Chapel (see p. 490).

ments. The origins of great art must always remain a mystery to the historian, but certainly intelligent patronage and public appreciation have much to do with them, and these the Italian artist had in fullest measure during the Renaissance. Ghiberti's marvelous bronze doors for the Baptistery in Florence (1425–52), worthy to be the gates of Paradise, in Michelangelo's words, are a good example of how a public contest, popular appreciation, and individual genius combined to produce a work of art.

St. Peter's church in Rome is in some ways the culmination of the art of the Renaissance. Here three of the finest artists of their day—Bramante, Raphael, and Michelangelo—were put to work by Julius II (1503–13), a pope with grandiose ideas, furious energy, and an instinct for artistic greatness. The result was a monument that perfectly expresses the Renaissance yearning to reconcile the best in the classical and Christian traditions.

The third characteristic of Italian art is its overwhelming concern with actual human beings here and now, precisely located in time and space, and represented in their full individuality. Byzantine and early medieval art was thoroughly symbolic. Figures and objects were meant to suggest theological truths, such as the Incarnation, or moral ideas, such as sacrifice. Important persons were pictured as larger than others or nearer heaven. Historical figures and contemporary figures were intermingled, all in contemporary dress, because the passage of time meant little in the face of eternity. Late medieval artists, however, became more and more interested in representing people and objects as they actually appeared to the eye. As their skill increased, they posed themselves, and their even more skillful Renaissance followers, a serious problem: how can an artist suggest an eternal spiritual truth by a photographic technique? Renaissance painters studied

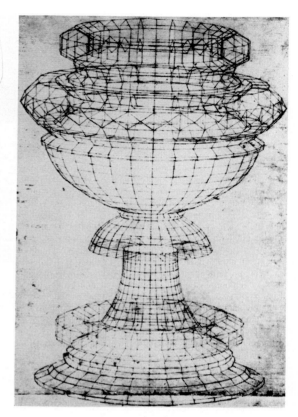

Drawing of a chalice by Paolo Uccello (1397–1475). Uccello devoted almost all his life to working out the rules of the fascinating new science of perspective, the art of picturing objects in three-dimensional space. This is an example of his numerous studies.

the laws of spatial perspective about the same time that Humanists were restudying the temporal or historical perspective of their day. As a result the artists pictured real persons whom they knew, in recognizable space, and living at a particular time, as shown by their costume. Some of them spent their lives in probing the psychological depths of human beings and trying to put on canvas what they found. The chief of these was the lonely scientific and artistic genius, Leonardo da Vinci (1452–1519), whose curiosity about the secrets of nature was as insatiable as his curiosity about the

487

Leonardo da Vinci's *The Last Supper* (1495–98). The original, on a wall of the church of Santa Maria delle Grazie in Milan, has been almost destroyed by moisture.

nature of man. In painting *The Last Supper* he chose not the moment when Christ breaks the bread and remarks, "This is my body . . . ," as a medieval artist might have done, but the more humanly dramatic and startling moment when He announces, "One of you will betray me." The resulting psychological crisis in each disciple is carefully portrayed. The climactic episode of the Creation, as Michelangelo painted it on the ceiling of the Sistine Chapel in St. Peter's, was the creation of Adam—an almost superhuman man at the threshold of self-consciousness, languid, wondering, awakening—almost as if he were a symbol of the man of the Renaissance. If some interpreters are correct, the same artist chose to portray Moses at the moment when he has caught sight of his people's idolatrous Golden Calf and is struggling to control himself.

These few examples out of many that might be chosen make the Renaissance point of view evident. The central concern is man here in this world, troubled, striving, with unknown possibilities. Thus Renaissance art is humanistic in the broader, more philosophical meaning of the word. Not that the artists rejected God or ignored nature. God is still there, and Renaissance landscapes are charming. But God is seen *through* man, through his heroism and his tragedy; and generally nature is of interest only as background or setting to the human drama. The most important question is what is to become of man. Pico della Mirandola, in a famous *Oration* on man's dignity (1486), pictured God as giving man something he had given to no other creature, the unique gift of freedom:

> Thou, constrained by no limits, in accordance with thine own free will, in whose hands We have placed thee, shalt ordain for thyself the limits of thy nature. . . . We have made thee neither of heaven nor of earth, neither mortal nor immortal, so that with freedom of choice and with honor, as though the maker and molder of thyself, thou mayest fashion thyself in whatever shape thou shalt prefer.

Every other creature had its pattern and its

limits, but to Pico man's nature and destiny were in his own hands. The men of the Renaissance had not lost belief in God, but they were convinced, in a way their medieval ancestors would not have understood, that man was on his own.

The greatness of Italian art lay in the fact that it reflected all the tensions and contradictions in the prevailing attitudes toward man. There was no party line in Renaissance art; there were no premature solutions of sharp differences, no accepted syntheses. Some artists were realists, others idealists. Donatello modeled despots as he saw them, with hard and observant realism, while Raphael (1483–1520) a generation later idealized the peasant girls he knew as calm and self-possessed Madonnas of ethereal beauty. Some artists were scientists and psychologists like Leonardo, who tried to peer into the souls of men and women, while others were like the Venetian Titian (1477–1576), who was more

interested in the external marks of character and the glorious play of color on the objects about him. Michelangelo, perhaps the most typical as well as the greatest artist of them all, gave his life to attempting the impossible: to reconciling the classical ideal of harmony, balance, and "nothing in excess," with the limitless strivings and boundless love of Christian piety. This attempt to reconcile the Greco-Roman and Hebraic-Christian worlds was the central striving of the Renaissance. It failed,

❖❖❖❖❖❖❖❖❖❖❖❖❖❖❖❖❖❖❖❖❖❖❖❖❖❖❖❖❖

Freud
on Michelangelo's Moses

The Moses of legend and tradition had
a hasty temper and was subject to fits of passion.
It was in a transport of divine wrath
of this kind that he slew an Egyptian who
was maltreating an Israelite, and had to
flee out of the land into the wilderness; and it
was in a similar passion that he broke the
Tables of the Law, inscribed by God
Himself. . . . But Michelangelo has placed a
different Moses on the tomb of the Pope,
one superior to the historical or traditional Moses.
He has modified the theme of the broken
Tables; he does not let Moses break them in his
wrath, but makes him be influenced by the
danger that they will be broken and calm that
wrath, or at any rate prevent it from becoming
an act. In this way he has added something new
and more than human to the figure of Moses;
so that the giant frame with its tremendous
physical power becomes only a concrete
expression of the highest mental achievement
that is possible in a man, that of struggling
successfully against an inward passion
for the sake of a cause to which he has
devoted himself.

From Sigmund Freud, "The Moses of Michelangelo," 1914, *On Creativity and the Unconscious* (New York: Harper, 1958), p. 37.

❖❖❖❖❖❖❖❖❖❖❖❖❖❖❖❖❖❖❖❖❖❖❖❖❖❖❖❖❖

Moses, by Michelangelo.

The Creation of Adam, by Michelangelo, from the ceiling of the Sistine Chapel, Rome. Michelangelo considered himself primarily a sculptor, but from 1508 to 1512 Pope Julius kept him at the task of painting this ceiling. His subject matter was the Book of Genesis, but his theme was really the glory of the human body, as this panel of the creation of Adam suggests. In both conception and execution the Sistine ceiling is one of the greatest masterpieces of western painting.

but the failure left an imperishable record in the arts.

Natural Science

The Renaissance contributed relatively little to the progress of natural science, but this little was important. The Humanists in general were more interested in man than in nature, more absorbed in literature than in science, more fascinated by form and style than by content. For several generations the more adventurous young minds in Italy were attracted to art and literature rather than to mathematics and physics. "From the scientific point of view," writes George Sarton, "the Renaissance was *not* a renaissance." The Humanists "created beauty, plenty of it, but not truth." Nevertheless the northern Italian cities of the fourteenth and fifteenth centuries contrib-

uted significantly to the scientific tradition that reached and influenced Galileo in the seventeenth.

In mechanical techniques and in the sciences that directly concerned man and his comfort the Italians made important progress, as might have been expected. As craftsmen, mechanics, and engineers, they were the best in Europe. In the science of perspective, their painters worked out the mathematical principles of representing figures in space. Their artists and doctors together advanced the knowledge of human anatomy beyond where it had been left by the Greeks. The *Notebooks* of Leonardo da Vinci are a landmark in the history of both art and science, and show how closely the two interests were related in a fifteenth-century mind. His studies of anatomical detail, for instance, are of equal interest to painters and doctors. Machiavelli sketched the anatomy of man in society with something of the same aesthetic feeling and scientific detachment as Leonardo, a fact that has persuaded some later historians to call him "the father of social science." Furthermore, the northern Italian universities, particularly Padua, where academic freedom was jealously guarded by Venice after 1404, fostered the study of mathematics, carried on the arguments over Aristotelian science that had been begun at the University of Paris, and eventually passed on to Galileo a theory of scientific method in something like its modern form.

The Example of Italy

Enough has been said to suggest how pervasive Italy's influence was on the rest of Europe during the Renaissance. This influence began as early as the thirteenth century and continued through the sixteenth. At first it was the economic institutions and practices of Italians that influenced other peoples. In the thirteenth and fourteenth centuries the business and banking practices of the northern Italian cities spread throughout much of Europe. In the fifteenth, Italians developed and passed on the device of double-entry bookkeeping, which gave businessmen a ready check on profits and stimulated the development of capitalism. The political practices of the despots and the political speculations of Italian thinkers had influence outside the peninsula, although differences of scale between a feudal monarchy like France and a city-state like Florence prevented direct imitation.

From the fifteenth century on, however, it was Italian Humanism and Italian art that spread most widely. By 1500 there were classical scholars in Germany and France who owed their enthusiasm for their new pursuits directly to Petrarch and

his successors in Italy. In the next century Humanism took root in Spain, England, and Poland. The first national histories of France and England on the model of classical histories were written by professional Italian Humanists. These were later imitated in Latin and the vernaculars by native writers. Ciceronian style, neoplatonism, the Italian concept of a liberal education, the ideal of "the gentleman," Renaissance architecture, Italian taste and technique in painting—all these spread to Augsburg and Antwerp, to London, Paris, and Madrid, either through Italians abroad or through northerners who came to study or fight in Italy.

The other countries of Europe, of

Studies in the anatomy of the neck and foot, by Leonardo da Vinci, showing how closely related were the viewpoints of "art" and "science" in the mind of a great genius of the Renaissance.

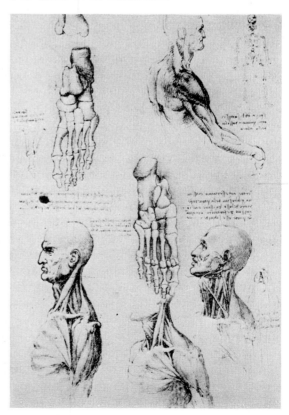

course, had their own traditions in literature, art, and thought. Albrecht Dürer (1471–1528), the most versatile and profound northern artist of the age, owed much to Italy, but he was thoroughly rooted in the tradition of his native Germany. The splendid Flemish painting of the fifteenth and sixteenth centuries owed little to Italian example, and the Flemish were able to teach the Italians something in their technique of painting with oils. French and English literature of the sixteenth century, culminating in Montaigne and Shakespeare, were essentially original developments. But it was typical of the century that Montaigne had traveled in Italy and that Shakespeare drew on Italian sources for some of his plots. Italian influence did not penetrate very far north of the Baltic or east of Poland and Hungary. But elsewhere the upper classes were all affected in one way or another by Italian styles and tastes, Italian ways of living, Italian ways of thinking. The result might be imitation, or it might be revulsion from "Italianate" manners. But everywhere the influence of Italy was felt during her golden age.

The Councils and the Papacy

Italy's golden age was not a golden age of the Church, whose capital was Rome. Three problems faced churchmen at the opening of the fifteenth century: (1) how to heal the Great Schism and restore the damaged prestige of the papacy resulting from the election of two popes; (2) how to stop the accelerating growth of heresy throughout western Christendom; (3) how to reform the administrative, financial, and moral abuses in the Church. By the end of the fifteenth century there was only one pope in Rome, but the prestige of his office had been sadly tarnished. The most dangerous heresies had been walled off or driven underground, but the religious atmosphere was heavy with discontent and revolt. Italy's age of light was an age of gathering darkness for the medieval Church.

The Great Schism (see p. 378) constituted an almost intolerable financial and psychological burden on Europe. It was hard enough to support one luxurious papal court, at Avignon; it was even harder to support two. In theory there could not possibly be two true Vicars of Christ, yet there was no way of being sure which of the two claimants was the real successor. Men felt as if they were in a sinking ship: "If we remain in it," a contemporary wrote, "we must perish with it, and if we stray outside, salvation escapes us, since outside the ship there is no salvation." Many Lollards and other heretics had strayed outside. Those who remained on board tried desperately to find some solution.

The two lines of popes at Rome and Avignon acted stubbornly, refusing to resign, to submit to arbitration, or even to meet each other. Their behavior served to increase antipapal feeling among both clergy and laity throughout Europe. In 1395 the French became so exasperated with their own pope that the French clergy, egged on by the government, withdrew their obedience from him for five years. This was the first sign of a policy which was to have an ominous future: secession from papal jurisdiction by the clergy of a large nation under the pressure of the secular government. There were already signs that the Babylonian Captivity and the schism might result in the dissolution of Christendom into independent national churches.

The Conciliar Movement

As early as 1379, the year after the schism developed, conscientious scholars at the university of Paris had suggested a more conservative and practical scheme than withdrawal of obedience. They urged that a general council of the Church be called. The leading advocates of the idea at the university worked out a revolutionary conception of the Church to support their proposal. The Church, they argued, was not the papacy, but the whole body of believers. Thus the Church's authority was embodied in a council representing all the faithful, with the pope as a limited monarch responsible to this representative assembly. The so-called fullness of power, which canon lawyers claimed for the pope, was a usurpation. Authority in the Church came from the bottom up, not from the top down. This conciliar theory of the constitution of the Church was to have strong appeal to secular rulers who were looking for a club to hold over the papacy. It was also to have a strong attraction for conscientious reformers during the next century.

In 1408 most of the cardinals of both sides deserted their popes and summoned a general council to meet at Pisa the next year. For a moment, a group of cardinals without a pope stood facing two popes without any cardinals, but the result was simply the election of a third pope. Unfortunately neither the Roman nor the Avignonese pope resigned as they were expected to. After five more years of confused negotiations, the new emperor, Sigismund, looking for prestige, compelled the Pisan pope, John XXIII, to summon a genuinely representative assembly.

This great council, which met at Constance in Switzerland from 1414 to 1418, made a strong impression on the imagination of the age. It healed the schism by bullying John XXIII into resigning, persuading the Roman pope to resign after he had gone through the formality of summoning and approving the council himself, and deposing the Avignonese pope, who by now had fled to the Spanish border and was supported only by Aragon. In 1417 it elected a new pope, Martin V, who soon commanded the allegiance of all western Christendom. The council was not so successful, however, in its other two tasks of suppressing heresy and instituting reform. The English and German delegates worked hard but unsuccessfully to have reform considered *before* the election of a new pope; the Latin nations were more anxious to heal the schism first and let reform come later. Once Martin V was elected, interest flagged in even the mild report of a committee to study abuses, and the council dispersed without ever really facing the complicated malpractices in the hierarchy. The bishops and doctors who were most eager to depose the schismatic popes and thus unite the Church were most severe and shortsighted in dealing with heresy.

John Hus

The danger-spot in 1414 was Bohemia. Here during the preceding century the emperor Charles IV had helped to foster a great national and cultural awakening among the Czechs. This awakening had run head-on into two obstacles: a corrupt and leaderless Church, and a steady influx of Germans into the cities and into the University of Prague. Since the Germans tended to support the status quo in the Church, the gifted group of Czech reformers who began to preach against ecclesiastical abuses toward the end of the fourteenth century soon found themselves leading a movement that was as much patriotic as it was religious. And this gave it its strength. In 1402 a brilliant young leader appeared in John Hus (1369?–1415). The burden of his preaching was that the Bible was the sole ultimate rule of faith, that Christ, not the pope, was the true Head of the Church, and that a man is saved by God through Christ, not by trusting in ceremonies and in a mediating priesthood now thoroughly corrupt. Hus had absorbed the ideas of Wiclif, whose books had been brought to

Bohemia by Czech students returning from England. By 1414 Hus himself had been excommunicated by the Roman pope, but he was at liberty, his movement was growing, and it looked as if Lollardy had struck fresh roots in Bohemia.

Hus eagerly seized the opportunity to journey to Constance to present his case before the council. He was almost immediately imprisoned for heresy. The emperor, who had granted him a safe-conduct, withdrew his protection the moment the dreaded charge of heresy was made. The conciliar leaders would have preferred a public recantation which could have been publicized throughout Bohemia, but Hus stood firm. In the dramatic trial that followed, the essential issue was whether the Bible and a man's conscience are the ultimate religious authority, as Hus argued, or whether the Catholic Church represented

John Hus on his way to the stake, from the 15th-century *Chronicle of the Council of Constance*.

by the clerical hierarchy is the sole authority, as the council declared. Hus was condemned and burned at the stake outside the walls of Constance in May 1415. His follower, Jerome of Prague, was burned on the same spot the following spring.

Civil and religious warfare broke out in Bohemia before the council disbanded. It lasted for almost twenty years. The upshot was an agreement in 1436 between the more conservative of the Hussites and the Church. This agreement recognized a national church in Bohemia with local control over ecclesiastical appointments and with liturgical differences, notably the right to offer the cup as well as the bread to the laity in the Eucharist. For the first time the Church had made an agreement on equal terms with condemned heretics after solemnly preaching a crusade and calling down the curses of Heaven upon them. Wiclif's Lollards had been driven underground in England, but the Hussite heresy had simply been walled off in Bohemia.

The restored papacy, which owed its existence to the Council of Constance, was more successful in defeating the conciliar movement than it was in extirpating heresy. The fathers had decreed at Constance that general councils must be summoned regularly, eventually once every ten years. The popes reluctantly complied with the letter of the decree but worked skillfully to control the councils they called. The Council of Basel (1431–49), which negotiated the agreement of 1436 with the Hussites, got out of hand for a time, deposed the Roman pope, and elected another. But in the end the superior diplomacy and more efficient administrative machinery of the Roman papacy won out. The leading churchmen and the most powerful secular rulers deserted the council, and by the time Nicholas V became pope (1447–55), the threat that the Church might be transformed into a limited monarchy was over.

Never again was there a general council of the Church that the pope could not control.

The popes' triumph over the councils left the papacy stronger in some respects, but weaker in others. Within the Church itself there was no longer any ecclesiastical body able to challenge the papal "fullness of power," but the victory had been bought at the price of further concessions to powerful secular rulers. In opposing the reforming element in the councils, the popes had isolated themselves still further from clerical and lay leaders of opinion, particularly in the north of Europe. As a result the popes had little defense when lay rulers announced that *they* would promulgate the decrees of the councils and reform the clergy within their own realms. In 1438 the king of France summoned an assembly of the French clergy and issued a solemn decree known as the Pragmatic Sanction of Bourges. This decree asserted the superiority of council to pope and strictly limited the pope's power of appointment and taxation in France. The effect was practically to set up a national, or "Gallican," Church, as it was called. In later years the popes were able to persuade the French monarchs to modify this one-sided action by "concordats," or agreements, between the papacy and the French crown. But in these agreements the monarchy always retained its control over appointments to the higher clergy. With some differences, the kings of England and Spain established similar limitations on papal power during the fourteenth and fifteenth centuries. In Germany, where there was no central government strong enough to stand up to the pope, papal rights of appointment, taxation, and jurisdiction were not limited as they were in the stronger monarchies. The popes had eliminated all rivals for power within the Church, only to be faced by much more greedy and formidable rivals outside the Church, the monarchs.

Julius II, "the warrior pope" satirized by Erasmus, patron of Bramante, Raphael, and Michelangelo, in a marvelous portrait study by Raphael.

The Renaissance Papacy

The eighty years between the accession of Nicholas V to the papacy (1447) and the sack of Rome (1527) are often called the period of the Renaissance Papacy. It was a brilliant but tragic era in the history of the Church. Some of the popes of the period were patrons of Humanism and the arts, notably Nicholas V, founder of the Vatican Library, and Julius II (1503–13), builder of St. Peter's. One, Pius II (1458–64), was Aeneas Sylvius, a celebrated Humanist, before his election. Two were particularly noted for their wars: Sixtus IV (1471–84), who was rumored to have died of rage at the conclusion of a peace settlement; and Julius II, who was also known to his generation as "the Warrior Pope." More than one was notorious for his nepotism, or favoritism to relatives. Roderigo Borgia, Alexander VI (1492–1503), was by far the worst of the lot. His mistresses lived openly with him, his voracious relatives from Spain got whatever they asked for, and his notorious son, Cesare Borgia, made a bloody attempt to become the ruler of all northern Italy with his father's help. Under Renaissance popes Church offices were offered to the highest bidders, a bank for the sale of pardons was set up in Rome, and a papal chancellor was said to have remarked, "God wills not the death of a sinner, but rather that he should pay, and live." All the accumulated evils of many years seemed to become intensified in the papal court, or Curia: simony, nepotism, immorality, involvement in secular politics and warfare. Innocent III two centuries before had been immersed in secular diplomacy, but it had been on a European-wide scale and the excuse had always been the advancement of the Church's cause. Now the scale of involvement was limited in effect to the Italian peninsula, and the popes were generally motivated by a narrow family interest. As time went on, Italians acquired an increasing material stake in the papacy and the papacy became more thoroughly Italianized, perhaps out of fear of another schism. (Since the end of the schism in 1417, only one non-Italian pope has been chosen, in 1522.) Most secular rulers came to assume that as ruler of the Papal States the pope would act like any secular despot, at the dictates of his own personal and family interests—with the unfair competitive advantage, of course, that he was considered to be the Vicar of Christ. In fact, for a time in the fifteenth century it looked as if the papacy might actually lose its spiritual character entirely and become simply another Italian principality.

Nothing could better illustrate the involvement of the papacy in the whole tangled web of Italian society and politics than the lurid incident known in Florentine history as the Pazzi Conspiracy (1478). This was a plot to murder the ruler of Florence, Lorenzo de' Medici, and his brother Giuliano. It was engineered by half a dozen persons, each of whom had a different reason to hate the Medici. The ringleader, Girolamo Riario, nephew of Pope Sixtus IV, had been prevented by Lorenzo from carving out a principality for himself in central Italy with the pope's backing. His chief accomplice was Francesco de' Pazzi, a young scion of a Florentine family whose bank was the chief competitor of the Medici bank (they had just persuaded the pope to transfer his account to them from the Medici). A third conspirator was Francesco Salviati, whom Sixtus had recently appointed archbishop of Pisa, where he was at odds with Lorenzo over his ecclesiastical rights. Some young men had recently murdered the duke of Milan, their imaginations fired by what their Humanist Latin teacher had told them about the approval of tyrannicide found in classical writers, and it may have been this incident that suggested assassination of the Medici to the conspirators. They told the pope of their plans. Sixtus was shocked at the idea of bloodshed, though he hotly supported wiping out the rule of the hated Medici in Florence. His nephew went ahead with the plot, confident that his uncle would approve after the deed was done. The plan called for the conspirators to set upon the two Medici brothers in the cathedral of Florence beneath Brunelleschi's great dome, at the most solemn moment in the ceremony of the mass when the host is raised for the adoration of the worshipers. This was too much for even the tough mercenary soldier who had been hired to do the job with his men—he objected to murdering the victims in church. So two priests were found who were "more familiar" with the scene and had no such scruples. Young Pazzi and an accomplice successfully dispatched Giuliano de' Medici, stabbing him twenty-nine times, but the priests bungled their job and Lorenzo managed to escape. The conspirators' failure to rouse the people of Florence against their "tyrants" only proved how popular the Medici were. The mob tore some of the conspirators to pieces and compelled the city officials to hang Francesco de' Pazzi and Archbishop Salviati from the windows of the town hall. This so enraged Sixtus that he excommunicated Lorenzo and laid the whole city of Florence under an interdict. It was not till the Turks attacked the southern tip of Italy two years later that the greater danger from abroad induced the pope to lift the interdict and restore Lorenzo to communion with the Church.

All the typical weaknesses of the Renaissance Papacy—simony, nepotism, secular involvement—were evident in the complications of the Pazzi Conspiracy. And yet the papacy survived. Deep at the heart of medieval Catholic belief was the conviction that the office is greater than the man, that the moral character of the priest or pope does not affect the validity of the sacraments he administers or the spiritual authority he wields. (The basic principle was laid down at the synod of Arles in 313 A.D.) It was this conviction in the hearts of ordinary people throughout Europe that carried the papacy through its darkest hour. "Thou art Peter," Christ had said, "and on this rock will I build my church; and the gates of hell shall not prevail against it" (Matthew 16:18).

The open corruption of the papal Curia during the fifteenth century, however, had much to do with the Protestant revolt that began in 1517. As one historian has put it, the popes of the Renaissance tried to substitute splendor for reform. In the hands of an intelligent and devoted Humanist like Nicholas V this was not an unworthy ideal. To him it meant reconciling Christianity with the best in ancient civilization and rebuilding Rome as the capital of a revived Christendom. But this ideal did not satisfy the mystical and moral strivings of thousands of the faithful, particularly those outside Italy. Significantly it was under a cultivated son of Lorenzo de' Medici, Pope Leo X (1513–21), that most of Germany was lost to the papacy, and under an illegitimate son of Lorenzo's brother, Pope Clement VII (1523–34), that England was lost.

The End of Italian Leadership

In 1494 King Charles VIII of France, with an army that was enormous by Italian standards, invaded Italy and occupied Naples, to which he laid claim as heir of the Angevins (see p. 355). The vigorous world of small city-states that had grown up over three centuries or more soon came to an end. The French claim to Naples and later to Milan drew the king of Aragon into Italy, and before long the peninsula became a battleground for the armies of France, Spain, and the Empire in what were called the Italian Wars (1494–1516). War continued sporadically throughout the first half of the sixteenth century. France had been the first to intervene, but it was Spain that came out on top. By 1529 she was in control of Naples and Milan, and so of the whole peninsula. Italy's cultural creativity continued for a time—the "High Renaissance" which saw the greatest work of Raphael, Titian, and Michelangelo coincided with the Italian Wars—but not for long. The heel of Spain and of the revived Inquisition (see p. 535) was heavy, and the cities of northern Italy never again recovered that rare combination of economic vigor, political independence, and intellectual excitement that made them the wonder of Europe. Italy continued to live magnificently for some time on her accumulated economic and intellectual capital, but the future belonged to the regions north and west of her.

Suggestions for Further Reading

1. General

J. Burckhardt's great "essay," *The Civilization of the Renaissance in Italy* * (1860), is still the starting point for study. J. A. Symonds, *The Renaissance in Italy,* * 7 vols. (1875), is more readable but less scholarly than Burckhardt. W. K. Ferguson, *The Renaissance in Historical Thought* (1948), traces the development of the idea of "rebirth" from the humanists themselves through Burckhardt to the present. The same author has also written a good brief survey, *The Renaissance* * (1940). The introductory volume to the *Rise of Modern Europe* series (edited W. L. Langer), by E. P. Cheyney, *The Dawn of a New Era: 1250–1453* (1936), treats economic, political, and cultural phenomena which were to have significance for later centuries. The next volume in the series is M. P. Gilmore, *The World of Humanism: 1453–1517* (1952). Both make excellent use of recent monographic material and offer critical bibliographies. W. Durant, *The Renaissance* (1953), is readable narrative history but not much concerned with historical explanation.

2. Italian Society and Politics

A. W. O. von Martin, *Sociology of the Renaissance* (1941), is a good example of the approach to the Renaissance of modern social historians. There is interesting material on Renaissance businessmen and bankers in M. Beard, *A History of the Business Man* (1938), and R. de Roover, *The Medici Bank* (1948). G. Mattingly, *Renaissance Diplomacy* (1955), traces the origins of modern diplomacy in Italy in a fascinating way. There are histories of all the major Italian states, but the most important for an understanding of the Renaissance are those on Florence. F. Schevill, *A History of Florence* (1936), is the best brief treatment in English. Based on this is the same author's briefer *The Medici* * (1949). H. Baron, *The Crisis of the Early Italian Renaissance,* 2 vols. (1955), is an important recent study of Florentine politics and culture in the early fifteenth century. Perhaps the best single volume on Machiavelli is F. Chabod, *Machiavelli and the Renaissance* (1958). D. Merejkowski's novel, *The Romance of Leonardo da Vinci* * (trans. 1902), gives a vivid and unforgettable picture of Italian society based on sound historical scholarship.

3. Literature and Art

Most of the general works listed above contain discussion of the literary and artistic achievements of the age. The classic literary history, still well worth reading, is F. de Sanctis, *History of Italian Literature* (1870; trans. 1931). G. Highet, *The Classical Tradition* (1949), traces Greek and Roman influences on western literature. The best introduction to the educational theories of the humanists is W. H. Woodward, *Vittorino da Feltre and Other Humanist Educators* (1905). Of the many works on Italian Renaissance art, two by masters of their subjects may be mentioned: B. Berenson, *The Italian Painters of the Renaissance* * (rev. ed., 1930), and E. Panofsky, *Renaissance and Renascences in Western Art,* 2 vols. (1959). An older handbook, still useful, is H. Wölfflin, *The Art of the Italian Renaissance* (1903; edited as *Classic Art,* 1952). A. C. Krey, *A City That Art Built* (1936), is an interesting brief attempt to relate cultural flowering to economic and political circumstances in Florence.

* Available in paperback edition.

4. Contemporary Writings

It is easy to become acquainted with the thought of Renaissance writers because of the number of readily available translations. Two source collections are particularly good: *The Renaissance Philosophy of Man* * (edited E. Cassirer, 1948), which includes Pico's *Oration,* and *The Portable Renaissance Reader* * (edited J. B. Ross and M. M. McLaughlin, 1953), which includes a selection from Alberti's *On the Family.* There are many editions of Boccaccio's *Decameron,* Cellini's *Autobiography,* and Castiglione's *The Courtier.* N. Machiavelli, *The Prince and the Discourses* * (trans. 1940; Modern Library), is the most convenient edition. C. B. Coleman has edited *The Treatise of Lorenzo Valla on the Donation of Constantine* (1922), and E. A. McCurdy has edited *The Notebooks of Leonardo da Vinci,* 2 vols. (1938). *The Vespasiano Memoirs* * (trans. 1926) offer contemporary thumbnail sketches of humanists, artists, and princes. B. Burroughs has recently edited Vasari's *Lives of the Artists,** (1961).

5. The Church

There is a full account of the Councils of Constance and Basel and of the Renaissance popes in the five-volume work by an Anglican bishop, M. Creighton, *A History of the Papacy from the Great Schism to the Sack of Rome* (1882–94). The best account, however, based on the Vatican archives, is the still larger work of the Swiss Catholic, L. Pastor, *History of the Popes,* 40 vols. (trans. 1891–1953). A. S. Turberville, *Medieval Heresy and the Inquisition* (1932), is a brief, popular account, including chapters on Wiclif and Hus.

* Available in paperback edition.

EX vetulis pannis tenuem contexo papyrum,
   Vertitur in gyros dum mola scabra suos:
In tabulis olim sua scripsit verba vetustas,
   Quas rudis ex cæra dextra liquente dabat.

EXimias Regum species, hominumq́ Deumq́
   Omnia Phidiaca corpora sculpo manu.
Deniq. pictoris quicquid manus æmula ducit,
   Id digiti possunt arte polire mei.

17

Reform and Revolution

in Western Christendom

Typographus. Der Buchdrucker.

ARte mea reliquas illuſtro Typographus artes,
Imprimo dum varios ære micante libros.
Quæ prius auſta ſitu,quæ puluere plena iacebant,
Vidimus obſcura noſte ſepulta premi.

Concinnator librorum. Buchbinder.

QVifquis in Aonijs ſtudioſus obambulat hortis,
Et ſtudijs tempus mitibus omne locat.
Huc properet,vigili ferat atq volumina dextra,
Edita Calcographus quæ prius ære dedit.

The art of bookmaking: the papermaker, the woodcutter, the printer, and the bookbinder. Four engravings from a book illustrating the arts, published in Frankfurt, 1568.

The century that followed the end of the Hundred Years' War and the fall of Constantinople to the Turks in 1453 witnessed revolutionary changes in the economy, the political structure, and, above all, the religious organization of Europe. While the Italian cities were generally enjoying their wealth rather than increasing it, trade and industry in western and central Europe were undergoing an expansion amounting to a revolution. This expansion went hand in hand with the appearance of enlarged and strengthened monarchies, in France, Spain, and England, and of stronger principalities on a smaller geographical scale in Germany. Economic expansion and political consolidation in turn accompanied a movement to reform the Church in the West—a movement that ended in revolt against the authority of the Roman papacy. The development of capitalism, the formation of strong monarchies, and the Protestant Reformation were separate and distinct movements, but each was intimately related to the others in the century between the close of the Hundred Years' War and the Religious Peace of Augsburg in 1555.

Technological Development and Economic Expansion

There were no revolutionary changes in Europe's sources of power at the close of the Middle Ages. Windmills and water mills were used to grind grain and cut timber; horses and oxen were used to till the soil; plodding mule trains carried goods over roads which were no better, and often worse, than they had been in Roman times. The chief source of power was still the strength of men's arms and legs, extended by various tools, machines, and weapons: hammers, saws, lathes, swords, lances. Several inventions which became widely used in the fourteenth and fifteenth centuries, however, were to have important effects on European society and economy. The introduction of the longbow and the pike had the effect of democratizing warfare by bringing the feudal knight literally down off his high horse. Each was cheap to manufacture, and each when properly used by infantrymen had devastating effect upon feudal cavalry. A rain of arrows from quick-shooting longbows, or the relentless advance of a phalanx of pikemen, their eighteen-foot weapons held out before them like the quills of a giant hedgehog, could throw a troop of heavily armed mounted knights into confusion and panic. The introduction of gunpowder from China (see p. 400) and its use in siege cannon from the early fifteenth century on heralded the end of the feudal castle as a key factor in warfare. The longbow and pike made the mounted knight's heavy armor obsolete, while the stone and iron balls shot from the first clumsy cannon pulverized the walls of the nobles' strongholds. Cavalry and castles did not disappear overnight, but infantry (and the common man who served in it) became more important, and the military superiority of the nobility was destroyed, never to reappear.

[handwritten margin note: common man more important]

The upper classes still commanded the armies and reaped the profits from war, but more and more it was the common man who did the fighting.

Printing

The invention of printing from movable type about 1450 (see p. 401) was even more revolutionary in its ultimate effects. So long as books had to be laboriously copied by hand, learning remained the possession of a comparative few. And yet more city-dwellers were learning to read and becoming conscious of the need for education, and the demand for books was growing. A new class of professional copyists arose to meet the demand, but their product was still very expensive. Europeans had already learned from the Moslems (who had learned from the Chinese) how to make paper, which was cheaper than parchment, and they had also learned, probably from the Chinese, how to print a whole page of reading matter or pictures from a carved block of wood. The next step was to cut up the separate letters and print them from metallic type which could be used over and over. We do not know exactly when and where this step was first taken, but it is associated with the name of John Gutenberg in the city of Mainz about the middle of the fifteenth century.

Printing presses spread rapidly from the Rhine Valley to Italy, the Netherlands, France, Spain, and England. By the early sixteenth century Europeans had a flood of books available at prices that would have been unbelievable a century earlier: "standard editions" of the Bible, the Fathers, and the classical writers, in both Greek and Latin, scientific works, devotional treatises, and popular manuals in the vernacular languages. Like all mechanical inventions, printing brought both good and evil in its train. The "standard editions" could multiply errors as well as correc-

A page from the oldest printed book in the West, the Gutenberg Bible, *ca.* 1456, showing the beginning of the Book of Proverbs, with hand illumination of initials and margins.

tions, and the pamphlets which were now so easy to print and circulate in large numbers could mislead as well as inform. But one thing was clear: learning, like warfare, would never again be the monopoly of a small upper class in European society, at least not for technological reasons. Anything human beings had written could now be multiplied and placed quickly and cheaply in the hands of anyone who could read.

Industry and Agriculture

Printing was one of several significant new industries. Others were silk-weaving, cannon-founding, and mining operations so extensive as to constitute practically a new industry. All required large initial investment in plant and machinery and so were organized from the start as capitalistic enterprises—that is, enterprises in which accumulated wealth was deliberately used to produce more wealth. In addition to capi-

The thyrd chappitre of the first tractate treteth Wherfore the playe Was founden and maad? Capitulo ij

He causes Wherfore this playe Was founden ben ij f. The first Was for to correcte and repreue the kyng for Whan this kyng enplmewdach saWe this playe / And the barons · knyghtes and gentilmen of his court playe Wyth the phylosopher / he merueylled gretly of the beaultc and noueltee of the playe. And desired to playe agaynst the phylosopher / The phylosopher ansWerd and sayd to hym that hit myght not be Won / but yf he first lernyd the play The kyng sayd hit Was reson and that he Wold put hym to the payn to lerne hit / Than the phylosopher began to

A page from the first book printed in England, *The Game and Playe of Chess*, printed by William Caxton.

tal, these industries needed and attracted free laborers from town or country who could be employed for a wage and dismissed when business slacked off.

Even in the country capitalistic methods calculated to produce a profit were occasionally being applied to the land. Some landlords were quick to see that raising sheep for wool was more profitable than accepting a customary share of a food crop. Legally or illegally, many of them, particularly in England, managed to fence off or "enclose" lands formerly reserved for the common use of villagers, or to convert ploughed land to pasture. Since tending sheep required far fewer man-hours than raising food on the same amount of land,

many families were displaced from the soil. Occasionally "improving landlords" turned to more intensive cultivation of the soil in order to produce a larger cash crop of food for the growing urban markets, often riding roughshod over the preference of villagers for time-worn methods.

In short, capitalism was being applied to industry and agriculture wherever individual entrepreneurs saw profit to be made in producing books, weapons, clothing, or food for sale in the open market. For some peasants and workers this meant new opportunity. Many an ambitious peasant was able to better his position, as Martin Luther's father did by becoming a miner, for instance. But a great deal of misery and unemployment also resulted from the breaking down of customary economic relationships, the eviction of peasants from their holdings, and the movement of population to the new industrial centers. "Sturdy beggars" and "vagabonds" were a constant problem to sixteenth-century town governments.

Commerce

Even more important than the increased production of European industry and agriculture, however, was the revolutionary expansion of European trade. Law and order were being established over larger areas of Europe, and voyages were linking European ports by all-water routes with India to the east and the Americas to the west (see Chapter 18). By 1500 commerce and finance were far more thoroughly capitalistic than either industry or agriculture. Venetian merchants had already learned to risk capital on fleets which ventured as far as Egypt or Flanders on voyages that might last for months. Merchants in Lisbon or Seville or Antwerp were becoming accustomed to speculating on the profits that might come from a voyage to Calicut or the Caribbean. Such expeditions might not pay off for many months or even years. Losses were sometimes large, but profits were often prodigious, attracting further investment in overseas trade. By 1550 the spices and silks of the Orient as well as the gold and silver of America had become normal elements in Europe's pattern of trade. We have no way of determining exact figures, but we know that the total volume and value of European trade was much larger in 1550 than in 1450.

Growing commerce meant more luxuries on the tables of the well-to-do and more employment opportunities for the many. But it also meant uneven distribution of the new wealth, both among individuals and among the regions of Europe. A few bankers and merchants managed to make fortunes which seemed fabulous to their contemporaries. Jacques Coeur (1395?–1456) invested the profits he had made from trading in the Levant in mining and land. His money, lent to King Charles VII of France, helped equip the armies that finally expelled the English from French soil by 1453, but Coeur was ruined in the end when the French nobles who had also borrowed money from him became jealous and fearful of him.

Jakob Fugger (1459–1525) of Augsburg was more fortunate. His family had begun as weavers, invested in Austrian mines and Spanish land, and served as bankers to the pope. Out of his enormous capital Jakob provided the money that bought the election of Charles V as Holy Roman Emperor in 1519 and, though he complained of Charles' ingratitude, his family's banking firm was the most powerful in Europe for almost a century, until Philip of Spain repudiated his debts.

Sections of two pages from books printed by Aldus Manutius of Venice. *Above,* the opening of Dante's *Divine Comedy,* 1502. *Below,* stanzas from a collection of early Christian poetry, 1501–04.

INFERNO.

El mezzo del camin di nostra uita
Mi ritrouai per una selua oscura;
Che la diritta uia era smarrita:
Et quanto a dir qual era, è cosa dura
Esta selua seluaggia et aspra et forte;
Che nel pensier rinuoua la paura.
ant'è amara; che poco è piu morte.
Ma per trattar del ben, ch'i ui trouai;
Diro de l'altre cose, ch'i u'ho scorte.
I non so ben ridir, com'i u'entrai;
Tant'era pien di sonno in su quel punto,
Che la ueraca uia abbandonai.
Ma po ch'i fui al pie d'un colle giunto
La, oue terminaua quella ualle,
Che m'hauea di paura il cor compunto;
Guarda'in alto; et uidi le sue spalle
Uestite gia d'e raggi del pianeta,
Che mena dritt'altrui per ogni calle.
Allhor fu la paura un poco queta;
Che nel lago del cor m'era durata
La notte, ch'i passai con tanta pieta.

ELEGIA.

Te ueniente deus mundanus cócidit error,
  concidit hic mundus te ueniente deus.
Gratia plena dei est, quæ totis gentibus extat.
  Abscedant sectæ. gratia plena dei est.
Sola columba redit, quæ totum circuit orbem.
  Discedant corui, sola columba redit.
Adueniet dominus dare digna piis, mala prauis.
  Credite iam miseri adueniet dominus.
Uisio Christe tui tormentum & pœna malorum est,
  Gloria cuncta bonis uisio Christe tui.
Gloria magna patri semper tibi gloria nate.
  Spiritui & nato gloria magna patri.

Sedulii epigramma.

Hæc tua perpetuæ quæ scripsi dogmata uitæ.
  Corde rogo facias Christe manere meo.
Ut tibi quæ placeant tete fauente requirens,
  Gaudia cœlorum te duce Christe metam.

C. Sedulii presbyteri hymnus de Christo succincte
  ab Incarnatione usque ad Ascensionem.

A solis ortus cardine   intacta nesciens uirum
ad usque terræ limitem   uerbo concepit filium.
Christú canamus pricipé   Enixa est puerpera,
natum Maria Virgine.   quē Gabriel prædixerat.
Beatus author seculi   quem matris aluo gestiēs
seruile corpus induit,   clausus Ioānes senserat.

Wealth tended to concentrate in a few hands in a few places. From about 1476 to 1576 Antwerp was the Wall Street of northern Europe, with Lyons not far behind. Then, for a century after 1576, it was Amsterdam. The wealth that poured in from the Orient and the New World had a way of gravitating to the commercial centers of the Netherlands. Where the investment market was the freest, where the largest and most aggressive firms transacted most of their business, here were the nerve centers of European finance.

Like the limited application of capitalism to industry and agriculture, the growth of trade and the spread of commercial capitalism resulted not only in new economic opportunities but also in social stress and psychological confusion. A businessman who had amassed a fortune might fear for his future because the feudal nobility despised him, the common people thought him a monopolist, and the Church frowned on his avarice. The capitalist of 1500 had acquired great power, the power of money to buy influence as well as goods, but he had not yet been able to buy social prestige or an easy conscience. He was still a new man in European society, struggling to find his place and justify his existence.

This brief review of economic expansion and of the social dislocation and psychic tensions that accompanied it will help explain many of the political and religious developments of the age.

Political Consolidation and Centralization

The monarchies of western Europe had undergone a severe crisis in the fourteenth century (see Chapter 13). The kings of

The Financial Empire of Jakob Fugger *ca.* 1485-1525

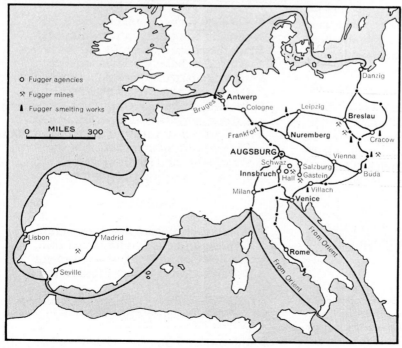

The house of Jacques Coeur in Bourges. A palace worthy of a king, built by a wealthy merchant.

England and France in 1300—Edward I and Philip IV—were strong feudal monarchs, but their successors allowed their political ambitions to outstrip their financial resources. Their ambitions were "modern," as one historian remarks, but their revenues were still "medieval." The Hundred Years' War (1338–1453) exhausted both France and England, and plague and social revolt added their toll of misery to war. The monarchs were not equal to the strain. As the fifteenth century opened, France was ruled by a king who had periods of insanity (Charles VI), England was ruled by a usurper who owed his throne to his fellow barons and to Parliament (Henry IV), and the imperial throne of Germany was occupied by a drunkard (Wenceslaus). The future did not seem very bright for the monarchies which had been so painfully built up in the twelfth and thirteenth centuries.

The later fifteenth century, however, saw a remarkable recovery of monarchical institutions in western Europe. As people grew more and more weary of war, violence, and anarchy, the forces striving to restore some semblance of law and order rallied to the support of the monarchs in France, the Spanish kingdoms, and England. And even mediocre monarchs were able to become powerful rulers by paying heed to the demand for peace and strong government.

Jacob Fugger the Rich with his secretary in his office, surrounded by filing cabinets labeled with the names of cities in which branches of his firm are located: Rome, Venice, Buda, Cracow, Milan, Innsbruck, Nuremberg, Antwerp, and Lisbon.

France

At times during the Hundred Years' War the authority of the French king had almost disappeared, but there had been considerable recovery even before the war ended in 1453. Charles VII (see pp. 391–93) was *pretty good* not a great king, but he was clever enough to make use of the widespread longing aroused by Joan of Arc to expel the English and to restore law and order to the French countryside. In 1438, by the Pragmatic Sanction of Bourges (see p. 495), he asserted his authority over the French clergy. In the 1440's he solved the financial prob-

lem of the crown by getting the consent of the Estates General to a new national tax on land called the *taille* and then continuing to levy it on his own authority. He organized a standing army under direct royal control, gained the support of wealthy merchants who supplied him with a siege train of heavy artillery, and methodically ousted the English from all their strongholds on the Continent except Calais.

Louis XI (1461–83) carried on his father's work and left the monarchy stronger than it had been since Philip IV. Louis, a slovenly and superstitious man with a morbid fear of death, had none of the outward attributes of kingship. He was called "The Spider" because he preferred to trap his enemies in a diplomatic web of his own spinning rather than to fight them. But Machiavelli admired him, with reason. The greatest threat to the French monarchy was the powerful state which the dukes of Burgundy had built up during the later stages of the Hundred Years' War on France's eastern frontier, including the wealthy cities of the Netherlands as well as Burgundy proper. Louis never actually defeated his rival, Charles the Bold, duke of Burgundy (1467–77), but he shrewdly helped Charles defeat himself. In the end the duke was killed in battle against the Swiss. The richest part of his inheritance, the Netherlands, fell to the Emperor Maximilian (1493–1519) through his marriage with Mary, daughter of Charles the Bold; but the rest was divided between the Empire and France, Franche-Comté falling to the emperor, the Duchy of Burgundy to the king of France. At home, Louis encouraged trade, developed an espionage network, and kept a firm rein on the feudal nobles and higher clergy. His successor Charles VIII (1483–98) married the heiress of Brittany and so brought the last great remaining feudal duchy under direct royal control. When Charles invaded Italy in

1494 (see p. 497) he was ruler of the largest and most powerful national monarchy in Europe.

Spain

The Iberian Peninsula had suffered almost as severely as France from war and feudal anarchy in the early fifteenth century. From 1085 to 1212 the petty Christian kingdoms of northern Spain had fought heroically to reconquer the peninsula from the Moslems in a movement known in Spanish history as the *Reconquista*. By the fifteenth century these kingdoms had coagulated into three monarchies: Portugal in the west, Castile in the center, and Aragon (including Catalonia and Valencia) on the Mediterranean coast. The kingdom of Granada, a small strip in the south, was the last remnant of Moslem rule. In 1469 a momentous marriage took place between Ferdinand of Aragon (1479–1516) and Isabella of Castile (1474–1504). The marriage brought no organic fusion of the political institutions of the two states, but husband and wife followed a common foreign policy and their heir could properly be called king of "Spain." A new national monarchy had been born from a dynastic union.

Isabella reestablished the authority of the crown in Castile and with her husband led a successful "crusade" to expel the Moors (as the Moslems in Spain were called) from Granada in 1492. The victory touched off a wave of national patriotism and religious intolerance which had been slowly gathering force during the later fifteenth century. In 1492 all Jews in both kingdoms were ordered to either become Christians or leave the land, and ten years later, in spite of promises of toleration when Granada fell, all Moors in Castile were offered the same choice. In 1478 some Dominicans had persuaded the pope to authorize Ferdinand and Isabella to set up the Spanish In-

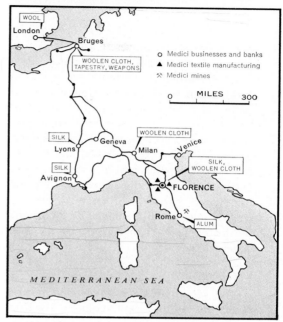

The Financial Empire of the Medici 1429-69

WOOL — London
Bruges
WOOLEN CLOTH, TAPESTRY, WEAPONS

o Medici businesses and banks
▲ Medici textile manufacturing
⚒ Medici mines

0   MILES   300

SILK — Lyons
Geneva
WOOLEN CLOTH
Milan
Venice
SILK — Avignon
SILK, WOOLEN CLOTH
FLORENCE
Rome
ALUM

MEDITERRANEAN SEA

quisition. This dreaded instrument became a powerful weapon of national unification when the monarchs directed it against the "converted" Jews and Moors. There was thus a note of religious fervor and racial hatred, which was lacking elsewhere, in the birth of Spain as a great power.

A second marriage was greatly to affect Spain's European destiny in the sixteenth century. The Emperor Maximilian and his wife, Mary of Burgundy, had a son, Philip, who was heir to Austria through his Hapsburg father and to the Netherlands through his mother. This son married Joanna, the daughter of Ferdinand and Isabella. Their son Charles, born in 1500, eventually became king of Spain (1516–56) and ruler of the Netherlands, Austria, Milan, Naples, and the Spanish possessions in America (see map p. 552). In 1519 he was also elected emperor as Charles V. Thus Spain was born by the union of Castile and Aragon and was then thrust out into the full stream of European politics and world empire by coming under the Hapsburg dynasty in 1516.

The Spanish monarchy was not wealthy, nor were its two halves, Castile and Aragon, ever thoroughly amalgamated. Even today Catalonia is markedly different from Castile. But the Spanish people had a crusading zeal born of the long conflict with the Moors, their armies soon proved themselves the best in Europe during campaigns in Italy and the Netherlands, and Columbus' discoveries brought in a stream of gold and silver from the new world that surpassed all earlier European dreams of wealth. As a result Spain was to become the leading power in Europe by the later sixteenth century.

England

The Hundred Years' War had been a heavy burden on a small country like England. But her most severe trial followed the end of the war, when her restless nobility and professional soldiery returned from France to plunge into thirty more years of intermittent civil war and feudal anarchy in the Wars of the Roses (1454–85) (see pp. 388–89). When it was all over, Henry, duke of Richmond, the first of the Tudors, was on the throne as Henry VII (1485–1509), by right of conquest and a dubious hereditary claim. The bloodshed and violence of the wars had sickened the people, and in the process a good many noble families had killed each other off. Taking advantage of the opportunity to restore the monarchy, Henry proved himself one of the ablest rulers in English history. He kept England out of foreign wars, encouraged trade, restored the sources of royal revenue, and cleverly eliminated threats from pretenders to the throne. His son, Henry VIII (1509–47), inherited a full treasury, a united nation, and (for its day) an efficient administration. Henry VIII soon wasted the treasury surplus in war with France, and his overbearing minister, Cardinal Wolsey, managed to alienate both nobles and clergy in his attempts to gather all the threads of power in Church and state into his own and his monarch's hands. But Henry VIII's England could compare well with either France or Spain in governmental efficiency and potential military strength, in spite of the fact that it had only about half Spain's population and a fifth that of France.

The Monarchs and the Nobility

Louis XI, Ferdinand and Isabella, and Henry VII all had certain common problems and they met these problems in strikingly similar ways. The chief obstacle in the path of rebuilding royal authority in the later fifteenth century was the military, political, and economic strength of the great feudal nobles in each country (the kings were wise enough never to attack the purely social prestige of the nobility). The monarchs used various expedients in their cold war with overmighty subjects. The key to success was to develop a supreme court which was able to overawe the haughtiest noble in the land. In France it was the *conseil privé,* or privy council, acting as a court; in Spain it was the *audiencia real;* in England, the Court of Star Chamber. These courts dealt with feudal breaches of the peace and recaptured royal rights and revenues that had fallen into noble hands. Feudal rights to hold courts, own castles, and command troops were examined and often annulled. Attempts to subject the nobles to taxation failed in France and Spain, but in England the nobles had always been taxed and continued to be. In order to undermine the long-standing political influence of the nobility, the kings brought more and more middle-class lawyers into their councils. The nobles were not excluded, but the real work was done by secretaries and clerks who owed their positions to the king's favor alone, not to their status as large landowners. In France and Spain bourgeois agents were also used to carry out the royal will in the towns and provinces; in England, members of the gentry, a class between the yeomanry and the hereditary nobility, were used as unpaid representatives of the crown. The economic policies of the monarchs tended to favor the bourgeoisie, and in general these policies had the solid support of the business classes, even when high taxation by arbitrary royal decree was the rule. For a merchant or a craftsman, law and order were always preferable to feudal anarchy and civil war, even when accompanied by royal tyranny.

The Monarchs and the Representative Assemblies

The second obstacle to royal absolutism was the representative assemblies: the Estates General in France, the Cortes in the Spanish kingdoms, and Parliament in England. These assemblies had reached the peak of their influence in the fourteenth century. In the fifteenth century, everywhere but in England, they declined. In France, as we have seen, the king persuaded the Estates General and the provincial assemblies to grant taxes to expel the English. He then simply continued to levy these taxes by royal authority alone. Often he would bargain separately with provincial Estates and thus play off province against province in settling the amount of a tax. As a result, the French crown attained virtual financial independence from the Estates during the fifteenth century. In Spain the monarchs played off class against class by summoning only the representatives of the cities when they needed money, thus depriving the townsmen of the possible aid of the great nobles. Anxious to support royal authority, the town representatives usually consented readily to whatever taxes the king demanded. The Cortes of Castile, Aragon, Catalonia, and Valencia, like the Estates General of France, met less and less frequently after the end of the fifteenth century and gradually lost all political importance. In England, Henry VII tried to move in the same direction by getting along without Parliament. But the English Parliament represented a nation with fewer important geographical and class divisions than France and Spain, and so was more difficult to ignore. Furthermore, the House of Lords and the House of Commons had a longer tradition of working together and a firmer grip on the purse-strings of the nation. When Henry VIII got into trouble with the pope (see p. 531), he summoned Parliament to give him support, and his use of Parliament as an accomplice had important and unanticipated results. By 1600, thanks to the frequent and important use Henry Tudor's successors made of it, Parliament had become a more powerful force in English government than ever before. By the same time, representative assemblies on the Continent had become hollow forms in states governed by absolute monarchs.

The Monarchs and the Church

The final obstacle to the development of monarchical power was the Church. Here the kings moved cautiously. Louis XI was proud to be called "Most Christian King" of France, Ferdinand and Isabella were proud to be known as the "Catholic Kings," and Henry VIII was especially proud of his title "Defender of the Faith," granted him by the pope in 1521. But on the three crucial questions of appointment of the higher clergy, taxation of the clergy, and the appeal of ecclesiastical cases to Rome, not one of the monarchs admitted the full papal claims. The English Parliament had limited papal appointments and papal jurisdiction rather strictly as early as the 1350's, while the papacy was at Avignon and England at war with France. The kings of England and France had successfully established their right to tax their own clergy still earlier. The French kings had asserted their right to control clerical appointments in the Pragmatic Sanction of Bourges, and the pope had granted Francis I the right to nominate the higher clergy and to settle the bulk of ecclesiastical disputes in France in the Concordat of Bologna in 1516. Even the "Catholic Kings" of Spain asserted and maintained their right to appoint, to tax, and to reform the clergy within their kingdoms, in spite of papal objections. We have already mentioned the independent status won by the Bohemian Church in 1436 (see p. 494). Thus long before the Protestant Reformation there were "national churches" in Europe which looked to the authority of the secular ruler in matters of appointment, taxation, and even jurisdiction, although not in doctrine.

To summarize, the foundations of the new European monarchies were efficient royal councils and supreme courts, middle-class civil servants, standing armies (except in England), and, above all, systems of national taxation which tapped the new sources of wealth and enabled the kings to build the bureaucracies and armies that overthrew the great feudal magnates. In England this new taxation was still under the control of Parliament; in France and Spain it came under the crown's control. In either case, it was recognized that the king could no longer "live of his own."

These tendencies in western Europe toward consolidation of territory and centralization of political power also appeared here and there in other parts of Europe in the sixteenth century. They appeared, for instance, in the kingdoms of Norway and Sweden, and in Russia where Ivan the Dread (1534–84) ruthlessly broke the

power of the aristocracy. In Italy there was no central government and therefore no movement toward union, to the despair of observers like Machiavelli.

In Germany there was some strengthening of central authority on a local scale, though not on the scale of the Empire. The emperor's office was elective, not hereditary; he had no traditional capital city, no core of royal lands from which his authority might spread outward as royal authority did in France; the office was traditionally supranational rather than national. There was no imperial army, no system of imperial taxation, no imperial supreme court with overriding authority. An attempt at the close of the fifteenth century to give the Empire these advantages was almost a total failure. When Charles V became emperor in 1519, his real strength lay in the fact that he was duke of Austria, lord of the wealthy Netherlands cities, and king of Spain, with its well-equipped armies and overseas treasure. Becoming emperor added something to his prestige, much to his responsibilities, but little to his power. Many dukes and princes of lesser rank in Germany expanded their territories at the expense of weaker neighbors and increased their authority within their principalities by methods very similar to those of the kings of western Europe. But in 1500 there was no central authority in Germany strong enough to resist papal exactions, foreign intervention, or the spread of heresy, if it should break out again as it had in Bohemia a century earlier. This lack of central authority was to be of crucial importance for the future.

Western Christendom, Eastern Orthodoxy, and the Turks

In 1500 Roman Christianity did not include all of Europe. To the east there was

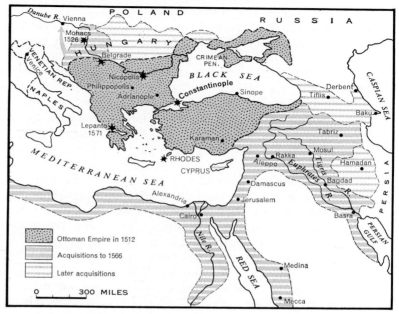

Orthodox Christianity, to the south there was Islam.

The Ottoman Turks were Moslems, but they were not fanatics. Usually they were more interested in taxing their Christian subjects and in learning from them than they were in converting them. Their highest military and civil officials were technically "slaves," sons of Christians taken from their parents, converted to Islam, and trained for their jobs. Their armies were the largest and hardiest in Europe, and their navies were a match for any other fleet in the Mediterranean. Half a century after their conquest of Constantinople in 1453 (see p. 434), the Turks were threatening the very heart of the European continent. They had taken over what was left of the Byzantine Empire in the Balkans and Asia Minor and had conquered Egypt. The greatest of their sultans, Suleiman the Magnificent (1520–66), captured Belgrade and the island of Rhodes, totally defeated a Christian army at Mohacs in Hungary in 1526, and almost captured Vienna in 1529.

These conquests were made easier by the fact that the Turks faced a divided Christendom. The schism in 1054 between the Greek Orthodox and Roman Catholic Churches (see p. 410) had never been healed. The Turkish peril stimulated the Churches to attempt a union at a council held at Florence in 1439, but it was a failure. Christendom had remained divided into two great halves, one owing allegiance to the patriarch at Constantinople, the other to the pope at Rome. Even within the two divisions Christian rulers and peoples were unable to unite against the infidel, preferring their own wars to "crusades."

The Byzantine emperor had always had greater control over the Orthodox Church than the western emperor had over the

Roman Church. And after 1453 the patriarchs at Constantinople accepted the Turkish sultans as the true successors of the Byzantine emperors. This disturbed the rulers of Russia. Under Ivan III (1462–1505) and Ivan IV (1534–84), as we have seen (p. 430), the theory began to spread that Moscow was "the Third Rome," successor to the Roman and Byzantine empires. "Two Romes have fallen, but the Third stands fast; a fourth there cannot be." In a logical extension of this theory, a new patriarch of the Orthodox Church, independent of the patriarch at Constantinople, was set up in Moscow in 1589. And so, as a result of the Turkish conquest, Eastern Christendom became divided administratively into a Greek Orthodox Church subject to the Turkish sultan and a Russian Orthodox Church subject to the Russian tsar. The Russian Church claimed spiritual leadership of *all* Orthodox believers.

The Roman and the Orthodox Churches had much in common: belief in the major Christian dogmas, in an authoritative priesthood, in the importance of the seven sacraments, and in the veneration of saints and relics. The rock upon which they split was the pope's claim to be the Vicar of Christ and sole head of the Church on earth. Between the Orthodox Church and Islam there was at least this much in common: both were extremely conservative. Eastern Orthodoxy was firmly grounded on fixed dogma and liturgy, and the Turkish state was based on immutable Islamic law, jealously guarded by jurists who opposed all change. While Western Christendom was on the verge of a religious upheaval, therefore, the other two main religious divisions of Europe showed a singular stability, which was to continue into the nineteenth century. There were no "reformations" (though there were some attempts at reform) during these centuries in the Orthodox Church or in Turkish Islam.

The Need for Reform in the Western Church

At the opening of the sixteenth century, the Roman Church was in the most perilous position it had been in since the Great Schism. Faced by the growing power of secular rulers who were limiting the papacy's powers of taxation, jurisdiction, and even of appointment in many countries, and caught in the maelstrom of Italian power politics, the popes of the fifteenth century had found themselves increasingly threatened by factions of Roman nobles, leagues of Italian princes, and pressure from more distant and more powerful rulers. The prestige of the papacy had been damaged by its long residence away from Rome in the fourteenth century and by the schism of 1378–1417. The administration of the Church had become increasingly decentralized as a result of these events. The popes had no military power of their own, and by 1500 they were regularly in debt, with little prospect of an easy way out of their financial straits in an era of rising prices. Even able and devoted Vicars of Christ—even an Innocent III—might have had difficulty defending the independence of the papacy and raising its moral prestige. But this was the era of the Renaissance popes—at best, worldly-minded administrators, at worst, corrupt and immoral men, caught up in secular tastes and interests.

From 1492 to 1503 the worst of the Renaissance popes, Alexander VI, was on the papal throne. The condemnation of Catholics and Protestants alike has fallen upon this Borgia from Spain who kept his mistresses in the Vatican, enriched his innumerable Spanish relatives, and used the money contributed by pious pilgrims to Rome in the jubilee year, 1500, to further the attempts of his son, Cesare Borgia, to carve out a powerful principality for himself in northern Italy. Sensitive and conscientious persons who visited Rome were appalled by what they saw and heard. Most of the cardinals were no better than the pope; the highest offices in the Church were bought and sold; and justice in ecclesiastical lawsuits seemed to be reserved for the wealthy who could buy it.

The state of the higher and lower clergy elsewhere in Christendom also troubled conscientious clergymen and laymen.

Bishops and archbishops throughout Europe were generally of noble blood, many of them nominated by monarchs or by the pope for reasons of personal obligation rather than for reasons of piety or administrative ability. Some held more than one bishopric, although this was contrary to canon law, and some rarely visited their sees (one never visited his except to be buried there). Even conscientious bishops found that their power to appoint the clergy and to reform abuses within their dioceses had eroded away with the years. Many powers that properly belonged to the bishop had either fallen into the hands of local laymen or had been "reserved" by the pope. The ignorance and immorality of the parish clergy were bywords among contemporary writers. The parish priest in general was no better or worse than he had been for centuries, and probably he was a cut above the level of his parishioners in literacy and sense of responsibility. But moral sensitivity to clerical misconduct had been rising. Furthermore, the tithes that the priest levied and the fees that he charged for baptisms, marriages, and burials were burdensome on laymen. Dislike of the clergy was widespread, ranging from amused contempt to bitter hatred. Most of the monastic orders of both monks and friars were in need of reform. The religious fervor of the age was not going into the monastic life, as it had several centuries earlier. Monasteries now had to search out recruits to keep their numbers up. Few new orders were being founded, and in spite of serious efforts at reform the moral tone of many of the older orders was low.

The most dangerous abuses were those practices which could be interpreted as the selling of spiritual benefits. The Church was by far the largest institution in Europe. It was rich in land, but poor in the newer forms of wealth. To maintain it cost money, and the clergy had a right to ask for a fair share of the growing wealth of Europe. But the methods used to raise money and the purposes for which the money was spent (such as waging war to add territory to the Papal States) outraged many believers. The pope demanded more and more payments from his appointees among the higher clergy. They in turn passed on the burden to the parish clergy, and they to the people. To make ends meet, some priests demanded the best garment of a deceased parishioner as a "mortuary fee," bishops squeezed all they could out of the revenues of their office, and the pope fostered jubilees, raised fees for legal judgments, and allowed abuses to creep into the sale of indulgences.

Indulgences

Indulgences, in fact, were the raw nerve of the Church's whole financial system. An indulgence is a remission of the temporal penalty for sin imposed by a priest in the sacrament of penance. It is granted on condition of true contrition for the sin and in consideration of some pious deed performed, such as going on a crusade or pilgrimage. During the Middle Ages a money "contribution" became the normal consideration, and the necessity of contrition was often forgotten by the believer. In the fourteenth century the popes developed the doctrine that there was a "treasury of merits" accumulated by Christ and the saints, from which Christ's Vicars could dispense benefits to the faithful through indulgences. In the fifteenth century Sixtus

A cartoon by Holbein makes the point that the handing over of the indulgence letter was timed so as not to anticipate the dropping of the money into the coffer. We see in this cartoon a chamber with the pope enthroned. He is probably Leo X because the arms of the Medici appear frequently about the walls. The pope is handing a letter of indulgence to a kneeling Dominican. In the choir stalls on either side are seated a number of church dignitaries. On the right one of them lays his hand upon the head of a kneeling youth and with a stick points to a large ironbound chest for the contributions, into which a woman is dropping her mite. At the table on the left various Dominicans are preparing and dispensing indulgences. One of them repulses a beggar who has nothing to give in exchange, while another is carefully checking the money and withholding the indulgences until the full amount has been received. In contrast he shows on the left the true repentance of David, Manasseh, and a notorious sinner, who address themselves only to God.

From R. H. Bainton, *Here I Stand* (Nashville: Abingdon-Cokesbury Press, 1950), pp. 72–73.

✠✠✠

IV, on the strength of this doctrine, claimed the power to release the souls of the dead from the penance they were undergoing in Purgatory as the temporal penalty for their sins. This claim helped make the indulgence trade even more lucrative. It was hard to refuse a contribution which would release the soul of a dead parent from years of suffering in the next world. In theory, contrition was still necessary, and the money was a "contribution." But it was too easy for laymen to conclude that the Church was selling salvation at a price— and then wasting the money on petty Italian wars and luxurious living.

There was nothing really new about the criticism of abuses in the Church. The Church was universally considered a divine institution, but everyone knew that it was administered by fallible human beings— that is, by sinners. There is no evidence that the moral state of the clergy was worse in 1500 than, say, in 1100. But the world of 1500 was far different from that of 1100, and it is well to review some of the main differences in order to understand why abuses now constituted a real danger to the Church.

Secularism

The European world of 1500 was more secular in its interests and ideals, as we have seen. The ascetic life preached by the Church and practiced by its monastic orders no longer seemed so heroic as it once had. The artist, the despot, the sea captain, and the businessman were carving out careers that seemed more exciting than sainthood, and the medieval interpretation of life in this world as a pilgrimage to the life after death seemed unsatisfying, even though it was not yet openly rejected. Granted that salvation was the goal of mankind, some men began to ask, why was renunciation of the world the only, or even the surest way, to gain the goal?

Religious Complexity

At the same time, the fifteenth century was an age not merely of increasing secular interests among some, but also of heightened religious sensitivity and piety among others. Both the worldly-minded and the devout were becoming critical of the growing complexity of the Church's sacraments and ceremonies. The popular religious impulse of the late Middle Ages had lost itself in a luxuriant growth of religious practices which seemed to many to verge on superstition and idolatry. The cult of the saints reached its peak, and the veneration of relics became a kind of obsession. Sacred symbols and ceremonies seemed to multiply in response to popular demand, but their religious significance sometimes almost disappeared. A fifteenth-century French artist painted a sensual, photographic portrait of the French king's mistress as the Virgin Mary, apparently without being conscious of any blasphemy. The line between the sacred and the secular seemed blurred in the popular mind. As a modern historian has put it, the religious atmosphere of the later Middle Ages was "supersaturated," and the most observant church leaders of the fifteenth century were worried. They saw that the Church was becoming dangerously vulnerable to radicals who might ask:

What is the core of Christianity? Is it to venerate an image of St. Anthony, to avoid meat on Fridays, and to go on a pilgrimage? Or, rather, is the heart of the matter to love one's neighbor and to live a Christlike life? If so, some might ask, what is the need of so many sacraments and ceremonies?

Reform by the State

A final reason why ecclesiastical abuses were so dangerous to the Church in 1500 was that there were now secular rulers strong enough to use the cry for reform for their own selfish purposes. We have seen how strictly the monarchs of western Europe had limited papal rights to appointment, taxation, and jurisdiction in their own realms. Powerful princes, landlords, and merchants all over Europe coveted the wealth of the Church. If secular rulers should decide to confiscate the Church's lands, buildings, and revenues, many of them now had the power to do so. The Church had failed to reform itself. The cry had already been raised that the state must do what the Church could not or would not do. Reform by royal command *might* have good results. In Spain, Cardinal Jiménez de Cisneros, strongly backed by Ferdinand and Isabella, worked wonders in reforming the Spanish clergy at the opening of the sixteenth century. But there was always the danger that reform by the secular power might result in control of the Church by the state and confiscation of its property.

Reformers and Reforming Movements

This account of the state of the Church must not obscure the fact that there were able critics and devoted reformers within the clergy. In the fourteenth century great mystical preachers led a remarkable religious revival in the Rhineland. And in the next century the Brethren of the Common Life, a group of laymen who devoted themselves to communal living and biblical piety (see p. 380), continued to emphasize direct, intimate communion with God in their communities and schools. In Florence between 1494 and 1498 one of the most remarkable preachers of the age, the Dominican monk Girolamo Savonarola, moved multitudes to repentance and for a time had the crowds making bonfires of their wigs, make-up, and other "vanities." These men still represented the medieval conception of reform, which assumed that the Church itself was divinely constituted and so could not be "reformed," but that the individuals who composed it could and should be regenerated. The leaders at the councils of Constance and Basel (see pp. 492–95) were reformers of a more modern sort. They meant to reform the institution itself. They wished to transform the constitution of the Church into a limited monarchy and believed that this would benefit the Church as a whole. Wiclif and Hus wanted to reform both the individual and the institution by returning to the Bible as the standard of Christian living and of ecclesiastical practice.

Each of these differing conceptions of reform was to take root and bear seed in one way or another during the sixteenth century. But none of them was successful before 1500. Mystics and preachers aroused crowds and individuals for short periods of time, but the impetus was soon spent and the institutional abuses remained untouched. Savonarola was hanged and his body burned by ecclesiastical authority in 1498. Wiclif was condemned as a heretic after his death, and Hus was burned at the stake. We have seen how and why the councils failed to reform the Church. Whenever attempts at reform threatened to undermine the status of the clergy as mediators between God and man, or the power of the pope as the Vicar of Christ—as they often did—they were declared heretical and

stamped out. It looked to some as if nothing would ever happen to shake the Church out of its complacency. The strength of vested interest and the dead weight of authority were too strong.

Christian Humanism

The most hopeful and significant reform movement of the late fifteenth and early sixteenth century was Christian Humanism. Under the inspiration of the classical revival in Italy (see pp. 477–79), a number of scholarly reformers in northern Europe came to feel that what was needed was to get back to the best in both the classical and the Christian traditions and to start afresh from the classics and the Bible. They argued that if men could only appreciate the ethical perfection of Socrates and Jesus, of Plato and Paul, then the absurdities of scholastic hair-splitting and the irrelevance of many ecclesiastical practices would become evident. Reform would inevitably follow from better understanding of the simplicity of primitive Christianity—and of the noble ideals of the Greeks and Romans, which they felt to be complementary rather than antagonistic to Christianity. Let the Church take the Bible and the early Fathers for its guides, not the scholastic theologians of the Middle Ages. Abuses would disappear if only laymen and clerics alike would recognize that Christianity was an attitude of mind and a way of life, not a complex set of dogmas to be believed and ceremonies to be gone through.

This was the program of a group of eminent individuals scattered widely over Europe. It was fundamentally conservative, designed to save the Church from itself. Its leaders were almost without exception loyal to Rome. It was obviously optimistic in its estimate of human nature. It rated the power of reason and education very high. It assumed that historical and literary scholarship could lead to ecclesiastical reform by

17 / Reform and Revolution in Western Christendom

Portrait of Erasmus, by Holbein. The painter has caught the rapt concentration of a scholar absorbed in his work. Attention is focused on pen and paper, the scholar's weapons. Both the Renaissance and the Reformation were the work primarily of scholars and writers, a point which is captured in this fine study of the greatest Christian Humanist.

Erasmus' Preface to his Edition of the New Testament

I utterly dissent from those who are unwilling that the sacred Scriptures should be read by the unlearned translated into their vulgar tongue, as though Christ had taught such subtleties that they can scarcely be understood even by a few theologians, or, as though the strength of the Christian religion consisted in men's ignorance of it. The mysteries of kings it may be safer to conceal, but Christ wished his mysteries to be published as openly as possible. I wish that even the weakest woman should read the Gospel—should read the epistles of Paul. And I wish these were translated into all languages, so that they might be read and understood, not only by Scots and Irishmen, but also by Turks and Saracens. To make them understood is surely the first step. It may be that they might be ridiculed by many, but some would take them to heart. I long that the husbandman should sing portions of them to himself as he follows the plough, that the weaver should hum them to the tune of his shuttle, that the traveller should beguile with their stories the tedium of his journey.

From Erasmus, "Paraclesis," *Novum Instrumentum,* trans. by Frederic Seebohm, in *The Oxford Reformers,* (New York: Dutton, 1914), p. 203.

✤✻✤✻✤✻✤✻✤✻✤✻✤✻✤✻✤✻✤✻✤✻✤✻✤✻

revealing earlier and purer practices. Cardinal Jiménez founded the University of Alcalá to raise the intellectual level of the clergy in Spain. He set its scholars to producing a monumental edition of the Bible, completed in 1522, which presented the original Hebrew and Greek texts in parallel columns with the Latin. In Germany Johann Reuchlin defended the study of Hebrew literature for the better understanding of the Old Testament against the violent attacks of a group of Dominicans who wished to destroy all Hebrew books but the Old Testament as dangerous to Christianity. In France, Lefèvre d'Étaples studied the Epistles of Paul and translated the New Testament into French (1523) as part of a program of education to enlighten his contemporaries and further the cause of reform. To John Colet and Sir Thomas More in England, study and reform were also closely related. Colet laid the groundwork for a program of clerical reform by lecturing on Paul and the Gospels. In his famous *Utopia,* More wrote a searching analysis of the most glaring social, political, and ecclesiastical evils of his day from the point of view of a scholar steeped in Plato and the Gospels, as well as in the monastic tradition of the Middle Ages.

Erasmus

The acknowledged leader of these Christian Humanists was Erasmus of Rotterdam (*ca.* 1466–1536). Erasmus had an equal enthusiasm for the Greco-Roman classics and for the Bible and early Christian writings. He devoted his life to scholarship in the conviction that sound learning would help save the Church. He edited the New Testament in the original Greek (1516)

with a preface urging that it be translated into all the vulgar tongues, and he published editions of the early Church Fathers. His hundreds of letters and his briefer books were even more influential. In them, with marvelous humor, underlying seriousness, and an unsurpassed command of the Latin language, he argued for what he called "the philosophy of Christ," that love of God and neighbor which he saw as the essence of Christianity in contrast to all the stupid and ridiculous perversions of Jesus' commandments which struck him in the Church of his day. In a typical passage

The Spread of Protestantism 16th century

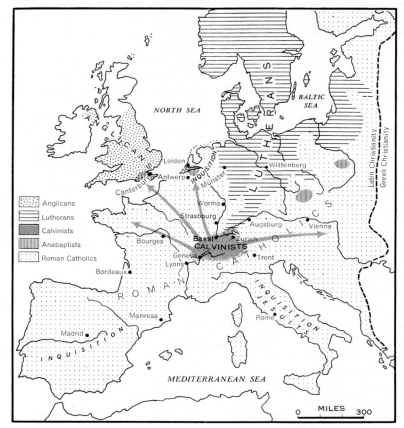

Anglicans
Lutherans
Calvinists
Anabaptists
Roman Catholics

NORTH SEA
BALTIC SEA
Leiden
Antwerp
Canterbury
Münster
Wittenberg
Worms
Strasbourg
Augsburg
Vienna
Bourges
Basel
CALVINISTS
Zurich
Geneva
Trent
Lyons
Bordeaux
Manresa
Rome
Madrid
MEDITERRANEAN SEA
Latin Christianity
Greek Christianity
ROMAN CATHOLICS
INQUISITION
JESUITS

MILES
0   300

he ridiculed the monks who call themselves "the religious" but keep "as far away as they can from religion." When the final reckoning comes, one monk will point to his fastings and ceremonies for credit, "another will boast that for sixty years he never touched money, except when his fingers were protected by two pairs of gloves." Christ will interrupt their boasts and say, "Whence comes this new race of Jews? I promised the inheritance of my Father, not to cowls, prayers, or fasts, but to works of charity." This device of imagining how Christ himself would judge the world of the 1500's was especially characteristic of Christian Humanism.

Christian Humanism was the most hopeful program of reform at the opening of the sixteenth century. But it was at best a scholars' movement that needed time, patience, and understanding to be successful. It was to influence every effort to reform the Church during the next century, both Protestant and Catholic, but as a practical program it was doomed to failure. It was too exclusively intellectual. The times were revolutionary and the remedies that over half of Europe was to adopt were both sterner and simpler than Erasmus' "philosophy of Christ."

Luther in 1520, by Lucas Cranach the Elder. This portrait appears on the title page of a German translation of Luther's pamphlet, On the Babylonian Captivity of the Church, published at Strasbourg, in 1520. It represents the reformer at the peak of his powers in the year he openly broke with the whole sacramental system of the medieval Church, as he did in this pamphlet.

Luther's Revolt from Rome

On October 31, 1517, an Augustinian friar who served as Professor of Bible in the little University of Wittenberg in Saxony posted ninety-five theses or propositions for academic debate on the subject of indulgences. The author, Martin Luther (1483–1546), was outraged by the unscrupulous salesmanship of a Dominican monk named Tetzel who had been hawking indulgences across the border in Magdeburg. "So soon as coin in coffer rings," Tetzel was reported as preaching, "the soul from Purgatory springs." The proceeds from this particular indulgence were meant to go toward the building of St. Peter's church in Rome, though most of it actually ended in the pockets of the archbishop of Mainz and of the Fugger banking firm. Luther's theses were immediately printed and debated not only in Wittenberg but all over Germany. The sensation they caused was the start of the Protestant Reformation.

"Out of love and concern for the truth and with the object of eliciting it," the theses began, a debate would be held under the presidency of the reverend father Martin Luther, Augustinian Friar and Master of

Sacred Theology, on the propositions that followed. Some of these were:

> There is no divine authority for preaching that the soul flies out of purgatory immediately the money clinks in the bottom of the chest. . . . It is certainly possible that when the money clinks in the bottom of the chest, avarice and greed increase. . . . All those who believe themselves certain of their own salvation by means of letters of indulgence, will be eternally damned, together with their teachers. . . . Any Christian whatsoever, who is truly repentant, enjoys plenary remission from penalty and guilt, and this is given him without letters of indulgence.

At the time, Martin Luther was a strong-willed, keen-minded, high-strung monk in his early thirties. He had had a severe spiritual crisis and had come through it with the conviction that a man is saved by his faith alone, not by his good works. He had been taught that good works were important: man must do his part to deserve God's favor by performing the ceremonial and sacramental acts commanded by the Church. Luther had been a most strenuous and conscientious monk. If good works could win a man salvation, surely they would win it for him, he thought. He had become a monk, which was a great good work in itself; he had fasted and prayed and confessed without end; he had become a

Pope Leo X, by Raphael. Leo was Giovanni de' Medici, son of Lorenzo the Magnificent of Florence. Raphael's brush suggests how difficult it was for this wealthy and cultured son of a Florentine banking family to understand the storm raised in Germany by Luther's protest against indulgences.

priest and a Professor of Bible. Yet he had no inner sense of forgiveness, only a growing sense of guilt and despair—and he demanded inner assurance. Peace came to him in what he felt was a revelation of what St. Paul had meant when he said that a man is saved by his faith in Christ, not by doing the works of the Jewish law. The ceremonies and religious practices of the medieval Church seemed to Luther a new Jewish law. Man is too corrupted by sin to meet the demands of such a law by his own efforts, and so he must rely on God's mercy in faith and trust. It is unthinkable that a man can buy God's favor by doing a good deed or performing some sacramental act. In the matter of saving a man's soul, Luther concluded, God does everything, man can do nothing.

It took Luther some time to work out the revolutionary implications of this thought. If a man is saved by his faith alone, then all the ceremonies and sacraments, all the pilgrimages and indulgences, everything the medieval Church called good works, were at best irrelevant and at worst dangerous. Indulgences were the first good work at which he struck. Within a short time after his attack their sales dropped off sharply in Germany. When the Dominicans, chief sellers of the indulgences, persuaded Pope Leo X to condemn his theses, Luther was gradually driven to deny the authority of the pope. Soon afterward, he denied the authority of a general council as well, since he came to believe that John Hus had been right on certain matters in spite of his condemnation by the Council of Constance. By April 1521 Luther found himself standing up before the Emperor Charles V at an imperial diet at Worms, saying that he was bound by the authority of the Scripture and his own conscience rather than by that of either pope or council. He could not recant any of his writings, he added, because his conscience was "captive to the

Word of God" and because it was "neither safe nor right to go against conscience."

The Bible and conscience—these were to be the two chief pillars of Protestant Christianity. Luther was not burned at Worms, as Hus had been at Constance. His safe-conduct was respected and he was allowed to return to the protection of his ruler, Frederick, the elector of Saxony. For twenty-five more years, till his death in 1546, he taught, preached, and wrote at Wittenberg, while the revolt against the papacy which he had touched off gathered momentum and spread over northern Europe. In the end, the unity of Western Christendom was permanently destroyed.

Lutheran Principles

In breaking with the papacy, Luther had been guided by three main principles: salvation by faith, not by works; the ultimate authority of the Bible; and the priesthood of all believers. The three were closely related to each other. It was through study of the Bible that Luther came to his belief in salvation by faith, and it was to the Bible that he always appealed against the authority of tradition or of the human institution, as he considered it, of the papacy. In 1522 he began and in 1532 he finished his greatest literary work, his German translation of the Bible, written in order that God's Word might be put into the hands of every devout person in Germany who could read. There was no essential difference between a priest and a layman, he insisted. A dedicated layman reverently reading the Scripture was closer to divine truth than a worldly pope proclaiming dogma for the Church. Christ had meant every believer to be a priest to his neighbor; He had not intended a special few to act as mediators between man and God. A Christian can serve God as well by being an honest merchant or a faithful housewife as by becoming a monk or a nun.

523

Thus Luther encouraged the dissolution of the monastic orders, and in order to dramatize his convictions he married a nun and became the happy father of six children.

Luther's original protest had been a purely religious matter, rooted in his own spiritual experience. But he soon learned to appeal skillfully to the thwarted patriotism and pecuniary grievances of his fellow Germans. "What has brought us Germans to such a pass that we have to suffer this robbery and this destruction of our property by the Pope?" he asked in 1520. "If the kingdom of France has resisted it, why do we Germans suffer ourselves to be fooled and deceived?" Luther appealed to princes anxious to confiscate church property, to businessmen restive under papal taxation and canon law, to German patriots resentful of the Italians who dominated the papacy and the College of Cardinals, as well as to devout laymen and conscientious priests who were shocked by the corruption in the Church and troubled by the confusion in its practices between the material and the spiritual. Above all, his principles of salvation by faith and of serving God in one's secular calling appealed to laymen of all walks of life, who found in them a way of reconciling Christian devotion with an active concern about worldly affairs. High-minded and low-minded motives were inextricably mixed in the minds of those who accepted Luther's arguments.

Luther had no intention of breaking away from the true Church of Christ nor of setting up a rival organization. But after 1520 he was convinced that the Church founded by Christ and the Apostles had got off the track somewhere in the Middle Ages, and that the bishop of Rome was not the Vicar of Christ, but rather the Anti-Christ. Much of the dogma and ritual of the Church of his day, Luther believed, was the work of men, not of God. These additions to Christianity must be stripped away, leaving only the pure faith of the Apostles and the early Church Fathers. In practice this meant setting up a new church under the protection and control of the various secular rulers in Germany. In this church there were two sacraments (Baptism and Holy Communion) in place of seven, a simplified ritual in German rather than

---

Luther on the Church

Thus it may come to pass that the Pope and his followers are wicked and not true Christians, and not being taught by God, have no true understanding, whereas a common man may have true understanding. Why should we then not follow him? Has not the Pope often erred? Who could help Christianity, in case the Pope errs, if we do not rather believe another who has the Scriptures for him? Therefore it is a wickedly devised fable— and they cannot quote a single letter to confirm it —that it is for the Pope alone to interpret the Scriptures or to confirm the interpretation of them. They have assumed the authority of their own selves. And though they say that this authority was given to St. Peter when the keys were given to him, it is plain enough that the keys were not given to St. Peter alone, but to the whole community. . . . Moreover, if the article of our faith is right, "I believe in the holy Christian Church," the Pope cannot alone be right; else we must say, "I believe in the Pope of Rome," and reduce the Christian Church to one man, which is a devilish and damnable heresy. Besides that, we are all priests, as I have said, and have all one faith, one Gospel, one Sacrament; how then should we not have the power of discerning and judging what is right or wrong in matters of faith?

From Martin Luther, "Address to the Christian Nobility of the German Nation," *Luther's Primary Works,* ed. by H. Wace and C. A. Buchheim (London: Hodder and Stoughton, 1896), pp. 170–71.

Latin, and more emphasis on the congregation's participation in the service. In spite of his main principles, however, Luther retained a rather high view of the sacraments and of the priesthood. Above all, he never wavered in his belief that he was not setting up another "church," but that he was purifying *the* Church. There could be only one true Church Catholic, into which all men were received in Baptism. Either the pope was right when he excommunicated Luther as a heretic in 1520, or else Luther was right when he burned the bull of excommunication. At first there were not two churches, one "Catholic" and the other "Lutheran," but an irreconcilable argument about the nature of the one true Church.

The Spread of Lutheranism

Luther's ideas were spread by his students and by his books, which poured from the new printing presses in both German and Latin. Many priests and monks were among his first converts, and his views were particularly popular among the middle classes of the German cities and the princes of northern and central Germany. The Humanists at first greeted his attack on indulgences with joy, but as Luther became more violent most of them retreated and stayed within the fold of the Roman Church. They wanted reform, not revolution, as Erasmus made clear when he finally and reluctantly broke with Luther in 1524. To Erasmus, Luther was a fanatic; to Luther, Erasmus was only half a Christian.

The peasants were excited by Luther's message at first, but he lost most of them after the Peasants' Rebellion of 1524–25. This was the largest and bloodiest of the many peasant uprisings resulting from complex economic and social causes during the later Middle Ages. The rebels' chief aim was to abolish serfdom and the burdens of the manorial system. "Therefore do we find

Luther on Good Works

Good works do not make a man good, but a good man does good works. A bishop is not a bishop because he consecrates a church, but he consecrates a church because he is a bishop. Unless a man is already a believer and a Christian, his works have no value at all. They are foolish, idle, damnable sins, because when good works are brought forward as ground for justification, they are no longer good. Understand that we do not reject good works, but praise them highly. . . . When God in his sheer mercy and without any merit of mine has given me such unspeakable riches, shall I not then freely, joyously, wholeheartedly, unprompted do everything that I know will please him? I will give myself as a sort of Christ to my neighbor as Christ gave himself for me.

From Martin Luther, "On the Freedom of a Christian Man," trans. by R. H. Bainton, *Here I Stand,* (Nashville: Abingdon-Cokesbury, 1950), pp. 230–31.

in the Scripture that we are free," they argued, "and we will be free." Luther was close enough to his peasant origins to sympathize with their demands, but the freedom he was interested in was an *inner* religious freedom, freedom from an ecclesiastical system, not from social or political bondage. At last, the atrocities committed by the peasants turned him against them, and he wrote a bitter condemnation of the uprising. The rebellion itself was finally put down with atrocities that went beyond even those of the rebels. The peasants felt that Luther had betrayed them, but the middle and ruling classes welcomed his social conservatism. After 1525 he and his followers fought as hard against radicals on their left, who wanted to carry the religious revolt too far, as they did against the Roman Catho-

Emperor Charles V, by Titian. Calm determination and lack of imagination are suggested in this portrait of the man who struggled for over thirty years to hold his scattered dominions together, to stamp out Protestantism, and to stem the Turkish tide.

advantage of ruling a relatively compact national monarchy. The result was almost a stalemate, except that the emperor gained control of Milan and of Italy in general, while the French made some permanent gains along their northeastern frontier. Meanwhile Charles V and his brother Ferdinand were also involved in efforts to stem the tide of Turkish conquest in the Mediterranean and the Danube Valley. The French in the West and the Turks in the East, sometimes in actual alliance with each other, allowed the emperor only a few intervals of peace in which to turn his attention to the religious division of Germany.

By the time of Luther's death in 1546, the German cities and principalities were about evenly divided between the two faiths. In 1547, during a peaceful interlude in his international struggles, Charles V finally found an opportunity to attack the Lutheran states. A confused war followed which proved that neither side could destroy the other, and in 1555 the emperor reluctantly allowed his brother Ferdinand, who was ruler of Austria and later Charles' successor as emperor, to conclude the Religious Peace of Augsburg. This peace allowed the rulers of the city-states and principalities of the Empire to choose between Lutheranism and Catholicism as they pleased and bound them to respect each other's rights. *Cuius regio, eius religio,* as someone later summed up the principle: the ruler determines the religion for the region. Individuals who disliked the ruler's choice might migrate to another state. Lutherans were allowed to keep all church lands which they had seized before 1552, but it was agreed that every Catholic bishop or abbot who turned Protestant in the future would have to resign his title and leave his lands in Catholic hands. This last clause was difficult to interpret and caused trouble later. The chief flaw in the settlement, however, was the exclusion of Calvinists, who

lics on their right, who wished to carry out the decrees of pope and emperor condemning Lutheranism.

Before Luther's death the emperor made almost no effective resistance to the spread of his ideas. Charles V never wavered in his orthodoxy, but the task of holding together his scattered dominions (see map, p. 552) proved so difficult that he was unable to bring political or military pressure to bear on his cities and states which had turned Lutheran. From 1522 to 1559 he and his son, Philip, were periodically engaged in a series of conflicts with France known as the Hapsburg-Valois Wars. In these wars the Hapsburgs had the greater resources, but the Valois of France had the

were growing rapidly, from the benefits of the peace.

The Peace of Augsburg was the first, grudging, official recognition, however, that Western Christendom had been rent asunder and would have to continue as a house divided. It was not religious toleration, but it was a step on the way. In the end, northern Germany became mostly "Protestant" (as Lutherans had been called since 1529, when they presented a "protest" at an imperial diet); southern Germany remained mostly "Catholic." The division remains today about as it was in 1560. Outside Germany Lutheran ideas spread widely but took root only in Scandinavia, where the kingdoms of Denmark, Norway, and Sweden became Lutheran before mid-century. Perhaps because Luther spoke so forcefully in the German idiom to his fellow Germans, his teaching was not so well adapted to export as was the teaching of Calvin (see below).

Luther had broken with the Roman papacy and had carried half of Germany with him. But after 1521 he was never in full control of the movement he had begun. Other leaders, sometimes with quite different ideas, shaped the revolt from Rome in ways that Luther often deplored. And forces which Luther and they only half understood—such as capitalism, social discontent, national sentiment, and monarchical absolutism—drove the movement into unexpected directions.

Calvinism

Luther's University of Wittenberg was not the only center from which reforming ideas were radiating. Other important centers were Zürich, Basel, Strasbourg, and especially Geneva. In these southern German and Swiss cities there developed a type of Protestantism closely related to Lutheranism, but at the same time different in emphasis—more rational and systematic, more organized and disciplined, laying more stress on moral conduct and political action, less on the inner relation of man to God. The members of this second family of Protestant churches are generally called "Reformed" churches, in contrast with the "Lutheran."

Ulrich Zwingli (1484–1531), the reformer of the church in Zürich, was a secular priest of good education, much influenced by Erasmus. He began his reforming career before he had heard of Luther, but was later deeply influenced by Luther's writings. The two broke over the proper interpretation of the Communion service. Luther maintained that Christ was truly present in the bread and wine, though not by transubstantiation (in Catholic dogma the "substance" of the bread and wine is transformed into the body and blood of Christ, while the "accidents" of taste, smell, and appearance remain the same). Zwingli maintained that the sacrament was essentially a memorial service commemorating the Last Supper.

Martin Bucer (1491–1551), the reformer of the church in Strasbourg, had been a Dominican who was inspired by hearing Luther defend himself at a disputation in 1519. He spent a good deal of his life trying to reconcile the various groups into which the Protestant movement tended to divide. He tried to find common ground between Catholics and Protestants as well as between Lutherans and Zwinglians. He was more tolerant of Anabaptists and radicals in general (see p. 530) than any of the other Protestant leaders; and he had a share in shaping the compromises represented in the Anglican Book of Common Prayer.

John Calvin (1509–64) had been trained as a lawyer and Humanist in his native France before he became converted to Protestantism and settled down as pastor in Geneva. He learned much from Luther, as well as from Zwingli and Bucer, whom he knew at Strasbourg. Through these influences and through his early training, he became the chief theologian and organizer of second-generation Protestantism. His *Institutes of the Christian Religion* served as the great handbook of Protestant principles for two centuries. It was a clear, well-organized, well-written book in both its Latin and its French versions, and its argu-

✣✣✣✣✣✣✣✣✣✣✣✣✣✣✣✣✣✣✣✣✣✣✣✣✣✣✣✣✣✣✣

Calvin on Predestination

Predestination we call the eternal decree of God, by which he has determined in himself, what he would have to become of every individual of mankind. For they are not all created with a similar destiny; but eternal life is foreordained for some, and eternal damnation for others . . .

In conformity, therefore, to the clear doctrine of the Scripture, we assert, that by an eternal and immutable counsel, God has once for all determined, both whom he would admit to salvation, and whom he would condemn to destruction. We affirm that this counsel, as far as concerns the elect, is founded on his gratuitous mercy, totally irrespective of human merit; but that to those whom he devotes to condemnation, the gate of life is closed by a just and irreprehensible, but incomprehensible, judgment. . . .

How exceedingly presumptuous it is only to inquire into the causes of the Divine will; which is in fact, and is justly entitled to be, the cause of everything that exists . . . For the will of God is the highest rule of justice; so that what he wills must be considered just, for this very reason, because he wills it.

From John Calvin, *Institutes of the Christian Religion,* trans. by John Allen (Philadelphia: Westminster Press, 1930), book III, Ch. 21, pars. 5, 7; Ch. 23, par. 2.

✣✣✣✣✣✣✣✣✣✣✣✣✣✣✣✣✣✣✣✣✣✣✣✣✣✣✣✣✣✣✣

ment had all the logic a trained lawyer could give it. Calvin's two polar principles were the absolute sovereignty of God and the radical depravity of man. The God he pictured was constantly in action, constantly working to bring in His Kingdom on earth. To Calvin, both salvation and damnation are predestined by God's inscrutable will. The effect of this doctrine on Calvin's readers, however, was not to induce resignation and despair but to stimulate moral activity and strenuous effort as God's instruments. Good works could not save a Calvinist—but they might be good evidence that God was working through him. Good works were a "sign" that a man was probably one of the Elect.

As time went on, Calvin's strict and authoritarian church in Geneva became the model for Presbyterian or Reformed churches in France, England, Scotland, the Netherlands, the Rhineland, Bohemia, and Hungary—later in North America and Dutch South Africa. Calvin advocated a ruling body in each local congregation composed of both ministers and laymen (presbyters or elders) who were to watch carefully over the moral conduct and beliefs of their congregation. These officials formed synods to link up the Reformed congregations of a whole district or nation. Thus in place of the Roman Catholic hierarchy of bishops and priests under the pope, and in place of Luther's state-churches, Calvin devised a peculiarly tough and flexible system of church government which resisted control by the state, maintained strict discipline, and, in the power of the laity, included a potentially democratic element. Unlike Lutheranism, Calvinism met the two conditions for successful export all over Europe: it possessed a systematic theology and it offered a practical substitute for medieval church organization.

By the 1550's Calvinism was spreading

rapidly. Except in a few cities like Geneva, the nerve center of the movement, and in Scotland, however, Calvinists never became a majority. But the Calvinist minorities were stubborn, well-organized, and widely distributed over Europe. Calvinism hardly touched Italy and Spain. And it was eventually rooted out of Bohemia, Poland, and much of Germany by the Jesuits. But it left a deep imprint on English society in the form of Puritanism, on France through the Huguenots, on Hungary, and on the Dutch Netherlands. Calvinist minorities formed a kind of revolutionary international society throughout Europe in the later sixteenth century. Like their chief rivals, the Jesuits, the Reformed ministers were often able to elicit a religious loyalty which transcended loyalty to secular rulers and nations. Calvinism was the militant, international form of Protestantism.

The Radicals

Some reformers wanted to move much further and faster along the road of religious revolution than Luther or Zwingli or Calvin. Here and there throughout Europe, in the cities, in weaving districts, and around mines, workers and peasants had been hard hit by the economic changes of the fourteenth and fifteenth centuries. As often as not, their discontent took on a religious coloring, combining easily with what survived of many earlier heresies—Waldensian, Lollard, and Hussite, for example. These were generally uneducated men and women who felt themselves to be the underdogs of society. They took most of Luther's ideas at face value—the Bible as authority, the priesthood of all believers, the freedom of true Christians from man-made ecclesiastical laws and ceremonies. During the 1520's in Switzerland and in the upper Rhine Valley particularly, little groups of such people came together proclaiming that

Sketches of Calvin drawn by a student, perhaps during a lecture.

a true Church of Christians was a voluntary association of converted believers, not the official or established institution believed in by Lutherans, Calvinists, and Catholics alike. Most of them believed that until a man came of age and knew what he was doing, he should not be admitted to the church through baptism. Thus, since their converts had usually already been baptized as infants, they were called Anabaptists, or rebaptizers, by their enemies. Their ritual was simple and generally they took the Bible literally. Most of them would not take an oath in a law court, accept public office, or serve as a soldier, and some practiced communism of goods on the model described in the second chapter of Acts. They were cruelly persecuted by Catholics and conservative Protestants alike as dangerous heretics and social radicals. A small but violent minority gave temporary excuse for such persecution when they captured the city of Münster and set up a reign of terror there for over a year (1534–35). But generally they were pacifistic and eager to suffer cruelty as their models, the Apostles, had done. After the 1530's the Anabaptists were to be found mainly in the Netherlands, Bohemia, Poland, and England, having been stamped out in southern Germany where they had originated.

In addition to such "evangelical" groups which tried to return to the first-century Gospel even more literally than Luther, there were other religious radicals. Some, following in the medieval mystical tradition, believed in following an inner voice rather than the letter of the Scripture, as did the Quakers in the next century. Others were more rationalistic, anticipating the doctrine which the nineteenth century was to call Unitarianism, the belief that there is only one God, not a Holy Trinity, and that Jesus was man at his best, not God. No one in the sixteenth century went quite this far, but the most interesting father of Unitarian ideas, the physician Michael Servetus (1511–53), combined an emphasis on the humanity of Christ with mystical and rationalistic ideas in a way characteristic of several sorts of religious radicals in his day. He was imprisoned by the Catholic Inquisition, escaped, and in 1553 was burned at the stake in Geneva as a result of Calvin's influence.

The ideas of these religious radicals, who went too far not only for Roman Catholics but also for Luther and Calvin, were of great importance in the religious history of the Anglo-Saxon peoples. It was in England during the seventeenth century and in the English colonies in America later still that Anabaptist ideas came to full flower. There the full implications of the church as a voluntary association, "a free church in a free state," organizing itself and electing a pastor, were fully worked out. Modern Baptists (who believe in adult baptism only), Congregationalists (who emphasize the autonomy of local congregations of Christians), and Quakers (who rely on the "inner light" and tend toward pacifism) all look back to the religious radicals of the sixteenth century as their remote ancestors. American Protestant conceptions of the place of the church in society owe more to Anabaptism than to either Luther or Calvin.

Anglicanism

The peculiarity of the English Reformation is that it was initiated by the king for reasons that had almost nothing to do with religion. Henry VIII cut England off from the papacy much as the king of France had cut his realm off from the papal obedience in 1395 (see p. 492). But in England the jurisdictional breach with Rome was followed by a decisive religious change.

In 1527, ten years after Luther had posted his ninety-five theses, Henry VIII was known as one of the pope's strongest supporters against the new heresy. Parliament had restricted papal rights of appointment and jurisdiction in England, but that had been two centuries before, during the captivity of the papacy at Avignon. Since then, England had not gone so far toward developing a national or "Anglican" Church as France had done in "Gallicanism." Lutheran ideas had taken only slight root in England among a few merchants, monks, and university scholars. There was a great deal of anticlericalism among the people and some patriotic dislike of the pope, but no organized movement of revolt. Henry, however, found himself in a personal quandary which was to lead him into direct conflict with the pope, Clement VII. After eighteen years of married life, Henry had only one living child by his wife, Catherine of Aragon, and that was a daughter. He knew that the lack of a male heir might well throw England into a new War of the Roses, and he knew that Catherine could bear him no more children. Furthermore, he was infatuated with a lady of the court named Anne Boleyn. Henry therefore asked the pope to annul his marriage with Catherine so that he might marry Anne. It was not hard to find technical grounds for the annulment (Catherine had been briefly married to Henry's older brother), but it was hard to persuade the pope to acquiesce, because he was in the power of the emperor, Charles V, and Charles was Catherine's nephew.

Henry was a proud and strong-willed man who could generally persuade himself that he was in the right, and he had a sure instinct for the best political means of achieving his ends. In 1529 he summoned Parliament in order to make the nation his accomplice in whatever he might have to do. He and his chief minister, Thomas Cromwell, skillfully turned the anticlerical sentiment in Parliament against the English clergy and forced them to acknowledge that the king was "Supreme Head of the Church in England." Then Henry threatened to withdraw all revenue and obedience from the pope. When Clement finally refused to grant the annulment, Henry carried out his threat. He had the marriage annulled in England by Thomas Cranmer, his new archbishop of Canterbury, married Anne, and then had Parliament cut all ties between the Roman papacy and England by a series of statutes in 1533–34. Conscientious monks, priests, and laymen who resisted this separation of England from obedience to Rome were executed; the most prominent martyr was Sir Thomas More (1478–1535), author of *Utopia*, chancellor of England from 1529 to 1532, and proclaimed a saint in the twentieth century. Henry was now in the pope's shoes so far as the Church in England was concerned, except that as a layman he never claimed the priest's power to administer the sacraments. All the rights of appointment, taxation, jurisdiction, and reform that had once been the pope's were now his. Between 1535 and 1539 he and

resisters were killed

Henry head of Church.

Henry VIII, by Holbein. The artist has captured something of Henry's imperiousness, his love of display, and his inflexible will in this portrait of 1540, six years after the breach with Rome became final.

ANNO · ETATIS ·   · SVÆ · XLIX ·

his agents demonstrated how wide this power was by dissolving the 550 monasteries in England, turning their inmates out into the world, and confiscating their revenues. Because Henry needed ready money to carry on a war with France, the bulk of these lands were eventually sold to nobles, gentry, and merchants. The result, probably unforeseen, was to bind a whole new class of landowners to the English crown and to the new religious settlement.

In breaking with the papacy Henry had no intention whatever of breaking with orthodox Catholic belief and practice. Cromwell tried to maneuver England into an all-Protestant alliance with the Lutheran princes, but Henry made it clear to his people that the breach with Rome was not to mean a letting down of the bars against heresy, whether Lollard, Lutheran, or Anabaptist. It was impossible, however, to seal England off against the influx of Protestant tracts and ideas, and even Henry himself approved the distribution to churches of an English translation of the Bible. By the time of his death in 1547, the Protestant wing of the English clergy led by Archbishop Cranmer was growing in power, and during the brief reign of Henry's sickly son Edward VI (1547–53), the government moved rapidly toward building a church more Protestant in doctrine and ritual. Cranmer gathered together the best rites he could find out of the ancient liturgies of the Catholic Church and translated them into majestic English in the Book of Common Prayer, which became the rallying point of Anglicanism as Luther's hymns were to Lutherans and Calvin's *Institutes* to Calvinists. There were Lutheran influences in Cranmer's work, also Zwinglian and even Lollard, but the chief influence was that of Martin Bucer, who crossed the Channel to work with Cranmer and died in England during Edward's reign.

This new official Protestantism had no time to take root among the people. In 1553 Catherine of Aragon's daughter Mary, the most honest and least politic of all the Tudors, came to the throne. She tried to vindicate her mother and atone for her father's sins by turning the clock back to 1529, abolishing all antipapal legislation, and restoring England to the papal obedience. But she outraged her people's patriotism by marrying a foreigner, Philip II of Spain, son and heir presumptive of Charles V, and she shocked their humanity by allowing three hundred Protestants to be burned for heresy in about three years. The courage with which Cranmer and more obscure victims went to their deaths, together with the arrogance of Philip's courtiers while they were in England, left an indelible impression on the English people. Patriotism and Protestantism became entangled in the public mind. When Anne Boleyn's daughter, Elizabeth I (1558–1603), came to the throne, there was little possibility that she would keep England in the Catholic camp. Elizabeth cautiously guided her Parliaments and her bishops into a religious settlement that was a moderate compromise between extreme Protestantism and obedience to the pope. In the Statutes of Supremacy and Uniformity of 1559, the queen accepted the title of "Supreme Governor" of the church in England, but she saw to it that the Book of Common Prayer could be read and used by both Catholics and Protestants who were not fanatics, and for the rest refused "to make windows into men's souls," as she put it. After the pope excommunicated her in 1570 she was forced to treat zealous Catholics in England as traitors, but she was not so severe with them as her Parliament wished her to be. When "Puritans," who wished to go much further than she in purifying the Anglican Church of "popery," became obstreperous in Parliament, she had to clap some of them in prison or in the stocks. But Protestantism and patriotism slowly fused during her reign, and England ended by becoming the largest single state to secede permanently from the Roman obedience. The secession cost less in bloodshed than it did in any other area of the same size, largely because of the firm control which Henry VIII and Elizabeth exercised over the pace of religious change in England.

Anglicanism was the most conservative form of Protestantism. In fact, many Anglicans today follow Henry VIII in insisting that their church is not "Protestant" at all. In Anglican theory it was the Roman papacy which in effect had "seceded" from the Catholic tradition during the Middle Ages, while Henry VIII and Cranmer restored the true continuity between the church of the Fathers and the church of the sixteenth century. In England itself, the Anglican position was a broad middle ground between a Catholic minority that wished to bring England back to Rome and a more important Puritan minority that wished to build a more radically Protestant church in England.

The Catholic Reformation — Church reforms itself

Luther, Calvin, Cranmer, and the radicals thought of what they were doing as a "reformation" of the Church, and to this day the movement is generally called the Protestant Reformation. To Roman Catholics, however, the movement was a "revolt" against the divine authority of the Vicar of Christ, a religious revolution. From this point of view the only true "reformation" was the successful effort finally made by the Roman Church, partly in response to the Protestant attack, partly as a result of internal pressures, to reform itself. Historians call this movement the Catholic Reformation, sometimes the Counter Reformation.

This movement was both a religious revival and a counterattack on Protestantism. Before Luther appeared on the scene, less violent men than Savonarola had been concerned about reviving the spiritual life of priests and monks. In 1516 a group of distinguished members of the clergy founded the Oratory of Divine Love at Rome with the purpose of deepening their own reli-

❖❖❖❖❖❖❖❖❖❖❖❖❖❖❖❖❖❖❖❖❖❖❖❖❖❖❖❖❖

A Catholic, Sir Thomas More, on the Church

The true Church of Christ is the common known church of all Christian people not gone out nor cast out. This whole body both of good and bad is the Catholic Church of Christ, which is in this world very sickly, and hath many sore members, as hath sometime the natural body of a man. . . . The Church was gathered, and the faith believed, before any part of the New Testament was put in writing. And which was or is the true scripture, neither Luther nor Tyndale [translator of the New Testament into English] knoweth but by the credence that they give to the Church. . . . The Church was before the gospel was written; and the faith was taught, and men were baptised and masses said, and the other sacraments ministered among Christian people, before any part of the New Testament was put in writing. . . . As the sea shall never surround and overwhelm the land, and yet it hath eaten many places in, and swallowed whole countries up, and made places now sea that sometime were well-inhabited lands, and hath lost part of his own possession in other parts again; so though the faith of Christ shall never be overflown with heresies, nor the gates of hell prevail against Christ's Church, yet in some places it winneth in a new people, so may there in some places by negligence be lost the old.

From *The Workes of Sir Thomas More*, 1557, pp. 527, 852, 853, 921.

❖❖❖❖❖❖❖❖❖❖❖❖❖❖❖❖❖❖❖❖❖❖❖❖❖❖❖❖❖

gious understanding and so of starting a wider reform among the clergy. Some members of the Oratory later began reforms of several monastic orders, others were prominent in reform efforts at the Council of Trent (see p. 535) and at the papal court. It took time, but in the course of the sixteenth century the whole atmosphere at the Vatican changed. After the bloody sack of Rome in 1527 by undisciplined imperial troops, the moral tone slowly improved and better popes were chosen, who in turn appointed better cardinals. In the second half of the century, several of the popes were zealous, almost fanatical persons, men who would have seemed utterly out of place in the Renaissance Papacy a century earlier. Religion and politics continued to be mixed at Rome and not all the ancient administrative abuses disappeared, but the popes of the later sixteenth century had a far better claim to the title of Vicar of Christ than had those of 1500.

The driving forces behind the Catholic Reformation, especially the political forces, originated in Spain. Years of crusading against the Moors had given Spanish Catholicism a peculiarly intense quality lacking in the rest of Europe. King Philip II of Spain (1556–98), the son of the Emperor Charles V, was a devoted Catholic who felt that it was Spain's destiny to become the bulwark of Roman Catholicism against Moors, Jews, and Protestants in Europe as well as the means of converting the aborigines of America. He tended to give orders to the popes rather than to take orders from them, but during his reign Spanish armies and navies, Spanish diplomacy, and Spanish saints constituted the hard core of a revived and militant Catholicism all over Europe.

The most important single agency in restoring papal power, in rolling back the tide of Protestantism, and in carrying Catholic missions overseas, was a new order founded by one of the most single-minded and influential saints in Christian history, a Spaniard of Basque descent named St. Ignatius of Loyola (1491–1556). While he was fighting the French in the service of his king, Ignatius' leg was fractured by a cannon ball. During a long and painful convalescence, he devoured the lives of the saints, which were the only reading matter at hand, and conceived the project of enlisting as a kind of Christian knight in the service of the Virgin Mary. During a lengthy period of trial and temptation he perfected the "spiritual exercises" which he later passed on to generations of followers. These exercises consisted in the believer's concentrating his imagination upon the most vivid details of Hell and of the life and death of Christ in order to strengthen his will and to direct it toward his salvation. While Ignatius was a student at the University of Paris (about the same time as Calvin), he enlisted the ten friends who became the nucleus of a new order which was approved by the pope in 1540. This was the Society of Jesus, whose members became known as Jesuits.

Everything in the rules of this new order was designed to develop a flexible, disciplined, and efficient body of ecclesiastical shock troops for the papacy. The Jesuit wore no distinctive habit, but dressed as his job might require, as priest, teacher, missionary, or secret diplomatic agent. He swore a special oath of obedience to the pope. He was carefully selected and trained for the most dangerous and difficult tasks the Church might require, from serving as confessor to a king, to venturing into Protestant countries where he might be executed as a traitor, or into foreign lands as remote as Brazil or India. The Jesuits were spectacularly successful. They strengthened the pope's control over the Church itself, they ran the best schools in Europe, and during the late sixteenth century they won back most of Bohemia, Poland, Hungary, and southern Germany from Protestantism.

The Roman Church strengthened itself against the Protestant attack in other ways as well. A general council was held at Trent in three sessions between 1545 and 1563 to define Catholic dogma and to reform abuses. The papal representatives and the Jesuits controlled the deliberations from the beginning so there was no danger of a revolt against the papacy as there had been in the councils of a century before. In reply to the central doctrines of Protestantism, the council declared that salvation is by both faith and works, and that final religious authority is in the Bible and tradition as interpreted by the Roman Church. The worst financial and administrative abuses in the ecclesiastical organization were reformed, and seminaries were set up for the training of priests. The council defined the Church's teachings much more sharply than they had ever been defined before, and re-established the absolute supremacy of the pope over the clerical hierarchy. Rome had lost much in the struggle with heresy, but the Catholic Church of 1563 was far better able to cope with future heresies than it had been in 1500. New forms of the Inquisition had been established in Spain (1480), the Netherlands (1523), and Italy (1542), and a system of censorship of printed books was instituted for the Church as a whole in 1559 and approved by the Council of Trent, which issued an "Index" of books whose reading was forbidden to the faithful. Local bishops and secular rulers had previously made efforts to censor the products of the new printing presses, but this was the first church-wide effort to keep immoral or heretical reading from the laity.

The Roman Church had found a new religious vitality and had closed its ranks

Cardinal Guevara, a Spanish Inquisitor of the 16th century, by El Greco. This portrait suggests some of the qualities of Inquisitors in general: seriousness, conscientiousness, and inflexible purpose.

against the Protestant threat. By the second half of the sixteenth century a relatively monolithic Catholic Church, reorganized from within and backed by Spain, the strongest military power in Europe, faced the divided Protestant states and minorities on something better than even terms.

Summary and Significance

It is not easy to sum up briefly the significance of all the complex, interrelated developments of the century after 1453. The

Protestant and Catholic Reformations were religious movements, phrased in theological terms, rooted deep in the religious experience of individuals like Luther and Loyola, and resulting in a religious fragmentation of Western Christendom which has lasted to the present day. But Luther's angry protest against indulgences would not have had such far-reaching results had not the economic, social, and political conditions been just right. The advance of capitalism, the insecurity of social groups which were either rising or falling in the social scale, the concentration of political power in the hands of kings and princes, the new enthusiasm for Greco-Roman civilization, the increasing this-worldliness in the concerns of men—all were part of the complicated world into which Luther's words fell. The medieval Church had already begun to disintegrate before Luther appeared, as the growth of state churches, the success of the Hussite movement, and the administrative confusion within the clerical hierarchy demonstrated. The religious upheaval was intensified by the growth of capitalism, of secularism, of national sentiment, and of absolutism in government. In turn, the Protestant Reformation accelerated the growth of these secular phenomena. It is very difficult to say precisely what was cause and what was effect. We can only say that while German princes, for example, took advantage of purely religious protests to confiscate church property for their own interests, religious reformers also took advantage of purely secular events like Henry VIII's desire to get rid of his wife, to advance the Protestant cause.

One thing is clear. The era of reform and revolution in the Church temporarily arrested the trend toward the general secularization of culture which had begun at the close of the Middle Ages and was intensified in Renaissance Italy. The century that followed Luther's death was a religious age, its most important arguments were religious arguments, its wars were intensified by religious fanaticism, and most of its leading figures were either men of religion or men considerably affected by religion. There are exceptions to this statement as to all generalizations, but on the whole it is true. The intensified interest in religion introduced a new and intolerant "ideological" element into the usual economic and political causes of conflict in European society. Venetian galleys fought the Turks for commercial reasons, of course. Feudal nobles fought private wars and monarchs led national armies for purely personal or dynastic reasons. But the deepest and most irreconcilable distrust was that engendered by religion. The hatred among Catholic, Lutheran, Calvinist, and Anabaptist was as profound in the sixteenth century as the hatred among fascist, communist, and democrat in the twentieth, and for somewhat the same reasons. None could believe that he or his family or his society was safe so long as the others were allowed to exist. Only in time did it become evident that a state could continue to exist even though its people differed in their religious beliefs. Religious toleration was the eventual result of the Reformation, it has been said, but not of the reformers.

The long-run effects of the Protestant Reformation on the economic, political, and cultural development of Europe have been vigorously debated by historians for over a century, without any wide measure of agreement. It has been argued and denied that Protestantism, with its emphasis on serving God in one's secular calling and with its appreciation of the bourgeois virtues of honesty, thrift, and self-discipline, provided the necessary religious sanction for the development of capitalism. It has been argued and denied that Lutheranism aided the growth of divine-right monarchy while Calvinism provided a spur toward the development of constitutionalism, and Anabaptism toward the development of modern socialism. It has been argued and denied that Protestantism wrecked the development of art by attacking the idolatry in contemporary worship and by rejecting most religious symbolism. And it has been argued and denied that by dissolving monasteries and thus destroying educational foundations Protestants set back elementary education many years. Both the good and the bad in modern capitalism, modern nationalism, and modern secularism have been attributed to Protestantism by one historian or another.

The historical data are far too complex for dogmatic judgments in such matters. The permanent schism of Western Christendom and the temporary intensification of the religious factor in European affairs can justly be attributed to the Protestant movement. Beyond this, all that can be said surely is that Protestantism allied itself with developments that had their origins far back, sometimes intensified them and accelerated their growth, occasionally blocked or countered their expansion. The history of capitalism, democracy, nationalism, and the secularization of culture must all deal with Protestantism, but in no case can any of these phenomena be explained by a simple chain of causes leading back to Luther and his revolt from Rome.

Suggestions for Further Reading

1. Technological and Economic Development

L. Mumford, *Technics and Civilization* (1934), is always stimulating but often inaccurate in detail. H. Heaton, *Economic History of Europe* (rev. ed. 1948), is a good general account. On printing, see: P. Butler, *The Origin of Printing in Europe* (1940); D. C. McMurtrie, *The Book: The Story of Printing and Bookmaking* (3rd rev. ed., 1943); and E. P. Goldschmidt, *The Printed Book of the Renaissance* (1950). R. Ehrenberg, *Capital and Finance in the Age of the Renaissance* (trans. 1928), is a study of the Fuggers. The Fugger Newsletters of the later sixteenth century are available in *News and Rumor in Renaissance Europe.**

2. Political Centralization

The best brief account in English is in M. P. Gilmore, *The World of Humanism* (1952). There are informing chapters on this and other related subjects in both the *Cambridge Medieval History,* Vols. VII and VIII (1932, 1936), and the *New Cambridge Modern History,* Vols. I and II (1957, 1958). There is a good popular biography of Louis XI by P. Champion (1927). R. B. Merriman, *The Rise of the Spanish Empire in the Old World and in the New,* Vol. II (1936), is the best account of Spanish consolidation. H. A. L. Fisher, *The Political History of England, 1485–1547* (1928), is the most reliable older account of early Tudor history, and S. T. Bindoff, *Tudor England* * (1950), is a good introduction to more recent interpretations. On Germany, see G. Barraclough,

* Available in paperback edition.

The Origins of Modern Germany (1952), and H. Holborn, *A History of Modern Germany: The Reformation* (1959). On the Turks, see Paul Wittek, *The Rise of the Ottoman Empire* (1938).

3. The Religious Upheaval

The best attempt at a synthetic treatment of social, political, and religious developments is still P. Smith, *The Age of the Reformation* (1920), a lively and opinionated book. H. J. Grimm, *The Reformation Era* (1954), does religious developments fuller justice than Smith and is abreast of recent scholarship, particularly on Luther. There are briefer treatments of the period in general in R. H. Bainton, *The Reformation of the Sixteenth Century* * (1952), G. L. Mosse, *The Reformation* * (1953), and E. H. Harbison, *The Age of Reformation* * (1955).

The mental and emotional climate of the fifteenth century is vividly described in J. Huizinga, *The Waning of the Middle Ages* * (trans. 1924); the piety of the period is examined in A. Hyma, *The Christian Renaissance* (1924). There are two perceptive biographies of Erasmus, by P. Smith (1923) and J. Huizinga (trans. 1952). Erasmus' best-known writings are available in modern editions: *The Praise of Folly* (edited H. H. Hudson, 1941) and *Ten Colloquies of Erasmus* * (edited C. R. Thompson, 1957).

The best short biography of Luther in English is R. H. Bainton, *Here I Stand* * (1950). H. Boehmer, *Road to Reformation* (1946), is another excellent Protestant account of Luther's development to 1521. H. Grisar, *Martin Luther: His Life and Work* (1935), is the best brief Catholic biography. There is no better biography of Calvin in English than W. Walker, *John Calvin* (1906), but this older account may be brought up to date by using the fine, broader survey of J. T. McNeill, *The History and Character of Calvinism* (1954). Modern translations of the writings of Luther, Calvin, and other reformers are appearing fast—for instance, in the *Library of Christian Classics*. These are too numerous to list here. H. E. Fosdick's anthology, *Great Voices of the Reformation* (1952), is a useful selection of passages from the works of the reformers from Wiclif to Wesley.

There is no standard work on the radicals. Good introductions to different aspects of the "left wing" of the Reformation are offered in F. H. Littell, *The Free Church* (1958), R. H. Bainton, *The Travail of Religious Liberty* * (1951), and N. Cohn, *The Pursuit of the Millennium* (1957).

On the origins of the Anglican Church there are two brief and authoritative accounts: F. M. Powicke, *The Reformation in England* (1941), and T. M. Parker, *The English Reformation to 1558* (1950). G. Mattingly, *Catherine of Aragon* (1941), is a very perceptive and readable biography.

The best general treatment of the Catholic Reformation is P. Janelle, *The Catholic Reformation* (1949). The best biography of St. Ignatius is by the Jesuit, P. Dudon (1949). For a less favorable treatment, see R. Fülöp-Miller, *The Power and Secret of the Jesuits* (1930). H. Jedin is engaged in writing a definitive *History of the Council of Trent*, the first volume of which has appeared in translation (1957).

4. Results of the Reformation

On the economic, political, and cultural consequences of the Reformation there are wide differences of opinion. A famous essay of M. Weber, *The Protestant Ethic and the Spirit of Capitalism* * (1905), became the starting point of a long controversy about the economic significance of Protestantism, which still continues sporadically. *Prot-*

* Available in paperback edition.

estantism and Capitalism: The Weber Thesis and Its Critics * (edited R. W. Green, 1959), is a convenient collection of selections from the literature of this controversy. R. H. Tawney, *Religion and the Rise of Capitalism* * (1926), is a stimulating essay in the Weber tradition; H. M. Robertson, *Aspects of the Rise of Economic Individualism* (1933), is severely critical of Weber. E. Troeltsch, *Social Teaching of the Christian Churches,* * 2 vols. (1912), is difficult but rewarding reading on the economic, social, and political theories of Catholics, Lutherans, Calvinists, and "the sects." The same author's *Protestantism and Progress* * (1906) maintains that the Reformation was still largely "medieval" and that the Enlightenment was the true beginning of "modern" times. K. Holl, *The Cultural Significance of the Reformation* * (1911) is more inclined to view Luther as the prophet of modern Germany and of twentieth-century culture in general.

* Available in paperback edition.

18

The Age of Discovery and the Greatness of Spain

The Protestant Reformation struck a Europe which was already in the throes of an entirely different sort of revolutionary movement. This was the maritime exploration which began with the fall of Ceuta across the Strait of Gibraltar to the Portuguese in 1415, accelerated enormously in the generation between Columbus' discovery of America in 1492 and the return of the first ship to circumnavigate the globe in 1522, and was still continuing unabated when the Peace of Augsburg in 1555 brought a breathing spell in the religious strife. The fifteenth and sixteenth centuries were an age of geographical discovery without parallel in the world's history. After the middle of the sixteenth century, these discoveries began to have a pronounced effect on the economy, the politics, and the diplomacy of Europe.

The Age of Discovery

About 1400 Europeans knew scarcely more than the Romans about the globe on which they lived. Scandinavia, England, Spain, and Egypt were on the outer fringes of the surface of the earth as they knew it. The rivers and inland seas were busy highways, but the oceans around the periphery of the Continent were still impenetrable barriers. Franciscan friars and the Polos of Venice had crossed the great steppes in the

thirteenth century and had returned with circumstantial knowledge of Cathay (China) and Cipangu (Japan), as well as parts of India and the Islamic Near East. Their journeys demonstrated that the great civilizations of China, India, and Islam were linked with each other and with Europe—so far as they were linked at all—mainly by caravans moving over the open grasslands which stretched like a dry ocean across the Asian continent. But after the collapse of the Mongol Empire in the fourteenth century (see p. 432), the highway across the steppes was no longer safe for missionaries or merchants. The Turks, who now straddled Asia Minor and the Balkans, encouraged neither travel nor trade, and it was the Arabs to the south and east who became the middlemen between the Orient and Europe. Arab ships plied the Indian Ocean, the Red Sea, and the Persian Gulf, bearing the spices and textiles of India and the East Indies to Alexandria and Beirut, whence the Venetians distributed them to the rest of Europe. But the Europeans themselves had no direct contact with the East.

By the end of the sixteenth century an almost incredible geographical revolution had taken place. Arnold J. Toynbee defines this revolution as "the substitution of the Ocean for the Steppe as the principal medium of world-communication." Europeans had mastered both the technological and the psychological problems of making long voyages over the sea. Their ships had crossed and recrossed the Atlantic Ocean, rounded the southern extremities of Africa and South America, pushed into the Indian Ocean, and crossed the Pacific. Men had hitherto believed that there was far more land than water on the surface of the globe. It was now dawning on European explorers that there was far more water than land, and that this water could become a kind of universal highway to any coast in the world for men who learned how to use its winds and ride its waves. The Mongol Empire had rested on mastery of the steppes. The important empires of the immediate future would rest on mastery of the oceans. When the first ship to circumnavigate the globe finished its voyage in 1522, Europe had begun to cast a web of communication and influence around the earth. During the next four centuries this web was to grow thicker and stronger until it had drawn all the other civilizations of the world under the direct influence of the civilization of Europe.

Conditions for Maritime Discovery

Norsemen had ventured out onto the North Atlantic as early as the eighth century in small open boats, and by about the year 1000 they had coasted North America in expeditions from Iceland and Greenland. Their numbers were too few and their

A 16th-century sailing ship, with its navigator (left center) sighting the sun to determine his latitude. The foremast (right) is square-rigged for running with the wind. The mainmast and the mizzenmast astern (left) are lateen-rigged for better tacking against the wind.

Toynbee
on the Age of Discovery

Since A.D. 1500 the map of the civilized world has indeed been transformed out of all recognition. Down to that date it was composed of a belt of civilizations girdling the Old World from the Japanese Isles on the north-east to the British Isles on the north-west. . . . The main line of communication was provided by the chain of steppes and deserts that cut across the belt of civilizations from the Sahara to Mongolia. For human purposes, the Steppe was an inland sea. . . . This waterless sea had its dry-shod ships and it quayless ports. The steppe-galleons were camels, the steppe-galleys horses, and the steppe-ports "caravan cities.". . . The great revolution was a technological revolution by which the West made its fortune, got the better of all the other living civilizations, and forcibly united them into a single society of literally world-wide range. The revolutionary Western invention was the substitution of the Ocean for the Steppe as the principal medium of world-communication. This use of the Ocean, first by sailing ships and then by steamships, enabled the West to unify the whole inhabited and habitable world.

From Arnold J. Toynbee, *Civilization on Trial* (New York: Oxford U. Press, 1948), pp. 67–70.

home bases too insecure, however, for them to make any permanent settlement on the new continent, and their discoveries were unknown to the rest of Europe. Before Europeans could make a sustained drive to push out across the Atlantic they needed (1) better ships, (2) surer aids to navigation, (3) firmer bases from which to operate, and (4) stronger motivation to brave the unknown.

The development of better ships was a long, slow process. Oar-propelled galleys had mastered the Mediterranean, and after 1314 the Venetians had even sent a fleet of galleys out into the Atlantic and around to the Netherlands once a year. But on the open seas sails were more efficient than oars, and broader, rounder hulls safer than the long narrow galleys. Toward the end of the fifteenth century the Portuguese had found the answer to long ocean voyages: the squat, three-masted caravel, with two masts generally square-rigged and one mast lateen-rigged. This combination preserved the advantage of both the European square-rig, which was better for running before the wind, and the Arab lateen-rig, which was better for sailing close to the wind. The caravels were slower than galleys, but they gave more space for cargo and more elbowroom for seamen on long voyages.

The galleys had generally stayed close to land, hugging the shoreline. Before ships could venture straight out to sea, shipmasters needed some way of determining their direction and their whereabouts. The compass gave the masters a sense of direction in dark weather and the astrolabe enabled them to determine their latitude with fair accuracy, while the improved portulan charts gave them the confidence that they could return to port (see pp. 401–02). (No precise way of determining longitude was to appear until the eighteenth century.)

City-states were the original bases from which Italians and Catalans set forth to explore and trade in the Mediterranean. The city-state of Venice had built a considerable trading empire in the eastern Mediterranean by 1400. The cities of northern Germany, bound in a loose federation known as the Hanse, were able to build a parallel empire in the Baltic and North seas. Like the Venetian, this Hanseatic empire reached the peak of its power in the fourteenth century. But transoceanic exploration, trade, and colonization required a broader base for support. The new monarchies of western Europe were better situated geographically than the Italian or German cities to open up the Atlantic. They also had advantages in man power, resources, and political centralization over the smaller city-states and even over leagues of cities like the Hanse. After 1400 the larger monarchies and republics gradually replaced the cities as the major units of commercial enterprise.

It is not easy to determine the motives that induced Europeans—rather than Chinese or Hindus or Moslems—to "discover" the rest of the world by taking to the sea. Certainly the fact that Christianity is a missionary religion had something to do with the European impulse. Zealous Christians eager to spread the Gospel have been in the forefront of nearly every phase of European expansion from the crusades to nineteenth century imperialism. The spirit of the crusades, a mixture of religious and political motives, continued longer on the Iberian Peninsula than elsewhere in Europe. By 1400 the Portuguese and Castilians and Aragonese had been fighting the Moors for three centuries, and the impetus of their attack on Islam seemed likely to carry beyond the shores of the peninsula. A great legend had grown out of Christendom's long struggle with the Moslems, the legend of Prester John, a Christian ruler of fabulous wealth and power who lived somewhere beyond the Islamic lands. At first he was located vaguely in Asia, but when the land-travelers from Europe failed to find him there, he was placed in Abyssinia (where in truth there was a Christian ruler). To find Prester John and thus to outflank Islam by discovering a powerful Christian ally in the Moslem rear—this was the persistent dream of Portuguese and Spanish explorers. Crusading zeal was not the primary impetus of the great discoveries, but mixed with more worldly motives it often played a large role.

Of these more worldly motives, the thirst for gold was the most compelling. Europe in 1400 was short of gold and silver. In an age without refrigeration, the spices which helped preserve meats and make them more palatable—pepper from India, cinnamon from Ceylon, ginger from China, nutmeg and cloves from the East Indies— were luxuries that verged on being necessities. These spices were expensive, thanks to their long journey from India or the Moluccas to European dinner tables, and thanks also to the Arab-Venetian trade monopoly. Europeans needed the spices more keenly than Asians needed anything Europe had to offer except gold and silver, so there was a steady flow of the precious metals from Europe eastward. This drain limited the supply of specie (hard coins) in Europe at a time when it was increasingly needed as currency. Before credit systems became widely developed in the seventeenth and eighteenth centuries, the only practical way to provide the credit needed by burgeoning commerce and industry was to increase the actual supply of bullion. Fifteenth-century rulers hardly saw the problem in these terms, but they were acutely aware of their need for gold. They knew that they had to have hard cash in their treasury to hire soldiers, equip navies, and pay bureaucracies.

By the late fifteenth century Europe had developed a competitive system of states and a competitive class of merchants. There was a restless, energetic, and bold seafaring population scattered along the Atlantic coastline. These sailors, fishermen, and merchants were slowly developing the techniques and the ships for making longer and longer voyages. They had religious and economic motives strong enough to overcome their superstitious fears of what lay beyond known waters. And their governments were usually ready to back them for glory and gain. Because of the desire

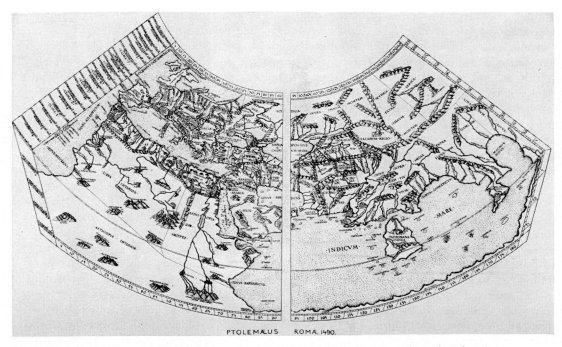

PTOLEMÆUS   ROMÆ 1490.

A map based on Ptolemy and published at Rome in 1490 which shows the effect of Ptolemy's overestimation of the extent of the Eurasian continent: China comes closer to Europe across the Atlantic than it is in reality. Ptolemy's error was one of several factors which led Columbus to believe that Japan was only some 2400 miles west of the Canary Islands. Note the general assumption of the map that the land area of the earth is greater than the water area.

for spices, Europe needed Asia more than Asia needed Europe. And Europeans, acting on an ancient geographical error, felt sure that they could reach Asia by sailing due west. Ptolemy in the second century had underestimated the size of the globe and overestimated the span of Asia, and the geographers of the fifteenth century, accepting his miscalculations, were convinced that Cipangu and Cathay lay only a very few thousand miles west of Europe. These were the conditions, material and psychological, which produced the great age of discovery. As one historian of the expansion of Europe has put it, the motives of European explorers may be summed up in these words: "Gospel, Glory, Gold."

Portuguese Exploration

Perhaps the greatest figure of the whole age stands at its very beginning, the figure of Prince Henry the Navigator (1394–1460), younger son of King John I of Portugal. In 1415 Henry helped persuade his father to cross the Strait of Gibraltar, capture Ceuta, and hold on to it as a base for further operations. From 1415 until his death in 1460, Prince Henry devoted his life to organizing, equipping, and sending out fleets which pushed farther and farther down the west coast of Africa. He was the first to bring together the scientific and the seafaring knowledge of his day, in the remarkable observatory which he set up at Sagres on Cape St. Vincent, the southwestern tip of Portugal. We know almost

18 / The Age of Discovery and the Greatness of Spain

nothing of his personality or appearance. We know that he had vague notions of outflanking Islam by discovering a water route from West Africa to Prester John or to the Nile River, but his dominant objective was to find gold. Curiously enough, he never sailed on any of the ships he sent out.

After Henry's death, the impetus of exploration was lost for a time. But his grand-nephew, King John II (1481–95), who had a hunch that Africa could be rounded, gambled shrewdly on the chance of finding an all-water route to India which would short-circuit the Venetian-Arab monopoly of the Red Sea route to the Spice Islands. By 1488 Bartholomew Dias had discovered the Cape of Good Hope, and in 1497 Vasco da Gama rounded the Cape with four ships, reached Calicut on the Malabar Coast of India in 1498, and was back in Lisbon with two of his ships in 1499. In 1500 a larger fleet commanded by Cabral and heading for India in Da Gama's wake happened on the coast of Brazil.

For the first time Europeans were in direct touch by sea with the older civilizations of the East. This first contact was to have momentous consequences in the end, but neither side was particularly impressed by the other on first meeting. The Hindus had only contempt for the bedraggled sailors who had spent months aboard Da Gama's ships, and the Europeans soon made it clear that they found nothing to respect in the older civilization of Hindustan. When the Hindus asked Da Gama what he sought in India, he is said to have replied laconically, "Christians and spices."

During the sixteenth century the Portuguese did their best to build a solid commercial empire in the Indian Ocean. Affonso de Albuquerque, their brutal but able governor from 1509 to 1515 and the real founder of this empire, saw the relation between trade, sea power, and strategic bases.

He seized Goa on the west coast of India to serve as his headquarters, Malacca on the Strait of Malacca to control the trade between the Spice Islands and the Indian Ocean, and Ormuz to dominate the Persian Gulf. He failed to capture Aden, which would have strangled the Arab-Venetian trade through the Red Sea. He was as ruthless in disciplining his own men as he was in terrorizing local Hindu princes and fighting Arab seamen. At Albuquerque's death in 1515 the Portuguese had a large share of the spice trade (though not a monopoly) and controlled strategic bases all the way from Africa to the East Indies. It was easy for the Portuguese and other Europeans to seize footholds in India because there was no central power that extended into the southern part of the peninsula (see p. 445). The Moguls had set up an empire in the north, but the Moslem and Hindu princes of the coastal districts were weak, divided, and powerless to resist the better-armed and better-disciplined Europeans. The Portuguese, however, made almost no impact on the teeming millions of India, in spite of a few spectacular efforts like those of the Jesuit St. Francis Xavier to convert some of the Hindu population to Christianity. They established "factories," or trading posts, but no colonies of settlement. And even their trade failed to grow. Individual voyages, especially the early ones, made large profits for their backers. But the cost to the Portuguese government of equipping fleets and maintaining fighting forces soon ate up what profits there were. Portugal was a relatively small and poor country, with a small merchant class. Italian, German, and Flemish bankers soon dominated the Portuguese trade, and the spices which arrived at Lisbon were soon being sent on directly to Antwerp, which proved to be a better point from which to distribute them to Europe. The burden of empire was already proving heavy when

Portugal, as we shall see, fell into the grip of Spain in 1580.

Columbus and Spanish Exploration

In 1484, before the Portuguese had reached the Cape of Good Hope, a Genoese sailor named Christopher Columbus had tried in vain to persuade King John II of Portugal to back him in a voyage of exploration to the west. Columbus was convinced by all the evidence at hand—Marco Polo's book, Ptolemy's geography, and an enthusiastic letter from a Florentine math-

ematician named Toscanelli—that it would be comparatively easy to reach Cipangu (Japan) by sailing due west. But for years he was unable to persuade any monarch to back him. At last the rulers of Spain, who had conquered the Moorish kingdom of Granada in January 1492, were free to turn their attention elsewhere. And so it was under Castilian auspices that Columbus sailed on his famous voyage. It took the Portuguese almost a century of patiently organized effort to reach the Old World eastward, while the Spanish reached the

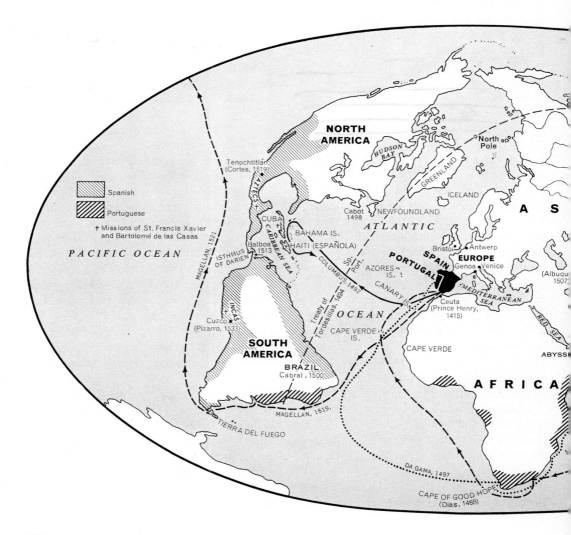

New World westward in one brilliant voyage. Castilian and Catalan sailors were perhaps as skillful as Portuguese, and their governments had colonized the Canary and Balearic Islands. But there was a larger element of luck in the founding of Spain's empire in the New World than in the establishment of Portugal's in the Old.

Columbus touched land in the Bahamas on October 12, 1492, thinking he had struck some small islands in the Japanese archipelago. Throughout four voyages and until his death in 1506, he remained convinced, in the face of increasingly puzzling evidence, that it was the Old World of Cipangu and Cathay which he had discovered. And so, although it was Columbus who named the "Indians" he found on the shores of Haiti and Cuba, it was the Florentine Amerigo Vespucci who gave his name to the continent Columbus had discovered. Amerigo, director of the Medici branch bank in Seville, sailed on both Spanish and Portuguese voyages and described what he saw in letters which were widely read throughout Europe. In one

The World of the Voyagers 1415-1550

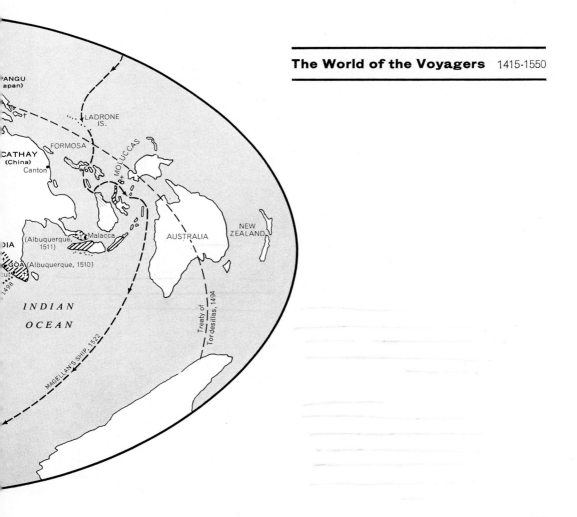

A map of Africa published by Sebastian Münster in 1544, showing the new route around the Cape of Good Hope which the Portuguese traveled to found their empire in the East.

he referred to the great southern continent in the west as *Mundus Novus,* a New World. Later map-makers labeled the two new continents "America," for the man who first realized that it was a New, not an Old, World that was opening up to view.

The Treaty of Tordesillas, 1494

Columbus had to put in to Lisbon on his return from his first voyage, and his stories naturally worried the king of Portugal. Soon both Spain and Portugal appealed to the pope for an adjudication of their rival claims to unoccupied and heathen lands around the globe. The pope, Alexander VI, was a Spaniard, and the line of demarcation which he drew in 1493 a hundred leagues west of the Cape Verde Islands was favorable to Spain. Portugal, however, gained a diplomatic victory through a treaty with Spain in 1494—the Treaty of Tordesillas. By this treaty a line was drawn from pole to pole 370 leagues west of the Cape Verde Islands separating Portugal's claims to the east from Spain's to the west. The Portuguese interpreted this as applying only to the Atlantic (it gave them Bra-

zil, but they did not know this in 1494). The Spanish preferred to believe that the line extended round the world, cutting it in half as a knife cuts an orange. They hoped that the settlement might give them the Moluccas, the heart of the Spice Islands, but later (1527) Spain sold all her claims to these islands to Portugal.

Magellan

By 1512 the Portuguese were in the Moluccas and had discovered the Pacific Ocean; in 1513 the Spaniard Balboa discovered the Pacific from the Isthmus of Darien in Central America. In the years to come, the Spanish, the English, and others tried again and again to discover a strait through the New World by which they might sail westward into the Pacific and reach the Spice Islands. The Portuguese navigator Magellan was convinced that he could do just that by rounding the southern tip of South America. He knew, of course, that Portugal would never back him in such an expedition, so in 1519 he sailed with Spanish backing. It was the third of the truly great voyages—along with those of

548   18 / The Age of Discovery and the Greatness of Spain

Columbus and Da Gama. Magellan negotiated the straits that are named for him and got across the Pacific after incredible hardships, only to be killed by natives in the Ladrone Islands. His navigator, Sebastián del Cano, brought one of the five original ships back to Lisbon by way of the Cape of Good Hope in 1522, the first ship to sail round the world.

What Europeans Knew of the World in 1522

The contrast between what Europe knew of the rest of the world in 1415 when Ceuta fell and in 1522 when Magellan's ship returned to the Tagus was startling. By the end of this century of discovery the Portuguese naval maps showed the outlines of Africa's coastline in considerable detail. Portuguese navigators were at home in the Indian Ocean, and their advance guard had pushed into the East Indies, coasted Formosa, and reached Canton. They were soon (in 1542) to visit the fabled Cipangu itself. In the west the Spanish had explored the Caribbean and the Gulf of Mexico, penetrated parts of Central America, coasted the northern shore of South America, touched on parts of the western shore by way of the Strait of Magellan, and visited islands in the Pacific all the way to the Philippines. The outlines of North America were still almost unknown, although the Italians John and Sebastian Cabot, sailing in the service of the king of England, had coasted parts of the continent near the mouth of the St. Lawrence between 1496 and 1509. The interiors of the great continents were still almost entirely unknown, but Europeans now had a fairly clear idea of the shape of Asia, Africa, and South America—and a growing sense of the vast extent of the oceans of the earth.

The Spanish Empire in the West

The years from 1500 to 1515 saw the building of Portugal's empire in the East.

The period from 1520 to 1550 was the "age of the conquistadors" who carved out an empire for Spain in the West. The Spanish explorers moved from the islands of the Caribbean to the shores of the mainland in search of gold or of a passage to the Pacific, and, as they began to hear exciting tales of wealthy, half-civilized empires, they turned from exploration to conquest. The most notable of the conquistadors were Hernando Cortes, who in 1519–21 conquered the formidable Aztec Empire in Mexico with six hundred men, sixteen horses, and a few cannon, and Francisco Pizarro, who in 1533–34 conquered the Inca Empire in Peru with even fewer followers. Their firearms, steel swords, and horses gave the Spaniards an advantage over the more primitive armed groups that faced them, but it was primarily their daring, their discipline, and their fanatical faith in the truth of their religion that accounted for their fantastic successes.

Within a generation Spanish soldiers and lawyers and friars unexpectedly found themselves the undisputed rulers of vast stretches of territory and hundreds of thousands of human beings. Often the new ruling class simply stepped into the place of former conquerors like the Aztecs and Incas, living on the tribute from subject populations which had supported their predecessors. Sometimes the Spanish devised new ways of exploiting the labor of the Indians, as they did on the islands. In the uplands the chief occupation became stock-raising to produce leather, which was much in demand in Spain. In the coastal lowlands, sugar was the chief product. This production called for large capital investment in land and refineries and demanded the forced labor of free Indians or of Negro slaves from Africa. The industry most favored by the Spanish government, however, was the mining of gold and silver. After the discovery of enormously rich silver mines in

Las Casas
on the American Indians

It has been written that these peoples of the Indies, lacking human governance and ordered nations, did not have the power of reason to govern themselves—which was inferred only from their having been found to be gentle, patient and humble. It has been implied that God became careless in creating so immense a number of rational souls and let human nature, which He so largely determined and provided for, go astray in the almost infinitesimal part of the human lineage which they comprise. From this it follows that they have all proven themselves unsocial and therefore monstrous, contrary to the natural bent of all peoples of the world.

. . . Not only have [the Indians] shown themselves to be very wise peoples and possessed of lively and marked understanding, prudently governing and providing for their nations (as much as they can be nations, without faith in or knowledge of the true God) and making them prosper in justice; but they have equalled many diverse nations of the world, past and present, that have been praised for their governance, politics and customs, and exceed by no small measure the wisest of all these, such as the Greeks and Romans, in adherence to the rules of natural reason.

From Bartolomé de las Casas, *Apologética historia de las Indias,* in *Introduction to Contemporary Civilization* (New York: Columbia U. Press, 1954), 2nd ed., Vol. I, p. 499.

****

both Mexico and Peru about 1545, the extraction and shipment of silver plate became the main business of the Spanish Empire as a whole. Every spring after 1564 the plate fleet of twenty to sixty vessels gathered at Havana harbor to be convoyed by from two to six warships to Seville. And every year the Spanish government waited anxiously until the bullion, which everyone agreed was the key to national strength, was safely in harbor.

The empire which grew out of these exploits and these economic activities was a kind of compromise between what the Spanish settlers, the Christian friars, and the Spanish government at Madrid would each have liked to see develop in America. The settlers, many of them ex-conquistadors, would have liked to set up a purely feudal system, with themselves as manorial lords living on the forced labor of the natives, unmolested by any political direction from Madrid. The Franciscans and other friars, particularly the great Dominican, Bartolomé de las Casas, would have liked to see the natives treated as fellow Christians and fellow subjects of the Spanish crown. Las Casas worked tirelessly to protect both the legal and the moral rights of the Indians in the face of relentless pressure from the settlers to exploit them. The government in Spain was determined to crush feudal independence, whether in the colonies or at home, to centralize all decision-making in Seville or Madrid, and to protect the natives so far as possible, as urged by the friars.

The theory of the Spanish Empire, as it had unfolded by the end of the sixteenth century, was remarkably sensible and humane by contemporary standards. The settlers were allowed to command the forced labor of the subject Indians, but this labor was regulated by public authority, not by private right. There were abuses, sometimes serious, and the long arm of the home government was often awkward and exasperatingly slow in dealing with local problems. But as time went on the Spanish came close to accomplishing what the Portuguese failed to accomplish in the East and what the English never attempted in North America: the Christianization and Europeanization of a whole population. The Spaniards took seriously the papal bulls of 1493 which gave them the heathen peoples of the New World to convert and nurture in the faith. In theory, the natives were considered Christians and subjects of the king (unlike the unfortunate Negroes, who were dismissed as the slaves of West African kings). The gulf between Spaniard and native was never entirely closed, in either religion or culture. But Spanish and Portuguese in the end became the languages of all Latin Americans, and Roman Catholicism the dominant religion. Intermarriage was so common that the mestizos, or descendants of mixed marriages, eventually became more numerous than the pure-bred of either race. It was significant that Mexico was named "New Spain" and Peru "New Castile." The Spanish (and the Portuguese in Brazil) made a serious attempt to convert a New World to western civilization.

Spain under Philip II

In the later sixteenth century Spain was the dominant power in Europe as well as in America. European politics and diplomacy revolved around the Spanish monarchy, and in what follows we shall view events from Madrid.

The accession of the Hapsburg Charles to the throne of Spain in the early sixteenth century (see p. 509) had thrust the Spanish into the full stream of European politics and diplomacy at a moment when the Protestant heresy was beginning to spread, the Turks were expanding in the Mediterranean and up the Danube Valley, and the job of exploring and colonizing America was demanding a huge expenditure of energy. To roll back the threats of heretics and infidels while conquering a new world was a heavy task for a state so recently formed. But for a brief and brilliant time,

the Spanish under the Emperor Charles V (1516–56) and his son, King Philip II (1556–98), were almost equal to the challenge. The sixteenth and early seventeenth centuries were the golden age of Spain.

Charles I & Philip II

In 1555–56 Charles V divided his family holdings between his brother Ferdinand and his son Philip. To Ferdinand went the Hapsburg possessions in Austria and the imperial crown (still elective in theory, but by now always bestowed on a Hapsburg). To Philip went the crowns of Castile and Aragon, with Castile's possessions in the New World, the Kingdom of Naples and the Duchy of Milan (which meant control of Italy), the Free County of Burgundy, and the Netherlands. Thus for a century and a half after 1556 there were "Austrian Hapsburgs" and "Spanish Hapsburgs," separate ruling houses but houses that cooperated closely in matters of dynastic policy. Except for the Netherlands, which might well have gone to Ferdinand because of their close cultural and geographical ties with the Empire, the possessions of Philip II formed a more tight-knit and centralized state than his father's holdings.

Philip II was thoroughly Spanish in speech, thought and character. After the death of his wife, Mary Tudor of England, in 1558, and the conclusion of peace with France in 1559, he returned from the Netherlands to Spain to remain until his death almost forty years later. He caught the imagination of his people as few of their rulers had done. To them he is still "Philip the Prudent," one of their greatest kings. Distrustful of his advisers, unable to delegate authority even in minor matters, slow beyond belief in coming to a decision, strongly Catholic in religion (his enemies would have said "bigoted"), convinced of his divine right to govern Spain as an absolute ruler strictly accountable to God but to no one else, Philip made his country the

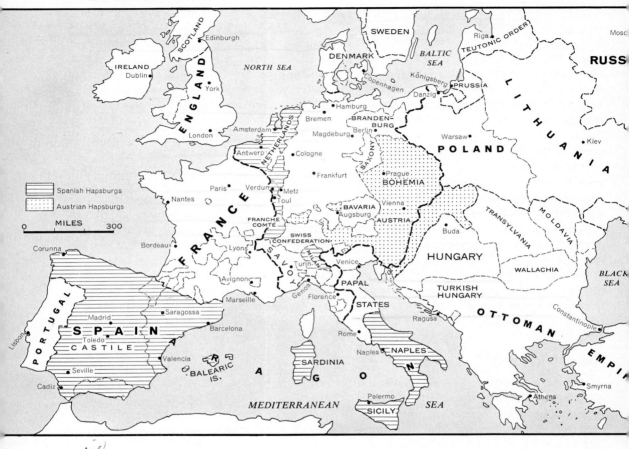

Phil. II VERY catholic

bearer of an ideal in which the secular and the religious were curiously blended.

This was the ideal of a restored Catholic Christendom with the Spanish monarchy as its leading power and defender. For centuries the Spanish had fought the Moors. To Philip, the crusade would continue against half-converted Jews and Moors at home and against Turks and Protestants abroad until the Christian Commonwealth of the Middle Ages had been restored. Meanwhile the Catholic faith would be carried to the New World. Since Spain was the divinely chosen agent of this mission,

what was in the interest of Spain was naturally in the interest of Christendom as a whole. Or so it appeared to Philip and to most of the Spanish nobility. If ever there was a monarchy and a ruling class with a sense of destiny, it was the Spanish of the sixteenth century. This spirit was evident in the Spanish Jesuits who guided the Council of Trent and helped to reconvert much of central Europe to Catholicism, in the Spanish friars who labored to convert the American Indians, in the conquistadors who toppled native empires in the New World, and in the tough Spanish infantry who for over a century defeated every foe they met in Europe. Philip II's Spain was the strongest military power on the Continent, the strongest naval power in the Atlantic, and the wealthiest state in Europe in terms of ready money. Spain was the nerve center of the Catholic Reformation. No wonder the terror of the Spanish name lived on into the seventeenth century long after Spanish strength had begun to waste away.

Economic Policy

The economic basis of Spain's predominance was the gold and silver which flowed to Seville in a swelling stream from the New World. Early in the sixteenth century it was almost entirely gold. But after the discovery in 1545 of the rich mines in Peru and Mexico, the bullion imported was mostly silver. The value of the treasure that reached Spain rose enormously between 1500 and 1600. In very round figures the average yearly value of bullion imports at the beginning of the century was something under $300,000; by about 1550 this had increased 15 times; and by 1600 over 40 times, to about $12,000,000. Then a steady decline set in, until about 1660 the average was down to around $1,200,000. The Spanish crown received about a quarter of the total as its share.

This influx of precious metals led to a steep rise in prices. In the first half of the sixteenth century, the rise was slow and generally stimulating to Spanish industry and commerce. But it became precipitous after the middle of the century, amounting to a severe inflation which struck Andalusia first, then the rest of Spain, and then the rest of western and central Europe as the metal flowed out of the Iberian Peninsula (in spite of all government prohibitions). It has been estimated that prices quadrupled in Spain in the course of the century. Since prices rose faster than taxes could be increased, Philip II was three

times forced to repudiate his government's debts, in 1557, 1575, and 1596. (His successors had to follow the same course in 1607, 1627, and 1647.) The effect of inflation on Spanish industry was eventually disastrous. Since prices always rose faster in Spain than elsewhere, it was relatively more expensive to manufacture goods in Spain than in other countries. This meant that Spanish producers could not sell their goods abroad and that cheaper foreign products captured the Spanish market. In the short run, Spain's silver enabled her to maintain her supremacy in Europe by paying her armies in cash and buying what goods she needed abroad. In the long run, this policy, combined with heavy taxation at home, helped to ruin her industry and commerce, and even to undermine her agriculture. There were other reasons for Spain's rapid economic decline in the seventeenth century, although historians differ about their importance: the contempt for work among her large class of nobles; the large proportion of the adult population who became priests, monks, and nuns; emigration to the New World; and expulsion from Spain of her best farmers, the Moriscoes, or converted Moors. But the influx of precious metals was probably the major reason for both the rapid rise and the equally rapid decline of Spain as the leading power in Europe. Spain lived for a century on the windfall of American treasure, and when the supply of bullion dwindled in the seventeenth century she found that the real sinews of her national strength—native industry and agriculture —were ruined.

Religious Policy

Philip II's religious policy was the most narrowly intolerant of his time. He abhorred heresy and unbelief with a holy hatred and said he would rather be king in a desert than in a land of heretics. He feared Islam as the ancient enemy both of Christendom and of his people. He hated Protestantism as a doctrine subversive of all order, religious and political. He would never compromise with either, at home or abroad. There were few Protestants in Spain, and they were easily dealt with by the Inquisition.

The Moriscoes in the southern part of the peninsula were more of a problem. In Philip's eyes and in those of most of his countrymen, these Moors who had been forcibly Christianized after the conquest of Granada in 1492 were still Moslems at heart. Furthermore, they were more prosperous than most Spanish farmers, and they were reputedly in league with the Moslems of North Africa. In 1566 Philip ordered them to stop using the Arabic language and learn Castilian, to give up their Moorish dress, and to stop taking hot baths

King Philip II of Spain by Tintoretto.

****

On Philip II of Spain

The pallor of his complexion was remarked on by all observers, and most of them drew the proper conclusion, namely, that it indicated a weak stomach and lack of exercise. Reddened eyes were a penalty of his excessive devotion to the written word both day and night. . . . Reading and writing occupied the major portion of Philip's day. . . . He had taken deeply to heart his father's injunction to direct everything himself, and never to give his full confidence even to the most faithful of his ministers, and the natural result was that his time was completely occupied with receiving and answering reports and letters. . . . Reports, reports, and even more reports; Philip was literally submerged with them in his later years, and moreover he did not stop at reading them; he annotated them, as he went along, with comments on matters as absurdly trifling as the spelling and style of the men who had written them—all in that strange, sprawling hand of his, one of the most illegible hands of an age more than usually replete with chirographical difficulties.

From R. B. Merriman, *The Rise of the Spanish Empire* (New York: Macmillan, 1934), Vol. IV, pp. 21–24.

****

as was their custom. In 1569 the exasperated Moriscoes broke into a revolt, which was savagely suppressed. As a result they were driven out of Andalusia and scattered over the rest of Spain. From there they were finally hounded out of Spain entirely in the years after 1609. Their numbers and importance to the Spanish economy have sometimes been exaggerated, but there is no doubt that their loss helped to weaken the Spanish economy.

At the height of the revolt of the Moriscoes in 1570, the Turks captured Cyprus from the Venetians and Europe again trembled before the threat of Islamic expansion. Philip II immediately allied with the pope and the Venetians to counter the danger, and in October 1571 a Spanish and Venetian fleet won a glorious victory over a large Turkish fleet at Lepanto in the Gulf of Corinth. Nothing decisive came of the battle, because the Christian forces were unable to follow up their victory. But the event had considerable importance for European morale, because it was the first time a Turkish fleet had been defeated.

The Apogee of Spanish Prestige

Philip's prestige probably never stood higher in Europe than in the years immediately following Lepanto. His suppression of heretics was popular at home and his defeat of the Turks gave him the undisputed political leadership of Catholic Europe. The pope was under his thumb much of the time. Philip tolerated no papal interference with the royal control of ecclesiastical appointments and jurisdiction in Spain, and he curbed the power of the Jesuit Order. But as the most powerful champion of Catholicism in Europe, he could generally count on papal support. France, potentially the strongest monarchy in Europe, was torn by civil war during most of his reign and so was unable to contest his leadership. England had just undergone a serious feudal rebellion in 1569 and her queen had been excommunicated by the pope in 1570. Meanwhile the Empire was safely in the hands of Philip's Hapsburg cousins. It seemed as if his dream of a resurgent Catholic Christendom dominated by Spain was about to become a reality.

This dream was shattered during the last quarter of the sixteenth century by the revolt of the Netherlands, the rise of English sea power, and the accession of a Protestant to the throne of France. In his struggle with the embattled forces of Protestantism in northern Europe, Philip overreached

himself, exhausted his resources, and started his nation on its long decline.

The Revolt of the Netherlands

The Netherlands were the wealthiest and most densely populated of Philip II's dominions. The three million people dwelling beside the mouths of the Rhine and the Meuse had lived by their industry and commerce since the early Middle Ages. The looms of the southern provinces turned out great quantities of linen and woolen cloth. The fisheries of the northern provinces provided most of Europe with pickled herring. Fishing stimulated shipbuilding, and windmills supplied the power for sawing timber as well as for other industrial processes. The comfortable houses of Bruges, Ghent, Antwerp, and Amsterdam were built with the profits of this flourishing industry and trade.

The seventeen provinces of the Netherlands had been united in a personal union by the dukes of Burgundy, who had also instituted an Estates General which met infrequently. But when Charles V inherited the territories in 1519 through his grandmother, Mary of Burgundy, there was little in the way of national feeling or common institutions to bind them together. Charles, who was brought up in Flanders and spoke Flemish as his native language, was the closest thing to a native ruler the Netherlands had ever had, but he inevitably sacrificed their interests to his broader imperial aims. During his reign the faint beginnings of a Netherlandish national consciousness appeared. The provinces were a crossroads for ideas as well as for commerce. The Humanism of Erasmus as well as the teachings of Luther took early root in the Netherlands, to be followed by Anabaptist ideas. But in the 1550's a militant, disciplined Calvinism spread rapidly and soon became the dominant form of Protestantism. Calvinists constituted tight-knit minorities in most of the cities of the seventeen provinces when Philip II took over the rule from his father in the fall of 1555.

Within ten years after his accession, Philip had alienated most of the nobility and bourgeoisie of the provinces. Native nobles were displaced in favor of Spaniards in the governing council, a policy which aroused the feudal pride and latent patriotism of the upper classes. A threat to enforce the laws against heresy with new efficiency and severity sent a thrill of terror through the Calvinist merchants and ministers. Madrid was almost a thousand miles away from Brussels, and Philip's Spanish Catholic mind was even more remote from the interests and concerns of his busy, prosperous Dutch and Flemish subjects, whether they were Calvinist or Catholic. The revolt which ensued was partly a feudal reaction against centralization, partly a patriotic movement directed against foreign rule, and partly a religious protest against an inquisitorial Catholicism.

In 1566 Calvinist mobs began to break images of the saints and smash stained-glass windows in Catholic churches throughout the Netherlands. Philip decided to make a frightful example of the iconoclasts. He sent the duke of Alva and about ten thousand Spanish regulars to the Netherlands with orders to bring the troublemakers either to the block or to the stake. Alva set up what came to be called a "Council of Blood" and boasted (with some exaggeration) that within the six years of his residence in the Netherlands (1567–73), he had executed upwards of eighteen thousand persons. In addition to spilling so much blood, Alva and his council confiscated large amounts of property and imposed a 10 per cent sales tax which almost strangled the trade of the country during the year or two it was in force. The Netherlanders never forgot these six years.

Instead of crushing the opposition to Philip, Alva's policy solidified their resistance, at least for a time.

William the Silent and Dutch Independence

By 1572 the resistance movement had found a leader in William the Silent, prince of Orange, the wealthiest landowner in the provinces. William was no military genius —he lost almost every battle he fought against the Spanish—but he had political wisdom, integrity, and patience, a rugged kind of patriotism, and a deep hatred of religious fanaticism, whether it was of the Calvinist or Catholic variety. He tried his best to hold the Calvinists in check, keep all seventeen provinces united against the Spanish, and still find a solution that would leave Philip as titular ruler. For a few years it looked as if he might succeed. In 1576 Calvinist excesses provoked a frightful sack of Antwerp by Spanish troops known as the "Spanish Fury." This was enough to frighten all seventeen provinces into an agreement to stick together called the Pacification of Ghent.

Within three years, however, both Protestant and Catholic radicals had got out of hand, moderates had lost influence, and animosity between Catholics and Protestants had begun to undermine the universal hatred of Spain. The almost unanimous opposition to Alva gradually gave way to a savage civil war in which the Calvinists, as the best-disciplined minority, took over leadership of the opposition to Philip and most of the Catholics rushed back into the arms of Spain for protection. The seventeen provinces split in two as Calvinists fled to the Dutch provinces in the north beyond the great rivers, where they were better able to defend themselves, and Catholics fled to the Walloon provinces in the south, where Spanish troops could be maintained and supplied from the upper Rhine. In 1579 the Dutch provinces in the north formed the Union of Utrecht. This Union ultimately became the foundation of the United Provinces, or Dutch Netherlands, which formally declared their independence of Philip II in 1581. And so the unanticipated result of the revolt of 1566 was that the seven northern provinces broke away from Spanish rule while the ten southern provinces remained "the Spanish Netherlands," until 1715 when they became "the Austrian Netherlands," and finally in 1830 "Belgium."

The Rise of the United Provinces

The Dutch Netherlands had to fight for their independence for two generations after 1581. They got some help from German, French, and English troops at various times, but the price that the French duke of Anjou and the English Queen Elizabeth asked for their help was often dangerously high. In the long run it was dogged determination, geography, and the rivalry of their enemies that won the Dutch their independence. William the Silent was assassinated in 1584, but his descendants carried on his tradition of able and disinterested leadership as "stadtholders" of one or more of the seven provinces and in 1688 another William of Orange was called to the throne of England. The "United Provinces" never formed more than the loosest sort of political federation, but the Dutch fought with stubbornness when they had to. The duke of Parma, who became Philip's representative in the Netherlands in 1578, was one of the best military commanders of his day, but he was unable to reconquer the provinces beyond the bend of the Rhine and Meuse, especially since he lacked control of the sea. The Dutch "Sea Beggars," or privateers, won as many battles against the Spanish on the water as William's armies lost on the land, and when Philip's Invincible Armada was broken up in 1588

by the English and the weather (see p. 561), it looked as if the Dutch would win. In 1609 they made a truce with the Spanish, then fought them again through most of the Thirty Years' War (1618–48). In the treaties that settled the war in 1648 the king of Spain finally recognized the independence of his former Dutch subjects.

By this time the new Dutch state had miraculously become one of the great powers of Europe. Most long wars exhaust even the victors, but the Dutch came out of their war with Spain the most powerful industrial and commercial nation in Europe. By the early seventeenth century they were building more ships each year than all other nations combined (two thousand, it was said), and they were better ships than any others—more economical to build and operate, able to carry more cargo more safely with less human labor, and equipped with a better rig, the

The Division of the Netherlands 1581

fore-and-aft. During the first half of the seventeenth century the Dutch captured more and more of the carrying trade not only of Europe but of the world. Their rates were cheaper, their business methods more efficient, their handling of cargo more skillful. The goods of their own which they offered for exchange were constantly being improved, thanks partly to the influx of skilled textile workers from the impoverished Spanish Netherlands. Antwerp (in the Spanish Netherlands) had been ruined by the Spanish soldiery and blocked off from the sea through the closing of the Scheldt River by the Dutch themselves,

Amsterdam harbor, detail of an engraving by Pieter Bast, 1597. A good impression of this busy center of world-wide trade.

and had thus lost to Amsterdam (in the United Provinces) her position as the commercial and financial center of Europe. Until their own vulnerability to attack by land became evident after 1660, the Dutch had no rivals who could contest their power.

The sheer geographical extent of Dutch commercial operations was remarkable. Their ships dominated the river trade of northern Germany and handled much of the grain trade of the Baltic. A large part of the carrying trade of England, France, Italy, and Portugal was in their hands. When Philip II seized the crown of Portugal in 1580 and stopped the Dutch from visiting Lisbon (whence the Dutch were accustomed to distribute Portuguese spices to the rest of Europe), the Dutch with characteristic daring went out to the source of the spices themselves in the Moluccas. In 1602 the Dutch East India Company was formed, amalgamating into one all the companies trading with the East. Company headquarters were soon established at Batavia on the island of Java, and by the middle of the century the Dutch had ousted the Portuguese from the Moluccas, Malacca, and Ceylon. For over a century the company was occasionally able to pay very large dividends, mainly by ruthlessly monopolizing the production of spices and limiting it to keep up prices. In 1652 the Dutch founded a colony at the Cape of Good Hope. A few years earlier they had come within an ace of ousting the Portuguese from Brazil. By 1614 they had a settlement on Manhattan Island named New Amsterdam which became the center for a large Dutch carrying trade in the New World. Before the Portuguese revolted against Spain in 1640 to regain their independence, the Dutch had seized most of Portugal's empire in the East. And when the French and British embarked on overseas trade and colonization, they found not only the Spanish and Portuguese but also the Dutch ahead of them all over the world.

So it was an industrial and commercial giant that Philip II conjured up when he set out to crush his rebellious subjects in the Netherlands. The revolt of the Netherlands may be considered as a kind of dress-rehearsal-in-miniature for those larger popular and patriotic revolts against absolute monarchy, beginning with the Puritan Rebellion in England and continuing through the American and French revolutions, which marked the next two centuries. There are many differences between these movements, but also many similarities in the mixture of economic, patriotic, and religious grievances, the blindness of the monarchs, and the ultimate triumph of "middle-class" interests.

The "Armada Portrait" of Queen Elizabeth I by Marc Gheeraedts, at Woburn Abbey. In the left background the English ships sail victoriously away from some burning wrecks of Spanish ships, and in the right background the Spanish fleet is battered by a terrifying storm in the North Sea.

Elizabethan England

Philip of Spain was almost as unfortunate in his dealings with England under Queen Elizabeth I as he was in his dealings with the Netherlands. England was crucial to his plans. His father, Charles V, knew that if he could add control of England to his control of Spain, Milan, Burgundy, and the Netherlands, France could be encircled and the vital sea routes between Spain and the Netherlands could be protected. For a few years (1554–58), while Philip, still prince, was married to Queen Mary of England, it seemed as if the Emperor's dream would be realized: England had been brought within the Hapsburg orbit and restored to Roman Catholicism. But the accession of Elizabeth to the throne in 1558 changed everything.

Queen Elizabeth I (1558–1603) is generally accounted the greatest of the Tudors and one of England's ablest rulers, though to some of her critics she was simply a woman of petty emotions and limited vision who did her best to cramp the expanding energies of her people. Whatever the judgment, she left England immeasurably stronger at her death than she had found it at her accession, and she died beloved of the great majority of her people. At twenty-five when she came to the throne she had already lived through a great deal: disgrace, humiliation, and even danger of execution during her sister Mary's reign. She had seen how Mary had lost the love of her people by marrying a foreigner and burning heretics. She came through these early experiences a strong-willed and shrewd young woman, aware of how precarious both her own situation and that of her nation were, determined to put politics before religion and follow a purely national policy.

Her instinct was always to temporize

and compromise. As the daughter of Henry VIII and Anne Boleyn, she could never allow England to submit to papal authority. But she wanted a religious settlement which would not alienate patriotic Catholics, and she hoped she could deceive the Catholic powers of Europe for a time into thinking that she could be won back to Rome. On the other hand, she resented the attempt of the Puritan minority to dictate a radical religious settlement to her, and she rejected the schemes of some of her Protestant councilors to support Protestant parties and Protestant revolts all over Europe. But she never completely broke with her patriotic Puritan subjects and never lost their loyalty, even when she clapped some of them in jail for speaking too boldly in Parliament. Elizabeth's policy was nationalist first and Protestant second, but the long-term result was to encourage that fusion of patriotism and Protestantism which became a permanent characteristic of English public opinion after her death.

In the same way she compromised and temporized in her foreign policy. Her instinct was to avoid clear-cut decisions, to keep a dozen intrigues afoot so that there were always avenues of escape from any policy, and to avoid war at almost any cost. The chief danger at her accession was from French intrigue in Scotland. The Frenchwoman Mary of Guise was regent for her daughter Mary Stuart, who was married in 1558 to the heir to the French crown. When in 1559 the fiery reformer John Knox returned to his native Scotland from Geneva, where he had imbibed the purest Reformed doctrine from Calvin, his preaching had an immediate and striking success. A religious revolution led by Knox was soon under way, and the whole French position in Scotland was undermined. The French connection with Scotland went back several centuries, and

since Mary Stuart's husband was now king of France, it was clear that France would make every effort to restore Catholicism and French dominance. For once Elizabeth made a rapid decision to ally with the Calvinist party in Scotland and keep the French out. By 1560 Knox, the Kirk (Church), and the pro-English party were in control, and Scotland was never again to become a dangerous foothold for French intrigue. The way was paved for the ultimate union of the English and Scottish crowns in 1603.

Mary Queen of Scots

Mary Stuart—or Mary Queen of Scots, as she is known to history—returned to Scotland in 1561 after her husband's death. She was a far more charming and romantic figure than her cousin Elizabeth, but she was no stateswoman. A convinced Catholic, she soon ran head-on into the granitelike opposition of Knox and the Kirk. Her marriage to her cousin Lord Darnley turned out badly and she became involved in a plot resulting in his murder. In 1567 she was forced to abdicate, and in the following year she fled from Scotland and sought protection in England from Elizabeth. No visitor could have been more unwelcome. Mary, as Henry VII's great-granddaughter, had the best hereditary claim to be Elizabeth's heir, but she was a Catholic and a foreigner. Elizabeth would never formally recognize her as her successor, nor would she marry in order to produce another heir, nor would she do anything to harm her fellow sovereign, except keep a close watch on her through her agents. This policy exasperated Elizabeth's Puritan advisers and left Mary free to become the center of almost every French or Spanish plot against Elizabeth's life during the next twenty years. In 1569, for instance, the Catholic nobility in the north of England rose in revolt in an effort to oust Elizabeth and put Mary on the throne with foreign aid.

The Anglo-Spanish Conflict

Philip of Spain had made cautious offers of marriage to Elizabeth at her accession, but she had rejected them. For over twenty-five years the governments of Philip and Elizabeth remained on good terms, determined to preserve the peace in the face of increasing friction. But conflict was almost inevitable. England was a small country with perhaps half the population of Spain, but during the quarter century of peace which Elizabeth's cautious temporizing gave her people, English industry, commerce, and shipping expanded considerably. For reasons we have already suggested, the Spanish were unable to produce the goods needed by their colonies. And Spanish shipping was not equal to supplying the insatiable colonial demand for African slaves. An aggressive merchant named Sir John Hawkins was the first Englishman to carry both goods and slaves direct to the Spanish settlements in the Caribbean in 1562. It was profitable but dangerous work. In 1569 he and his cousin, Sir Francis Drake, were almost wiped out by a Spanish fleet. In revenge, Drake seized the annual silver shipment from Peru on its way across the Isthmus of Panama. In 1577–80 he followed Magellan's route around the world and demonstrated the vulnerability of the Spanish Empire. By the 1580's he had become the terror of the Spanish Main. Meanwhile English sailors were boldly probing the coasts of North America in a vain search for a Northwest Passage which would short-circuit the Portuguese route to the Indies. In 1553, in a search for a Northeast Passage around the top of Europe, they entered the White Sea, landed at Archangel, and visited the tsar of Russia, Ivan the Dread. By 1600 English ships

and merchants were joining their fellow Protestants, the Dutch, all over the world in contesting the Spanish-Portuguese monopoly of overseas trade.

It was the revolt of the Netherlands, however, which finally brought England and Spain to blows. For years the economic ties between England and the Low Countries had been close. The English people sympathized with the victims of Alva's tyranny, and English Sea Dogs cooperated informally with Dutch Sea Beggars and Huguenot privateers to prey on Spanish shipping and to cut Spanish communications by sea with the Netherlands. Philip's ambassadors in England became deeply involved in one plot after another against Elizabeth's life, usually with the object of setting Mary Stuart on the throne. In 1587 Elizabeth reluctantly consented to Mary's execution when confronted with unmistakable evidence of her complicity in these plots. Now the way was cleared for Philip to attack England in his own interest (to put Mary on the throne of England might have benefited France even more than Spain), and in 1588 he sent his "Invincible Armada" north to hold the Channel while Parma ferried his Spanish veterans across to conquer England for Spain.

The story of the defeat of the Armada has become an allegory of the triumph of the young, vigorous nation over the old and senile. The Spanish ships were large and slow, equipped with inferior cannon, and commanded by a landlubber. The fleet was conceived as a means of transporting troops, not of fighting battles at sea. The English ships that put out from Plymouth to harry the Spanish up the Channel were smaller and more maneuverable, trained to fire their cannon at longer range. Parma was not ready when the Spanish reached Calais and anchored there. The English sent in fire ships among the Spanish ships

The Armada

When the Spanish Armada challenged the ancient lords of the English on their own grounds, the impending conflict took on the aspect of a judicial duel in which as was expected in such duels, God would defend the right. . . . So when the two fleets approached their appointed battleground, all Europe watched. For the spectators of both parties, the outcome, reinforced, as everyone believed, by an extraordinary tempest, was indeed decisive. The Protestants of France and the Netherlands, Germany and Scandinavia saw with relief that God was, in truth, as they had always supposed, on their side. The Catholics of France and Italy and Germany saw with almost equal relief that Spain was not, after all, God's chosen champion. From that time forward, though Spain's preponderance was to last for more than another generation, the peak of her prestige had passed. . . . So, in spite of the long, indecisive war which followed, the defeat of the Spanish Armada really was decisive. It decided that religious unity was not to be reimposed by force on the heirs of medieval Christendom, and if, in doing so, it only validated what was already by far the most probable outcome, why, perhaps that is all that any of the battles we call decisive has ever done.

From Garrett Mattingly, *The Armada* (Boston: Houghton Mifflin, 1959), pp. 400–01.

as they lay at anchor, drove them northward in panic, and attacked them fiercely off Gravelines. Stormy weather completed what the English had begun. Hardly half the galleons which left Spain made their way back northward and westward around Scotland and Ireland. The victory gave a lift to the morale of Englishmen and of Protestants everywhere. It ended all further thought of Spanish conquest of England—or reconquest of the Netherlands, for that matter. It did not mean the end of Spanish sea power. During the Anglo-Spanish war that began in 1585, English troops were heavily involved in suppressing a rebellion in Ireland, which was backed by some Spanish help, and in supporting Dutch Protestants and French Huguenots. England had neither the resources nor the ships to crush Spain at sea, and Spanish land armies were still the best in Europe. War lasted till 1604, when a peace was signed by the successors of Philip and Elizabeth. The only thing that was clear by then was that the English and the Dutch had taken their places beside the Portuguese and the Spanish as major powers on the sea.

The French Wars of Religion

One obvious reason for Spain's ascendancy in the later sixteenth century was the inability of any other power except the Ottoman Empire to challenge Philip's monarchy, until the rise of the Dutch and English at the close of the century. A divided and dispirited Italy had fallen under the heel of Spain. The Empire was too disunited to qualify as a great power. After the Religious Peace of Augsburg the states of Germany relapsed into a state of uneasy quiet. Lutheranism ceased to spread, but both Calvinism and the Catholic Reformation made increasing numbers of converts. The mounting religious tension was to burst out into civil war within the Empire early in the next century. Meanwhile, the Austrian Hapsburg emperors were generally friendly toward their Spanish cousin, Philip. Finally, the chief obstacle to Hapsburg expansion, France, was torn by a series of civil and religious wars which prostrated the monarchy, revived feudal anarchy, and devastated large areas of the country between 1562 and 1593. Almost overnight France was transformed from an aggressive national mon-

The Spanish Armada, by an unknown artist. Some of the Spanish ships, like the galleass in the foreground, had both oars and sails.

archy into an object of intervention by neighboring states.

The Causes of the Civil War

France, with a population about double that of Spain, was the largest nation in Christian Europe under a single, centralized government. The development of absolute monarchy in France, impressive as it was, was by no means complete or irreversible. Like other European monarchies from the fifteenth to the eighteenth centuries, France had grafted monarchical institutions on to older feudal customs. There was still a powerful and turbulent feudal nobility in France, and a new "nobility of the robe" composed of wealthy lawyers was pushing its way into the ranks of the privileged. Many of the provinces of France, particularly around the southern and western periphery of the country, had local rights and privileges which they cherished jealously in the face of royal encroachment. In France class differences and local differences cut deeper than they did, for instance, in England, and there was no national representative institution quite like the English Parliament. The French *parlements* were essentially higher courts of law, and there were not one but several of them. The French Estates General had never established its control over taxation, and met only at infrequent intervals.

Into this half-established absolute monarchy the strong irritant of religious conflict was injected about the middle of the century in the form of a militant Calvinism. Lutheran ideas had taken only shallow root in some French cities, but the rational theology and disciplined organization of Reformed Christianity—not to mention the superb French style of Calvin's writings—appealed widely to many nobles and bourgeois throughout France. The French Calvinists were nicknamed Huguenots. On the eve of the civil wars they boasted about twenty-five hundred churches. They probably never numbered more than a sixth of the population (some scholars say as low as a twelfth), but they were an aggressive and well-organized minority, sure of their faith, and confident of the support of a few nobles at the very top of the social hierarchy such as Admiral Coligny. Arrayed against them were strongly Catholic noble families like that of Guise, but, more important, the whole dead weight of monarchical institutions was against them. The Concordat of Bologna in 1516 had given the king full control over the appointment of the higher clergy in France as well as considerable indirect control of papal taxation and jurisdiction. With such power in their hands, French kings thereafter had none of the usual inducements to go over to Protestantism. The monarchy remained stanchly Catholic until the very end of the century. So also did the University of Paris and the Paris *parlement*. The weight of central authority was thrown consistently against religious change and consequently the Huguenots remained a permanent minority in France.

The Course of the Wars

The wars that broke out in France in 1562 were at once social, political, and religious. When Henry II died in 1559, the royal authority fell first into the hands of the Guise family, then into the hands of his wife, Catherine de' Medici, during the reigns of her three weakling sons, Francis II (1559–60), Charles IX (1560–74), and Henry III (1574–89). Catherine was an astute woman who put politics before religion and did her best to keep the feuding factions at court and the religious fanatics throughout the country from flying at each other's throats. But she had a hard time of it because she lacked formal authority and by now the animosities had become bitter. Calvinism allied itself with the forces of feudal unrest and local separatism. This alliance often made for strange bed-fellows—on one side, high-minded Calvinists, discontented nobles, and antimonarchical lawyers—on the other, sincere Catholics, royal agents, and defenders of the status quo. Fanatics on both sides appealed for foreign aid, the Huguenots to the English, the Dutch, and the Germans, the Catholics to Spain. Both England and Spain sent troops, mostly at the beginning and again at the end of the wars.

Fighting was of the savage and bitter kind that characterizes civil wars. The Catholics won most of the pitched battles, but were unable to wipe the Huguenots out. In 1572 Catherine was persuaded by the Catholic fanatics that one sharp blow might end all the trouble. At two o'clock in the morning of St. Bartholomew's Day, Catholic armed bands set upon the Huguenots in Paris, where many of their leaders were gathered for the wedding of the king's sister to the Protestant, Henry of Navarre. Coligny and many others were killed. The slaughter spread quickly to other French cities, and before it was over probably ten thousand Protestants had been massacred. This was the most spectacular of innumerable atrocities on both sides. It horrified Protestants throughout Europe and, according to one story, made Philip II

A contemporary impression of the Massacre of St. Bartholomew's Day, August 24, 1572.

laugh aloud. But it had little if any effect in settling the conflict in France.

Henry of Navarre

The wars dragged on for twenty more years, becoming more and more confused and purposeless until the Huguenot Henry of Navarre came to the throne in 1589 as Henry IV (1589–1610). He had a difficult time making good his claim to the crown against a Catholic League which held Paris and against troops of Philip II which intervened from the Spanish Netherlands under Parma. In the end he found that the only way he could capture Paris was to renounce his faith and become a Catholic, which he did in 1593. He did not forget his former fellow Protestants, however. By the Edict of Nantes in 1598 the Huguenots were granted freedom of conscience, freedom of worship in specified places, equal civil rights, and the right to control some two hundred fortified towns throughout France. This last provision,

which left a kind of "state within a state," showed that the edict simply recognized a religious stalemate. The zealous on both sides of the religious fence considered it only temporary. But it constituted the first formal recognition by a European national monarchy that two religions could be allowed to exist side by side without destroying the state, and growing numbers of Frenchmen who preferred civil peace at any price to the anarchy and fanaticism of the past forty years supported it. With the conclusion of peace with Spain and the publication of the Edict of Nantes in 1598, France was ready to resume the building of a strong monarchy.

The General Character of the Later Sixteenth Century

The age of Philip II and Elizabeth of England had several marked characteristics: (1) It was an age of civil and international war. (2) It was an age in which

565

politics were religious and religion was political. (3) It was an era strongly colored by expansion overseas. (4) Finally, it was a "golden age" of culture for Spain, England, and the Dutch Netherlands.

War

The civil and international wars of the period were the result of economic changes, social tensions, and religious hatreds. The steep rise in prices throughout most of Europe hurt those nobles and bourgeois who lived on relatively fixed incomes and aided those more adventurous businessmen and landowners who were in a position to profit by the inflation. The result was increased social instability and restlessness. The contemporary literature of Europe insisted that rank, order, and de-gree were the God-given pattern of society, but perhaps this very insistence was a sign of uneasiness about how long the old feudal hierarchy would last. In any case, the economic situation produced men who were touchy and insecure, ready to fight in defense of old rights or to acquire new. There were combustible materials, in other words, which could easily be fanned into war. The spark that set these materials aflame was religion—the Spanish hatred of Moslems and Protestants, the Dutch and Huguenot hatred of Roman Catholicism, the fear that hovered over religious minorities and religious exiles of the torture chamber, the stake, and the headsman's axe. And so the century following Luther's death in 1547 is often called the Age of Religious Warfare.

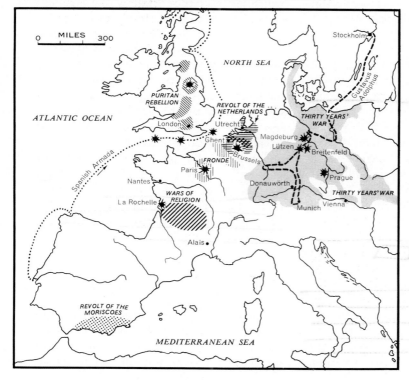

Centers of Revolution and Civil War 1560-1660

18 / The Age of Discovery and the Greatness of Spain

The Escorial, Philip II's monastery-palace near Madrid.

Religious Politics

A more precise description might be the Age of Religious Politics. Until the Reformation, European politics and diplomacy had grown slowly less religious and more secular. Now for a century, thanks to the religious schism, politics and diplomacy became once more strongly motivated and embittered by religion. The monarchies were faced by religious ideologies which often commanded fiercer loyalties than could the dynasties themselves. A Jesuit schemed and worked and often died for an ideal that obviously transcended all state boundaries. In the same way a Scottish Presbyterian, a Dutch Calvinist, and a French Huguenot often had more in common with each other than did subjects of the same king. Thus religious differences sometimes undermined the power of monarchs, as they did in France and the Netherlands. Sometimes religious zeal reinforced loyalty to the dynasty, as it did in Spain and among English Protestants. Perhaps the best symbol of this Age of Religious Politics was the Escorial, half-palace and half-monastery, which Philip II built for his residence near Madrid. The plan of the building was that of a grid, in grisly memory of the way St. Lawrence was roasted to death, and the private chamber of the king was connected directly with the chapel of the monastery. A century later a palace would be built at Versailles which would express the spirit of a quite different age.

The Expansion of Europe

During the later sixteenth century oceanic trade, overseas colonies, and sea power acquired new importance in the calculations of European statesmen. Undeclared war could still go on overseas without involving European mother countries in war. But by 1600 every European state along the Atlantic seaboard was involved in the scramble for gold, slaves, spices, sugar, and tobacco. Sooner or later the home country was drawn into seizing bases, sending out settlers, expanding shipping yards, and building warships. New products flowed into Europe, a new stimu-

567

Religion and Patriotism

A Spanish ambassador reporting the words of a French Catholic in 1565:

Nowadays Catholic princes must not proceed as they once did. At one time friends and enemies were distinguished by the frontiers of provinces and kingdoms, and were called Italians, Germans, Frenchmen, Spaniards, Englishmen, and the like. Now we must say Catholics and heretics, and a Catholic prince must consider all Catholics of all countries as his friends, just as the heretics consider all heretics as friends and subjects whether they are their own vassals or not.

An English Protestant writing in 1589:

All dutiful subjects in this land desire with all their hearts the continuance of God's religion; the preservation of Queen Elizabeth; and the good success of the English navy. These particulars, I grant, are not expressed in flat in the Lord's Prayer; but they are contained within the compass of, and may be deduced from the petitions of that excellent prayer. Whosoever doubteth of this is void of learning.

As quoted in Erich Marks, *Die Zusammenkunft von Bayonne* (Strassburg: K. J. Trübner, 1889), p. 14; as quoted in Benjamin Hanbury, *Historical Memorials Relating to the Independents* (London: Congregational Union of England and Wales, 1839–44), Vol. I, p. 71.

lus to European industry appeared in colonial markets, and new problems developed in financing and organizing overseas trade and colonization. Conflicts in jungles thousands of miles across the sea could now affect the relations of European nations, as in the case of Spain and England. There were even a few faint indications in the writings of the sixteenth century of the profound effects that the discoveries were beginning to have on the European mind and imagination. Sir Thomas More's *Utopia* (1516), Michel de Montaigne's *Essays* (1580–1595), and Sir Francis Bacon's *The New Atlantis* (1627) are examples of writings affected by Europe's exciting discovery of civilizations in the East far older than its own and of societies in the West more primitive than its own.

"Golden Ages"

Finally, the later sixteenth and early seventeenth centuries witnessed a "golden age" of literature and the arts in three of the nations we have been considering. Shakespeare's plays and Spenser's poetry in Elizabethan England, Cervantes' *Don Quixote* and Velasquez' paintings in Spain of the early seventeenth century, and Vondel's poetry and Rembrandt's portraits in Holland of the mid-seventeenth century represent a kind of summit of achievement in the history of the arts in these three nations. Shakespeare (1564?–1616), Cervantes (1547–1616), and Vondel (1587–1679) are still the greatest figures in the literary history of their native countries, and, though England produced no great painter, Frans Hals (1580?–1666) and Rembrandt van Rijn (1606–1669) are the towering figures in Dutch painting, as El Greco (1548?–1614) and Velasquez (1599–1660) are in Spanish.

In each case the artistic flowering accompanied or, as in Spain, immediately followed a period of heroic national struggle, effort, and achievement. It is tempting to say that ages of national expansion and excitement, times of heroism and "crusade," provide great artists with the stimulation and the receptive audiences they need. On a more mundane level, it is clear that "golden ages" depend on the existence of a class of people with enough education, wealth, and leisure to appreciate luxuries like books and paintings. The historian can

Rembrandt's visualization of the whole of Chapter 19 of the Gospel according to St. Matthew. On the right are the sick who look to Christ for healing; on the upper left, the Pharisees who show their contempt for him; below them the rich young man who is unable to give up his wealth to follow him, sitting with chin in hand, and the children eager to come to him, in spite of Peter (left of Christ), who thinks his Master has more important things to do. The figure of Christ is undistinguished, except that all the action of the picture flows toward and away from him. All the men and women —sick and well, rich and poor, young and old—reveal themselves by their reaction to the central figure. The bulky figure at the lower left probably suggests the indifference of the unconcerned onlookers. Protestant concern with the Bible reaches its artistic climax in Rembrandt's drawings of biblical scenes.

record the existence of such classes and the occurrence of heroic national effort in England, Spain, and the Dutch Netherlands during these years. But he cannot account satisfactorily for Shakespeare's extraordinary appreciation of the complexities of human motivation, Cervantes' sympathy for all sorts and conditions of men, or Rembrandt's penetration of the depths of the religious soul. All these are mani-festations of purely individual genius. Nor can he account for the appearance in France during a time of troubles of three writers who have profoundly influenced the French mind: Montaigne (1533–92), Descartes (1596–1650), and Pascal (1623–62). The historian can explain something about the conditions and characteristics of "golden ages." He cannot explain the appearance of genius.

Suggestions for Further Reading

1. Geographical Discovery

Two brief general studies provide a good introduction to the subject: J. H. Parry, *Europe and a Wider World, 1415–1715* (1949), and C. E. Nowell, *The Great Discoveries and the First Colonial Empires* * (1954). W. C. Abbott, *The Expansion of Europe,* 2 vols. (1918), is an older but still valuable general account, including consideration of the effect of the discoveries upon Europe. *The Great Age of Discovery* (edited A. P. Newton, 1932), is a collection of reliable articles by various authors. Sir Percy Sykes, *A History of Exploration* (1934), surveys the whole subject from ancient times on; H. H. Hart, *Sea Road to the Indies* (1950), describes the Portuguese exploits; J. B. Brebner, *The Explorers of North America, 1492–1806* (1933), and A. P. Newton, *The European Nations in the West Indies, 1493–1688* (1933), treat exploration in particular areas. E. Sanceau has written a good modern biography of Henry the Navigator (1947). S. E. Morison, *Admiral of the Ocean Sea,** 2 vols. (1942), is the best account of Columbus. C. McK. Parr, *So Noble a Captain* (1953), is a reliable account of Magellan. E. Sanceau, *The Land of Prester John* (1944), traces Portuguese interest in Abyssinia. The best correctives for older Anglo-Saxon notions of Spanish colonizing are C. H. Haring, *The Spanish Empire in America* (1947), and L. Hanke, *The Spanish Struggle for Justice in the Conquest of America* (1949). Two novels offer colorful impressions of the age: C. S. Forester, *To the Indies* (1940), about Columbus, and S. Shellabarger, *Captain from Castile* (1945), about Cortes.

2. Spain

R. B. Merriman, *Rise of the Spanish Empire in the Old World and in the New,* 4 vols. (1918–34), is a superbly written and scholarly account of Spain in Europe and overseas to the death of Philip II. R. Trevor Davies, *The Golden Century of Spain, 1501–1621* (1937), and *Spain in Decline, 1621–1700* (1956), are well-informed, interesting, sometimes controversial accounts. J. H. Parry, *The Spanish Theory of Empire in the Sixteenth Century* (1940), studies the effect of empire upon the Spanish monarchy. E. J. Hamilton, *American Treasure and the Price Revolution in Spain, 1501–1650* (1934), is the starting point for study of sixteenth-century inflation.

3. The Netherlands

The most scholarly brief account of the Dutch rebellion and its consequences is in the two books of P. Geyl, *The Revolt of the Netherlands, 1555–1609* (1932), and *The Netherlands Divided, 1609–1648* (1936). There is a beautifully written popular biography of William the Silent by C. V. Wedgwood (1944).

4. Elizabethan England

There is a wealth of well-written, scholarly books on the period. Sir John Neale, author of three brilliant volumes on the parliamentary history of the reign, has written the best biography of Queen Elizabeth (1934); but E. Jenkins, *Elizabeth the Great* (1959), adds insight on the purely personal side. C. Read's thorough biographies, *Mr. Secretary Walsingham,* 3 vols. (1925), and *Mr. Secretary Cecil* (Lord Burghley), 2 vols. (1955, 1960), provide intimate knowledge of the politics of the period. A. L. Rowse has written with zest on Elizabethan society in *The England of Elizabeth* (1950) and *The Expansion*

* Available in paperback edition.

of Elizabethan England (1955). J. A. Williamson, *The Age of Drake* (3rd ed., 1952), is by a master of naval history; and G. Mattingly, *The Armada* (1959), is one of those rare books, a definitive treatment of its subject which is at the same time magnificent reading.

5. France

It is more difficult to find good reading in English on France than on England in the sixteenth century. L. Batiffol, *The Century of the Renaissance* (trans. 1916), is an older general account of France in the sixteenth century. There are good biographies of Catherine de' Medici by P. Van Dyke, 2 vols. (1922), and of Henry of Navarre by Q. Hurst (1938). There is a brief modern account of the period in F. C. Palm, *Calvinism and the Religious Wars* (1932). J. W. Thompson, *The Wars of Religion in France, 1559–1576* (1909), is older but still useful. A. J. Grant, *The Huguenots* (1934), is both scholarly and brief. W. F. Church, *Constitutional Thought in Sixteenth Century France* (1941), discusses with discernment the conflict of medieval and modern ideas of government during the civil wars.

19

The Making of the Modern State, 1600-1660

The seventeenth century saw the culmination of a long, slow process which has engaged our attention many times in preceding chapters: the emergence out of the feudal and ecclesiastical society of the Middle Ages of the modern sovereign, territorial state, supreme over all persons and groups within its frontiers, and independent of all control from beyond its borders. This process began with the building of strong "feudal monarchies" in the twelfth century. After a lapse in the fourteenth century, it made further headway in the "new monarchies" of the later fifteenth century. After a further lapse marked by the civil and religious wars after the Reformation, it culminated at the end of the

S. PAULES CHVRCH

THAMESIS

seventeenth century in two contrasting types of modern state: the absolute monarchy of Louis XIV in France, and the constitutional monarchy of William III in England. The making of the modern state was a process of defining and concentrating political power—that is, the power to make law, to carry out the law, to make war and peace. From a theoretical point of view, it meant defining the concept of "sovereignty" ever more clearly. From the practical point of view, it meant fixing supreme power in some organ of the state, either in the monarchy (as in France and most other states) or in the representative assembly (as in England and a few other states).

The history of European civilization from the close of the Middle Ages is first and foremost the history of sovereign, territorial states. The rise and fall of these states, the predominance of some and the decay of others, give each century of modern western history its peculiar character and explain the particular influence of the West, at any given time, on the rest of the world. The seventeenth century witnessed the slow but decisive decline of Spain, the rise of France to European hegemony, the

View of London in 1616, showing the old St. Paul's Church (note the windmill to the left), the Globe Theatre, where many of Shakespeare's plays were performed (lower right of left-hand panel), and London Bridge.

FLUVIUS

South Warke

Hobbes' Leviathan

When Thomas Hobbes published his tough-minded book on the state in 1651, he chose his title from the Book of Job. "Leviathan" is the fearful and powerful aquatic beast, either a crocodile or a whale, described by Job in Chapter 41. The crowned ruler pictured above is likened by the artist to this beast, described in the verse of Job quoted above his head: "There is no power on earth that may be compared to him." The book and its title page are good landmarks of the making of the modern state. Hobbes calls the sovereign power of a state, usually conferred on one man, "that great Leviathan, or rather (to speak more reverently) that mortal God, to which we owe under the immortal God, our peace and defence."

heyday of Dutch prosperity and power, the appearance of England as a major power with revolutionary political ideas, the final disintegration of the German Empire, and the appearance of Sweden and Russia on the stage of European diplomacy. It saw the last of the "religious" wars and the first of the more purely "commercial" wars. Europe continued to expand abroad, but now it was the Dutch, the English, and the French who were the leaders, not the Spanish and the Portuguese. Economic motives became more prominent than religious in this expansion, and for the first time a conscious economic theory of the national interest began to influence statesmen. Finally, a "scientific revolution" gave Europeans a radically new way of understanding and controlling natural processes (see Chapter 21).

The Mercantile Economy of Early Modern Europe

Before we turn to the political and intellectual developments of the seventeenth century, we shall first summarize the economic and social changes which we have observed taking place from the fifteenth century on, and then sketch, very briefly, the economic development of Europe from 1600 to 1700.

Historians often refer to economic changes from about 1450 to 1750 as the "Commercial Revolution." It was Adam Smith, writing in 1776, who first called the economy of this period the commercial or mercantile system. Smith thought that Europeans had had two "systems" of enriching themselves: the system of agriculture (through the Middle Ages), and the system of commerce. He did not say so, of course, but he himself was living on the threshold of a third system—one in which industry was to be the dominant element and which would be ushered in by an "Industrial Revolution." Let us follow his lead and call the economy of the fifteenth through the seventeenth centuries a mercantile economy, one in which the dominant figure of the merchant overshadowed both the farmer and the manufacturer.

Several general features of this period are immediately evident. First, the volume and value of European trade increased enormously. Second, the geographical area covered by European trade routes expanded very widely after the great discoveries. Third, the nerve centers of this trade moved in the fifteenth century from Venice in the Mediterranean and the Hanse in the Baltic and North seas, to Portugal and Spain along the Atlantic. Finally, by the early seventeenth century these nerve centers were shifting once again—this time from Lisbon and Seville to Amsterdam, London, and Paris. After 1600 Europe's economic center of gravity was somewhere in the triangle formed by the capitals of France, England, and the Dutch Netherlands.

We have already noted some of the more obvious causes of the expansion of trade: the establishment of law and order over wider areas by stronger governments, improvements in navigation, expansion of the medium of exchange through the discovery of new sources of gold and silver, and the growth of accumulated surpluses of wealth which men could invest in the production of more wealth. Now we shall note changes in the economic institutions of Europe which resulted from this quantitative expansion of trade and at the same time aided further expansion.

Gild Economy vs. Capitalist Economy

The gild system was not adapted to meet the constantly growing demand of towns for food and clothing, of royal and noble courts for luxuries, and of armies for weapons and supplies. The gild was an

❖❖❖❖❖❖❖❖❖❖❖❖❖❖❖❖❖❖❖❖❖❖❖❖❖❖❖❖❖

Europe's Growing Population

This chart is an attempt by a historian to show at a glance the changes in population density per square mile in certain European countries during a period of four hundred years. Since there was no census anywhere in Europe before the nineteenth century, the author is careful to point out that "the estimates are rough approximations only." Such charts are helpful, but since they are based on very inadequate data, the reader must always remember that they convey an undue sense of definiteness and precision.

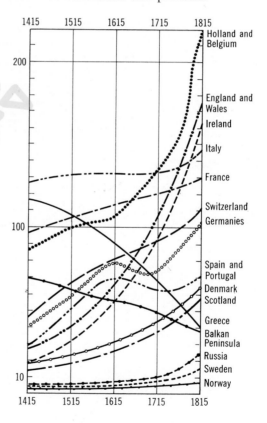

Redrawn from Geoffrey Bruun, *Europe in Evolution, 1415–1815* (Boston: Houghton Mifflin, 1945), pp. 240–41.

❖❖❖❖❖❖❖❖❖❖❖❖❖❖❖❖❖❖❖❖❖❖❖❖❖❖❖❖

The Center of European Economy early 17th century

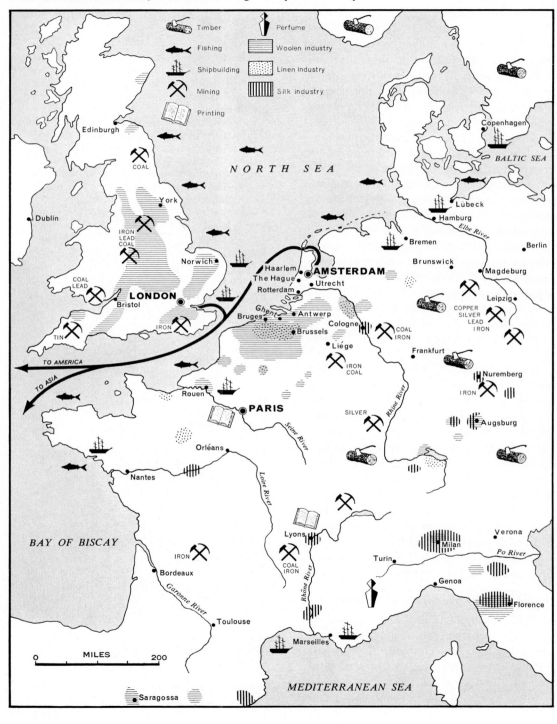

Timber
Fishing
Shipbuilding
Mining
Printing

Perfume
Woolen industry
Linen industry
Silk industry

Edinburgh
COAL
York
Dublin
IRON
LEAD
COAL
Norwich
COAL
LEAD
LONDON
Bristol
IRON
TIN
TO AMERICA
TO ASIA
Rouen
PARIS
Orléans
Nantes
BAY OF BISCAY
IRON
Bordeaux
Garonne River
Toulouse
Seine River
Loire River
Lyons
COAL
IRON
Rhône River
Marseilles
Saragossa
MEDITERRANEAN SEA

NORTH SEA

Haarlem
The Hague
Rotterdam
AMSTERDAM
Utrecht
Ghent
Bruges
Antwerp
Brussels
Cologne
Liége
IRON
COAL

Copenhagen
BALTIC SEA
Lübeck
Hamburg
Bremen
Brunswick
Berlin
Magdeburg
Elbe River
Leipzig
COPPER
SILVER
LEAD
IRON
COAL
IRON
Frankfurt
Nuremberg
IRON
SILVER
Rhine River
Augsburg

Verona
Milan
Po River
Turin
Genoa
Florence

MILES
0   200

BAY OF BISCAY

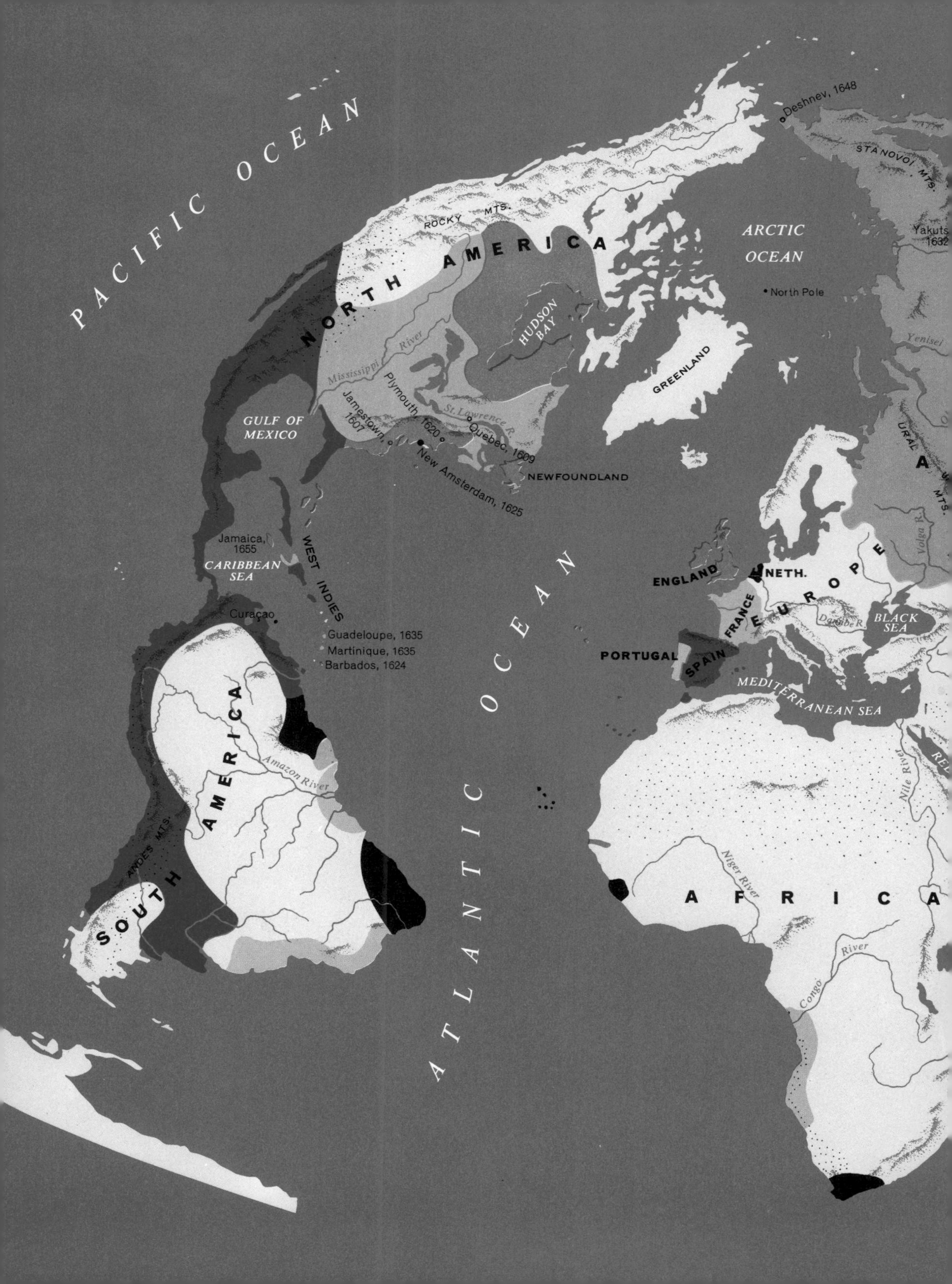

PACIFIC OCEAN

ARCTIC OCEAN

Deshnev, 1648

STANOVOI MTS.

Yakuts, 1632

Yenisei R.

North Pole

NORTH AMERICA

ROCKY MTS.

River

Mississippi

St. Lawrence R.

HUDSON BAY

GREENLAND

URAL MTS.

A

Plymouth, 1620

Jamestown, 1607

Quebec, 1609

New Amsterdam, 1625

NEWFOUNDLAND

GULF OF MEXICO

Jamaica, 1655

CARIBBEAN SEA

WEST INDIES

Curaçao

Guadeloupe, 1635

Martinique, 1635

Barbados, 1624

ATLANTIC OCEAN

ENGLAND

NETH.

FRANCE

EUROPE

Volga R.

BLACK SEA

Danube R.

PORTUGAL

SPAIN

MEDITERRANEAN SEA

Amazon River

SOUTH AMERICA

ANDES MTS.

Nile River

RED

Niger River

AFRICA

Congo River

Colonization 17th century

☐ English	☐ French	■ Dutch	▫ Desert
■ Spanish	▨ Russian	☐ Portuguese	

PACIFIC

OCEAN

JAPAN

sk,
3

Yeniseisk, 1618

Amur River

Lake Baikal

EAST
CHINA
SEA

A S I A

C H I N A

Yellow River

Yangtze River

PHILIPPINE
IS.

SOUTH
CHINA
SEA

SPICE IS.
(MOLUCCAS)

AMBOINA

EAST INDIES

AUSTRALIA

ARAL
SEA

ASPIAN
SEA

Brahmaputra
HIMALAYA MTS.

Ganges R.

Indus River

Calcutta,
1690, 1700

INDIA

BAY OF
BENGAL

JAVA

ARABIAN SEA

Bombay,
1661, 1665

Madras, 1639
Pondicherry, 1674

INDIAN OCEAN

association of merchants or craftsmen aimed at stabilizing and regulating trade or production in the interest both of the gild members and of the local community. It was designed to divide the available business or the available work as fairly as possible among the gild members, and to grant the community strict control over gild activities in return for a monopoly. It was not intended to stimulate unlimited expansion of trade or production. In order to supply the growing demands of cities, courts, and armies, however, individual entrepreneurs (contractors, we would call them) began, on their own, to organize large-scale commerce and production outside the gilds. Sometimes the gilds themselves underwent a subtle transformation whereby a few masters would take over as owners of the business, reducing journeymen and apprentices to the status of workers without any hope of rising to ownership. In either case, it was the merchant who served as the moving force. It was the merchant, the man who knew what to buy and where to sell, who organized the economic activity of Europe during these years in response to the demands of kings, nobles, and bourgeois.

Putting-out and Gathering-in Systems

A typical example is what happened in the cloth trade. In Florence the merchant gild which marketed finished cloth managed to organize and subordinate the various craft gilds which worked on the cloth at different stages. The result was the great *Arte di Lana,* or cloth gild, which took on more and more the look of a complex capitalistic enterprise organized by merchants. In England, as in other parts of Europe, individual entrepreneurs began to buy wool, pass it out to peasants to be spun into thread, carry the thread to others to be woven into cloth, take the cloth to fullers and dyers, and finally sell the fin-

ished product. This "putting-out system," as it came to be called, had the double advantage of bypassing the older gild restrictions in the towns and of tapping new sources of cheap labor in the countryside. It was clearly "capitalistic," since the entrepreneurs retained ownership of the product at all stages, and sometimes even supplied the tools. In the same way English merchants bought Swedish iron, gave it out to Sheffield tool-makers, and sold the product abroad (the English were the best precision-tool makers in Europe). The "putting-out system" dominated the textile industry from the sixteenth to the eighteenth centuries.

Other industries followed the "gathering-in system" (we call it the factory system). In industries like printing, cannon-founding, mining, and shipbuilding, for example, and even in some textile processes like silk-weaving and calico-printing, it was more efficient to gather workers together at some central place where their work could be directly supervised and coordinated. But in both the putting-out and the gathering-in systems, it was almost invariably the merchant, not the manufacturer or the technician, who did the organizing.

Joint Stock Companies

When the merchants of a country wanted to obtain a monopoly of trade in some one product, they at first formed what the English called "regulated companies." These were simply associations of individual merchants trading on their own within the limits of a government-regulated company, on the model of medieval merchant gilds. The regulated companies were associations of men, not of capital. What was needed, however, was some sort of association which would tap both the human and the financial resources of a nation more effectively, an association that would attract investors, both great and small, who themselves could never qualify as active traders in a regulated company. The answer was the "joint stock company," an amazingly flexible institution which was to be the parent of many other economic and political institutions on both sides of the Atlantic in future years.

The joint stock company was an association of capital, not of individuals as such. Individuals bought shares in a venture, like a trading voyage, and shared in the profits in proportion to their investment. When the association continued beyond a single venture, it became a joint stock company. This device had two advantages: it enabled anyone from a modestly wealthy man to a Queen Elizabeth to invest in a business enterprise like Drake's voyages, and it associated businessmen with courtiers and statesmen at a time when both business sense and influence at court were necessary to the success of commercial ventures. The joint stock idea originated in southern Europe, but it was applied to large-scale overseas enterprise first in England in the Russia Company of 1553 and then in the Netherlands, France, and elsewhere. The English and Dutch East India Companies, the companies which founded Virginia and Massachusetts, and the Bank of England were all joint stock companies.

The quantitative expansion in trade, then, brought about the change from gild to joint stock company as the dominant form of commercial organization. This same expansion brought about a still more striking change: the change from town to king as the regulator of economic activity. The unit of economic activity in the Middle Ages, apart from agriculture, was the town or the city-state. As stronger monarchs appeared at the end of the Middle Ages, urban economy was steadily absorbed into the national economy throughout much of Europe, except Italy and Germany. The monarchs stepped into the shoes of the medieval town officials and began to regulate trade, encourage production, grant monopolies, and balance the interests of producer and consumer much as municipal governments had done, but now on a much larger scale. In both municipal and monarchical government, the aim was theoretically to advance the good of the community, never the good of the individual, to increase the "common wealth" by regulating trade and industry.

Mercantilism

The system of political economy developed by the leading governments of Europe in the sixteenth and seventeenth centuries is generally called mercantilism. It was a program for increasing the wealth of a country by regulating its trade. It assumed that there is a certain stock of wealth in the world at any given time and that one country's gain is another country's loss. It assumed further that by regulating trade in the proper way one could increase a country's industrial and agricultural production and so add to its wealth. The main aim of mercantilism was to increase the country's war potential by building up a large reserve of the precious metals, fostering home industries, expanding shipping, and encouraging colonies which could supply raw materials unavailable at home. In the sixteenth and seventeenth centuries when modern credit devices were still in their infancy, a country had to have a good reserve of gold and silver to pay its armies and fight its wars.

The easiest way to build up such a reserve—short of discovering new mines or capturing a Spanish plate fleet—was for a nation to export more than it imported and thus to compel foreign buyers to pay in cash for the excess. And so, in practice, mercantilism called for tariffs to discourage imports and various benefits to encourage export industries, in order to gain a favorable balance of trade. It forbade the export of gold and silver, tools and machines, and important raw materials, and it also forbade the emigration of skilled laborers. Logically mercantilist theory called for the abolition of all internal tariffs and all internal barriers to trade, but it was impossible to accomplish this except in England. Government tended, however, to accept paternalistic responsibility for the whole economic system. They regulated gilds in the national interest, set maximum wage levels, and devised laws (particularly in England) for setting the unemployed to work and for taking care of the unemployable. But the core of mercantilism remained the conviction that trade is the most important of all economic activities and that the regulation of trade is the government's most important economic concern.

Mercantilists favored the acquisition of colonies as sources of raw materials and as markets for home manufactures—colonies, in short, that enhanced the strength of the mother country. But they had no use for colonies that raised crops or produced manufactured goods that competed with the home country's products, nor for colonies that traded directly with other nations or with the colonies of other nations. To subordinate colonies to the home country and to integrate them into the home economy were cardinal principles of mercantilists.

We have necessarily made mercantilism seem more clear-cut and consistent than it actually was in practice. It differed from one country to another, in response to the concrete interests of the ruling group. In France the system is often called *Étatisme,* or state-ism. The hand of the government was very heavy in France, government intervention in commercial enterprise was

An Englishman on the Importance of Trade

ca. 1630

Although a kingdom may be enriched by gifts received, or by purchase taken from some other nations, yet these are things uncertain and of small consideration when they happen. The ordinary means therefore to encrease our wealth and treasure is by foreign trade, wherein we must ever observe this rule; to sell more to strangers yearly than we consume of theirs in value. For suppose that when this kingdom is plentifully served with the cloth, lead, tin, iron, fish and other native commodities, we do yearly export the overplus to foreign countries to the value of twenty-two hundred thousand pounds; by which means we are enabled beyond the seas to buy and bring in foreign wares for our use and consumptions, to the value of twenty hundred thousand pounds; by this order duly kept in our trading, we may rest assured that the kingdom shall be enriched yearly two hundred thousand pounds, which must be brought to us in so much treasure; because that part of our stock which is not returned to us in wares must necessarily be brought home in treasure. . . .

Behold then the true form and worth of foreign trade, which is, the great revenue of the king, the honour of the kingdom, the noble profession of the merchant, the school of our arts, the supply of our wants, the employment of our poor, the improvements of our lands, the nursery of our mariners, the walls of the kingdoms, the means of our treasure, the sinews of our wars, the terror of our enemies.

From Thomas Mun, *England's Treasure by Foreign Trade* (New York: Oxford U. Press, 1933), p. 5.

direct and positive, regulation was minute, and relatively little initiative was left to individual enterprise. "Government" in

France meant the king, a third force above both nobility and bourgeoisie, and the king only occasionally represented the interests of one or the other of these classes. In England mercantilism also meant regulation of the economy in the government's interest. But both before 1688 and especially afterward, the English government was more responsive to the pressures of businessmen than the French. It is often very difficult to tell whether English economic policy represented the interest of the state as a whole or the interests of individual entrepreneurs. In the United Provinces, where the federal government was in effect a government of businessmen, the interest of the state and the interests of the business community practically coincided, as they often did in the medieval town run by and for its gilds. Dutch mercantilism was not so much the regulation of trade by the state as it was the control of economic policy by organized business. In the rest of Europe, however—in Spain, Portugal, Austria, Prussia, Sweden—mercantilism represented primarily the interest of the monarchy and so followed the French model more than the Dutch.

The Rise in Prices

The rise in prices continued in the seventeenth century, though not so rapidly as in the later sixteenth century. The rise was not uniform in all parts of Europe, and in the present state of research it is hard to generalize. But a reasonable estimate is that prices more than doubled between 1500 and 1600 in Europe as a whole, then rose another 20 per cent by 1700, and another 10 per cent by 1800. This inflationary tendency had both social and political results. The social results are much disputed by historians, but there is agreement that the classes which lived on relatively fixed incomes—great nobles, lesser gentry, or members of medieval craft gilds—were hard hit, while the classes that lived by trade, large industry, or capitalistic farming did well. During the later sixteenth and early seventeenth centuries, there were always many impoverished nobles and gentry in England, France, and Spain who were ready to join an overseas voyage or a continental war. On the other hand, wealthy merchants and lawyers were constantly gaining titles of nobility and buying land as a symbol of their new status. And so, while many members of older noble families were being driven down in the social scale, a "new nobility" was pushing its way into the ranks of the privileged and taking its place beside the older families. The number of nobles, in relation to the rest of the population, was very large in Spain and was rapidly increasing in both France and England, thanks to the monarchs' constant temptation to add to their revenue by selling patents of nobility. Thus at least one reason for the many civil and international wars of the seventeenth century was the social mobility and restlessness evoked by economic change.

We have seen something already of the political effects of the rise in prices. Generally speaking, prices tended to rise faster than government income, and almost every major government in the seventeenth century had to face severe financial crises. The Spanish government was least successful in meeting these crises. In Spain the price rise was more severe than elsewhere, and the burden of military commitments was very heavy. The result was, as we have seen, that the government was forced to repudiate its debt about every twenty years from 1550 to 1650. The French government was somewhat more successful in raising the money it needed for its wars and its court, but the taxation system was antiquated and trouble was simply postponed to the eighteenth century. In England the Stuarts were never able to build a sound system of government finance because they lost the confidence of Parliament, which controlled the major part of the royal revenue. But after 1688 a monarchy which had gained the confidence of Parliament as well as the business community was able to construct an exceptionally strong system of public finance which included parliamentary taxation, a national bank, and a permanent public debt. In large measure this system was modeled on Dutch governmental finance, the most successful of the age. Since the rulers of the United Provinces were representatives of the business community, they had little difficulty, at least for a century, in raising the money and credit they needed for their overseas empire-building and their wars. In an age dominated by trade, a state which had a flourishing commerce and could command the confidence of its merchants could weather any financial storm. A state which had little commerce or was at odds with its merchants was in for trouble.

European Expansion in the Seventeenth Century

Europe continued to expand overseas in the seventeenth century. We have seen how the Dutch were drawn by their war of independence to take to the sea (see p. 557). By the end of the seventeenth century they had ousted the Portuguese from their empire in the East. The Portuguese successfully defended their colony in Brazil, and the Spanish Empire in Central and South America remained as large and imposing as ever. But early in the century two new competitors for commerce and colonies appeared beside the Dutch in India, the Caribbean, and North America. These were the English and the French. They were not strong enough to attack the

Spanish directly. Rather, they went where the Spanish were not and developed a new and rival kind of empire. Meanwhile the Russians moved overland to stake out their claim to the northern half of Asia.

The East

First the English and then the French followed Vasco da Gama's route to the East. The English East India Company was founded in 1600, the Dutch in 1602, the French in 1664. The English found that the Dutch were too firmly established in the Spice Islands to be dislodged, so after a Dutch "massacre" of ten English merchants at Amboina in 1623, they withdrew to India. Here they set up "factories," or trading posts, on the Portuguese model. Until the break-up of the Mogul Empire in central India early in the eighteenth century, it was never possible for Europeans to establish sizable colonies or penetrate very far into the interior of the teeming subcontinent of India. Their footholds on the coast depended entirely on sea power for support, and as Portuguese sea power declined in the seventeenth century and the Dutch busied themselves farther east, the English moved in. By the end of the century they were established at Bombay, Madras, and Calcutta. Meanwhile, the French at Pondicherry had become their most important potential rivals. The stage was set for a struggle in the next century between the British and the French East India Companies over the commerce and riches of India.

The Caribbean

In the Caribbean the story was somewhat the same. Early in the seventeenth century the Dutch, the English, and the French were all searching for footholds in the Greater Antilles and on the mainland around the periphery of the Spanish settlements. After an unsuccessful attempt to

American Indians performing a ritual harvest dance around seven posts which probably represent minor deities. Four women and ten men in various attire take part in the dance, using "the strangest gestures that they can possibly devise. . . . Three of the fairest virgins of the company are in the middle, who, embracing one another, do, as it were, turn about in their dancing." Water color by John White, an artist who accompanied the English expedition of 1585 to Roanoke Island.

take Brazil from the Portuguese, the Dutch seized Curaçao as a base from which to raid Spanish commerce. The English settled Barbados in 1624 and acquired Jamaica in 1655. Meanwhile, the French settled Guadaloupe, Martinique, and St. Dominique. All these islands rapidly became rich sugar-producing areas, thanks to slave labor. So the English and French, who came to the Caribbean to trade and buccaneer on the Dutch model, stayed on to become plantation-owners on the Spanish model. The English and French sugar islands in the Lesser Antilles were the darling of mercantilists at home. The planters cultivated a crop which could not be grown in Europe, they developed no industries to compete with home industries, and they were entirely dependent on their mother countries for manufactured goods, shipping, and protection. Not surprisingly, the sugar islands were the center of attention among financiers and diplomats for over a century.

The chronic dearth of manufactured goods and slaves in the Spanish colonies meant that foreign smugglers who could slip by the Spanish navy were always welcome. As Portuguese control of the slaving stations on the western coast of Africa relaxed, the Dutch and English stepped in to supply the Spanish West Indies with the Negroes needed on their sugar plantations. The brutality of this trade has become a byword, but it aroused no protest whatever in any European nation during the seventeenth and early eighteenth centuries.

North America

To the north, a new kind of colonial expansion was beginning which was to have more far-reaching results than West Indian sugar-planting, though it was overshadowed for the moment by the economic success of the tropical islands. This was the settlement of North America. There were many reasons why the Dutch, the English, and the French at the opening of the seventeenth century should think of settling North America. For some time their sailors had been searching for a Northwest Passage to the Indies. Their ships were already engaged in cod-fishing on the Newfoundland Banks. It was evident that North America could supply vast quantities of furs and timber. There might be precious metals to be mined, and it might turn out that sugar could be grown farther north than the Caribbean. Permanent settlements could support all these economic activities and at the same time help turn the flank of the Spanish in the New World. The Dutch, the English, and the French all had reason to hate the Spaniards, though none yet had the power to attack the Spanish colonies directly.

Sir Walter Raleigh's unsuccessful attempt to found a colony in Virginia during the 1580's, however, had suggested some of the difficulties of settling the land the Spanish had left unoccupied. The climate was more rigorous and the soil not so rich as in the Caribbean. The natives were more hardy and more hostile, and they were too few to be organized into a working force to support a European ruling class, as in the Spanish colonies. To plant a permanent colony in North America a whole labor force had to be transported and supported, perhaps for years, until the settlement became self-sufficient. This called for a large investment of capital and a large number of settlers. Furthermore, it called for strong belief and determination.

The Dutch, the French, and the English

It was the English and, to a lesser degree, the French, not the Dutch, whose determination proved strongest. The Dutch explored the Hudson in 1609 and settled New Amsterdam on Manhattan Island in 1621, but their colony of New Netherland never became more than a center for maritime trade and the export of furs. Unsupported by the company that founded it, it fell to the English in 1664. The French were more successful. From Cartier, who discovered the St. Lawrence in 1535, to La Salle, who coursed the Mississippi in 1682, their explorers were more adventurous, their fur-traders better able to adapt to the country, and their Jesuit missionaries more determined, than the representatives of any other European nation in the New World. In 1605 there were French settlers in Acadia and in 1608 Champlain founded Quebec. By 1640 there were perhaps 3000 Frenchmen in Canada, by the end of the century about 10,000. The growth was slow for several reasons. The settlement of French Canada was marked by paternalism and relatively little individual initiative. Only when the French government actively encouraged Frenchmen to emigrate, as it had under Colbert in the 1660's and 1670's, did the colony grow appreciably. Since land was granted in large blocks or *seigneuries* to a few proprietors under semifeudal conditions, there was little inducement for peasants to emigrate. The government strictly prohibited the Huguenots, who wanted to emigrate, from going to Canada (they went to the English colonies instead). A "New France" was established in the New World, it is true, directly governed from home in the Spanish manner. The St. Lawrence Valley was settled and the Mississippi was explored to its mouth. But the slow-growing colony of *seigneurs* and *habitants,* as the peasants were called, was soon far outdistanced by the English settlements to the south.

The founding of the English colonies in North America was the result of a peculiarly favorable set of historical circumstances in the mother country. The idea of colonization—as a means of turning the Spanish flank and bringing new economic strength to England—had been skillfully sold to ordinary Englishmen by enthusiasts and businessmen before Queen Elizabeth's death. London and Bristol merchants were wealthy, ready for colonizing ventures, and able to organize them by means of joint stock companies. The constitutional and religious conflicts that troubled England through most of the seventeenth century provided many people with both material and idealistic motives for wishing to emigrate. Finally, the English government, whether it was that of the Stuarts or of their revolutionary opponents, was generally favorable to colonizing projects. It encouraged but did not direct these projects, and put no bar in the way of religious minorities that wished to emigrate.

The first successful colony, planted at Jamestown by the Virginia Company in 1607, had a difficult time of it until the settlers discovered that by concentrating on a single crop, tobacco, they could buy the goods they needed from England. The little band of religious dissenters who landed at Plymouth in 1620 lost half their number during the first winter and survived only by sheer heroism. But the Massachusetts Bay Company, which founded Boston, was able to profit by the Pilgrims' experience. In 1630 it transported 900 settlers across the ocean in a large and well-planned operation. Within ten years the population had increased to about 14,000 in Massachusetts and within twenty years there were about 20,000 in New England as a whole. This population had developed a surplus of food for export, and had plenty of fur, fish, and timber to ship back to the mother country. By the end of the century more colonies had been established, either as offshoots from the original settlements or by royal grants to "proprietors," until there were twelve in all (the thirteenth was added in 1732). By 1700 it has been estimated that there were almost 200,000 English settlers in North America, as compared with about 10,000 French. It was already clear that North America would some day be predominantly English-speaking.

English and French Colonies

The English colonies were more divided and less well controlled by the home government than the French. New France was under one central administration at Quebec while the English colonies were under twelve separate governments. Each of the twelve eventually elected representative assemblies which controlled local legislation and taxation. The royal governors were not responsible to these assemblies, but, since they were generally dependent on the assemblies for their salaries, their power was strictly limited. After the Restoration in 1660 (see p. 597), the government of Charles II made serious efforts to tighten its administrative control of the colonies' economic life, along the lines of orthodox mercantilist theory. In a series of statutes known as the Acts of Trade (1663–73) Parliament did its best to compel the colonies to produce only what England could not produce and to send all exports directly to England in English or colonial ships. Every attempt was made to keep the colonists from trading directly with the colonies of other nations. In return, the settlers were granted a monopoly of the English market for their special products, and the home country developed a large merchant marine and navy to supply and protect the colonies.

Naturally there was resistance to these measures in the colonies. When colonial assemblies objected to having their trade regulated by a Parliament in which they were not represented, the English government annulled some colonial charters and tried for a time in the 1680's to govern the colonies through royal officials alone. The Revolution of 1688 in England was followed by a return to the older, easy-going treatment of the American colonies, however. The English colonists submitted to the theory of parliamentary regulation of their trade so long as the regulations were not too strictly enforced, but they became more and more accustomed to running their own local affairs to suit themselves. This meant that in any possible major conflict with the French in North America, the English government would have a hard time mobilizing and unifying the war effort of twelve separate and self-willed colonies. But the English settlers would have the inestimable advantage of outnumbering the French by about twenty to one.

Without conscious design, the English in the seventeenth century fashioned a new kind of colonial empire in North America, quite different from either the Portuguese or the Spanish. The Portuguese Empire (and, to a large degree, the Dutch) was based on armed trade. The Spanish Empire was based on the efforts of a ruling class of soldiers, planters, and missionaries to convert the natives and exploit their labor. But the Protestant English (and Protestant Dutch) were never particularly interested in converting the natives. They never felt responsible for the Indians as the Spanish did, partly because there was no possibility of exploiting their labor. So they simply displaced the natives from the land on which they settled. The English transferred a whole European population to a new environment and permitted it to blend the traditional institutions it brought from home with the innovations and improvisations evoked by the new surroundings. Not surprisingly, these innovations tended toward economic, political, and religious freedom. The breeze was blowing in this direction in England, and it was blowing even more strongly in the colonies.

The Russians in Siberia

While the French and British in North America were pushing westward from the Atlantic seaboard toward the Pacific, the Russians were pushing eastward from the Ural Mountains across Siberia toward

A Cossack with the head of a Tartar. The first Cossacks were fugitives from the Grand Duchy of Moscow or from Poland who became hunters or fishermen on the frontier and, later, farmers, ranchers, or bandits.

the Pacific. The two movements were strikingly similar in many respects, but the Russians had no ocean to cross at the start and they reached the Pacific first. In 1581 groups of Cossacks—"pioneers," or "frontiersmen," who had earlier pushed back the Tartars and Turks and had settled in the lower valleys of the Dnieper, the Don, and the Volga—began to move eastward from the Urals under a leader, Ermak, who became famed in song and story. Like the French in Canada, they were mainly in search of furs, particularly sable, and so they followed the dark pine-forest, not the steppe to the south. The great rivers of Siberia—the Obi, the Yenisei, and the Lena —flow north into the Arctic Ocean, but in their upper reaches they branch out so as almost to touch each other, thus enabling the Cossacks to move easily across the continent by water. The movement was not planned or organized. The settlers simply flowed eastward through the sparsely settled wastes of Siberia in search of furs, occasionally stopping to form widely separated settlements, and reached the Pacific in the early 1640's, barely two generations after the movement began. The distance covered was greater than that across North America, but there were no great mountain barriers until near the end and no serious resistance from natives until the Cossacks met the Chinese in the Amur Valley. Here the Russians were checked by a superior civilized state, and in 1689, by the first treaty concluded between Russia and China, the Russians withdrew from the Amur basin. They remained behind the Stanovoi Mountains for the next 170 years.

Like the English, the Cossacks were in search of freedom as well as furs, and their early communities in Siberia were often wild and lawless, like later towns of the American "Wild West." But the tsar's government soon reached out across the vast distances to establish its administration and tax the lucrative fur trade—more like the French than the English government in North America. By 1700 there were perhaps half again as many Russian settlers in Siberia as there were French and British in North America, and by 1711 there were governors of West Siberia and of East Siberia. In the eighteenth century the fur trade gradually gave way to mining, lumbering, and farming in Siberia. By the end of the century, Russian traders were venturing across the Bering Strait into Alaska and down the North American coast line in search of seals. Thus long before the English colonists in America had reached the Pacific, the Russians, by a combination of individual daring and government backing, had staked out a claim to the northern half

of Asia and had even reached out to touch the shores of the Western Hemisphere.

France: In Search of Order and Authority, 1598–1661

Seventeenth-century France still felt the effects of the anarchy and violence that had prevailed for almost a half century before the Edict of Nantes in 1598. Political necessity had obliged Protestantism to ally itself with the antimonarchical forces of feudalism and provincialism, and the large nobles had come out of the religious wars more powerful and unruly than before. Three weakling kings had tarnished the prestige of the monarchy. Merchants and manufacturers had been hard hit by the wars, and the peasants had suffered heavily from the ravages of undisciplined soldiers. The mass of the people had grown tired of religious fanaticism and were now ready to submit to any authority which would restore law and order.

Jean Bodin, the most penetrating political thinker of the tragic years just past, had seen what was needed in his book *The Republic*, which he published in 1576. He argued that in any well-ordered state, supreme power or *sovereignty* must be clearly lodged somewhere in some organ of the state, preferably the monarchy. Sovereignty he defined as the power "to lay down the law to subjects in general without their consent." Bodin did not think of this power as arbitrary or capricious: the sovereign was still subject to the laws of God and of nature. But he insisted that sovereign power must not be limited by any human agency —that is, it must be "absolute" to be effective. He insisted that it cannot be divided, for instance among king, Estates General, and *parlements*. It must be recognized as legitimately residing in one person or one political institution. No one had defined sovereignty so clearly before, or argued so persuasively for it as the only remedy for feudal anarchy and civil war. Bodin's prescription for France's ills was fulfilled in general by Richelieu and Louis XIV, who built an absolute monarchy that became the model and envy of most of Europe.

Henry IV and Sully

The first steps toward restoring the power of the monarchy and the prosperity of the land were taken by Henry IV and his minister, Sully. Henry, first of the Bourbon dynasty, was a popular king—courageous, vigorous, humorous, tolerant, sensitive to the condition of the peasants, and sound in his judgment of men. But he spent much of his time in hunting and love-making and left the routine business of government to Sully and others. Sully was a puritanical Huguenot with a keen sense of economy and a hatred of dishonesty. He put the monarchy into fairly sound financial condition for the first time in half a century, mostly by limiting the expenditures of the court, recovering the rights and revenues of the crown which had been lost during the wars, and discharging dishonest tax collectors. The French taxation system was inefficient, corrupt, and inequitable. The taxes were "farmed"—that is, the right to collect them was granted to private collectors who paid the government a fixed sum and then collected all they could. The burden fell most heavily on the peasant, since the nobles were exempt from major taxes. Sully could do nothing to make the system more just (nor could any French minister down to the Revolution), but he could make the ramshackle system work better by supervising the farming of the taxes more carefully. (It has been estimated that as a rule hardly half the taxes collected in France at this time reached the treasury). Moreover, the re-establishment of internal peace and order, which allowed the agriculture and commerce of the country to recover, helped to increase the government's revenues, especially from customs duties. Within twelve years after the Edict of Nantes Sully had amassed a sizable surplus in the treasury, and Henry IV was about to squander it on a war against the Austrian and Spanish Hapsburgs when he was assassinated by a Catholic fanatic in 1610.

The Estates General of 1614

Within a few years the work of Henry and Sully was in ruins. Under the regency of Henry's widow, Marie de' Medici, the government fell into the hands of a Florentine adventurer, the treasury surplus was sopped up by rapacious courtiers, and Spain began once more to intervene in French affairs, sometimes in a strange alliance with the Huguenots. In 1614 the Estates General were summoned (they had met only very infrequently during the preceding century in times of national crisis), but the deliberations soon turned into a kind of class war between the nobility and the Third Estate (the bourgeoisie). The assembly dissolved with a strong declaration that "the king is sovereign in France, and holds his crown from God only." It was not to meet again until 1789, on the eve of the Revolution. Clearly the medieval French Estates had neither the power nor the *esprit de corps* to stand together and reform the monarchy. Torn by class differences, they resigned the task to the monarch himself and strengthened his claim to the divine right to rule.

Richelieu

In 1614 Henry IV's son, Louis XIII, was still only fourteen years old, a neurotic youth passionately addicted to hunting. He was soon to be married to Anne of Austria, daughter of Philip III of Spain, as a symbol of France's subjection to Hapsburg influence. So there was not much to be hoped

from the monarch himself—except that he might choose and support some able first minister. The man was already in sight—a brilliant young bishop named Richelieu who had been chosen to compose the address to the throne by the Estates General —but it took him several years to become a cardinal (in 1622) and head of the king's council (in 1624). From 1624 to his death in 1642 Richelieu was the real ruler of France. In the end it was he rather than any member of the Bourbon dynasty who founded absolute monarchy in France.

There is no mystery about Richelieu, as there is about many other great figures in history. He had the clearest and most penetrating mind of any statesman of his generation. And he made his purpose perfectly plain: to enhance the power and prestige of the French monarchy beyond any possibility of challenge, either by Austrian and Spanish Hapsburgs abroad, or by Huguenots and feudal nobles at home. He came to his task with a marvelous grasp of political and diplomatic possibilities, an infallible memory, and an inflexible will unhampered by moral scruples. Richelieu admired Machiavelli's writings and the heart of his political creed was *raison d'état*—the doctrine that the good of the state is the supreme good, and that any means may be used to attain it. He would coolly send an innocent man to his death in order to frighten other troublemakers, enhance the authority of the monarchy, and so save bloodshed in the end. "In judging crimes against the state," he argued, "it is essential to banish pity." He was not irreligious, but the workings of his mind were overwhelmingly this-worldly. "Man is immortal; his salvation is hereafter," he once argued against some conscientious scruples of the king, but "the state has no immortality, its salvation is now or never." While his cardinal's robes helped protect him against assassination, his policy was that of an astute secular statesman who put public order before religious zeal. His reputation for diabolical cleverness went even beyond the reality and helped him to terrorize his enemies and gain his ends.

Richelieu had three concrete objectives

which had to be carried out more or less simultaneously: First, he meant to break the political and military power of the Huguenots. Second, he meant to crush the political influence of the great nobles. And finally, he meant to destroy the power of the Hapsburgs (often in alliance with Huguenots and unruly aristocrats) to intervene in French internal affairs.

The Edict of Nantes had allowed the Huguenots to garrison about two hundred towns, the chief of which was La Rochelle on the west coast. Richelieu persuaded Louis XIII that he would never be master in his own house until he had wiped out this "empire within an empire." Rumors that the government had decided to attack provoked the Huguenots to rebel and Richelieu proceeded to besiege La Rochelle. He had no navy, and the city was supported in the later stages by English ships. But with characteristic determination Richelieu built a stone jetty to shut the harbor off from the open sea and in 1628 the inhabitants surrendered. At the Peace of Alais in 1629, which settled the dispute, Richelieu was unexpectedly generous in his terms. He had no respect whatever for what he contemptuously called "the allegedly Reformed religion," but he allowed the Huguenots the right to worship as they pleased once he had attained his primary objective of eliminating their political and military control over a large part of France. He did not wish to alienate Protestants abroad who could help him in a war with Spain and Austria, and he hoped he could make loyal and useful citizens out of the Huguenots. In this he was successful. The Huguenots served the crown in the war that followed against the Hapsburgs and stuck loyally by the monarchy in the crisis of the Fronde. An indirect result of the siege of La Rochelle was Richelieu's successful effort to recover control of the French coast from local nobles—a success that enabled him to build up an effective royal navy.

Richelieu's attack on the political power of the nobility was less successful than his attack on the Huguenots, but it was just as determined. Until the very end of his career, he was constantly threatened by aristocratic intrigues which usually revolved around the queen mother, Marie de' Medici, or Louis XIII's brother, Gaston. In response to this threat, he developed a network of spies, set up a special tribunal to try noble lawbreakers, and sternly forbade dueling, an aristocratic privilege which symbolized feudal anarchy. He gradually weeded the great nobles out of provincial governorships, and put more local administrative responsibilities on direct representatives of the crown. These representatives, called *intendants,* were usually of middle-class origin and therefore more dependent on the monarchy. Richelieu did nothing to attack the economic or social status of the French nobility, but he began the process, which Louis XIV completed, of destroying their political independence.

To raise the prestige of France abroad, Richelieu rebuilt the French army as well as the navy and recruited an efficient corps of spies and diplomats who kept him informed and carried out his tortuous diplomacy all over Europe. He was no financier, nor did he have any interest in bettering the condition of the common people. Thanks to his war against Spain after 1635 he left the government's finances and the nation's peasants in worse state than he had found them. But after eighteen years of subtle diplomacy, then active intervention in the Thirty Years' War (see p. 601), he enabled France to replace Spain as the leading power on the European continent.

Mazarin and the Fronde

At Richelieu's death in 1642 (Louis XIII died a few months later in 1643) the prestige of the French monarchy both at home and abroad was very much higher than it had been when he became first minister. The test of his work was to come in the next few years. Louis XIV was a child of five when his father died, and so his mother, Anne of Austria, was appointed

A wax medallion of Cardinal Mazarin.

regent. Fortunately she left the business of government to the man whom Richelieu had picked and trained to succeed himself, an Italian cardinal named Mazarin. Mazarin had the subtlety and political skill of his master but not his inflexible will; he was both more adaptable and, as a foreigner, even less popular than Richelieu. His two main objectives were to continue the war against Spain until the Hapsburgs were beaten and to maintain the prestige of the monarchy at the level to which Richelieu had raised it. The nobility hated him as a foreign upstart, however, and the bourgeoisie hated him for the high taxes he imposed in order to carry on the war. The result was the last serious rebellion that was to take place against the monarchy until the French Revolution, a complicated and purposeless movement known in French history as the Fronde (1648–52).

The word "Fronde" referred to a game of slinging clods at passing coaches played by the more unruly children of Paris. The two rebellions that were nicknamed the first and second Frondes were almost as senseless as the game. Mazarin made the mistake of reducing the interest paid by the government on its large public debt, thereby outraging the wealthy bourgeois who were heavy investors in government offices and large buyers of government bonds. The *Parlement* of Paris, backed by the other high courts of the realm, made itself the spokesman for the middle classes, protested Mazarin's financial expedients, and drew up a scheme for limiting the government's right to tax. The *Parlement* of Paris, like the six provincial *parlements,* was a closed corporation of lawyers, not a popular representative assembly. It represented the selfish interests of the bourgeoisie, but little else. When discontented nobles began to take up the standard of revolt for even narrower and more selfish reasons, the lawyers in the *parlements* took fright and the first Fronde of the bourgeoisie gave place to the second Fronde of the nobles. For three years some of the worst elements among the French nobility stood in rebellion against the government in the name of feudal privileges. It was soon clear to the middle classes, who had started the trouble, that victory for the aristocratic rebels could only mean a return to feudal anarchy. And so the *parlements* and the bourgeois threw their weight behind the government. By the end of 1652 the rebellion had disintegrated and Mazarin, who had had to flee the country, was once more back in the saddle. It was more evident than ever to most Frenchmen that the only alternative to a strong monarchy in France was civil war and feudal license. The violence of these years left an indelible impression on the mind of the young king, Louis XIV, who came to hate Paris, despise the mob, and fear the nobility when they were unrestrained by a firm royal hand.

In spite of the Fronde and the tax burden that continued to oppress the common people, Mazarin carried on the war with Spain until the proud Spaniards were forced to ask for terms in 1659 (see p. 604). Maria Theresa, daughter of Philip IV of Spain, was married to Louis XIV in the secret French hope that she might some day give the Bourbons a claim to the Spanish crown. Unlike the marriage of Louis XIII and Anne of Austria a generation before, this marriage symbolized the humiliation of Spain and the triumph of France as the leading power in Europe. Mazarin died in 1661, and Louis XIV announced to his ministers that he would henceforth be his own prime minister. Now the work of Richelieu had come to full fruition. The French monarchy no longer had anything to fear from Huguenots and nobles at home or from Hapsburgs abroad. It was an absolute monarchy, endowed with a fuller sovereignty than any other yet seen in European history.

England: In Search of Civil and Religious Liberty, 1603–60

While Richelieu and Mazarin were laying the foundations of absolute monarchy by divine right, leaders in England were slowly working out the implications of constitutional, parliamentary monarchy. Richelieu could see clearly where he was going, but the goal was never so clear to the English leaders during their century of conflict with the crown. Englishmen groped their way toward a conception of sovereignty as something rooted in law rather than in personal authority, something to be lodged in the hands of an assembly that represented the community, or at least its more wealthy and influential members. In spite of the widespread trend toward absolute monarchy, medieval Estates occasionally won victories over monarchies elsewhere in Europe in the seventeenth century. But the result was always anarchy and confusion, as it was in Poland and some German states. Only in England was a representative assembly able to broaden the base of its political power and at the same time to concentrate and increase that power. When Queen Anne came to the throne in 1702, the English government was both a stronger and a more popular government than it had been in 1603 when James I succeeded Elizabeth. The example of what England did, particularly as reflected in the writings of John Locke, was to have enormous influence in western history during the next two centuries.

England, on the periphery of European civilization, had always been peculiar in her political development. For instance, although the strong monarchy of the Tudors (1485–1603) was part of a general European trend toward the strengthening of kingship, the survival and strengthening of Parliament under the Tudors was without parallel elsewhere. The Tudors continued to use Parliament in legislation and taxation while rulers on the Continent were doing their best to get along without representative assemblies. Parliament, particularly the House of Commons, slowly acquired a corporate feeling and a sense of being an integral part of the national government. The House of Commons, it will be remembered, represented both the mercantile classes in the towns and the gentry in the country. The knights and squires had been increasing in numbers, in wealth, and in political influence since the dissolution of the monasteries. They governed England at the local level as justices of the peace (the English monarchy had no paid bureaucrats like the French *intendants*), and they dominated the lower house of Parliament by sitting as representatives not only of the counties but often of the boroughs as well. The House of Commons in which they sat had grown steadily in wealth and influence, until one member could boast in 1628 that the lower house could buy the House of Lords three times over.

Thus the English Parliament in the early seventeenth century represented the nation, above class differences and local interests, in a way no other representative assembly in Europe did. There were no provincial estates in England as there were in France, and the class lines between peers, gentry, and wealthy burgesses were not so sharply drawn as the line between nobility and Third Estate on the Continent. English merchants were continually buying land and becoming gentlemen, while younger sons of the nobility often went into the professions. This meant that if the monarch should ever fall out with Parliament—and with the social groups it represented—he would not be able to play class against class or district against district.

The Tudors

Queen Elizabeth had had trouble with her Parliaments, particularly at the beginning of her reign and again at the end. But the dangers from abroad—from Philip of Spain, from Mary Queen of Scots, and from the Catholic Reformation—were always serious enough to quiet opposition when it threatened to endanger the national safety. It was generally recognized that only Parliament could make a law or approve a tax above and beyond the customary revenues of the Crown. It was also recognized that other matters, such as foreign policy, lay outside the competence of Parliament and within the sphere of what was called the royal prerogative.

There was considerable doubt about religion. The Tudors consistently claimed for the crown exclusive control of religion, but Henry VIII had confirmed the breach with

Rome by parliamentary statute, Mary had asked Parliament to restore England to the Roman obedience by statute, and Elizabeth had broken with the pope once more by statute. Elizabeth's Parliaments made more than one effort to reform the Church in a Puritan direction and to nudge the queen on foreign policy, presumptuous acts for which Elizabeth scolded them sharply. But she was too popular for Parliament ever to make a real issue of the conflict and too astute ever to demand a clear definition of her prerogative. Tudor "despotism" was a popular despotism, and Tudor Parliaments on the whole did more to increase than to diminish the power of the monarchy.

James I and Parliament

It has been said that the Stuarts, who occupied the English throne from 1603 to 1714, were the unwitting authors of English political liberty because of their stupidity and stubbornness, which provoked first the Puritan Rebellion (1640–60) and then the Glorious Revolution (1688–89). In spite of the sympathy of many recent historians for the Stuarts, there is much in this view. James I (1603–25), the son of Mary Queen of Scots, was a well-meaning but pedantic intellectual who never had the imagination to understand the people he was called on to govern at Elizabeth's death. His aims were praiseworthy—peace with Spain, toleration of the Catholic minority in England, union of England and Scotland, a strong but benevolent monarchy—but he was insensitive to criticism, extravagant, and fatally inclined to let worthless favorites run his government. Unlike Elizabeth, who had a thousand ways of covering up what she really meant in cloudy and ambiguous language, James liked to have things clear. He had written a book, *The True Law of Free Monarchies,* in which he made it clear that kings owed their position to God alone, were responsi-

Divine Right

James I, king of England, by an unknown artist.

ble only to God, and in fact were themselves a little like gods on earth.

His belief in a monarchy "free" of all restraint, free to do as it pleased for the good of the people, did not appeal to his Parliaments. With all real danger of a revival of feudal anarchy gone in England, the middle classes were coming to be more afraid of monarchical tyranny than they were of aristocratic violence. And the end of the Elizabethan war with Spain in 1604 removed any reason James' Parliaments might have had for restraining their criticism of the monarchy. Parliament was as much to blame as the first two Stuarts for upsetting the delicate Tudor balance between parliamentary power and royal prerogative, but the monarchs offered plenty of pretexts for parliamentary aggression.

Early in the reign of James I friction developed over three interrelated issues: re-

ligion, finance, and foreign policy. The Puritan majority in the House of Commons wished to "purify" the Anglican Church of everything that savored of Catholic practice, from "popish" ritual to the authority of bishops. James was clear-sighted enough to see that if Presbyterian synods of ministers and laymen should replace royally appointed bishops in England, as they had in his native Scotland, the authority of crown over church would be destroyed. "No bishop, no king," he remarked within a year of his arrival in England. Parliament, with its eye on the extravagance of James' court, but blind to the rising cost of government everywhere in the early seventeenth century, kept James short of money. James replied by devising various ways of raising money without parliamentary approval, such as increasing the customs duties on his own authority. A conflict arose among the judges and lawyers over the exact limits of the king's prerogative, a conflict in which the main decisions went in the king's favor. The subservience of the courts to the royal will further disturbed Parliament.

Meanwhile James was following a foreign policy that exasperated the Puritan majority in Parliament. He was too friendly with Spain for the Puritan taste, he did little to defend Protestants abroad against the rising tide of Catholicism, and he finally tried to marry his son Charles to the Spanish Infanta. When James chided the House of Commons in 1621 for even discussing his foreign policy, the House bristled and passed a unanimous Protestation defending its right to discuss "the arduous and urgent affairs concerning the King, State, and defence of the realm, and of the Church of England." This was revolutionary talk. James tore the resolution from the Commons' *Journal,* but he could not undo what had been done. The House of Commons, which Queen Elizabeth had kept under the control of her privy councilors, was now taking the initiative under leaders of its own. An aggressive and powerful element among James' subjects was demanding political rights which he was utterly unwilling to grant.

Charles I and the Puritan Rebellion

The situation rapidly worsened during the first four years of the reign of Charles I (1625–29). Charles' worthless favorite, the duke of Buckingham, led two disastrous expeditions abroad, one to attack the Spanish at Cadiz, another to try in vain to relieve the Huguenots at La Rochelle (see p. 589). To raise money for its wars, the government tried a forced loan or "benevolence" and arbitrarily imprisoned those who objected to paying. Parliament in 1628 drew up a formal protest in the form of a Petition of Right, which they finally compelled Charles to approve. Its two main provisions were that no one should henceforth be compelled to pay any tax or loan "without common consent by Act of Parliament," and that no one should be imprisoned without cause shown. The House of Commons threatened to impeach Buckingham, who was murdered shortly afterward.

Next year the House of Commons was roused to fury before Charles dissolved it. It declared that anyone who introduced anything savoring of Catholic practices in the Anglican Church was "a capital enemy to this kingdom and commonwealth," and that anyone who advised or submitted to the levying of taxes without parliamentary consent was "a betrayer of the liberties of England." The issue of "sovereignty" had finally been raised, and the word itself was being debated by lawyers and parliamentary orators. Where did the supreme power in England lie—in the king or in Parliament? The old answer, that it lay in the "king-in-Parliament," would no longer do.

Archbishop Laud, a modern caricature by Jean Charlot, drawn from a contemporary portrait.

The royal prerogative and "the liberties of England" were no longer reconcilable.

Charles I now took things into his own hands and ruled without Parliament for eleven years (1629–40). He was less intelligent, more stubborn, and less honest than his father. James had always yielded before conflict became irreconcilable. Rather than yield, Charles was to resort to duplicity and falsehood in the crises ahead of him, and as a result he ended his life on the scaffold, trusted by almost no one. He tried to duplicate Richelieu's brilliant work across the Channel (1624–42). He chose tough-minded advisers: Thomas Wentworth, earl of Strafford, in political affairs, and William Laud, archbishop of Canterbury, in ecclesiastical affairs. With them and others, Charles devised new methods of nonparliamentary taxation which provided enough money to run the government so long as it stayed out of war. Laud began a movement back toward more ritual and formality in the Anglican service, which looked to the Puritans like an attempt to restore Catholicism. All opposition, whether to arbitrary taxation or to innovations in worship, was sternly suppressed by the courts. Everything went well until Laud tried to force the Anglican Book of Common Prayer on stubbornly Presbyterian Scotland. Before long an angry and well-led Scottish army was encamped in northern England. Charles and Strafford, finding themselves unable to raise an army to fight the Scots, had to summon Parliament to get the money to buy them off.

The Long Parliament, which met in November 1640 and was not dissolved until 1653, became the workshop of a revolution. It sent Strafford and Laud to the scaffold. It passed an act stating that a Parliament must be summoned at least every three years. It outlawed all unparliamentary taxation and abolished the prerogative courts (the Court of Star Chamber and the Court of Ecclesiastical Commission), which had been the chief instruments of the "Eleven Years' Tyranny." In other words, in less than a year (1640–41) it had abolished absolute monarchy in England. This much of its work won unwilling approval from Charles, since sentiment for it was virtually unanimous. But when the more radical Puritans in Parliament went on to abolish bishops from the Anglican Church, a party began to form around Charles in opposition to the parliamentary majority. And thus a civil war broke out in 1642 which lasted until 1649.

Enough has been said to suggest that the Puritan Rebellion was primarily a war of ideas, not of classes or of districts or even of interests, though the interests of merchants and gentry who were outraged by nonparliamentary taxation were certainly involved. Generally the towns, the middle classes, and the southeast of England supported Parliament, while much of the country, the aristocracy, and the north-

west supported Charles. But nobles, squires, and artisans from all parts of England were to be found on both sides. Unlike the Fronde, the Puritan Rebellion involved genuine ideals which would inspire loyalty on both sides: on the one hand, benevolent monarchy—on the other, a parliamentary monarchy; on the one hand, a strong Anglican Church governed by bishops appointed by the crown—on the other, a Presbyterian Church governed by a national assembly of elected "presbyters" or elders, or even Congregational Churches governed by the members of independent congregations.

Parliament was better able to raise mon-

England During the Puritan Rebellion 1642-46

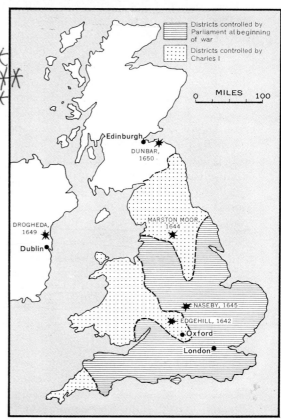

ey than the king. Furthermore, the parliamentary side proved better able to recruit an army with strong morale. This was the work of a brilliant cavalry officer named Oliver Cromwell, a deeply religious man, who proved that his fellow Independents, or Congregationalists, made better fighters than any others. These Independents were generally of lower economic status than either Anglicans or Presbyterians, who were strong in London among the business classes. They were unsophisticated Bible-reading Puritans of strict morals who believed in independent congregations democratically organized, with none of the strict clerical discipline and national organization that the Presbyterians had. The "New Model Army" which Cromwell recruited and trained finally defeated the king's forces in 1645, only to fall out with their political masters, the Presbyterians, who had dominated Parliament since the Anglicans withdrew in 1642 to join Charles. With Parliament and the army at loggerheads about what to do with the king and about what sort of government to set up in England (many in the army wanted a truly democratic regime), the king was able to escape and make one last bid for victory before being finally defeated by Cromwell in 1648. Cromwell and the Independents in the army were determined now to get at what they considered the root of the trouble. They "purged" Parliament of its Presbyterian members, executed King Charles I in 1649, abolished monarchy and the House of Lords, and set up a republic, or "Commonwealth," with the "rump" of the Long Parliament as its government and Cromwell as its moving spirit.

Cromwell

Cromwell proved to be a revolutionary leader unlike almost any other in western history. He tried in vain to avoid becoming a dictator. He ruthlessly suppressed a

Oliver Cromwell, by Samuel Cooper.

Catholic rebellion in Ireland, defeated the Scots when they intervened in favor of the son of Charles I, fought a commercial war with the Dutch in 1652–54, and boldly dissolved what was left of the Long Parliament in 1653. In a few short years he had decisively won a civil war, united the British Isles under one government for the first time, made England again the terror of the seas, and apparently wiped the slate clean for any political experiment he wished to try. The rest of his career until his death in 1658, however, was a tragic search for an answer to an insoluble problem: how to guarantee religious toleration of all kinds of Protestants except determined Anglicans, and at the same time how to develop some constitutional basis for his government. The English people were not ready for toleration, he found—unless compelled by a strong government.

By the Instrument of Government in 1654, the first written constitution in the history of a major European nation, a "Protectorate" was set up with a "Parliament" elected by wealthy landowners and with Cromwell as protector. It did not work. Parliament and protector quarreled with each other as earlier Parliaments had quarreled with the Stuarts, and Cromwell was forced to set up an open military dictatorship of major generals to prevent the representative assembly he had instituted from disbanding his army and persecuting his coreligionists. The plain fact was that most Englishmen were not ready for religious toleration, especially toleration of the radical religious minorities that composed Cromwell's army.

Furthermore, it became more and more evident that it was impossible in England to break utterly with history and to set up a new sort of government simply by writing a constitution. There was already a "constitution" deeply ingrained in the English political tradition, although it was nowhere written down in full. Soon after Cromwell's death even his own supporters saw that the only possible remedy for military dictatorship was to restore Parliament, and that the only way to restore Parliament was also to restore the monarchy. In 1660 the monarchy, Parliament, and the Anglican Church were all restored by an invitation from a "Convention Parliament" to Charles II to return from France and take up the crown which he was assumed to have rightfully held since his father's head rolled in the dust in 1649.

The Restoration

At first glance nothing more remained in England after twenty years of civil war and revolutionary experiment than had remained in France after the defeat of the Fronde. To this day Englishmen refer to the events we have described as the "Puritan Rebellion," not a revolution, because it was succeeded by the "Restoration." But one thing at least had been decided: there was to be no absolute monarchy in Eng-

land. All legislation of the Long Parliament which had received the signature of Charles I before the outbreak of civil war was preserved at the Restoration. The balance of power between king and Parliament was still not finally settled, but it was clear that the king no longer had a free hand. Strafford and Laud had tried to do for Charles I what Richelieu and Mazarin had done for Louis XIV, but all three Englishmen died on the scaffold while all three Frenchmen died in their beds. The attempt of the first two Stuarts to set up a royal despotism, followed by the attempt of Oliver Cromwell to set up a military dictatorship of Puritan "saints," left most Englishmen with certain half-expressed convictions whose effects can be

A royalist pamphlet of 1659. Charles I is in Heaven, Cromwell in Hell.

THE
Court Career,
DEATH
Shaddow'd to life.
OR
SHADOWES OF
LIFE and DEATH.

A Pasquil Dialogue
Seriously perused and highly
approved by the clearest Judgments.

Printed in the Year 1659.

traced in English history for over two centuries. Among these convictions were a fear of allowing any one individual to acquire too much political power, a deepened respect for government by law rather than by personal command, a reverence for Parliament as the defender of individual rights against arbitrary despotism, and a distaste for standing armies.

The early seventeenth century was a brilliant age in the history of English literature, including Shakespeare's mature work, the Authorized, or King James, Version of the Bible (1611), and Milton's formative years. It was also a brilliant period in political thinking, as statesmen and pamphleteers argued the case for king or Parliament or some more radical solution in hundreds of tracts. But no one was yet able to express the full meaning of the English experience during these sixty years.

Perhaps Thomas Hobbes' *Leviathan* (1651) best represented the political insights and fears of these turbulent years, if

❖❖❖❖❖❖❖❖❖❖❖❖❖❖❖❖❖❖❖❖❖❖❖❖❖❖❖❖❖

Hobbes on Might and Right

The Laws of Nature (as Justice, Equity, Modesty, Mercy, and in sum doing to others as we would be done to), of themselves, without the terror of some Power to cause them to be observed, are contrary to our natural Passions, that carry us to Partiality, Pride, Revenge, and the like. And Covenants, without the Sword, are but Words, and of no strength to secure a man at all. Therefore notwithstanding the Laws of Nature (which everyone hath then kept, when he has the will to keep them, when he can do it safely), if there be no Power erected, or not great enough for our security, every man will and may lawfully rely on his own strength and art for caution against all other men.

From Thomas Hobbes, *Leviathan,* 1651 (New York and London: Everyman, 1914), p. 87.

❖❖❖❖❖❖❖❖❖❖❖❖❖❖❖❖❖❖❖❖❖❖❖❖❖❖❖❖❖

not the greatest hopes. Writing in the midst of civil war, Hobbes pictured the life of man without government as "solitary, poor, nasty, brutish, and short." Without some authority to enforce law, there is no society, no order, only "a war of every man against every man." Men in general are inclined to "a perpetual and restless desire of power after power." So they set up a sovereign power by agreement or contract (it makes no difference whether the sovereign is a king or a Parliament), by which all men agree to obey the sovereign, but only so long as he is able to maintain order. The sovereign is not bound by anything in the contract. No clearer argument for might as the necessary basis of all right had ever been written. Hobbes took Bodin's argument for a legitimate sovereign authority (see p. 586) and subtly transformed it into justification of sheer arbitrary power. His book could be used equally well to support Charles I or Cromwell. In a sense the main effort of Englishmen during the seventeenth century was to find some way to *refute* Hobbes—to subject political power to the restraint of law and to increase its responsibility to the governed. They finally succeeded in 1688.

Germany: Disintegration and Disaster, 1618–1648

While France was building the strongest monarchy in Europe and England was undergoing a constitutional crisis from which she was to emerge with new strength, the German-speaking peoples were caught up in one of the most futile and destructive wars in the history of Europe. The Thirty Years' War (1618–48) was really four successive wars which began in Bohemia, spread to the rest of the Empire, and finally involved most of the major powers on the Continent. It was a savage and demoralizing conflict which put "Germany" still further behind the political development of the western European states.

The Causes of the Thirty Years' War

The war sprang out of a complicated mixture of religious and political issues. At the opening of the seventeenth century the religious atmosphere in Germany was calm but sultry. Lutherans and Catholics had not fought each other since the Peace of Augsburg (1555), but the Catholics were disturbed by the fact that, in spite of the provisions of the peace, most of the Catholic bishoprics in northern Germany had fallen into Lutheran or secular hands (see p. 526). This gave some grounds for a rising tide of Catholic reaction headed by the Jesuits and the German Catholic princes, particularly Maximilian, duke of Bavaria. The spread of Calvinism had introduced a militant element into German Protestantism, partly because Calvinists had been excluded from the Peace of Augsburg. When Maximilian roughly disciplined the Protestant town of Donauwörth, the Calvinist ruler of a small state on the middle Rhine called the Palatinate, the elector Frederick V, took the lead in forming a Protestant Union among the German princes and cities in 1608. In reply a Catholic League was organized the next year under the leadership of Maximilian. So by 1609 two illegal military alliances faced each other within the Empire, each afraid of the other and each determined to keep the rival religion from making any further gains.

Political issues were inevitably mixed with religious since the underlying principle of the Peace of Augsburg was taken to be *cuius regio, eius religio:* the ruler of a region determines its religion. This power over religion was only one sign of the growing independence of the three-hundred-odd political units of all sorts and sizes which composed the "Holy Roman Empire of the German People," as the Empire had come to be called. It was the ambition of the Austrian Hapsburgs, particularly Ferdinand, the archduke of Styria, to consolidate and extend what was left of the imperial power. As a first step toward this objective it was necessary to establish firm control over what had been Hapsburg family domains—Austria, Bohemia, and Hungary—and so in 1617 Ferdinand got himself elected king of Bohemia.

Revolt in Bohemia

Bohemia was a flourishing kingdom in which two nationalities (Germans and Czechs) and several religions (Catholicism, Lutheranism, Calvinism, and remnants of the Hussite movement of two centuries earlier) lived fairly peaceably together under a promise of toleration by a previous Hapsburg ruler in 1609. Ferdinand, a zealous Catholic, began systematically to undermine this toleration and to re-Catholicize the country. This action provoked rebellion by the Bohemian Estates, which were dominated by a strong Protestant majority. In May 1618 two of Ferdinand's councilors were tossed from a castle window in Prague ("defenestration" was a Bohemian way of showing displeasure dating back to Hussite days) and civil war in Bohemia broke out between the Hapsburg ruler and the Estates. The Estates set up a dictatorship of the assembly, raised an army, deposed Ferdinand, and offered the crown of Bohemia to Frederick V of the Palatinate. When Frederick unwisely accepted, the Protestant Union became involved in defending the Bohemian Estates while Maximilian of Bavaria brought the Catholic League to the support of Ferdinand. In 1619 Ferdinand was elected emperor. Thus a war that might have remained a local affair soon spread through the Empire.

The Bohemian phase of the war was soon ended. The forces of the emperor and the League overwhelmed those of Frederick and the Bohemian Estates near Prague in 1620. Frederick fled, and the emperor proceeded to work his will on the prostrate Bohemians. Half the property in the country changed hands through confiscation. The Jesuits were given free rein to reconvert the country to Catholicism and within ten years, with the strong backing of the state, they had succeeded. The prosperity of the country was ruined, Protestantism was stamped out or driven underground, and the rising national spirit was crushed for two centuries to come. The first round of the struggle had gone decisively to the Hapsburgs and their Catholic allies.

Danish Intervention

The spectacle of what the Hapsburgs, the troops of the Catholic League, and the Jesuits had accomplished in Bohemia terrified Protestants elsewhere in Germany. Maximilian's troops soon overran Frederick's own dominions, the Palatinate. With Spanish help from Franche-Comté, the imperial half of Burgundy, the armies of the League were everywhere triumphant. In spite of the common danger, the Protestants could not unite. The Lutherans had been more afraid of a rebel Calvinist victory in Bohemia than of an imperial triumph, and so Lutheran Saxony had actually helped Ferdinand put down the revolt. Frederick V was the son-in-law of James I, but Protestant England gave no help because James and Charles I were too involved in difficulties at home.

In 1625 the Protestant king of Denmark intervened, partly to save the cause of his coreligionists but primarily to pick up some territory in northern Germany. Within a year he was beaten in battle by a large army raised by the most inscrutable figure of the war, a wealthy war profiteer and professional soldier named Wallenstein, who had

Wallenstein, by Van Dyck.

offered the emperor his services. Wallenstein had no religious convictions whatever, and his political aims have puzzled generations of historians. His immediate aim seems to have been to build an imperial Hapsburg military machine of such strength that it could not only eliminate all Protestant opposition but also operate independently of all other forces in the Empire, including the Catholic League. Before long Wallenstein and the League were as much at loggerheads on one side as Calvinists and Lutherans were on the other, and religion slowly receded in significance.

The Edict of Restitution, 1629

The high-water mark of Hapsburg triumph and Catholic reaction was reached in 1629. Denmark withdrew from the war, leaving Wallenstein's army supreme. Bohemia had already fallen under the Hapsburg heel. The electoral vote of the Palatinate had been taken from Frederick and given to Maximilian of Bavaria, thus ensuring a Catholic majority among the seven imperial electors.* And now the Catholic League and Jesuit advisers persuaded Ferdinand to issue the Edict of Restitution in 1629, which restored to Catholic hands all ecclesiastical lands lost to Protestantism since 1552. It was evident that this edict could not be carried out without more bloodshed, because it meant that Catholic bishops were to be restored throughout northern Germany and that the rough balance already established in Germany between Catholicism and Protestantism was to be destroyed. This finally roused the Lutherans inside and outside Germany to a sense of their peril.

Swedish Intervention: Gustavus Adolphus

In 1631 the Protestant cause was saved from disaster by the intervention of Sweden, a country that had not appeared before on the stage of international politics. Gustavus II (Gustavus Adolphus) was the ablest ruler of his generation. His country was sparse in population and resources, but he had cultivated its iron and timber industries, united the nation behind him, and built the best army of the day. It was not large, but it was well equipped (with the first uniforms and an improved musket), well disciplined, and inspired by high morale. Gustavus had already come close to making the Baltic a Swedish lake in wars with Denmark and Poland. He now stepped into the fray as the sincere champion of Lutheranism, hoping apparently to set up a federation of Protestant states in Germany under Swedish control (his aims are not altogether clear).

Gustavus arrived too late in 1630 to save Magdeburg from a terrible sack by the

* See p. 395. In 1648, at the Peace of Westphalia, an eighth electoral vote was created for Frederick's heir, the count palatine, to restore the vote taken from Frederick and given to Bavaria. In 1692, Hanover became a ninth electorate.

Gustavus Adolphus, king of Sweden, by Van Delft after Mierevelt.

Imperialists in May 1631, but in the fall of 1631 he overwhelmed the Imperialist armies at Breitenfeld in Saxony. He then marched triumphantly to the Rhine. Wallenstein, whom the emperor had dismissed under pressure from the Catholic League, was recalled, only to be beaten by Gustavus at Lützen in 1632. Gustavus himself was killed in the battle, however, and by 1634 his army had finally been outnumbered and beaten, Wallenstein had been murdered by one of his staff, and another phase of the war had come to an end. Swedish intervention had saved German Protestantism but had not gained a decision. The most powerful state of all had been watching the course of events closely and was now to intervene with decisive results.

French Intervention: Richelieu

Since he came to power in 1624, Richelieu had kept in close touch with the prog-

MAGDEBURG.

ALBIS FLUVIUS   Die Elbe Flu.

The siege of Magdeburg, 1631, with Tilly's imperialist troops advancing to the attack across the Elbe River.

The Sack of Magdeburg——May 1631

Then was there naught but beating and burning, plundering, torture, and murder. Most especially was every one of the enemy bent on securing much booty. When a marauding party entered a house, if its master had anything to give he might thereby purchase respite and protection for himself and his family till the next man, who also wanted something, should come along. It was only when everything had been brought forth and there was nothing left to give that the real trouble commenced. Then, what with blows and threats of shooting, stabbing, and hanging, the poor people were so terrified that if they had had anything left they would have brought it forth if it had been buried in the earth or hidden away in a thousand castles. In this frenzied rage, the great and splendid city that had stood like a fair princess in the land was now, in its hour of direst need and unutterable distress and woe, given over to the flames, and thousands of innocent men, women, and children, in the midst of a horrible din of heartrending shrieks and cries, were tortured and put to death in so cruel and shameful a manner that no words would suffice to describe, nor no tears to bewail it.

From Otto von Guericke, in *Readings in European History*, ed. by James Harvey Robinson (Boston: Ginn, 1906), Vol. II, pp. 211–12.

ress of the war through his ambassadors and agents, but for ten years he did not feel that the French army was strong enough to intervene in Germany. His major purpose was to crush the Hapsburgs, both Austrian and Spanish, and he was ready to ally with anyone, Protestant or Catholic, who was opposed to them. The Dutch, who went back to war with their old enemies the Spanish in 1621, were his first allies. He made overtures to Maximilian of Bavaria and encouraged the Catholic League in its opposition to Wallenstein's schemes of imperial expansion. He subsidized Gustavus Adolphus' invasion in 1631, but was embarrassed when Gustavus attacked Bavaria and other members of the League. When the Swedes were finally defeated in 1634, Richelieu saw that he would have to intervene directly if he was to check Hapsburg expansion in central Europe. And so in May 1635 he sent a French herald to Brussels to declare war on the king of Spain.

The Thirty Years' War had lasted for seventeen years with no decisive result, and it was to continue for thirteen more dreary years while French and Swedish and Dutch armies fought against the Spanish and Imperialists. In 1643 the French finally destroyed the legend of Spanish invincibility by crushing a Spanish army at Rocroi in the Netherlands. It was the first time in a hundred and fifty years that a Spanish army had suffered a major defeat. Two years later the emperor lost his last allies, Saxony and Bavaria, to the Swedes and the French. By 1648 the Swedes were threatening Vienna and storming Prague. The dream of Emperor Ferdinand II (who had died in 1637) of re-Catholicizing Germany and establishing a strong Hapsburg monarchy in central Europe lay in ruins.

The Peace of Westphalia, 1648

Peace negotiations dragged on for over five years (1643–48) because of the complexity of the problems involved and because each side was still hoping for a last victory in the fighting, which still continued. The Congress of Westphalia was Europe's first great peace conference and the first international gathering of comparable importance since the Council of Constance (1414–18). But it was a far different gathering from that of two centuries earlier. The atmosphere and the business at hand were now entirely secular, and the communities represented were sovereign territorial states which recognized no earthly superior. In order to embarrass the emperor, the French insisted that each petty German state which so desired should be represented at the congress. The result was a kind of caricature of what Europe was becoming: a collection of absolutely independent states, jockeying for power and prestige, each making war or peace according to its own interest, and recognizing only the most shadowy common interest. "Christendom" had dissolved, and the word "civilization" was not coined till the next century to express in secular terms what "Christendom" had once meant to Europeans in religious terms. The appearance of the modern sovereign state was formally recognized at the congress which settled the Thirty Years' War.

The Peace of Westphalia of 1648 recognized the right of each German principality to make alliances and to declare war on its own. This constituted practical recognition of the disintegration of the Empire into over three hundred separate sovereignties. France and Sweden were left free to intrigue and interfere in the proceedings of the Imperial Diet, which they did without scruple in the years to come. Switzerland and the Dutch Netherlands were finally recognized as sovereign states, independent of all ties to the Empire. France acquired some very ambiguous rights to Alsace, Sweden acquired important German territory along the shores of the Baltic and the North Sea, and the two German states of Brandenburg and Bavaria ended up with increased territory and prestige. As for religion, the old principle of *cuius regio, eius religio* was reaffirmed. Calvinism was simply added to Catholicism and Lutheranism as one of the recognized faiths. The ownership of church lands was settled as of 1624, meaning in general that northern Germany remained Protestant and southern Germany Catholic. France and Spain were unable to reach agreement, so their war continued until French victory was finally recognized in the Peace of the Pyrenees in 1659. France received some territory along the Pyrenees and in Flanders, and the Spanish princess, Maria Theresa,

Europe in 1648

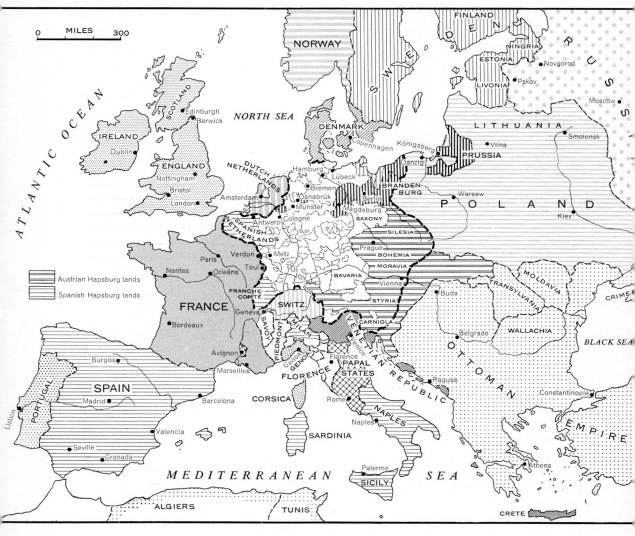

****

War Casualties
and Internal Disturbances

This diagram is an attempt by a sociologist to reduce to graphic form a very complex mass of data covering nine centuries. The lower figures represent war casualties per million of the populations involved, the upper figures represent the extent, duration, and intensity of internal disturbances such as revolts and civil wars. Note the generally *inverse* relationship between the two curves, suggesting that as the power of the state increases foreign wars increase and civil disturbances decrease, and vice versa. The one exception is the seventeenth century, in which *both* war casualties *and* internal disturbances increase. Historians tend to be skeptical about such diagrams, arguing that they give a false impression of assurance about both the accuracy of the data and the validity of the interpretation of a very complicated problem.

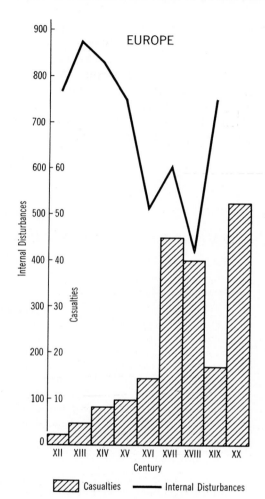

Redrawn from P. I. Sorokin, *The Crisis of Our Age* (New York: Dutton, 1942), p. 214.

****

married Louis XIV. In general, the peace settlements of the middle of the century left France the strongest power in Europe, Spain prostrate, the Empire shattered, and a kind of power vacuum in the center of Europe.

The Social Results of the War

The Thirty Years' War was one of the most brutal and destructive wars of which we have record until the twentieth century.

Armies robbed, raped, and murdered their way back and forth across Germany. The lack of any modern supply system meant that they had to live on the land. We have gruesome records of towns totally wiped out, cities reduced to a small fraction of their original population, and cultivated land reverting to waste. Starvation and disease killed more than the sword. It is impossible to be sure of the total decline in population, but some historians believe that Germany may have lost a third of its inhabitants. Others insist that the destruction was not so great as contemporary sources would suggest, and that recovery in farming districts was rapid. The social and psychological effects, however, were certainly frightful. A whole generation grew up accepting violence and brutality as normal. Superstition and witchcraft increased in influence. Feudalism was strengthened rather than weakened by the decline in population, and the fragmentation of the Empire into practically independent states hampered economic recovery. Cultural and political provincialism were to go hand in hand for the next two centuries in German history. In fact, it is almost impossible to find any good result that came out of the generation of aimless fighting in Germany known as the Thirty Years' War.

Suggestions for Further Reading

1. General Works on the Seventeenth Century

There are three very successful attempts at a synthetic treatment of the period: D. Ogg, *Europe in the Seventeenth Century* (5th ed., 1948), is a sound and interesting narrative of the major developments on the Continent, arranged by country. G. N. Clark, *The Seventeenth Century* (1931), is a more analytical discussion of different aspects of the period: for instance, population, industries, military organization, political thought, science, religion. C. J. Friedrich's volume in the *Rise of Modern Europe* series, *The Age of the Baroque, 1610–1660* (1952), combines narrative and analysis and makes use of recent interpretations of baroque style. C. J. Friedrich and C. Blitzer, *The Age of Power* * (1957), is a brief and thoughtful survey of the century, based on Friedrich's larger work.

2. Mercantilism and Economic Growth

L. B. Packard, *The Commercial Revolution, 1400–1700* (1927), is the briefest reliable treatment of mercantilism. J. W. Horrocks, *Short History of Mercantilism* (1925), and P. W. Buck, *The Politics of Mercantilism* (1942), are somewhat longer studies. The fullest and best treatment is E. F. Heckscher, *Mercantilism*, 2 vols. (1935). H. Sée, *Modern Capitalism* (trans. 1928), is the best extensive discussion of the subject. F. L. Nussbaum, *History of the Economic Institutions of Modern Europe* (1933), summarizes the work of the great German historian of capitalism, W. Sombart. D. Hannay, *The Great Chartered Companies* (1926), is a good introduction to its subject. J. U. Nef, *War and Human Progress* (1950), argues that war is a detriment, not a stimulant, to technological and economic progress, particularly in this period.

3. Expansion Overseas

In addition to the works cited for Chapter 18 on geographical discovery, the following are useful on special topics: B. H. M. Vlekke, *The Story of the Dutch East Indies* (1945); L. B. Simpson, *The Encomienda in Spain* (1929); and H. A. Wyndham, *The*

* Available in paperback edition.

Atlantic and Slavery (1935). On the rivalry of France and England in America, the many fascinating volumes of Francis Parkman dating from the 1860's are still worth reading, especially the earlier ones. G. M. Wrong, *The Rise and Fall of New France,* 2 vols. (1928), is the standard modern account. *The Cambridge History of India,* 5 vols. (1922–37), is useful for reference.

4. France

J. Boulenger, *The Seventeenth Century* (trans. 1920), is a standard one-volume account in English. F. C. Palm, *The Establishment of French Absolutism, 1574–1610* (1928), and P. R. Doolin, *The Fronde* (1935), are good special studies. Of the many books on Richelieu, the most trustworthy short account is C. V. Wedgwood, *Richelieu and the French Monarchy* (1949). Richelieu's France is the setting of Alexander Dumas' famous novel *The Three Musketeers* and of the two others about D'Artagnon which followed; all three books are based on thorough knowledge of the period.

5. England

The classic one-volume account, Whiggish in sympathy and brilliantly written, is G. M. Trevelyan, *England under the Stuarts* (1904, 1946). The standard modern account is G. Davies, *The Early Stuarts, 1603–1660* (1937), in the *Oxford History of England* series. The detailed narrative history of S. R. Gardiner, published in 18 volumes (1863–1903) and covering the years 1603–56, is a major achievement of English historical scholarship to which all later accounts are indebted. C. V. Wedgwood has published two volumes of a projected new history of the Puritan rebellion, *The King's Peace, 1637–1641* (1955) and *The King's War* (1958). D. L. Keir, *The Constitutional History of Modern Britain, 1485–1937* (4th ed., 1950), and J. R. Tanner, *English Constitutional Conflicts of the Seventeenth Century* (1928), together constitute a good introduction to some of the more technical constitutional issues of the period. There are many biographies of Cromwell, but the best is still C. H. Firth, *Oliver Cromwell and the Rule of the Puritans in England* (1900, 1925). W. Notestein, *The English People on the Eve of Colonization, 1603–1630* (1954), is a good introduction to the social history of the period, and B. Willey, *The Seventeenth Century Background* (1934), a good introduction to its intellectual history. A. S. P. Woodhouse, *Puritanism and Liberty* (1938), is a selection of sources illustrating the ferment of democratic ideas during the rebellion.

6. Germany

There are good chapters on the Thirty Years' War in Ogg and Friedrich (Section 1, above), also in H. J. Grimm, *The Reformation Era* (1954), and H. Holborn, *A History of Modern Germany: The Reformation* (1959), both listed after Chapter 17. Far and away the best general account in English is C. V. Wedgwood, *The Thirty Years War* (1938), though S. R. Gardiner's older brief account (1897) is still worth reading. The scholars' argument over how destructive the war was may be followed in S. H. Steinberg's criticism of Wedgwood in *History,* Vol. 32 (1947), pp. 89–102.

Source of Illustrations

Key to Credits

A Fratelli Alinari
B The Bettmann Archive
BM Trustees of The British Museum, London
C Culver Pictures, Inc.
G Giraudon
MFAB The Museum of Fine Arts, Boston
MMA The Metropolitan Museum of Art, New York
NYPL New York Public Library
PML The Pierpont Morgan Library, New York

Title Page
ii: *left,* Leonard von Matt; *right,* Ken Domon, from *The Muro-ji,* Bijutsu Shuppan-Sha. iii: *left,* Trinity College Library, Cambridge; *right,* G.

Chapter 1
6: MFAB. 8: French Cultural Services. 14: MMA, Excavations of the MMA, Rogers Fund, 1930. 15: *top,* Historical Pictures Service; *bottom,* MMA, Carnarvon Collection, gift of Edward S. Harkness, 1926. 16, 17: Ewing Galloway. 19: MMA, Fletcher Fund, 1940. 20: C, in Louvre. 21: The Chase Manhattan Bank Museum of Moneys of the World. 25, 30, 31: all, B. 32: The Oriental Institute, University of Chicago.

Chapter 2
40, 41: BM. 44: A, in Vatican Museum. 46: BMFA. 47: G, in Munich Museum. 49: Museum at Delphi. 52: American School of Classical Studies, Athens, Agora Excavations. 57: BM. 58: G, in Naples Museum. 59: Alison Frantz Collection, American School of Classical Studies, Athens. 60: FPG. 61: A, in Vatican Museum. 62: MFAB. 66: A. 69: A, in National Museum, Naples.

Chapter 3
76: K. Gullers, Rapho-Guillumette. 78: A, in Villa Giulia Museum, Rome. 79: A, in Archaeological Museum, Florence. 83: MFAB. 97: B. 98: A, in Uffizi, Florence. 104: MFAB.

Chapter 4
116: American Numismatic Society. 117: B. 120, 121: American Numismatic Society. 122: J. A. Cash, Rapho-Guillumette. 123: B. 126: *top,* L. S. Davidson, FPG; *bottom,* Jean Roubier, Rapho-Guillumette. 132: Anderson, in Borghese Gallery, Rome. 133: Dumbarton Oaks Collection.

Chapter 5
138: Ewing Galloway. 139: American Numismatic Society. 142: G, in Louvre. 143: MMA, Gift of Henry G. Marquand, 1897. 145: B. 154: Dumbarton Oaks Collection. 157: G, in Academy of History, Madrid. 162, 163: American Numismatic Society. 165: B.

Chapter 6
168: Eliot Elisofon, *Life.* 170: Archaeological Survey of India, Mrs. A. K. Coomaraswamy. 171: © Dept. of Archaeology, Govt. of India, in National Museum, New Delhi. From Zimmer, *The Art of Indian Asia.* 177: Archaeological Survey of India, in Sarnath Museum, Mrs. A. K. Coomaraswamy. 179: Mrs. A. K. Coomaraswamy, in Chicago Natural History Museum. 181: Eliot Elisofon, *Life.* 182, 183: all, Freer Gallery of Art, Smithsonian Institution. 186: both, Chiang Yee, *Chinese Calligraphy: An Introduction to Its Aesthetic and Technique,* Harvard University Press, 1938. 187: C. 188: © BM. 189: A. C. Cooper, Penguin Books, in Scientific Academy, Leningrad.

Chapter 7
192, 195: BM. 197: MMA, Purchase, 1895, Administrative Funds. 201: G, in Cluny Museum, Paris. 203: B, in University Library, Upsala. 204: PML. 206: BM. 207: Dumbarton Oaks Collection. 210, 211: all, MMA, Gift of J. Pierpont Morgan, 1917.

Chapter 8
214: Jean Roubier, in Cabinet des Medailles, Bibliothèque Nationale, Paris. 216: B. 220: Turkish Info. Service. 221: C. 222: A. 226: G, Rossano Cathedral Treasure. 229: C. 231: Freer Gallery of Art, Smithsonian Institution. 237: Spanish Nat. Tourist Dept.

Chapter 9
240: Photo Millet-Connaissance des Arts, in Louvre. 247: Osterreichische National-Bibliothek, Vienna. 248, 249: all, Green, by permission of the Board of Trinity

College, Dublin. 250: *top,* Dr. Harold Busch, Frankfurt; *bottom,* A. 251: Radio Times Hulton Picture Library. 253: PML. 255: Nithard, *Historia* (facsimile, NYPL). 257: Universitetets Oldsaksamling, Oslo. 265: P. E. Schramm, *Die Deutschen Kaiser und Könige in Bildern,* 1928. 267: Staatsbibliothek, Munich. 270, 271, 272: BM.

Chapter 10
276, 277: G. 279, 280: BM. 284: Ewing Galloway. 286, 287: Sir Frank Stenton: The Bayeux Tapestry, Phaidon Press, London. 289: BM. 293: Vatican Library. 294: Jean Roubier. 297: Municipal Library, Dijon. 298: Ewing Galloway. 300: Adapted from drawing by K. Conant, in Koehler, "The Third Church at Cluny," *Medieval Studies in Memory of A. Kingsley Porter,* Harvard University Press. 301: Jean Roubier. 302, 303: all, F. S. Lincoln. 304: Jean Roubier. 306: BM.

Chapter 11
312: Jean Roubier. 317: G. 318, 319: Jean Roubier. 320: *top,* B; *bottom,* Peter Martens. 321: Curators of the Bodleian Library, Oxford. 323: PML. 325: B. 326: University Library, Bern. 327, 331: Master and Fellows, Corpus Christi College, Cambridge. 332: Vatican Library. 339: A, Church of San Francesco.

Chapter 12
344: BM. 349: MMA, The Cloisters Collection. 354: Masters and Fellows, Corpus Christi College, Cambridge, purchase 1954. 357: PML. 359: Bibliothèque Nationale, in Bibliothèque de l'Arsenal. 360: A. 361: BM. 364, 365: Radio Times Hulton Picture Library. 366: PML. 367: Bibliothèque Nationale. 368: A. 370: Jean Roubier. 371: Foto-Marburg.

Chapter 13
374: G, in Louvre. 376, 377: all, B. 382: G, in Musée Condé, Chantilly. 385: PML. 387: BM. 388: B. 390: NYPL. 391: PML. 392: G. 396: NYPL, Rare Book Room. 398: *top,* G, Musée Condé, Chantilly; *bottom,* NYPL, Print Room, from Lübecker Totentanz, 1489. 399: Royal Library of Belgium. 401: B.

Chapter 14
407: A. 408: both, Cooper Union Museum. 411, 412: MMA, Rogers Fund, 1913. 414: Ewing Galloway. 416, 420, 425: B. 428: Historical Pictures Service. 430: C. 431: from Charol, *The Mongol Empire,* 1941. 432: Catalan Atlas, NYPL Map Room. 433: Radio Times Hulton Picture Library.

Chapter 15
439: Eliot Elisofon, *Life,* in Amsterdam Museum of Asiatic Art. 441: Victoria & Albert Museum. 442: *top,* Ernst Haas, Magnum; *bottom,* Eliot Elisofon, *Life.* 447: MMA, Gift of Alexander Smith Cochran, 1913. 450: © Museum Rietberg, Zürich. 451: Fogg Art Museum, Harvard University. 452: both, from Chiang Yee, *Chinese Calligraphy, An Introduction to Its Aesthetic and Technique,* Harvard University Press, 1938. 453: BM. 456, 457: Freer Gallery of Art, Smithsonian Institution. 460: MMA, Gift of Edgar Worch, 1950. 461: from D. T. Suzuki, *Zen and Japanese Culture,* Bollingen Series LXIV. 462: from Ken Domon, *The Muro-ji,* Bijutsu Shuppan-Sha. 463: from D. T. Suzuki, *Zen and Japanese Culture,* Bollingen Series LXIV.

Chapter 16
468, 471, 472: A. 474: woodcut by Jacopodi Barbari, NYPL, Print Room. 475: A. 482: B. 485: C. 486: B. 487: John Pope-Hennessy, *Uccello,* Phaidon Press, London, 1950. 489: Brown Brothers. 490: A. 494: NYPL, Spencer Collection. 495: A.

Chapter 17
500, 501: BM. 503: Art Institute of Chicago. 504, 505: all, NYPL, Rare Book Room. 507: Radio Times Hulton Picture Library. 508: B. 516: MMA, Dick Fund, 1936. 519: Archives Photographiques, in Louvre. 520: NYPL, Print Room. 521: A. 526: C. 529: NYPL, Print Room. 531: Historical Pictures Service. 535: MMA, Bequest of Mrs. H. O. Havemeyer, 1929.

Chapter 18
541: B. 544, 548: NYPL, Map Room. 554: B. 558: Royal Library of Stockholm. 559: Woburn Abbey, Residence of His Grace the Duke of Bedford. 563: B. 565: Bibliothèque Nationale. 567: C. 569: Art Institute of Chicago.

Chapter 19
572, 573: NYPL, Print Room. 574: NYPL, Rare Book Room. 582: William T. Clements Library, University of Michigan. 588: Trustees, National Gallery London. 590: Trustees of the Wallace, Collection, London. 593: National Portrait Gallery, London. 594: by Jean Charlot from Hilaire Belloc, *Characters of the Reformation,* Sheed & Ward. 596: B. 597: BM. 600: C. 601: NYPL, Print Room. 602: C.

608

Index

Illustrations and maps are indicated by italicized page numbers.

Armada, *563;* defeat of, 557, 561–62
Arminius, 112
army: Anglo-Saxon, 271–73; of Arab Empire, 236–37, 415; Assyrian, 30; of Byzantine Empire, 415, *416,* 420; English, 384–85, 387; Hittite, 25; Italian mercenary, 472; Macedonian, 63; medieval, 261, 502; Persian, 34, 35; Roman, 83–84, 95, 112, 116, 118, 123, 132–34, 139–41, 150–51; Spartan, 53; Swiss, 395 (*see also* warfare)
art: Anglo-Saxon, *192, 206;* Byzantine, *407, 408, 409;* Chinese, *182–83;* 185, 187, *189,* 460, *460;* early Christian, 164–65; in Eastern Roman Empire, *214, 216,* 219–21; Egyptian, *14,* 16–18; in Germanic kingdoms, *192, 197, 201, 204, 206, 207, 210–11;* Greek, 48, 57–60; Hellenistic, 70; Italian Renaissance, 469, 484–91; medieval, *253, 276–77, 286–87,* 317–21; Minoan, 36; Persian, 35; prehistoric, 7, 9; Roman, 78, *132,* 162–63 (*see also* architecture; drawing; miniatures; painting; sculpture)
Arthurian legends, 322, *323*
artisans: medieval, 316–17; in Roman Empire, 152 (*see also* gilds)
Asia: European trade in, 542–45, 549, 581 (*see also* China; India; Japan; Middle East; Near East)
Asia Minor, 24–25, 31, 42, 43, 69; in Byzantine Empire, 226, 406, 418; in Eastern Roman Empire, 215, 219, 225; under Persians, 32, 34, 54, 56; under Rome, 91, 96–97; under Turks, 416, 420–21, 424, 433, 513
Asoka, 175–77
Assurbanipal, *31*
Assyrian Empire, 28–32, *29*
astrolabe, 402, 542
astronomy: Babylonian, 21; Greek, 130; Indian, 179–80; medieval, 266–67, 336; Moslem, 412, *412*
Athena, statue of, *47*
Athens, 50–52; during Age of Pericles, 56–61; in Peloponnesian War, 61–63; in Persian War, 54–56
Attica, 50, 54–56
Attila, 160
Augsburg, Religious Peace of, 526–27, 562, 599
Augustine (St.), Archbishop of Canterbury, 206
Augustine (St.), Bishop of Hippo, 158, 163–64; quoted, 82, 164
Augustus, 110–16; Pompey and, 101–02; quoted, 111 (*see also* Octavian)
Aurelian, 134, 139, 141
Austria, 395, 512, 526, 599
Austrian Netherlands, 555
Avars, 225, 246
Averroës, ibn-Rushd, 413
Avicenna, ibn-Sina, 413
Avignon, papacy at, *370,* 371–72, 378, 492–93
Aztec Empire, 549

B

Babur, 445
Babylon, 19
Babylonia, 19, 31 (*see also* Mesopotamia)
Babylonian Captivity, 371, 378, 492
Bacon, Francis, 568
Bacon, Roger, 359
Baghdad, 236, 238, 411, 423

Balboa, Vasco de, 548
Balkan states: Bulgars in, 406; Byzantine Empire and, 410; in Eastern Roman Empire, 215, 219, 225, 226; Ostrogoths in, 160, 161, 215; under Turks, 433, 513
banking, medieval, 314–16, 505 (*see also* money)
Bannockburn, battle of, 363, 383
Baptists, 530
barbarians: in Eastern Roman Empire, 215; in Roman Empire, 149–50, 160–61 (*see also* Germanic tribes; Goths; Huns; Mongols; nomads)
barons, English, 287–88, 327–28, 350–52, 364–65, 383, 386, 388 (*see also* counts; earls; nobility; patricians)
Basel, Council of, 494, 518
Basil I, 406
Basil II, 415
basilica, 165, *165, 222*
Bavaria, 599, 604; in Frankish kingdom, 244–45; in German empire, 262–63
Bayeux tapestry, *286–87*
Beauvais cathedral, 317–18
Becket, Thomas, *325,* 326
Belgium, beginnings of, 557 (*see also* Flanders; Netherlands)
Benedict (St.), 202, *204*
Benedict, Ruth, quoted, 23
Benedictine Rule, 203–04, 297
Beowulf, 271, *271*
Berbers, 218, 236, 237
Bernard (St.), 297–99, 304–05, 333; quoted, 299
Bernini, Giovanni Lorenzo, 486
Bhagavadgita, 173
Bible: Alcalá edition of, 519; Christian Humanism and, 518–20; English translation of, 532; Gothic, *203;* Gutenberg, *503;* King James version, 598; Latin translation of, 164, 482; Lutheran, 523; reproduction of, in Middle Ages, 247–48; Wicliffe translation of, 381 (*see also* New Testament)
bishops, 201–02, 205, 208–09, 242; appointment of, 333; at end of Middle Ages, 515; investiture of, 202–95; organization of, 145
Black Death, 381–82
Black Prince, 384–85
Boccaccio, Giovanni, 477, 481
Bodin, Jean, 586–87, 598
Boethius, 195–97, 267
Bohemia, 313, 395, 512; Hussites in, 493–94; Protestantism in, 528–30; Thirty Years' War in, 598–600
Boleyn, Anne, 531, 532, 560
Bologna: Concordat of, 512, 564; University of, 306–08, 338
Bonaventura (St.), 359
Boniface (St.), 244
Boniface VIII (Pope), 368–71, *368;* quoted, 369
Book of Common Prayer, Anglican, 527, 532, 595
Book of Kells, 248
Book of the Dead, 14
bookmaking, *500–01*
books: Chinese, *453;* printed, 502–03, *503, 504, 505* (*see also* manuscripts; miniatures; printing)
Borgia, Cesare, 496, 514
Boston colony, 584
bourgeoisie, 314, 316–17, 471, 511 (*see also* burgesses; plebians)
Bourges, Pragmatic Sanction of, 508, 512

Charles V (Holy Roman emperor), king of Spain, 505, 509, 512, 523, 526, *526,* 531, 534, 551, 555, 559
Charles Martel, 212, 237, 241, 242–44
Charles of Anjou, 355
Charles of Orléans, 396
Charles the Bold, duke of Burgundy, 508
Charles the Great (see Charlemagne)
Chartres cathedral, *320;* nave of, *304;* sculpture in, *336;* stained-glass windows in, *317,* 319–21
Chaucer, Geoffrey, 362, 385, 396, *396*
Chin dynasty, 455, *455*
China: ancient, 169, 181–91, *184, fol. 176,* European explorations in, 458–59, 540, 543, 544, 549; Japan and, 450, 454, 463; during Middle Ages, 448–61, *455, 459;* Mongol Empire in, 423, 426, 431–32
chivalry, 470, 476 (*see also* courtly life)
Chola kingdom, 439
Chou dynasty, 182–86
Christendom, 603 (*see also* Christianity; Roman Catholic Church)
Christian Humanism, 518–21, 525, 527; of Erasmus, 555
Christianity, 4; beginnings of, 114–15; in Eastern Roman Empire, 215, 221–23; exploration and, 543, 545, 549; in Germanic kingdoms, 194, 196; Mohammedanism and, 232–33, 235; persecutions of, 117, 144, 146; in Roman Empire, 130–31, 138, 142–49, 152–54, 157–58, 161, 163–65; spread of, *fol. 336;* Zoroaster and, 34 (*see also* Greek Orthodox Church; Roman Catholic Church; Russian Orthodox Church)
Chronicles of Moissac, quoted, 252
Chu Hsi, 455, 460
Chuang Tzu, quoted, 185
Church (*see* Christianity; Greek Orthodox Church; Roman Catholic Church; Russian Orthodox Church)
churches (*see* architecture)
Cicero, 98–99, *98,* 105, 118
Cipangu (*see* Japan)
circumnavigation, Magellan's, 548–49
Cistercian Order, 297–99, 346
cities, in Roman Empire, 134–35 (*see also* city-states; towns)
City of God, 158, 164; quoted, 164
city-states, 91; Greek, 3, 46–63; Italian, 77, 469–76, *473,* 491, 497; Mesopotamian, 19–22; trade and exploration by, 542–43 (*see also* cities; Roman Republic; towns; *specific city-state*)
civil service: under Charlemagne, 252–53; in China, 449, 457, 460; in Mauryan Empire, 175; in Roman Empire, 123, 131–32, 138 (*see also* bureaucracy, government)
Civil War, Italian, 95
civil wars: in France, 562–65; in Roman Republic, 95–96; war casualties and, *605* (*see also* rebellion; revolution)
civilization, 2–5; definition of, 2
class, social (*see* social class)
classical antiquity (*see* Humanism)
classical revival (*see* Renaissance)
Claudius, 116, 118
Cleisthenes, 52
Clement V (Pope), 371, *371*
Clement VII (Pope), 378–79, 497, 531
Cleopatra, 105–06

clergy, at end of Middle Ages, 515 (*see also* bishops; monasticism; Roman Catholic Church)
Clermont, Council of, 295
clocks, invention of, 402
Clovis, 207–08
Cluny, monastery of, 291, *300,* 301
Coeur, Jacques, 505; house of, *507*
coined money (*see* money)
coins: Anglo-Saxon, *270, 272;* Greek, *62;* Ostrogothic, *195;* Roman, *116, 120–21, 139, 162–63,* 163
Colbert, Jean Baptiste, 583
Colet, John, 519
Coligny, Gaspard de, 564
Colleoni, Bartolommeo, *472*
coloni, 152 (*see also* serfdom)
colonization: in the Americas, 581–85; of Greeks, 42–43, *43;* mercantilism and, 579; of Phoenicians, 27, *43;* in seventeenth century, *fol. 576;* in Siberia, 585–86 (*see also* exploration)
Columban (St.), 209
Columbus, Christopher, 546–49
commerce (*see* mercantile economy; trade and commerce)
commercial revolution, 574
Commodus, 133
common law (*see* law, English common)
Commons, House of, 591–92, 593–94; formation of, 389–90; origins of, 352, 364–65
Commonwealth, of Cromwell, 596
companies, commercial, 577–78
compass, 542; invention of, 455
compurgation, in medieval law, 198
condottieri, 472
Confessions of St. Augustine, 164
Confucianism, 183–88, 450, 455, 460
Confucius, 182–86; quoted, 183
Congregationalists, 530 (*see also* Puritans)
conquistadors, age of, 549
Constance, Council of, 493, 494, 518, 523
Constantine (Roman emperor), 147–49; Arch of, *138;* Donation of, 243–44, 482; quoted, 147, 243
Constantine VII (Byzantine emperor), 408
Constantine XI (Byzantine emperor), 434
Constantinople, 148–49, 154, 313; attacks on, by Swedes, 258; in Byzantine Empire, 225–26, 237–38; in Eastern Roman Empire, 215, 219; schools at, 408; sack of, 419, 421; under Turks, 434, 513–14 (*see also* Byzantine Empire)
Constantius, 149, 153
constitution: of Cromwell, 596–97; of Greek city-states, 48, 52; Roman, 81 (*see also* Magna Carta)
constitutional monarchy, 573, 591, 595, 597–98
consuls, Roman, 81–82, 91
Copernicus, 400
Coptic Church, 153, 235
Cordoba, mosque at, *237*
Corinth, 45, 51
Corpus Juris, 224, 225, 306–07
Cortenuova, battle of, 354
Cortes, Hernando, 549
Cortes (Spanish courts), 511
Cossacks, 585–86, *585*
cotton-growing, in China, 460
councils, papacy and, 492–95
Counter Reformation (*see* Catholic Reformation)

counts, feudal, 260–62 (*see also* barons; earls; nobility; patricians)
county, in Carolingian period, 252, 260 (*see also* shire)
court: as aid to monarchy, 510–11; English, 269, *390;* French, 348, *392, 563;* Spanish, 511 (*see also* justice)
courtly life, in Middle Ages, 323 (*see also* chivalry)
Cranmer, Thomas, 531–32, 533
Crassus, 97–101
Crécy, battle of, 384, *385*
Crete, 23, 36, 406
Cromwell, Oliver, 596–97, *596*
Cromwell, Thomas, 531–32
crusades, 295–97, 299, 326, 348–49, 354, 417–23, *417, 420,* 433; against heretics, 335
cuneiform writing, 20–21, *21*
Cybele, *143*
Cynicism, 71–72
Cyrus, 32

D

Dacia, 123, 135
Damascus, 27, 234–35
Dance of Death, 398, *398*
Danes, invasion of England by, 258, 259, 268, 271–72 (*see also* Denmark)
Dante Alighieri, 359–61, *360, 478,* 482; *Divine Comedy, 505;* quoted, 360
Danube, as Roman frontier, 111, 149, 154–55
Darius, *32,* 33, 54
Decameron, 477, 481
Deccan, 438–39, 443–44, 445
Delhi sultanate, 443–45
democracy: in Athens, 51–52; in Rome, 81–82
Denmark: Protestant Reformation in, 527; in Thirty Years' War, 600 (*see also* Danes)
Descartes, René, 569
Despenser, Hugh le, 383
Dias, Bartholomew, 545
dictatorship: in Italian city-states, 472–73, 474; in Roman Empire, 102–03, 133 (*see also* absolute monarchy; tyrants)
Diocletian, 135, 139–42, *139,* 146
diplomacy, in Italian city-states, 473–74
Discovery, Age of, 540–51, *546–47, 567–68*
Divine Comedy, 359–61, *505;* quoted, 360
divinity of ruler, 12, 68, 102, 142 (*see also* absolute monarchy)
Domesday Survey, 288–89; quoted, 288
Dominic (St.), 340
Dominican Order, 339–40, 345, 358–59; in Spanish Empire, 550
Domitian, 121
Donatello, 485, 489
Donation of Constantine, 243–44, 482; quoted, 243
Drake, Francis, 561
drama: English, 568, 598; Greek, 59–61, 67, 71; Indian, 180
Dravidians, 171, 172, 439
drawing: German, *517, 521;* Italian Renaissance, *487, 491;* Japanese, *463* (*see also* miniatures)
Dürer, Albrecht, 492
Dutch East India Company, 558, 578
Dutch Netherlands: Calvinism in, 528–29; formation of, 556–59, *557;* Japan and, 464; North American colony of, 583; in seventeenth century, 574, 575, 578, 580–82, 596, 603

E

Earls, medieval English, 270, 272–73 (*see also* barons; counts; nobility; patricians)
East India Companies, 558, 578, 581
East Indies, 545, 581
Eastern Europe (*see* Byzantine Empire)
Eastern Roman Empire, 158, 161, 193–94, 215, *218;* under Justinian, 215–24 (*see also* Byzantine Empire)
economy: of China, 188; of Egypt, 16; of Greece, 42–43, 53; of India, 176; of Italian Renaissance, 491; late medieval, 345–47, 375–78, 388–89, 469, 501, 504–06; medieval, 200, 278–83; of Roman Empire, 118, 125–27, 134–35, 141, 151, 161–62; of seventeenth-century Europe, 574–81, *576;* of sixteenth-century Europe, 566; of sixteenth-century Spain, 553 (*see also* trade and commerce)
Edict of Nantes, 565, 587, 589
education: Chinese, 184, 186, 187–88, 338, 449, 451, 460; in Germanic kingdoms, 197; in Greek city-state, 47; in Italy's golden age, 469, 478–79; in Japan, 463; in medieval Europe, 241, 246–48, 253, 266; printing and, 502–03; Protestantism and, 537; in Roman Empire, 162; during twelfth century, 303–08
Edward I, 362–67, *364, 365,* 369, 377, 383, 507
Edward II, 383
Edward III, 375, 383–85, 389
Edward VI, 532
Edward the Confessor, 272–73, *272,* 286
Egypt, chronological history: ancient, 12–18, *12, 24;* under Hyksos, 22; Hittites and, 25–26; decline of, 31; under Persians, 33; in Hellenistic period, 68–70, 88; under Rome, 90, 105–06; in Eastern Roman Empire, 222–23, 225–26; under Moslems, 233, 235, 416, 418–20; under Mamelukes, 421–24; under Turks, 434, 513
Egyptian scribes, *15*
Elagabalus, 134
Eleanor of Aquitaine, 323
Elizabeth I, 532, 557, 559–61, 592
emperor: German, authority of, 512; as Roman title, 103, 109 (*see also* monarchy)
England, chronological history: Anglo-Saxon, 204–07, *205,* 269–73; invasion of, by Northmen, 258, 259; under Norman conquest, 287–90; late medieval, 323–28, *324,* 350–53, 355, 362–65, 367–69, 375, 379; in Hundred Years' War, 382–88, *384;* in fifteenth century, 388–90, 491–92, 510–12; in sixteenth century, 510–12; Elizabethan, 555, 559–62, 568–69; in seventeenth century, 574–75, 577–79, 580–82, 591–98, *595* (*see also* Britian)
England: Anglicanism in, 530–33; India and, 447–48; North American colonies of, 583–85; Protestantism in, 528–30, 532
English language, in medieval literature, 321
English literature (*see* literature, English)
English Peasants' Rebellion, 381, 386
engravings, *500–01, 558*
Epictetus, 131
Epicureanism, 71–72
Erasmus, Desiderius, 380, *519, 520–21,* 525; quoted, 519

Ghent, Pacification of, 556
Ghiberti, Lorenzo, 487
Gibbon, Edward, 121
gilds, medieval, 316–17, 338, 375–76, *376*, 469, 470; mercantile economy and, 471, 575–78
Giotto: *Dante, 360; St. Francis, 339*
Glorious Revolution (*see* Revolution of 1688)
Godwin, 272, 286
gold: as money base, 543; Spanish acquisition of, 549–50, 553
Golden Bull, 395
Gothic architecture, 300–03, *300, 303, 304,* 318–21, 357, *358,* 395, 470 (*see also* stained-glass windows)
Gothic Bible, *203*
Gothic sculpture, 318–19, *318–19, 336,* 361
Goths, 156–58 (*see also* Ostrogoths; Visigoths)
government: in Arab Empire, 235; Byzantine, 227, 415; Carolingian, 246, 252–54; Chinese, 182, 187–88; in Eastern Roman Empire, 217; Egyptian, 13; English, 268–70, 272, 323–28, 350–53, 362–65, 367–68, 383, 386, 389, 560; feudal, 262–63; French, 330, 347–50, 365–68, 393, 563; in Germanic kingdoms, 197–201, 211; German, 268, 331, 353–55, 512, 598–99, 603; Greek, 41–49; Indian, 175–76, 181–82, 441, 445–46; Italian city-state, 472–74, 475; Japanese, 463–64; late medieval, 376–78; Mesopotamian, 19; Moslem, 415; municipal, 282–83; Norman, 285–86, 287–90; of North American colonies, 584–85; Persian, 33–34; Roman, 78–83, 91–95, 102–04, 108–11, 122–23; Russian, 428, 430; in seventeenth century, 573, 580–81, 598; Swiss, 395 (*see also* law; monarchy)
Gracchus, Caius, 93–95
Gracchus, Tiberius, 93–95
Granada, 509
Gratian, 307; quoted, 307
Great Schism, 378–80, *379,* 468, 492
Great Wall of China, 187, *187,* 189
Greco, El, 568; *Cardinal Guevara, 535*
Greece, chronological history: early, 32, 35–37, 40–46; city-states of, 46–54; in fifth century B.C., 54–63; in fourth century B.C., 63–67; in Hellenistic period, 67–73; under Rome, 89–90, 130–31 (*see also* Byzantine Empire; Eastern Roman Empire)
Greek civilization, 3; influence of, 67, 77, 89, 169–70, 196, 226, 469, 479–80
Greek colonies, 42–43; in Italy, 85
Greek fire, *416*
Greek language: in Byzantine Empire, 408; in Eastern Roman Empire, 162, 216; in Ostrogothic kingdom, 196; during Renaissance, 478
Greek Orthodox Church, 223, 225–26, 410, 421; in Russia, 424–25, 427 (*see also* Christianity, in Eastern Roman Empire; Russian Orthodox Church)
Greeks, 25
Greenland, 258
Gregory, Bishop of Tours, 208; quoted, 208
Gregory I (Pope), the Great, 205–07
Gregory VII (Pope), 292; quoted, 292
Gregory X (Pope), 357
Gregory XI (Pope), 378
Grosseteste, Robert, 359
Guericke, Otto von, quoted, 602
Guevara (Cardinal), *535*

guild (*see* gild)
Guillaume de Lorris, 361; quoted, 362
Guillaume le Breton, 321
Guiscard, Robert, 285
Guise family, 564
gunpowder, 455–56, 502
guns (*see* firearms)
Guntram, 208
Gupta Empire, 178–81, *180,* 440
Gustavus Adolphus, 601, *601,* 603
Gutenberg, Johann, 502

H

Hadrian, 122, 123, 129
Hadrian's Wall, *122,* 123, 149
Hals, Frans, 568
Hammurabi, 20, *20*
Han dynasty, 176, 181, 187–91, *fol. 176, 189,* 449
Hanbury, Benjamin, quoted, 568
handwriting (*see* calligraphy; writing)
Hannibal, 87–88; route of, *87*
Hanseatic League, trade and exploration by, 542, 575
Hapsburg Empire, 395
Hapsburg-Valois Wars, 526
Hapsburgs, 395, 509–10, 551; French monarchy and, 587–89, 590; in Thirty Years' War, 599, 603
Harold, 286–87
Harsha, 181, 438, 439
Harun al-Rashid, 415
Hastings, battle of, 286–87
Hawkins, John, 561
Hebrew, study of, 519
Hebrews, 27–29 (*see also* Jews)
Hellenism (*see* Greek civilization)
Hellenistic period, 67–73
Héloïse, 305
Helots, 53–54
Henry I (of England), 289–90, *289,* 323
Henry II (of England), 323–26
Henry III (of England), 350–53
Henry IV (of England), 386–87, 389, 507
Henry V (of England), 387, 391
Henry VI (of England), 387–88, 391
Henry VII (of England), 510, 511
Henry VIII (of England), 510, 511, 530, *531,* 560
Henry II (of France), 564
Henry III (of France), 564
Henry IV (of France), of Navarre, 564–65, 587
Henry I (of Germany), 263–64
Henry IV (of Germany), 293–94, *293*
Henry V (of Germany), 294
Henry VI (of Germany), 333–34
Henry the Lion, 332
Henry the Navigator, 544–45
Heraclius, 225–26
heresy: Arian (*see* Arian heresy); in fifteenth century, 468, 492–93, 494; in late Middle Ages, 335–37, 345, 380–81 (*see also* Protestantism)
Herodotus, 66–67
Hideyoshi, *463,* 464
hieroglyphs, 15–16, *15,* 18 (*see also* writing)
Hildebrand, 292
Hincmar, quoted, 199

Hinduism, 179, 438, 440–41, 443; in Southeast Asia, 441; Mohammedanism and, 443–46 (*see also* Brahmans)
Hippo, 163
historical studies, of Italian humanists, 479–80
history, writing of: Anglo-Saxon, 270; Byzantine, 409; Chinese, 188, 451, 455; Greek, 66–67, 71; in Middle Ages, 321; Roman, 118–21, 128
Hittite Empire, *24*
Hittites, 22, 24–26, 32; Greeks and, 36
Hobbes, Thomas, 574, 598; quoted, 598
Hohenstaufen dynasty, 331–34, 353–56
Holbein, Hans: cartoon, *519; Erasmus, 519; Henry VIII, 531*
Holland (*see* Dutch Netherlands)
Holy Roman Empire, 599, 603 (*see also* German-Roman Empire; Hapsburgs)
Homer, 49; quoted, 42
Honorius, 158
Horace, 120
House of Commons (*see* Commons, House of)
Huguenots, 528, 529, 564–65, 587, 588–89; emigration of, 583
Huizinga, J., quoted, 383
Humanism, 469, 477–82, 487, 490, 491
Hundred Years' War, 383–88, *384, 385,* 393, 469, 470, 507–08, 510
Hungary: in Hapsburg Empire, 395, 599; Magyars in, 259; Mongols in, 425; Protestantism in, 528–29; Turkish attacks on, 433, 434
Hunnish ornaments, *154*
Huns, 438; in China, 189, *190,* 448; in Eastern Roman Empire, 219; in Europe, 154–56, 160; in India, 181, 438
Hunyadi, John, 434
Hus, John, 381, 493–94, *494,* 518, 523
Hussite Wars, 470, 494
Hussites, 529, 599
Hyksos, 22, 25

I

Iberian peninsula (*see* Portugal; Spain)
Ibn-Khaldun, 435; quoted, 435
Iceland, 258
iconoclasm, 243
icons, Byzantine, *407,* 409
Ikhnaton, 18
Iliad, 49; quoted, 42
illuminated manuscripts (*see* manuscripts, illuminated; miniatures)
illustrations, book, *453, 500–01, 503, 504, 505, 574, 597* (*see also* miniatures)
Illyria, 87
imperator (*see* emperor)
Inca Empire, 549
India: ancient, 169–82, *175, 177, fol. 176;* Arab Empire and, 236, 411–12; China and, 187, 448, 450; English traders in, 581; European settlements in, 447–48, 545, 581; in Middle Ages, 438–48; Mohammedanism in, 443–46, *444*
individualism, and Renaissance, 476–77
Indo-Aryans, 171–73
Indochina, 458; Indian influences in, 441
Indo-Europeans, 23–26, 77
Indonesia, 441
indulgences, 515–16, *516*
Indus Valley, 170–71

industry: of Dutch Netherlands, 557–58; at end of Middle Ages, 501, 503–04; medieval, 281–82, 284–85, 400–01; in Roman Empire, 125–27, 131 (*see also* capitalism; trade and commerce)
inflation: in seventeenth century, 580; in sixteenth century, 553
Innocent II (Pope), 298–99
Innocent III (Pope), 333–35, 338, 345, 353, 354, 421
Innocent IV (Pope), 347, *354,* 355–56
inquest, trial by, 288, 324
Inquisition, 335, 345; revival of, 497, 535
investiture conflict, 292–95, 331, 333
Ionia, 49–50
Ireland: Catholic rebellion in, 596; Christianity in, 205–06; invasion of, by Northmen, 258
Irnerius, 306
iron: Hittite use of, 25; in western Europe, 77
Iron Age, 9
Isabella of Castile, 509, 510, 511, 517
Isis, 143–44
Islam (*see* Mohammedanism)
Islamic Caliphate (*see* Arab Empire)
Israel, 28 (*see also* Jerusalem; Palestine)
Istanbul, 148 *n.* (*see also* Constantinople)
Italian language, 359
Italy, chronological history: ancient, 77, *80;* under Ostrogoths, 160, 193, 195; under Eastern Roman Empire, 209–10, 217–19; in Carolingian period, 243–45, 248–49, 256; in Byzantine Empire, 243, 285, 409; invasions of, in Middle Ages, 258–59; in German-Roman empire, 264–66, *264,* 276, 330–35, 353–56, *353;* Norman conquest of, 285–86, *285;* in fifteenth century, 469–97, *473,* 512; in sixteenth century, 526, 551 (*see also* Roman Empire; Roman Republic)
Italy: towns of, 281, 332, 375 (*see also* city-states, Italian); trade and commerce of, 313, 409, 425, 432
Ivan III (the Great), 429–30, 514
Ivan IV (the Dread), 430–31, 512, 514, 561
Iyeyasu, Tokugawa, 464

J

Jacobite Church, 153
James I, 591–94
Jamestown colony, 584
Japan, 461–64; age of discovery and, 540, 544, 546, 549; China and, 450, 454, 462; Mongols and, 458
Jean de Meung, 362; quoted, 363
Jerome (St.), 164
Jerome of Prague, 494
Jerusalem, 33; Crusades and, 296, 348–49, 355, 417–21
Jesuit Order, 529, 552, 555, 567; in Bohemia, 600–01; founding of, 534–35; in North America, 583
Jesus of Nazareth, 114
Jews: Christianity and, 114, 144; conquest of, 28–29, 31, 33; in Hellenistic period, 69; Spanish Inquisition and, 509
Jhering, Rudolph von, quoted, 306
Jiménez de Cisneros, 517, 519
Joan of Arc, 387–88, *388,* 391–93, 508
John (of England), 326–28, 329–30, 334, 350–51
John II (of France), 391
John I (of Portugal), 544

Magdeburg, Siege of, 601–02, *602*
Magdeburg cathedral, ivory carving from, *265*
Magellan, Ferdinand, 548–49
Magna Carta, 327–28, 350; quoted, 328
Magna Mater, 143, 144
Magyars, invasions by, *256, 258*–59, 264
Mahabarata, 173
Mahmud, 443
Maimonides, 413
Malay Peninsula, Indian influence in, 441
Mamelukes, 421–22, 423–24
man: prehistoric, 7–9; Renaissance, 479, 488 (*see also* gentleman)
Manichaeans, 144, 335
manuscripts, 247; Anglo-Saxon, *271;* Arabic, *231, 411, 412;* illuminated, *203, 209, 247*–49, *446* (*see also* calligraphy; miniatures; writing)
Manutius, Aldus, printing of, *505*
Manzikert, battle of, 296, 416
maps, development of, 402
Marathon, battle of, 54
Marcus Aurelius, 122–23, *123,* 131
Maria Theresa, 591, 604
Marie de' Medici, 587, 589
Marius, 95, 96
Marks, Erich, quoted, 568
Marshal, William, 326–27, *327*
Marsilius of Padua, 380
Martial, 128
Martin V (Pope), 493
Mary I (of England), 532, 551, 559
Mary of Burgundy, 508–09, 555
Mary Stuart (Queen of Scots), 560–61, 592
Masaccio, 485
Massachusetts Bay Company, 584
Massacre of St. Bartholomew's Day, 564, *565*
masters, in gilds, 316–17
mathematics: Babylonian, 21; Greek, 50; Hellenistic, 72–73; Indian, 179–80; Italian Renaissance, 491; in Middle Ages, 196, 266–67; Moslem, 412
Matthew Paris, *Historia, 289, 327, 331, 354*
Mattingly, Garrett, quoted, 562
Mauryan Empire, 174–77, *176*
Maxentius, 147
Maximian, 140–41
Maximilian (duke of Bavaria), 599–603
Maximilian (Holy Roman emperor), 508–09
Mazarin, Jules, 590–91
measurement, technology of, 402
Mecca, 229–31
Medes, 31, 32
Medici, Cosimo de', 475–76, 482
Medici, Giuliano de', 496
Medici, Lorenzo de', 475–76, *475,* 482, 496–97
Medici family, financial empire of, *509*
medicine: in Eastern Roman Empire, 130; Moslem, *411,* 412, 413; during twelfth century, 305–06, *306*
Medina, 230–31
Mediterranean Sea: Italian trade in, 281, 313–14, 425, 475; Turkish control of, 434
Mediterranean world, 3–4, *218,* 238, 241 (*see also* Arab Empire; Byzantine Empire; Eastern Roman Empire; Roman Empire)
mendicant orders (*see* Dominican Order; Franciscan Order)
mercantile economy, 574–81

merchants, medieval, 282, 315–16 (*see also* bourgeoisie; burgesses; plebeians)
Merovingians, 207, 210–12
Merriman, R. B., quoted, 554
Mesopotamia, 12, 13, 18–22, *18;* in Arab Empire, 234, 235, 237, 238; in Mongol Empire, 423; under Roman Empire, 123; under Turks, 434
metallurgy, 400–01 (*see also* bronze; iron)
Mexico, 549
Michelangelo Buonarroti, 485, 486, 487, 489, 497; *The Creation, 468,* 488, *490; Moses,* 488, 489, *489*
middle class (*see* bourgeoisie; burgesses; merchants; social class)
Middle East, Alexander's empire and, 67–70 (*see also* Near East)
Milan, 473, 474, 497; under Spanish Empire, 526, 551
Milton, John, 598
Ming dynasty, 432, 459–61, *459*
miniatures (from manuscripts), *226, 267, 279, 280, 289, 293, 297, 306, 323, 327, 331, 332, 344, 349, 354, 357, 359, 361, 364, 366, 367, 371, 376, 377, 382, 385, 387, 390, 391, 392, 396, 398, 399, 401, 416, 420, 425, 494;* Indian, *441, 447*
Minoans, 23, 36, 40
Mithra, *142*
Mithraism, 34, 143–44
Mithridates, 96
modern world, beginnings of, 469 (*see also* state, modern)
Mogul Empire, in India, 445–48, *445;* Portuguese and, 545
Mohammed, 227–32
Mohammed Ghori, 443
Mohammedanism, 229–33, 235; conversion of Mongols to, 432; conversion of Turks to, 416; in fourteenth century, 434–36; and Greek culture, 70; in India, 443–46, *444;* Orthodox Churches and, 514 (*see also* Arab Empire; Moslems)
Mohenjo-Daro, 170–71
Moissac, Chronicles of, quoted, 252
Moluccas, 548
monarchy: absolute (*see* absolute monarchy); constitutional (*see* constitutional monarchy); in England, 269–73, 350–53, 362–65, 367–68, 386, 591–98; during fifteenth century, 501, 506–07, 510–12; in France, 328–30, 347–50, 365–68, 390–93, 563, 586–87; in Germany, 200, 263–68; in Greece, 41, 45; growth of, 468–69
monasticism, 202–07, 209; mendicant orders of, 339–40; reform of, 291, 297; in sixteenth century, 515 (*see also specific order*)
money: Charlemagne's system of, 254; gold basis of, 543; invention of, 43–44; lending of, 314–16; regulation of, by Diocletian, 141 (*see also* banking)
Mongol Empire, 423–28, *426,* 431, 434–35; in China, 457–60; conquest of Turks by, 433–34; end of, 540
Mongolia, 427
Monophysites, 222–23
monotheism: in Egypt, 15, 18; Jewish, 28
Montaigne, Michel de, 492, 568–69
Montfort, Simon de, 351–53
Mont-Saint-Michel church, *302–03*
Moore, Charles A., 184 *n.*

Moors, (see Moslems, in Spain)
More, Thomas, 519, 531, 568; quoted, 533
Moriscoes, 553–54
Moscow, 425
Moslems: in Byzantine Empire, 406; crusades and, 417–23; invasions of Europe by, 256, 258–59; in Spain, 210, 238, 245, 415, 509, 543; Turkish (see Turks); Visigoths and, 193 (see also Arab Empire; Mohammedanism)
Mun, Thomas, quoted, 579
Münster, 530
Muscow, Principality of, 428–31, 429
Mycenae, 37
Mykerinus, 6
mystery religions, 72
mythology, Greek, 45 (see also religion)

N

Nantes, Edict of, 565, 586
Naples, 473, 497
nationalism: in thirteenth century, 351; vernacular language and, 322 (see also monarchy; state, modern)
natural science (see anatomy; science)
naturalism, in Gothic art, 484
Near East, 7–39, 11, 26 (see also specific countries)
Nebudchadnezzar, 31
neoplatonism, 131
Nero, 116–17, 116, 118
Nerva, 121
Netherlands, 394–95; Dutch (see Dutch Netherlands); during fifteenth century, 471, 506, 508; in Hapsburg Empire, 551; revolt of, from Spanish Empire, 555–57, 557, 559, 561 (see also Flanders)
New Amsterdam, 558, 583
New England, 584
New Stone Age, 7–9
New Testament, 115
New World, discovery of, 547–49
Nicaea, creed of, 148
Nicholas V (Pope), 494, 495, 497
Nicopolis, battle of, 433
Nineveh, sculpture at, 31
nobility: monarchs and, 510–11; in seventeenth century, 580, 587–90 (see also barons; counts; earls; patricians)
Nogaret, Guillaume de, 369–71
nomads, in China, 188–90 (see also barbarians; Huns; Mongols)
Norman conquests, 284–90, 285
Normandy, 258–59, 262, 283–85, 291, 327, 328, 330
North Africa: under Arabs, 236, 415; under Eastern Roman Empire, 217–19; under Turks, 434; under Vandals, 159–61 (see also Carthage; Carthaginian wars)
North America: Dutch settlement of, 558, 582–83; early exploration of, 547, 549, 561; English settlement of, 582–85; French settlement of, 582–85; Russian exploration of, 586; Scandinavian exploration of, 258
Northmen, invasions of, 256, 257–58; voyages of, 541–42
Northwest Passage, 561, 583
Norway, 512; Protestant Reformation in, 527
Norwegians, 258

Notre Dame cathedral, Paris, 319, 320; rose window, 312
Notre-Dame-du-Port, Clermont-Ferrand, portal of, 294
Novgorod, Church of the Savior, 428
Nureddin, 419

O

Ocean voyaging, 540–43, 546–47 (see also exploration)
Octavian, 105–06, 108–10 (see also Augustus)
Odo (count of Paris), 260
Odo of Deuil, quoted, 419
Odovacar, 160
Odyssey, 49
Omar (Moslem caliph), 230, 233
Omar Khayyám, 412
Ommiad dynasty, 234–38
Oppenheim, assembly at, 293
Optimates, 95–96, 104
ordeal, in medieval law, 198–99
ornaments: Anglian, 192, 206; Germanic, 197, 201, 210–11; Hunnish, 154; medieval, 253
Orthodox Church (see Greek Orthodox Church; Russian Orthodox Church)
Osiris, 143–44
Osman I, 433
ostracism, Greek, 52
Ostrogoths: in Balkans, 215; in Italy, 160, 193, 195, 208–09, 217–18
Othman, 230, 232, 233–34
Otto I, the Great, 264–67, 265
Otto III, 267, 267
Otto IV, 334
Otto of Freising, 321
Ottoman Empire, 433, 513, 513
Ovid, 120

P

Pacific Ocean, discovery of, 548–49
Padua, University of, 491
pagans, 153
painting: Chinese, 456, 456–57; Cretan, 37; Dutch, 568–69, 569; early Christian, 145, 165; English, 582; Flemish, 374, 398, 399, 471, 484, 492, 600; German, 519, 531; Greek, 44, 46, 61; Hellenistic, 69; Indian, 168, 181; Italian Renaissance, 468, 475, 478, 484–85, 487–89, 488, 490, 495, 522, 526, 554; late medieval, 339, 360, 368, 397–98, 399; prehistoric, 8; Spanish, 535, 568 (see also drawing; miniatures)
Pakistan, 444
Palatinate, 395, 599, 600
Palestine, 27; conquest of, by Arabs, 233 (see also Jerusalem)
Panchatantra, 180
papacy: in Carolingian Empire, 242–44, 248–51; early, 154; and German-Roman Empire, 264–68, 353–56; Lutheranism and, 523; power of, 202, 204, 292–95, 333, 368–72; during Renaissance, 492–97 (see also Roman Catholic Church)
Papal States, 243–44, 334, 354–56, 371, 378, 473, 496
paper: invention of, 187, 452; making of, 500, 502

Q

Quakers, 530

R

Radical Protestants, 529–30
Rajputs, 438, 443, 445, 446; code of, quoted, 440
Raleigh, Walter, 583
Ramayana, 173
Raphael, Sanzio, 487, 489, 497; *Pope Julius II, 495; Pope Leo X, 522*
rationality, in medieval philosophy, 357–59 (*see also* logic)
Ravenna, 210, 219
rebellion: English Peasants', 381, 386; German peasants', 525; Puritan, 592, 595–96 (*see also* civil wars; revolution)
Reconquista, 509
reform (*see* Roman Catholic Church, reform in)
Reformation (*see* Catholic Reformation; Protestant Reformation)
Reformed churches, 527–29
Reims cathedral: nave, *358;* sculpture, *319*
religion, 12; of Akbar, 446; Chinese, 181, 182–83 (*see also* Buddhism; Confucianism); Christian (*see* Christianity); Egyptian, 13–16, 18; Greek, 45–46, 47–48; Hittite, 25; Indian, 171–73 (*see also* Buddhism; Hinduism); Jewish, 28–29, 34, 114–15; in medieval literature, 397; Mesopotamian, 22; mystery, 143–44; Persian, 34–35; prehistoric, 8, 9, 12; Roman, 78, 113; Shinto, 462 (*see also* Coptic Church; Greek Orthodox Church; Mohammedanism; Roman Catholic Church; Russian Orthodox Church; secularism)
religious freedom, in Lutheranism, 525
religious toleration, 536, 596–97
Religious Warfare, Age of, 566
religious wars: in Bohemia, 470, 494; in France, 562–65; in sixteenth-century Europe, 566–67, *566* (*see also* Thirty Years' War)
Rembrandt van Rijn, 568; *Christ Healing the Sick, 569*
Renaissance, 480–81 (*see also* Italy, in fifteenth century)
representative assembly: in England (*see* Parliament); in France (*see* Estates General)
Republic, 64; quoted, 65
republican government: in Italian city-states, 472, 475; Roman (*see* Roman Republic); Swiss, 395 (*see also* Parliament)
Restoration, 584, 597–98
Reuchlin, Johann, 519
revolution: in Netherlands, 555–59; in sixteenth-century Europe, *566;* war casualties and, *605* (*see also* civil wars; rebellion)
Revolution of *1688, 584,* 592, 598
Rhine, as Roman frontier, 111, 149, 154
Riaris, Girolamo, 496
Ricci, Matteo, 461
Richard I, Lionheart, 326, *326,* 329, 419
Richard II, 386–87, *386*
Richelieu, Armand de, 588–90, *588,* 594; and Thirty Years' War, 601–03
Robert de Courçon, quoted, *337*
Rocroi, battle of, 603
Roman Catholic Church: and Carolingian Empire, 242–51, 255; Catholic Reformation of, 533–36 (*see also* Protestant Reformation); crusades of (*see* crusades); financial system of, 346–47, 514–16 (*see also* tithing); in Germanic kingdoms, 201–09; German-Roman Empire and, 264–68, 331–35, 353–56; Great Schism of, 378–80, *379,* 513; heresy and (*see* heresy); indulgences of, 515–16; during Italian Renaissance, 492–97, 514–15; in Japan, 464; medieval towns and, 282; monarchy and, 511–12; monasticism in (*see* monasticism); Mongols and, 431–32, 459; reforms of, 291–95, 297, 339–40, 380–81, 469, 501, 514–21; revival in, during eleventh and twelfth centuries, 290–308; in Scotland, 560; secularism and, 345–47, 356, 361–62, 368–72; Spanish Empire and, 549, 552–55, 556–57; taxation of, 356, 369, 511–12; and Thirty Years' War, 599–604 (*see also* Anglicanism; Christianity; papacy; Protestant Reformation; Protestantism)
Roman civilization: Humanism and, 469, 477–80; Ostrogoths and, 195–97; provinces and, 124–25
Roman Empire, early, 3, 108–37; under Augustus, 108–16; at height of power, 121–31; in third century, 131–35
Roman Empire, late, 138–65; decline of, 154–62; under Diocletian, 139–42; East Asia and, 169–70, 187, *fol. 176;* in fourth century, 149–54
Roman Republic, 3, 77–106; decline of, 96–106; early, 77–88, *80;* expansion of, 89–90, *101;* second century B.C., 88–96
Romance of the Rose, 361–62, *361;* quoted, 362, 363
Romanus IV, 416
Rome, 77–79, 486, 492 (*see also* Papal States; Roman Empire; Roman Republic)
royalist pamphlet, *597*
Rumanians, 410 *n.*
Runnymede, 327
Russia, 512; Byzantine Empire and, 406, 410; Empire of, 429–31; English communication with, 561; Mongols in, 423, 424–29; settlement of Siberia by, 585–86; in seventeenth century, 574, 581; Swedes in, 258
Russian Orthodox Church, 514 (*see also* Greek Orthodox Church, in Russia)

S

Sailendra dynasty, 441
St. Albans historians, 321
St. Bartholomew's Day Massacre, 564, *565*
St. Basil cathedral, Moscow, *430*
St. Denis, monastery of, 299–302, 305; stained-glass window, *276–77*
Ste. Chapelle church, Paris, 318
St. Mark's church, Venice, *221*
St. Peter's cathedral, Rome, *486,* 487
St. Pierre church, Moissac, sculpture in, *318*
St. Rémy-de-Provence, Roman arch and mausoleum in, *126*
St. Savin church, *301*
St. Sophia church, Constantinople, 220, *220*
Saladin, 419, 421
Salamis, battle of, 55–56
Salerno, 305
Salic Law, 390
Salviati, Francesco, 496–97
Salvius Julianus, 130
Samnite wars, 84–85

San Vitale church, Ravenna, *250;* mosaic of, *216*
Sant' Appollinare Nuovo church, Ravenna, *222*
Sargon's palace, sculpture in, *30*
Sarnath, sculpture of, *177*
Sarton, George, 490
Saul of Tarsus, 115 (*see also* Paul)
Savonarola, Girolamo, 518, 533
Saxons (*see* Anglo-Saxons)
Saxony, 263–64; Lutheranism in, 521–23
Scandinavia, invasions from, 257–58 (*see also* Denmark; Norway; Sweden)
scholarly class, Chinese, 449, 457
scholarship, in Renaissance, 482 (*see also* education; Humanism; philosophy; science)
scholasticism, 305, 470
Schoolmen, 482 (*see also* scholasticism)
schools, medieval (*see* universities)
science: Chinese, 400, 413; Egyptian, 17–18; Greek, 49–50, 66, 130; Hellenistic, 72–73; Indian, 413; Italian Renaissance, 490–91; medieval, 196, 336–37, 359, *359*, 398–400; Mesopotamian, 21; Moslem, 411–13, 435–36; Roman, 127, 162 (*see also* astronomy; mathematics; physics)
scientific revolution, 574
Scipio, Publius Cornelius, 88
Scotland, 193; Calvinism in, 528–29, 560, 595; as French ally, 379, 383, 560–61; wars with England, 363, 383, 595–96
sculpture: Assyrian, 30, *30, 31;* Chinese, *188, 450, 451;* early Christian, 165; Egyptian, *15,* 16–18; Etruscan, *78, 79;* Gothic, 318–19, *318–19, 336,* 361; Greek, *40–41, 47, 57–58, 57, 58,* 177; Hellenistic, *66;* Hittite, 25, *25;* Indian, *170, 171,* 176–77, *177, 178, 179, 439;* Indochinese, *442;* Italian Renaissance, *472, 482, 484–89, 485, 489;* Japanese, *462;* medieval, *240, 251, 265,* 397–98; Mesopotamian, *19, 20,* 21; Persian, *32;* Roman, *83, 117, 133, 142, 143,* 163; Romanesque, *294, 298, 318;* viking, *257*
sea power, 541–44, 557–58, 562, 567
secularism: during fifteenth century, 516–17; in Italian city-states, 477; during late Middle Ages, 345–47, 356, 361–62, 368, 371–72; Protestant Reformation and, 536
Seleucus, 68
Semites, 19 (*see also* Aramaeans; Hebrews; Phoenicians)
senate, Roman, 81–83, 92–98, 100–102; under Augustus, 108, 111, 112; under emperors, 121, 122
Seneca, 117
Septimius Severus, 133
Serbs, 410; conquest of, by Turks, 433 (*see also* Slavs)
serfdom: end of, 386; in England, 287; in Roman Empire, 152, 162; in Russia, 428, 430 (*see also* agriculture; farmers; peasant)
Servetus, Michael, 530
Severi, 133–34
Shang dynasty, 182
Shakespeare, William, 492, 568–69, 598
Sheng, 186–87
sheriff, in medieval England, 269–70
Shi-ites, 415
Shinto religion, 462
shipping: Chinese, 460; at end of Middle Ages, 401; Dutch, 555, 557–58; English, 389; German, 313 (*see also* trade and commerce)

ships, sixteenth-century, 541–43, *541*
shire, English, 270 (*see also* county)
Shiva (*see* Siva)
shoguns, Japanese, 464
Shotuku, 463
Siam, 441
Siberia, 585–86
Sicily, 354–55; in Carthaginian wars, 85–86; Moslems in, 258; Norman conquest of, 285–86
Sidon, 27
Sigismund, 493
silk, Chinese, 187, *189*
silver, Spanish acquisition of, 549–50, 553
Sistine Chapel, *486;* painting in, *468, 488, 490*
Siva, 180, *439*
Sixtus IV (Pope), 495, 496–97, 515–16
slavery: in American Spanish Empire, 549–51, 561, 582; in Greece, 48, 51, 52, 53; in Roman Empire, 92–93, 127, 152
Slavs, 205; in Byzantine Empire, 410; in Eastern Roman Empire, 219, 225; German expansion and, 313; Magyars and, 259 (*see also* Bulgars; Serbs)
Sluys, battle of, 384, *385*
Smith, Adam, 574
social class: in Italian city-states, 471–72; in Roman Empire, 114; seventeenth-century economy and, 580
Social War, 95
Socrates, 64
Solon, 51–52
Song of Roland, 321–22; manuscript, *321;* quoted, 322
Sophists, 63–64
Sophocles, 60–61
Sorokin, P. I., 605
South America, exploration of, 548–59 (*see also* Americas)
sovereignty, 586, 594, 598 (*see also* monarchy)
Spain, chronological history: in Carthaginian wars, 87–88, 90; under Rome, 91, 96–97, 101, 118, 124; under Visigoths, 159, 193–95, 207, 210; under Eastern Roman Empire, 217, 219; Moslems in, 236–38, 245, 276, 413, 415; during fifteenth century, 497; at end of Middle Ages, 509–11, 512; Catholic Reformation and, 534–35; exploration by, 543, 546–49; under Philip II 551–58, 561–62, 565, 568–69; during seventeenth century, 573, 575, 580, 587, 589–91, 593, 594, 600, 603–05 (*see also* Hapsburgs; Spanish Empire)
Spanish Empire, in Americas, 509–10, 549–52, 581–83, 585
Spanish Netherlands, 557, *557* (*see also* Flanders; Netherlands)
Sparta, 51, 53–54; in Peloponnesian War, 61–63; in Persian War, 54–56 (*see also* Greece; Hellenistic period)
Spenser, Edmund, 568
Sphinx, 16, *17*
Spice Islands, 545, 548, 581
spices, commerce in, 543–44, *545*
Ssu-ma Kuang, 455
stained-glass windows, *276–77, 312, 317,* 318–21
state, modern, 572–74, 603; conceptions of, 368 (*see also* nationalism)
Stephen II (Pope), 243
Stilicho, 158

Stoicism, 71–72, 131, 142–43; and Roman law, 129
Stone Age, New, 7–9
Strafford, Thomas Wentworth, earl of, 594–95, 597
Strasbourg, 527
Stuarts, 592–93
stupa, *178*
Suger (Abbot), *276–77, 299–303*
Sui dynasty, 448
Suleiman the Magnificent, 513
Sulla, 96
Sully, Maximilien, 587
Sumerians, 19, *19*
Sung dynasty, 423, 455–58, *455*
suttee, 179
Sutton Hoo treasure, *192, 206*
Sweden, 512, 574; Protestant Reformation in, 527; in Thirty Years' War, 601, 603
Swedes, 258
Switzerland, 395, 603; Protestant Reformation in, 528–29
Sylvester II (Pope), 266
Syracuse, 51, 62
Syria, chronological history: ancient, 19, 25, 31; during Hellenistic period, 68–70; in Roman Empire, 101; in Eastern Roman Empire, 215, 219, 222–23, 225–27; in Arab Empire, 233, 235; in Byzantine Empire, 406; under Turks, 416, 418, 434; Mongol attack on, 423

T

Tacitus, 128
Tamerlane, 433, *433,* 445
Tamils, 439–40
T'ang dynasty, 448–55, 463
Taoism, 184–85
Tarentum, 85
tariffs, mercantilism and, 578–79
Tarik, 236
taxation: in Arab Empire, 235; in Carolingian Empire, 252; by Church, 346–47, 514–15 (*see also* tithing); of Church, 356, 369, 511–12; in Eastern Roman Empire, 217; in England, 326–28, 351, 363–65, 386, 587, 591–95; in France, 366–67, 393, 508, 563, 587, 590–91; monarchy and, 510–12; in Roman provinces, 91, 94, 151–52
tea: in China, 450; in Japan, 463
technology: of Italian Renaissance, 490; in late Middle Ages, 400–02, 502–03
Tertullian, 145, 154
Tetzel, Johann, 521
textile industry: in England, 389, 577; in Flanders, 281–82, 316; in Italy, 470–71, 475, 577
Thales, 50
Thebes, 63
Themistocles, 55, 56
Theodora, 216–17, *216*
Theodoric, 160, 195, *195*
Theodosius, 156–58, *157*
Theologia Germanica, 380, 397
theology: of Abelard, 304–05; early Christian, 145–46, 148, 153–54, 163–64; late medieval, 399; of Thomas Aquinas, 357–59
Theotocopuli, Domenico (El Greco), 568; *Cardinal Guevara, 535*
Thermopylae, battle of, 55

Thierry, 209
Thirty Years' War, 557, 589, 598–605
Thomas a Kempis, 397
Thomas Aquinas (St.), 340, 357–60, 399, 400, 413
Thousand and One Nights, A, 413
Thucydides, 66–67; quoted, 53
Tiberius, 114, 116, *162*
Tigris-Euphrates Valley, 10–11, 18
Tintoretto, *Philip II, 554*
tithing, 245, 249
Titian, 489, 497; *Charles V, 526*
Titus, 121; Arch of, *117*
Tordesillas, Treaty of, 548
Toscanelli, Paolo, 546
tournament, *323*
towns, medieval, 281–83, 313–14, 375, 377, 578 (*see also* cities; city-states)
Toynbee, Arnold J., 540; quoted, 541
trade and commerce: of Arab Empire, 228, 236, 241; of Byzantine Empire, 409; Chinese, 188, 189, 450, 458, 461; in Eastern Roman Empire, 215; Greek, 42–44, *43,* 50–51; in India, 176, 178; of Italian city-states, 470–71, 475; Japanese, 464; medieval, 241, 281–83, 313–16, *315,* 501, 504–06; Mesopotamian, 20; Persian, 34–35; Phoenician, 27, *43;* Portuguese, 545; in Roman Empire, 125–27, 131; during seventeenth century, 575–81 (*see also* industry; mercantile economy)
trade unions (*see* gilds)
Trajan, 121–22, *121,* 123
Trajan's Column, *108–09*
Trent, Council of, 534, 535, 552
trial (*see* courts; jury trial; justice)
tribe: Arabian, 228–29; Germanic (*see* Germanic tribes)
Tribonian, 224
tribunes, Roman, 81, 94, 96
Trinity, Christian doctrine of, 145–46, 148, 410
Triumvirate, First, 98–100
Triumvirate, Second, 105–06
Tu Fu, 453; quoted, 454
Tudors, 388–90; 510, 592
Turks: in Arab and Byzantine Empires, 416–17, 421; in China, 448, 454–55; conquests by, 433–34; crusades against, 296, 417–22, 431, 433; in Danube Valley, 526, 551; defeat of, at Lepanto, 554–55; in India, 443–45, *444*
Tuscany, 333
tyrants: Greek, 45, 52; in Italian towns, 356, 377 (*see also* absolute monarchy; dictatorship)
Tyre, 27

U

Uccello, Paolo, drawing, *487*
Ulfila, 157, 203
Ulpian, quoted, 136
Unitarianism, 530
United Provinces (*see* Dutch Netherlands)
universities, medieval, 305–08, *308,* 337–38
Upanishads, 172
Urban II (Pope), 295–96; quoted, 295
Urban VI (Pope), 378–79
Urdu language, 444
Utopia, 519, 531, 568
Utrecht, Union of, 557

V

Valens, 156
Valla, Lorenzo, 482
Van Dyck, Anthony, *Wallenstein, 600*
Vandals, 159, 161, 193, 217–18
vassalage (*see* feudalism)
vassals, 260–62
Vedas, 171; quoted, 172
Velasquez, Diego, 568
Venice: and Byzantine Empire, 409; in Eastern Roman Empire, 210, 219; exploration and trade by, 313–14, 504, 542, 575; Fourth Crusade and, 420–21; government of, 377; during Renaissance, 471, 474, *474,* 475, 486, 491; Turkish battle with, 554–55
Vercingetorix, 100
Verdun, Treaty of, 255
Vergil, 112, 120
vernacular, 359
vernacular literature (*see* literature, medieval vernacular)
Verrocchio, Andrea del, sculpture of, *472*
Vespasian, 117, *120,* 121, 123
Vespucci, Amerigo, 547–48
Vézelay church portal, *298*
Vienna, siege of, 434
Vigilius (Pope), 223
Vijayanagar kingdom, 440, 443, 445
vikings (*see* Northmen)
village: Indian, 440; medieval, 279–81, 469
Villard de Honnecourt, 358
Villon, François, 396–97; quoted, 397
Vinci, Leonardo da, 487–91; drawing, *491; The Last Supper,* 488, *488*
virtù, 476
Visconti, Gian Galeazzo, 474–75
Vishnu, 180
Visigoths, 158–59, 193–95, 207, 210, 215 (*see also* Goths)
Vision of Piers Plowman, The, 397
Vondel, Joost van den, 568

W

Waldensians, 335, 529
Wales, 193; conquest of, 363
Wallace, William, 363

Wallenstein, Albrecht von, 600, *600,* 601, 603
Wang An-shih, 456–57
war casualties, *605*
warfare: in Japan, 463–64; technological changes in, 502 (*see also* army; firearms)
Wars of the Roses, 388–89, 470, 510
Wenceslaus, 507
Westphalia, Peace of, 601 *n.,* 603–05
Wiclif, John, 380–81, 493, 518
William I (of Dutch Netherlands), the Silent, 556–57
William I (of England), the Conqueror, 273, 286–89, *289,* 325
William II (of England), William Rufus, 289, *289*
William III (of England), 557, 573
witchcraft, 382; and Thirty Years' War, 605
Wittenberg, University of, 521–23
Wolsey, Thomas (Cardinal), 510
woolen cloth (*see* textile industry)
Worms, Concordat of, 294
Worms, Diet of, 523
writing: Chinese, 182, *186;* Egyptian, 15–16; Japanese, 461–62, *461;* medieval, *203, 209, 247, 247–49, 255, 297;* Phoenician, 27; Roman, *108–09;* Sumerian, 20 (*see also* calligraphy; manuscripts)
Wycliffe, John (*see* Wiclif)

X

Xerxes, 54, 56

Y

Yangtze Valley, 448
Yoritomo, 464
York, House of, 388

Z

Zacharias (Pope), 242
Zangi, 419
Zeno, 160
ziggurat, 22
Zoroaster, 34
Zoroastrianism, 144
Zürich, 527
Zwingli, Ulrich, 527, 528, 529